Research Guide to U.S. and International Interest Groups

Research Guide to U.S. and International Interest Groups

Edited by Clive S. Thomas

Westport, Connecticut
London

Library of Congress Cataloging-in-Publication Data

Research guide to U.S. and international interest groups / edited by Clive S. Thomas.
    p. cm.
  Includes bibliographical references and index.
  ISBN 0–313–29543–3 (alk. paper)
  1. Pressure groups—United States. 2. Lobbying—United States. 3. Pressure
groups—Research. I. Title: Research guide to U.S. and international interest
groups. II. Thomas, Clive S.
JK1118.R47   2004
322.4'3—dc22   2003059625

British Library Cataloguing in Publication Data is available.

Library of Congress Catalog Card Number: 2003059625
ISBN: 0–313–29543–3

First published in 2004

Praeger Publishers, 88 Post Road West, Westport, CT 06881
An imprint of Greenwood Publishing Group, Inc.
www.praeger.com

Printed in the United States of America

The paper used in this book complies with the
Permanent Paper Standard issued by the National
Information Standards Organization (Z39.48–1984).

10 9 8 7 6 5 4 3 2 1

This book is dedicated to the hundreds of elected and appointed public officials and their staffs, lobbyists, civil servants, interest group leaders, group activists, and political journalists around the world, who, over the past thirty years, have found the time to share with me their observations, experiences, and insights about interest groups and lobbying.

Contents

CONTENTS

Contents

CONTENTS

Contents

CONTENTS

12 *Interest Groups in Selected Nonpluralist Regimes, Transitional Democracies, and Developing Societies*   *323*

13 *Interest Groups in International and Transnational Politics*   *341*

Contents

Preface

This *Guide* is intended primarily for undergraduate and graduate students who need an initial and comprehensive overview of the major research on various aspects of interest group studies. The book will also be useful for political scientists and other academics for reference in their research. It will be helpful to those who teach courses on interest groups and need a succinct explanation of particular aspects of interest group studies. The book may also be used for course preparation and developing class assignments. As with most handbooks on academic literature, the entries in this book do not provide an in-depth review of each subject. What they do provide is an overview of major publications and the status of knowledge on a wide range of subjects within the field of interest groups. As a primer for more in-depth study and generating ideas for research projects, three important points need to be explained about this book.

First, while this book includes reference to recent research on virtually all areas of interest group studies published in English, the time lapse between submitting the manuscript and the date of publication means that, like most political science books, it is not completely up-to-date. However, the book provides information on the major works, authors, and trends in research across the gamut of topics within interest group studies, equipping the reader with the essential background knowledge and information about where to look for more in-depth studies and more recent research. This broad, long-term focus will give the book a longer shelf life, rendering timeliness less important.

Second, because much of the literature and research on interest groups has been conducted on the political system in the United States, and because the major readership of this *Guide* will likely be American, much of the material focuses on various aspects of U.S. interest group activity.

The goal of this book, however, is to be comprehensive and cover the entire field of interest group studies. Accordingly, as browsing the book's contents will reveal, about half the material in this *Guide* covers aspects of interest group activity outside the American system, such as neocorporatism, the study of comparative interest groups, an overview of interest groups in particular countries and regions, and the role of groups in international politics. Other entries deal with general theories and explanations that claim to be applicable beyond the bounds of one political system, such as why people join interest groups and what shapes lobbying strategies and tactics.

Third, regarding the language and type of sources cited, although this *Guide* seeks to include research on interest groups from around the world, for reasons of practicality, readership, and the market for the book, it confines its sources predominantly to those in English. Furthermore, this book generally confines source references to published books or articles found in libraries, as these are easily available. Some reference is also made to sources available on-line. But because they are not so readily available, few references are made to papers presented at academic conferences. However, where a conference paper is the major or only source on a subject or where it is particularly valuable, it is cited.

Many of the over one hundred and twenty topics covered in the book are closely related or overlap with other topics. Therefore, the book has been formatted to facilitate cross-reference. This is done by dividing the fifteen chapters into sections and further dividing some sections into subsections. The simple cross-reference system is explained in the introduction to chapter 1.

As this reference guide is intended for those at several levels of academic knowledge on interest groups, some guidance on how to use this book is in order. For the undergraduate or graduate student or anyone else coming to the study of interest groups for the first time, it is strongly recommended that they first read chapter 1 in its entirety. The chapter provides a short explanation of the special features of this *Guide*; an overview of the study of interest groups, including American approaches and others; and a review of the problems faced by researchers. It also explains the structure of the *Guide* and provides guidelines on using the book. In addition, students embarking on their first research project on interest groups should also read chapter 15 ("Conducting Research on Interest Groups") before consulting entries on specific areas of interest group studies. Those more knowledgeable on interest groups should first read the last section of chapter 1 (section 8—designated in the cross reference system as 1.8.) to get direction on using the book to most efficiently meet their needs.

Of all the people I have to thank for making this *Guide* possible, at the top of the list are the seventy-eight contributors. Many of them will be recognized as authorities on their subjects and have been drawn from around the world; others are up-and-coming—the prominent interest group scholars of the future. Laura Savatgy worked as my research assistant dealing mainly with the bibliography and proofing the manuscript and made many valuable suggestions on content and organization. Michael Boyer also worked as my research assistant on the latter stages of this project; Steffi Walter, of the University of Passau in Bavaria, helped check references when she was an exchange student at the University of Alaska. Beatrice Franklin of the University of Alaska Southeast Library was of tremendous help in locating reference materials and tracking down citations. Michael Hermann of Greenwood Press was a first-rate editor and a great source of encouragement during the long, tedious process of producing a book of this type. My former Dean, Mary Lou Madden, was very supportive, as was Chancellor John Pugh of the University of Alaska Southeast.

Most importantly, I thank my wife Susan and my faithful feline companions Reggie, Miranda, Hamilton, and Wellington, whose support, encouragement, and love was so important during those many times when this project wasn't going quite the way I'd planned.

Clive S. Thomas
Juneau, Alaska
September 21, 2003

Chapter 1

Introduction: The Study of Interest Groups

Clive S. Thomas

1.1. SPECIAL FEATURES OF THIS BOOK AND THE PURPOSE OF THIS CHAPTER

Since the academic study of interest groups emerged in a significant way in the 1950s, it has been dominated by research on the U.S. political system. For several reasons, explained at various points in this book (see, for example, chapter 11, section 1 [11.1.], 12.1., and 13.1.), much less research has been conducted on group activity in other liberal democracies, in authoritarian regimes, and in international politics. As the United States is in many ways the most advanced political system in terms of the development of interest group activity and a large portion of the world's interest group scholars reside there, this primacy of the United States in interest group studies is understandable. As a consequence, much of the material in this *Guide* either relates directly to the U.S. political system or is based on research upon the United States.

However, largely because of its separation of powers system, its weak political parties, and low level of ideological politics, the United States is an aberrant political system in regard to interest group activity (C. Thomas 1993b). Thus, to understand only the U.S. situation provides a blinkered and rather distorted view of interest group activity as it operates in the various political systems throughout the world and in global and world regional politics. With this in mind, the primary purpose of this *Guide* is to provide a comprehensive overview of the literature and research on all aspects of interest group studies and not just work relating to the U.S. political system. Given this broader focus, the following five special features of this *Guide* are important to note.

First, this book is the first one-volume, comprehensive reference detailing the major literature and research on the entire gamut of interest group studies, from the internal organization and maintenance of interest groups to their role in the public policy process. In reaching beyond work on the United States, it includes reference to comparative interest group studies, groups in pluralist and nonpluralist political systems and in international politics.

Second, since the major use of this book will be by students and scholars in the United States, and because of the importance of research on the U.S. system to interest group studies, numerous references are made throughout the book to place the U.S. experience in perspective with other group systems and group activity. For example, when an overview of group strategies and tactics is provided (see section 7.2.), an explanation is given of how these tactics differ in the United States from those in other liberal democracies.

Third, the book fills a gap in interest group studies that will be of use to newcomers to the subject and those with various levels of existing knowledge. Newcomers, particularly students, will find this a useful primer. Those with some background on interest groups will find literature reviews of topics to refresh their knowledge and the treatment of topics with which they may not be familiar.

Fourth, in reviewing the extent of research and literature on each topic, reference is made to the major gaps that still need to be filled on the topic. This information will be useful to students and academics alike searching for research projects.

Fifth, this first chapter provides a succinct overview of the academic study of interest groups, which, in terms of the holistic study of the subject, is not available in any other source. As will be shown, however, the academic study of interest groups is far from holistic in regards to being a coherent academic subject but is rather fragmented, with scholars studying one area of the subject, often having very little knowledge of other areas.

Turning now to the specifics of this chapter, it is intended for those coming to interest group studies for the first time, those familiar with the literature on U.S. interest groups but who are seeking an overview of the field in general, and those needing a succinct refresher course on the terminology, scope, methods, and problems of interest group studies. The last section of the chapter will also be useful to those who want suggestions on how to use this *Guide*.

The chapter is divided into seven major sections. Section 1.2. defines interest group, interest and related terms, and explains the distinction between interest groups and the closely related political organizations of political parties and social movements. In section 1.3. the functions of interest groups are explored. Section 1.4. explains the problems facing those undertaking research on interest groups. Then in section 1.5. the theoretical approaches to interest group studies, mainly pluralism and corporatism or neocorporatism, are briefly explained. Section 1.6. identifies the categories of subject matter of interest group studies, divided into two broad categories of groups as organizations and group involvement in the public policy process. Section 1.7. identifies the major approaches used in studying interest groups. Finally, section 1.8. provides information on what this *Guide* does and does not cover and pointers on how to get the best use out of it.

To facilitate further investigation of the topics covered in this and other chapters in the book, several cross-references are given to chapters and sections of chapters in this *Guide*. As can be deduced from cross-references in this chapter so far, the first number in these cross-references is the chapter number and the second is the section. For example, the entry on the relationship between interest groups and political parties is in chapter 4, section 5 and is designated as section 4.5. As with all chapters, complete references of works cited in the text are found in the reference section following chapter 15.

1.2. DEFINING *INTEREST GROUP* AND RELATED TERMS

Interest Group, Interest, and Lobby

There is no single agreed-upon definition of an *interest group* among scholars. The broad diversity of definitions is well encapsulated by Baumgartner and Leech (1998, 25–30). Definitions range from the very narrow to the very broad. Many scholars studying interest groups at the national and state level in the United States use a narrow, legal definition confining their focus of study to those groups required to register under national or state lobby laws and exclude those not required to do so. Yet, many groups and organizations engage in lobbying but are not required to register. This is not only the case in the United States, where registration of interest groups and their lobbyists is extensive, but more so in many other countries where registration laws are much less comprehensive and in many places do not exist.

The most important of these nonregistered interest groups are those representing government itself—particularly government agencies (including the federal and state governments in the United States). Where registration laws exist, most do not require public officials at any level of government to register as lobbyists. Thus, to confine the definition of an interest group to a narrow, legal definition would exclude many interests. So a broader definition is more appropriate in many instances and certainly for use in this book, which covers interest group activity in its many forms and across many different types of political systems. A useful definition in this regard is as follows:

An *interest group* is an association of individuals or organizations or a public or private institution that, on the basis of one or more shared concerns, attempts to influence public policy in its favor.

This definition embraces the three broad categories of interest groups operating in political systems around the world, past and present.

The first category, often referred to as the traditional membership group, is made up of individuals such as doctors, gun owners, farmers, students, and so on. However, some groups composed of individuals may not have a formal organization or an official membership. In all societies there are many informal groups that operate as interest groups but would not be included under a narrow definition. For example, a group of influential citizens in Finland may be concerned about the lack of computers available in elementary schools and may lobby their friends who are government officials to deal with the problem. Perhaps a more important example of informal groups is anomic groups. These are short-lived, often spontaneous groups such as those organized to demonstrate against unpopular policies. French farmers are renowned for this by blocking the streets of Paris with tractors and livestock to protest agricultural policies they dislike. In developing countries there are informal groups of elites, tribal leaders, or other informal social structures that can influence public policy as much as any formal group, but would not be covered by a narrow definition of interest group. Similarly, in authoritarian systems, including communist regimes, there are influential groups of political and professional elites that the system does not recognize as formal groups but that, nevertheless, often work informally to influence public policy.

The second category of interest groups, usually called organizational interests, is composed not of individuals but of organizations—they are actually organizations of organizations. These can be public or private organizations that represent for-profit or nonprofit entities. In the economic sphere many of these are narrowly based trade associations representing such businesses as car manufacturers, oil companies, or railroads. Some are more broadly based: for example the Confederation of British Industry (CBI), which includes all types of industries, or the Australian Council of Trade Unions (ACTU), a general trade union organization composed of individual unions. Examples of nonprofit organizational interests are national associations of public universities and public hospitals. Public interest and social issue groups, such as environmentalists and consumer groups, also often join together in national organizations. Organizational interests representing all or a substantial number of the groups in a broad area of economic or social activity—business, labor, agriculture, local government, education, the handicapped, and so on— are called peak associations (see section 4.10.).

The third category is that of institutional interests, which are not really groups at all. As Walker (1983), Salisbury (1984), Gray and Lowery (1995, 2001), and Thomas and Hrebenar (2003) have pointed out, many organizations that lobby are, in fact, institutions, both public and private: such as individual business corporations, think tanks, and the multitude of government agencies and levels of government (including departments of national governments), cities and towns, public universities, public corporations (like nationally owned airlines), and, in some countries, special districts for services like education and water supply. Moreover, in many countries the armed forces are important in lobbying for their budget and shaping public policy. Overall, probably the most important lobbying forces in any society are the various elements of government. Most of these institutional interests, while having employees, staff, or governing boards, are not membership organizations (composed of individuals or other organizations) in the traditional sense of an interest group.

As with all definitions of an interest group, the broad definition set out above has its own problems, particularly those of delineation. Thus, this definition is not used by every contributor to this *Guide*. But the definition is worth bearing in mind as it will help to make sense of many of the entries that deal with informal lobbying activity.

The terms *interest* and *lobby* used as nouns are often used synonymously and interchangeably with the term *interest group*; but they are more general terms and are used in a variety of ways. The term *lobby* always has political connotations (usually referring to a collection of interests such as business groups), but *interest* may or may not. It may simply refer to a part (a sector) of society with similar concerns or a common identity that may or may not engage in political activity, such as farmers or minorities. It is from these similar concerns and common identities of interests and sectors, however, that interest groups and lobbies are formed. Furthermore, the distinction between an interest or lobby and a formal interest group is sometimes difficult to make in practice. This is partly because organized groups, such as antitax groups, often act and are perceived as representing a broader political interest than their official membership. The term *interest* instead of *interest group* is often used when considering government entities working to influence other governments, because of the broader and less formalized nature of the constituencies represented. Interest is also used to designate other broader interests such as government elites and tribal leaders.

To embrace both these registered and nonregistered lobbies and the broader political groupings represented by the terms interest and lobby, one study of interest groups suggested the term *organized interest* instead of simply interest group (Schlozman, Lehman, and Tierney 1986, 9–12). Indeed, this is a more accurate term. However, as the authors who develop it admit, this is rather a clumsy label and the term interest group is more commonly used and accepted. For this reason we will use interest group here, bearing in mind our broad definition of the term.

Lobbying and Lobbyist

Interest groups work to achieve their goal of influencing public policy through the activity of *lobbying*. The process of lobbying involves three stages that may overlap in practice: first, gaining access to policy makers; second, creating an attitude among policy makers conducive to the group's goals; and third, influencing policy makers in the group's favor. Not all lobbying activity is directed to influence immediate policy decisions. Some is intended to gain access or create an atmosphere—involving trust, credibility, and maybe even dependence of public officials on a group—that will be conducive to the group in shaping future government policy. This includes providing information to policy makers—technical and political—that is unsolicited or by request.

Lobbying also takes many forms: from direct contact of group representatives with policy makers (known in the United States but not in most other countries as insider lobbying tactics), to the connection of a group with officials of the political party in power, to indirect interaction through demonstrations and protests (known in the United States but, again, not in most countries as outsider lobbying tactics). Thus, we can define lobbying for comparative analytical purposes as:

> The interaction of a group or interest with policy makers, either directly or indirectly, that has a view to influencing current policy or creating a relationship conducive to shaping future policy to the benefit of that group or interest.

This definition says nothing about what constitutes effective lobbying. It is simply a definition of the fundamental activity. The elusive question of what constitutes effective lobbying or interest group power is addressed in section 7.17.

Interest groups operate mainly by using one or more lobbyists. In essence, a *lobbyist* is a person who represents an interest group in order to influence government decisions in that group's favor (but see section 7.6. for a more comprehensive definition). The decisions most often targeted by lobbyists are those concerning public policies. Consequently, lobbyists also target decisions about who gets elected and appointed to make those policies. As can be deduced from what has been said already, lobbyists include those required to register by law and those representing non-registered groups and organizations, particularly government as well as informal groups (see sections 7.6., 7.7., 7.8., and 7.9.).

Interest Group System

An *interest group system* is the array of groups and organizations, both formal and informal, and the lobbyists who represent them, working to affect public policy within a country or on the international or regional level. As one element of the socioeconomic and political life of the country, how an interest group system's characteristics—size, development, composition, methods of operating, etc.—relate to a country's economy, society, and government is particularly important. The idea of an interest group system is an abstraction, of course, because even though there are relations between various groups and lobbyists representing various interests, never do all the groups in a political system act in concert to achieve one goal. However, the holistic concept of an interest group system vis-à-vis other elements of the political system—such as the executive, the parliament, bureaucracy, or political parties—is useful for understanding the relative importance of the elements of a political system in policy making and the distribution of political power (see chap. 4).

Differentiating Interest Groups, Political Parties, and Social Movements

Finally, it is important to distinguish an interest group from a political party and a social movement. The distinction is not entirely clear and there is overlap, but for our purposes we can make the following differentiation. Interest groups are usually concerned with a narrow issue or range of issues and try to promote these for their members, their organization, or society as a whole but they do not want to formally control the machinery of government. Social movements try to champion grand visions of social change (usually for a large, dispossessed segment of the population) or broadly defined issues (such as in the United States in the 1960s with African Americans, women, and environmentalism). Political parties, which can be seen as a collection of interest groups, seek to direct the energies of groups and movements through the electoral process to win control of government in order to implement a broad-based political platform (C. Thomas 2001a, 4–10).

1.3. THE FUNCTIONS OF INTEREST GROUPS: THEIR PRIVATE GOALS AND PUBLIC ROLES

It is important to place the political role of interest groups in perspective. Unlike political parties, which originate and exist primarily for political purposes, as Mancur Olson (1965) pointed out, most interest groups are not primarily political organizations. They develop from a common economic or social interest, as, for example, farmers forming a cooperative, automakers forming a business trade association, the blind forming a self-help association, or tennis enthusiasts forming a club. Such organizations promote programs and disseminate information to enhance the professional, business, social, or avocational interests of their members. Much of this activity is nonpolitical, as when the American Dental Association publishes its journal or provides cut-rate life insurance for its members.

However, many nonpolitical interest groups are forced to become politically active because there is no other way to protect or promote the interests of their members or an organization such as a business. Thus, Mancur Olson (1965) saw entry into the political arena as a by-product of a group's or organization's fundamental nonpolitical role. Workers' movements in Western Europe entered the political arena in the late nineteenth century to establish the legality of trade unions and to promote child labor and worker safety laws. Employers' organizations became politically active to counter both union power and to resist government regulation. Farm groups in many parts of the world used the political process to secure and preserve import tariffs and farm subsidies. Increased government involvement in the economy and in society in the Western world since the 1930s has brought a plethora of new groups into the political arena to protect themselves from government regulation, to secure a piece of the government budget, or to promote some value or belief.

Many scholars used to make a distinction between nonpolitical and political groups by designating the former as interest groups and the latter as *pressure groups*. This distinction is still used by many scholars in Britain, British Commonwealth countries, and in continental Europe. Some scholars also use the term *special* interest groups to designate groups operating in the political arena (see, for example, Morehouse 1981, chap. 3; Makielski 1980; and S. Miller 1983). In general, however, *interest groups* is the generic term used today to designate groups (whether or not they are politically active) that have the potential to engage in politics.

Therefore, while most interest groups have many nonpolitical goals, they have one overriding goal when they become politically active: to influence the political process—particularly public policy—in their favor. In addition to promoting the political interests of their members or organization, interest groups perform several important functions for political systems, though the importance of any particular function will vary from system to system, particularly between liberal democracies and nonpluralist systems.

The Aggregation and Representation of Interests. Together with political parties, interest groups are a major means by which people with similar interests and concerns are brought together, or aggregated, and their views articulated to government. Thus, interest groups are an important vehicle for political participation. This is especially the case in liberal democracies between elections.

Facilitating Government. Groups contribute to the substance of public policy by being significant sources of both technical and political information for policy makers. This is because interest groups and their leaders are often the most knowledgeable sources of information on their topic of concern. Ideas put forward by interest groups are often the source of legislation. In many instances groups help to facilitate the process of bargaining and compromising essential to policy making in pluralist systems. They often perform this role in authoritarian regimes as well, albeit in a less officially recognized, more informal way. And groups sometimes aid in implementing public policies: for example, when the Kansas Farm Bureau distributes information about a state or about a U.S. federal government agricultural program.

Political Education and Training. To varying degrees, interest groups educate their members and the public on issues. They also provide opportunities for citizens in democratic countries to learn about the political process and to gain valuable practical experience for seeking public office. In authoritarian regimes they also provide a training ground for party operatives and other people with political ambitions.

Candidate and Public Official Recruitment. In democracies, groups often recruit candidates to run for public office, both from within and outside their group. In authoritarian regimes, groups can be an important source for future leaders, like the Communist youth organizations in many countries.

Sources of Campaign Finance and Sources of Political Party Electoral Support. Increasingly these days in democracies, particularly in the United States and Western Europe, groups help to finance political campaigns, both candidate elections and ballot measure elections (initiative, referendum, and recall). Interest groups are also important sources of campaign workers, such as union members helping to get the Social Democrats elected in Germany. This funding and campaign support function is not confined to democracies, however. Mass parties in authoritarian regimes often rely on interest groups for support.

However, there is a contradiction between the relationship of the private political goals and the public roles of interest groups: their positive public roles are purely incidental. With the minor exception of good government groups, like Common Cause, the League of Women Voters, and some think tanks, interest groups in their private capacity do not exist to improve democracy or to improve the functioning of the political process. Thus, the positive public role of interest groups is a paradoxical by-product of the sum of their selfish interests. Consequently, the actions of many interest groups and their lobbyists, which often appear against the public interest, produce many negative attitudes toward them among the public and can have negative effects on democracy. It was James Madison, way back in 1787, in *Federalist Number 10* (Brock 1965) who set out what is the classic explanation of both the positive and negative role of interest groups or, as Madison referred to them, factions. Jeffrey Berry refers to this as "Madison's dilemma" (J. Berry 1997, chap. 1). In many countries these concerns and problems have led to the regulation of interest group activity (see chap. 14).

1.4. PROBLEMS OF STUDYING INTEREST GROUPS

Anyone coming to study interest groups for the first time will soon discover that there are several problems in attempting to advance knowledge in this field. In fact, there is an irony in our knowledge about interest groups. Thousands of pieces of literature exist, including a myriad of original research studies, as the entries in this *Guide* attest. Yet, in many aspects of interest group studies there is little definitive knowledge. What most characterizes the study of interest groups, as is the case in other areas of political science and the social sciences in general, is not definitive knowledge but various interpretations and perspectives by scholars. This will become evident in reading the various entries in this book. There are, for example, various interpretations of the effects of corporatism (see section 3.4. and chap. 10), of how groups originate and survive (see chap. 5), of what determines group influence (see section 7.17.), and of the consequences, advantages, and disadvantages of regulating interest groups (see chap. 14), among many other areas of group studies.

Major reasons for the dearth of definitive information on various aspects of interest group activity are similar to those in the social sciences in general: the number of variables involved in many situations—such as a decision-making process—many of which may not be known and thus go unidentified (see section 15.2. for an explanation of *variables* as used in social science); different methodologies used by different researchers that yield different results in investigating the same phenomenon, such as whether or not media campaigns are effective for interest groups; and the cost of doing extensive survey research is often a barrier to producing a statistically viable study, among many other problems faced by social scientists. Specific to interest group studies, the following are problems facing researchers.

Defining Terms and Delineating Categories. It was noted above that there is dispute about exactly what is and is not an interest group. There is also dispute about several other terms in interest group studies such as pluralism, power, and public interest group. Then there are disputes about categorizing, such as how to classify various types of groups and organizations (For example, do we classify professional groups under business or in a separate category?), and disputes about who is and who is not a lobbyist (Do we, for example, include individuals lobbying on their own behalf?). This lack of agreement on terms and categories leads to their use in different ways, which often produces different results in studying virtually identical subjects.

The Boundary Lines of Interest Group Activity. A similar problem arises in attempting to determine what is and what is not interest group activity. Prominent American interest group scholar Robert Salisbury tells a story of a job interview where he was asked if he would teach a separate course on interest groups, to which he replied no, as interest groups are all-pervasive in the political system. Thus, researchers are faced with deciding what is and is not interest group activity and different delineations often produce different results in similar studies. A good illustration of this problem is the broad definition of an interest group set out in section 1.2. This definition, embracing more elements of the political system than a narrow one—particularly government and informal entities—will produce different results in all sorts of studies, including those on what constitutes the makeup of the interest group community and what to include when studying lobbying tactics.

Differing Approaches and Methodologies. There are two aspects to this. First, there are various ways to study the same aspect of interest group activity. These range from highly empirical approaches, such as rational choice and public choice approaches (see section 3.5.), to normative approaches and combinations of the two, which may include mail surveys or structured interviews. These varying methods often produce different results on the same subject. The influence of political action committees (PACs) on voting in the U.S. Congress is a good example (see sections 2.5. and 7.4.). Chapters 3 and 15 explain various methods of researching into interest groups.

Second, there are varying approaches to studying interest groups in different political systems. There are three main reasons for this. One is that the operation of parliamentary systems—like Britain, Sweden and New Zealand—with their strong parties, make interest groups less obvious than in the United States, and so for many years the study of these groups in parliamentary systems was neglected. A second is that, even though interest groups exist in all countries, many societies do not recognize their activities in the way that scholars of U.S. politics do. There is, for example, no word in German, Swedish, or Czech for lobbyist. Third, countries at different levels of development display different forms of interest group activity, and the less formal activity in less developed political systems is often not recognized as interest group activity in the way that scholars of more advanced countries define it. Thus, in studying interest groups across political systems, comparisons can be difficult. In the next section (see 1.5.) more is said about the schools of focus of scholars, which has bearing on the type of studies and knowledge available on interest groups.

Identifying the Numerous Variables in a Specific Situation. As stated above, problems in identifying the numerous variables in certain situations is a major barrier to definitive studies of interest groups. In addition, there is the dynamic nature of interest group activity over time when circumstances may change and new variables come into play. A prime example of the problems associated with identifying the variable involved in a specific situation and over time is determining group power or influence (see section 7.17.).

Problems of Gathering Data. Most academic studies of interest groups apply some form of scientific method and thus need data from which to work. Many barriers exist to gathering data, particularly original data, on interest groups. One is cost. It costs a lot of money to conduct a mail survey and much more to do personal interviews. Consequently, most studies are based on fairly narrow target populations that limit their applicability in some instances. Another barrier is securing enough returns to make the study statistically significant. A third problem is getting accurate information on subjects that are highly politically sensitive, such as the role of lobbyists in killing a piece of legislation. Researchers have developed various approaches to deal with these problems, including developing ways to test for the accuracy of returns and focusing on case studies as opposed to comprehensive studies of group activity in an attempt to tailor their study to available funds. Chapter 2 deals with the issue of how to acquire data in the study of U.S. interest groups, and chapter 15 deals with the issue of limited data sources.

However, these problems of studying interest groups should be placed in perspective. Not all areas of group studies are equally affected by them. Moreover, many methodologically rigorous and enlightening studies have been produced that have considerably advanced the knowledge of interest group activity as illustrated throughout this *Guide.* And a major advantage of being aware of these problems and the need for their solution can provide students and scholars with ideas for research projects.

1.5. THEORETICAL APPROACHES IN THE STUDY OF INTEREST GROUPS AND THE SCHOOLS OF FOCUS OF SCHOLARS

This section is divided into two parts. The first identifies the major theoretical approaches that scholars have used to explain the role of interest groups within political systems. The main focus is on approaches as they relate to liberal democracies because these are the most developed. The second part identifies the groupings within the community of interest group scholars with regard to what might be called their schools of focus and methods of study, which is partly a reflection of the theoretical approaches considered in the first part.

Theoretical Approaches

Scholars have developed two major theoretical explanations of how interest groups in liberal democracies relate to the public policy making process. These are the *pluralist* model and its modifications, and the *neocorporatist* or *corporatist* model. Other explanations have also been developed.

Pluralism. Pluralism is the most widely accepted explanation of how interest groups relate to the political system in liberal democracies. Foley stated: "The pluralist conception of society . . . sees a vast profusion of group interests represented and embodied by political groups, none of which has the power to prevail over the rest" (Foley 1991, 87). In this process the government is neutral, disengaged from interest group conflicts, all are free to organize for political purposes, and there is equal access to policy makers. All western democracies exhibit some degree of pluralism; but the United States is perhaps closest to this pure pluralist model. However, much criticism has been leveled at pluralism. The two major criticisms are that the distribution of economic resources is uneven and that the government is not neutral in the resolution of this conflict process, both of which undermine the basic assumption of pluralism. Pluralism and its modification are considered in section 3.2.

Neocorporatism and Corporatism. Whereas the pluralist policy environment is a free-flowing system, neocorporatism is a structured, cooperative relationship between government and certain interest groups; the goal being to provide stability and predictability in the development and implementation of certain policies, most often economic policies. Because of its focus on economic policies, those interests most often participating in neocorporatist arrangements are producer groups: mainly business and labor.

Neocorporatism as a theory of interest groups in liberal democracies originated in the 1970s and so is much younger than pluralism. However, corporatism has a long history that is particularly associated with conservative nationalist and authoritarian regimes, such as Hitler's Germany, Franco's Spain, and Austria in the 1930s. As with neocorporatism, corporatism uses employer organizations and trade unions as agents of state economic and social regulation. The major difference between corporatism and neocorporatism is that in the former these agreements are imposed by the state, but in the latter, in liberal democracies, they arise from societal pressures and participation and compliance is voluntary. Since World War II, Western European countries—particularly those in Scandinavia, Germany, Switzerland, and Austria—have exhibited the most extensive neocorporatist interest group activity. However, like pluralism, neocorporatism has been subject to numerous criticisms. Neocorporatism and corporatism are considered in section 3.4. and in chapter 10.

Although they are the major models of interest group activity in liberal democracies, pluralism and neocorporatism are not the only models. Two others are important to understand.

The Responsible or Strong Political Party Model. This model sees strong, disciplined parties that dominate the policy process as the major determinants of interest group activity—interest groups that are dependent on the party in power for access and ultimately influence. This model is considered in section 3.6.

The Neo-Marxist Model. Although a less commonly accepted explanation, the neo-Marxist model offers a major critique of pluralism and neo-corporatism. It holds that interest group influence is less the product of politics or societal agreements than it is of class consciousness. This is particularly true, neo-Marxists hold, in explaining the influence of business and the capitalist class. See section 3.8. for a fuller explanation of this model.

In practice, explanations of the role of interest groups in public policy making in liberal democracies is probably best described as a combination of two or more of the above explanations, depending on the country concerned.

Explanations of Interest Group Activity in Nonpluralist Societies. The explanation of interest group activity in policy making in authoritarian and nonpluralist regimes is far less easily categorized. In old style communist regimes, like those of the Soviet Union and Eastern Europe, the so-called transmission belt system operated by the various communist party organizations transmitting what the party wanted to the people. In other systems, a version of the strong party model may determine interest group activity, as was the case for many years with the Institutional Revolutionary Party (Partido Revolucionario Institucional or PRI) in Mexico. In yet other societies, like Egypt and several countries in Latin America, a form of corporatism operates (see chap. 12).

Schools of Focus of Interest Group Scholars

Like many academic subjects, the study of interest groups did not develop systematically. As with several other fields of study, it received its impetus from particular scholars who recognized a phenomenon, researched it, and published material. Early pioneers included Arthur Bentley (1908), Pendleton Herring (1929), David Truman (1951), Samuel Finer (1958), and Joseph LaPalombara (1964). It was not until the early 1960s that interest group research began to gain a wide following among scholars—mainly scholars of U.S. politics. The study of interest groups outside the United States took longer to develop, in part because interest groups were seen as much less significant than in the United States.

This piecemeal development and greater interest in the United States, plus the fact that interest groups operate in different ways in different political systems, has resulted in a fragmentation of the scholarly community studying interest groups in terms of theoretical tradition, focus of group activity, and often in approach and methodology. While the divisions within the scholarly community are not hard and fast and are not coherent enough to be labeled school of thought, they do, in effect, represent different schools of focus. Broadly, five of these can be identified.

1. The American School. As indicated at the beginning of this chapter, those studying interest groups in U.S. politics are by far the largest contingent of interest group scholars. Moreover, perhaps as much as two-thirds to three-fourths of the literature produced on interest groups either focuses on the American system or is based on research conducted on that system. Scholars of American interest groups tend to: fall within the pluralist tradition or one of its various modifications; divide the study of interest groups between the internal organization of groups and their role in the public policy making process; have moved more and more into highly empirical techniques of analysis; and, because of the nature of U.S. politics, focus considerable attention on the role of interest groups in the electoral process, legislatures, and courts.

Understandably perhaps, some American interest group scholars have been rather parochial and are often not concerned about or familiar with interest group activity outside the United States. Most interest group courses in American universities, for example, focus only on U.S. interest groups. Allan Cigler (1991b) has provided an excellent overview of the development and focus of American interest group studies (see also Crotty, Schwartz, and Green 1994 and section 2.5.). An insightful critique of the American approach is provided by F. Davis and Wurth (1993).

2. The Parliamentary Democracy and Neocorporatist School. This is an even broader catch-all category than the American school and includes scholars who study interest groups in liberal democracies, predominantly parliamentary systems. Most of these scholars reside outside the United States. Because of the nature of parliamentary systems, with their strong political parties and often social democratic traditions, these scholars have employed a combination of theoretical traditions: particularly neocorporatism (especially in Continental Europe) often in combination with various forms of modified pluralism, the strong party model, and other statist and neo-Marxist approaches. Furthermore, the differences in governmental structure and the policy process in these countries compared to the United States have meant less emphasis on lobbying strategies and tactics in the electoral process, in legislatures, in the courts, and on lobbyists, and more emphasis on lobbying the executive (see section 11.1.).

3. The Nonpluralist School. For several reasons, much less research has been conducted on interest groups in nonpluralist societies than in liberal democracies. This is mainly because interest group studies developed first among scholars studying western liberal democracies, due to the ability of groups to freely form and operate in the open. It is also because, as mentioned earlier, interest group activity in nonpluralist societies is often manifested differently and usually less formally than in pluralist societies, and because other aspects of the politics and government in nonpluralist systems seem more important (see section 12.1.). However, there is a body of research on nonpluralist systems with some work being conducted by applying similar techniques to studying groups in pluralist societies. Most information on group and interest activity, however, has to be gleaned from general studies of individual countries or phenomena such as political development.

So this is a disparate group of scholars using eclectic techniques, their commonality being an interest in how organizations, elites, and broadly defined interests, including social movements, achieve their goals in societies where representation and the right to organize is restricted or even banned. With a few exceptions, most scholars publishing on nonpluralist groups and interests would not see themselves first and foremost as interest group scholars, but as specialists in a particular country or region or in some other aspect of the politics of these societies.

4. The Comparative School. The focus here is the comparison of national group systems, individual interest groups and interests (sectors), among other topics, across liberal democracies. Some work also exists on comparisons across nonpluralist societies (particularly former communist regimes) and between pluralist and nonpluralist societies (for example, Ball and Millard 1987). Although there is no separate group of scholars conducting comparative research (most comparativists also conduct research on individual countries), since the late 1970s many comparativists have been from outside the United States and have been schooled in the neocorporatist tradition. The shift from a pluralist to a neocorporatist approach in comparative interest group studies can be traced, in large part, to Schmitter's influential article "Still the Century of Corporatism?" published in 1974 (see chapter 10).

5. The International Perspective. There is no clearly defined subfield of interest group studies within the academic subject of international relations. Furthermore, like scholars of nonpluralist systems, few scholars of international politics would consider themselves primarily interest group specialists. Nevertheless, a growing body of literature exists covering the activities of a host of international organizations, like Greenpeace (an environmental group) lobbying international organizations such as the United Nations (UN) as well as lobbying national governments. When these studies use a theoretical approach, it is often based on a theory taken from the field of international relations, such as regime or transnational theory, as the traditional theoretical approaches considered above (particularly pluralism and corporatism) are less applicable to group activity outside of the nation state and its subdivisions (see chap. 13).

1.6. THE TWO MAJOR CATEGORIES OF SUBJECT MATTER OF INTEREST GROUP STUDIES

Having outlined the major theoretical traditions of interest group studies and the broad categories of focus of scholars, we now briefly identify the types of subject matter that have been studied. As indicated above, in the United States this subject matter has been divided into two broad categories: one is concerned with groups as organizations and their internal dynamics; the other is concerned with interest group activity in the public policy process. These categories do overlap, and many studies combine both. Furthermore, as also indicated above, there is criticism of this division of the subject matter (F. Davis and Wurth 1993) for a variety of reasons. One of these is that it tends to exclude certain types of groups from study—mainly informal and certain governmental interests. Nevertheless, this categorization is a useful starting point for understanding the subject of interest group studies. And the broad definition of interest group used by several contributors to this *Guide*, plus the comprehensive subject matter covered, effectively deals with the shortcomings of this twofold division.

The Internal Dynamics of Interest Groups: Origin, Organization, Maintenance, and Demise

This area of study includes: how and why interest groups develop; how they are organized, including the role of group leaders and members; how groups make decisions about strategy and tactics; how groups are able to maintain their existence, even after their original goals may be achieved or no longer relevant; and why some groups disappear while others survive.

The major research in this area has been conducted by American scholars, and probably the most important work in this regard is Mancur Olson's *The Logic of Collective Action* (1965). However, the findings from this area of group studies has general application to the origin, organization, maintenance, and demise of organized interest groups throughout the world. Many entries in this *Guide* deal with aspects of this subject area, but the major examination is in chapter 5.

Interest Groups in the Public Policy Process

In contrast to the study of the internal dynamics of interest groups, the subject matter of this aspect of group studies is concerned with the public political activity of interest groups. It includes a wide range of topics such as: how the socioeconomic and political system affects interest group activity and lobbying; how interest groups organize for political purposes and the strategies and tactics they use; factors determining group success; and issues regarding the effects of interest groups on the political system, such as how they advance or inhibit representation and democracy in pluralist societies.

Studies of interest groups in public policy making fall into five categories, regarding the type of political system studied.

1. The Study of Individual Countries. Most scholarship has focused on the activities of interest groups in the public policy process in individual countries, particularly liberal democracies, but there is also some work on nonpluralists societies (see chap. 12). The country most studied has been the United States, for the reason explained in the last section. Studies of individual countries cover a wide range of subjects: from general studies of the country's interest groups as a whole, to the study of individual groups, to the study of policy communities (a number of groups in the same policy area, such as education), to studies on the details of particular strategies and tactics.

2. State, Provincial, and Local Interest Group Activity. The least existing scholarship, though the amount is increasing, deals with interest groups and the public policy process in states, regions, and local jurisdictions. Again, most of this work, perhaps 90 percent or more, has been conducted on jurisdictions in the United States, particularly on U.S. state politics; but some also exists on Canada and Australia.

3. Comparative Interest Group Studies. This subject area was covered above in identifying schools of focus of interest group scholars. In terms of volume, it likely places second to work on individual countries. Like studies on individual countries, comparative studies cover a gamut of topics.

4. Interest Groups in Nonpluralist Societies. This subject area, as also mentioned above, is a catchall for a very disparate and eclectic body of literature, much of which only incidentally deals with interest groups and interests in the public policy process.

5. Interest Groups in International Politics and Policy Making. Unlike the subject area of nonpluralist interest activity, the studies in this subject area are often directly concerned with interest groups and their effect on public policy. However, in terms of the number of studies and the extent of literature, this area, like that of nonpluralist studies, is relatively small and offers much opportunity for new research.

1.7. TYPES OF STUDIES AND METHODS OF STUDY

Now that we are familiar with the subject matter of group studies, one more important aspect to explain has to do with the types of studies and methods that interest group scholars use in conducting research. Regarding their methods, as explained in reviewing the problems of group studies above, scholars use a wide range of systematic techniques, often various techniques in combination, that extend from normative analysis to various levels of empirical analysis employing social scientific methodology. It is not necessary to explain these approaches in detail at this point in the *Guide*, but rather to be aware that various methods are used. Chapter 15 is devoted to the methods and techniques of research on interest groups. Before consulting the individual entries in this book, it is useful, however, to be familiar with the types of approach or focuses of study that form the body of literature on interest groups.

Four Approaches and Their Combination

Broadly defined, there are four major approaches to interest group studies.

1. Theoretical Studies. This type of study attempts to develop an explanation of some aspect of interest group activity. These studies stem from very ambitious attempts to develop grand theory (general theories of interest groups) such as: Mancur Olson's (1965) attempt to develop a general explanation of group formation and maintenance; Gray's and Lowery's (1996a) work, built on Olson's, that explains the composition of the range of groups (the so-called group universe) in U.S. state politics; work by Bianchi (1986b) that attempts to explain interest group activity in the Third World; and transnational theory regarding the activities of interest groups in international politics.

2. Comprehensive Studies of Interest Group Activity. Here the goal is to develop a broad understanding—the big picture of interest group activity in its various dimensions (a sort of Charles Darwin approach of identification), such as: which groups operate in a particular jurisdiction, the strategies and tactics that they use, the extent of their influence, as well as many other topics. Schlozman and Tierney (1983) and Heinz et al. (1993) have attempted to do this for Washington, D.C., while Thomas and Hrebenar (2003) have attempted it for U.S. state politics. The British Interest Group Project, organized through the University of Aberdeen in Scotland, attempts to do this for Britain. And there have been several comparative studies that attempt to do this across Western democracies (for example, Ehrmann 1958; van Schendelen 1993). Although their numbers are increasing, there are relatively few comparative studies because of the large resources of money and time required. Often these projects are supported by large grants from public agencies, like the National Science Foundation (NSF), or private bodies, like the Pew Charitable Trusts. Some of these studies last for years, including periodic updates. The ongoing Gray and Lowery study on U.S. state politics, for example, began in the mid-1980s. Like theoretical studies, comprehensive studies of interest group activity are best left to scholars well versed in the literature and who have experience in various research techniques.

3. Studies of a Particular Aspect of Interest Group Activity. This approach takes one aspect of interest group activity—such as the origin of groups, lobbyists, the role of groups in the electoral process, the relationship between political culture and interest group activity, legislative lobbying, interest group power, and so on—and examines it in various ways. This could include examining the aspect over time, across jurisdiction in a country (such as states or cities), and even examining it across countries. As the entries in this *Guide* indicate, this is the focus or approach of many interest group scholars. This type of study is also best left to experienced scholars; such studies are also often supported by public or private funds.

4. Case Studies. These comprise by far the largest category of work in the interest group literature. Case studies can include: a detailed analysis of a particular interest group or interest; the circumstances surrounding an incident in a group's history, such as a decision to enter a political coalition with another group or groups; or the examination of a particular policy issue and the groups involved in it, such as President Clinton's attempt to enact national health legislation in 1993–94. Case studies are useful for three reasons.

First, they are "essential for description, and are, therefore, fundamental to social science" (King et al. 1994, 44). Second, they can be used to demonstrate general arguments and to test hypotheses and theories. Finally, they allow for an "intensive examination of [a phenomenon] even with limited resources" (Collier 1993, 107). As Collier also noted, "the decision to analyze only a few cases is strongly influenced by the types of political phenomena under study and how they are conceptualized" (Collier 1993, 105). Interest groups are particularly amenable to case studies. They are discrete organizations: it is easy to study the National Rifle Association (NRA), Greenpeace, the American Federation of Labor-Congress of Industrial Organizations (AFL-CIO), or the AIDS Coalition as individual units, whether the focus is on organizational, electoral, or policy making issues. Moreover, case studies allow a researcher to examine groups over time (longitudinal studies) and thus to focus on continuities and changes. A case study is the best type of study to embark on as a student or newcomer to interest group research.

While it is important to be aware of these four major approaches to interest group studies, in the practice of research, rarely does a study fall within one approach but usually combines approaches. That is, most studies have more than one goal. For example, many case studies have been conducted to test certain general theories. These include several studies of specific groups to test Mancur Olson's (1965) general theory of why people join groups. And comprehensive studies of group activity are rarely undertaken simply to gather factual data (though these are, in themselves, very useful); but more often studies are done to develop general theories or explanations of such phenomena as group influence, the strategies and tactics that groups use, how lobbyists spend their time, or how partisanship might affect the role and success of groups, as well as many other phenomena.

1.8. GUIDELINES FOR USING THIS BOOK

The overview of interest group studies in this chapter shows that there is a vast body of literature on various aspects of interest groups and their role in political systems. Consequently, this presents a challenge in regard to what should be included and excluded from this *Guide* and how to organize the entries. This concluding section explains the rationale behind the content and organization of this book, plus the more or less common format of individual entries.

The major factor determining this organization and content was the intended readership for this *Guide*. It is primarily intended for undergraduate and graduate students who need an initial and comprehensive overview of the major research on various aspects of interest group studies. The book will also be useful to political scientists, other academics, and those teaching courses on interest groups; those who need a succinct explanation of particular aspects of interest group studies (for course preparation, for developing class assignments, or for reference in their own research) will also find this *Guide* helpful.

Content: Coverage, Types of Sources Cited, and the Content of Entries

In terms of the general content of the book, because much of the literature and research on interest groups has been conducted on the U.S. political system, and as the major readership of this *Guide* will likely be American, much of the material focuses on various aspects of American interest group activity. However, a review of the contents pages reveal that this reference book covers the entire field of interest group studies as explained in the overview above (see section 1.6.). As with most handbooks on academic literature, the entries do not provide an in-depth review of each subject. The book is a primer for more in-depth study and for generating ideas for research projects.

Regarding the language and type of sources cited, although this *Guide* seeks to include research on interest groups from around the world, for reasons of practicality, readership, and the market for the book, it confines its sources to those in English. However, the sources in this book are not confined to those in political science or to academic works. Works from other disciplines, such as history, economics, sociology, and several areas of popular writing, are cited when they are important or the only sources available in a particular field of interest group studies. For the most part, the book does confine source references to those published in book or article form found in libraries, as these are easily available. Some references are also made to sources available on-line. But because they are not so readily available, few references are made to papers presented at academic conferences (see section 2.4.). However, when a conference paper is the only source or major source on a subject (or when it is particularly valuable), it is cited.

Each entry more or less includes the following information: first, an explanation of the concept or area of interest group studies; second, an overview of the status of knowledge on the subject; third, a review of the major literature on the topic, including various interpretations when they exist; and fourth, an evaluation of the literature regarding its extent, the gaps that exist, problems of analysis manifested, fruitful areas for further study, and so on. The sections of each chapter are self-contained but are also intended to integrate with other parts of the chapter. The introduction to each chapter provides an overview of its contents to facilitate this integration. The final chapter of the book, chapter 15, provides an introduction to conducting research on interest groups and will be useful both to the newcomer to political science research and those needing a refresher on the basic element of research.

Organization of Material

Many approaches could be taken to organizing the vast amount of material available on interest groups, none of which would be perfect or entirely avoid overlap. The organization adopted here is intended to facilitate easy access to the material, to avoid as much overlap as possible, and to serve the needs of the intended readership. In addition to the detailed subject listing in the contents of the book, the following points will be useful in tracking down subject matter.

One aspect of the book's organization is that it more or less uses the division of interest group studies set out in section 1.6. above. Thus, there are chapters, containing several entries, that devote themselves to major topics: such as the origin, maintenance, organization, and mortality of interest groups (chapter 5); the role of interest groups in the public policy process (chapter 7); the comparative analysis of interest groups (chapter 10); interest groups in pluralist systems (chapter 11); interest groups in nonpluralist, transitional, and developing societies (chapter 12); and interest groups in international politics (chapter 13).

A second organizational aspect is to include specific entries on the major theories associated with interest group studies and how interest groups affect the socioeconomic environment in political systems in general, including concerns about interest groups. This is covered in chapters 3, 4, and 14 respectively.

A third aspect is to provide extensive reference to interest groups in U.S. politics. This is done in chapter 2, covering sources of information in U.S. interest group studies; chapter 6, on interest group activity in U.S. national, state, and local politics; and in chapters 8 and 9, which deal with individual interests and interest groups in U.S. politics (with some reference to these interests in other countries), such as business, labor, education, environmentalists, senior citizens, and gun control.

Inevitably, there is overlap with some topics being covered by two or more entries, either because they are central to the understanding of several aspects of interest group studies, such as policy networks or peak associations, or because they are referred to in the overview in one place, as in this chapter and in chapter 2, but are dealt with in more detail in another part of the book.

However, where overlap occurs, such as with the topics of pluralism and corporatism, great effort has been made to integrate the treatment of these topics, including the use of cross-referencing, and to prevent repetition of explanation and of reference sources. In fact, by following up on these cross-references, the reader can acquire a more extensive under-standing of the topic. In the case of corporatism and neocorporatism, for example, the concept is explained and the major literature is reviewed in section 3.4.; an in-depth review of how the concept is used in comparing interest group activity across countries is provided in chapter 10; its importance in the interest group politics of several individual Western European democracies is treated in various entries in chapter 11; and its use and adaptation in several transitional and authoritarian systems is cov-ered in some entries in chapter 12.

Chapter 2

Sources of Information on Interest Groups in the American Political System: An Overview

Anthony J. Nownes

2.1. INTRODUCTION

Where does a student or researcher go to find information on interest groups? What are the major sources—popular and academic—to consult? Mainly by explaining the major research on interest groups in American politics, this chapter provides an overview of these sources. In doing so it also provides insight into two questions regarding the academic study of American interest groups: (1) What has been the focus or concern of interest group studies and who have been the major scholars working in these areas?; and (2) What have been the major academic trends in this field and what are the major scholarly works that they have spawned? Even though the emphasis of the chapter is on interest groups in American politics, much of the material, especially that on group origin, maintenance, and mortality, has relevance for understanding group activity in other political systems.

The five major sources on group studies explained here are (1) popular writing, (2) textbooks, (3) conference papers, journals, and monographs, (4) major interest group studies contained in monographs and journal articles, and (5) primary data sources.

2.2. POPULAR WRITING: NEWSPAPERS, MAGAZINES, AND BOOKS

By far the largest body of writing on interest groups is found in the thousands of newspapers and magazines throughout the world. The authors of these articles may simply interview one or two people with different views on an issue, as might be the case for a reporter on a small newspaper; or they may conduct an in-depth investigation, such as those frequently found in *The New York Times, Newsweek*, and the political watchdog group Common Cause's publications. In the early 1990s, for example, the Associated Press (AP) published a series of articles on lobbying in all 50 U.S. state capitals. But even the most comprehensive studies by newspapers and magazines must be selective in their research. Moreover, to the extent that such pieces are subject to editorial policy, their objectivity may suffer.

Book authors who aim for a wide, popular readership also employ a variety of information-gathering techniques. Some, like Geoffrey Birnbaum, a journalist and author of *The Lobbyists: How Influence Peddlers Get Their Way in Washington* (1992), and Birnbaum and Murray, *Showdown at Gucci Gulch: Lawmakers, Lobbyists and the Unlikely Triumph of Tax Reform* (1987) base their work on their own observations of the political scene. Others, like Pat Choate, whose *Agents of Influence* (1990) analyzes the power of the Japanese lobby in Washington, D.C., produce mild exposés based on preconceived notions. These authors are selective about their research and its presentation.

Still other authors aim to write how-to books on lobbying or organizing interest group campaigns. Examples include: Wolpe and Levine, *Lobbying Congress: How the System Works* (1996); Donald deKieffer, *How to Lobby Congress* (1981) and his *The Citizen's Guide to Lobbying Congress* (1997); and on lobbying at the state level, Dorothy Smith, *In Our Own Interest* (1979), and Guyer and Guyer, *Guide to State Legislative Lobbying* (2000). These authors rely on their own or others' expertise as practitioners to write their books.

Despite its often unsystematic and selective research methods, and its advocacy of particular causes or points of view, popular writing is often the only available source of information on some aspects of interest group activity. This was the case, for instance, with information on interest groups in many states until the late 1980s. Thus, popular writing can be a starting point for research and can also provide examples and anecdotes to illustrate academic work.

2.3. TEXTBOOKS

Textbooks are intended for a nonexpert, but more informed readership than newspapers, magazines, and popular books. There are two types of interest group textbooks: standard textbooks and readers. In addition, some texts combine a treatment of interest groups and political parties.

Standard Textbooks

Standard textbooks are a mix of the often ad hoc, unsystematic research of popular writing and the structured, systematic methods used in scholarly writing such as in a monograph, which is a book presenting the results of research, usually on a narrow subject. In essence, a textbook on interest groups is a synthesis of various types of information on the subject, both popular and scholarly. Thus, the authors of textbooks draw upon a range of sources in varying combinations, including some that contain extensive original scholarly research, which makes their text more like a monograph and often useful as a reference source. Other textbooks are simply a collection of essays presenting various types of academic and popular information and explaining basic principles with some insights from the author.

Four examples of early standard textbooks are: Zeigler, *Interest Groups in American Society* (1964); Zeigler and Peak, *Interest Groups in American Society* (1972); Ornstein and Elder, *Interest Groups, Lobbying and Policy Making* (1978); and Wootton, *Interest-Groups* (1970). Since the mid-1980s the major textbooks have been: J. Berry, *The Interest Group Society* (1997); Browne, *Groups, Interests and U.S. Public Policy* (1998); Hrebenar, *Interest Group Politics in America* (1997); Mahood, *Interest Group in American National Politics* (2000) and his *Interest Group Politics in America* (1990); Mundo, *Interest Groups: Cases and Characteristics* (1992); Nownes, *Pressure and Power: Organized Interests in American Politics* (2001); Wootton, *Interest Groups: Policy and Politics in America* (1985); Ainsworth, *Analyzing Interest Groups: Group Influence on People and Politics* (2002); Wright, *Interest Groups and Congress: Lobbying, Contributions, and Influence* (1996); Schlozman and Tierney, *Organized Interests and American Democracy* (1986); and Lowery and Brasher, *Organized Interests and American Government* (2004). The latter four contain considerable original research.

Because of the relatively small number of textbooks on American interest groups, besides Birnbaum (1992) cited above, the following popular texts provide useful supplements: Phillips, *Arrogant Capital: Washington, Wall Street, and the Frustration of American Politics* (1994); Rauch, *Demosclerosis: The Silent Killer of American Government* (1994); Simpson and Sabato, *Dirty Little Secrets* (1996); and Silverstein, *Washington on $10 million a Day* (1999).

Readers

Readers are edited volumes of articles by different authors that often contain the results of research conducted by the authors. Two of the early, pioneering readers were Zisk, *American Political Interest Groups: Readings in Theory and Research* (1969), and Salisbury, *Interest Group Politics in America* (1970). Since the mid-1980s there have been three major interest group readers: Cigler and Loomis *Interest Group Politics* (2002), Petracca, *The Politics of Interests* (1992), and Herrnson, Shaiko, and Wilcox, *The Interest Group Connection* (1998 and 2003). The Herrnson, Shaiko, and Wilcox reader has been published twice and the Petracca reader only once, while the Cigler and Loomis volume is in its sixth edition; serious students of group politics should consult earlier editions (1983, 1986, 1991, 1995, and 1998).

The National Focus of Textbooks and Readers

With few exceptions, textbooks and readers on U.S. interest groups focus primarily on groups at the national level in Washington, D.C. A few include some references to or contributions on interest groups in the states (see, for example, Hrebenar 1997; Lowery and Brasher 2004; Nownes 2001; Petracca 1992; Cigler and Loomis 1991 and 1995); but there is virtually no treatment of local interest groups in texts and readers. This bias toward national group activity is likely due to the higher profile of politics in Washington, D.C., perhaps a belief—true or false—that students will not be interested in state and local group activity, and probably the academic training of the authors and editors which focusing mainly on national politics.

However, an understanding of the activities of state and local interest groups reveals much about group behavior and the development of interest group systems and provides a more balanced view of group activity in U.S. politics and government. Several scholars have recognized this. As a consequence, since the late 1960s and particularly since the mid-1980s, there has been increasing scholarly attention to state and local interest group activity, as well as intergovernmental lobbying in books, chapters and articles. To acquire a more comprehensive perspective on the extent and type of interest group activity in the United States, textbooks and readers must be supplemented with these additional sources on state, local and intergovernmental group activity. For some initial direction in this regard, see sections 2.5., 6.4., 6.5., and 6.6.

Texts Combining Interest Groups and Political Parties

As explained in chapter 1, interest groups and political parties are the most important political organizations linking citizens to government in liberal democracies (like the United States). They are closely interrelated in that parties are, in effect, an umbrella organization for several interest groups. For this reason, many colleges in the United States—though rarely in other countries—have a course titled, "Political Parties and Interest Groups" and texts covering both parties and groups serve the needs of such a course. The classic work combining the two organizations is V. O. Key, *Politics, Parties & Pressure Groups* (1964). Key was a pioneer in the study of parties and groups at both the national and state levels and the first edition of his book appeared in 1942. Two other examples of such texts are Ippolito and Walker, *Political Parties, Interest Groups, and Public Policy: Group Influence in American Politics* (1980) and, more recently,

Hrebenar, Burbank, and Benedict, *Political Parties, Interest Groups, and Political Campaigns* (1999). Unlike most texts devoted solely to interest groups, the Key and Hrebenar, Burbank, and Benedict volumes include several examples from the American states. To varying degrees, these parties and interest group texts also treat the important interrelationship and interdependence of parties and groups. This relationship is dealt with in some detail in section 4.5.

2.4. CONFERENCE PAPERS, JOURNAL ARTICLES, AND MONOGRAPHS

In contrast to textbooks, the major sources containing original research on interest groups are found in academic papers presented at conferences, in journal articles, and in monographs. The nature of monographs was outlined above. Here we explain the purpose and sources of conference papers and identify the major journals publishing interest group research.

Conference or Convention Papers

Conference (sometime called convention) papers (generally 5,000–6,000 words in length, about thirty double-spaced, typed pages) usually include initial findings of a research project and are presented at a professional conference for feedback from other scholars with a view to developing them into a journal article or monograph. Each year interest group scholars (as well as other political scientists) gather at conventions across the United States and in other countries to disseminate and obtain the latest research on interest groups. The largest meetings in the United States at which interest groups are considered are the Western Political Science Association (March), the Midwest Political Science Association Meeting (March/April), the American Political Science Association (APSA) Meeting (late August/early September), and the Southern Political Science Association Meeting (November). Several other regional conferences are also held. Each association publishes a preliminary program, usually sent only to association members, in which papers on interest groups can be identified. Those not attending these conferences can usually obtain the papers by contacting the author(s). The APSA now has its papers posted on a Web site. However, as stated in chapter 1, since these papers are not available through libraries and bookstores, they have been largely excluded from the sources cited in this *Guide*.

Political Science and Other Journals

Articles presenting original research on interest groups are published in several academic journals in the social sciences and sometimes in business journals and law reviews. Articles from these numerous journals form a major source of the research and literature on interest groups presented in this *Guide*. The political science journals that most often include articles on group politics are the *American Political Science Review* (*APSR*), *American Journal of Political Science* (*AJPS*, formerly the *Midwest Journal of Political Science—MJPS*), the *Journal of Politics* (*JOP*), the *Political Research Quarterly* (*PRQ*, formerly the *Western Political Quarterly—WPQ*), the *Social Science Quarterly* (*SSQ*), the *American Politics Quarterly* (*APQ*), *Polity*, and *Legislative Studies Quarterly* (*LSQ*).

An extensive, sometimes long-drawn out review process by scholars is involved regarding articles submitted to these refereed journals, resulting in most manuscripts submitted being rejected. Thus, ideally, only the most thorough and cutting-edge research is published. However, because of the extensive review process, by the time many articles are published they are two to three years old.

2.5. MAJOR CATEGORIES OF RESEARCH AND THEIR FINDINGS

The major sources of interest group studies are the numerous research projects conducted by interest group scholars. Using a similar classification of the areas of interest group studies set out in chapter 1, here we divide these studies into: (1) group formation, organization, maintenance, and mortality; and (2) several aspects of groups in the public policy process.

Group Formation, Organization, Maintenance, and Mortality

Interest group scholars have spent more time on the topic of group formation, organization, and maintenance than any other topic, but only recently have come to study group demise. To the earliest scholars, the issues of formation and maintenance were not particularly vexing. Truman (1951), for example, concluded that group formation was the natural result of people with shared interests coming together to protect these interests—especially if they were threatened. However, this pluralist demand-side notion of group organization was decimated by Mancur Olson in his landmark book, *The Logic of Collective Action* (1965). He argued that because most political interest groups seek collective goods, rational individuals will *not* spontaneously join groups that serve their interests. For Olson, the key to successful mobilization is either coercion (such as mandatory membership in a trade union) or the provision of selective incentives (such as a magazine or reduced cost life insurance) that accrue only to members.

Mancur Olson's work became popular just as groups proliferated in the late 1960s and early 1970s. As such, it spawned a number of critiques and extensions. This body of literature suggests that while Olson's basic framework is valid, the barriers to group formation may not be quite as daunting as he concluded. Many scholars have suggested, for example, that individuals do not engage in the type of cost-benefit analysis Olson suggests (for example, Frohlich and Oppenheimer 1978; Moe 1980; Kerry Smith 1985). Others argue that Olson's theory ignored a number of non-material benefits of collective action including fun, prestige, status, conviviality, and even altruism and morality. To support these claims, a number of empirical studies confirmed that individuals often join groups for reasons other than narrow economic self-interest (for example, Axelrod 1984; Chong 1991; Godwin and Mitchell 1982; Rothenberg 1988).

One crucial element in group development that Olson ignored is the group leader. As Salisbury (1969) notes, the empirical study of group formation has shown that a group entrepreneur—someone who designs a group's incentive structure and stimulates group membership—is often crucial to group success. To Salisbury, the entrepreneur is an important part of the formation puzzle that Olson identifies, because members do not spontaneously join together to protect their interests.

Though they tinker with his basic framework, most of Olson's critics implicitly accept it. Jack Walker (1983) is an exception, however. He argues that the key to group formation is not the ability to attract individual group members, but rather the ability to procure patron support. Walker concludes that wealthy patrons, especially private foundations, wealthy individuals, the federal government, corporations, and other interest groups, "play a crucial role in the initiation and maintenance of groups" (Walker 1983, 402). Patrons are so important, Walker concludes, that they are often the impetus for group formation. They seek out entrepreneurs and provide them with "seed money" and a raison d'être.

In addition to his work on the origin and maintenance of groups, Walker (1983) sparked an interest in the demise or mortality of groups; but in the absence of data, he only speculated on the subject. However, in an extensive study of interest groups in the American states, Gray and Lowery (1996a) gathered considerable data on group mortality. They show that the demise of groups can affect the composition of the range of groups operating and can skew it toward business or public interest groups. Their findings and the consequences of these results, as well as an extensive review of research on group origin and maintenance, are covered in chapter 5.

Interest Groups in American Politics and the Public Policy Process

A host of studies have been conducted on the role of groups in the public policy process in America, mainly at the national level but increasingly at the state level and, to a lesser extent, at the local level. Here we outline five major categories of studies, those relating to: (1) the makeup of the interest group universe; (2) groups in the electoral process; (3) lobbying and lobbyists; (4) interest groups in states and communities; and (5) the question of group influence.

1. The Make-up of the Interest Group Universe. The types of groups operating at the national level, or the composition of the *group universe*, as it is termed in interest group studies, has been of interest to political scientists since the 1950s. Not until the 1980s, however, was an empirically based portrait of the group universe developed. Two landmark studies, Jack Walker (1983) and Salisbury (1984), first defined the broad contours of the Washington group universe. Walker found that since the 1960s the number of politically active interest organizations had skyrocketed. The most pronounced growth was in the number of public interest (citizen), or what he called "non-occupational," groups. Walker's study confirmed the conventional wisdom that business, occupational, and labor groups dominated the interest group universe.

Following Walker's research, Salisbury (1984) conducted a large-scale study of Washington-based interests and concluded that the last few decades had witnessed an astounding increase in the political activity of *institutions*. Churches, states and local governments, foundations, public interest law firms, colleges and universities, hospitals, and think tanks, he found, had become ubiquitous. Perhaps the only thing Walker and Salisbury missed was the astounding expansion of political activity by individual corporations since the 1960s (Vogel 1978; Ryan, Swanson, and Bucholz 1987; G. Wilson 1981).

Overall, the research suggests that the traditional membership group, characterized by face-to-face interactions between individual members, shared goals and interests, and regular meetings, constitutes a minute portion of the group universe, which is now dominated by institutional interests (see section 4.3.).

What Walker and Salisbury did for understanding the composition of the group universe at the national level, Hrebenar and Thomas (1987, 1992, 1993, 1993a, 2003; see also Thomas and Hrebenar 1991a, 1992a, 1996b, 1999a, and 2003), and Gray and Lowery (1995 and 1996a; Lowery and Gray 1998) have done for understanding the group universe in the American states. These studies show that developments in the states reflect national trends with variations in the makeup of the group universe determined by the socioeconomic composition and other factors of a particular state (see sections 6.2. and 6.4.).

2. Interest Groups in the Electoral Process. There are many ways that interest groups can become involved in the electoral process, including: endorsing candidates, providing campaign workers, working to pass or defeat referenda, initiatives and recall petitions, helping to get out the vote on election day, and contributing money. In the United States, the most common and well-studied aspect of group electoral activity is the role of political action committees (PACs) in funding candidates for election to office. There are several texts that provide a basic overview of

PACs and their activities (Magleby and Nelson 1990; Sabato 1984 and 1990; Sorauf 1988b and 1992) as well as numerous articles. Scholarly attention to PACs has focused largely on three topics: (1) the variety of PAC organizational forms; (2) patterns of PAC giving; and (3) the effect of PAC money. Because PACs are a relatively new phenomenon in American politics, much of the early attention focused on describing them and their activities (see Sabato 1984; Sorauf 1988b). The question of most interest to students of PAC giving is: What is the effect of PAC money? The literature on the relationship between PAC giving and congressional voting is far from definitive with some studies saying PACs do have influence, some concluding that they do not, while others are inconclusive. The role of interest groups in elections and the controversy about the influence and role of PACs is covered in sections 7.3. and 7.4., respectively.

3. Lobbying and Lobbyists. The period since 1980 has seen major advances in research on lobbyists and the activity of lobbying. Thomas and Hrebenar (1996b, 124) have given us the best generic definition of a lobbyist: "a person designated by an interest group to represent it to government for the purpose of influencing public policy in that group's favor" (but see section 7.6. for a more extensive definition). Most lobbyists (between 75–80 percent) work for, and are employed by, a single organization. Thus, the popular portrait of the lobbyist as a hired gun who works for the highest bidder and moves from client to client, is inaccurate (Rosenthal 2001; Salisbury 1986; Thomas and Hrebenar 2003).

Much of what we know about *what lobbyists do* in Washington, D.C. comes from Schlozman and Tierney (1983) and from Heinz et al. (1993). At the state level much of the knowledge comes from Rosenthal (2001), Hrebenar and Thomas (1987, 1992, 1993a, 1993b; see also Thomas and Hrebenar 1999a and 2003), and Nownes and Freemen (1998a and 1998b). The Nownes and Freeman research has shown that much of what lobbyists do is not directly contacting public officials but monitoring what is happening to legislation. Nownes and Freeman have also advanced our knowledge on the role of female lobbyists in the states. And Nownes and Giles (2001) and Nownes, Cooper, and Giles (2002) have begun to explain the role of lobbyists at the local level.

Building upon work by Bauer, Pool, and Dexter (1963), Milbrath (1963), and James Q. Wilson (1973), Schlozman and Tierney (1983) examined the range of advocacy activities in which groups engage. They conclude that while classic forms of lobbying such as testifying at legislative hearings and helping to draft legislation continue to predominate, more groups than ever before seek influence through unconventional activities such as grassroots lobbying, protest, and litigation. They also conclude that Washington lobbying "has become both more sophisticated and more professional" (Schlozman and Tierney 1983, 365). Unfortunately, no one has conducted a follow-up study, and thus we do not know precisely how much lobbying has changed in the last 20 years. We do know, however, that grassroots lobbying is more prominent than ever before (Cigler and Loomis, 1995a).

4. Interest Groups in the American States and in Communities. Although the vast majority of interest group research on the American political system concerns Washington-based groups, there is a growing body of literature on interest groups in the states and on group activity in local politics.

Since the mid-1980s there have been two major comprehensive studies of interest groups in the fifty states. One is an ongoing study organized by Hrebenar and Thomas drawing on interest group scholars from across the United States, published in four volumes—the West, South, Midwest and Northeast—(Hrebenar and Thomas 1987, 1992, 1993a, 1993b, 2003) and in several articles and chapters (e.g., Thomas and Hrebenar, 1991, 1992a, 1996b, 1999a, and 2003). The other is a much more empirically based study by Gray and Lowery (1996a) concerned with the diversity and density of interest group systems and how this relates to economic complexity and development of a state. Other important studies on state interest groups and lobbying include Rosenthal (2001) and Nownes and Freeman (1998a and 1998b) cited above; and Brunk, Hunter, and Wilson (1991) and Brace (1988) on interest groups and economic development. For an overview and critique of this state in interest group literature and its relationship to interest group theory, see Gray and Lowery (2002).

The major problem with studying local interest groups is, of course, that there are literally thousand of cities, towns, and counties, plus special districts across the nation. Consequently, no equivalent to the Hrebenar and Thomas and the Gray and Lowery studies on the states has been conducted on local interest groups. Neither is there a general textbook on local interest groups. However, one way to get an overview of group activity at the local level is to consult texts on urban and local politics such as Brian Jones (1983, chap. 7) and Christensen (1995, chap. 11). Much of the research on groups at the local level has centered around questions as to the extent or lack of pluralism in local politics (Abney and Lauth 1985; Paul Peterson 1981). In this *Guide*, sections 6.4. and 6.5, respectively, examine state and local interest group studies in more depth.

5. Interest Group Influence. Assessing the influence of groups on public policy poses several analytical challenges. First, many variables affect any given policy decision. Second, group visibility and access do not necessarily translate into influence. Third, what looks like influence is often just agreement. All the same, many scholars have grappled with the question of how much influence groups have over policy outcomes. There have been several different explanations and several different approaches to analyzing group influence.

The earliest works saw groups as important players in so-called subgovernments or networks of policy-making (Cater 1964; Freeman 1965), particularly those entities known as iron triangles (see section 7.16.), composed of legislative committee members, program administrators, and interest group representatives. The argument went that these subgovernments resolve their differences without interference from outsiders and render policy decisions that benefit all three elements, often at the expense of the public at large (Garceau 1941; Charles O. Jones 1961; McConnell 1953 and 1966). However, in a breakthrough study still widely cited, Heclo (1978) argued that, by the 1970s, in the wake of congressional reforms, group proliferation, and the wide availability of technical information, the iron triangle metaphor was seriously incomplete. Heclo argued that coherent subgovernments had given way to amorphous issue networks characterized by permeable boundaries, unstable coalitions of interests, a lack of centralized control, and a large roster of active and interested participants. His formulation continues to resonate because it helps explain a number of recent developments in group activity in the policy process, including group proliferation. Others argue that subgovernments have given way not to wide-open issue networks, but rather to narrow issue niches (Browne 1988 and 1990).

Perhaps the most important study of group impact yet conducted is Heinz et al. (1993) which maps the terrain of four policy domains and gives coherence to the issue network concept. Rather than tight triangle-like structures, the authors discover permeable networks of policy-making. Overall, this study describes a system of policy-making that seems to approach pluralism (albeit an imperfect, elite pluralism—see sections 3.2. and 3.3.). In many policy domains a multiplicity of groups compete for policy gains, active interests are varied and reflective of a wide variety of policy alternatives, and there are no central players to mediate or integrate disparate group demands.

As part of their study of state interest groups, Hrebenar and Thomas identified ten major factors that determine the power of individual interest groups, the most important of which appear to be the extent to which the group is needed by government and the relationship between the group's lobbyists and public officials (Thomas and Hrebenar 1999a). For a more extensive review of the research and approaches to interest group power and influence see section 7.17.

2.6. PRIMARY SOURCES OF DATA ON INTEREST GROUPS

Primary information is data about an interest group provided by the group or obtained from some other source, such as a state public disclosure agency, which has not been edited or interpreted by some person or organization not associated with the group. Primary data is of various kinds, including: membership figures past and present, the group's budget, lobbying expenditures, issue and position papers, annual reports, newsletters, magazines and pamphlets, and tax returns.

One way to gather primary data about individual interest groups is to contact a group directly. Not all groups and organizations are willing to share their data with the public (private businesses, trade, and professional associations are usually very reluctant to do so), but several are, particularly public interest groups. Materials from these organizations can provide a good sense of what a group does, how much money it has, how it spends its money, what its policy goals are, who constitutes its membership, how it recruits members (if it has any), what it offers supporters, and how successful it is.

How does one find out how to contact a group? Most university libraries and many public libraries contain directories of interest groups. The most comprehensive and useful directory is the annual *Encyclopedia of Associations* (2003), which contains basic information on virtually every membership organization in the United States. The annual editions of *Washington Representatives* (2003) contain an extensive list of lobbyists active in Washington politics. They also contain information on whom each individual listed represents, and how he or she can be contacted. There are several other volumes that contain information on specific *types* of groups. For example: the *National Trade and Professional Associations of the United States* (2001); *Public Interest Profiles 2001–2002* (2002), which is an index of citizen groups; the *2001 National Directory of Corporate Public Affairs* (Steele 2001); and the *Annual U.S. Union Sourcebook* (2001). In addition, the Federal Election Commission's (FEC) various materials on PAC contributions and other campaign information not only provide the names and addresses of interest groups but are also valuable sources of primary data. For a profile of over three hundred major interest groups in the United States that combines secondary and primary data, see Ness, *Encyclopedia of Interest Groups and Lobbyists in the United States* (2000).

Most of the volumes mentioned above focus on Washington-based groups and representatives. However, information is also available on how to contact state groups and lobbyists. First, the publisher of the *Encyclopedia of Associations* (which focuses on national organizations) also publishes a companion volume *Encyclopedia of Associations: Regional, State and Local Organizations* (2001). Second, because every state in the United States requires that lobbyists and interest groups register (though the criteria for whom must register vary across states—see section 14.4.2.), the states are excellent sources of information on groups and their representatives. Most states publish annual—sometimes quarterly—lists of registered lobbyists and organizations. Some publish much more extensive data on PAC contributions, conflict of interest information, etc. These lists are generally available to the public either free or for a small fee.

Finally, a tremendous amount of primary source material is available on the Internet. Several interest groups have their own websites (home pages) on the Internet, and dozens more create sites every day. Most Internet search programs (for example, Internet Explorer or Netscape) will enable you to access a group's Internet site simply by typing in the group's name and choosing the search option. The typical group site contains basic information on group policies, goals, and membership, as well as details on how to contact and join the group. An increasing amount of data from the FEC and state lobby regulation agencies is also available on-line.

2.7. CONCLUSION: LOOKING BEYOND THE AMERICAN PERSPECTIVE

This chapter has focused mainly on sources of interest group studies on the American political system. Anyone studying interest groups, both Americans and those from outside the United States, should certainly be well acquainted with these major sources, since in many ways the United States is the classic interest group system and the most advanced in terms of the development of interest group organization and lobbying techniques. A good argument can be made that a gradual *Americanization* of lobbying techniques is taking place in many capitals around the world from Canberra to Ottawa to Brussels. However, as chapter 1 points out, in some ways the American system is atypical of interest group activity across the Western world. This is especially the case with the role of groups in the policy making process. For example, the role of PACs is virtually nonexistent in other countries, and lobbyists are far less visible publicly and often have different roles.

To acquire a comprehensive understanding of interest groups we need to look beyond the American system. In fact, by doing so we can obtain new insights into the American system itself. Just as learning a foreign language forces a person to learn new things about the structure and usage of their own language, so studying interest group activity in other political systems provides insights not otherwise obtainable and helps place one's own system in a new light. In this regard, several chapters and entries in this book are particularly useful, as well as being valuable in broadening knowledge on interest groups in general. Chapter 10 on comparative interest groups, chapter 11 on interest groups in pluralist systems, chapter 12 on groups in nonpluralist systems, and chapter 13 on interest groups in international and transnational politics are especially recommended for broadening this understanding. In the next chapter, the contrasting perspectives between the entries on pluralism (see section 3.2.) and corporatism and neocorporatism (see section 3.4.) will also aid in this regard.

Chapter 3

General Theories of Interest Group Activity: Pluralism, Corporatism, Neo-Marxism, and Other Explanations

3.1. INTRODUCTION

Clive S. Thomas

The entries in this chapter outline the major theories developed by scholars to explain the overall relationship between interest groups and political systems and to show how groups interact with the policy process. As such, these theories, explicitly or implicitly, offer an approach, or methodology, for understanding interest group activity in the broad, or macro, context of political systems.

   The theories and explanations considered here apply primarily to pluralist or liberal democratic systems. There are three reasons for this. First, these systems are the subject of well-developed theories based upon extensive research. Second, the vast majority of the work on interest groups has been conducted on groups and group systems in pluralist democracies. Therefore, a focus on macro explanations of groups operating in these systems is a prerequisite for understanding many aspects of interest group studies. Finally, no general theories of interest group activity apply to a wide range of nonpluralist systems in the way that pluralism and neocorporatism apply to virtually all pluralist systems. Perhaps this is because nonpluralist regimes cover such a gamut of systems, from mild forms of authoritarian regimes such as Franco's Spain to extreme totalitarian systems like communist Albania. The lack of applicable theories may also stem from the fact that, for a variety of reasons, scholars who study nonpluralist systems have not been as concerned with interest groups as scholars of pluralist democracies have been (see section 12.1. and chap. 12 in general). Therefore, a general explanation or explanations of interest group activity in nonpluralist systems awaits development.

However, elements of the explanations in this chapter do apply to some nonpluralist systems. This is particularly true of corporatism (see section 3.4.) in many of its manifestations. In fact, all the models and explanations considered here apply somewhat to the relationship of interest groups to nonpluralist systems. Even pluralism (3.2.) is relevant from the practical perspective of a competition of interests in some nonpluralist regimes, even though the official ideology of a regime may deny such competition.

The two major explanations considered in this chapter are "Pluralism and its Modifications" (see section 3.2.) and "Corporatism and Neo-corporatism" (see section 3.4.). Pluralism is not only the major theory explaining the interaction of interest groups in pluralist systems—it is also the major theory in political science in the Western world. Neocorporatism, a much more recent theory, dates from the 1970s, though its derivations go back much further. It is associated primarily with the social democracies of Western Europe and is much less applicable to the United States. However, although pluralism and neocorporatism are the most widely accepted and well-documented theories of interest groups operating in pluralist systems, both are wanting in theoretical rigor and thus are inadequate explanations of group activity.

Of the other theories and explanations considered here, Elitism (see section 3.3.), the major modified form of pluralism, is important enough to warrant its own entry. Three entries, "The Responsible or Strong Political Party Model" (3.6.), "Statist-Centered Approaches" (3.7.), and "Neo-Marxist Approaches" (3.8.), are further variations on the pluralist model and, to some extent, the neocorporatist model, emphasizing certain elements in the political system (political parties, the government, business, etc.) as key in understanding the role of interest groups. The other two entries, "Political Economy Approaches" (3.5.) and "New Institutionalism" (3.9.), were primarily developed as methodological approaches and not as macro explanations but are still relevant to the macro role of interest groups. Economic approaches, through schools of thought such as rational choice and public choice, provide a perspective on how groups are affected by and affect the political system and society. Such approaches also offer insights into the internal operations of interest groups. New institutionalism attempts to explain how institutions—such as legislatures, executive departments, and so on—affect how interest groups operate and the role of this interaction in shaping policy outcomes.

None of the theories and approaches examined here offer a complete explanation of the way that interest groups relate to and are affected by pluralist political systems. Another important factor to note is that each theory or approach has been subject to the ebb and flow of academic fashion—a once-prominent theory may become unpopular because it seems less applicable, or simply because it does not agree with a current academic fad. Neocorporatism is one example. Its popularity in the 1970s gave way to a sense that it was less relevant by the 1990s. Likewise, the *new* in new institutionalism emphasizes its proponents' belief that institutions do matter, whereas for a long time scholars believed that institutions had little influence on interest group activity. Despite these caveats, each theory or explanation offers its own important insights. And, either directly or indirectly, each provides a critique of the others. In the absence of an existing grand theory of interest groups, the explanation of group activity at the system level in a particular pluralist system—Germany, Japan, the European Union, for example—likely lies in a combination of two or more of the theories presented here.

3.2. PLURALISM AND ITS MODIFICATIONS

Grant Jordan

Pluralism is often seen as the dominant paradigm—the theoretical orthodoxy—in political science and the most realistic description of how interest groups relate to the political system in liberal democracies, especially in the United States. The basic elements of pluralism are encapsulated by Dye and Zeigler (1970, v):

> Pluralism portrays the American political process as competition, bargaining and compromise among a multitude of interest groups . . . the modern pluralist accepts giant concentrations of power as inevitable . . . The pluralist realizes that the unorganized individual is no match for giant corporate bureaucracy, but he hopes that countervailing centers of power will balance each other and thereby protect the individual from abuse. Groups become the means by which individuals gain access to the political system. The government is held responsible not by individuals but by organized groups and coalitions of groups (parties). The essential value becomes participation in, and competition among, organized groups.

However, few, if any, concepts in political science and interest group studies have been as subject to debate as pluralism.

First, although it is the prevailing ideology, few scholars actually identify with pluralism. Dye and Zeigler (1970) point out the irony that while most American textbooks are founded on a pluralist perspective, challenging the orthodoxy of pluralism is common in these texts. Second, there is a major debate about what actually constitutes pluralism and whether it is a realistic description of the policy process and the role of interest groups in liberal democracies. Third, the nebulous nature of a core concept of pluralism and the dispute over whether it is an accurate description of policy making has led to several modifications of pluralism. And fourth, scholarly perspectives on pluralism have emphasized different interpretations and elements at different times.

Vaguely Defined Orthodoxy: The Debate about the Essence of Pluralism

Pluralism is a remarkably ill articulated idea. It has primarily been associated with Robert Dahl, but even he noted that once he had used the term:

> Later . . . the concept took on a life of its own. . . . In fact, a good deal of the "theory" consisted of interpretations by hostile critics who sometimes constructed a compound of straw men and inferences from the work of assorted writers who by no means held the same views. (Dahl 1984, 232)

Pluralism has often been discussed, as in the *Federalist Papers* numbers 10 and 51 (Brock 1965), without the use of the actual term. It is also a label that is applied to very different concepts. It has been repeatedly rediscovered, but as Gunnell (1996, 254) puts it, "the continuities are less evident than often assumed." In this vein, Polsby (1980, 112), while noting the relevance of writers such as Tocqueville (1835), Bentley (1908), Herring (1929), and Truman (1951) to the rediscovery of pluralism in the 1960s, also observes that there really was no core body of work on pluralism to be refurbished. What existed was a set of loosely connected ideas and assumptions labeled *pluralism*. However, since James Madison, its central proposition has been that competing interests should be encouraged in order to prevent an overly powerful government. This general orientation to interest groups regards them as "generally beneficial, or at least benign" (M. Olson 1982, 35).

The main post–World War II criticism of pluralism was that it was too uncritically descriptive and too optimistic in assuming some kind of fair contest among protagonists. Pluralist scholars were well aware of these shortcomings. Lindblom (1979, 523), for one, responded emphatically, "Who can deny so obvious a point?" to the criticism that not all interests are equally represented in the process. And Dahl's complacent-sounding argument that the United States had a "political system in which all the active and legitimate groups in the population can make themselves heard at some critical stage in the process of decision" has been regularly misquoted by critics of pluralism. Dahl's claim was not that all interests were equal. He went on to say:

> To be "heard" covers a wide range of activities . . . Clearly, it does not mean that every group has an equal control over the outcome. In American politics . . . control over decisions is unevenly distributed; neither individuals nor groups are political equals. (Dahl 1956, 145)

The key to Dahl's argument was not that power was held *equally* but that is was *dispersed.* Dispersal of power among the institutions of government (national, state, and local; bureaucratic and elected; presidential and legislative) facilitates access by different sorts of groups. In this vein, Dunleavy and O'Leary (1987, 13) point to what Sartori (1976) termed the "value belief dimension" to pluralism. Sartori (1994) argues that this feature of liberal democracy grew out of religious toleration—a formula invented by minorities to assure their own freedom, not to protect the freedom of others. A concomitant of the respect for different values has been a suspicion of authority (Dahl 1984, 235, 238).

Imprecision about the nature of pluralism stems in part from the term's variety of uses and manifestations. Here the work of Polsby (1980) is particularly instructive. Pluralism-as-methodology he termed *Pluralism 1*, defining it as eclectic methods of gathering data. This is a research strategy that examines how decisions are made and how conclusions are drawn. Pluralism 1 was an explicit challenge to the stratification, or elitist, perspective on pluralism that Polsby charged built its conclusions into the research design. In a similar vein, Bachrach and Baratz (1962) say, "the pluralists' . . . approach to and assumptions about power predetermine their findings and conclusions."

Pluralism 2 is pluralism as conclusions about the distribution of political power. It involves propositions purporting to describe a certain state of affairs in one or more local communities. Polsby writes:

> Pluralists . . . see American society as fractured into congeries of hundreds of small special interest groups, with incompletely overlapping memberships, widely differing power bases, and a multitude of techniques for exercising influence on decisions salient to them. (Polsby 1980, 118)

> The pluralist 2 state of affairs . . . has one or more characteristics . . . dispersion of power among many rather than a few participants; competition or conflict among political leaders; specialization of leaders to relatively restricted sets of issue areas. . . . (Polsby 1980, 154)

Less clearly, Polsby also identifies *Pluralism 3*. This is the broad intellectual tradition that accepts some human nature assumptions that predict that individuals act out of self-interest.

Pluralism Modified and Qualified: The Variety and Imprecision of Neopluralisms

Terms like *neopluralism, reformed pluralism, critical pluralism,* and even *anti-pluralism* are repeatedly coined by scholars seeking to draw distinctions from earlier variants (Jordan 1990). One widely used term that embraces many of these forms of modified and qualified pluralism is *elitism* (see section 3.3.). Yet there is no consensus on how to label these modified or qualified forms. Nor is there much detail on how they differ from actual (as opposed to caricatured) pluralism, which is, broadly speaking, portrayed by its critics as being a system of open competition. But this is an unfair oversimplification. Dunleavy and O'Leary (1987, 23) correctly observe that "pluralists know that citizens do not and cannot directly control policy-making in polyarchies." Furthermore, those writing in a pluralist vein see a clear pattern of segmentation in the policy process.

This segmentation was clearly expressed in the 1960s and 1970s by the use of the term *subgovernment:* the idea that within the political system there exists close, often closed arrangements between powerful entities that have a symbiotic relationship. An extreme form of this was the "iron triangle" (see section 7.16.). Here policy was made through closed sectoral arrangements between the relevant civil servants, politicians, and cliental interest groups.

The issue network school (see section 7.16. and chap. 10) revision of pluralism—whose proponents see a web of loosely related government agencies, politicians, and groups in the same issue area—suggests that since the 1980s a pattern of conflict and confusion has superceded the neatness of iron triangles with their clearly identifiable subgovernments (Gais, Peterson, and Walker 1984; Heclo 1978). Salisbury et al. (1992, 149) also suggest that the subgovernment approach is too rigid. Jeffrey Berry (1989, 245) concludes that "the majority of recent empirical studies are critical of the traditional subgovernment thesis." This is a return to the image of the structureless conflict of competitive pluralism.

In their study of British interest groups, Richardson and Jordan (1979) focus on the idea of policy communities. These are clusters of interests and policy makers around policy areas that tend to be more permanent than issue networks. In these communities interest relations are often institutionalized, and certain groups are excluded from the policy process. This is a form of pluralism where there is no single united elite in all policy areas. For example, the privileged elite in the arms industry is not the same elite as in the tobacco industry. M. Smith (1990) characterizes the work of Richardson and Jordan, with its central idea of policy communities, as *reformed pluralism.*

McFarland (1987, 130) sees Lowi (1979), Schattschneider (1960), and McConnell (1966) as anti-pluralists, while Nordlinger (1981, 157, 223) describes this school as neopluralist. Neopluralism, Nordlinger argues, is unlike the original form in that these writers believed that resource inequalities are dispersed cumulatively. Dunleavy and O'Leary (1987, 293) note that neopluralists "are prepared to concede what conventional pluralists always denied, that business interests occupy a position of special importance compared with other social interests." Their neat distinction is undermined, however, by the fact that no pluralists are cited espousing such a naïve position.

Three Generations of Pluralism

Since the turn of the twentieth century, the concept of pluralism has undergone various permutations. McClure (1992) identified three broad generations of pluralism.

1. Anglo-American, Mainly Philosophically Oriented Pluralism. This developed at the turn of the twentieth century as a philosophical reaction against the monistic state—the superior and most politically legitimate entity in society and in public policy–making. Perhaps the definitional weakness of pluralism can be explained by its origins as an anti-theory. This first interpretation of pluralism denied, on normative grounds, the exclusive legitimacy of the sovereign state and argued that churches, trade unions, and other groupings were not inferior. The state, according to British historian Harold Laski, "is only one among many forms of human association and, as compared with other associations, has no superior claims" (Coker 1924, 93). Conjoined with this normative belief about legitimacy was a descriptive body of literature that sought to describe how the political machine really worked. This literature argued that policy making was not confined to official institutions, a notion which discredited legalistic and constitutional accounts of how policy was made and replaced debates about the desirability of particular policies with descriptions of policy making.

2. American Empirical Pluralism. Roughly spanning the period from the 1920s to the 1960s, McClure's second category could equally be labeled *Pressure Group Pluralism/Mainstream Pluralism.* From Odegard (1928) to Herring (1929) to Truman (1951), authors looked at empirical practice and found groups active in the process. Pluralism, now less philosophical in orientation, was transmuted into an anti-theory challenging elitism, as in Dahl (1961). Gunnell (1996, 259) notes that, like Madison, Herring and his successors once more transformed a disease of democratic government into a theory of democracy. Dahl (1956) developed this orientation into a sort of empirically derived democratic theory.

Besides generating an academic critique, this generation of pluralists also produced another reaction. As McLennan (1995, 1) notes, for many during the 1970s *pluralism* was a term of abuse. American pluralism was taken by many radicals as representing little more than an apology for corporate capitalism, a Western Cold War ideology parading as mature social science. In another sort of critique pluralism was presented in a simplified, caricatured form, which set the stage for neocorporatism to appear as what was perceived by many as a novel discussion of interest group-governmental cooperation (Almond 1988). In fact, neocorporatism was not entirely distinctive when judged against the subgovernment approach to pluralism (see section 3.4. and chap. 10).

3. Multiple Identity or Postmodern Pluralism. As McClure (1992, 112) writes: "For the third time this century, arguments for 'pluralist politics'

45

are beginning to command attention." Thus, to use the words of Schlosberg (1998), this third generation might also be labeled *Resurrected Pluralism*. In this variant there is no longer a zeal for empirical understanding, but instead a normative reformism. Apart from an acceptance of the irreducible complexity of society and the sheer multiplicity of valid differences, such sources see politics as a process involving the construction of identities by, and in, organizations. Regarding the resurrection of pluralism, Schlosberg observed:

> After years of thorough critique, a purge of sorts, and, finally, relative obscurity, political and social theorists have begun to resurrect pluralist themes, even if they often do not acknowledge the term. . . . [and]. . . . only a few would consciously label themselves "pluralist." (Schlosberg 1998, 583, 591)

While there is an endorsement of pluralism from these postmodern quarters, the links should not be exaggerated. If there is a willingness to endorse the anti-monist theme of the first generation and the beneficial effects of organizational proliferation, there is also, as Schlosberg notes, a remarkable reluctance to be seen as endorsing the work of pluralists. Dahl and Lindblom are commended only for shifting away from early pluralism. The current sentiment is that the earlier pluralists were right, but the later pluralists were wrong. However, suspicion of the notion of the state provides a linking thread—though few authors even loosely attached to a pluralist position use the term *the state* with much frequency. Instead, they find all kinds of alternatives: *government, administration, elected politicians,* and *civil servants,* among others. Descriptive pluralists find major divisions in what others see as a unified state. They particularly focus on the friction between government departments and the divisions within capitalist representation (Vogel 1996).

Schlosberg (1998, 608) has portrayed the re-emergence of this philosophical interest as rescuing pluralism from the land of the theoretical untouchables. However, the new pluralism is normative, whereas mainstream pluralism was primarily empirical. Pluralism has been transformed as well as disinterred. There is a return to abstract conceptualization that predates the first pluralist generation (see also Eisenberg 1995).

Conclusion: A Practical Perspective

Logically, pluralism as a practical system cannot deliver satisfactory outcomes for all interest groups. Pluralism is a political arrangement that recognizes that interest groups have different needs, which they may legitimately pursue. Resources do matter in determining access and influence for a group, as do institutional structures (see section 3.9.), including the role of government (see section 3.4.) and political arrangements such as the strength of political parties (see section 3.6.). And even the promise that different views can be addressed given time is little compensation for frustrated organizations, as there is no guarantee that their political position will improve in an acceptable period of time. If a group is a political loser, it is only a small consolation that many other groups with equally few resources have, at different times over different issues, had satisfactory outcomes.

3.3. ELITISM

Andrew S. McFarland

Here, *elitism* refers to a school of interest group analysis, one that replaced the pluralist school and that, since 1980, has been giving way to neopluralism. Some of the writers on elitism, cited below, would likely not have considered themselves part of a particular school, but in retrospect this appears to be the case. And if this school's influence is now waning, its impressive accomplishments have left a permanent mark upon political science.

In regard to interest groups, elitism might be better termed *multiple elitism*, because it refers to the perspective that the American political system is largely controlled by multiple separate elites, each dominating a particular area of public policy. Multiple elitism agrees with pluralism in rejecting the concept of a single power-elite in control of the important issues of American politics. However, while elitism regards policy areas as controlled by an elite particular to that area, pluralism sees policy as being influenced by a much wider range of individuals and interests.

The most enduring contribution to elitist theory is Mancur Olson's *The Logic of Collective Action* (1965). Olson argues that many widely shared but diffuse interests will not organize into groups because successful lobbying provides a collective benefit to all interested parties regardless of whether they contributed to the group. Many public policy benefits, such as national defense or reducing air pollution, contribute not just to the individual but to the public good. Olson argues that we cannot expect rational people or organizations to contribute to an interest group because they will receive the benefit of the group's actions anyway. On the other hand, rather small groups sharing a few interests—often a group of several business corporations—will organize because each corporation will see that its contribution is necessary to the political success of the group. Such a well-organized economic interest will then constitute a well-organized elite in some area of policy, overcoming more widely shared and diffuse interests that do not organize into groups.

A second extremely influential elitist theory work is Lowi's *The End of Liberalism* (1969, 1979). In an analysis parallel to Olson's, Lowi argued that vaguely specified legislation has invited particularistic interest groups to form coalitions with friendly members of Congress and agencies of the executive branch. Such coalitions, or "little governments," separately control many policy areas because congress and the president lack the political will and means to intervene, and widely shared interests cannot organize to provide countervailing power.

Another extremely influential writer of this school was Schattschneider, who argued in *The Semisovereign People* (1960) that manipulation of the scope of conflict is the basic variable of politics. Consequently, cliques of particularistic special interests constantly work to prevent the public from knowing about some issues and thus prevent wide participation in decision making on those issues. Schattschneider believed that American politics tends to be dominated by multiple-elites, which need to be balanced by stronger political parties. See section 3.6.

A fourth elitist theorist was Edelman, who wrote *The Symbolic Uses of Politics* (1964). He argued that small groups that have a continuing economic interest in a given public policy would pursue this interest continually in an effective, rational manner. On the other hand, the wider public is less informed about many public policies and easily convinced that reform legislation has dealt with an issue when in reality it has not. The legislation is a symbol of the public's concern about a problem; the legislation, however, may not be effectively implemented because interests affected by the reform will organize to undermine the legislation. The general public does not understand this, regards the legislative symbol as operating according to design, and loses interest in the matter, thereby leading to renewed elite control. Given the many policy areas, Edelman argues, this process leads to multiple elitism.

A fifth multiple elitist theory is Stigler's (1975) theory of regulation. Stigler argued that governmental regulatory laws act in the interest of the regulated, who mobilize interest groups to pass and maintain such laws to serve their own narrow interests, not those of the general public.

Other writers on elitist theory are discussed in McFarland (1991), which includes a useful bibliography.

3.4. CORPORATISM AND NEOCORPORATIST THEORY

Peter J. Williamson

Corporatism (and its recent variant, neocorporatism) is a cooperative relationship between government and certain interest groups, the goal of which is to provide stability and predictability in the development and implementation of policies, most often economic policies. Because of corporatism's focus on economic policies, economic interests and producer groups are the most common participants in corporatist and neocorporatist arrangements. The two major producer groups are business and labor.

Agriculture and the professions are often included under business or labor as employers or members of the labor force. Because three sectors of society—government, business, and labor—are generally involved, negotiations are often referred to as *tripartite negotiations* and outcomes as *tripartite agreements*. And this institutionalized and authoritative process of negotiations between the key sectors of society is referred to as *neocorporatist* or *interest group intermediation* and sometimes as *concertation* (C. Thomas 1993a, 9).

Neocorporatism as a model of interest group activity in pluralist democracies is just thirty years old. However, its predecessor, corporatism, has a lengthy pedigree. Under the influence of Catholic moral philosophy (as well as secular conservative nationalist strands), corporatist economic and social theory advocated using employer organizations and trade unions as agents of state economic and social regulation. This placed corporatism somewhere between the free market and administration by a state bureaucracy. Peter Williamson (1985, Part 2) provides an overview of this aspect of corporatism, which was influential in continental Europe from the middle of the nineteenth century to World War II. During the twentieth century corporatist ideas were adopted by a number of authoritarian regimes (Williamson 1985, Part 3), including Nazi Germany and Fascist Italy and in the Latin-Iberian world (Malloy 1977; Pike and Stritch 1974).

Despite its historical association with reactionary thought and authoritarian practice, from the mid-1970s corporatist studies of interest groups in Western industrialized democracies became an important field. To distinguish this type of corporatism from its authoritarian forms, the prefixes *liberal* (liberal corporatism) and *neo-* (neocorporatism) were usually attached. The launch of neocorporatism can largely be attributed to Schmitter's (1974) essay "Still the Century of Corporatism?" He argued that in liberal democracies the institutional structures of organized interests displayed similarities to some non-democratic regimes; however, in democracies these similarities arose from societal pressures rather than state imposition. For this reason, corporatism in authoritarian and non-pluralist regimes is sometimes labeled *state corporatism*, while in liberal democracies *societal corporatism* serves as a synonym for neocorporatism.

Central to Schmitter's thinking was the idea of organized interests being structured into a limited number of peak associations (see section 4.10.) for each function or interest—ideally one peak association for business, one for labor, one for agriculture, and so on. This single representation limited competition among groups, and membership took on features of compulsion, which reduced the possibilities of membership breakaways. The state granted groups a representational monopoly in return for certain compliant behaviors. In setting forth an ideal model, Schmitter explicitly provided an empirical and theoretical alternative to the predominant pluralist view of interest group politics. Schmitter and the neocorporatist generation of scholars raised the status of *corporatism* within democracies beyond a casual label for any structured, close relationship between interest groups and public authorities. The usage of *corporatism* in this less structured form of developed pluralism in describing the Western European experience is found in Beer (1956, 7), Eckstein (1960, 427–28), LaPalombara (1964, 222–46 and 283–84), Rokkan (1965, 113), Lowi (1969, 70), and Heisler (1974, 42).

Elements of Neocorporatist Theory and Phases in Their Development

In the 1970s, following Schmitter's lead, corporatist studies addressed the idea of interest intermediation in contrast to interest representation (Schmitter and Lehmbruch 1979). The idea of intermediation suggested that interest groups ceased to be merely representative bodies and became agencies through which member interests were mediated with the state. Similarly, interest groups could assume responsibility for implementing public policy, thereby regulating the economic behavior of their members. At the time, most attention focused on incomes and prices policies. Such policies—negotiated by and often implemented through trade union and employer organizations—highlighted the possibility that members would sacrifice some of their autonomy for a wider public interest (Lehmbruch 1979a and 1979b).

This emphasis on institutional structures was not the exclusive approach of early neocorporatist theory, although it has remained predominant. In effect, two variants of neocorporatism emerged from the outset (Schmitter 1982). The second, as represented by Lehmbruch (1979a and 1979b) and Panitch (1979), concentrated on participation in policy making and implementation—an emphasis that makes this variant difficult to distinguish from corporate pluralism as developed by Rokkan (1965) and Heisler (1974). However, the vast majority of corporatist theorists did not share pluralist assumptions about politics and society. This was most obvious in discussions of the proactive role of the state under corporatism (Cawson 1978; Jessop 1979; Panitch 1979). Neocorporatist writers spent much of the 1980s trying to firm up a theoretical distinction from conventional pluralism (Cawson 1986; Schmitter 1985; P. Williamson 1989).

The essential element in the development of corporatist theory was the need for a theory of the state. The state was seen as serving institutional interests of its own, which influenced the nature of corporatist structures and the political decisions they produced. There was, however, no agreement within corporatist writings about state theory and neo-Marxist class-based theories (Jessop 1979; Offe 1981, 1984; Panitch 1979, 1980) and perspectives based on the state as a powerful organization in its own right (Schmitter 1979, 1985) were developed Cawson (1986 and 1988).

Scholars who provided the most coherent and considered view of the state and corporatism, argued that the state should not be viewed as a unified whole. The failure of corporatist theory to clarify the position of the state meant that corporatist conclusions remained broadly speculative, often based more on a scholar's own values than on a validated analysis of the evidence.

Corporatism was concerned not just with intermediation and political representation, but also with the involvement of interest associations in implementing public policies agreed upon with state bodies. This posed the question of whether private interest groups were effectively being given public authority as agents of the state. This would involve consequences for interest representation not considered in conventional interest group analysis.

Many empirical examples of this "private interest government" were identified and analyzed in the corporatist literature. Streeck and Schmitter (1985) highlight the issues effectively, and reveal the breadth of such arrangements in all types of sectors, although the principal example was self-regulation by unions and employer organizations of prices and incomes policies. However, while these developments challenged traditional views about private interest groups and public authorities and, in the British case, generated considerable debate about accountability (C. Crouch and Dore 1990), the broader significance remained ambiguous. In one way such developments could be seen as an extension of pluralist interest representation into the state's administrative machinery itself, while an alternative, less favorable, view was that this was a state takeover of private interest groups to its own ends. The studies were never quite able to provide the answer to this fundamental question.

Lehmbruch and Schmitter (1982) decisively took corporatism into the area of comparative politics. This analysis ranked countries on a corporatism league table and then measured the association between the ranking and political and economic outcomes. The hypothesis tested was that corporatist arrangements, through facilitating stable management of the economy, improved "governability" (Schmitter 1981) and economic performance (Schmidt 1982).

Studies did not stop here, but extended to consideration of what socioeconomic (especially class divisions and conflicts) and political characteristics supported the development of corporatist arrangements (Goldthorpe 1984; Scholten 1987a). The conclusion was that for corporatism to be adopted and operate successfully, features like a predominance of social democratic or labor parties and restricted socioeconomic differentiation were required (Lehmbruch 1982; Schmidt 1982; Schmitter 1981).

The study of macro-corporatism, or corporatism at the national level, was not the only dimension of corporatism studied in the 1980s. Wassenberg (1982) suggested that a national focus alone gave the misleading impression that corporatism had a monolithic, society-spanning presence. For him, corporatism was more relevant to the study of arrangements at the sectoral or industrial level—*meso-corporatism*. From this viewpoint many comparative studies of different industrial sectors were born. Cawson (1985) provides a comparative review of institutional arrangements of interest organizations in the same industries across several countries from a corporatist perspective.

Neocorporatism As an Explanation of Interest Group Activity: Strengths and Weaknesses

Corporatism opened up an important debate about the wider nature of close and structured relationships between public authorities and seemingly independent organized interests. The traditional pluralist picture was challenged, although it also counter-challenged in turn (Almond 1983; Heisler 1979; A. Jordan 1984). In this respect, corporatism posed, and continues to pose, many interesting questions. However, answering these questions requires both sophisticated theories of interest determination (organizational power in relation to the state) and considerable detailed empirical data. Corporatism produced the latter, but has been unable to deliver the former in a way that would allow the empirical data to be understood by means other than placing it alongside broad theoretical stances about the state and democracy (Cox and O'Sullivan 1988).

Corporatism has never represented a complete alternative to pluralism. From the outset it was recognized that polities were not exclusively corporatist, but had to be placed on a continuum between ideal corporatism and ideal pluralism. Moreover, there were major variances among Western democracies in their ability to achieve neocorporatist arrangements. The United States had not embraced corporatism (Salisbury 1979; G. Wilson 1982), though see Shaiko (1998) for an alternative explanation. Japan had a form of corporatism, but it did not involve labor organizations (Hrebenar 2001; Pempel and Tsunekawa 1979). And Britain had little success in embracing corporatism (Lehmbruch 1982, 21). Corporatism, therefore, appeared to be linked to specific socioeconomic, political, or cultural phenomena and was not a universal development of interest group activity in liberal democracies. This appeared to be the case not only at the national level but also at the sectoral level (Atkinson and Coleman 1989b; W. Grant 1991a and 1991c). Furthermore, Lijphart and Crepaz (1991) contend that corporatism should simply be seen as a product of a consensual democratic political system (as opposed to an adversarial system). This view doubts the centrality of corporatism in creating a consensus to manage the economy. Such doubts are magnified by the inconsistent definition of *corporatism* across corporatist studies (Keman and Pennings 1995).

In addition, by the end of the 1980s corporatist theory faced two empirical challenges. First, the increasing shift to market-based policies by most

Western governments and higher rates of unemployment began to dictate a new agenda for research that was less concerned with regulation involving trade unions and employer organizations. Even where regulation persisted, the state often preferred to deal directly with individual firms (Cawson et al. 1990). Second, there was evidence that organized interests were changing both in terms of their attractiveness as a means of representation and their actual ability to deliver members' compliance. (Schmitter 1989; see also Micheletti 1990b examining the Swedish case).

Given such developments, in 1989 Schmitter published an article provocatively titled, "Corporatism is Dead! Long Live Corporatism!" Interestingly, this article displayed a downgrading of theory and a generally less assured approach. Since then the flow of literature with an exclusive corporatist focus has declined. Yet corporatism as an analytical concept is far from receiving its last rites. There remains a considerable interest regarding corporatist relations in industrial policy, including its relation to the internationalization of markets (Greenwood, Grote, and Ronit 1992a; Martinelli 1991). Likewise, attention has returned to corporatism and macro economic performance in the context of Economic and Monetary Union (EMU) in the European Union (Schmitter and Grote 1997) and questions of governance (Gorges 1996; Marks et al. 1996; Streeck and Schmitter 1991).

Thus, while corporatism has become caught up in addressing the complexity and diversity of advanced polities and economies and has moved on from the greater certainties surrounding the corporatist model in the 1970s and 1980s, there is still mileage in its central question of how democratic pressure politics are given particular institutional arrangements. Corporatism continues to offer insights beyond historical analysis, but does so much more as one piece in the analytical toolbox for exploring empirical data. But today it is much less explicitly presented as *the model* of a system (W. Grant 1991c, 113–14).

See chapter 10 (especially sections 10.2., 10.3., and 10.4.) for the place of the neocorporatist perspective in comparative interest group studies and a critique of its strengths and weaknesses as an explanatory theory.

3.5. POLITICAL ECONOMY APPROACHES AND EXPLANATIONS

Paul Brace and Kellie Butler

Economic theories of interest groups provide insights into both the internal dynamics of groups—particularly the reasons for group membership and its consequences for representation—and the effect of interest groups on the public policy process and on society as a whole. A good example of a general theoretical study of interest groups using an economic approach is Grossman and Helpman, *Special Interest Politics* (2001).

In most areas of political inquiry, studies employing economic approaches have left an indelible mark on contemporary research. For example, Downs (1957) reoriented thinking about the interplay of voters and parties; Buchanan and Tullock (1962) pointed to dysfunction of democratic institutions and processes. These and other studies illustrate the analytical value of accepting human behavior as purposive, leading to less-than-obvious conclusions arrived at through intuition disciplined by logic and precision in theory. While it is difficult to gauge the overall impact of economic approaches, modern political science would be vastly different without them.

Economic approaches have been used to understand interest groups from the early years of the study of political science. Bentley (1908) used an economic approach that focused on political pressure groups. His work helped stimulate the large amount of literature in political science on pluralism. Yet despite Bentley's early efforts, interest groups received scant attention in economic models of political processes until the mid-1960s. In Downs's (1957) model, for example, collective organizations are conspicuously absent. And Buchanan and Tullock (1962) give them only slight attention.

Economic Explanations of the Internal Dynamics of Groups

Mancur Olson's Contribution—Rational Participation in Interest Groups. Olson's *The Logic of Collective Action* (1965) altered the direction of scholarship to include collective organizations by focusing on the incentives for group formation and the biases this may create in the representativeness of groups. Applying the simple logic of the provision of public goods to the outcomes achieved by interest groups, Olson showed that groups face significant obstacles to their formation. The largest impediment is the free rider problem: individuals who may share a group's collective goals have an incentive to be a rational non-contributor to the group because the group cannot deny them the benefits of the policy goals the group seeks. According to Olson, group goals are insufficient to stimulate collective action and not all groups will be able to surmount the free rider problem. Small groups facing lower organizational costs and benefiting from a single large member (one receiving so much benefit to be willing to cover all or a majority of the costs of collective action) and groups with access to selective incentives (material inducements that depend on an individual's contribution to the group, such as a journal or newsletter) that only members receive have special advantages that allow them to form. Because individuals join these groups for reasons besides the group's collective aspirations, this raises fundamental questions about the ability of such groups to represent member interests.

Pluralist theories that viewed groups as natural extensions of member interest were fundamentally contradicted by Olson's theory. By focusing on the necessary and sufficient conditions under which a utility-maximizing individual would join a group, Olson laid bare the precarious and biased organizational footing on which groups form. In so doing, he also questioned the normative interpretations of political scientists that underscored the corrective give and take of interest group participation over the long run. However, one obvious weakness of his explanation is that the material rewards for participation in many groups are quite minor; yet some such groups have large memberships, often without the aid of selective incentives. Olson (1965, 2, 108) allowed that groups may contain "altruistic" or "irrational individuals," and selective incentives may not always be necessary. He proposed that psychology, particularly social psychology, may be more appropriate for studying "groups that are characterized by a low degree of rationality" (M. Olson 1965, 160, 161).

Subsequent studies have identified other motivations besides material gain as reasons to contribute to or participate in interest groups (see, especially, Moe 1980a and 1980b). Purposive and solidary goals have been added to material gain as incentives. Purposive goals as incentives suggest that individuals join a group to achieve the group's ends, while solidary incentives suggest that there are direct benefits from participating in the group that lead some to join. Any single group is likely to offer some mix of all three incentives. Moe suggests that the mixture of incentives can influence a group's internal politics, stability, resilience, and effectiveness over time.

Economic Explanations of the Effect of Groups on Public Policy and Society

Economic Theories of Regulation and the Effects of Groups. In a later work, Mancur Olson (1982) argues that the biases in group formation retard a society's economic development by concentrating resources in the hands of the organizationally advantaged. The dynamics of collective organization confound the efficiencies of the market economy over the long run, although the details and empirical support for this argument have been subject to debate (Brace and Cohen 1989; Gray and Lowery 1988).

Where Olson was preoccupied with the conditions for group formation and their organizational and political consequences, some work by other economists focused on the role of groups in the regulatory process. Specifically, these economists sought to provide explanations for the behavior of regulated industries, regulatory agencies, and the consequences of their interactions in the market and the political system.

These theories challenge the ostensible public interest basis for regulation. A basic premise of these theories is that the primary source of regulation is the regulated industry itself. Contrary to conventional interpretations that view regulations as minimizing negative externalities or prohibiting monopoly, regulation is promoted by industries that, unable to regulate competition privately, seek regulation to create barriers to entry and to punish recalcitrant producers. Thus, industries secure government regulation to overcome free rider problems among competitors and to protect and even increase profits. This phenomenon is referred to as *capture*—an interest group dominating a policy area within an agency. Captured regulatory agencies work to further the interest of industries, not those of the public at large (Demsetz 1968; Stigler and Freidland 1962).

The Public Choice School. Some economists have placed interest groups at the center of their interpretations of government and politics. Theorists such as Buchanan, Tollison, and Tullock (1980) and Tollison and McCormick (1980 and 1981) see government as an arena where wealth transfers and rents (monopoly rights granted by the government) are conferred. The pursuit of economic rents drives much of the political activity of interest groups. The government is organized to supply rents (e.g., licenses, permits, and tariffs) in a manner that allows it to provide entitlements and still maintain the political decision maker's position and power. From this perspective, both government size and organization are largely the result of demand for and supply of economic rents.

Strengths and Weaknesses of Political Economy Approaches

Taken together, economic theories of interest groups provide an understanding of both the internal dynamics of groups and the policy process, helping to explain why the "pluralist choir sings in an upper class accent" as Schattschneider (1960) observed. But the political economy explanation of interest groups in the public policy process is incomplete. It provides a theory of political action that reduces public sector interests primarily to economic interests that are organized. There is clearly much more going on that needs to be addressed.

The economic interpretation of interest groups suggests that large interests organize, support politicians who promote key programs, and thereby extract collective benefits from government. While a satisfactory interpretation on many levels, this view is at variance with some central facts. For example, we know that government is more than a cipher for special interests. We know also that politicians have goals that are not all facilitated by pandering to groups. Furthermore, some interests are created by public policies. In addition, we know that institutional procedures that affect agenda setting and structures that affect preference aggregation can alter the influence of interest groups on public policies.

Ultimately, a more satisfactory picture of interest groups must reconcile the incentives of politicians with those of groups and the manner in which the two interact within political institutions. From such an enriched vantage point, we may better understand the influence of groups relative to public authority, enhancing our understanding of the role of the state in the policy making process.

3.6. THE RESPONSIBLE OR STRONG POLITICAL PARTY MODEL

David J. Sousa

The responsible political party model, sometimes referred to as the strong party model, is used to distinguish the relatively weak, non-programmatic parties operating in the United States from the stronger, more programmatic parties in other Western democracies, especially Great Britain. Epstein (1980) observed that American scholars summarizing the British party model for Americans often used a dated and idealized conception of the realities of British party politics. Still, the responsible party model—which makes clear predictions about the deleterious consequences of party weakness and links interest group power to "overload" and "ungovernability," immobilism, and rising popular alienation from politics (Fiorina 1980)—has shaped scholarly debate on the nature of change and the role of interest groups in democratic nations.

The responsible party model was advanced by scholars and politicians frustrated by the barriers to progressivism caused by the internal diversity of the Democratic Party in the United States and by the growing power of what Schattschneider (1942) called "pressure groups." Advocates of this model typically characterize interest group power as undemocratic, arguing that the "sovereign majority" can rule only through political parties that meet the basic test of responsibility. The argument is that responsible/strong parties: (1) take clear issue positions; (2) choose candidates on the basis of loyalty to the party program, and make renomination contingent upon loyalty to that program; and (3) when in power, work to enact their electoral programs (Lawson 1980). In the absence of strong political parties, interest groups short-circuit majority rule, developing close ties to politicians and party factions in ways that allow them to prevail over the will of the majority.

Schattschneider (1942, 190), the most ardent supporter of the responsible party model, saw pressure groups as "a parasite living on the wastage of power exercised by the sovereign majority" and argued:

> [P]arty government is better than government by irresponsible organized minorities and special interests. The parties are superior because they must submit their fate to an election, and they are responsible to the public. By every democratic principle the parties, as mobilizers of majorities, have claims on the public more valid and superior to those asserted by pressure groups which merely mobilize minorities. Government by interest groups who have never dealt successfully with the majority and never submitted

themselves to the judgment of the public in an election is undemocratic and dangerous. (Schattschneider 1942, 193)

Another ardent endorsement of the responsible party model came in a report by the American Political Science Association's Committee on Political Parties (APSA 1950; for a strong critique of this report, see Kirkpatrick 1971). The argument for greater party responsibility is explained well in Fiorina's (1980) analysis of the problems of governance in the United States during the Carter years.

Advocates of the responsible party model also assert a simplistic (though theoretically interesting) inverse relationship between the effectiveness of political parties versus that of interest groups and the power relationship between parties and groups. The failure of political parties (defined as their inability to adequately represent the interests of large numbers of citizens, effectively respond to emerging issues, and use governmental power effectively to address pressing problems) creates openings for alternative organizations aimed at transmitting group demands and linking citizens to government. Among these alternative organizations are interest groups. Lawson and Merkl (1988) provide a theoretical discussion of the relationship between party decline and the political role of interest groups, social movements, and alternative political parties in addition to case studies of developments in Europe (Denmark, France, Germany, Great Britain, Italy, Poland, Sweden, Switzerland), Ghana, India, Israel, Japan, Taiwan, and the United States.

A prime example of a new organization filling the party power void is the rise of the political action committee (PAC) in the United States. Sorauf (1980 and 1988a) argues that PACs did not begin the process of party decay in the United States, but they have thrived in a legal, technological, and political environment in which parties have struggled to maintain their positions. PACs challenge parties by offering alternative sources of financial and organizational support to politicians, and by pressing issue demands that may conflict with the wishes of party leaders. The rising role of PACs and lobbying groups, coupled with the diminishing position of party organizations, creates a political system far better at "articulating" than "aggregating" or "adjusting" citizen demands (Sorauf 1980).

Sorauf also suggests that there is a "natural cycle in the lives of parties," in which they exercise substantial influence in the early years of democratization and then "lose it in the much greater political literacy, wider political involvement, and newer political agendas of those societies and economies as they mature" (Sorauf 1988a, 284). J. M. Hansen (1991) shows that when interest groups provide electorally valuable resources more efficiently than parties, politicians value ties with groups more than ties with parties. Politicians may also find that they can more effectively define themselves for activists through close alliances with particular interest groups. The proliferation of groups also allows citizens to express their preferences through organizations more effectively than they can through weak, diverse, and aggregative political parties.

Lawson (1980) adds layers of complexity to this analysis, but the body of literature on parties and interest groups suggests that the rise of groups is a common occurrence in countries where political parties are faltering. The complexity of the party-group relationship across Western democracies and some transitional political systems is extensively explored in Clive Thomas (2001a; see also section 4.5.). The conclusion is that parties are not going to disappear because they perform functions not performed by interest groups and other organizations. Instead, as Thomas suggests, they are working to redefine their roles, including their role with interest groups (Thomas 2001a, chaps. 1 and 15).

Some scholars—particularly those studying U.S. state politics (Key 1964, 154–65; Zeigler 1983, 111–17; Zeller 1954, 190–93), but also others, such as Graham Wilson (1990a)—have argued that there is an inverse power relationship between parties and groups: strong parties, such as those in Britain, mean weak interest groups, while weak parties, such as those in the United States, result in strong interest groups. Thus, the interests of certain minority constituencies—those represented by strong interest groups—will triumph over the majority will because there are no strong parties to represent that majority will. Recent research shows that the relationship is much more complex (Thomas and Hrebenar 1999a; C. Thomas 2001a, 95–96, and chap. 15). Strong parties and strong interest groups can coexist as they do in most Western European countries and in some states in the United States, such as New York and New Jersey. This is further evidence that the responsible party model is far more complex than its original advocates understood.

In recent years scholars of rational choice and principal-agent theories have rethought the question of party strength and weakness. They have elaborated, mainly in the U.S. context, on a theory of "conditional party government." The argument is that partisan elections tend to produce legislators "whose policy preferences are similar within and differentiated between" (and perhaps among) parties (Aldrich and Rohde 1997–98, 546). Where elections produce party caucuses with relatively homogenous preferences, those caucuses will endow legislative party organizations and party leaders with the resources necessary to realize collective goals. Where elections produce party caucuses that are sharply divided (e.g., the U.S. Democratic Party in the 1950s and early 1960s), those caucuses will not be willing to grant significant resources and authority to leaders. In the U.S. context the increasing ideological homogeneity of legislative party caucuses, driven particularly by the growing strength of the Republican Party in the South, is thought to have enhanced the power of party leaders and created the conditions of a kind of party government in the U.S. Congress (Aldrich and Rohde 1997–98; Rohde 1991).

3.7. STATIST-CENTERED APPROACHES

David J. Sousa

There is no simple state-centered or statist theory of interest groups or a definable body of literature in the field. Instead, there is a literature that emphasizes one or more of the following four perspectives: (1) The limits of pluralistic, society-centered explanations of outcomes, emphasizing the ways that the autonomy of the state, grounded in a set of policy ideas and the interests of state managers, enables it to pursue its own goals independent of interest group claims; (2) Questions about institutional capacity and the problem of state building; (3) The effects of evolving ideas about the proper relationship between state and society on the ways that interest groups are integrated into the policy process; and (4) Interest groups as a dependent variable—the ways that laws, societal norms, institutions, and political processes may shape the formation, structure, and nature of interest groups and group claims on society.

State Autonomy

The major argument here flows from the observation that "the state is not only affected by society but also affects it" (March and Olsen 1984). Political institutions do not merely provide arenas in which interest groups compete; and public policies do not simply reflect social forces. Institutions and policies shape interest group politics in fundamental ways. Public policies themselves, once adopted, become endowed with separate meaning and force by having an agency established to deal with them. Nordlinger (1981, 1) contends that state preferences are at least as important as group preferences in driving policy, and that "the democratic state is not only frequently autonomous insofar as it regularly acts upon its preferences, but also markedly autonomous in doing so even when its preferences diverge from those of the most powerful groups in civil society."

Institutional Capacity and State-Building

Skowronek (1981) brought a historical perspective to questions about problems of state capacity and advocates broader conceptualizations of the context in which interest groups formulate objectives and press demands. He demonstrated that in mid-nineteenth-century America, courts and parties were incapable of meeting rising societal demands for regulatory action because their very structure, norms, and settled practices "presumed the absence of national administrative capacities" (Skowronek 1981, 248). Settled structures and processes may interfere with the adoption of rational solutions to emerging problems; they may block effective responses to interest group demands. Students of interest group politics must attend to the "fit" between the demands placed upon governments and the state's capacity to meet those demands and be attentive to periods in which it becomes necessary to reconstruct governing ideas and institutions in order to facilitate effective state action to meet emergent demands.

Ideas Have Consequences

The literature on groups has been so focused on the role of interests that it has paid little attention to the role of ideas in motivating group activity and shaping group strategies, tactics, and prospects. Still, the importance of ideas has not been entirely neglected (Landy and Levin 1995). Lowi (1969) focuses on the enormous significance of a "public philosophy" in shaping the role of interest groups in the polity and defining the relationship between state and society. McConnell (1966) offers a compelling analysis of the ways that key tenets of American ideology shaped thinking about the place of interest groups in the political system. More recently, Weir (1992) emphasized the importance of ideas in shaping U.S. employment policy. And in a work focused on explaining differences in natural resources policies, Klyza (1996) emphasizes the importance of ideas in shaping relationships between the state and private power. He demonstrates that without an understanding of the dominant political-economic ideas in a given time, it is impossible to understand either the kinds of demands that private interests place upon the state or the ways that the state defines its (or the public's) interest. Once established and institutionalized, these patterns of demands and definition of interests are difficult to break. Public policy outcomes cannot be understood simply as a reflection of the present constellation of group and institutional forces because of the long shadow that the past—the institutionalized past—casts over contemporary action.

Interest Group Politics As a Dependent Variable

Another, somewhat fragmented, body of literature treats interest group politics (and social movements) as dependent variables affected by state structures, events, and established patterns in public policy (Chubb 1983; Skocpol and Finegold 1982; Tilly 1978). An exemplary work in this tradition is Hattam's (1993) study of the American Federation of Labor's (AFL) "voluntarism" in the United States. Hattam dismisses explanations of the AFL's pursuit of "business unionism" that focus on the heterogeneity of the American labor force as a fundamental barrier to class-based political action. Instead, she contends that the "divided" structure of the American state, and especially the dominance of courts within that divided structure, induced labor leaders to abandon political strategies and focus on economic action. In this case, state structure, coupled with the hostility of judges to labor's political agenda, shaped union strategy in fundamental ways. Thus, it is impossible to understand labor strategy without reference to the nature of the state.

In the social movement tradition, scholars applying the political process model (Costain 1992b; Costain and McFarland 1998; McAdam 1985) emphasize the role that state action plays in triggering social movements and shaping movement strategies and potentials.

3.8. NEO-MARXIST APPROACHES

David J. Sousa

Neo-Marxist theories center on understanding and explaining the role of the state in capitalism. These theories are Marxist because they assume the centrality of class and class conflict in the political economy; they are neo-Marxist because they focus on the state apparatus and on exploring the mechanisms that lead state managers to act in the interests of capital. This theoretical debate among Marxists emerged in the face of the "class compromise" of the post–World War II era, growing affluence in the West, and then the stagflation crisis of the 1970s. The best summary of the major neo-Marxist perspectives on the state is Skocpol's (1981) critical analysis of neo-Marxist explanations for important pieces of New Deal legislation. There are also excellent overviews in Carnoy (1984) and Jessop (1982).

There are three basic neo-Marxist models: (1) The instrumental Marxist or corporate liberal model; (2) The functionalist model; and (3) The structural dependence or class struggle model.

The instrumental model is usually associated with Miliband (1969 and 1977). Instrumentalists see the direct translation of class power into state power, and contend that capitalists control the state by three means: by holding powerful positions themselves, by directing state action, and by dominating normal political processes through the control of politically valuable resources. State policy reflects the interests of the dominant fraction of the capitalist class, but it will not always reflect naked class power. That is, the instrumental model holds that where reforms are necessary for maintaining the stability of the system and the dominance of the capitalist class, those reforms will be forced by the leaders of the capitalist class.

The functionalist model is associated with Poulantzas (1969, 1974, 1975), who argued that the capitalist state, while in some respects autonomous from the capitalist class, performs two vital functions for the reproduction of capitalism. First, the state works to unite the capitalist class, taking and enforcing decisions that at times hurt some sectors of the capitalist class in the interest of maintaining long-term stability. Second, the state works to block the development of working-class consciousness and unity by purveying an ideology of universal citizenship and, at times, by exacerbating racial, ethnic, and occupational divisions. This model was powerfully criticized by Skocpol (1981). She questioned why we should expect that states will always have the institutional capacity, technical knowledge, and prescience necessary to enact policies to serve the long-term interests of capital.

The structural dependence or class struggle model is most closely associated with Block (1977) and Lindblom (1977 and 1982). This school recognizes that capitalists and their allies can assume positions of power in the state, and that business interests will be quite powerful in normal political processes through the effective use of campaign contributions and control over the instruments of persuasion. But the essence of the model is that capitalists do not need direct control of the state, or "ownership" of state managers, to exercise dominant influence. Instead, capitalists' control of decisions about production and investment—and the power to disinvest in the face of unfavorable state policies—ultimately constrains state managers (whatever their ideologies or constituencies) to serve the interests of capital. Since elected officials need a healthy economy to stay in office, and because the state is dependent upon tax revenues generated by business activity and investment, policy making and the policy agenda itself are fundamentally constrained in liberal democracies.

The structural dependence model is difficult to test, though Skocpol's (1982) critique of its applicability to the New Deal case in the United States is provocative. And Przeworski and Wallerstein (1988) find some significant limitations to the model. They suggest that under some circumstances market discipline will indeed constrain demands on the part of social groups for greater consumption (or regulation), but that it is possible for states to largely escape the constraints associated with a structural dependence.

Students of interest groups may find these models (particularly the structural dependence model) useful for orienting their thinking about key developments in the political economies of the West, especially the weakening of labor movements. If union strength contributed to the growth of the welfare state and of economic regulation—if it weakened the structural dependence of the state on capital, what will be the implications of union decline? Can emergent environmental and consumer groups play the same role in challenging the privileged position of business?

3.9. THE NEW INSTITUTIONALIST PERSPECTIVE ON INTEREST GROUPS

Michael J. Gorges

New institutionalism (sometimes referred to by European scholars as *neoinstitutionalism*, see section 10.2.) is "concerned with illuminating how institutional arrangements shape political outcomes by structuring the relationships among contending societal groups" (Thelen 1991, 22). Consequently, new institutionalist analyses of interest groups attempt to elucidate the relationship between institutional structures, interest intermediation, policy choice, and policy impact.

Although there is no one new institutionalism, the approach can be summarized in the fundamental insight that institutions matter, and that political phenomena cannot be understood using rational choice explanations alone, which are criticized for underestimating the importance of institutional context (DiMaggio and Powell 1991, 5). For new institutionalists, institutions—organizational structures, conventional procedures, legal-administrative rules, organizational incentives, and informal institutional structures such as roles and norms, all of which persist over time—are independent variables that influence political choices. Structures and rules influence decisions by shaping actors' goals, and by mediating among actors, leaving their own "imprint on political outcomes" (Thelen and Steinmo 1992, 9). Consequently, the choices of political actors are strongly constrained by institutional norms and rules and "existing institutional arrangements are powerful forces in shaping political interests and the conflicts between them" (Zysman 1983, 295).

Two debates divide new institutionalist scholars: the definition of institutions; and the role institutions play in political and social life. While most definitions include both formal organizations and institutional rules and procedures that structure conduct, others include factors such as norms and class structure (Thelen and Steinmo 1992, 19). North (1990, 3), for example, has defined institutions as "the rules of the game in a society, or more formally, . . . the humanly devised constraints that shape human interaction." The more intense debate is over the degree to which institutions matter; there are three major schools of thought: historical, sociological, and rational choice institutionalism.

Rational choice institutionalists argue that institutions are created by utility-maximizing individuals with clear intentions. Historical institutionalists argue that one of the shortcomings of rational choice institutionalism is that it excludes preference formation from the analysis. They do not deny that individuals attempt to calculate their interests but argue that outcomes are the product of the interaction among various groups, interests, ideas, and institutional structures, and these preferences evolve and should not be viewed as fixed. Sociological institutionalists contend that individual decisions are a product not only of the institutional setting but also of a much larger environment. Individuals find themselves "embedded" in cultural and organizational "fields" or "sectors" that determine "self-interest" and "utility" (Koelble 1995, 232).

In general, new institutionalist scholars focus on two aspects of politics: (1) The conditions under which the institutional environment has an effect; and (2) Institutional change and institutionalization. In their studies of policy making, for example, new institutionalists argue that institutional features of the environment shape the goals and means of participants in the policy making process. In turn, this environment is shaped by two primary actors: the state and professional bodies. Studies of institutional change focus on how and why institutions evolve, and on the processes of institutional reproduction (DiMaggio and Powell 1991, 63–66; North 1990).

Institutionalization, on the other hand, can be defined as "the process whereby social processes, obligations, or actualities come to take on a rule-like status in social thought and action" (Meyer and Rowan 1977, 341). Institutionalization is also seen as a constraining process that forces actors or organizations to "take on the formal and substantial attributes of organizations within which they interact and upon which they depend" (DiMaggio and Powell 1983, 147). This "institutional isomorphism" can be brought about through the coercive action of a state, by one organization recognizing the success of another and attempting to copy it, or when an organization adopts the "conventional wisdom" that certain forms are more "modern, appropriate, and professional" (W. R. Scott 1987, 504).

Turning to the application of new institutionalism to the study of interest groups, as Immergut (1998, 21) notes, "the structure of political opportunities will shape the strategies of organized interests and their beliefs regarding the efficacy of different types of political action." Thus, any study of interest groups that takes into account the role of institutions in accounting for outcomes could plausibly be labeled new institutionalist. Neocorporatist theory, however, provides a particularly insightful new institutional perspective. An explanation of neocorporatism is provided above (see section 3.4.). In regard to its being a new institutional approach to interest group studies we can make the following brief comments.

Neocorporatist theory is part of a new institutionalist approach to politics because of its fundamental assumption that behavior cannot be understood entirely through rational choice or pluralist theoretical frameworks (Schmitter 1989, 62). Initially offered as an alternative to the dominant pluralist paradigm, neocorporatist theory provided new insights into the relationship between the state and civil society as represented by interest groups. Indeed, the theoretical contribution of neocorporatism is that "it takes as a starting point the role of the state in shaping interest representation" (Collier and Collier 1979, 967). The state plays an active role as the "architect of political order," favoring and promoting some groups at the expense of others and thereby profoundly affecting group dynamics. In Schmitter's words, the state is "a constitutive element engaged in defining, encouraging, regulating, licensing and /or repressing the activities of associations" (Schmitter 1982, 260). Neocorporatist theories focus on the institutional devices facilitating the cooperation of private actors in policy formulation and implementation (Schmitter 1974).

From the corporatist perspective, corporatization is the institutional-ization of a pattern of interest intermediation involving an increase in the participation of the official group(s) at the expense of unofficial or unrec-ognized groups. It also emphasizes an increase in the degree to which interest associations can be considered monopolistic, hierarchical, and authoritative. It "entails a fundamental alteration of the manner in which the favored interest groups relate to both the state and their members" (Keeler 1981, 185).

For a new institutionalist perspective on U.S. interest group activity see Ainsworth (2002). For the place of the new institutionalist perspective in comparative interest group studies and a critique of its value as an explanatory theory, see chapter 10 (esp. sections 10.2., 10.3., and 10.4.).

Chapter 4

Interest Groups and the Socioeconomic and Political System

4.1. INTRODUCTION: A MINIMALLY INVESTIGATED TOPIC

Clive S. Thomas

Interest groups do not develop or operate in a vacuum. The development of an interest group system, the types of groups and interests that exist, and the way they attempt to influence public policy are determined by historical, geographical, cultural, social, economic, political, governmental structural and other factors. In turn, interest group activities help shape and define the nature of a political system. Consequently, knowledge of the operating environment is crucial for understanding the fundamental influences that shape such specifics as the make-up of the group system, how groups are viewed in the society, how they organize internally for political purposes, and the strategies and tactics that they employ in a particular country, state, or locality.

Different operating environments produce different interest group systems and the variations in strategies and tactics they use (see sections 3.1. and 7.2.). This is not only the case between diverse environments, such as agricultural and industrial societies and liberal democracies and totalitarian regimes, but also among systems with less obvious differences, such as the states in the U.S. (see section 6.4.). Thus, the knowledge of differences in the interest group operating environment also facilitates comparison between interest group systems and helps explain specific variations in the organization and operation of interest groups and interests.

In particular, this knowledge can facilitate an understanding of how and why the general explanations of interest group activity reviewed in chapter 3 apply to some political systems and not in others, and why some systems combine the elements of several of these explanations.

Although the influence of the socioeconomic and political environment is very important in understanding interest group systems and the activity of individual groups and interests, the subject is a vast one, and its boundary lines broad and nebulous. Mainly for this reason, plus the prohibitive costs and organizational problems of conducting research on such a large and broad subject, there is no general text focusing specifically on the subject for any country, including the United States, and certainly nothing comparing different political systems. In fact, the subject of the operating environment is one of the least researched in the field of interest groups. Thus, the various aspects of this topic provide many opportunities for future research.

The existing research on this broad topic is of two types. First, some scholars have focused on specific elements of the environment, such as the influence of political party systems and of public opinion, in shaping interest group activity. Second, several studies deal with aspects of the operating environment, usually incidentally as part of research on other subjects, and information can be gleaned from these studies. For example, those studying legislative lobbying tactics in the United States have to do so in the context of the structure of the legislature being studied, including its political party system, its formal organization, and political subculture. Thus, through a synthesis of work from specific studies on elements of the environment, with material extrapolated from other relevant studies, we can begin to piece together a partial picture of the influence of the operating environment on interest group activity.

In combination, the entries in this chapter provide a partial understanding of the influences of this environment. As with much of the material in this *Guide*, most of the findings are based upon the U.S. political system with some research from other liberal democracies. There is little on the influence of the operating environment in nonpluralist group systems in this chapter. This is because much less work has been conducted on these systems in general (see section 12.1.), and thus much less is known about environmental influences on their interest group systems.

An overview of the functions and roles of interest groups within the political system and society as a whole can be found in chapter 1 (see section 1.3.). Regarding the specific entries in this chapter, the most research both on the United States and other liberal democracies has probably been conducted on the relationship between political parties and interest groups (see section 4.5.). In terms of the volume of research, both specific and incidental studies, next would come research on public opinion (most of which is on the U.S. system) and on peak associations (see sections 4.8. and 4.10.). Most of the research on the important influence of political culture on interest group activity has been acquired incidentally from projects focusing on other topics (see sections 4.4. and 4.9.). As the entry in section 4.4. points out, we know very little about the broader influence of political culture on interest group activity. Some research considers the influence of the social structure (see section 4.6.), but this research focuses mainly on the U.S. political system. Since the late 1980s, a specific body of research on interest groups and economic development has begun to appear (see section 4.7.). Most of the knowledge on the structure of the political system and its affects on interest group activity has to be synthesized from other studies (see section 4.3.).

Despite the dearth of research on the operating environment and the fact that most of what exists focuses on the U.S. political system, some fascinating and enlightening findings have been produced. These may well have broader implications for other liberal democracies as these political systems have similar patterns of socioeconomic and political development. These findings may also have some relevance for other interest group systems—such as those in transition to democracy and even the group systems in third world countries—as they develop more formal elements of interest group activity. For example, extrapolating from the entry on the development of interest group systems (see section 4.2.) suggests that there are some common influences at work across western systems that have wrought changes in the type and range of interest operating in liberal democracies over the past 50 years. The entries on political culture and cultural influences on lobbying (see sections 4.4. and 4.9.) imply that culture is likely a major influence on group strategies and tactics. The entry on public opinion (see section 4.8.) leads to a conclusion that across the Western world, and perhaps beyond, there is an essentially negative attitude toward interest groups and their representatives, which has important implications for group strategies and tactics. And extrapolating from the entry on social structure (see section 4.6.), it may be that social change, among other factors, particularly the development of a middle class, has important lessons for understanding all interest group systems in terms of the types and range of groups that come and go. All these possible implications await testing by future research.

4.2. INTEREST GROUP SYSTEM DEVELOPMENT AND VARIATION: AN OVERVIEW

Clive S. Thomas

How, and under what circumstances, do interest group systems develop and vary? How are they transformed from the informal interests and processes of contact and influence predominant in tribal and developing societies, as well as authoritarian regimes, to the wide range of formally organized interest groups and the use of sophisticated processes of access and influence operating in liberal democracies? Are there some common environment factors that influence this development and the way it determines such elements as the types of interests and interest groups that emerge and the way they attempt to influence government? Are there distinct stages of development in the progression from informal to highly formalized interest group systems? If so, is this development a common linear one with each system going through the same stages in a particular order? Or do some systems develop in a nonlinear way? Moreover, why do political systems at the same level of development often manifest major differences in elements of their interest group system, as is the case in some post-industrial democracies between pluralist and neocorporatist systems?

The present state of knowledge means that we can provide only partial answers to most of these and many other questions about how and why interest group systems develop and why they vary. There is a body of research on the recent developments of interest groups in the United States, particularly the so-called *group universe* (the types and number of groups operating) and the development of lobbying techniques (see chapters 6 and 7), but little research on other systems, pluralist or non-pluralist, is available. However, by extrapolating from several studies, observations can be made about various aspects of the development of and variation among group systems.

General Factors

As part of the socioeconomic and political development in a society, the development of an interest group system involves the gradual differentiation, professionalization, and formal organization of the processes of aggregation and articulation of political interests. That is, it involves a progression from a court official affiliated to a king or a confidant or close friend affiliated to a dictator informally pushing a cause or benefit for themselves, their family or group, to the formal groups in the capitals of the Western world. The latter manifest business, labor, public interest groups, and a host of other causes, using hired lobbyists or consultants and other professional staff, and maybe highly organized grassroots public relations and media campaigns to bring pressure to bear on an array of elected and appointed public officials. Many variables influence this development, either advancing, impeding, and in some cases, retarding it. Among the most important of these appear to be the type of political system, and the variations within the same type of political system including differences in governmental structure, socioeconomic and political development, and political culture and subculture.

Extent of the Legality and Acceptance of Interest Group Activity

In advanced liberal democracies, there is a general right to form groups whereas authoritarian regimes usually place major restrictions on, and may even ban, group formation and lobbying. Thus, a far wider range of formally organized groups exists in liberal democracies using a wider range of lobbying techniques than in nonpluralist societies. Furthermore, in many societies, interest groups are viewed as detrimental to the functioning of society. Consequently, they are seen as illegitimate, as they place special or sectoral interests above those of the nation as a whole. This view is not only expressed in the official ideology of Communist countries; it is unofficially recognized in many authoritarian and developing countries as expressed in the attitudes of elites in countries like Bangladesh and Taiwan (see sections 12.2. and 12.4.). Even in transitional regimes, where the development of formal interest group activity is an essential element, interest groups can be viewed as antithetical to the success of a society. For example, in Argentina there is a skepticism of interest groups among the public, a hangover of the fear of belonging to banned groups in the old regime, and among some politicians who see interest groups as impeding the transition to democracy by promoting their special interests (D. Johnson 2001). Such skepticism may stymie the development of an informal into a formal interest group system. In contrast, even though interest groups are viewed with skepticism and distrust in many developed pluralist societies, such as in the United States (Petracca 1992a, xix-xx), they are still seen as necessary to the functioning of the political system, and such societies develop extensive formal interest group systems.

However, despite freedom to organize in liberal democracies, it should not be assumed that groups will automatically develop to represent all interests in society as was once believed by Bentley (1908), Truman (1951), and other scholars. Mancur Olson's (1965 and 1971) classic work on collective action showed that interests have varying abilities to organize, and thus, the group system does not fully reflect all interests of a society. For a review of Olson's work and that of his critics, see section 5.2.

Nor should it be assumed that as underdeveloped societies become more developed and authoritarian societies become more pluralist, the increase in group activity will follow some linear pattern that will ultimately result in most group systems resembling those of post-industrial, pluralist democracies. Padgett (1999) has some interesting observation in this regard about the pattern of interest group developments in the transitional regimes of Eastern Europe in general and the former East Germany in particular since 1989. In some developing societies and transitional ones too, if existing patterns of representation—such as personal networks of informal representation as well as institutional representation—are not replaced by effective formal interest groups, some societies may lapse back into authoritarian rule, as has often been the case in Latin America.

The Political Culture and Political Subcultures

Political culture, which is the values and beliefs about politics—what government should and should not do, what are and are not legitimate ways for political leaders to act, and so on—varies from country to country (and often within a country) and influences the role of interest groups. The level of acceptance of interest groups just considered above is one manifestation of how political culture can affect the group operating environment; but there are several others. Political cultural differences have also led some countries to regulate interest group activity extensively, as in the United States, while in others it is much less stringently regulated, as in Britain and Germany (see chapter 14). Of particular importance is the extent of political ideology within the political culture. In both democracies and authoritarian regimes, deep-rooted ideology can lead to certain patterns of interest group involvement or exclusion from the policy process, which is not the case in less ideological political cultures. In Sweden, for example, the social democratic belief of including all interests in the policy-making process, leads to the government organizing and funding groups, such as immigrant workers who might not form otherwise (Micheletti 1993). In contrast, in communist regimes the ideology does not officially recognize interest groups, and so they have to operate unofficially. See section 4.4. for an in-depth review of the importance of political culture.

The Level of Socioeconomic Development

The more economically advanced the society, particularly if the society is a liberal democracy, the more formalized and extensive the number of interest groups with more people belonging to them. The development of a middle class is particularly important as a basis for the development of many professional and cause groups, especially in post-industrial societies. In less developed, particularly authoritarian, third world countries with rural economies and low levels of education, the range of interest is much narrower and the forms of representation are largely informal, with a very small segment of society gaining access to government.

The extent to which the business community and trade unions are united through peak associations is another factor. In liberal democracies, the greater the extent of trade union membership and the fewer the number of peak associations representing business and labor, the greater the potential for neocorporatist arrangements—for government, labor, and business to determine major economic and social policies (see section 3.4.). Thus, the interest group systems in many continental European countries, especially Scandinavia, Germany, Switzerland, and Austria, have developed neocorporatist characteristics whereas neocorporatism is generally not a feature of the U.S. interest group system (C. Thomas 1993a; see sections 3.4. and 4.10.).

The General Decision-Making Process of a Political System— Where Is Political Power Located?

The location of power will determine the access points and methods of influence used by interest groups. The political and governmental structure also likely influences the extent of the formal and institutional development of the interest group system and the extent of the regulation of interest groups and lobbying. The influence of political and governmental structures on the development and variation in interest group systems is covered in section 4.3.

Major Political Developments

Besides the gradual process of political development of a society, such as developing more formalized political institutions and perhaps expanding participation in the policy-making process, major political developments such as wars, major policy changes, the coming to power of new leaders, and changes in control of government by a political party, among other factors, can have an important long-term effects on the development of an interest group system. While the once popular disturbance theory of interest group system development is no longer held, and Mancur Olson (1965 and 1971) and his critics have shown that not all interests have the capacity to organize equally for political purposes (see section 5.2.), major political developments do affect current groups politically active and often bring others not previously active into the political arena either to promote or protect their political interests. For example, the Vietnam War and the Great Society program of the 1960s had such an effect in the United States. In Western Europe, the Single European Act of 1986, which moved the European Community (EC, now the European Union, EU) toward a more politically powerful entity by transferring many policy functions from national capitals to the EU headquarters in Brussels, caused a major expansion in groups operating within the EC/EU and expanded the range and sophistication of the techniques they used. Such major political events often produce waves, or surges, of development in interest group systems followed by lulls. For example, the major expansion in activity precipitated by the Single European Act lasted until the mid-1990s. Since then there has been a period of consolidation and the expansion has slowed considerably (C. Thomas, Hrebenar, and Boyer 2001).

Future Development of and Variation in Interest Group Activity

As a natural and indispensable part of politics and policy making, the role of interest groups is likely to increase in all political systems in the future. A major reason for this is that interest groups are among the most, if not the most adaptable, resilient and effective of all political institutions and generally much more so than their major counterparts of political parties and social movements (see section 1.2.). In part, this is because interest groups coalesce around natural or specific and usually narrow communities (such as cattle ranchers, computer manufacturers, and animal-rights advocates) and thus have a more common identity and community of interest among their membership. In contrast, parties and social movements often embrace a wide range of perspectives and have organizational structures that are often very cumbersome (as with many parties) or very loose (as with many social movements), which makes it much harder for them to adapt to changing political circumstances.

Thus, interest groups are more enduring and, over the long-term, they are the most likely vehicle to be used by those seeking benefits from government. And the broader the range of demands placed on government, the more interest groups are likely to develop. In fact, the major reason for the future expansion of interest group activity will likely be that in all types of political systems, government activity is likely to expand, thus causing disturbances, which will affect politically active interests more extensively and force individuals and organizations not politically active to enter politics.

The specific reasons for expansion in group activity and the particular form it will take will vary among types of systems. In political systems that are in transition from authoritarianism to liberal democracy, as in Eastern Europe and parts of Africa and Latin America, a combination of factors will be at work, including the lifting of restrictions on the right to organize, the increasing importance of business and business interests (especially in former communist countries), and an increasing presence of foreign and international interests. In developing countries, such as India, Mexico, and Indonesia, the factors at work will be an expanding economy, the rise of a middle class, and a consequent increase in political efficacy on the part of the population in general.

In post-industrial liberal democracies, interest group activity will likely expand due to the increasing breakdown of political ideology and the increasing pragmatism, or *Americanization*, of these systems where interest groups are seen as more able to deliver political benefits than political parties; an increasing international and transnational presence of interests in individual countries and organizations such as the EU; an expansion in the so-called *nonprofit*, or *third sector*. and the increasing use of this third sector by government to deliver services and the need of this sector to obtain government funds.

With the increase in interest group activity, the distinction between groups, political parties, and social movements is likely to become increasingly blurred and the definition of interest group set out in chapter 1 (see section 1.2.) may need modification. More interest groups will become *interest parties*—narrowly based organizations often focusing on a single issue that attempt to gain seats in a parliament and become part of a governing coalition in order to push their cause. Some of the religious parties in Israel can be considered interest parties as could Solidarity in Poland in the 1980s when it could also be considered a social movement, as well as many parties in post-communist Eastern Europe such as the Independent Smallholders' Party in Hungary.

This expansion, in particular the internationalization of interest group activity, will produce some homogenization in the organization of interests, their role in political systems, and the techniques they use to gain access and exert influence. However, specific governmental structures, political culture, deep-rooted ideology, historical practice, and short-term political circumstances will likely always work to give interest group activity many unique elements in each country.

4.3. INTEREST GROUPS AND THE STRUCTURE OF THE POLITICAL AND GOVERNMENTAL SYSTEM

Clive S. Thomas

Together with socioeconomic factors and political culture, variations in political processes in institutions and governmental structure, in particular the policy-making process, provide important insights into the differences between interest group systems (see section 4.2.). These factors advance an understanding of group operating techniques—their strategies and tactics. This is because, as their major goal is to influence public policy in their favor, all but the most unsophisticated groups and interests will orient their operations to access and influence the power points within the political and governmental system. Knowledge of the differences in political processes and governmental structures is useful for understanding the contrast between the operation of interest groups in the United States and in parliamentary democracies and between pluralist systems and nonpluralist regimes.

Scholars comparing interest group systems across countries and regime types have been most interested in the differences within political and governmental structures; though there has been some interest from scholars concerned with variations within individual countries particularly the United States (Gray and Lowery 1996a; Thomas and Hrebenar 2003). For the most part, however, scholars have only addressed the factor of differences in political and governmental structure incidentally and not as a major focus of research. Consequently, insights into the influence of this factor must be extrapolated from various studies. Extrapolation reveals that four factors are particularly important: (1) the constitutional structure, particularly the contrast between the parliamentary and separation of powers systems and federal and unitary systems; (2) the strength of political parties; (3) the power and independence of the bureaucracy; and (4) the degree of centralization or fragmentation of a political system and the extent of corporatism or neocorporatism.

The Constitutional Structure: Parliamentary versus Separation of Powers Systems and Federal versus Unitary

The formal structure of a government is important in determining the strategies and tactics of groups because it is a major—though not the only—determinant of the policy-making power structure. In parliamentary democracies power is held by a cabinet, which represents the majority political party or coalition of parties in the parliament. In such systems, while some lobbying focuses on parliaments (P. Norton 1999), the parliament and the courts have little power in day-to-day policy decision making, and thus, groups rarely focus their attention on these bodies. Instead, virtually all day-to-day lobbying takes place on the executive branch (though preparatory work may be done within a political party—see below). In contrast, the separation of powers systems in the United States, with power distributed between the Congress, president and the courts, provides many more options in strategy and tactics for groups, with a major focus on legislative lobbying and increasingly on the courts, as well as lobbying the executive.

Potentially, as least, a federal system, with its sharing of major policy domains between national and state or provincial governments, also provides more access points for interest groups. This is certainly the case in the strong federal system in the United States, and to a certain extent in Canada. However, in some federal systems, other factors may work to reduce the fragmenting effects of federalism on policy-making and thus reduce the options open to interest groups. For example, this is the case in Germany because of the existence of strong political parties and neocorporatist policy-making (Gellner and Robertson 2001). The reasons for this will become clearer when considering strong political parties and neocorporatism.

The Strength of Political Parties

A key factor in determining the policy-making power structure in a liberal democracy is the strength of political parties. (This may also be the case in a nonpluralist system, though the party in this system is, in general, a tool for a dictator and his close friends and allies.) When political parties are strong, they can determine who their candidates will be and enforce strict party discipline in voting in a legislature, as in many liberal democracies such as Germany, Sweden, and Britain; they are the dominant force in determining what policies get enacted. In such systems, a party's support of a policy issue, particularly a major economic or social policy, is often a prerequisite for getting it on to the policy agenda. Consequently, in these systems, certain economic, social, and ideological groups often ally themselves with major parties—for example, business with conservative parties and labor with socialist or liberal parties. Thus, key lobbying efforts take place at party conferences and meetings.

In contrast, political parties in the United States are generally weaker, especially at the state level in the South and in the West. While there is certainly some affinity between the Democratic Party and labor and liberal causes such as environmentalists, and between the Republican Party and conservative causes such as business and certain religious groups, party-group affiliation is much less structured and ideological than in other liberal democracies (C. Thomas 2001b). This policy power vacuum left by parties provides more strategy and tactic options for interest groups, including lobbying powerful individual legislators, and gaining a powerful position with key legislative committees. The decline of ideology across the Western world, and particularly Western Europe, is making the factor of parties less significant and more akin to the situation in the United States by increasing the strategy and tactic options for many groups (C. Thomas 2001a; chapters 1 and 15; see sections 3.6. and 4.5.).

The Power and Independence of the Bureaucracy

Whether the political system is a liberal democracy or some form of authoritarian system, the vast majority of decisions affecting interest groups are not made by politicians but by bureaucrats or civil servants. This is because the bulk of decisions affecting groups are mundane, low-profile decisions regarding issues such as the writing of regulations for occupational licensing (such as of doctors, lawyers, and accountants) and health and safety rules for factories, and so on. Government bureaucracies in all societies are important to interest groups; but they become particularly important as targets of groups and determinants of their success the more developed the society. In some post-industrial liberal democracies, such as France (Appleton 2001; F. Wilson 1993) and Japan (Hrebenar 2001; Hrebenar and Nakamura 1993), the bureaucracy is particularly important because of the long tradition of government centralization and the close relationship between governments and senior civil servants as with Liberal Democratic Party governments and the civil service in Japan. Such bureaucratic power tends to produce more closed interest group systems with establishment groups—those favored by the governing party and the bureaucracy—having a distinct political advantage. Bureaucracies tend to be of particular importance to economic peak associations in neo-corporatist societies (see below and section 3.4.).

The role of a bureaucracy in shaping interest group strategies and tactics in nonpluralist societies defies easy categorization. Much depends on the relationship of the particular department or agency and its top personnel with the king, dictator, politburo, party apparatus, or other key decision-making centers. However, societies with corporatist arrangements give particular power to certain elements of the bureaucracy, particularly those dealing with business and labor; and thus business and labor orient much of their efforts to dealing with these departments

(Bianchi 1986a, 1986b; Castles 1967; Schmitter 1971; Skilling and Grif-fiths 1971; and see chapter 12).

The Degree of Centralization or Fragmentation of the Policy Process and the Extent of Corporatism/Neocorporatism

The three factors considered above indicate that the major structural characteristic of a political and governmental system influencing interest group strategy and tactics is the degree to which it has a centralized or fragmented policy-making process. This is, in fact, the case whether the system is nonpluralist or pluralist. Highly centralized political systems, such as totalitarian regimes like the U.S.S.R. under Stalin, contemporary authoritarian regimes such as those in the Persian Gulf, and liberal democracies like France, Japan, and Germany, have highly centralized power structures—the dictator, king, or his close associates in non-pluralist systems, the cabinet and political party, and perhaps the bureaucracy in many parliamentary liberal democracies. This considerably restricts the access points available to interest groups and limits the strategies and tactics available to them. Such highly centralized systems also have the potential to use a corporatist or neocorporatist policy-making process (see section 3.4.) where government gives preference in lobby representation to key peak associations (see section 4.10.) on major economic and social issues. In contrast, the highly fragmented power structure at the U.S. federal and state levels, where neocorporatist arrangements are not feasible, provide many more access points and increase the range of options of strategies and tactics. A theoretical framework comparing the affects of political and institution structure on interest group activity in western democracies can be found in Clive Thomas's *First World Interest Groups: A Comparative Perspective* (1993a, 16–21).

The combination of the separation of powers, weaker parties, and relatively strong federalism in the United States also likely contributed to the early public emergence and institutionalization of interest group activity in general, particularly lobbying and its professionalization, and probably to early attempts to regulate lobbying. A lobbying corps had developed in Washington, D.C., by the early twentieth century and in the states by the late 1930s. This is in contrast to Western Europe and other parliamentary systems where lobbying was not seriously acknowledged by academics or politicians until the late 1950s and in some countries much later (see section 11.1.). This was largely because the political and governmental structure of these systems, and particularly the overwhelming dominance of political parties in the policy process, kept lobbying much more informal and generally far from the public eye at private meetings of party officials, and in the offices of cabinet members and senior civil servants. Furthermore, the regulation of group activity in liberal democracies outside the United States is minimal (*Parliamentary Affairs* 1998;

see also chapter 14). While this is, in part, a product of political cultures that have not recognized lobbying as *lobbying* (see sections 4.4. and 11.1.), it is likely as much to do with the structure of parliamentary systems, particularly dominant parties, which can prevent the enactment of stringent regulations either because they see them as unnecessary or detrimental to their interests.

As indicated, political and governmental structure is only one, albeit an important influence on interest group activity, particularly upon group strategy and tactics. This factor works in combination with other important elements, such as political development (see section 4.2.) and political culture (see section 4.4.) plus the other topics covered here in chapter 4 to shape the form of an interest group system and how groups attempt to influence public policy.

4.4. INTEREST GROUPS AND POLITICAL CULTURE

Martin A. Nie

In essence, a national political culture (and a regional or local political subculture) is a community's values and beliefs about the quality, style, and extent of political processes and government operations. The extent or lack of constraints placed on interest groups is largely determined by political culture. This relationship of groups and political culture is a reciprocal one—each influencing the other and thus each can be either an independent or dependent variable.

In fact, it appears that political culture is the most significant environmental factor shaping both group organization and the methods that groups use to achieve their goals. However, this assertion, inferred as a by-product of several general studies of political culture, is speculative, as very little direct research has been conducted on the relationship between interest groups and political culture. There is no comprehensive study of the relationship in the U.S. political system, or that of any other country or comprehensive comparative analysis across political systems. The limited information that exists on this relationship has to be extrapolated from the general research on political culture. These studies are the major source of information in this entry.

Two of the few scholars who explicitly address the relationship of interest groups and political culture are Wootton (1985) and Castles (1967). Wootton argues that the study of political culture is very important to explaining interest groups in U.S. politics. Understanding political culture, he argues, provides essential background on why the United States has become a special-interest nation. Castles addresses the importance of political culture in comparative interest group studies. Even though Castle's book is dated, as it covers both pluralist and nonpluralist political systems and emerging nations, it offers valuable insights for explaining differences between interest group systems.

Of the many general studies on political culture, the following are useful either because they set out the basics of the concept of political culture or because they offer important explicit or implicit insights into the relationship between interest groups and political culture. These studies focus predominantly on political culture in advanced liberal democracies. Beyond generalities, very little is known about political culture in nonpluralist and developing countries, and thus, its affect on the relationship between interest groups and political culture.

Almond and Verba (1963, 14–15), who popularized the study of political culture, define it as "the particular distribution of patterns of orientation toward political objects among the members of the nation." They cite three dimensions of political culture: The *cognitive* refers to knowledge and information about government and its politics, the *affective* refers to feelings toward political objects, and the *evaluative* dimension, which refers to judgements about political objects that combine cognitive and affective elements (see also, Almond and Verba 1980). Verba (1965, 513) redefined political culture as "the system of empirical beliefs, expressive symbols, and values which defines the situation in which political action takes place." Political culture can thus be seen as a way in which boundaries are set on the actions of interest groups.

Devine (1972) examines political culture as a value system that can influence political and social behavior by serving as a screening mechanism filtering perceptions of reality (see also S. Welch 1993). Lipset (1990 and 1996) contends that this screening mechanism is comprised of historically constructed ideological values. Thus, a nation's historical background offers guidance in understanding its present political, and hence, its interest group system. Lipset (1990), for instance, uses the disparate histories, including class structure and religious experiences, to show how Canada is more collectively oriented than the United States.

Evidence suggests that group activity, both of individual groups and the group system as a whole, is either facilitated or constricted by the prevailing political culture. This culture is a mind-set shaping the political context in which groups operate. For example, could the National Rifle Association (NRA) be as successful anywhere but in the United States? Moreover, U.S. environmental interest groups must work within a cultural context accentuating the importance of private property, Lockean liberalism (which emphasizes individualism and a minimal role for government), and often unfettered economic growth. Bayes (1982, chapter 3) examines this unfettered influence of American culture and ideology on interest group activity, especially in U.S. foreign policy. In contrast, in some former communist countries, such as the Czech Republic, the political cultural legacy of circumscribing group activity lives on expressed in a deep skepticism of interest groups and lobbyists and, ironically, inhibiting the transition to liberal democracy (Evanson and Magstadt 2001). Even in some liberal democracies, political culture may place major constraints on interest group activity. In Israel, for example, the need for national consensus and nation building has long placed group activity in a negative light (Yishai 2001). And the differences in political culture among the nations of the EU considerably influences the nature of lobbying in each country and leads to major challenges for those lobbying the EU Commission and parliament (see section 4.9.).

Inglehart's (1977, 1990, 1997) study of value changes in post-materialist societies has important implications for the development of interest group systems. He contends that citizens in countries such as the United States, Japan, Britain, Norway, Greece, and Germany are undergoing significant cultural change. As older (materialist) generations are being replaced by younger ones (post-materialist), a simultaneous change in values is taking place. In short, younger generations tend to be more concerned with quality of life issues than with a materialist emphasis on economic and physical security. These value changes affect the groups that people join or those with which they identify. The emergence of environmental, civil rights, gender-oriented, peace, and other post-materialist groups may be a result of this value change (see also, Pierce, et al. 1992).

Political culture has also been studied at the regional and state level within countries, particularly in the United States. Those such as Elazar (1972, 1975, 1994) and Ellis (1993), for example, contend that a nation such as the United States consists of numerous and often divergent political subcultures. As Key (1949, 36) contended, "the political distance from Virginia to Alabama must be measured in light years." What these and other scholars recognize is the cultural diversity prevalent in any large heterogeneous society and its impact on politics including interest group activity. Elazar (1972), for instance, identifies three political cultures within the United States. According to Elazar, these individualistic, moralistic, and traditionalistic subcultures are patterned throughout the nation and ultimately affect subnational politics and policies, and thus, interest group activity. However, Elazar's classification has been subject to a barrage of criticism (see, for example, Erikson, Wright, and McIver 1989).

In their extensive 50-state study of interest groups, Hrebenar and Thomas (1987, 1992, 1993a, 1993b) show how regional and state contexts within the United States, such as history, demographics, and natural resources, ultimately influence interest group activity (see also, Thomas and Hrebenar 1992a). There is, for instance, a major difference in interest group activity in the upper Midwest (the Dakotas, Iowa, Minnesota, Wisconsin, and Michigan) where group activity is far more constrained and reflects a moralistic political culture from that of the states of the South where the less restrained element of a traditionalist political culture are in evidence (Hrebenar and Thomas 1992, 1993b). A large part of group success depends on societal support or sympathy, and this public backing is dependent on political culture and subcultures. Groups must be cognizant of the culture within which they function or they run the risk of alienating the constituencies they need most (Erikson, Wright, and McIver 1993). Simply transplanting the standard methods of influence from one nation, region, state, or city to another will not necessarily be successful.

This brief discussion shows the value of the concept of political culture for understanding interest group activity. There is certainly a need in interest group studies to more rigorously and systematically apply the political culture concept or at least recognize the larger cultural variables at play. While there are formidable barriers to extensive original research in this area in terms of the broadness of this relationship and the costs of conducting such a project, a valuable first step would be to synthesize existing research dealing with this relationship.

4.5. INTEREST GROUPS AND POLITICAL PARTIES

Allan J. Cigler

In liberal democracies, political parties and interest groups are the principal institutions linking citizens to their governments. A major problem in studying the relationship is that of distinguishing between a party, an interest group, and a social movement (C. Thomas 2001a; see chapter 1). In some countries, some parties and interest groups are so intertwined organizationally and financially, such as the religious parties and religious groups in Israel, that it is difficult to consider them as separate entities. In the United States, parties and interest groups are typically viewed as distinct and engaging in different political activities, with interest groups being particularly important in the policy-making arena and parties of particular significance in elections.

Even in the United States, however, party-group relations are increasingly difficult to disentangle in a world in which *organized interests* replace *interest groups* as the preferred terminology (the group in question may be a loosely knit group of issue activists with no formal membership); and what constitutes a political party is also not clear. Parties today look like and are largely defined by law as special interest groups of their own, whose major purpose is less to mobilize voters and aggregate interests and more to raise campaign funds. And although the vast majority of interest groups do not engage in electoral activities, some engage in traditional party activities, from recruiting candidates for public office to funding campaigns to mobilizing voters, further muddying the party-group distinction.

The literature on party-group relations in U.S. politics is more normative than empirical, and the relationship has been as much the concern of state politics specialists as those studying national politics (C. Thomas 2001b); and general textbooks that combine the studies of parties and groups, such as Key (1964), Ippolito and Walker (1980), and Hrebenar, Burbank, and Benedict (1999), treat the intricacies of the interrelationship of parties and groups only cursorily. Much of the early research simply mentions the party-group relationship in passing. The literature reflects the bias among political scientists that parties are a positive democratic force, reconciling society's diverse elements, providing policy direction, and representing the vulnerable and unorganized elements of society, while interest groups tend to exacerbate divisions by pursuing narrow, upper-class, and selfish concerns. The underlying assumption is that when strong parties control the political agenda, the influence of groups is lessened, benefiting the broad public interest (see section 3.6.).

The supposed inverse relationship between party and group power has been subjected to few precise tests. V. O. Key, Jr.'s (1949) study of 13 southern states in the 1940s still represents the most convincing example of how interest groups fill the political vacuum in U.S. state policy making when parties are weak organizationally. Later comparative state studies by Zeller (1954) and Morehouse (1981) confirmed that in states with strong parties, interest groups are less influential. A more contemporary, comprehensive study of party-group relations in the U.S. states (Thomas and Hrebenar 1999a) suggests that generalizing about the relationship needs qualification: While weak party systems are typically accompanied by extensive group domination of the policy process, a number of states have strong parties along with a dynamic, influential interest group system.

Research on the party-group relationship at the national level in the United States is particularly scarce; though Clive Thomas (2001a) provides an extensive synthesis of the major work. The most illuminating historical study dealing with party-group competition in the policy process is J. M. Hansen (1991) focusing on the evolution of the farm lobby from 1919 to the early 1980s. According to Hansen, the theoretical basis for the competitive, inverse relationship between parties and interest groups can be found in the desires of elected officials to win election and their willingness to grant policy access to those who can reduce electoral uncertainty. Since officials are often unclear about constituent concerns, cooperation and consultation with mediating institutions like parties and interest groups become strategies for dealing with such uncertainty. Compared to parties, interest groups, with their knowledge of constituent issue positions and their ability to influence constituents on a lawmaker's behalf, may be more reliable agents of political intelligence for risk-averse officials.

When group perspectives dominate elections, close working relationships are encouraged with interest groups, usually at the expense of parties. The tremendous rise in political action committee (PAC) numbers in recent decades has intensified interest in party-group relations. Early studies suggested that PACs had the potential to usurp the parties' role in campaign finance, especially independent/ideological PACs that damaged party coalition-building efforts (Sabato 1984). One study of PAC contributors, however, found that few PACs harbor antiparty orientations (J. Green and Guth 1986), while another (Sorauf 1991) found that PACs have not had great success in registering and mobilizing voters and remain specialized conveyers of cash to candidates, not threatening parties. More recently, researchers have begun to explore the implications of *soft money*, interest group contributions to parties that are not limited and that may exceed one million dollars by some groups (Magleby 2000). There is a growing public concern about what groups receive in return for such contributions.

Overall, recent research on party-interest group relations in U.S. politics suggests that the connection is best viewed as symbiotic (A. Cigler 1991a): partly competitive, partly cooperative, and partly accommodating. Parties and interest groups may share electoral aims and cooperate in electioneering activity, illustrated by the Democratic Party-organized labor connections since the 1930s. Parties may be energized by organized interest, issue activists, such as gays in the Democratic Party and Christian Right adherents in the Republican Party, who in return for their efforts gain a forum for their views and access to the political process they could not have achieved otherwise. Finally, studies of PAC-party relations illustrate how parties have accommodated themselves to potentially rival organizations, by forming loose fundraising alliances with prominent PACs, emerging as brokers by assisting such PACs in directing contributions to particular campaigns, and aiding party candidates in soliciting funds from donor PACs (Herrnson 1988).

An early work combining the role of parties and groups in a comparative political context is Duverger (1972). However, for the most part, this volume treats parties and groups separately paying little attention to the complexities of their interrelationship. The most extensive work comparing party-group relations across liberal democracies is Clive Thomas (2001a). This edited volume includes chapters on 13 countries: traditional democracies (Britain, France, Sweden, and the United States); new democracies (Germany, Italy, Israel, and Japan); and transitional democracies (Spain, the Czech Republic, Poland, Argentina, and Mexico). The concluding chapter includes two theoretical frameworks: One sets out the factors that influence party-group relations in liberal democracies; the other provides a seven-part classification of the various types of party-group relations from *integration* (the closest), through *noninvolvement* (the most common), to *conflict and confrontation*. Contrary to what is generally believed, the book finds that it is not the relationship between socialist parties and labor interest groups, common in many Western European and neocorporatist system, that is the strongest and most interdependent party-group relationship but that between the two major parties and major interest groups in the United States.

4.6. INTEREST GROUPS AND THE SOCIAL STRUCTURE

Laura A. Wilson

Interest group scholars have long realized that social structure influences the development of interest group systems. However, for many years research involving social structural variables and interests, such as class, education, age distribution, and income, faced one significant barrier—obtaining databases sufficiently large and varied to permit meaningful analysis. With the advent of comparative state studies of interest groups in the United States, it became possible to identify and systematically study interests existing in the same period but under different social conditions. Other scholars have employed historical research to trace the evolution of the relationship of social structures and interests. The vast majority of research on interest groups and social structure focuses on the U.S. political system, mainly at the state level. However, these findings may be applicable to other political systems, especially liberal democracies, and can provide insights into how social structure influences the development of interest group systems in general.

The study of the influence of social structure on interest groups began when Schattschneider (1960) first argued that the U.S. interest group system was biased in favor of the upper classes. Zeigler and Peak attempted to explain the paradox of how interests flourish in a governmental system that distrusts them through analysis of class status. The middle class tend to be supportive of interests while lower-class members are highly mistrustful of interests and refuse to participate in these organizations (Zeigler and Peak 1972, 39–41). In addition, the work of John Sullivan (1973) in studying U.S. state population characteristics and their relationship to state political systems led to the study of social complexity and heterogeneity of the population and how this affected interest groups.

The attempt to develop more inclusive theories of interests and social variables came with the work of Morehouse and Zeigler on comparative state interest group systems. Premised on the disturbance theory concept that interests can serve as adaptive mechanisms when social change occurs, these authors attempted to identify the elements of social structure and complexity which promote the emergence of interest group systems.

Morehouse (1981; see also Morehouse and Jewell 2003) correlated three measures of social complexity with the emergence of strong interest group systems. Strong interest group systems tended to be associated with states lacking complex economies and the attributes of modern affluent societies such as low levels of professional employment and advanced education. Strong interest group states were found in the South while weak interest groups were characteristic of northeastern states.

Zeigler (1983, 112) furthered the work of Morehouse by analyzing additional social variables related to the development of interest group systems. Noting that a paradox exists in that weak interest group states contain more wealth, Zeigler isolated state government spending as opposed to overall government spending (state and local). He found that strong interest group states tended to be more centralized organizationally and spend more state funds, thus confirming the concept that wealthier states promote interest group activity.

More recent work includes Hrebenar and Thomas's (1987, 1992, 1993a, 1993b) study of interest groups in all 50 states. They have developed an analytical framework for understanding interest group activity, which includes levels of social and economic development. The social development variable includes levels of urbanization, middle-class status and professional employment; the economic development variable includes economic diversity and decreased income inequalities (Thomas and Hrebenar 1999a, 123–24; 2003). Although Hrebenar and Thomas's research is based on state case studies, the rich contextual information provided by this methodology is without peer in the study of state interest groups.

More quantitative research which contain social structural variables include Hunter, Wilson, and Brunk (1991) and Lowery and Gray (1993a, 1993b, 1998; Gray and Lowery 1996a). Hunter, Wilson, and Brunk analyzed more than 39,000 lobbying registrations across 49 states to ascertain the effects of social variables on lobbying. Using data related to economic diversity, per capita income, and population as well as data related to lobbying regulation and governmental size across four types of interests, this study found no significant relationships between either the economic or income variables and lobbying. However, population size did appear to be significant for industry and financial lobbies as well as single issue lobbies.

Lowery and Gray (1993a; 1993b; Gray and Lowery 1996a) analyzed the creation of additional interest groups due to increased social complexity. Arguing that economic variables are most critical in promoting interest group formation, they found a relationship between the economic variables employed and the number of interest groups. However, the relationship is the opposite of that hypothesized—as economies grow in size, the number of interests decline. Their work also suggests that increased economic diversity rather than economic size may be the critical economic factor in determining the number of interests in a state. In addition, these authors argue that institutions will tend to dominate when state economies are either stressed or are smaller in size (Lowery and Gray 1998).

Not all studies of social structural variables and interests have focused on the U.S. states. There are some studies on Washington, D.C., and on comparative interest groups. The work of Jack Walker and his associates on Washington, D.C., explicitly explored changes in social structure as the basis for interest group changes in the post–World War II period. Using a historical approach, Walker identified the emergence of a large, educated middle class, and the development of institutionally supported interests as the basis for increased mobilization of previously uninvolved segments of the population in the interest group arena (Walker 1991).

In the field of comparative interest group studies what Hrebenar and Thomas did for state interest group politics with their theoretical framework, Clive Thomas (1993a, 16–21) has done for the study of interest groups across advanced liberal democracies. His analysis includes such social structural variables as union membership, the extent of social and religious homogeneity, and the extent of social class in society.

While research into social structure and interests continues to be of concern to scholars, this approach is not without its critics. Moe (1980) and Salisbury (1984) argue that such research, while informative, does little to explain the formation of specific groups or the reason why individuals choose to join certain groups. As noted by Lowery and Gray (1993a), one future direction of research might be to explain links between the study of macro-level social variables and macro-level studies of the motivations leading individuals to join groups.

4.7. INTEREST GROUPS AND ECONOMIC DEVELOPMENT

Kennith G. Hunter

Research into the relationship between interest groups and economic development policy has not been as extensive or systematic as it has been for many areas of interest group studies. Consequently, the specific role of interest groups in this policy area is still unclear despite extensive anecdotal evidence suggesting that many interest groups work to shape economic development. The most comprehensive review of scholarship in this field is Hunter (1999).

Although scholarship is scanty and inconclusive, there is no doubt that, particularly since the 1970s, officials in the U.S. states have been greatly concerned about economic development. For this reason, business interests often enjoy privileged access to state leadership regarding economic development issues, especially in states dominated by Republicans and conservative Democrats (Thomas and Hrebenar 1999a). This situation skews the public agenda to where economic development becomes the dominant policy area pursued in many U.S. states. Even seemingly unrelated issues—such as the training of prisoners in new job skills, the preservation of small rural hospitals, creation of a state lottery, and so on—are touted as examples of economic development. This tendency to label so many things as economic development makes it extremely difficult to separate true economic development policy from those policies claiming to be such, and this impedes scholarly analysis.

At a more specific level, although scholars can only speculate about the relationship between interest groups and economic development policies, recent research follows two paths. One is that interest groups are very protective of their self-interests and tend to promote specific policies (Dye 1990; M. Olson 1982; Shelley et. al., 1990). Individual firms or associations of firms (such as the Chemical Manufacturers Association and the American Plastics Council) have little vested interest in advocating general policies that benefit all businesses or society in general. Doing so invites competition for market share and for scarce public dollars to subsidize business operations. Instead, firms or associations argue for public policies that will benefit a particular firm or economic sector such as chemical manufacturing. The second view is that interest groups may produce both industry and society-wide benefits (for example, Hoenack 1989; Gray and Lowery 1988). Individual firms or associations of firms, such as the American Bankers Association or the Farm Bureau, may advocate general government policies that have benefits for society. Given that firms want to expand their market share while reducing costs, the attraction of having general benefits for future use may outweigh concerns that the policy may promote some competition within an economic sector. This may have additional importance if a firm has no immediate plans for expansion but wants to establish public policies that facilitate state-funded growth for them in the future.

Perhaps the most important milestone in the relationship between economic development and interest groups are Mancur Olson's (1982, 97–98) ideas regarding the relationship between interest groups and economic growth. He contends that when nations experience long periods of stability, they will have greater opportunity to accumulate "growth retarding organizations," and as a result, they will have lower rates of growth. Olson argues that distributional coalitions of interests (particularly strong trade unions) slow down a society's capacity to adopt new technologies and to reallocate resources in response to changing conditions, thereby reducing the rate of economic growth. Most scholars now dismiss Olson's work as inaccurate (for example, Ambrosius 1989; S. M. Davis 1996; Garand 1992; Gray and Lowery 1988; Jordan and Maloney 1996; Lange and Garrett 1985; W. Mitchell and Munger 1991).

Although many scholars have found little evidence to support Olson's propositions, efforts to test his ideas are the basis of recent theories about the relationship among interest groups, other variables, and economic development. These studies use various combinations of economic, political, and socioeconomic variables including legislative professionalism, changes in gross state product, economic diversity, and the types of interest groups to more fully examine the relationship between interest groups and economic development (Hunter 1999). Moving the study of the relationship or interest groups and economic development from the realm of anecdotal information to empirical analysis is the most urgent need, and these recent research developments are a step in that direction.

4.8. INTEREST GROUPS AND PUBLIC OPINION

Ken Kollman

When referring to the relationship of interest groups and public opinion, the reference may be to one of two separate but usually interrelated elements: (1) the general public's and sometimes public officials' knowledge and attitudes toward interest groups, which is part of the political culture or subculture of a country and, in specific circumstances, can both constrain and aid group activity; or (2) how specific interest groups are constrained by or enlist public opinion through such activities as grassroots lobbying, media and public-relations campaigns, and even demonstrations, in advancing their goals (see sections 7.13., 7.14., and 7.15.). This delineation is not always made clear and some studies refer to both elements without distinction. But it is important to bear the two elements in mind for understanding both the general context in which interest groups operate and the specific strategies and tactics that they use.

The small amount of literature that exists focuses primarily on the second element, and most of this is based upon the U.S. experience and takes the form of case studies. There is no general study—not of the United States or any other country or a cross country comparison—of the role of public opinion on interest group activity in regard to its political cultural element. However, opinion-poll data is available on the knowledge and attitudes of Americans toward interest groups and lobbyists (see section 6.7.).

In regards to the importance of general public attitudes to interest groups, empirical evidence available on the United States (see section 6.7.) reveals a tension between the realization that groups are necessary and the concerns about their detrimental affects on democracy (Petracca 1992a, xix-xx). Although knowledge of public attitudes to interest groups in other liberal democracies, including transitional democracies like those in Eastern Europe, must be gleaned from secondary sources, all indications are that, where such public attitudes exist, they tend to be negative (Van Schendelen 1993; Evanson and Magstadt 2001; see chapter 14).

Thus, across the Western world, interest groups and lobbyists are generally viewed unfavorably. In the United States, in particular, they are often accused of thwarting popular policies. Mass media feed these accusations with stories not only of graft, but also of strikes, demonstrations, large campaign donations, and logrolling within the government and across major social interests. One consequence of these negative attitudes in the United States, and to a lesser extent in other western democracies, has been the regulation of interest group activity and lobbying (see chapter 14). These regulations are attempts by institutional reformers to respond to public concern (even outrage) over the supposed inequality in access and power granted to certain interest groups.

However, while surveys demonstrate the hostility that the public feels toward *special interests*, these surveys also indicate that citizens appreciate the work that *their* particular interest groups do to represent them and are often willing to participate in interest group activities. Furthermore, while elected officials complain about lobbyists, they also value the information lobbyists provide, and they respond to lobbyists who can credibly claim to represent the views of many constituents.

These general attitudes held by the public and public officials have an important affect on the way that interest groups operate on a day-to-day basis. Public opinion is both a constraint on interest groups and a powerful force they try to harness in their lobbying efforts. There is little sense in lobbying in favor of policies that no elected officials from any major political party will support because to do so endangers their reelection prospects, and thus what is realistic often comes down to how elected officials perceive the popularity and salience of policies among the mass public. Interest group leaders not only react to negative public opinion by making particular choices about strategies, but they also try to present public opinion in compelling and advantageous ways to elected officials and even seek to influence that opinion directly.

In fact, one consequence of the unpopularity of lobbyists and interest groups is that interest group leaders strive to cloak their lobbying efforts in populist clothing. Group leaders use outside lobbying, or targeted mobilization of citizens, to convince elected officials of the popularity of their proposed policies. They can generate letter writing and e-mail campaigns, organize demonstrations, run advertisements, and publish polling results. Sometimes the outside lobbying effectively, and genuinely, represents the actual views of large numbers of constituents on an issue. Other times the group pays a lot of money to manufacture the participation by members of the public, and the outside lobbying is misleading in overstating popular support for the group's goals (see sections 7.13., 7.14., and 7.15.).

To understand the state of research, a good starting point is V. O. Key's classic work *Public Opinion and American Democracy* (1967). Major recent works are Lupia (1992) on advertising in referendum elections, and Ainsworth and Sened (1993) on lobbying strategies, both of which are representative of rational choice approaches to studying interest groups in the context of battles over public opinion. J. M. Hansen (1991) on agricultural lobbies offers an important theoretical contribution. Kenneth

Goldstein (1998) and Kollman (1998) focus on outside lobbying and grassroots mobilization. Browne (1995a) and Jeffrey Berry (1999) focus on local interest groups and how they mobilize to influence politicians. Studies of European interest groups and public opinion have been conducted by Imig and Tarrow (2001) and by Greenwood (1997, 2003a). Gerber (1999) deals with interest groups and direct legislation in California including references to group attempts to influence public opinion on ballot propositions. Finally, Andsager (2000) and M. Welch, Leege, and Woodberry (1998) have published compelling empirical papers on the topic.

Some important results from this recent research are that intense lobbying in favor of a particular policy cannot overcome overwhelming public opinion against that policy (Lupia 1992; Gerber 1999; Kollman 1998), that interest groups spend a lot of resources trying to determine the importance of specific policy issues to the public (Browne 1995a; J. M. Hansen 1991; Kollman 1998), and that groups taking unpopular positions have a difficult time gaining access to lawmakers (Imig and Tarrow 2001; J. M. Hansen 1991).

Clearly, much more research needs to be done to provide a comprehensive understanding of the important role of public opinion as it affects interest groups in general and in their day-to-day operations in particular. Among the key research questions to be pursued are: How does the public view the institutions that lobbyists represent? What does the public conceive the purpose of lobbyists to be? Does the public's view parallel James Madison's conception of faction, where groups unite for some purpose adverse to the general interest? And how does the public evaluate the activities of specific interest groups?

4.9. NATIONAL CULTURES AND LOBBYING: THE CASE OF THE EUROPEAN UNION AND ITS IMPLICATIONS

Rinus Van Schendelen

An interesting question for students of comparative and transnational lobbying is the extent to which national cultures affect lobbying styles. The conventional wisdom is that national culture is very important; but there is little evidence to support this. Minimal as it is, some academic and popular work on the EU offers insights in this regard that have broader implications for comparing lobbying styles and techniques.

Spinelli (1966) analyzed different styles of political behavior in Brussels, the European capital, by people from the then six member-states of the European Economic Community (EEC): Belgians behave at ease, Dutch obstinately, Italians detached, Germans serious, and French bureaucratically. The smallest state of Luxembourg was not mentioned.

Since then, the different styles of political behavior in what is now the EU have become a major topic of jokes and cynicism among practitioners, but less the subject of systematic research by scholars. Most of the academic evidence has to be extrapolated from other studies on the EU.

Network studies, such as Glenda Rosenthal's (1975), suggest some culturally determined differences of networking and bargaining in Brussels. Policy studies, by H. Wallace et. al. (1989) and Lodge (1983 and 1989), reveal differences of policy values, which especially relate to different regional and sectoral backgrounds of the various officials and lobbyists. Institutional studies, such as those by Nicoll and Salmon (1994) and Nugent (1994), stress national cultural factors as being paramount in shaping the character of EU institutions. Case studies of EU lobbying by Greenwood, Grote, and Ronit (1992a), Mazey and Richardson (1993), and Pedler and Van Schendelen (1994) deal implicitly with the variety of cultural styles of interest group formation and lobbying behavior. Other studies, such as Van Schendelen's (1993, 2002), relate public or private lobby behavior at the EU level to domestic factors, including cultural ones.

Extrapolation from these sources reveal the following: British and Danish lobbying are more aggressive than that of most EU members during the formulation of policy, but very compliant once policy has been made and must be implemented. The French are good at using procedures and committees. The Germans, more than others, see litigation before the European Court of Justice as a tool of lobbying. The Dutch like to run European federations of national interest groups. The Italians preferably operate through their Brussels-based clan or *apartenenza*. And the member states with strong regions or regionalism at home, for example Italy, tend to speak in Brussels with many voices. Another observation is that the phenomenon of the professional, and particularly the contract lobbyist (often referred to in Brussels as a political consultant), has entered the Brussels scene mainly from the United Kingdom and from a few continental multinational companies, but is spreading to other northern countries, and these consultants are being increasingly used by smaller businesses and government organizations.

These findings are small beginnings; but they do offer insights into the challenges and problems that result from transnational lobbying and beg for a greater understanding as organizations like the EU and as globalization increases lobbying across national borders. The reason why styles of lobbying needs systematic research is not just for academic purposes. An understanding of national styles of lobbying within and beyond the EU and what elements do and do not transfer across countries has a very practical application. Such knowledge is a precondition for lobbying effectiveness in transnational lobbying. Lack of knowledge of the styles and techniques of the opposition is detrimental to one's own interest as Gardner (1991), C. Thomas (1998b), and C. Thomas, Hrebenar, and

Boyer (2001) have demonstrated with regard to U.S. groups and interests lobbying in the EU.

4.10. PEAK ASSOCIATIONS
Ronald G. Shaiko

The term *peak association* is used most in the analysis of economic organizations in corporatist or neocorporatist political systems (see section 3.4.); though the generic use of the term is applicable to certain types of economic groups in the United States. Peak associations are organizations of organizations. They are usually economically-based umbrella groups representing the broad economic forces in society, most often business, labor, and agriculture; though increasingly, there are peak associations in noneconomic areas such as in environmental and women's issues. In Western Europe, examples of economic peak associations are: the Schweizereische Handels-und Industries-Verein (VORORT) for Swiss business; the Trade Union Congress (TUC) in Britain for labor unions; and the Lantbrukarnas Riksförbund (LRP), the farm peak association in Sweden. In the United States, major peak associations include: the U.S. Chamber of Commerce, the Business Roundtable, the National Association of Manufacturers, and the National Federation of Independent Business (representing the business sector); the American Federation of Labor-Congress of Industrial Organizations (AFL-CIO; representing labor); and the American Farm Bureau Federation (representing agricultural interests).

From the neocorporatist perspective, peak associations represent the "sectoral-unspecific aggregation and organization of [economic] interests" that work together with government to formulate economic policies (Lanzalaco 1992). The sectoral-unspecific nature of peak associations refers to the breadth of inclusion of the various economic components that comprise the business sector, organized labor, and farm interests. For example, within the membership of the U.S. Chamber of Commerce are Fortune 500 corporations representing the entire spectrum of business enterprises as well as small businesses. Similarly, the AFL-CIO represents more than 80 unions that include workers in an array of occupations.

The distinction between a peak association and a coalition, whether in the American context or from the corporatist perspective, is important. Peak associations are permanent organizations that represent the aggregate interests of business, labor, or agriculture on a wide variety of policy issues. As a result, they are often constrained by the diversity of opinions found within the autonomous organizations that comprise the peak association's membership (corporations that belong to the VORORT or individual labor unions that comprise the TUC, for example). In contrast, political coalitions are usually formed on an ad hoc basis and are focused on a specific policy issue upon which the coalition members agree. They may also include components of both business and labor as well as citizen groups (C. C. Campbell and Davidson 1998; Hula 1995 and 1999; Shaiko 1998; Shaiko and Wallace 1999).

The roles of peak associations in the U.S. policy-making process are less clearly defined than they are in neocorporatist or corporatist political systems such as Japan, Austria, Norway, and Sweden. The degree to which a nation has a coherent industrial policy, derived from collaborative links between government and industry, is an indication of the existence of a neocorporatist system aided by peak associations. The key distinction between the roles of peak associations in the United States and in Japan, for example, lies in the facilitation of a system of interest intermediation in which organizations representing the major interests in society enjoy a monopoly of representation that is recognized and encouraged by the state in Japan but not in the United States. In Japan, the Ministry of International Trade and Industry (MITI) has developed, with the input of peak associations, industrial policies that provide a long-term view of economic development (C. Johnson 1982; Wilks and Wright 1987; Hrebenar 2001; Zeigler 1988).

In the United States, there are no systematic mechanisms to grant such monopoly representation to business, labor, or farm peak interests in the policy process. This is due, in part, to the fact that the interest group system is not as encompassing as in neocorporatist societies: The United States has low membership density (the number of potential members belonging to groups, such as labor), and sectors are represented by more than one peak association (as with business). On the other hand, in most neocorporatist countries, membership density is high, and usually one peak association represents a sector (C. Thomas 1993a, 16–21). Perhaps because of the lack of macro-level neocorporatism in the United States (G. Wilson 1982; Salisbury 1979; Schmitter 1981), peak associations have received little attention by scholars studying U.S. politics. While this lack of attention may have some validity in comparing the U.S. with other countries, it has also resulted in few analyses that attempt to apply neocorporatist perspectives to the study of organized interests within the U.S. policy-making process, which can produce valuable insights. In the United States, corporatist relationships often evolve at the micro-policy level (Cater 1964; J. Berry 1988; Heinz et al., 1993; Shaiko 1998).

In contrast, because the role of peak associations in neocorporatist systems is such an integral part of policy making, scholars focusing on European systems have produced extensive literature exploring the complex relationships between peak economic interests and government. This not only includes work at the national level but also at the transnational level (Berger 1981; Joan Campbell 1992; W. Coleman and Grant 1988; Keeler 1987; Greenwood, Grote, and Ronit 1992a; Peddler and Van Schendelen 1994; and see section 3.4.).

Chapter 5

The Origin, Maintenance, Organization, and Mortality of Interest Groups

Frank R. Baumgartner and Beth L. Leech

with an entry by
Virginia Gray and David Lowery

5.1. INTRODUCTION

This chapter focuses on the research and literature conducted on the internal dynamics of interest group activities in contrast to the role that groups have in the public policy-making process. It specifically deals with the origin, maintenance, organization, and demise of groups. The bulk of the research cited is work on the U.S. political system; but much of it has relevance for understanding interest group activity and group systems in liberal democracies in general.

As section 1.5. points out, there is no water-tight distinction in subject matter between the study of the internal dynamics of groups and their role in the public policy-making process—some subjects and aspects of others can be included under both. This is the case, for example, with the composition and development of the group system in a country, or in other jurisdictions, which includes the range and number of groups operating (the so-called *group universe*) and of interest group *subsystems* (how interest groups organize and operate within particular policy areas, such as agriculture, healthcare or child welfare). For this reason, the group universe, group subsystems, and other subjects (which cannot be neatly compartmentalized into one of the two main areas of group studies) are partly covered in this chapter with cross-references to other entries in this *Guide*.

5.2. THE ORIGIN AND MAINTENANCE OF INTEREST GROUPS

Theories of group politics once depicted the creation, growth, and death of interest groups as a natural and unbiased process that reflects the emergence of interests in a society at large. However, while scholars recognized the dominance of certain special interests such as business, the origins of interest groups and its consequences for political power was seldom seen as an important topic for research. This changed with the 1965 (and 1971) publication of Mancur Olson's *The Logic of Collective Action: Public Goods and the Theory of Groups.* The current thought on the origins of interest groups theorizes that institutions and concentrated economic groups are advantaged, and that noneconomic interests need the help of entrepreneurs and patrons in order to organize. A group's attempts to maintain its memberships and budget are presumably affected by similar processes, and therefore, group origins and maintenance have usually been studied in tandem.

No exhaustive bibliography on group origins and maintenance exists, but books by Jack Walker (1991; chaps. 2, 3, and 5), Knoke (1990; chap. 2), and Baumgartner and Leech (1998; chaps. 4 and 5) are useful starting points. Knoke examines the individual-level decisions that affect groups; Walker analyzes the societal and governmental forces behind group origins and maintenance; and Baumgartner and Leech provide a general overview of the literature.

Disturbance Theory

The idea that the creation of interest groups is natural and unproblematic is most often attributed to Truman (1951). According to Truman, the interest group system in equilibrium accurately reflects the multiple and conflicting beliefs and desires of the people, thus ensuring political stability. In this system, every person is a member of multiple, overlapping groups, and every conceivable interest is represented.

This group-based theory of politics, under which organizations spring spontaneously from all individual interests, had its modern origins in the work of Bentley (1908). While Truman provided detailed historical description of interest group activity in the United States to support his argument, Bentley's work is primarily theoretical. Although Bentley did not argue that all groups were fairly represented within government, he did believe that all human interaction was group based—groups were demographic, and social categories that might or might not be formally organized. Bentley defined group so loosely that virtually any belief or desire held by more than one individual qualified. Under such a vague definition, the question of the origins of groups is not an issue.

Groups exist because *interests* exist. Early empirical works by scholars such as Herring (1929) reflect this view. Describing the Washington interest group scene in the 1920s, Herring wrote:

> Not only are almost all sorts of interests and classes represented but also all sides of most questions as well. For example, the motorists have the Amer-

ican Automobile Association; the manufacturers are represented by the National Automobile Chamber of Commerce, while the distributors speak through the National Automobile Dealers Association. Makers and sellers of accessories, tires, batteries, and parts have their national associations. What of the poor pedestrian? There is the American Pedestrian Protective Association, organized in 1926. (Herring 1929, 22)

For Bentley, Herring, Truman, and many other scholars, a group theory of politics was *the* theory of politics because all relevant interests seemed to be represented. Truman saw the creation of groups as a natural reaction to social and economic disturbances. Although he made it clear that not all interests would be formally organized at a given time, he believed that unorganized, shared attitudes constituted potential groups that *would* organize if disturbed. This equilibrium state of interests would be altered from time to time by societal disturbances such as economic shifts or demographic changes. Similarly, any increase in political activity that conflicts with another interest would prompt activity by a countervailing group. Disturbance theory seemed to guarantee that the constellation of organized interests would never be far from the set of potential interests in society.

Disturbance theory is largely discredited today. While certainly everyone has interests, as Bentley and Truman saw, the organization of those interests is far from automatic, even when societal disturbances occur. Salisbury (1969 and 1975) provides a discussion of the logical and empirical problems with the theory, as well as useful bibliographies of older related works. Garson (1974 and 1978) provides a detailed review of how group theories of politics came to be widely held and subsequently discarded.

Olsonian Rational Choice Theory

Mancur Olson's *The Logic of Collective Action* (1965 and 1971) sounded the death knell for disturbance theory. Olson logically showed why some interests would be less likely to organize than others, and in doing so, he provided an explanation for the empirical findings of business dominance in the interest group system that had been noted by so many before him (e.g., Cater 1964; Maass 1951; Schattschneider 1935 and 1960). Olson's book also prompted a shift in interest group scholarship, and the collective action dilemma and its limitations became the most written-about aspect of the field of interest groups. Many of these studies have been theoretical extensions of Olson's work, supported by formal mathematical models rather than detailed data collection. Hardin (1982) provides a good example of these theoretical developments. Knoke (1986; 1990, 35–38) provides a good bibliography of empirical research inspired by Olson.

Olson's theory begins with the observation that by Bentley's definition, groups have interests and goals in common. Disturbance theory and other traditional approaches lead one to expect groups to work toward furthering those goals; but Olson argued that the traditional approaches are wrong. He pointed out that many of the common goals of groups are what economists call *public goods*—they represent benefits, which, if attained, are shared by those who worked to attain them as well as those who did not. A manufacturer, for example, benefits from a tariff on foreign goods, regardless of whether that manufacturer contributed to the lobbying effort for the tariff. Everyone benefits from breathing cleaner air regardless of whether they joined an environmental group. Olson's theory holds that rational, self-interested individuals will not voluntarily work together to attain a communal goal if that goal is for the public good.

Olson hypothesizes that small groups have an easier time overcoming the collective-action dilemma. This may be for three reasons. First, they can exert social pressure on members. Second, each individual contribution affects the likelihood of achieving the collective goal: In a large group, the withdrawal of one person's contribution may affect total revenues minimally; in a small group, it may be substantial enough to render unlikely the achievement of the group's goals. In this case, there is no dilemma: either all contribute or none reap the benefits. There is no temptation to be a free rider here, and there may be considerable pressure to conform to the contribution levels of others in the group. And third, the collective good may be valuable enough that one or a few members may be willing to bear the cost even in the presence of free riders. This last situation leads to what Olson called the exploitation of the large by the small because members with less to gain from the collective good may rely on those with much to gain to provide the collective good for everyone.

According to Olson, large groups can overcome the collective action dilemma only by providing selective incentives. These selective incentives can take the form of coercion to join, as is the case in a closed union shop, or, more commonly, it can take the form of benefits, such as low-cost insurance rates, opportunities for professional advancement, or a subscription to a magazine or journal. Olson argued that the political power of most large interest groups is really a by-product of the group's primary, nonpolitical functions. That is, groups like the American Medical Association (AMA) and the Veterans of Foreign Wars (VFW) came into being and continue to exist because they provide selective benefits—in these examples, professional services and social opportunities—to their members and only to their members. Once a group is firmly established for nonpolitical purposes, it is able to expend some of its excess organizational capital toward lobbying for collective goods, but this is a by-product of the organization, not its reason for being. Many of the most powerful interest groups in Washington, D.C., such as the National Rifle Association

(NRA) and the American Association of Retired Persons (AARP), came into being through by-product mechanism. The by-product theory of political action is one of the most potent explanations of lobbying in Washington, D.C., and other liberal democracies. Ironically, it points toward nonpolitical explanations for political behavior by interest groups.

Research Based on Olson's Hypotheses

Empirical tests of hypotheses that group origins are derived from collective action are primarily of two types: surveys of group members and experiments. Tillock and Morrison (1979), Moe (1980a), Rothenberg (1992), and Knoke (1990) surveyed members of different interest groups and analyzed their reasons for joining. Tillock and Morrison, and Rothenberg based their work on the surveys of a single noneconomic interest group, while Moe surveyed members of five economic groups in Minnesota. Knoke surveyed nearly 9,000 members of 35 professional, recreational, and women's groups. While selective benefits were cited as important by many members, as would be predicted by Olson's theory, a significant number of members also said that political or ideological concerns (which are collective benefits) played a role in their decisions to join.

Moe (1980a, 1980b, 1981) and Rothenberg (1988 and 1992) question Olson's assumption that individuals possess accurate information about the benefits of group membership. Moe argues that people join groups in part because they overestimate the importance of their contribution to the provision of the collective benefit. His survey of Minnesota group members found that people who reported strong feelings of efficacy also were more likely to cite political reasons (a collective good) rather than material or solidary (social) reasons for joining a group. In effect, these people joined groups because they misjudged their ability to influence group actions: had these members obtained more accurate information about the importance of their own contribution, they would not have joined.

Rothenberg studied membership decisions within Common Cause. He concluded that people may join a group they know little about, since the investment in time and money is usually nominal, then, through a process of "experiential search," decide whether to remain a group member. Although Rothenberg's data is cross-sectional, he did show that long-time members knew more about the group and were more committed to remaining with the group than newer members. Membership recruitment and retention are often discussed interchangeably, but Rothenberg's work suggests that the processes affecting them may be different.

J. M. Hansen (1985) took a slightly different tack, analyzing changes in the overall memberships of three national associations over time. His findings were closer to what one would expect from disturbance theory than from an Olsonian perspective. Membership increased during times when collective group interests were threatened by social and economic factors.

Whether these findings constitute valid tests of the Olsonian theory has been questioned in part because the samples included only those who defied the collective action dilemma and decided to participate in a group, without a comparable sample of potential members who did nothing. (Rothenberg, however, compares member characteristics to characteristics of the population at large.) In response to Tillock and Morrison's (1979) study of members in the Zero Population Growth (ZPG) group, Olson (1979) argued that what was striking was the millions of believers in population control who chose not to belong to ZPG, not the few thousands of "deviants" who did.

Unlike the member surveys, experimental studies consider both joiners and nonjoiners. Results have been mixed, but again tend to show that people will indeed join groups to further collective goods. However, the level of joining is often seen as *suboptimal*, meaning that not everyone who would benefit from a public good agrees to contribute to creating that good. In these experimental studies, subjects are typically given tokens representing a small amount of money and offered the opportunity to invest it in a public good that will only be provided if enough people agree to invest in it. If the collective action succeeds and the public good is provided, all subjects receive a benefit. If the collective action fails, those who contributed to the collective good lose their original investment, while free riders keep theirs.

A series of experiments by Marwell and Ames (1979, 1980, 1981) using high school students indicated that most would not choose to free-ride, while Dawes et al. (1986) found that free ridership decreased when researchers promised that free riders would be forced to pay their share should the collective action succeed. Isaac, Walker, and Thomas (1984) found widely varying degrees of free ridership within their set of eight experiments, and they suggest that group size and marginal per capita returns may explain at least part of the variation. Although the results of these studies are provocative, the question is often raised whether the results from a laboratory setting would be replicated in the real world.

Researchers have rarely sampled both activists and free riders in a nonlaboratory setting. Two exceptions involve studies that analyzed community mobilization stemming from the Three Mile Island (TMI) accident of 1979 (Walsh and Warland 1983) and from environmental threats to Lake Tahoe (Sabatier 1992; see also Sabatier and McLaughlin 1990). Free riding was found to be more widespread than first indicated by experimental studies: Only 12 percent of residents who described themselves as discontented contributed a token amount of time or money to antinuclear efforts, and only 6 percent of people who owned second homes in the

Tahoe Basin area joined environmental efforts. Contrary to what Olson's theory would predict, however, the lack of information about the mobilization effort was seen as the primary reason for free riding in the TMI case, although calculations of self-interest were also important. The Lake Tahoe study found that joiners believed more strongly in group goals than nonjoiners, suggesting that collective benefits rather than selective benefits may explain membership decisions.

In general, research testing Olsonian hypotheses has provided support for his prediction that large groups pursuing collective goals will not organize to their full potential. However, this research has also shown that Olson's preferred explanation for why some individuals do join a collective action (to gain selective material benefits) fails to explain the motivations of all individuals. Olson's focus on suboptimality also brushes aside the question of whether the group, no matter how small in proportion to the number of people who agree with their goals, might still be large enough to achieve significant results. Both the environmental movement and the Civil Rights movement, for example, attracted few active members compared with the number of people who stood to benefit from their collective goals, and yet both movements were successful on a number of fronts.

Selective Benefits: Going beyond Economic Self-Interest

Critics of Olson often focus on whether economic self-interest is an adequate explanation of why people join and remain members of interest groups. This area of the literature is rooted in an article by Clark and Wilson (1961; see also J. Q. Wilson 1973) on the strategies groups adopt to maintain their membership bases. The typology set forth by Clark and Wilson distinguishes three types of membership incentives—*material, solidary*, and *purposive*. Material incentives are the same types of tangible selective benefits described by Olson. Solidary incentives arise from the act of associating and "depend for their value on how the recipient appears in the eyes of others" (J. Q. Wilson 1973, 40). They include such intangibles as social relationships with other group members and increased status in the eyes of nonmembers. Purposive incentives (sometimes also called *expressive* benefits [Salisbury 1969]) are even less tangible, involving the good feelings people get from contributing to a cause in which they believe.

Salisbury (1969) first adapted this typology to an Olsonian framework and illustrated how such incentives could help explain group origins as well as group maintenance. Moe (1980b and 1981) expanded and formalized this revised model, and other researchers have inquired about selective incentives in their surveys of interest groups and their members (e.g., J. Berry 1977; Knoke 1990; Rothenberg 1992; Schlozman, Verba, and Brady 1995; J. Walker 1983 and 1991). Solidary and purposive incentives are often cited as important by group members and leaders. Jack Walker's surveys of 1,500 interest groups showed that solidary and purposive benefits were offered by most of the groups and that personal material benefits, such as insurance and merchandise discounts, were less common.

Explaining individuals' decisions to join in terms of solidary and purposive incentives is problematic, however, because such benefits are difficult to measure and because the concept of a purposive incentive can be expanded to explain virtually every possible case. While Olson recognized that selective incentives need not be limited to material benefits, he believed that his theory was best applied to economic interest groups where the dominant forms of selective benefits were material. Olson wrote that stretching his argument to such types of organizations as philanthropies and charities would not be useful since the resulting theory would not be subject to any possible empirical refutation (Olson 1971, 160 n). Jack Walker (1991, 47) suggests that instead of trying to include purposive incentives within an Olsonian framework, researchers should focus on determining the conditions under which individuals will join groups to advance purposive or collective goals.

Other Explanations of the Origin of Groups

While researchers studying group members have focused on assessing the extent of free riding and describing the type of person who contributes to a collective good, other scholars have suggested ways in which groups might overcome or at least minimize the collective action dilemma. By turning the focus away from the rank-and-file member, they are able to note the importance to interest groups of patrons and entrepreneurs, and they find that many interest groups are not really groups at all. Institutions, professions, and social movements provide additional ways for organized interests to manifest themselves.

Patrons: One of the major findings from the surveys of interest group membership conducted by Jack Walker in 1980 and 1985 was the importance of patron contributions (J. Walker 1983 and 1991). While most of the previous empirical work applying Olson's theory focused on the problem of convincing individual members to contribute their fair share, Walker's surveys demonstrated the importance of large contributions from foundations, government grants, corporations, and wealthy individuals. His survey revealed that 34 percent of profit-sector groups and 89 percent of citizen groups received start-up money from some type of patron (J. Walker 1991, 78). Citizen groups reported that about 35 percent of their annual budgets were funded by patrons (J. Walker 1991, 82). He argued that an increase in patronage was the primary reason for the rapid increase in the number of interest groups during the 1960s and 1970s.

Walker emphasized that group formation could not be understood by looking solely at individual-level variables. Of crucial importance were "the incentives, constraints, and opportunities" created by governmental, economic, and social institutions (J. Walker 1991, 49). For instance, major social legislation often includes provisions to create citizen advisory groups and often creates a material benefit that encourages potential group members to work toward protection by joining a group.

Entrepreneurs: Mancur Olson discussed the use of selective incentives to overcome the collective action dilemma, but never suggested who or what would provide these initial incentives. Salisbury's classic article "An Exchange Theory of Interest Groups" (1969) proposed that it is individual entrepreneurs who create groups, then offer potential members selective incentives to join. In exchange, entrepreneurs whose groups succeed provide themselves with staff jobs and the chance to further their own political agendas. Since Salisbury's article, the role of entrepreneurs has, to some extent, been recognized by virtually every researcher of group origins and maintenance.

Occupational Groups: By far the most common type of interest group are associations representing various professions and trades. As Olson's by-product theory predicts, these associations first originate from non-political motives, then some of their excess organizational capital is used for lobbying. Walker's study of membership associations found that more than 75 percent of these groups were in some way associated with occupations. About half of these occupationally based groups were nonprofit groups such as the Association of American Medical Colleges and the National Association of State Alcohol and Drug Abuse Directors (J. Walker 1991, 59–60).

Many people with interests who do not mobilize on their own—such as children, the mentally handicapped, and the poor—nonetheless have organizations that lobby on their behalf. Social service professionals and other entrepreneurs sometimes form these clientele organizations to serve groups of people to which the entrepreneur does not belong. Walker (1983 and 1991) argued that broad-based organizations of this type tend to arise after a major piece of social legislation has been passed, creating bureaucratic patronage for the service providers in question.

Institutions: As Salisbury (1984) points out, many of the entities often referred to as interest groups are not really groups at all. In addition to the clientele groups serving various social groups, a large percentage of the organized interests represented before government are entities such as think tanks, local governments, universities, and corporations for which collective-action problems are either minor or nonexistent. This points to the question of whether the problems discussed by Olson may have been given more prominence in the interest group literature than they deserved.

Social Movements: The process through which social movements arise is essentially a membership process, and thus scholars of social movements often employ Olson's theoretical framework. Gamson (1990) presents data on 53 protest groups supporting Olson's by-product theory: Groups that offered selective incentives in addition to solidary benefits were more than twice as likely to succeed than those that offered only solidary benefits.

Jack Walker (1991, 52) and Oliver, Marwell, and Teixeira (1985) suggest, however, that Olson's work is an incomplete description of the creation of social movements. While Walker stresses the importance of patronage and the political environment, Oliver, Marwell, and Teixeira take issue with Olson's assumption that individuals make decisions about collective action independent of others. The authors argue that while this assumption may hold true in economic markets, it seldom is true in social group formations. In part, individuals make their decisions based on the actions of others. Oliver, Marwell, and Teixeira mathematically outline a theory that predicts the conditions under which an unorganized interest will succeed in compiling the critical mass of members needed to begin a collective action. Chong (1991) builds on this theory, using the case of the U.S. Civil Rights movement of the 1960s. His explanation stresses the importance of an individual monitoring the decisions of others and using social pressure to encourage cooperation.

5.3. THE INTERNAL ORGANIZATION OF INTEREST GROUPS

Studies of the internal organization of interest groups have focused primarily on issues of internal democracy and member participation. Since interest groups are often seen as vehicles for enhancing citizen representation, researchers have attempted to determine whether groups actually represent members' beliefs or whether Michels's (1958) "iron law of oligarchy" is a more accurate depiction of groups and their leadership. These questions, however, apply primarily to membership organizations; the internal organization of institutions and clientele groups has been largely ignored within the interest group literature. James Q. Wilson (1973, chaps. 11 and 12) provides a good bibliography of older works on the topic; Knoke (1990, chaps. 8 and 9) offers a more recent discussion of the literature; and Baumgartner and Leech (1998, chaps. 5 and 6) provide a general overview of the literature.

Internal Democracy

Group members have generally been found to place only loose constraints on the governance and external political activities of their organizations. Mancur Olson's by-product theory suggests that most members joined their group for reasons other than lobbying. And empirical studies indicate that most members are ill informed about their organization's political stances and about candidates for organization leadership. So, although democratic processes such as board elections often exist on paper, it is most often a small core of activists who set the agenda for group activities. These activists do not have free rein, however, just as legislators must concern themselves with public opinion and solicit constituency views, so must organizational leaders be concerned with the views of their rank-and-file members. Leaders must avoid alienating current and potential members with unpopular lobbying stands.

The advocacy group for responsible government, Common Cause, has been studied both through qualitative interviews (McFarland 1984a) and a broad-based membership survey (Rothenberg 1988 and 1992). Although members of the group elect the organization's governing board and are asked to share their views by completing an annual poll, only about one-fourth of the membership votes, and fewer still, fill out the poll (McFarland 1984a, 96). Rothenberg's survey shows a lack of knowledge among most members that prevents the group from functioning as a truly democratic organization. Leaders are, however, responsive to membership opinions that they hear. According to McFarland, the group is constrained by the possibility that members may leave the group, and avoids lobbying on any issue opposed by 20 percent or more of questionnaire respondents. Considering the case of lobbying against the MX missile, Rothenberg (1992, 186) concludes that while rank-and-file members may have veto power over group actions, it is the activists who set the agenda and leaders who maintain discretion over how that agenda is pursued and enacted.

Moe (1980a, 74 ff) argues that Olson's by-product theory implies that group political goals and individual political goals will not necessarily coincide. Under this version of the by-product theory, and since members join a group for its selective material benefits rather than its collective benefits, leaders can lobby for whatever they like without worrying about member beliefs. Moe introduces the idea of entrepreneurial bargaining to this discussion, and suggests ways that members, staff, and outsiders might influence an entrepreneur's policy decisions.

Knoke's surveys include responses from nearly 9,000 group members and 459 groups. He found that most associations have democratic structures (i.e., elected boards or officials) and decentralized patterns of influence, disputing the idea of inevitable oligarchy advanced by Michels (1958). Knoke concludes: "Numerous democratic structures exist that rein in tendencies toward power usurpation by leaders" (Knoke 1990, 160).

Public interest groups, which are created primarily to influence public policy, differ from the recreational and professional associations studied by Knoke. Leaders of national public interest groups surveyed by Berry indicated that their members are "supportive rather than participatory" (J. Berry 1977, 188). These groups tend to lack even pro-forma democratic structures, and most decision-making power resided with the staff.

Again, however, members were seen as wielding influence through their ability to withhold contributions.

Steven Rathgeb Smith and Lipsky (1993) provide a rare look at the internal organization of clientele groups. In a study of 30 nonprofit clientele organizations in New England, they find that because of the importance of government contracts and other funds for group operations, most are at least partially controlled by public officials. These researchers examine the tension between government influence on the one hand and the need to represent the disadvantaged before government on the other.

Members and Leaders

The tendency for most members to participate only minimally in group governance has led a few researchers to investigate the demographic and attitudinal differences among nonmembers, members, activists, and leaders. While members have been found to be more socioeconomically advantaged on average than nonmembers, few other definitive conclusions can be drawn from the data on the differences between members and activists.

Who belongs to interest groups? In answering this question we confine our answer to Americans as the vast majority of membership surveys have been conducted in the United States. Mass surveys indicate that the percentage of people who belong to at least one association is between 70 and 90 percent, depending on how strict a definition of membership is used and exactly what types of groups and organizations are included (Baumgartner and Walker 1988). A much smaller proportion of Americans are highly active in the group system. Baumgartner and Walker (1988, 919) found, for example, that only about 5 percent of their respondents to a 1985 survey had six or more organizational memberships. Participation in interest groups is clearly skewed by social class (Verba and Nie 1972; Baumgartner and Walker 1988). Verba et al. (1993) found that people who receive benefits for which poverty is not a requirement, such as Social Security and education loans, were much more likely to belong to an association dealing with that program than were people who received need-based benefits like food stamps and Medicaid.

Although a majority of Americans belong to some kind of association, most members do little more than donate money and add their names to the mailing list. Rothenberg, in his study of Common Cause (1992), divided members into *checkbook participants*, who pay their dues but do little else, *checkbook activists*, who donate additional money, and *temporal activists*, who donate time to the organization. Activists were more likely to be older, married, and from a less urban area than rank-and-file members. Although variations in race, education, and gender often are correlated with different levels of political participation, Rothenberg found no significant differences between activists and members for those characteristics. Rank-and-file members tended to be more politically conservative than activists, however.

Most large groups employ staff members who take charge of most of the organization's external political activities. James Wilson (1973, 226) uses anecdotal evidence to illustrate that staff members often hold more extreme views than rank-and-file members, although staff also have been known to moderate the views of group activists. Sabatier and McLaughlin (1990) present evidence from surveys of Lake Tahoe area business and environmental groups indicating that leaders tend to hold more extreme views than members.

Salisbury's (1969) exchange theory suggests that whatever the staff of a group does, it must reflect what members want, or they would not join the group. However, there is no guarantee that the benefits group leaders and staff offer members are the *political* benefits that they seek. An entrepreneur could potentially offer material benefits in order to attract supporters, then lobby on whatever topic he or she chose. Browne (1977) suggests, however, that such a situation would be unlikely. His study of four municipal interest associations indicates that organization staff feel pressure from members to provide individual services, but often must respond primarily with collective lobbying activities simply because they do not have enough employees to serve each member individually. The collective benefits are also meant to serve the members.

5.4. THE COMPOSITION AND DEVELOPMENT OF THE INTEREST GROUP SYSTEM AND GROUP COMPETITION

The Interest Group Universe

Research into the interest group universe has primarily concerned itself with questions about whether the system is biased and is rigidly closed to outsiders or more open and fluid (Baumgartner and Leech 1998, chap. 5). Some research has also been conducted on the changing composition of the group universe at the federal and state levels since the late 1960s (see section 6.2.). While business interests predominate, there is change in the system and other interests do sometimes prevail. Gray and Lowery (1996a) provide a good bibliography of research on the group universe at both the state and national levels, as well as a detailed discussion of related theoretical issues. Petracca (1992a) provides a useful bibliography of works related to the national interest group universe.

Gray and Lowery (1996a) make the point that we cannot completely understand interest group populations simply by studying individual-level incentives: The environment in which groups operate is also important. Borrowing concepts from population ecology and using data on interest groups within all 50 states, they present a theory in which the number and type of groups in existence is a function of the number of potential constituents, the degree and type of government activity in a given policy area, and government stability. The composition of and recent development in the group universe at the federal and state levels in the United States is covered in more detail in section 6.2. (see also section 5.5.).

Policy Subsystems, Subgovernments, and Interest Group Competition

To understand the group system, we must know more than how many groups there are, we must know how those groups are distributed across policy domains and the degree of competition among these groups. These topics are addressed in the study of policy subsystems, issue networks, and policy niches, all of which are often collectively referred to as subgovernments.

There have been many studies of subsystems within particular policy areas (e.g., Cater 1964; J. L. Freeman 1965; Fritschler 1975; Maass 1951). Many of these studies have been interpreted to suggest that the group system is closed, and that insiders are the only ones with influence in Washington, D.C. Heclo (1978) took issue with this view, arguing that policy systems are much more open, and today, they experience much more internal conflict. He preferred the term *issue network* to describe the interactions of interest group representatives, bureaucrats, legislators, and other interested parties.

Most empirical work in this area supports the idea that the interest group system is not monolithic. The surveys of lobbyists and government officials undertaken by Heinz et al. (1993; see also Salisbury et al. 1987) led those researchers to conclude that there is no single group of influential interest representatives in a given policy domain. Browne (1990), however, shifted the focus from the domain to the issue and concluded that conflict between groups is relatively rare. Using data from more than 200 interviews, he argued that groups find narrow issue niches in which they can dominate unchallenged. Baumgartner and Jones's (1993) longitudinal analyses of legislative hearings, media attention, and additional data for nine issue areas led them to conclude that while particular interests may predominate during a given period, such policy monopolies can and do break up, making way for other interests. A more detailed analysis of interest groups and policy subsystems is provided in section 7.16.

Overall, the research on the group universe and policy subsystems has tended to conclude that while business interests do make up a disproportionate percentage of the system, nonbusiness interests also play important roles. There is change over time and across issue domains, and there is no monolithic or permanent power structure.

5.5. THE MORTALITY OF INTEREST GROUPS

Virginia Gray and David Lowery

The scholarly emphasis on the mobilization of interests has produced a great deal of knowledge about how interest groups form but very little about how they disband. It is assumed that the same forces that govern mobilization govern dissolution: Groups that are hard to form are equally hard to maintain—but this is not known for certain. This question is critical because if different kinds of organizations die at different rates, then the population remaining will be different. For example, if citizens' groups disappear at a faster rate than business groups, the population of organizations may be skewed toward business even though new citizens' groups are being created all the time. Baumgartner and Leech (1998) are among those who emphasize the importance of group mortality in contributing to bias in the interest group system.

In the few attempts to study this question, scholars have found that it is important to keep the birth of an organization separate from its death (when it first came into existence and when it ceased to function). It is also important to keep an organization's entry into lobbying separate from its exit from the lobbying community (when it began and when it stopped lobbying). An organization might first be established, take up lobbying later on, and then become politically inactive (although it may still exist as an organization). From a political perspective, the beginning and end of an organization's lobbying activities is particularly significant.

On the national level, the first person to recognize the importance of the mortality question was Jack Walker (1983), who noted that in Washington, D.C., citizens' groups (often used as a synonym for *public* interest groups) were founded more recently than private groups. The explosion of citizen groups since the 1960s, he argued, meant that they constituted a larger proportion of the group universe than in the past. But he noted that without data on the mortality of different kinds of groups, his conclusions were speculative.

A few years later Schlozman and Tierney (1986) analyzed Washington-based interest organizations and, like Walker, they found that there had been an explosion in the number of citizens' groups. But contrary to Walker's survey, they found that citizens' groups actually decreased as a proportion of all active organizations between 1960 and 1980. This seemingly contradictory conclusion was explained when Schlozman and Tierney discovered that the mortality rate among citizens' groups was much higher than any other groups. Among all groups politically active in 1960, 60 percent were still active 20 years later; but for citizens' groups, only 33 percent were still lobbying. Thus, citizens' groups find it relatively easy to enter the lobbying world but also easy to exit from it. These findings are not definitive, however, because several problems marred Schlozman and Tierney's study.

At the state level, Gray and Lowery (1995 and 1996, chap. 6) carefully measured the entry and exit of lobbying in six states. They tracked 8,500 individual organizations and asked whether an organization listed on a state's lobby registration list in 1980 was still listed in 1990. In their sample, the survival rates were much lower than those recorded at the national level: The rates per state ranged from 36.6 percent to 56.7 percent.

Gray and Lowery reasoned that survival rates might differ among different types of organizations—institutions, associations, and membership groups. According to existing theoretical accounts such as Salisbury's (1984), institutions should be more durable and persistent whereas membership groups are thought to be riven with weakness and fragility. Contrary to these expectations, Gray and Lowery found that institutions have the lowest survival rates in the lobbying function, while associations and membership groups have higher survival rates.

Gray and Lowery next asked whether the failure to survive as a registered interest group signaled the death of the organization or if it is simply the cessation of the lobbying function. In one state, Gray and Lowery intensively investigated the life histories of more than 600 organizations; they found that institutions tended to withdraw from lobbying but still continue to exist, while for membership groups and associations, withdrawal from lobbying often coincided with the death of the organization. Lobbying is a more central activity for membership groups and associations while institutions can enter and leave the political arena as salient issues wax and wane. The authors concluded that the patterns of entry are about twice as influential as the patterns of exit in shaping the interest group universe. The population of organized interests is highly fluid; the fluidity critically affects the balance among organized interests whether the system is skewed toward business or consumer interests.

Many questions remain unanswered, such as what happens to organizations that withdraw from lobbying but do not dissolve as organizations. Do they monitor legislative activity and reenter the fray when needed? Do they form political action committees (PACs)? Furthermore, there is little or no comparative work that can facilitate a comparison of mortality patterns in the United States with mortality rates elsewhere.

5.6. CONCLUSIONS: SUBJECTS FOR FURTHER STUDY

The focus on individual membership decisions that has dominated interest group studies since Mancur Olson's path-breaking work leaves researchers to question whether the group system is half-empty or half-full. It is clear that noneconomic, collective interests are not organized to their fullest potential, and yet, many such interests do exist. Perhaps it is time to ask how effective groups are in spite of their *suboptimality*. After all, if a group representing a fraction of a larger community carries the full political weight of that community when it speaks out on political issues, the problem of collective action is minimized. On the other hand, if a small group is discounted because of all the potential members who declined to join, the problem of collective action seems insurmountable.

Clearly, questions about group origins, maintenance, organization, and demise remain important because of issues of political representation; but it is important to avoid studying groups from a solely membership-based point of view. The research described in this chapter points to the importance of the government, patrons, entrepreneurs, and institutions in group formation, maintenance, and governance. As yet, relatively little attention has been paid to these influences on group origins, maintenance, and organization, and how they are likely to affect the interest group system as a whole.

Chapter 6

Interest Groups in National, State, Local, and Intergovernmental Politics in the United States

6.1. INTRODUCTION

Clive S. Thomas

Chapter 2 of this *Guide* provides an introduction to the various sources of information and the major areas of research on interest groups in U.S. politics; and chapter 5 draws heavily from the U.S. experience in reviewing the work on the internal dynamics of interest groups. This present chapter focuses primarily on the major research on the operation of interest groups in the public policy process in the United States. Scholars studying group activity in the U.S. policy process tend to focus on one level of the federal system—national, state, or local. For this reason, this chapter is organized along these lines (sections 6.3. national, 6.4. state, 6.5. local, and 6.6. intergovernmental lobbying). Before reviewing work on the various levels of the system, section 6.2. traces the changing nature of the range and number of groups—the so-called group universe—in U.S. politics since the late 1960s. The chapter concludes with an entry (section 6.7.) on the public perceptions of interest groups and lobbying in the United States.

Several sources will be useful in supplementing or providing background to the entries in this chapter. Two sources, Allan Cigler (1991b) and Crotty, Schwartz, and Green (1994), provide good overviews of the state of research on U.S. interest groups. Although these sources are slightly dated and focus on the national and state levels only, they do cover both the internal dynamics and public policy aspects of U.S. interest group studies, provide useful critiques of the strengths and weaknesses of existing studies, and make suggestions for future research. A critique of the

American approach to the study of interest groups, particularly the way the subject matter is divided, is found in Frank Davis and Albert Wurth (1993). For those seeking information on specific U.S. interest groups, lobbyists, and political action committees (PACs), the two volumes by Ness (2000) are particularly useful. Besides chapter 2, other entries in this *Guide* that deal specifically with interest groups in the U.S. public policy process are sections 3.2. and 3.3. on pluralism and elitism respectively, section 4.3. on the political and governmental structure, several entries in chapter 7 on strategy and tactics (including section 7.17 on group power), and the various groups and interests covered in chapters 8 and 9. Finally, Clemens (1997) provides a historical perspective on the modern origins and development of the U.S. interest group system (1890–1925). This comprehensive analysis includes a treatment of the emergence of various strategies and tactics by farmers, labor, and women and the development of intergovernmental lobbying by state groups in Washington, D.C.

6.2. THE INTEREST GROUP UNIVERSE IN WASHINGTON, D.C., AND THE STATES

Anthony J. Nownes, Frank R. Baumgartner, and Beth L. Leech

The term *group universe* is used to describe the types and numbers of interest groups and interests operating in a country or at the subnational level (state, province, county, city, or town). Most of the research on the group universe in the United States has been conducted since the 1960s and focuses on the national level in Washington, D.C. There is also a growing body of comprehensive work on the states, but there is no comprehensive study of local jurisdictions. There are, however, numerous studies of local interest groups from which a picture of the group universe in various local jurisdictions can be gleaned (see section 6.5.). The overview provided here focuses on the group universe at the national and state levels and the recent changes in its composition.

At the national level, Jack Walker (1983 and 1991) and Schlozman and Tierney (1983 and 1986) produced two broad empirical descriptions of the Washington interest group population. Walker surveyed more than 1,000 groups in his two surveys, although his investigation was limited to membership groups. Schlozman and Tierney surveyed fewer than 200 groups, but their survey included corporations and some other nonmembership organizations. Two other surveys, Laumann and Knoke (1987) and Heinz et al. (1993), include all entities cited by informants as influential, including professional lobbying firms, but they limit their investigations to specific policy domains. Laumann and Knoke consider energy and health policy; Heinz et al. study agriculture, health, energy, and labor.

At the state level, the major work has been conducted by Thomas and Hrebenar (1990, 1996b, table 4.1, 1999a, 2003), Gray and Lowery (1995,

1996a, 2001), and Hunter, Wilson, and Brunk (1991). These are fifty-state studies that in combination provide a comprehensive picture of the group universe. The works by Thomas and Hrebenar and by Gray and Lowery provide a twenty-two year time series (1980–2002) that enables us to trace the changing group universe at the state level. See also section 6.4.

To understand the nature and limitations of the research on the group universe, four points are important to bear in mind. First, little is known about the group universe before the 1960s, which is when the first extensive interest in this topic arose among American interest group scholars. The assumption is that far fewer and a much narrower range of groups and interests operated in Washington, D.C., and the states; but no one knows for certain. Recent research, still in its early stages (Tichenor and Harris 2002), provides evidence that the range of groups, including the presence of many public interest groups, may not have been as narrow at the national level as previously believed. Second, the range of potential groups is a function of the constitutional and legal authority of a particular jurisdiction. In particular, the federal government has jurisdiction over foreign policy; thus a multitude of foreign lobbies operate in Washington, D.C., but few at the state level. Third, the more diverse the socioeconomic and political structure of the society, the wider the range of groups and interests (Thomas and Hrebenar 2003, table 4.1). California, for example, has a more diverse group universe than North Dakota. Finally, consulting only registration lists of interest groups at the national and state levels can be misleading in accurately conveying the number of active groups and interests. This is because some states use a very broad definition of *interest group* (such as Arizona and Florida) while others (Arkansas and Idaho, for example) use a narrow definition. See section 1.2. for problems associated with different definitions of the term *interest group* and section 14.4.2. for information about the state regulation of interest groups.

Six Major Characteristics of the Changing Group Universe

With these points in mind, we can move to identify six major characteristics of and developments in the interest group universe at the national and state levels since the 1960s.

1. The Proliferation of Interests. According to most researchers, the number of organized interests active in Washington, D.C., and the states has increased markedly since the end of World War II (Schlozman and Tierney 1983, 1986; J. Walker, 1983, 1991; M. A. Peterson and Walker 1986; Gray and Lowery 1995, 1996a; Thomas and Hrebenar 1999a). Group proliferation was especially pronounced in the 1960s and continued well into the early 1980s at both the national and state levels. There are probably close to 15,000 organized interests active in Washington, D.C., close to 40,000 at the state level (Hunter, Wilson, and Brunk 1991), and tens of thousands more in local jurisdictions. The reasons for group proliferation are manifold and include increased governmental activity in the 1960s and 1970s, the decline of political parties, unprecedented economic growth, and increasing levels of income and education (J. Berry 1997).

2. The Dominance of Business and Occupational Interests. What has the national and state interest group universe looked like since the late 1960s, and what does it look like in the early 2000s? Business and professional interests have predominated and continue to predominate at least in terms of numbers of organizations represented in Washington and the states. At the national level both Jack Walker (1983) and Schlozman and Tierney (1983, 1986) found that about three-fourths of groups were associated in some way with occupations. Heinz et al. (1993, 63), however, show that although overall business interests are the predominant type of organization, there is considerable variation across policy domains. For instance, trade associations are three times more common in agriculture (51 percent of the organizations) as in health (16 percent), and citizen groups are more common in the agriculture and energy domains (14 and 11 percent, respectively) than in health and labor (7 and 4 percent). Work on the states reveals similar findings; though the socioeconomic makeup of the state produces variation. For example, the group universe in Massachusetts is much more varied than in Alaska (Gray and Lowery 1995, 1996a; Thomas and Hrebenar 1996b, 1999a, 2003; Hunter, Wilson, and Brunk 1991).

3. The Rise of Public Interest Groups. Again, according to most research (e.g., Schlozman and Tierney 1986, 75), as late as the 1950s, public interest groups (also known as citizen groups) were barely visible in U.S. politics (but see Tichenor and Harris 2002 for a contrasting perspective). Schlozman and Tierney reported that 56 percent of the civil rights groups and 79 percent of the social welfare groups listed in a 1981 directory of lobbyists were founded after 1960, while only 38 percent of the trade associations and 14 percent of the corporations were that new. Jack Walker (1983, 1991) also found a rapid increase in the founding of citizen groups beginning around 1960. Public interest groups have also become regular players in state politics (Thomas and Hrebenar 1996b, 127; Gray and Lowery 1995, 1996a). The expansion of the public interest group universe is directly traceable to the rise of "movement politics" (environmentalists, consumers, women, and so on) in the 1950s and 1960s. Interestingly, the rise of liberal public interest groups in the 1960s spawned a conservative "counterattack" in the 1970s and 1980s (A. Crawford 1980; Moen 1992).

4. The Expansion of Corporate Activity. While business has always been well represented in Washington and in the states, since 1960 the number of individual corporations with both Washington and state capital offices has increased considerably, perhaps as much as tenfold at the federal level (Ryan, Swanson, and Bucholz 1987; G. Wilson 1986; Vogel 1989) and several times at the state level (Gray and Lowery 1995, 1996a; Thomas and Hrebenar 2003). The number of companies active in trade associations, peak associations, and coalitions has also increased. Two factors appear to be responsible for this expansion in business activity of the 1960s, 1970s, and 1980s: government regulation and the rise of liberal public interest groups (Herman 1981; Harris 1989; Vogel 1989).

5. *The Rise of Institutional Interests.* Businesses are not the only institutions that expanded their political activity in the 1970s. By the mid-1980s, a number of other types of institutions—many of which either did not exist previously or existed but avoided overt involvement in politics—including churches, think tanks, private foundations, hospitals, public interest law firms, colleges and universities, charities, individual state and local governments, and foreign countries had stepped up their political involvement (Salisbury 1984; M. Hayes 1986; Gray and Lowery 1995, 1996a, 2001; Thomas and Hrebenar 2003). As Allan Cigler (1991b, 102) points out, a large number of factors explain the great expansion of institutional political activity in recent decades, but "particularly important has been the expansion of government activity in virtually all aspects of business, cultural, and social life." In the early 2000s, institutions dominate the world of interest group representation at the federal level and are becoming increasingly important at the state level where they now constitute a majority of organized interests (Gray and Lowery 2001; Thomas and Hrebenar 2003).

6. *The Rise of Political Action Committees (PACs).* PAC activity has increased exponentially since 1970 at the federal level (Alexander 1984; Sorauf 1988b, 1992) and also in the states (Thomas and Hrebenar 1999a). At the federal level in 1970, there were fewer than 500 nationally active PACs. By 1980, largely due to changes in federal election laws, there were close to 3,000. By 1996 there were approximately 4,000 (Federal Election Commission 1995); but by 1999 the number had declined slightly to 3,778 (Federal Election Commission 1999). Comparable figures do not exist at the state level, but the increase has been substantial (Hrebenar and Thomas 1987, 1992, 1993a, 1993b). See also section 7.4.

The Expanding Group Universe and Group Power

In sum, the interest group universe is larger and more varied than ever before. Moreover, the trends described here suggest that the term *interest group* is increasingly archaic. As Allan Cigler (1991b, 103) notes: "To capture the essence of today's special interest process one must focus on all 'organized interests,' not simply membership organizations." This is also true at the state level (Thomas and Hrebenar 2003; see section 1.2.).

However, despite the major expansion in the group universe at both the national and state levels since the 1960s, the evidence suggests that this has not had a major effect on the groups and interests that are consistently effective, which are predominantly business and occupational groups (Heinz et al. 1993; Hrebenar and Thomas 2003; see sections 7.17. and 14.2.). In fact, at the national level, Schlozman and Tierney (1986, 87) conclude that despite the influx of citizen and public interest groups, things are more unbalanced than before; though Jack Walker (1983, 1991) draws a more positive conclusion. Generally, however, it is important not to assume that the increased activity or visibility of an interest group or interest is accompanied by increased influence. Being active and visible is one thing; being effective is quite another. Thus, many groups and interests that are very active, such as groups for the poor, for consumers, and for the arts, may not be particularly successful.

Further treatment of the development and composition of the group universe in the United States and in political systems in general and the consequences or lack thereof of this development and composition can be found in sections 5.4., 5.5., 8.1., and 14.2.

6.3. INTEREST GROUPS IN U.S. NATIONAL POLITICS

William P. Browne

The research and literature on interest groups in U.S. national politics is both extensive in volume and diverse in its perspectives. This cumulative literature is the product of varying purposes, including interpreting the policy process, explaining how groups evolve, and attempting to account for the effectiveness or lack thereof of interest groups. This literature includes studies that are empirical, normative, prescriptive, and some that are a mix of two or all three of these approaches. Thus, there is neither a common theme nor a shared agenda in this literature.

There is, however, a set of three partially answered questions that thread through much of that literature and concern most scholars. These questions are (1) What do interest groups do? (2) Why do they do it? and (3) Do interest groups matter in U.S. public policy? Addressing these three questions is the approach in this entry. It provides both a different and a supplementary approach to understanding the role of groups in U.S. national policy making provided elsewhere in this *Guide* (for example, section 2.5. provides an overview of the major work on groups in U.S. national politics). Readers can go to four bibliographies for a great deal of work not mentioned here: Harmon (1978), Heinz et al. (1993), Jeffrey Berry (1997), and Nownes (2001).

What Do Groups Do?

There are three different answers to this question. Each answer is based on its own perspective. The most basic answer is the constitutional one:

groups petition national government to redress their grievances (Eastman 1977). In the United States, lobbying is generally agreed to be a First Amendment right, one that can be only minimally regulated. The resulting lack of constraints on lobbying explains, in part, why so many interests organize nationally.

The second answer relates to representation. Bentley (1908), even while not specific in his theoretical analysis, has gotten most of the credit for portraying U.S. politics as that of group politics. He emphasizes that the common interest of those in a group accounts for its organization and activities—a group must be understood in terms of its own interests. Within constitutional bounds, groups do whatever they can to pursue their interests.

The key is in determining exactly what positions on public issues and policy are in the interest of the group. Empirical work shows that, in terms of their focus on issues, groups range on a continuum from those organized around the broadest array of goals to those focusing on a single and very specialized issue (Browne 1988, 55–63; Cook 1998). From other theoretical work scholars came to learn that no group can lobby effectively on every matter that its supporters may consider important (J. Wilson 1973). Resources and opportunities are too limited. So, as Truman (1951) showed, interest groups need to decide strategically what they can credibly and successfully represent. Mancur Olson (1965) demonstrates that small rather than larger sized groups can be more effective because their memberships can be more easily linked together and to a common lobbying goal. Also, as empirical work finds, the smaller the group the more likely it revolves around a specialized policy goal rather than several broad ones (Heinz et al. 1993).

The third answer relates to strategy and tactics. While U.S. interest groups do whatever is needed to win, they can only win when policy makers value what they do. Work on exchange theory by Michael Hayes (1981) and empirical research on Congress by Browne (1995a) makes that point. What policy makers want most is information, both about the technical aspects of workable public policy and the reactions of the public to any policy changes. As Milbrath (1963) notes from his large database on lobbyist opinions, this makes interest group politics mostly a communications process. But other things often need to be done to get policy makers to respond to available information. As Schlozman and Tierney (1986) and Jack Walker (1991, 103–121) demonstrate in their empirical analyses, the "full service" lobby may do everything from acting in coalition with other groups to mobilizing both its members and the public to litigating in court to distributing campaign funds. All of this is to gain listeners. Browne (1998) goes further, emphasizing that multifaceted, or all-directional, lobbying works better than simple communications.

As Gamson (1975) theorizes, some interest groups, especially those outside the political mainstream, must employ a much broader range of tactics than others—particularly establishment groups—to make their point. Protest and even violence, when used as a surprise tactic, have been employed strategically for getting previously inattentive policy makers to listen. The Civil Rights movement is the best example (J. Wilson 1973, 171–92). Protest also has been used, however, by political insiders such as teachers, mostly because of its shock value in mobilizing likely sympathizers within the general public (J. Walker 1991).

Why Do Interest Groups Do What They Do?

Politics is by nature an interactive process (Bentley 1908), necessarily involving other people. Thus, the literature consistently emphasizes that interest groups do the many things that they do for the single purpose of getting close to and influencing others.

This observation has led to numerous studies, some based on field research and some primarily theoretically oriented, that attempt to explain how groups establish relationships with key policy makers. One product of these studies was the category of literature concerning the iron triangle, subsystems, and subgovernments (see section 7.16.). Lowi (1969, 1979) provided the foremost theoretical work while Fritschler (1989) produced a thorough empirical analysis on the subject. Triangle theory portrays committees of Congress, executive agencies, and interest groups as the key players in policy making. The essence of the theory is simple. The three parts of the triangle become mutually autonomous decision makers: committees writing laws for a single policy area, agencies providing the policy's technical details, and specialized interest groups mustering political support in order to become insiders—indispensable to committees and agencies. With the triangle in agreement, so the story goes, the rest of government recognizes expertise and leaves triangle partners alone. However, this closed and expertise-based triangle theory has been seriously questioned for its overly simplistic treatment of politics. For example, in a study that spanned more than twenty years, Fritschler (1989) saw the range of participants in tobacco policy making expanding and involving increasingly contentious groups and officials. Heclo (1978) observes that this makes the resulting relationships appear more like an ever-changing cloud than a well-structured triangle.

John Mark Hansen (1991), in a historical work based on extensive documentary analysis, explains that the likelihood of a group gaining a competitive advantage over other sources of influence in U.S. politics does not depend on just getting inside the proper policy-making alliances. Rather, it depends on getting policy makers to see a group's issue as unlikely to go away and, therefore, politically unavoidable. Close relationships persist only as long as the issue has importance. Hansen, and the work of such state-building theorists as Skocpol (1979) and Skowronek (1982), shows that, unlike the conclusions of triangle theorists, gaining influence within U.S. politics has never been easy or simple. That explains why lobbying strategies and tactics are so numerous and varied but are most importantly about communicating information on the issue at hand and its implications.

Do Groups Matter in U.S. National Policy-Making?

This is both a question of contribution and of influence. Thus, there are two answers to this question. However, the answer regarding influence is the least satisfactorily answered question about groups in U.S. national politics.

The best way to assess the contribution of interest groups to national politics is by accepting a frequent observation that if interest groups did not exist policy makers would have to invent them. Groups not only inform; they also do such things as support the high costs of elections and raise social problems to new levels of political importance (J. Walker 1991). However, the proliferation of interests does slow down—and in some cases stymie—the policy process.

The question of influence is much more difficult to answer, and the present state of research is inconclusive. The decades-old debate over influence, as defined by two classic theoretical studies that were based on extensive field research, breaks down into two schools: the lobbyists-in-charge view (Schattschneider 1935) and the lobbyists-sharing-space perspective (Bauer, Pool, and Dexter 1972). Studies that support Schattschneider see groups dominating policy making and often subverting the democratic process (McConnell 1966). Economists who explain lobbying as rent-seeking behavior in their models also tend to this view, but primarily because of unnecessary costs being imposed on government (Stigler 1974; G. Becker 1985). However, their work suffers from unproven assumptions built into the analysis. The Bauer et al. proponents, often using transaction theory, see groups and policy makers as two among several types of independent influence agents in politics. Defenders of this perspective, such as the pluralists, see little or no normative harm in group activity.

No one is likely to resolve this debate (see, for example, John Wright 1990; R. Hall and Wayman 1990). However, recent empirically based theories generally take the Bauer et al. side. For example, Heinz et al. (1993) find influence to be both shifting and situational. Mucciaroni (1995) and Browne (1995a) both detail the limits of organized group influence. John Wright (1996) offers a similar view (see also Ainsworth 1993). It is J. M. Hansen (1991) who best sums up this debate. He concludes that both the in-charge and sharing-space views explain parts of national policy making. On occasion, groups are dominant because they sometimes can direct the attention of policy makers to some problems to the exclusion of others. Thus, there is a sort of group dominance, even in a competitive universe of free-agent interests and officials. Dominance is not, however, long term as another empirical analysis documents (Baumgartner and Jones 1993). Policy equilibrium can be expected to be disrupted when numerous forces, including interest groups, come together to create considerable policy attention.

A more extensive examination of power and influence in interest group studies is provided in section 7.17.

Directions for Future Research

The literature on groups in U.S. national politics may be vast, but the unknowns are also extensive. Virtually every aspect of group politics at the national level considered in this entry needs greater and more systematically detailed observation. Most attention is needed regarding the circumstances determining group influence or lack thereof. In looking more at this problem, attention should be paid to competing sources of influence: the media, political parties, sets of constituents, regional interests, and think tanks, among others.

Also important is that interest groups need to be studied in national politics more comparatively, with bigger data sets, both historically and longitudinally, and in conjunction with the changing fortunes of other organizations and institutions such as political parties. For example, Libby (1999) produced an excellent study of comparative and conflicting group influences. Only by developing larger, more comprehensive, and better comparative studies, including multidisciplinary studies like that of Heinz et al. (1993), will knowledge advance.

6.4. STATE INTEREST GROUPS

Clive S. Thomas

Although the quantity and range of research on interest groups in U.S. state politics is far less extensive than that on groups in U.S. national politics, there is a large and increasing body of literature. In particular, since the mid-1980s there have been major advances in knowledge made possible by the first fifty-state studies and by several smaller studies focusing on a select number of states. Even so, while there are several chapters in books and several articles (e.g., Thomas and Hrebenar 2003; Nownes and Freeman 1998a) that provide an overview of interest group activity across the states, there is no general text of the type that exists on national interest group politics such as J. Berry (1997) and Nownes (2001). Neither is there a general bibliography solely focusing on state interest groups. However, Gray and Lowery (2002) offer a critique of the major academic work and the following comprehensive review of both academic and popular sources provides a starting point for the researcher.

Literature and Research on State Interest Groups: Nine Types of Studies

Nine types of studies have treated, or more often touched upon, interest group activity in state politics. Many of these studies are dated but are useful for providing a historical picture of group activity across the states, in particular regions, or in individual states.

First, written for a popular readership, there are books that deal with state politics, and to some extent state interest groups, as part of a general treatment of the life of the states. John Gunther's (1951) survey of politics in America in the late 1940s contains valuable insights into group activities in the states at a time when major interests were beginning to emerge. A 1970s and early 1980s version of the Gunther approach was the nine-volume series by Neal R. Peirce and his associates on the people, politics, and power of the various subregions of the United States (1972a, 1972b, 1972c, 1973, 1974, 1975, 1976, 1980; Peirce and Barone 1977). A follow-up volume to this series was published by Peirce and Hagstrom in 1983. Despite their shortcomings, in the absence of comprehensive and comparative academic information before the early 1990s, scholars turned to these studies to piece together an understanding of state interest groups. Morehouse (1981, 112), for example, relied heavily on the books by Peirce in putting together the first list of the most effective groups in the fifty states.

Turning to academic works, the second category of literature is treatment in books on the government and politics of individual states or some aspect of state politics and government, such as the state legislature, and in books that include chapters on individual states as examples or case studies. Although about 45 states have had some text written on their politics or governmental institutions and the University of Nebraska Press has an on-going series that will eventually cover all fifty states, the treatment of interest groups in these various studies varies widely. Some books devote a separate chapter to interest groups while others do not. These treatments also display a wide variety of approaches from the purely anecdotal to the highly conceptual and quantitative. They also vary in scope and depth of treatment.

Third, beginning with V. O. Key, interest groups have received some treatment in texts on regional politics. Besides Key's (1949) classic work on Southern politics, other works on the South include Havard (1972), Bass and DeVries (1976), and Black and Black (1987). A subregion of the South, the border states, was covered in a book by Fenton (1957). Fenton (1966) later produced a volume on Midwest politics. Lockard (1959) and Milburn and Schuck (1981) produced volumes on New England politics. The West has been covered in books by Jonas (1961, 1969) and by Clive Thomas (1991, chap. 7), and the Rocky Mountain subregion of the West was covered by Donnelly (1940). Yet, with some notable exceptions (for example, C. Thomas 1991, chap. 7), the treatment of interest groups in these studies has usually been only incidental.

Fourth, there are several books focusing on specific aspects of regional politics that have included treatments of particular state interest groups. These include, for example, studies of religion in Southern politics (Baker, Steed, and Moreland 1983), and of water policy (Reisner 1986) and environmental policy (Z. Smith 1992) in the West.

A fifth category comprises studies that treat interest groups in a broader comparative study of some aspect of state politics. These include Zeller's (1954) and Wahlke et al.'s (1962) studies of the legislative system in the states and Francis's (1967) study of legislative issues in the fifty states. Luttbeg (1992) produced a comprehensive comparison of state (and local) politics and government including interest groups.

A sixth category includes a body of literature that has a public policy focus and has taken a case study approach to investigating the effect of individual groups. Some of these studies are comparative in nature. Two examples are Browne's (1988) book on agricultural interest groups and their role in national and state political, economic, and social life and Mansbridge's (1986) study of the failure of the Equal Rights Amendment. Other studies focus on a single state. These include Zeigler's (1963) study of the impact of the Florida Milk Commission (controlled by the dairy interests) on milk prices in that state and Joseph Stewart and Sheffield's (1987) study of the use of the courts by Black interest groups in Mississippi.

A seventh category of literature has taken what is in essence a micro approach to the study of state interest groups and group theory. These have examined either a specific aspect of the internal organization and operation of groups or how groups affect some part of the state political process such as the legislature. Sometimes these studies have been concerned with specific states such as Zeller's (1937) mid-1930s study of lobbying in New York State. Most often these studies have used two or more states in an attempt to provide comparative analysis. C. Bell, Hamm, and Wiggins (1985), for example, used three states in their study of group impact on several areas of public policy. Zeigler and Baer (1969) used four states in their study of lobbying in state legislatures. More recent studies include Rosenthal (1993, 2001) on lobbying and lobbyists in the states, drawing on six states, and Nownes and Freeman (1998b) who use data from three states to draw some general conclusions about the role of women lobbyists.

These seven categories are a useful starting point in a study of state interest groups, particularly group activity in individual states. Yet, with the exception of some studies in the sixth and seventh categories, because of their great variation in methodology and scope and depth of analysis, they are of very limited value for purposes of comparative analysis (and often for individual state analysis). However, the eighth category of literature has taken a macro approach to the study of state interest groups by developing theoretical explanations of group activity in relation to their political and governmental systems. These studies are intended both to offer explanations of group activity in individual states and to compare group activity among states. The most notable work here has been conducted by Zeller (1954), Zeigler (1983), Zeigler and van Dalen (1976), Morehouse (1981), Nice (1984), and Nownes and Freeman (1998a). None of these studies, however, conducted systematic research on all fifty states. Their attempts at comprehensive analysis were based upon original data from only a few states and drew upon other information (such as that referred to in the first seven categories above) that varied in its methodology from the impressionistic to the highly quantitative, a divergence far from ideal for comparative analysis. Yet these comments should not be interpreted as understating the significant contribution of these studies.

The ninth category of studies attempts to deal with these problems of extrapolation and methodology by studying all fifty states based upon a common set of questions and a systematic methodology. There are three such existing studies. These studies, particularly the Gray and Lowery study but also the Hrebenar-Thomas study, have generated an extensive literature.

The Fifty-State Hunter, Wilson, and Brunk Study

This project focuses on the role and impact of state interest groups, particularly their lobbyists, in various policy areas of state politics. The study's definition of an interest group is based upon state registration lists of interest groups and lobbyists, and the extent of the data is broad ranging. This includes one survey of 39,000 state lobbyists, based upon lobby registration lists for 1984, 1985, and 1986 and a second similar survey based upon 1989 and 1990 lists in all fifty states. From this research, several new theories have been developed that add to our understanding of state interest groups (Hunter, Wilson, and Brunk 1991; Hunter, Brunk, and Wilson 2002).

The goal of this research is to determine the extent to which theories that were developed to explain the role of interest groups in Washington, D.C., are both relevant and sufficient for explaining the behavior of interest groups at the state level. Among the findings are that lobby registration laws do not inhibit the growth of interest groups and that Mancur Olson's free-rider problem appears to be less relevant at the state level as interests may not be behaving in a rational manner. Indeed, quantitative evidence from this study shows that interests appear to engage in herd behavior, an irrational response to the obvious limitations of the policy process (K. Hunter 2001 and 2002). Currently, the authors are updating their data with 1996 figures to continue this project.

The Gray and Lowery Fifty-State Study

The most extensive empirical study conducted on state interest groups to date is by Gray and Lowery. They argue that a state's economy largely

125

governs the nature of its interest group system. Their research is based upon extensive data sets of registered interest groups in the states beginning in 1975.

As to the specifics of their research, Gray and Lowery (1996a) attempt to determine the ways by which interest groups and interest communities are constructed from distributions of interests in society. The states are ideal for such work given their substantial variation on two key traits. First are variations in *density*, or the extent to which interest communities are crowded. They explain this with the energy-stability-area (ESA) model, which suggests that state interest communities increase in size, but in a density dependent manner, as the numbers of potential constituents of organized interests grow and as political and policy uncertainty increases (Lowery and Gray 1995). The second element is *diversity* of interest communities. Lowery and Gray (2002) explain this by examining how the uniquely shaped density functions of different sectors or guilds of organized interests alter their relative contributions to the overall size of interest communities as state economies become larger. The authors then examine how the density and diversity of state interest systems influence the political process and policy outcomes.

As a by-product of their study, Gray and Lowery have also added to knowledge of other aspects of state interest group activity. These contributions include the role of contract lobbyists (Gray and Lowery 1996b), the significance of lobbyist and interest group registration lists for understanding the extent of lobbying activity in a state (Lowery and Gray 1997; Gray and Lowery 1998), the affect of national trends in interest group activity on the makeup of the group universe and strategies of interest groups in particular states (Lowery and Gray 1994; Wolak, Newmark, McNoldy, Lowery, and Gray 2002), and the importance of institutions in the makeup of state interest group communities (Gray and Lowery 1995, 2001; Lowery and Gray 1998).

The Hrebenar-Thomas Fifty-State Study

Whereas the Hunter, Wilson, and Brunk and the Gray and Lowery fifty-state studies focused on particular aspects of state interest group activity, the major goal of the Hrebenar-Thomas study was to provide the first general picture of state interest group activity by researching all fifty states. The major topics of focus were the range of groups and interests operating in the states, the relationship of interest groups and political parties, the types of strategies and tactics employed, the types and roles of lobbyists, the regulation of interest groups, intergovernmental lobbying as it affects state interest groups, and the influence of state groups based upon a three-fold categorization of group and interest power. The study was conducted between 1983 and 1990, with partial updates in 1995, 1998, and 2002.

Besides its broader focus, this study differs from the other two fifty-state studies mentioned above in other ways. Most importantly, the Hrebenar-Thomas study uses a broader definition of the term *interest group* than almost all existing studies by including "hidden lobbies" (those not required to register under state law), particularly government agencies. The study pays particular attention to lobbying the administrative branch of government and, more recently, the courts (Thomas and Hrebenar 1992b; Thomas, Boyer, and Hrebenar 2003), both of which have become increasingly important targets of lobbying in the states since the early 1980s. And this study uses a combination of qualitative and quantitative techniques, drawing on the expertise of specialists on state politics and interest groups in all fifty states. Over one hundred political scientists and other specialists have been involved in the study. This methodology contrasts with the Hunter, Wilson, and Brunk and the Gray and Lowery studies, both of which make more use of empirical data and use direct research and survey methods as opposed to using a team of individual state experts.

Even though the work on individual states from the Hrebenar-Thomas study is well over ten years old, it is still the only study that provides a state-by-state analysis of all fifty state interest group systems based upon a common methodology (Hrebenar and Thomas 1987, 1992, 1993a, 1993b). Fifty state syntheses of the study, including its updates, can be found in Thomas and Hrebenar (1990, 1991a, 1996b, 1999a, 2003) and a regional perspective based on the study is in Thomas and Hrebenar (1992a). One of the ongoing concerns of the Hrebenar-Thomas study is the assessment of interest group power in the states (Thomas and Hrebenar 1999b, 1999c). All of the above references include treatment of this, and an overview of trends in state interest group power since the early 1980s can be found in Hrebenar and Thomas (2003, table A). A more extensive review of the issues of group and interest power in the states can be found in section 7.17.

Further Research

Even though there has been a surge in research on state interest groups during the last twenty years, there remain many opportunities for further work. At the most extensive level, a need exists for a general text on the subject, which might be a synthesis of existing research. As the individual state chapters produced from the Hrebenar-Thomas study are now dated and many developments have taken place in state interest group systems in the last fifteen years, it would be very useful to have a new study of all fifty states.

On specific aspects of group activity, some important topics needing investigation are the increasing intergovernmental connection of state interest groups, including the increase in national organizations working through the states (see section 6.6.); the effects that new technologies, such as the Internet and e-mail are having on strategies and tactics, which has certainly affected the way that lobbyists can monitor legislative activity; the increasing importance of the role of the courts for interest groups and the role of interest groups in judicial elections and reconfirmations; and the ongoing issue of the effect of interest group and lobbyist regulations on the behavior of groups and their representatives, as well as on the conduct of public officials being lobbied.

Finally, although not specific to state interest groups, the states are useful laboratories for studying some broader questions regarding interest groups. Among many topics, of particular importance here are the continuing question of what constitutes group power (see section 7.17.), the affect of political action committee (PAC) contributions (see section 7.4.), how political culture affects lobbying decisions and styles (see section 4.4.), and the affects of the continuing expansion of the group universe on group activity and influence (see section 6.2.).

6.5. INTEREST GROUPS IN LOCAL POLITICS

Paul Schumaker

Even though reference to local groups is rarely made in general texts on American interest groups (see, for example, J. Berry 1997, Browne 1998, Hrebenar 1997, Nownes 2001), there is an increasing body of research on local group activity. In conjunction with work on national and state groups, this research helps to provide a more complete picture of group activity in the United States and can be used to test and advance explanations about interest group activity in general. Furthermore, because local groups are more accessible then state groups and national organizations, they offer perfect opportunities for original research, including interviewing group personnel and members and conducting participant observation and survey research (see chap. 15). For those not familiar with the dynamics of local group activity, a good starting point, including an overview of the local group universe and the nature and dynamics of group activity, are the works by Brian Jones (1983, chap. 7) and Christensen (1995, chap. 10). An alternative perspective on the importance of local groups (and parties) is provided by Paul Peterson (1981, chap. 6) and referred to later in this entry. The overview provided in these books can be supplemented by the following review of main sources, of explanation of the major trends in interpretation, and of the principal schools of thought on local interest groups.

The Pluralist School and Its Critics

Over a century after Tocqueville's (1835/1840) observations about the centrality of voluntary associations in communities in the United States, pluralism emerged as the dominant theory of urban politics. Orthodox pluralists (e.g., Dahl 1961; see also section 3.2.) argued that cities contained many organized groups representing diverse interests and that unorganized interests were easily mobilized into politically effective groups. From the pluralist perspective, power was distributed widely among groups, and group participation facilitated democratic governance.

An extensive body of research questioning this pluralist description of local group politics soon emerged. Following Floyd Hunter (1953), elite theorists acknowledged the role of civic groups but argued that economic influentials, not a heterogeneous array of ordinary citizens, dominated such groups. Other analysts argued that groups that might challenge dominant interests were inhibited from becoming active due to a "mobilization of bias" (Bachrach and Baratz 1970; see also section 3.3.) and that such "protest" groups that did emerge usually fared poorly in political struggles (Lipsky 1970).

A number of research projects sought to synthesize pluralist and antipluralist depictions of local group politics by estimating and explaining differences in the influence of various types of groups in a wide range of American cities (Abney and Lauth 1985). These studies typically showed that business interests were more organized and influential than such "countervailing groups" as unions, neighborhood groups, and civil rights organizations and that differences in political institutions explained little variance in group influence (Getter and Schumaker 1983).

During the 1980s, the debate between pluralists and their opponents subsided, and a number of other models of local politics emerged. According to the "state autonomy model," city officials act on the basis of their own interests independent of the demands of organized interests (Gurr and King 1987). Even more influential have been models stressing the dependence of cities on economic factors in formulating development policies. According to Paul Peterson (1981), local politics "is groupless politics," because group influence is confined to relatively unimportant issues involving "housekeeping services." Such models reinforced the findings of the San Francisco-Oakland Bay City Council Research Project that stressed the "irrelevance" of interest group activity for urban policy making (Zisk 1973, 151).

Four Major Interpretations of Local Interest Group Politics

As a result of these developments and challenges to the pluralist school, at least four strands of urban research continue to stress the importance of local interest groups: (1) revisionist pluralism, (2) the growth machine model, (3) studies of ascendant groups, and (4) regime theory.

Revisionist pluralists continue to stress group influence, but unlike orthodox pluralists, they employ empirical research to determine whether (and the conditions when) groups contribute to democracy or are treated fairly by democratic procedures (Schumaker 1991). According to Waste (1986), group politics can take deviant forms, ranging from "privatized pluralism"—in which interest groups appropriate public authority for private purposes—to "hyperpluralism"—where interest groups raise many competing demands and make coherent governance impossible. Perhaps the most consistent revisionist thesis is the prevalence of "stratified pluralism," where urban governments exhibit "systematic biases" against minority groups and other disadvantaged citizens (Pinderhughes 1987).

The growth-machine model (Logan and Molotch 1987) views urban politics as dominated by a coalition of groups—developers, realtors, financiers, construction interests, and others—who benefit from the enhanced "exchange value" of land that occurs if cities experience extensive economic and population growth. This model holds that the policies of the growth machine can be opposed by neighborhood organizations, environmentalists, NIMBYs (Not In My Back Yard groups), and others who are concerned with the "use value" of property. One offshoot of this model has been research on antigrowth groups and movements (e.g., Castells 1983).

A third focus of recent studies has been on newly prominent grassroots organizations (Boyte 1980), especially neighborhood groups. According to Dilger (1992), residential community associations have become prominent in affluent suburbs, fencing themselves off from the broader community and privatizing government functions. However, most neighborhood associations seek better municipal services and protection from disruptive forces. The organizational characteristics, representativeness, and effectiveness of neighborhood groups have been widely studied (e.g., J. Thomas 1986). Jeffrey Berry, Portney, and Thomson (1993) have concluded that neighborhood groups have furthered democratic practices in a number of cities in the United States.

Regime theory is perhaps the most influential strain of recent thinking on urban interest groups. While previous urban research viewed group politics as competitive, regime theory sees group politics as more cooperative. When no group has enough power to act alone, local politics involves groups forming cooperative regimes that produce social power and solve community problems. Economic-development regimes (Stone 1989), progressive regimes (DeLeon 1992), and human-resource regimes (Stone 1998) are just some of the different coalitions that have been identified and analyzed.

With the exception of the pioneering study by Putnam (1993), few studies have examined Tocqueville's belief that local voluntary associations play a critical role in developing civic-minded Americans who contribute to effective self-government. Comparative research on local groups in other countries suggests that Americans may be no more involved in local organizations than citizens of other Western democracies (Balme, Becquart-LeClercq, and Clark 1987) and that American groups are no different from those in most countries in that they usually promote and protect narrow interests at the expense of broader community interests.

6.6. THE INTERGOVERNMENTAL ACTIVITY OF INTEREST GROUPS

Clive S. Thomas

In most political systems, but particularly in liberal democracies, an increasing number of interest groups and interests operate at more than one level of government and across political jurisdictions at the same level for the simple reason that their interests are being increasingly affected by more and more government at various levels. This is particularly the case in the United States with its strong brand of federalism (federal and state) and extensive intergovernmental relations (IGR) between national, subnational (regional), state and local governments, between states, and between local governments—all of which can affect the fortunes of interest groups. Consequently, many organized interests have developed strategies involving some form of intergovernmental lobbying. This is the case, for instance, with the education lobby across the country. The nation's largest schoolteachers organization, the National Education Association (NEA), lobbies in Washington, D.C., in every state, and in most local jurisdictions; and U.S. universities lobby in their state capitals and in Washington, D.C. through such organizations as the American Council on Education (ACE), the American Association of State Colleges and Universities (AASCU), and the National Association of Independent Colleges and Universities (NAICU). The web of intergovernmental lobbying is illustrated in Figure 6.1.

Despite the increasing importance of this intergovernmental activity of interests groups and the fact that to some extent many groups have long been involved in lobbying at various levels, there is no general text or other general treatment of intergovernmental lobbying in U.S. politics. This can probably be explained by the fact that most scholars who study the general role of interest groups in the public policy process focus on one level (mainly Washington, D.C., or the states), and those who study IGR are more interested in the role of national and state agencies in the process, rather than that of individual private interest groups such as business and labor or public interest groups such as environmentalists. Therefore, information on intergovernmental lobbying in U.S. politics has to be gleaned from three main sources: (1) general texts on IGR, (2) case studies and work on individual interest groups and interests, and (3) work on the general intergovernmental influence of interest group activity.

General Texts on IGR

There are several general texts on the IGR relationship in government and politics and these are a good starting point for studying the IGR

Figure 6.1 The Interrelation of Interest Groups and Interest Activity in U.S. Politics

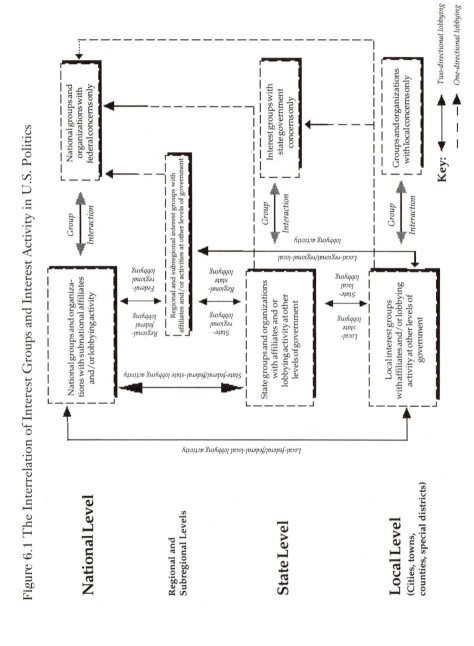

Source: Developed by the author.

activities of interest groups and interests. These texts include Nice and Fredericksen (1995, esp. 33–42), which pays the most attention of a general IGR text to lobbying both by governments and by private interests; O'Toole (2000), which contains several references to IGR lobbying; Deil Wright (1988), which is an extensive treatment of IGR from a structural perspective with some reference to lobbying; and Hanson (1998), which focuses on state-local relations.

Again, however, it is important to point out that, for the most part, these texts are concerned with government agency lobbying and much less with the IGR lobbying of private interests. In this regard, these texts are most useful for students and scholars in the field of public administration who are interested in the formal structures of lobbying by governments as opposed to the politics and informal aspects of IGR lobbying by both government agencies and private lobbying groups. Most of the works cited in the following two sections are more concerned with the political dynamics of IGR lobbying.

Case Studies and Work on Individual Interest Groups and Interests

There are several publications that in dealing with individual interest groups and interests (such as business and labor) deal with lobbying in an IGR context. There are also some studies that specifically focus on IGR lobbying by particular groups and interests.

General treatments of interests that contain an IGR component are Browne (1988) on agricultural policy making, Asher et al. (2001) on labor in the electoral process, Cook (1998) on higher education, and Baer and Bailey (1994) and Maurice Berube (1988) on K–12 education and teachers as an IGR lobbying force. As education policy is shared between federal, state, and local governments, it is a particularly fruitful area to pursue in regard to IGR lobbying (see section 8.11.), even though no text or monograph on IGR education lobbying has been produced. Work on business lobbying in an IGR context is less common; but see Vogel (1989). The general literature on the smoking issue (see section 19.18.) contains many references to IGR lobbying and the increasing attention paid by tobacco companies to the states (see also, Fritschler and Hoefler 1996). Clemens (1997) provides a historical perspective on the development of IGR lobbying activity by farmer, labor, and women's state organizations in Washington, D.C.

Sources that deal with specific groups and organizations engaging in IGR lobbying are predominantly concerned with government and organizations of governments or government officials lobbying other levels of government, particularly state and local governments lobbying in Washington, D.C. The most extensive work in this regard is by Cammisa (1995) who examines the activities and success of five state and local lobbying groups: the National League of Cities, the U.S. Conference of Mayors, the National Association of Counties, the National Conference of State Legislatures, and the National Governors' Association. Beverly Cigler (1995) provides a more general but comprehensive overview of organizations engaged in IGR lobbying with a good treatment of the political dynamics involved. She covers individual jurisdictions, institutional organizations such as the Council of State Governments, membership associations of officials such as the National Conference of Mayors, and support organizations like the U.S. Advisory Commission on Intergovernmental Relations (ACIR) and pays some attention to the role of public interest lobbies operating in an IGR context. Jonathan Walters (2000) provides an overview of the development of the state and local lobby in Washington, D.C. More dated, but still useful, treatments of specific IGR lobbying activity include Haider (1974) on governors and mayors lobbying in Washington, D.C., and Cingranelli (1983) who examines the role of the states lobbying in the nation's capital.

General Perspectives on the Intergovernmental Activity of Interest Groups

There are some studies that focus on the broader context of interest group activity in the policy process in an IGR context. Most of these are written from a state government and politics perspective. Three studies that are more general are Levine and Thurber (1986), which examines the IGR lobby, both its problems and its effectiveness, in the light of the Reagan revolution of the 1980s; Deil Wright (1972), which looks at the role of governors in obtaining grants for their states; and R. Allen Hays (1991), which examines priority setting by governments, groups, and organizations involved in IGR lobbying.

In the state politics literature, there has been a debate about the influence of IGR activity of interest groups on the strategies and tactics pursued by groups and interests across the states. Thomas and Hrebenar (1991a, 1992c, 1999a, 130–31) argue that a nationalization of interest group activity—including the types of groups operating and their strategies and tactics—is taking place across the states due to the increasing IGR activity of interest groups as politics become more and more national in content. Brian Anderson's (1997) study of interest group federations operating at the state and federal level (and sometimes at the local level) confirms this. In contrast, Wolak et al. (2002) argue that the makeup of state interest group communities and group activity in a state are largely determined by local state circumstances.

Future Research: Opportunities and Barriers

From the dearth of material cited in this entry, it is clear that few areas of the study of U.S. interest groups in the public policy process offer more opportunities for future research than that of the intergovernmental activity of groups and interests. Four suggestions that would considerably advance knowledge in this area are as follows.

First, a general text on American interest groups that covers group activity and lobbying activity at all three levels of government (plus perhaps the regional level) and includes a chapter or two on IGR lobbying would be a major contribution to the literature. Second, a long article, or preferably a book, synthesizing existing knowledge and identifying the various elements and perspectives on IGR lobbying would be an even greater contribution to the interest group literature. As can be deduced from this entry, the literature at present is very fragmented and disparate with neither an in-depth overview nor an explanation of IGR lobbying at the federal, state, and local levels. Third, a need exists for a general systematic, theoretical explanation of IGR lobbying in the United States that could include, among other topics, the application of theories of IGR to lobbying, the increasing trend in IGR lobbying, strategies and tactics that might be specific to IGR lobbying, the particular problems faced by groups lobbying in the IGR arena, and factors determining effective IGR lobbying. And fourth, several policy areas, including business and social issue group activity, need case studies on IGR lobbying. Such studies could help to enhance understanding and provide specific examples for the first three suggested areas of needed work on IGR lobbying.

However, what is likely to inhibit the advancement of knowledge in IGR lobbying is the present disciplinary focus among IGR scholars and scholars who specialize in U.S. interest groups. IGR lobbying is rarely the primary focus of IGR scholars. When it is treated, it is usually from the perspective of governments and agencies lobbying as opposed to private and public interest groups (business, education, environmental groups, and so on). As also indicated earlier, most scholars of U.S. interest groups specialize in one level of group activity, mainly the national level. Even those who cover more than one level of interest group activity in a general text on interest groups (for example, Hrebenar 1997) do so without making an IGR connection. Thus, it will take a major change in the approach to studying both IGR and U.S. interest groups before any major advances are made in understanding the IGR activity of interest groups in the United States.

6.7. PUBLIC KNOWLEDGE OF AND ATTITUDES TOWARD INTEREST GROUPS AND LOBBYISTS IN THE UNITED STATES

Robert C. Benedict

Important elements shaping group activity in the United States are the public's and public officials' knowledge (accurate or not) and attitudes (positive or negative) regarding interest groups and their representatives.

This is largely because interest group and lobbying activities are more subject to public disclosure laws (see sections 14.4.1. and 14.4.2.) and thus to more public exposure and scrutiny in the United States than in any other country, and because public opinion plays a particularly important role in shaping American public policy. The entry on interest groups and public opinion earlier in this book (see section 4.8.) provides general background on the various roles of public opinion in interest group activity and identifies the major literature. In this present entry the focus is specific to the United States and to public knowledge and attitudes as part of the American political culture as opposed to the specific effects of public opinion on interest group strategies and tactics (see section 4.8.). The information in this entry is based largely on public opinion polls over the past fifty years plus reference to the small amount of literature available on this topic.

Public Attitudes

There is no general study of the role of public opinion on interest group activity in the United States. However, generalizations about the affect of public opinion on interest group activity can be gleaned from several sources. V. O. Key's *Public Opinion and American Democracy* (1967) contains an extensive discussion of "pressure groups" and focuses on whether group efforts to influence the general public actually convert into public opinion. Key concludes that success depends on the general balance of power between groups and that its effects will be evident over the long run rather than the short term (Key 1967, 530–31). Of recent books on public opinion, Neuman (1986) has two brief references to the role of interest groups in structuring public opinion about politics, while most other treatments do not mention the subject (Stimson 1991; Abramson 1983; W. Mayer 1992; Zaller 1992). Furthermore, books specifically on interest groups and lobbying contain little, if any, discussion of public opinion (for example, Hrebenar 1997; Schlozman and Tierney 1986; J. Berry 1997). The few references to public opinion concern how groups use opinion as a tactic to achieve lobbying ends, rather than general public opinion about interest groups and lobbying.

The most valuable information about public attitudes to interest groups and lobbyists is found in national opinion surveys dealing with attitudes toward institutions including political institutions. Beginning in the mid-1970s, several polls, including Gallup, Louis Harris, and the National Opinion Research Center, conducted yearly surveys of public confidence in institutions (McAneny and Moore 1995; National Opinion Research Center 1993). While attitudes toward political institutions (particularly Congress and the president) have declined dramatically since the early 1970s, private sector interest groups began with lower levels of public confidence, and thus saw smaller declines. Combining Gallup responses of a "great deal" and "quite a lot" of confidence for both big business and organized labor in the 1970s, only one-third of Americans expressed confidence, and the percentage dropped to one-quarter in the 1990s (McAneny and Moore 1995). Similar patterns are found in the annual polls of the honesty and ethics of those in major institutions (McAneny and Moore 1995).

One important caveat in evaluating data about attitudes toward interest groups is that if the subject is of low salience to respondents, polls are measuring nonattitudes. When a 1949 Gallup Poll asked for the definition of "lobbyist," 43 percent gave either no answer or an incorrect answer, while thirty-five years later about half were "familiar" and nine percent "very familiar" with activities of lobbyists (Gallup Poll 1949; Roper Poll 1984). When lobbies are defined as "special interests," half of respondents could not name any group in this category, 15 percent cited minority groups, 11 percent unions, and 9 percent business groups (CBS/*New York Times* 1984).

When asked general questions about the impact of lobbyists on government, not surprisingly, the responses are overwhelmingly negative. (American Talk Issues Foundation 1993). Even when given the positive side of lobbying, that of providing information to help make better policies, Americans selected the negative choice by 45 percent to 32 percent. When asked about why the government is not working better and given six possibilities ranging from political party breakdown to voters' information levels, by a two-to-one ratio the response of "too much special interest influence on government" was selected (Roper Poll 1978).

Both Roper and Gallup polls have periodically asked about attitudes toward specific interest groups, although Roper framed the responses in terms of "two much" or "too little" influence by generic groups such as "doctors," while Gallup asked for four-fold "very favorable" to "very unfavorable" responses to specific groups such as the American Medical Association (AMA). In descending order, Roper finds labor unions, gay rights advocates, businesses, and doctors exercising "too much influence," while farmers, the disabled, and senior citizens led the "too little" category (Roper Poll 1987). While Gallup did not find a change in most groups' favorability rating over time, the National Rifle Association (NRA) did decline from a 55 percent "very" or "mostly" favorable rating in 1993 to 42 percent in 1995. Gallup's finding of a 75 percent "favorable" rating of the American Association of Retired Persons (AARP), tracks with the evidence from the Roper Poll (1987) of the public's desire to see senior citizens exercise more influence (Gallup Poll 1989, 1993, 1995; see also Time Yankelovich Poll 1985).

However, doctors are a good example of the phenomenon in polling where the public will hold one opinion on a general subject but reverse it when asked about the specifics of that subject (McCloskey and Brill 1983; Prothro and Grigg 1988; Roberts, Hite, and Bradley 1994). Thus, while "doctors" in general are seen as exercising too much influence over government in the Roper Poll, nearly two-thirds of respondents gave the American Medical Association a "very" or "mostly" favorable rating in 1993 and 1995 (Gallup Poll 1993, 1995).

A succinct summary of public attitudes toward interest groups and lobbyists in general and specific groups (such as business and labor) based on these several decades of polls and the implications of these attitudes for public policy making can be found in Benedict, Thomas, and Hrebenar (1996) and Thomas and Hrebenar (1995).

The Attitudes of Public Officials

As to the attitudes of public officials to interest groups and lobbyists, again, no specific study is available. Information has to be gleaned from various sources, most of which reveal a different perspective than that represented in the general public. Beginning with a study by Milbrath (1963) of Washington lobbyists and confirmed by more recent popular and academic studies (Birnbaum 1992; Schlozman and Tierney 1986; Heinz et al. 1993), it is clear that public officials have a much more positive view of both interest groups and lobbyists, seeing both as indispensable to their jobs. This ambivalent, though essentially positive view of groups and their representatives, also comes through in studies of state interest groups (Hedlund and Patterson 1966: Kolasa 1971; Patterson 1963; Teune 1967; Hrebenar and Thomas 1987, 1992, 1993a, 1993b).

Problems Inhibiting Past and Future Research

To be sure, there is much yet to learn about public and public officials' knowledge of and attitudes toward interest groups. However, progress in this area is hindered by both conceptual and data problems. The activities of interest groups are less salient to Americans than are other political institutions, and proliferating numbers of groups combined with their practice of operating behind closed doors provides little incentive for citizens to gain information about them. As for data collection, no set of common questions has been replicated over the last fifty years to provide an accurate time-series picture of public attitudes. Each poll is a snapshot—often reflecting special conditions of the moment and frequently unique questions asked in the poll. Seldom are survey questions asked in a way that allows the intensity of the feelings and the existing level of knowledge of respondents to be gauged and factored into the survey results. Only when these issues are dealt with can the research on this topic be systematically advanced.

Chapter 7

Interests and Interest Groups in the Public Policy Process: (I) Strategies and Tactics

7.1. INTRODUCTION TO CHAPTERS 7, 8, AND 9

Clive S. Thomas

Interest group scholars in the United States, and to a large extent, throughout the Western world, divide the study of interest groups into two broad categories: (1) the internal dynamics of group formation, organization, maintenance, and demise; and (2) interest group activity in the public policy process. This two-fold categorization certainly has its shortcomings (see section 1.6.). However, although these two categories often overlap in practice, it is a useful distinction for analyzing interest group activity from an academic perspective because it reflects the two major aspects of interest group life. In some chapters of this *Guide* (for example, chaps. 6 and 11), both categories are combined with little need to distinguish between them. Chapter 5, however, focuses primarily on the internal dynamics of groups. In this present chapter and the following two chapters we concentrate on interest groups in the public policy process.

Three points need to be addressed concerning the subjects covered in this chapter, chapters 8 and 9, and the sources used. First, the focus is not on the general (the macro) relationship of interest groups to the policy-making process. This subject is covered in chapter 3 in which pluralism and neocorporatism, among other general explanations, are reviewed. In chapters 7, 8, and 9, the focus is toward specific (the micro) aspects of group involvement in the policy process: the strategies and tactics that groups use and the major types of groups working to influence public policy. Second, the coverage is mainly on group activity in liberal democracies and includes very little on strategies and tactics used in nonpluralist systems or the treatment of specific groups in those systems. This is largely because there is a shortage of material on nonpluralist systems (see section 12.1.). Third, as is the case with much of the material in this *Guide*, most of the research and literature reviewed is on the U.S. political system. However, reference material for research and literature covering political systems in other countries, in particular parliamentary democracies, is included.

Turning to the specific content of the three chapters, this chapter focuses on the various strategies and tactics (the general approaches, specific techniques, and targets of lobbying) that are available to interest groups in most liberal democracies in their quest to influence government decisions. As the U.S. system exhibits the widest range of formalized strategies and tactics, this chapter includes treatment of some major American practices. However, many strategies and tactics common in the United States are either not used in most political systems, such as judicial lobbying, or they are in their infancy, such as grassroots lobbying. For this reason, a major purpose of this chapter is placing U.S. practice in perspective. The following section (see section 7.2.) in particular contrasts the various strategies and tactics employed in the United States with those used in most Western European and other parliamentary systems.

Chapters 8 and 9 examine the research and literature that cover various interests and interest groups active in the public policy process in the United States and across the Western world. The subject is divided based on the distinction made in the study of U.S. interest groups between the so-called *traditional interests* and the so-called *new interests*. Chapter 8 analyzes traditional interests including business, labor, and agriculture, which have been active in the public policy process for more than 100 years. Chapter 9 analyzes new interests, such as environmentalists, civil and human rights groups, senior citizens, and animal rights groups, that have developed and become active since the late 1960s. As the introduction to chapter 8 (see section 8.1.) points out, this is far from a water-tight distinction. But as there is no single agreed upon system or method of classifying interest groups, the distinction between traditional and new interests is a useful tool to categorize the so-called interest group universe for purposes of analysis.

7.2. STRATEGY AND TACTICS: PLACING U.S. PRACTICE IN PERSPECTIVE

Clive S. Thomas

As noted in chapter 1 (see section 1.2.), the process of lobbying involves three activities that often overlap in practice: (1) gaining access to policy makers; (2) creating an attitude among policy makers conducive to the group's goals; and (3) influencing policy makers in the group's favor.

These three activities are implemented through a group's strategy and tactics. The terms *strategy* and *tactics* are often used interchangeably because they are so interrelated in practice, but there is an important difference between them. A strategy is an overall plan for gaining access and influence and securing specific policy goals. In effect, it is the result of deliberate calculations that consider the cost-effectiveness of different possible means. Tactics are the specific means for achieving these goals.

A strategy may be more or less explicit and formalized depending upon the nature of the group and its available resources. Small community groups with few resources may only have vaguely-conceived strategies for approaching local public officials; whereas large, well-financed groups, such as the American Medical Association (AMA) and the Confederation of British Industry (CBI), develop extensive and sophisticated strategies. Ideally, a strategy will include elements such as (1) goals to be achieved and what are and are not acceptable fall-back positions, (2) identification of key policy makers to be persuaded, (3) ways that policy makers will be approached and persuaded by hired lobbyists, group personnel, group members (through the phone, letter, or e-mail, and so on), and an association with a political party if parties are important decision makers in the public policy arena. Much of a strategy is not related to immediate concerns. It is geared toward gaining access or creating an atmosphere that will be conducive to the group in influencing future government policy. This involves building up trust, credibility, and often obligation (perhaps through helping someone get elected) and maybe even creating dependence or *capture* (where a group effectively controls a government agency or policy area).

Group tactics are the specific ways in which strategy is implemented on a day-to-day basis. Tactics will include which public officials in which branches of government will be contacted, who will contact them and when, and how the message will be delivered. Tactics may also include a specific media or public relations campaign, even demonstrations and protests, aimed at influencing policy makers' stances. The combination and implementation of tactics may change as political circumstances change. Making such adjustments is a major factor in effective lobbying, which is why lobbying is considered an art, not a science.

Scholars often make a distinction between *insider* and *outsider* strategy and tactics and between *direct* and *indirect* lobbying. These terms do not lend themselves to precise definitions, but they are helpful in distinguishing types of lobbying activity. Insider strategies and tactics are those where lobbyists and group leaders confine their lobbying to the contacts that they have built up in the policy-making process and do not involve group members or utilize media, public relations campaigns, or public protests. Up until the late 1960s in the United States, virtually all strategies and tactics were geared toward insider lobbying, and it is still largely the case outside of the United States. Even in the United States, insider lobbying is still favored by long-established groups that are part of the political establishment, such as certain businesses and the professions. In contrast, many newer, nonestablished interests, such as some environmental groups and those for the poor and animal rights, often use outsider strategies and tactics that involve using pressure from their grassroots membership or using the media, public relations, and demonstrations to try and influence policy makers. This is mainly because they do not have governmental contacts or the positive reputation with policy makers to be able to use insider tactics. Such strategies and tactics are often described as indirect lobbying as they attempt to influence public officials through a third party such as the media or public opinion. In contrast, direct lobbying involves lobbyists, group leaders, or group members who contact public officials directly in person, by phone, letters, or e-mail.

In practice, while a lobbying campaign using only insider tactics can work, campaigns primarily involving outsider tactics and indirect lobbying must at some point involve direct lobbying in order to get the group's specific demands across to policy makers. Increasingly since the 1970s, particularly in the U.S. but also in other liberal democracies, even establishment interests have come to use a combination of insider and outsider tactics and direct and indirect lobbying. This is largely a result of the fact that many more interests have entered politics and the competition for the ear of policy makers and what it takes to influence their actions becomes more difficult. Thus, the developments in interest group activity since the 1960s has blurred the distinction between direct and indirect lobbying and insider and outsider tactics.

Evidence shows that there are some common elements to strategies and tactics across all political systems whether they are pluralist or nonpluralist or whether they are developed or developing societies; but there are also some wide variations in strategies and tactics (Ball and Millard 1987; Bianchi 1986b; Castles 1967; Thomas, Hrebenar, and Boyer 2001). To understand the reasons behind the similarities and variations, it is important to distinguish between the *activities* of lobbying and the *process* of lobbying. The activities of lobbying are universal; the process for achieving these will, to varying degrees, be affected by culture and institutional structures and mores.

Whether it is in Washington, D.C., a U.S. state capital, a national capital in Western Europe, an authoritarian country in the Middle East, or some totalitarian regime, there appear to be six fundamental strategies and tactics that are common to all political systems: (1) monitoring the activities of government and other interests as they affect the group, (2) making and maintaining contacts in government and with other groups, (3) building trust and credibility, and in some cases loyalty, with one's contacts, especially public officials, (4) creating a relationship with public officials where they will want to help one's group, (5) working to insure harmony within the group and with other group allies on key lobbying issues, and (6) continually refining the lobbying effort in the light of the changing political climate (Thomas, Hrebenar, and Boyer 2001). Furthermore, it is clear that the use of lobbyists in some form or another is the major tactic employed in all societies. (see section 7.6.).

Together, culture, institutional structures, and mores shape the forms and processes of the universal activities of lobbying and the way lobbyists go about their business. In effect, these factors determine the local "rules of the lobbying game." In many ways, cultural and institutional factors overlap and thus may be inseparable. However, for analytical purposes it is useful to distinguish between them because culture is more related to values and behavior, and institutions more related to formal structures and processes. Political culture, for example, can dictate the strategies and tactics that are acceptable and the ones that are not as acceptable. For example, the use of hired lobbyists to contact public officials directly is accepted more by public officials in the United States than by European public officials who prefer to hear from group leaders or members (Thomas, Hrebenar, and Boyer 2001). Institutional structure has much to do with where power lies and thus will dictate the channels that groups will use in attempting to influence public policy. The highly centralized parliamentary democracies of Western Europe, with power located in the cabinet and often a political party, means that lobbying a parliament is a low priority and in many cases unproductive (though see P. Norton 1999 for the use of parliamentary lobbying as part of a broad strategy). The major strategies and tactics in these systems focus on working with the bureaucracy and in some cases one or more political parties.

In contrast, the separation of powers system operating in the United States fragments power, and thus there are many more points of access. When this is combined with the relatively weak political party system, especially in many states, and that lobbying has been accepted for a longer period of time than in other countries, it can be understood why the processes of lobbying and the range of techniques used are much more extensive in the United States than in any other political system. Furthermore, this fragmentation of power and multiple points of access allow strategies that involve lobbying in many political venues simultaneously (Holyoke 2003). These options in strategies and tactics and the wide range of techniques employed make the United States an aberration among nations (Thomas 1993b). For example, as mentioned above, Europeans are much more likely to use insider or direct contact in lobbying, as opposed to outsider, indirect techniques.

This does not mean that the entire range of U.S. techniques are not known to European interest groups and lobbyists or that they are not being used in some instances. Rather, it is a case of many strategies and tactics not being part of the tradition of lobbying or being strategically or tactically inappropriate. For example, killing legislation is a common tactic in the United States, but in parliamentary systems, once the party or the cabinet has decided upon a policy, this tactic is rarely used. Perhaps the most obvious difference between the tactics in the United States, and most other liberal democracies, is the use of campaign fund contributions to candidates and parties by interest groups. Although this tactic is practiced increasingly in Europe, it is minuscule compared to the role of political action committees (PACs) in the United States. However, because of increasing pluralism in many Western democracies, in part ushered in by the declining importance of political parties and ideology, lobbying strategies and tactics in parliamentary democracies are taking on more and more of an American complexion (Thomas, Hrebenar, and Boyer 2001).

The entries in chapter 4, particularly sections 4.2. (interest group system development), 4.3. (political and institutional structure), and 4.4. (political culture), provide more in-depth analysis of why interest group activity, including strategy and tactics, vary among political systems.

7.3. NONFINANCIAL INVOLVEMENT OF INTEREST GROUPS IN THE ELECTION PROCESS

Ronald G. Shaiko

The bulk of research relating to the activities of organized interests in the electoral process in U.S. politics focuses on the financial contributions of interest groups through political action committees (PACs) to candidates for office as well as to political parties (see section 7.4.). Relatively little has been written on the nonfinancial aspects of group activity in the election process in the United States or elsewhere. However, by consulting a range of sources, mainly on U.S. politics, information can be gleaned on a variety of nonfinancial avenues of interest group activity in elections. These include: candidate endorsements, voter education, candidate recruitment and nomination, development of political party platforms, voter registration and get-out-the-vote (GOTV) efforts, campaign staffing support, and the provision of in-kind services to candidates.

Candidate Endorsements by Interest Groups

Candidate endorsements by interest groups are common and are often utilized by candidates to demonstrate their support from various constituent interests. Interest group endorsements are usually based on ratings generated through the analysis of the voting records of office holders on a range of policy issues (Fowler 1982; Krehbiel 1990; Poole 1981; Poole and Rosenthal 1991). The emergence of ratings such as those compiled by Americans for Democratic Action (ADA), the U.S. Chamber of Commerce (USCC), and the American Conservative Union (ACU) have been utilized by political scientists as surrogates for political ideology. The League of Conservation Voters ratings have also been useful in analyzing environmental issues. Little research, however, has linked these ratings and the resultant endorsements by some interest groups to electoral outcomes.

Voter Education

Related to endorsements are the production and dissemination of voter education materials by interest groups. The Christian Coalition, for example, produces and circulates hundreds of thousands of pieces of education material in the form of candidate scorecards that identify the policy positions of candidates without expressly endorsing or opposing specific candidates. While the intent of such materials is to identify candidates and their records that support Christian Coalition positions, there is no expressed advocacy of any candidate or party. As a result, neither the interest group nor the candidates for office must declare such voter education efforts as financial contributions to election campaigns (Rozell and Wilcox 1997; Wilcox 1996).

Similarly, internal communications between interest group leaders and their members have been ruled by the Federal Election Commission (FEC) to be exempt from being recorded as direct or indirect financial contributions to candidates or parties, even if these communications explicitly direct members to support or oppose a particular candidate for office. In the 1996 elections, for example, the National Federation of Independent Business (NFIB) spent as much money on internal communications with its 600,000 members as on direct PAC contributions and independent expenditures. Yet none of the money spent internally was recorded with the FEC (Shaiko and Wallace 1999).

Candidate Recruitment

Interest groups are also active in the candidate recruitment and nomination processes within both major parties in the United States (Crotty 1984; E. Epstein 1980; Fowler 1993; Herrnson 1995; Kazee and Thornberry 1990). A variety of organized interests, including single issue groups, have become increasingly active in the recruitment and nomination of like-minded individuals to run for public office (Crotty 1984; Goldman 1991; Hicks 1994; Sue Thomas 1994). Similar patterns of interest groups recruiting candidates are documented in Britain, Canada, and Mexico (Camp 1995; Kay, Lambert, and Brown 1991; Norris and Lovenduski 1995).

Input into the Formulation of Political Party Platforms

The growing activism of organized interests in the formulation of political party platforms has received wide coverage in the popular press, but less academic scrutiny. However, a few studies have analyzed the platform-building processes undertaken by the two major parties in the United States, and some of these allude to the roles of organized interests (e.g., Budge and Hofferbert 1990; Monroe 1983; L. Smith 1989, 1992; Walters 1990). Baer and Bositis (1988, 1993) and Baer and Dolan (1994) present a more comprehensive view of the nexus between organized interests and party activists.

Voter Mobilization

Voter mobilization by organized interest groups, through voter registration efforts and GOTV drives, has received considerable attention from political scientists, particularly from scholars focusing on minority representation. Following the passage of the Voting Rights Act in 1965, the political mobilization of previously disenfranchised voters became the goal of many interest groups, particularly in the South (Arrington and Taylor 1993; C. Davidson and Grofman 1994; Giles and Hertz 1994; Longoria, Wrinkle, and Polinard 1990; Timpone 1995). More recently, the efforts of organized interests in support of the Motor Voter legislation have been documented (J. Moss 1993).

The Provision of Election Campaign Volunteers

Another aspect of political mobilization of activists by organized interests is the provision of campaign volunteers and other support staff during the election cycle. Historically, organizations with strong grassroots memberships have activated their members for political purposes (see section 7.13.). Such groups include labor unions, citizens groups, church congregations, and a variety of membership associations. Due to the local nature of such mobilizations, there is little systematic research on the roles of organized interests in providing campaign support (but for an assessment of the grassroots electoral prowess of the National Rifle Association, see Shaiko and Wallace 1998). Some efforts, however, are organized at the national level. For example, the efforts of the American Federation of Labor-Congress of Industrial Organizations (AFL-CIO) since 1980 in organizing its membership at the congressional district level has resulted in the creation of more than 200 Legislative Action Committees across the country. Such efforts warrant future analysis by political scientists.

The Provision of Political Expertise

Finally, the provision of political expertise by organized interests to political candidates in the form of in-kind services are often as important as financial contributions. Herrnson (1995, 121) documents a variety of services provided to candidates by interest groups including: polls, campaign advertisements, issue research, fund-raising assistance, and strategic advice. The American Medical Association (AMA), in addition to being one of the largest contributors to congressional campaigns through AMPAC, its political action committee, serves a large number of candidates by providing benchmark polls at greatly reduced costs. Several interest groups also provide direct training for candidates and campaign staffers (Gimpel 1994) as well as technical assistance in the form of targeting, demographic profiles, and other computer-assisted data collection efforts (Herrnson 1995).

The nonfinancial support of political candidates by organized interests provides a great deal of fertile ground for the analysis of interest group influence in the political system. While gathering data in this area may be more onerous than analyzing PAC contribution data supplied by the FEC, the findings may provide greater insights.

7.4. POLITICAL ACTION COMMITTEES (PACs)

Ronald J. Hrebenar

Political action committees (PACs) are organizations set up to raise and distribute funds to candidates running for public office. PACs are usually connected to an interest group and are the major means used by many groups to create access to key politicians. As a consequence, PACs have become a major source of campaign finance in U.S. politics at the federal, state, and to some extent, at the local levels of politics. For example, in both the 1996 and the 1998 federal election cycles, PACs gave approximately $200 million to candidates (Willis 1999, 28).

The first PAC was the AFL-CIO PAC organized in the 1940s. The big explosion in the number of PACs occurred in the 1970s and 1980s. At the federal level, from just a handful in the early 1970, the total exploded to over 4,000 by 1990. By 1999, the total had declined to 3,778 with the largest number representing corporations (1,540). Other major categories included: non-connected or independent PACs, those not associated with an interest group (941); trade-membership and health (826); labor (318); and 153 others (FEC 1999).

Research on PACs

PACs are relatively easy to study. Original, raw data is quickly collected and made available by the Federal Election Commission (FEC), which maintains sites on the Internet with free access to its files. There are also several excellent directories of PACs, such as Fraser Associates (1980), Roeder (1982), Zuckerman (1998), and Ness (2000, 621–77). The academic study of PACs is largely grounded within political finance studies that began in the 1960s. The premier producer of these studies is Herbert Alexander and his series of election finance books (Alexander 1995). Alexander and other researchers have also produced more general studies of money in U.S. politics (Alexander 1992; Malbin 1984; Sorauf 1988b, 1992) while other scholars have produced more specific studies on aspects of money in politics such as congressional or presidential campaigns (C. Lewis 1996; Magleby and Nelson 1990).

The first major popular study of PACs was Sabato's *PAC Power* (1984). He explored several key and continuing research questions regarding PACs. First, what is the internal organization and decision making of PACs? Do PACs *buy* the votes of politicians? Do PAC financial contributions constitute an undesirable form of financial influence in the political system? Who are the recipients of PAC gifts? What are the linkages between PACs and political parties? How can PACs be reformed to make them less dangerous to the political system? Other early works include Sorauf (1984) in which the focus is on the effect of PACs on U.S. democracy; and Alexander (1983), which made a case for PACs.

Much of the early research concentrated on the explosion in the number of PACs and questions about their internal decision making. Since many PACs are simply allocating entities for their parent interest groups, perhaps the most important organizational decision-making process is how PACs decide to allocate their only important resource—money. Several case studies focused on this process (Biersack, Herrnson, and Wilcox 1994; Eismeier and Pollock 1988; Jacobson and Kernell 1983). A number of early studies show that PACs tend to support incumbent legislators (Malbin 1984). However, several other studies indicate that some PACs— especially nonaffiliated PACs and some corporate PACs—sometimes support challengers (Gopoian 1984; Latus 1984; W. Welch 1982; Ryan, Swanson, and Bucholz 1987). Many of these same studies find that PACs tend to support legislators in key positions, such as committee chairs and party leaders.

Inconclusive Evidence on the Influence of PACs

The most important PAC research question is that of the impact of PAC contributions on public policy decision making. In short, is the PAC campaign contribution the modern equivalent of the nineteenth century bribe? As pointed out in chapter 2 (see section 2.5.), the research is inconclusive running the gamut from PACs being influential to having some influence to having no influence at all.

What we are left with are three conclusions upon which most scholars of PACs agree. First, PAC money can buy access to legislators but does not necessarily buy votes (Magleby and Nelson 1990; Sabato 1984, 1989; Sorauf 1992; Wolpe and Levine 1996). Second, PAC money can influence congressional voting behavior when one or more of the following conditions are present: legislators have no strong preferences (Conway 1991;

Fleischer 1993; Magleby and Nelson 1990); an issue has very low visibility (Conway 1991; Denzau and Munger 1986; D. Evans 1986; Malbin 1984; Sorauf 1992); the public at large is inattentive or indifferent (Conway 1991; Magleby and Nelson 1990; Malbin 1984; Schlozman and Tierney 1986); or when an issue is technical and arcane (Sabato 1984). Third, PAC money may not influence congressional voting, but it does affect how legislators behave in other less visible parts of the legislative process, for example in a committee (Conway 1991; J. Wright 1996).

Obviously, with these different results, much work remains to be done on this topic. It is possible that different types of issues may produce different types of relationships. Also, additional work is necessary to identify the various other factors influencing voting such as ideology, constituency identity, party and personal background and, if possible, distinguish these from the PAC money variable.

Another important research question centers around the relationship between PACs and political parties. In the 1990s, the issue of so-called soft money contributions from interest groups to parties became a major topic for research. For a period in the 1970s and early 1980s, there was some concern about PAC replacing parties in terms of campaign financing. Parties made a come back in the late 1980s and the key question is how the two types of organizations complement each other in supporting candidates in election campaigns (Alexander and Haggerty 1984).

By the early 2000s, the increase in significance of so-called leadership PACs (organized around party and legislative leaders), PAC involvement in raising soft money for political campaigns, and the growing power of ideological PACs (in contrast to the traditional labor and corporate PACs), all indicate that the PAC world is always changing as new ways are found to channel money from interest groups to politicians and parties (Glasser and Eilperin 1999; Willis 1999).

7.5. INTEREST GROUP INVOLVEMENT IN DIRECT DEMOCRACY

Richard Braunstein

The procedures of direct democracy—the initiative, referendum, and recall—were primarily reforms of the Progressive Era. They were seen as ways to counteract the practices of political machines and the domination of the legislative process by special interests. As an ideal, direct democracy creates citizen-legislators to provide an external check on representative institutions. However, the question of whether this goal has been achieved through direct democracy remains largely unanswered (Bowler, Donovan, and Tolbert 1998; Low 1991).

Much of the research on direct democracy details the entrenched position of organized interest groups (Cronin 1989; Magleby 1984). Magleby

(1984, 189) notes that "for nearly a century the direct legislation process has been primarily a single-issue-group process." Furthermore, organized interests have greater access to the resources necessary to both initiate and win ballot campaigns than do unorganized citizen groups. As Cronin (1989, 5–6) notes, "although the direct democracy devices . . . are widely available, the evidence suggests it is generally the organized interests that can afford to put them to use." And well-financed groups are often able to block proposed legislation in ballot contests (Cronin 1989; Magleby 1984). This enables them to inhibit the passage of statutory and constitutional laws that oppose their interests. In a more empirically-based study, Gerber (1999) makes similar points to Magleby and Cronin.

Thus, the greatest concern raised by the influence of money on ballot issue outcomes is that it "gives too much of a head start to well-funded special [private] interests that can afford to hire specialized firms with computerized lists of likely supporters" (Cronin 1989, 217; see also Berg and Holman 1987, 29). However, although much of the existing literature focuses on the advantaged role of private interest groups, there has yet to be a comprehensive study of their dominance when compared to well funded and organized public interest groups that use similar strategies and tactics. There is no evidence to suggest that in the direct democracy process, private interests flourish over public interests or that liberal groups succeed more than conservative groups (Cronin 1989, 186–87). Groups like Common Cause and the League of Women Voters have been successful in ballot campaigns, suggesting that the public interest can also be served by direct democracy. What is evident is that organized interest groups tend to succeed over unorganized groups.

Groups with extensive resources are not always successful, however. Approximately 20 percent of ballot issue campaigns are won by underdog groups that spend considerably less than typical well-funding interests (Cronin 1989, 113). Grassroots campaigns have been successful, in part, because of the legitimacy they hold with the public and insofar as it involves *citizen-legislators*. Furthermore, ballot issue committees that raise a majority of their contributions from out of state, or from one or two large contributors, can create negative perceptions among voters, resulting in electoral defeats (D. Olson 1992).

Research has also shown that large contributions by well-funded organizations to ballot issue campaigns can lead to direct legislation with widely shared costs and benefits (Braunstein 1999). This is further evidence that the substantive outcomes of ballot issue elections are not determined solely by campaign spending of well-financed interests. Instead, a number of factors contribute, including the actual subject matter of a ballot proposition, existing social needs, media endorsements, and the ideological concerns of the electorate (Braunstein 1999; D. A. Smith and Herrington 1997).

7.6. LOBBYISTS: DEFINITIONS, TYPES, AND VARYING DESIGNATIONS

Clive S. Thomas

Although Deakin (1966) notes that the word *lobbyist* appeared in print in the United States as early as 1808, the origin of the term is subject to dispute. What the various explanations have in common, however, is that those seeking favors from government waited in a lobby (a foyer, waiting room, or entrance hall) to buttonhole, waylay, or importune public officials to take some action in their capacity as public servants to benefit the group or organization represented by the favor seeker.

One explanation about the term's origin is that favor seekers hung about the entrance hall (the lobby) to the House of Commons in England and *lobbied* Members of Parliament (MPs) before they went into session. Rosenthal (2001) provides another explanation. He argues that the term *lobby agent* was first used in the early 1800s to describe association representatives active in New York state politics. They literally waited in the corridors of power to impress their case on legislators. Later *lobby agent* was shortened to *lobbyist*. Still another explanation is that the term originated during the presidency of Ulysses S. Grant (1869–77), who kept a suite at the Willard Hotel not far from the White House where favor seekers would buttonhole him for favors in the hotel's lobby. A variation on this explanation also involves Washington D.C. and agents of companies that produced supplies that were needed during the Civil War (1861–65), such as munitions, uniforms, and food. Many top officials in the Department of War lived in hotels and rooming houses, and the company agents would wait in the lobbies and intercept the officials to lobby them for lucrative war contracts as they made their way to work.

Whatever the explanation, the media, especially in the United States, tends to use the term *lobbyist* in a generic way giving the impression that all lobbyists are similar in their backgrounds, methods, and operating styles. Consequently, this view is generally held by the public (Thomas and Hrebenar 1995). In fact, there are several types of lobbyists, and the distinction between them is important because it explains much about their mode of operation and their power base. In recent years among scholars of U.S. interest groups, a generally accepted nomenclature has been developed to distinguish between types of lobbyists. In other liberal democracies, however, there is no agreed upon nomenclature.

Definitions of Lobbyist

A *lobbyist* can be defined as "a person who represents an interest group in order to influence government decisions in that group's favor" (Thomas and Hrebenar 1999a, 124). This definition has gained some acceptance and has been used by several scholars (for example, Rosenthal 1993, 2001; Nownes 2001). However, the definition is too narrow to be used in comparative lobbying analysis across countries to embrace the roles played by group personnel designated to aid in affecting public policy (see sections 7.7. and 7.9.). Indeed, it may be too narrow a definition even for lobbyists in the United States. Therefore, a broader definition is needed to embrace the roles and differences between U.S. lobbyists and those in other countries who perform related roles. A more all-embracing definition of a lobbyist is:

> A person designated by an interest group to facilitate influencing public policy in that group's favor by performing one or more of the following for the group: (1) directly contacting public officials; (2) monitoring political and governmental activity; (3) advising on political strategies and tactics; and (4) developing and orchestrating the group's lobbying effort (Thomas, Hrebenar, and Boyer 2001).

Types of Lobbyists in the United States

For many years, varying and rather vague designations were used to distinguish between types of lobbyists (or *Washington representatives* as they are often referred to in Washington, D.C.). These included *independent* lobbyists and *professional* lobbyists, both of which were often also referred to as *hired guns* because they are paid specifically to lobby. These designations were sometimes contrasted with amateur lobbyists; though it was often unclear whether the term *amateur* meant unpaid or that amateur lobbyists were not well versed in lobbying techniques or a combination of the two (see, for example, Milbrath 1963; Zeigler 1983). Beginning in the late 1980s, a standard terminology on the types of lobbyist began emerging among scholars of U.S. interest groups. This divides lobbyists into five types (Thomas and Hrebenar 2003, table 4.2):

1. Contract Lobbyists. Those hired on a contract for a fee specifically to lobby. They often represent several clients and may be members of lobbying firms with several lobbyists. Although they constitute only about one-fourth of the federal and state capital lobbying communities, it is the contract lobbyist (sometimes referred to derisively as a *hired gun*) whom the public hears most about through the press. This is partly because some contract lobbyists, though only a small percentage, earn six- or seven-figure incomes.

2. In-House Lobbyists. Sometimes known as association or company lobbyists, this term refers to the executive directors, presidents, and employees of a host of organizations and businesses from environmental groups, the AFL-CIO, school board associations, trade groups, to telecommunications companies, and large corporations such as Microsoft. They represent only one client—their employer. They were the first type of lobbyists to appear on the political scene beginning in the mid-nineteenth century when big business, especially the railroads, became a significant part of the U.S. economy. As a group, they have probably always constituted the largest segment of the federal and state capital lobbying community, and today they account for one-third to one-half of all lobbyists. Probably because of the negative connotations raised in the public's mind by the word lobbyist, in-house lobbyists are often given a euphemistic title by their organizations, such as representative, agent, advocate, government relations specialist, or, more often, legislative liaison.

3. Government Legislative Liaisons. Employees of government agencies and local governments who, as part of their job, represent their agency or jurisdiction to other governments and the legislative branch. Possibly because lobbyists have a negative image, in addition to the fact that governments attempt to maintain at least a facade of unity, federal agencies and state and local governments do not officially refer to them as lobbyists. Instead, they often use the designation legislative liaison. However, these individuals are very much lobbyists in practice. They include heads and senior staff of federal and state government agencies, representatives of state universities, and elected and appointed officials of local governments. An estimate is that government lobbyists constitute between one-third and one-fourth of the federal and state capital lobbying communities. (See also section 8.12.2.)

4. Citizen, Cause, or Volunteer Lobbyists. Lobbyists who typically represent small nonprofit organizations, social welfare groups, or community organizations. These lobbyists are usually very committed to their causes. The only payment they receive (if they receive any at all) is for their expenses. They constitute about 10 percent of the state lobbying community, and about 75 percent of them are women. No figures exist for this type of lobbyist at the federal and local levels.

5. Private Individuals, "Hobbyists," or Self-appointed Lobbyists. They constitute only 1 to 2 percent of the state lobbying community (no figures are available for the federal and local levels). They lobby for pet projects, direct personal benefits, or against a policy or proposal they find particularly objectionable. Besides politically motivated members of the general public, this category includes prominent (often wealthy) individuals, such as Peter Angelos, owner of the Baltimore Orioles baseball franchise, working federal and state government to benefit their economic interests.

The Designation of Lobbyists in Other Western Democracies

Partly because many Western democracies have only recently come to recognize the role of interest groups and lobbyists (see section 11.1.), and many do so reluctantly, there is no agreed upon nomenclature for lobbyists outside the United States. These individuals are variously referred to as political consultants, government affairs representatives, public affairs representative, among other designations. One major difference is the role of the contract (or hired) lobbyist. First, the term contract lobbyist is a designation rarely used outside the United States; they are sometimes referred to as commercial lobbyists (Jordan 1991) as in Britain or simply as political consultants. Second, in most countries, including those in the European Union, Australia, and Canada, these individuals are less likely to contact government officials directly but act as group advisors, monitor activity affecting the group, and act as facilitators to set up meetings of group officials with policy makers (hence the broader definition of a lobbyist set out above). In fact, in some cases it is somewhat of a misnomer to call these individuals group representatives as some of them may rarely advocate the group's position directly to government. Nevertheless, they are intimately involved in the *process* of lobbying as defined above, and therefore should be considered as part of the lobbyist community in their respective country.

But should these people be referred to as lobbyists in comparative analysis if most countries do not use the term and, indeed, find it pejorative and that some countries, like France and the Czech Republic, do not have the word *lobbyist* in their language? These are, indeed, compelling reasons for using another term. The problem is that there is no widely accepted term that fits this need. Political consultant is probably the most general term used in Western democracies outside the United States to designate a hired lobbyist, and government affairs/public affairs representative is used most to refer to what Americans would call an in-house lobbyist. Both terms, however, are too general and can include other activities disassociated with lobbying, such as campaign organizing. The advantage in using the term *lobbyist* is that, even though it is shunned by many countries and primarily associated with the United States, it is widely understood and, while far from ideal, is the most appropriate term to use in comparative analysis of lobbyists and lobbying activity.

7.7. THE ROLE OF LOBBYISTS

Elizabeth A. Capell and Clive S. Thomas

What do lobbyists do? What is their role in a political system, in particular, a pluralist political system? At first sight, the answer to this question appears obvious: Lobbyists work to influence government policy to benefit their group or organization. While this is an accurate general description, there are specific activities that are subsumed under this generic role. And the roles vary somewhat between the types of lobbyists and even vary among the same type within the same country, state or local government (see sections 7.2. and 7.6.), and more so among political systems, particularly between the United States and parliamentary systems (see section 7.10.). While some reference in this entry is made to lobbyists in parliamentary systems, the focus is primarily on lobbyists' roles in the United States, where the bulk of the research (perhaps 90 percent) has been conducted.

Common Roles of Lobbyists and the Different Emphasis of These Roles Among Types of Lobbyists

Although there is no such person as a *typical lobbyist*, regardless of their type or country of operation, there are four roles that virtually all lobbyists perform either to government and/or to their client or employer: (1) connect an interest group with government; (2) communicate information; (3) persuade; and (4) monitor government activity.

First, all lobbyists perform the role of connecting an interest group with government. As an interface or facilitator, the lobbyist serves roles with both government and his/her client (contract lobbyist) or a group, association, or business (in-house lobbyist). The lobbyist shapes the relationship between the group and the government by identifying the decision makers to contact and by attempting to influence their views. Research on the U.S. states by Thomas and Hrebenar (1999a) argues that this group-government facilitating role of lobbyists is so crucial that (together with the extent to which government depends on a group) it is one of the two most important factors in determining group success, or lack thereof, in the policy process.

Lobbyists also often play an important role in the internal dynamics of a group in relation to the form and conveying of the group's message to government, including helping to plan and orchestrate their organization's strategy and tactics. In fact, in many parliamentary systems, contract lobbyists (often simply referred to as consultants) may not directly contact public officials but help plan and orchestrate the lobbying campaign including identifying the key officials to contact and leave the lobbying to the representatives of the business or organization (McGrath 2002; Thomas, Hrebenar, and Boyer 2001).

Second, the lobbyist acts as the communicator of information for both the government and his/her client or employer. This information can be technical (such as about the group he/she represents, or the likely effects of a policy) or it can be political (such as who is likely to oppose the group's goals or suggestions). This is all based upon the lobbyist's knowledge of the process and the players. Different types of lobbyists have different assets when it comes to providing information. In-house lobbyists and legislative liaisons have specific and often extensive knowledge about their group or business, often unequaled knowledge of their particular interest (business, cause, agency, etc.) that they represent. On the other hand, contract lobbyists are rarely experts in a particular field or business. They are much more likely to have knowledge of the political process—which is the main reason they are hired—and sometimes expert knowledge on particular parts of the governmental system such as the budget process or a department such as transportation. The degree of reliance of legislators and other government officials on information from lobbyists varies over time, issues, and political jurisdictions.

Third, is the role of the lobbyist as persuader mainly attempting to influence government in favor of their group's goals. Greenwald (1977, 65) encapsulates this role as follows: "lobbyists are salesmen for their groups, but they sell information and ideas instead of toothpaste." Similarly, Milbrath (1963) asserts that lobbyists are in business for two reasons—to communicate and to persuade. As pointed out above, what policy makers want most is information. Often, however, lobbyists need to use various means to get policy makers to respond to available information. As many scholars have clearly demonstrated (for example, Schlozman and Tierney 1986; J. Walker 1991, 103–21), the full service lobby may do everything from act in coalition with other groups, to mobilizing both its members and the public, to litigating in court, to distributing campaign funds. All of this is to gain listeners and advocates in government. Browne (1998) goes further, emphasizing that multifaceted or all-directional lobbying works better than simple communications.

However, the question of what constitutes the ability to persuade—the ability to exert power and influence—is one of the most elusive aspects, if not the most elusive aspect of interest group studies. The answer is much more complex than the simplistic view that power is determined by the amount of money or the political connections of an interest group, which is often the explanation given in the media and generally believed by the public. Insights on this question of group and lobbyist power are provided in sections 7.8., 7.10., and particularly in section 7.17.

The fourth common function of lobbyists is that they spend much of their time monitoring the actions of government and not actively lobbying. As Allan Cigler (1991b, 119) points out, the consensus among group scholars is that "actual lobbying may be only one of a myriad of activities" in which lobbyists engage. In fact, in general, most lobbyists spend much of their time doing things other than lobbying, such as planning, preparing materials, working with their clients or staff in preparing their lobbying effort. Monitoring the actions of government as it is affecting or may affect their group or organization is one of the major tasks they perform. This is true of contract and in-house lobbyists in Washington, D.C. (Harris 1989; Heinz et al. 1993; Salisbury 1990), in the U.S. states (Nownes and Freeman 1998a; Rosenthal 2001; Thomas and Hrebenar 2003), and of lobbyists in other Western democracies and particularly consultants (Thomas, Hrebenar, and Boyer 2001; McGrath 2002). Thus, most of the time many lobbyists are passively involved in politics rather than being active participants.

Having identified the four major common roles and the variations that may be the case for types of lobbyists within and across political systems, we move to make some brief comments about particular aspects of the role of lobbyists.

Lobbyists and the Government

As the face and voice of an interest group in the governmental process, the lobbyist's role involves representing a group before some part of the government, most often the legislature and the executive. The lobbyist serves as an advocate, an analyst and purveyor of information about the impact of policies and politics, and an informal aide de camp to legislators and other government officials.

Many scholars including Milbrath (1963), Schlozman and Tierney (1986), and Heinz et al. (1993) identify *tactics of advocacy* or *techniques of influence*, which include: testifying before official bodies; maintaining general relations with officials; maintaining informal, substantive contacts with officials; helping to draft legislation; alerting legislators to the effects of a bill on their district; the lobbyist writing letters to officials (now, of course, including e-mails); and preparing witnesses to testify. In his book on the California legislature, Muir (1982) also sees the lobbyist as a teacher in the school of politics, one who frames the intellectual issues, pointing out the subtleties in a situation, and implying a conclusion.

Many early empirical studies concluded that lobbyists direct their efforts toward legislators and other government personnel sympathetic to their concerns. Bauer, Pool, and Dexter (1972), Dexter (1969), Matthews (1960) and Milbrath (1963) concluded that the role of lobbyists was to not necessarily persuade but to reinforce or mobilize legislators already predisposed to a particular group's views. More recent research shows that this is not necessarily the case and that most lobbyists see their role as working on those opposed to their issue and the undecided officials (Austin-Smith and Wright 1994; Rothenberg 1992; Schlozman and Tierney 1986, 292). See section 7.10. for a more extensive review of the types of officials that lobbyists target in terms of an official's disposition on an issue.

Lobbyists and Their Client or Employer

With few exceptions, the literature on lobbyists focuses on the visible public relationship between the lobbyist and government rather than the less visible, internal relationship between the lobbyist and his/her group, organization, or business. However, as indicated above, and as Heinz et al. (1993) observe, "on average, though with substantial variation among organizational roles, interest representatives spend a surprisingly large proportion of their time on the internal affairs of their organizations." In addition, Milbrath (1963) observes that almost all lobbyists serve as information conduits between the government and their client and that some do this exclusively. Dexter (1969) notes that Washington lobbyists often instruct their clients on how to accommodate, adapt, and adjust to government (see also Ainsworth and Sened 1993). They do this by helping their clients and employers understand the positions of the government and other interests that the government has to take into account.

Lobbyists ignore this internal role at their peril. If they do not serve as an information conduit, the group or organization may think that the government is doing nothing of interest to them (and that the lobbyist is superfluous). If the lobbyist fails to influence the policy position and political strategy of the group, both are likely to be out of touch with the political realities facing the lobbyist. Lobbyists play a pivotal role in identifying for a group its interest in an issue and in framing responses to complex policy questions both because of the lobbyist's knowledge about policy options and about political feasibility. In addition, as explained below, lobbyists often have a great influence on the disbursement of campaign funds on behalf of their client or organization.

The Role of Lobbyists in Determining Strategies and Tactics

In the United States (but less so in other countries) it is often the role of the lobbyist, particularly the contract lobbyist, to attempt to shape the relationship between the group and the government. They do this by attempting to influence the selection of decision makers, mainly elected officials but sometimes appointed ones, or by attempting to change the opinions of those already in office. Thus, lobbyists play a role in campaign activities, grassroots activity, public relations and media strategies, and coalition building as well as direct contact with decision makers. Larger organizations may assign these responsibilities to persons other than the lobbyist who contact government officials directly, but the lobbyist usually decides on final strategy and tactics.

Artie Samish, the famous (or infamous) California lobbyist of the 1940s and '50s who was reported by California Governor Earl Warren to be more powerful than the governor on issues affecting his clients, said that the secret of great power was "Very simple, young man . . . I selected the candidates that I thought would be agreeable to my clients, and I saw that they got elected. And if they didn't behave, I saw that they got unelected" (Samish and Thomas 1971). Using similar criteria, lobbyists also attempt to influence who is appointed as a decision maker, whether it is a legislative committee chair or a department head.

Like campaign involvement, grassroots activity and public relations, or media strategies, are targeted, fomented, and often organized by lobbyists. Jeffrey Berry (1977) in his study of public interest groups identifies the community organizer as one variety of lobbyist. Whether generating preprinted postcards (Schriftgiesser 1951) or orchestrating meetings between key constituent and legislators, eliciting grassroots action that connects constituents with elected officials is an important element of the lobbyist's role (Sachs, Cantor, and Neale 1986; Schlozman and Tierney 1986).

Media-related activities appear repeatedly on the list of tasks of lobbyists (J. Berry 1977; Birnbaum 1992; DeGregorio and Rossotti 1995; Dexter 1969; Heinz et al. 1993). Historical accounts, including Sachs, Cantor, and Neale (1986) and Burdette (1950) describe lobbyists planting stories in newspapers and influencing the media.

Lobbyists also work with lobbyists representing other like-minded entities, sometimes in formal coalitions but most often in informal alliances. These alliances pool the efforts of lobbyists and enable them to bring more political pressure to bear and in some cases to specialize in an aspect of a campaign. In fact, the lobbyist will be a key decision maker and often *the* decision makes as to the range of venues in which to lobby (the legislature, executive, media, etc.), which often involves entering into coalitions or informal agreements with other groups. A decision on the range of venues in which to lobby simultaneously is often based on the lobbyist's assessment of the opposition to a group's goals and how to counter it (Holyoke 2003).

Do Lobbyists Specialize in Particular Tasks or Policy Areas?

The answer to this question depends on the type of lobbyist and the size of the jurisdiction in which they operate.

Most contract, in-house, cause lobbyists, and legislative liaisons perform the gamut of tasks that lobbyists have to perform as identified in this entry—contacting government, working with their client, group, or business, monitoring, planning strategy, and so on. Robert Nelson et al. (1987, 192) point out that organizational representatives "typically distribute their time among a number of substantive fields and contact many government institutions" and "pursue the interest of the client organization, wherever it may take them." Other studies have noted that many contract lobbyists are hired to provide technical expertise rather than advice on public policy questions (Salisbury 1986; Laumann and Heinz 1985).

As to whether lobbyists specialize in a particular policy area or related areas, this depends on the type of lobbyist and the size of the jurisdiction. Obviously, in-house lobbyists, cause lobbyists, and legislative liaisons focus on the specific policy areas of their business, organization, or agency. So it is only contract lobbyists who are in a position to be generalists in terms of the policy areas that they represent. In large jurisdictions like Washington, D.C., and states with large populations, such as California, New York, and Michigan, there is some specialization among lobbyists and some lobbying firms. Some Washington lobbyists, for example, specialize in mining, healthcare, or transportation (often as specialized as railroads) among many other policy areas (Heinz et al. 1993). One California contract lobbyist specializes in representing California's high tech interests; others specialize in representing agriculture (even as specialized as the agricultural chemical industry), education, and local governments (Michael, Walters, and Weintraub 2001; Syer 1987). However, in states with small populations, such as Alaska, Idaho, North Dakota, and Vermont, contract lobbyists are more likely to be generalists and may have a range of clients from businesses to hospitals to local governments (Thomas and Hrebenar 1991c).

7.8. LOBBYISTS IN WASHINGTON, D.C., AND THE AMERICAN STATES

Anthony J. Nownes

It is difficult to determine precisely how many lobbyists are currently active in Washington, D.C. Estimates range from 10,000 to 90,000 (Phillips 1994, 34). It is even more difficult to determine how many lobbyists are active at the state level, but the number certainly runs well over 20,000. Tens of thousands more are active in local politics. However, all these figures depend on how *lobbyist* is defined (see section 7.6.). And while some of what is said about lobbyists here will be applicable to lobbyists in local government, particularly large cities, this entry focuses on lobbyists in national and state politics. We first consider the major academic and popular sources for studying lobbyists. Then we examine the makeup of the lobbying community, the backgrounds of lobbyists, and the attributes of successful lobbyists. The previous two entries (sections 7.6. and 7.7.) explain the various types of lobbyists and the role of lobbyists in the political process, respectively, and provide essential background for understanding this present entry.

Major Academic and Popular Sources on Lobbyists

Much has been written by both scholars and popular writers on lobbyists in Washington, D.C., and there is an increasing body of work on lobbyists in the states. The following sources, including various directories of lobbyists and interest groups, are good starting points for studying lobbyists.

Washington, D.C. The first major academic study on Washington lobbyists was Milbrath (1963). Twenty years later Schlozman and Tierney (1986) conducted another extensive general study. The most recent comprehensive studies are Heinz et al. (1993) and the numerous articles that Heinz and his colleagues have published over the last 20 years. The most useful of these for studying lobbyists are Laumann and Heinz (1985) and Robert Nelson et al. (1987). An article by Salisbury (1986) is also very insightful. Three of the first popular studies of lobbyists were Burdette

(1950), Schriftgiesser (1951), and Deakin (1966); the most recent comprehensive popular study is Birnbaum (1992).

The most useful directory of Washington lobbyists is the annual publication *Washington Representatives* (2003). See section 2.6. for more information on Washington directories that include lists of lobbyists and their contact information.

Lobbyists in the States. Three of the earliest works on individual states were De Vries (1960) on Michigan lobbyists, Patterson (1963) on Oklahoma lobbyists, and Hedlund and Patterson (1966) on lobbyists in Illinois. The first major work was Zeigler and Baer (1969); this study focused on only four states, however. The most comprehensive study is Rosenthal (1993, 2001) with extensive work having been conducted by Hrebenar and Thomas (1987, 1992, 1993a, 1993b). These authors (Thomas and Hrebenar 1991c, 1999a) have developed a typology of lobbyists for the U.S. states (which has been adopted by most scholars) and have gathered information on the backgrounds and approximate percentages of each type in the lobbying community (this typology is also useful for understanding the lobbying community in Washington). Contract lobbyists have been studied by Gray and Lowery (1996b) and women as lobbyists by Nownes and Freeman (1998b). An insightful examination of lobbyists in California is Michael, Walters, and Weintraub (2001).

Probably because the number of state lobbyists is so large, there is no commercial publication equivalent to *Washington Representatives* listing all registered state lobbyists. There are, however, publications that list some contract lobbyists by state, some of which are available on the Internet (e.g., *State Contract Lobbyists Directory* at http://www.stateandfed.com/home/lobby1.asp.). See also section 2.6. for directories that include state organizations for help in locating lobbyists. Virtually every state has lobbyist lists. Most states make their lists available to the public and, increasingly, through their state Web site.

Two Significant Characteristics of the Washington and State Lobbying Communities

The Dominance of In-House Lobbyists and Government Legislative Liaisons. Media stories on lobbyists tend to focus on powerful contract (hired gun) lobbyists like Clark Clifford (who reportedly received over $1 million for some advice he gave the DuPont family), and Michael Deaver (who receives a retainer of approximately $250,000 from just *one* of his many clients). While these super lobbyists make for fascinating media attention, they are the exception rather than the rule in Washington politics and in the states. As Salisbury (1986) discovered about Washington, D.C., using a narrow definition of lobbyist to include only contract and in-house lobbyists as lobbyists, approximately 80 percent of these two types of Washington lobbyists are in-house (association or business) lobbyists.

161

Salisbury's study has not been duplicated at the state level. But as Hrebenar and Thomas (2003) and Rosenthal (2001) point out, there is little doubt that a large percentage (perhaps as high as 40 percent) of state lobbyists are association lobbyists—not hired guns (this figure is based upon legislative liaisons and volunteer lobbyists being included as lobbyists; see section 7.6.). Thomas and Hrebenar (2003) also point out that a large percentage of those who lobby state capitals on a day-to-day basis represent various federal, state, and local government entities—perhaps 30 to 40 percent—and certainly a greater number than contact lobbyists. No study of legislative liaisons in Washington, D.C., has been conducted, but they are also likely a very prominent part of that lobbying community.

The Rise of the Lobbying Law Firm. One reason the media focuses on contract lobbyists is because their numbers have increased in recent years. In fact, the recent proliferation of hired guns has produced a new player in Washington politics and in the larger states like California, New York, and Massachusetts. This is the lobbying law firm, which often brings together a number of contract lobbyists. The number of lobbying law firms (and public relations firms specializing on politics) is rising in Washington and in state capitals (Rosenthal 2001).

Today's all-purpose lobbying law firm provides a wide variety of services including public relations, grassroots lobbying, media services, political consulting, fund-raising, and direct lobbying. Unfortunately, few interest group scholars have studied lobbying law firms or public relations firms in detail. To learn about these new political players, one must look to journalistic accounts such as those of Hedrick Smith (1988) and Birnbaum (1992).

The Background, Motivation, and Salaries of Lobbyists

Who are lobbyists? What are their backgrounds? Why do they do what they do? And do they all earn astronomical salaries?

Lobbyists as Elites. Forty years ago, Milbrath (1963, chap. 5) found that lobbyists are generally well-educated, upper or upper middle class, 40 to 60 years old, white and male. Virtually every subsequent study of lobbyists has reached similar conclusions (for example, Rosenthal 2001; Salisbury 1986; Zeigler and Baer 1969). There is some evidence, however, that the lobbying community is becoming more diverse. For example, studies of state lobbyists show that women are increasingly well represented in the lobbying community (Nownes and Freeman 1998b; Rosenthal 2001).

Career Paths. Though lobbying is an elite occupation, few children grow up aspiring to become lobbyists. As Jeffrey Berry (1989, 85) notes, "people become lobbyists because previous jobs lead them to it." What types of jobs? Studies indicate that a majority of Washington contract lobbyists come from government service both elected and appointed. Salisbury et al. (1989), for example, found that 56 percent of a sample of lob-byists had prior government experience. This finding is confirmed in other studies of Washington lobbyists (Milbrath 1963; Salisbury 1986). Among the most common government positions previously held by lob-byists are legislative aide, member of Congress, White House aide, and executive agency official. Ex-government officials have advantages over other lobbyists, the most obvious of which are specialized knowledge about the policy process and access to key decision makers.

Government is also the primary training ground for state contract lob-byists. This is confirmed by Thomas and Hrebenar (1996b, 141–45; 1999a, 126–30). According to Rosenthal (1993, 30), former legislators "are among the most effective lobbyists in the state capital and are cer-tainly perceived as the most influential." Former state legislative staff and executive branch officials also often become state contract lobbyists. Why do so many national and state government employees/officials become contract lobbyists? Studies of lobbyists suggest that both the lure of money and the thrill of politics play a role (Rosenthal 1993; Zeigler and Baer 1969).

The prevalence of government officials who become contract lobbyists has caused concern among many who fear that the revolving door (mov-ing from government service to lobbying, and sometimes back into gov-ernment again) may harm the integrity of government. For example, many analysts feel that former government officials have special access to policy makers and that this access may translate into special favors (G. Adams 1981; MacKenzie 1987; Quirk 1981). This partly explains the move to reg-ulate lobbying (see chap. 14), which in many jurisdictions includes a wait-ing period—usually a year—before a former public official can lobby.

After public service, law is the occupation that produces most contract lobbyists. Many lawyer-lobbyists are in demand because of their special knowledge of the law and the law-making process.

However, while most contract lobbyists in both Washington and state capitals have prior government experience or are lawyers, many in-house lobbyists have no government experience nor are they lawyers. In Wash-ington Robert Nelson et al. (1987), for example, found that most associ-ation lobbyists serve their employers for many years in other capacities before they become lobbyists. In addition, some association lobbyists act as executive directors of the organizations for which they lobby, and many others engage in tasks other than lobbying (R. Nelson et al. 1987; Salis-bury 1986). The studies by Thomas and Hrebenar (1996b, 141–45; 1999a, 126–30) and Rosenthal (1993, 34) confirm that there is an almost identical career pattern for in-house lobbyists in the states. State in-house lobbyists are much more likely to have worked their way through their profession or business before becoming a lobbyist than to have been in government service.

Salaries. Largely because the media publicizes the large salaries of some contract lobbyists, there is a general belief that lobbyists make huge incomes. Certainly, they earn more than the average salary of an American, and some Washington lobbyists make well over $1 million (Nownes 2001, 121). Some state lobbyists are also well paid. Texas's top lobbyists make more than $1 million annually; and this would be true in many large states (Rosenthal 1993). Even in smaller states like Arkansas, a number of lobbyists make close to $100,000 per year. However, the large salaries (more correctly fees) are those paid to contract lobbyists and not to in-house lobbyists who work for a single salary. Moreover, many contract lobbyists make less than many in-house lobbyists who may be senior members of an organization or business. Rosenthal (1993, 32) estimates that the average state lobbyist (he does not specify contract or in-house) probably earns about $50,000 a year.

What Makes a Successful Lobbyist?

The main answer to this question is experience and contacts. As Salisbury et al. (1989) conclude, experience produces increased knowledge about policy issues, contacts, and familiarity with the policy process. Moreover, as Rosenthal (1993, 35) points out, because "it takes time for integrity and honesty to be demonstrated, for victories to be won, and for reputations to develop," experience is an important asset. Thus, it is not surprising that most lobbyists have a great deal of experience. In their pioneering study of state lobbyists, Zeigler and Baer (1969) found that the average lobbyist had between 8 to 12 years of lobbying experience. Lobbyists at the federal level also tend to be experienced (Salisbury et al. 1989).

People skills are also important to a lobbyist's success. As Wolpe (1990, 19) points out, effective lobbying "is a function of interpersonal relations." And Rosenthal (1993, 36) notes that lobbyists themselves feel that good social skills and a good attitude are crucial to a lobbyist's success. Again, Thomas and Hrebenar (1996b, 1999a, 2003) confirm this. Finally, because lobbying can be hard, arduous, and unrewarding work, persistence, a willingness to work hard and a thick skin are also important.

Gaps in the Literature

Although much has been written on lobbyists, this subfield of interest group studies still has much to be investigated. There is little understanding, for example, of how lobbying has changed with the advent of computer technology and the Internet. Moreover, there are few in-depth studies of state lobbyists. What is needed is a 50-state study of lobbyists. And despite some pioneering efforts by Nownes and Giles (2001) and Nownes, Cooper, and Giles (2002), we have very little knowledge of lobbyists at the local level—who they are, what motivates them, and what they may or may not have in common with lobbyists in Washington, D.C., and the states.

7.9. LOBBYISTS IN COUNTRIES OUTSIDE THE UNITED STATES

John Warhurst, Brian Hocking, and A. Paul Pross

There is relatively little literature, academic or popular, on lobbyists outside the United States. This is partly explained by lobbying being a larger industry and a more accepted activity in the United States. However, since the late 1960s there has been considerable growth in the lobbying profession in several Western democracies generating a small but increasing literature on lobbyists. Lobbyists were mentioned in works on interest groups in the 1960s and 1970s (e.g., Kirchner 1981; T. Matthews 1973; Stanbury 1978), but the major works come later.

There are now several books by practitioners, journalists, and academics on lobbyists and lobbying. These include studies on Britain (C. Miller 1990, 2000; Greer 1985); on Canada (Sawatsky 1987); on Australia (Cullen 1990; Sekuless 1991); and on the European Union (EU) (Gardner 1991; Greenwood 2003a; Pedler 2002; Van Schendelen 2002).

Academic studies appear mainly in journals. These include: S. Anderson and Eliasson (1991) on lobbying in the EU; A. Jordan (1989) on insider lobbying in Britain; and Warhurst's studies of lobbyists in Australia (1987, 1990). Books include: G. Jordan (1991), a study of British commercial lobbyists containing chapters by academics and practitioners; Rush (1990) also a discussion of commercial lobbying; Doig (1990) includes studies of lobbying in several countries; and Hocking (1990) on foreign interest lobbying. Van Schendelen (1993), Pedler and Van Schendelen (1994), and Mazey and Richardson (1993a) examine lobbying in the EU. The Mazey and Richardson volume, like G. Jordan's (1991), include studies by both academics and practitioners.

One area of literature on lobbyists discusses the government relations specialist: In-house lobbyists in large corporations who manage company relations with government. There are now enough studies (including W. Grant 1984; Litvak 1981; Streeck 1983) to enable recent work, such as W. Grant (1991a) on Britain, and Bell and Warhurst on Australia (1993) to begin comparing the differences between national styles.

Another source on lobbyists is the literature on lobby regulation. The move to regulation reflects unease about the ethics of lobbying and a perceived tension between lobbying and democratic processes. This is of concern in Britain, in particular, where it was a major focus in a 1995 report (Berrington 1995). Pross (1991) and Atkinson (1995) examined the regulation of lobbyists in Canada and Warhurst (1987, 1990) examined it in

Australia. An important study is Rush (1994), who focuses on Canada, but also provides a comparative analysis including the situation in Germany, Australia, Britain, and the United States. The most comprehensive study on regulation, which includes many insights on lobbyists in Western democracies, including Japan, Germany, Israel, Denmark, and the EU, is a special issue of *Parliamentary Affairs* (1998).

Part of the growing interest in lobbying results from its increase across national borders. In particular, foreign interest lobbying is an issue in the United States (Choate 1990; Hocking 1990, 1991). This is part of the development of complex policy environments that transcend national boundaries and span subnational, national, and international political arenas (Hocking 1993). Here, lobbyists are, in essence, agents of access acting on behalf of both governmental and nongovernmental interests that, stimulated by the pressures of regional integration and the globalization of politics and economics, see the need to exercise influence at a number of levels. One response to this is the growing international networks of lobbyists as, for example, U.S. lobbying firms establishing a presence in the EU (Gardner 1991; Thomas, Hrebenar, and Boyer 2001). Surprisingly, the international relations literature has cast little light on transnational lobbying activities (see section 1.6.; chap. 13). What is needed is work that builds on the insights offered by Moon (1988) who studied South Korean lobbying activities in the United States.

These studies point to important differences between lobbyists in the United States and elsewhere, which flow from systemic differences (see section 4.3.). First, the target of lobbying in parliamentary systems is primarily the executive's role (ministers and civil servants) rather than the legislature, as is Congress in the United States. Whereas the U.S. political system is open and individual members of Congress are less bound to their political party, parliamentary systems are more closed, the executives more powerful and political parties more highly disciplined. Second, the profession of lobbying is different and less developed. Lobbyists emerge primarily from careers in public service or in parliament (in Britain MPs can register as lobbyists for particular clients). Lawyers are far less prominent among the ranks of lobbyists outside the United States, though this is changing as the organization of the lobbying profession changes. Third, lobbyists have less status and professional recognition outside the United States (Lloyd 1991), though this, too, may be changing.

Obviously, the study of lobbyists outside the United States is an open field, and much remains to be done. A good beginning would be a comprehensive synthesis of the existing literature and a comparison between the types of lobbyists, their backgrounds and styles across Western democracies.

7.10. LEGISLATIVE LOBBYING

Keith E. Hamm and Robert E. Hogan

Placing Research on Legislative Lobbying in a Comparative Context

"What would politics in America be like without lobbies and lobbyists?" (Eulau 1964, 27). This rhetorical question posed four decades ago encapsulates a major difference between the legislative process in the United States and in parliamentary democracies.

Perhaps 95 percent of the research on legislative lobbying across the Western world has been conducted on the U.S. political system mainly focusing on Congress with an increasing body of studies on the states (see section 6.4.). In this case, the predominance of research on the U.S. system is not primarily due to the large percentage of interest group scholars who study U.S. politics, but to a simple fact of constitutional structure and its consequence for the power structure. In the United States, the separation of powers fragments decision making and gives power bases to both the legislature (Congress and state legislatures) and the executive (the president and state governors). In contrast, parliamentary systems locate power in the executive (the prime minister and the cabinet) and parliaments generally have little independent decision-making power. In the United States, interests groups and their lobbyists focus on the legislature as a key part of their strategy whereas in parliamentary systems the executive is the major focus of lobbying (though getting a provision into the ruling party's platform is key). Hence, there is minimal research on legislative lobbying in parliamentary systems. Consequently, this entry focuses predominantly on legislative lobbying in the United States with only a brief mention of parliamentary systems.

Two points will place the importance of legislative lobbying in the United States in a broader context than it is often viewed, given the predominance of legislative lobbying studies in the research on lobbying. First, rarely does a lobbying strategy involve only the legislature. Even most insider lobbying strategies (see section 7.2.) involve lobbying the executive; and increasingly both insider and outsider lobbying strategies involve a multifaceted approach that include grassroots lobbying, media and public relations campaigns, and even demonstrations and protests (see sections 7.2., 7.3., 7.4., 7.13., 7.14., and 7.15.). Thus, it is difficult to isolate legislative lobbying from other elements of strategy. Lobbyists certainly view their lobbying effort as holistically involving all the elements of a strategy. And many political scientists have recognize this holistic nature of lobbying, including those who have studied policy networks, iron triangles, and the like (see section 7.16.). However, perhaps because legislative lobbying is much more visible than executive lobbying and generally easier to study, plus the practical consideration that research projects must be limited in scope to be completed, has meant that many researchers have studied legislative lobbying without relating it to other elements of lobbying. This has often given the misimpression to students and others studying lobbying in U.S. politics that legislative lobbying is all that counts in the U.S. system. Second, and a related point, because it is impossible to compartmentalize legislative lobbying from other elements of a strategy, much of the work on legislative lobbying and the discussion about it has application to other aspects of lobbying, particularly to the question of what constitutes effective lobbying.

There is no seminal work on legislative lobbying that covers the gamut of issues in this field; nor is there any general text that encapsulates the findings of the wide range of research that has been conducted on the U.S. political system. Given this, the best way to provide an overview of the work on this subject is through the major research questions that have concerned researchers. Out of many, three stand out: (1) the activities and strategies of interest groups and lobbyists; (2) the focus of their efforts; and (3) the relative influence of lobbying and the factors that condition this influence. Considering these three questions will involve identifying the major studies that have been conducted on legislative lobbying at the federal and state level. Those interested in an extensive review of the literature and a more detailed bibliography, should consult Hamm (1983a) and Richard Smith (1995).

Activities and Strategies of Interest Groups and Lobbyists

Several studies focus on what interest groups actually do to influence the legislative process. Researchers have tried to categorize the strategies used by groups. One distinction is between *insider strategies* and *outsider strategies*. Insider strategies are what most writers consider the traditional lobbying activity—communicating with lawmakers within the legislative institution. Outsider strategies are attempts by interest groups to influence lawmakers by way of public opinion or the electoral process through such techniques as contributions to political campaigns and coordinated citizen letter-writing campaigns. Another way to categorize lobbying activity is to differentiate between direct and indirect lobbying. While most typical forms of lobbying entail contacting legislators directly, there are indirect forms of contact through intermediaries such as legislative leaders or legislative staff (see section 7.2.).

Insider and outsider strategies are often linked: Lobbyists may use the threat of an outsider strategy as a method of gaining access to individual lawmakers. Several studies have attempted to show empirical support for this link (e.g., Grenzke 1989; Herndon 1982; Langbein 1986) and have found campaign contributions to be useful in predicting access to lawmakers though not very effective in predicting their votes.

However, most legislative lobbying primarily involve insider strategies. Within this category, a variety of tactics can be distinguished. For example, some strategies can be described as formal, including scheduled presentations to legislators at committee hearings while others are more informal and involve one-on-one interactions with legislators.

What types of lobbying techniques are used most frequently? One survey of Washington-based interest groups finds that some techniques are used by almost all groups (99 percent reported testifying at hearings; 98 percent reported contacting officials directly; and 95 percent reported engaging in informal contacts with officials); while others are used much less often, only 27 percent reported engaging in protests or demonstrations, for example (Schlozman and Tierney 1986, 150). In his study of lobbying in state legislatures, Rosenthal (1993) finds that both direct and indirect forms of contact are used. He notes, however, that the nature of this contact has changed in recent years in part due to the changing nature, mainly the increase of professionalization, of many state legislatures. Today's lobbyists will almost invariably have to make an argument on the merits of an issue. Personal relationships still count, as do grassroots efforts and political campaigns, but lobbyists also have to present a reasonable case (Rosenthal 1993, 190).

What factors determine the lobbying strategies an interest group will pursue? The nature of the lobbying group can shape the type of strategy pursued. For example, Gais and Walker show that:

> The most important factors determining whether interest groups will engage in political action and the type of tactics they will adopt are the conflictual character of their political environment, the nature and extent of their internal resources, the character of their memberships, and the sources of their financial support. (Gais and Walker 1991, 120)

The type of lobbyist representing the group is also important. Rosenthal (1993) finds that contract lobbyists are more likely to work toward developing personal relationships with legislators by means of entertaining and socializing, whereas for cause lobbyists "theirs often is a fight for truth and justice and they rely more on outside strategies to influence legislators" (Rosenthal 1993, 41). This is also supported in the 50-state study of lobbyists by Thomas and Hrebenar who show that different types of lobbyists have different power bases and often emphasize different assets. Contract lobbyists are often facilitators between their clients and lawmakers whereas in-house lobbyists and legislative liaisons rely more on providing information (Thomas and Hrebenar 2003).

Where Interest Groups and Lobbyists Focus Their Efforts

The focus of lobbying efforts can refer to: (1) the types of legislators targeted in terms of their position, pro or con, on an issue; or (2) the part of the legislative process targeted. Both areas have been of interest to researchers.

Types of Legislators Lobbied. Many early empirical studies concluded that lobbyists direct their efforts toward legislators sympathetic to their concerns. Bauer, Pool, and Dexter (1972), Dexter (1969), D. Matthews (1960), and Milbrath (1963) concluded that the role of lobbyists was not necessarily to persuade but to reinforce or mobilize legislators already predisposed to a particular group's views. As Matthews (1960, 191) explains, "the principal effect of lobbying is not conversion but reinforcement." Dexter (1969, 63) notes that, "most lobbyists, most of the time, act to reinforce, strengthen, aid, and reassure congressmen and their staff who tend to be on their side." Lobbyists have the role of reinforcing existing policy positions of legislators. For Bauer, Pool, and Dexter (1972), lobbyists are disseminators of information to legislators and are acting as "service bureaus." What then is the rationale for interest groups lobbying at all? Several reasons have been suggested by scholars.

Milbrath (1963) argues that lobbyists realize that efforts to change the minds of legislators are largely unfruitful. He argues that legislators hold predispositions about certain political issues and only pay attention to those communication channels that send messages that they want to hear. Lobbyists understand this and direct their messages only to those legislators who are receptive. Dexter (1969) argues that pressing issues with opponent lawmakers may instigate stronger opposition than might otherwise have been the case. Michael Hayes (1981) points out that lobbyists primarily focus attention on sympathetic lawmakers because they are the ones who provide access. Access is important to the lobbyist not only for the purposes of influencing policy, but also for demonstrating their relevance to the larger interest group (Hayes 1981, 86). And R. Hall and Wayman (1990) show that supplying information to sympathetic lawmakers does not necessarily mean that this information lacks impact; on the contrary, it lowers the costs of obtaining information, which is then used by legislators to attempt to convince their colleagues to support a given policy position. The authors go on to say that, "by selectively subsidizing the information costs associated with participation, groups affect the intensity with which their positions are promoted by their legislative agents" (Hall and Wayman 1990, 815).

Recent studies have questioned not only the interpretation of these findings, but also the rationale behind why interest groups and lobbyists focus attention only on lawmakers who agree with them. Schlozman and Tierney note that:

> In selecting targets for legislative lobbying, representatives of organized interests ordinarily waste little effort attempting to convert diehard opponents. Rather, they concentrate on persuading those sitting on the fence and planning legislative strategy with allies. (Schlozman and Tierney 1986, 292)

Austin-Smith and Wright (1994) have even suggested that considerable lobbying efforts are focused on unsympathetic lawmakers and that the activity directed toward sympathetic ones are for the purpose of counteracting the efforts of opposing lobbyists. Rothenberg (1992) finds evidence that lobbyists often target much of their efforts toward undecided or uncommitted lawmakers.

Targets of Lobbying in the Legislative Process. Turning to research on the points in the legislative process where interest groups and lobbyists focus their efforts to promote or oppose legislation, these studies are of two major types. One type follows a piece of legislation through the legislative labyrinth and examines how interest groups have an influence at various points along the way. A second type examines interest group influence on a number of pieces of legislation at a particular stage of the legislative process.

Three major stages of the legislative process have been examined: the setting of the legislative agenda, the committee stage, and roll-call voting. One of the first places that interest group influence can be felt is on the development of the legislative agenda. Kingdon (1984) shows that interest groups can have a significant influence on setting the agenda in the U.S. Congress (see also Baumgartner and Jones 1993). In terms of the second stage, Rosenthal (1993, 184) notes:

> The standing committee is, perhaps, the lobbyists' principal focus. If a lobbyist is advocating legislation, it has to be reported out of committee favorably in both houses (although in some states, bills may not be referred to committee in the second house). (Rosenthal 1993, 184)

A prominent area of research involving targets of lobbying is subgovernments, or "iron triangles," that examines the interaction among executive agencies, legislative committees, and interest groups (see section 7.16.). Research shows that within the subgovernment a commonality of interests and goals often exists among legislators and interest groups (Shepsle 1978). Such an environment makes the task of lobbying much easier. A number of single policy studies have shown how some groups have been able to extract major benefits from these types of arrangements. In a quantitative analysis, John Wright (1990) examines the influence of lobbying activity on committee voting while controlling for a variety of other factors including campaign contributions. Overall, he finds that lobbying contact has a significant impact on voting in committees.

Several studies have examined the impact of interest groups on the final stage of the legislative process—the roll-call votes of legislators. While this is probably the most easily measured stage of the legislative process, it may be the least likely place to observe interest group influence due to its relatively high visibility. See Richard Smith (1995) for a review of the research on this target of the policy process.

Perspectives on the Influence of Interest Groups and Lobbyists

The question of interest group and lobbyist influence in legislatures is examined here by first identifying trends in how scholars have viewed this influence or lack of it. Then the question of the most effective techniques used by lobbyists is reviewed followed by the broader question of what constitutes an influential interest group in a legislature.

Trends in the Interpretation and Explanation of Influence. Early views of lobbying suggested that lobbyists played a large role in the legislative process—they were major players who wielded considerable power. Bentley (1908), Truman (1951), and Latham (1952) held that legislators adjusted policy to the demands of competing interest groups. Schattschneider (1935) argued that interest groups dominated the policy-making process in Congress. Revisions of this perspective were offered by Bauer, Pool, and Dexter (1972), Kingdon (1981), D. Matthews (1960), Milbrath (1963), and Wahlke et al. (1962). These authors argued that through their lobbying efforts, interest groups have only a minimal effect on legislative policy making. These revisionists justified their conclusions by noting that lobbyists rarely ever try to change the minds of legislators. More recent studies fall somewhere between these first two perspectives. Rosenthal points out that:

> Although communication is an important part of the process, lobbying is not simply the transmission of information. The purpose of the endeavor is persuasion. Legislators must be persuaded to support the particular position being presented by a lobbyist. Persuasion is not necessarily conversion, however. (Rosenthal 1993, 20)

John Mark Hansen (1991, 2) makes a similar point.

The Most Effective Lobbying Techniques. What types of lobbying techniques are most influential? Jeffrey Berry (1977) and Milbrath (1963) note that lobbyists feel that personal presentations to legislators are the most important activities for influencing policy decisions by Congress. Similarly, Zeigler, and Baer's (1969) study of lobbyists in state capitols find that lobbyists believe that personal communication with legislators is the most effective technique. This is borne out by the various contributions to the Hrebenar and Thomas's 50-state study (Hrebenar and Thomas 1987, 1992, 1993a, 1993b). While direct communication is believed by lobbyists to be the most effective form of lobbying, it is also probably the most costly to pursue (Schlozman and Tierney 1986).

Several empirical studies have focused on the framing of issues and the informational roles played by lobbyists in legislatures. Richard Smith (1984) makes the case that members of Congress base their voting decisions on their interpretations of issues surrounding a vote, and lobbying efforts can have a significant influence on the interpretations which members develop. While this ability to shape interpretation is rather unstable and coalitions will probably be quite volatile, lobbyists are able to frame many of the issues for legislators. Other work (for example, Ainsworth 1993; Ainsworth and Sened 1993; and Austin-Smith 1993) has focused on the information-sharing role of lobbyists and shows, through theoretical models, how lobbyists are able to use information strategically to reduce legislators' uncertainty concerning the electoral and policy consequences of pending legislation. However, in a review article, Richard Smith (1995) notes that many of the propositions derived from these theoretical models remain empirically untested.

Factors Conditioning the Influence of Interest Groups and Lobbyists. A number of factors can either enhance or inhibit the influence of an interest group and a lobbyist within a legislature: the receptivity of legislators to lobbying activity, the type of legislator being lobbied, the nature of the lobbying group itself, the other actors in the system, the nature of the issue under consideration, and the characteristics of the institution in which the lobbying group operate.

The receptivity of legislators to lobbying is largely determined by two factors: the role legislators perceive themselves as fulfilling with regard to interest groups and lobbyists and the information to which the legislators are exposed (Wahlke et al. 1962). Other factors make legislators either more or less receptive to information from interest groups and lobbyists. Zwier (1979) notes that specialists within a given area (subcommittee chairs, for example) rely more heavily on interest groups and executive agencies than nonspecialists who rely more on internal sources of information (such as fellow legislators) in making decisions. Hurwitz (1988) shows that the policy goals of legislators influence where they turn for information on a given issue.

The nature of the interest group or the lobbyists' tactics may condition their influence. For example, Rosenthal (1993) notes that some lobbyists are not able to have as much influence as others because they are less willing to compromise or to become part of the political process. Many cause lobbyists fit this category and often find great difficulty even in gaining access to lawmakers. Other scholars have noted that the extent of the lobbying effort and the amount of resources expended by an interest group are important predictors of lobbying success. Zeigler and Baer (1969, 35) find that, "... as the number of lobbyists representing the group increased, so did the legislators' perception of the power of the group."

Another factor that conditions the influence of an interest group is the nature of other actors within the legislative environment. Studies have shown that interest groups are just one source (and usually far from the most important) among many which inform and influence legislators (see Bradley 1980; Kingdon 1981; Kovenock 1973; Ray 1982; Songer et al. 1986). Other legislators, party leaders, constituents, personal beliefs, and the media are all potential sources of information and influence.

John Mark Hansen (1991, 7) notes that lobbyists are not only in competition with these sources, but also with each other saying that "lobbying groups gain and forfeit access to congressional deliberations as they win and lose their competitive advantage relative to rival informants and propagandists." These studies find that, for the most part, other legislators, constituency, and personal beliefs are of greater significance than interest groups.

The nature of the legislation being considered may also condition the influence of lobbying activity. Here Rosenthal (1993, 214) argues, "On minor issues, the lobbyist's influence is likely to be central, and may in fact carry the day. On major issues, other factors play a much greater role, and a lobbyist's influence is likely to be marginal." Denzau and Munger (1986) find empirical evidence that legislators will be more likely to respond to lobbying efforts when constituents are uninformed and unorganized about particular issues. Zeigler and Baer (1969, 212) come to a similar finding on the state legislative level saying that, "in general, the narrower the scope of a piece of legislation, the greater the opportunity for a lobbyist to intervene in the decision-making process." Lowi (1964a) as well as Michael Hayes (1981) developed typologies to explain the relative success of interest groups in different areas. Exploring the relative importance of lobbying groups on legislative decision making, Songer et al. (1986) find that the issue area is an important predictor of where legislators turn for information.

Finally, the nature of the institution may also condition the influence of lobbyists. The process of obtaining information by state legislators varies according to the professional research capabilities of the legislature (Wissel, O'Connor, and King 1976). In states where staff support is underdeveloped there is greater reliance by legislators on external sources of information of which lobbyists are one source. In states where staff support is more highly developed there is much less dependence on external sources of information and there the access of lobbyists to specialist legislators is diminished (Sabatier and Whiteman 1985). In addition, the nature of the power structure within the legislature is important. As Rosenthal (1993, 91) argues about legislatures in general: "Power is more dispersed just about everywhere today." However, this power structure still varies by institution. Lobbyists may have a more difficult task where power in a chamber is more diffuse. In such situations they cannot simply focus their efforts on a few key legislative leaders, but must broaden their appeal to rank-and-file members.

An attempt to encapsulate the various factors that constitute an influential interest group was part of the 50-state study conducted by Thomas and Hrebenar (2003). For a more general consideration of the power and influence of interest groups see section 7.17.

Research on Legislative Lobbying in Parliamentary Democracies

While legislative lobbying in parliamentary systems is still minimal compared with legislative lobbying in the United States, the gradual erosion of strong ideology and strong party control in Western Europe and a consequent loosening of centralized power have meant that lobbying parliaments is beginning to develop. This is reflected in the recent publication of academic studies plus increasing attention to parliamentary lobbying in texts on interest groups on individual parliamentary systems as well as some practical how-to books on the subject, which offer important insights for the researcher.

The best general academic treatment is Philip Norton (1999) which examines lobbying in eight Western European parliaments including the EU parliament. Insights on the development of parliamentary lobbying in 10 Western democracies—again including the EU parliament—can be found in a collection of articles on lobby regulation across the Western world (*Parliamentary Affairs* 1998). An edited volume examining the role of interests in parliaments in the transitional democracies of Eastern Europe is Agh and Ilonszki (1996). In regard to works focusing on individual countries, on Britain there is J. D. Stewart (1958), an edited volume by Rush (1990), and two practical but insightful guides by Dubs (1988) and Ellis (1998); on the EU parliament see Timmermann (1996). These two parliaments appear to be most receptive to lobbying. Additional information on lobbying in parliaments can be found in some of the entries in chapter 11, which deal with interest groups in parliamentary democracies.

Directions for Future Research

Despite this large body of research on legislative lobbying, several areas need further investigation. First, the specifics of decision making involved in lobbying needs further study: How do lobbyists decide on allocating their resources? What factors lead them to pursue certain types of strategies? What leads them to strive after certain policy goals? Second, more work is needed to provide a systematic understanding of the influence of lobbying at different points in the legislative process and over a wider range of individual legislator activities. Third, studies examining the influence of lobbying at the agenda building and committee stages of the legislative process would also be very enlightening. Fourth, more studies on lobbying in parliamentary systems would be useful both in themselves and for comparative analysis among Western democracies, including the United States.

7.11. EXECUTIVE BRANCH LOBBYING IN WASHINGTON, D.C.

Christopher Cooper and Brian Noland

As the entries on political and governmental structure (see section 4.2.) and strategy and tactics (see section 7.2.) point out, the executive branch is the major target of lobbying in most countries. Perspectives on lobbying the executive branch in parliamentary democracies can be found in the various entries in chapter 11.

In the United States, however, the separation of powers system operating at both the federal and state levels (which gives the legislature its own power base) means that legislative lobbying is of crucial importance (see section 7.10.). Perhaps because it is much more visible and more subject to regulation than executive branch lobbying, lobbying the legislature has received the bulk of attention by scholars of U.S. interest groups. However, many interest groups at the federal and state levels also lobby the executive branch as part of their lobbying strategy. A few groups, mainly those with highly technical concerns such as at the state level in occupational licensing of professions like beauticians and accountants, primarily lobby the executive and may not lobby the legislature for years. In section 7.16., the focus is on the various ways that interests, legislators, and executive branch officials interact in the policy process. Here we focus on executive lobbying at the national level in the United States and its two major targets: the president and the bureaucracy.

Lobbying the White House

The minimal scholarly attention paid to lobbying the presidency before the 1930s can be partly explained by the lack of a coherent and formal lobbying target within the White House prior to the presidency of Franklin D. Roosevelt (Pika 1991). In addition, many groups believed that the executive branch was not worth lobbying. Before the rise of the modern presidency, the president had little power over either the budget or policy, and most groups tended to concentrate their efforts elsewhere (J. Berry 1997; Pika 1991). Franklin Roosevelt was the first president to officially open his White House to group interests. His main goal was to establish relationships with interest groups that would help him win reelection. President Truman adopted Roosevelt's basic policy toward groups and sought to gain electoral support in exchange for help in the policy arena (Pika 1991).

President Eisenhower looked beyond electoral benefits and used group support to further his policy goals. President Kennedy behaved similarly. In 1963, Kennedy met with a number of prominent civil rights groups in an attempt to reduce racial tensions. This represented a new level of White House interaction and consultation with interest groups. The trend toward presidential "conferences" continued in subsequent administrations (Pika 1991).

President Johnson considerably strengthened the connection between the White House and interest groups by increasing the number of staffers acting as liaisons for interest groups (Pika 1991). President Nixon continued to expand the number of liaisons, but focused less on responsiveness and more on mobilizing group support for the administration's policies. However, Nixon ignored staffer William Baroody's proposal to reorganize the liaisons into a coherent, centralized structure. President Ford kept Baroody on in his administration and in 1974 established the Office of Public Liaison (OPL), which was created solely to confer with interest groups (M. A. Peterson 1992). Ford's approach to public liaisons continued the decline of presidential electoral oriented relationships with interest groups (Pika 1991). At first President Carter expanded the role of the OPL. But overwhelmed by the tremendous access allowed interest groups, he reduced their access during the second half of his administration and reconsidered his approach to the OPL. During the administrations of Presidents Reagan and George Bush, Sr., the OPL decreased in power (Pika 1991).

Even with recent changes, the OPL is now an institutionalized part of the White House. Presidents recognize the power of interest groups and understand that their own success as a president may hinge on a coherent policy toward group access (Pika 1991). However, as Pika (1993) points out, the centralization and institutionalization of the OPL may lead to divided loyalties. Some liaisons may be torn between serving the president's interests and the interests of their colleagues in various interest groups. In addition, the OPL produces managerial costs (Pika 1993).

Mark A. Peterson (1992) has identified four ways that the president can use the OPL. First is interest group liaison as *legitimization*, which attempts to use interest groups to influence the public. Second is *consensus building* in which presidents use interest group power to mobilize forces in favor of specific program goals. Third is *outreach* in which the OPL is used to contact and influence groups that are not generally part of the government establishment. And fourth is *coalition-building* in which interest group liaisons engage in partisan coalition building for achieving program goals.

Although the OPL is undoubtedly the most important liaison between interest groups and the White House, it is not the only connection. Often, ad hoc commissions meet with interest groups for various reasons. Generally, press coverage of these interactions is avoided (J. Berry and Portney 1994).

Lobbying the Bureaucracy

Interest groups generally lobby the bureaucracy by attending regulatory hearings, meeting personally with agency personnel, and helping to write rules and regulations (J. Berry 1997). Groups also use the "notice-and-comment" procedure (Kerwin 1994).

James Q. Wilson (1989) identifies four distinct types of group-agency interaction. In *client politics*, the benefits of a program are realized by a small group of people and the costs are incurred by a large majority of people. Here, any group support is largely one-sided, as the group receiving the benefits lobbies the appropriate agency strenuously, while no or few other groups lobby against the client group. An example is a large industry, like oil or mining, getting a major tax break or exemption, which has little or no benefit to the society as a whole, plus it reduces revenue in the federal or state coffers. In *entrepreneurial politics*, policy has a high cost for a small group and relatively small benefits are spread over a large population. In this case, opposing interests will fight against the proposed policy or its implementation. This would be the case with reducing aid to pork producers, which would marginally—at least theoretically—reduce the average U.S. citizens' tax burden. But many other farm groups might oppose this move fearing that they would be next in line for a cut in subsidies. In *conflictual politics*, there are high per capita costs as well as high per capita benefits. In this case, interest groups on both sides of the issue will be very active. This is most likely to result in some form of stasis, as each side holds the other in check. This would be the case, for instance, in a stand off in a state between the businesses and trade unions, and likely the trade union federation (the AFL-CIO), over right-to-work laws (anti-close shop union legislation). Finally, in *majoritarian politics*, an agency distributes relatively small benefits at a small cost. Interest group activity in this case is virtually nonexistent. The subsidization of school lunch programs by a state department of education is an example.

Lobbyists who attempt to influence administrative policies face a different situation than that of legislative lobbyists (J. Berry 1997). A major difference is that while members of Congress have an eye on reelection, bureaucrats and agency heads generally have job security. This situation necessitates different tactics by lobbyists. One major favor that lobbyists can offer agency personnel is that they often need interest group support to buttress budget requests and remain viable (Quirk 1980).

While excellent research has been conducted on executive-interest group relations, there is still much left to learn. Scholars have produced illuminating case studies of this dynamic (see Browne 1995a; Moe 1985; Rothenberg 1994; Scholz and Wei 1986) but have made few generalizations. Moreover, while scholars have produced theoretical works suggesting new models of agency-group behavior (Bendor and Moe 1985; Peltzman 1976; Posner 1974), more work needs to be done on testing the practical relevance of these theories.

7.12. JUDICIAL BRANCH LOBBYING IN THE UNITED STATES

Susan M. Olson

Although compared with legislative and executive lobbying, judicial branch lobbying is minimal, it is an increasingly important tactic used by certain interest groups in the United States. In contrast, judicial lobbying is rare in most other political systems largely because of the structure of those systems, which give a minimal political and policy role to the courts (see section 4.3.). For this reason, this entry focuses entirely on judicial lobbying in the United States. Lobbying the courts differs from lobbying the legislative and executive branches because the type of contacts permitted between the lobbyists and the decision makers is so constrained. Interest groups may approach judges only through established roles in litigation.

The two classic mechanisms for lobbying the judiciary are sponsoring test cases and submitting *amicus curiae* (friend of the court) briefs (Vose 1958). Sponsorship consists of providing the legal counsel and, if necessary, recruiting plaintiffs to raise an important legal issue. *Amici curiae* are third parties that believe the outcome of a case will affect its interests. Groups must have the permission from both direct parties or the court to file an *amicus* brief. Besides these two major avenues, groups may participate as a named party, intervenor, fund-raiser, expert witness, or advisor. And some interest groups work to get particular judges appointed who reflect the group's perspective or general philosophical orientation. Lee Epstein's (1991) thorough bibliographic essay on interest group activity in the courts is a good starting point for a review of the literature.

Studies Before 1980

Although interest group involvement in the courts was noted in early works on pluralism (Bentley 1908; Truman 1951), it received no specific attention until Vose (1959) produced his analyses of the National Association for the Advancement of Colored People's (NAACP) restrictive covenant cases and other interest group litigation (Vose 1957, 1966, 1972). Other early case studies by historians and political scientists examined case sponsorship by Jehovah's Witnesses, conservative business interests, labor unions, and the American Civil Liberties Union (ACLU) (Markmann 1965). Despite these studies, the first aggregate analysis of interest group litigation in the U.S. Supreme Court argued that these instances were isolated exceptions rather than part of the courts' normal environment (Hakman 1966, 1969).

Hakman notwithstanding, evidence of judicial lobbying mounted, and scholars attempted to generalize about the phenomenon. Richard Cortner (1968, 1970) first articulated what is known as the *political disadvan-*

tage theory—that groups mainly litigate because they are disadvantaged in majoritarian arenas. Since most case studies had been of litigation by minority, racial, and religious groups or other politically disenfranchised interests, this theory was widely accepted.

During this period *amicus curiae* activity was less studied than test case sponsorship, but two major contributions were Krislov's (1963) review of the historical evolution of the role of amici and Puro's (1971) dissertation, which examined amicus participation in the U.S. Supreme Court from 1920 to 1966.

Research Since 1980

Research since 1980 has produced more studies of group involvement at the Supreme Court on various liberal issues such as women's rights (O'Connor 1980), the environment (Wenner 1984), obscenity and free speech (Kobylka 1991), the poor (S. E. Lawrence 1990), separation of church and state (Ivers 1995), civil rights (Greenberg 1994), race relations (Wasby 1995), and Native Americans (Hermann and O'Connor 1996). But the topics of research have also broadened in several ways.

First, the rise of conservative interest group litigation received attention (L. Epstein 1985). Second, more aggregate analyses of *amicus curiae* briefs appeared. O'Connor and Epstein (1981–82) reanalyzed and extended Hakman's data and challenged his conclusions. Caldeira and Wright (1988, 1990) demonstrated the influence that *amici* play in case selection (see also Hermann 1997; McGuire and Caldeira 1993). Third, scholars studied interest group activity in lower courts (L. Epstein 1994; S. Olson 1981; Songer and Kuersten 1995; Stewart and Heck 1983). Among other things, these studies showed that interest groups sometimes have goals other than getting to a high court for a definitive constitutional interpretation. Fourth, scholars began surveying nonlitigating as well as litigating interest groups, asking if, when, and why they choose to use the courts (Bruer 1987; R. Nelson and Heinz 1988; Scheppele, Lane, and Walker 1991; Schlozman and Tierney 1986). This approach facilitates more accurate testing of competing hypotheses about why groups litigate.

Collectively, these research trends resulted in a questioning of the political disadvantage theory as too limited an explanation of interest group litigation (S. Olson 1990). Many types of groups use litigation as one weapon in an arsenal of political strategies, depending on the situation. Another perennial issue is whether and how groups influence court decisions. Depending on how the question is conceptualized and measured, scholars reach differing conclusions (Caldeira and Wright 1988; L. Epstein and Kobylka 1992; L. Epstein and Rowland 1991; S. E. Lawrence 1990; Rossotti, Natelson, and Tatalovich 1997; Songer and Sheehan 1993; Spriggs and Wahlbeck 1997; Stewart and Sheffield 1987).

Influencing Judicial Appointments

Another development since 1980 has been research on interest groups attempting to influence judicial appointments. These efforts include testifying on federal nominees at confirmation hearings and trying to influence senators' votes, especially on Supreme Court appointments (Caldeira and Wright 1995; Flemming, MacLeod, and Talbert 1998; Watson and Stookey 1995; Maltese 1995; Shapiro 1990; Silverstein 1994). Influence at the state level by interest groups other than bar associations (Sheldon 1994) is less studied (Bright 1997; Reid 1996; Thomas, Boyer, and Hrebenar 2003; Wold and Culver 1987) even though interest groups have more opportunities to influence judicial selection as most state judges serve renewable terms.

Related Literature

An area of research providing considerable information about interest group litigation, but focusing on different questions is the literature on courts and social policy and social change. Major works in this area include: Galanter (1974), Scheingold (1974), Horowitz (1977), Handler (1978), M. McCann (1994), Kessler (1990), G. Rosenberg (1991) and Brigham (1996). This literature is becoming more international through research on "cause lawyering" around the world (see Sward and Weisbrod 1978; Scheingold 1994; Abel 1995; S. Olson 1995; Epp 1998).

7.13. GRASSROOTS LOBBYING

Burdett A. Loomis

Grassroots lobbying, the solicitation of support from constituents that is targeted at elected officials—legislators and to some extent the president and governors—and other decision makers, has long been practiced in U.S. politics but is much less common as a group tactic in other liberal democracies. The structure of the U.S. political system, with its separation of powers and relatively weak political parties and consequent decentralization of power (see section 4.3.), facilitates such a tactic. In contrast, the weakness of parliaments and the strong centralized cabinet government buttressed by strong political parties in most liberal democracies largely precludes effective grassroots lobbying. For this reason, this entry focuses on grassroots lobbying in U.S. politics.

From the Anti-Saloon League letter-writing campaigns to well-financed corporate efforts, grassroots tactics were familiar elements of group politics in the 1880–1930 era (Schlozman and Tierney 1986, 197). Labor unions frequently adopted grassroots techniques in the 1950s and 1960s. More recently, business interests, cause groups, and specialized lobbying firms have taken advantage of advances in communications technology to solicit and direct grassroots appeals (A. Cigler and Loomis 1995a, 396; Shaiko 1991). A good example occurred in the mid-1970s when Congressman Roy Taylor of North Carolina received 15,000 letters from his district on an obscure provision in a piece of land use legislation. Much of this avalanche of mail resulted from the U.S. Chamber of Commerce urging its members to contact key legislators and convey their opposition to the provision. Taylor successfully opposed it in committee. Subsequently, when asked of the Chamber's influence, he professed surprise, insisting that "I never heard from the Chamber of Commerce. I responded to 15,000 letters I got from my district" (Loomis 1983, 170). Today members of Congress routinely pay more attention to information that comes from their own constituents than from almost any other source (Browne 1995a). This elementary political fact serves as the linchpin of the power of grassroots lobbying as organized interests seek to influence legislative decisions.

Despite its significance, there is no definitive analysis of grassroots lobbying; nor is there any comprehensive bibliography. Rather, research has: (1) included grassroots efforts as part of a broad study of interest groups (e.g., Schlozman and Tierney 1986; Browne 1988); or (2) been limited to a case study (e.g., Loomis 1983; Foreman 1995). Both approaches date back to Odegard's (1928) research on the Anti-Saloon League and Herring's (1929) work on group representation before Congress.

Given that grassroots lobbying includes a host of activities that range from national letter-writing and e-mail campaigns to a few telephone calls directed at a few key legislators, it is often difficult to determine either when such efforts have occurred or the extent of their success. Scholars have long wrestled with interpreting the impact of mail and other grassroots contacts generated by particular interests. In their study of interest groups, Zeigler and Peak (1972, 153) evaluate the letter-writing campaign as "probably the least effective and most relied-upon lobbying technique." From extensive congressional communications data, gathered in the 1950s, Dexter (1956) comes to a similar conclusion. These early studies view legislators as systematically discounting large-scale mail campaigns in which interest groups have clearly solicited constituents to send form letters (and today, e-mails), which are easily identifiable as not individually written.

Subsequent research found both the individualized nature and the volume of grassroots communication to be important (Rosenstone and Hansen 1993, 108–9). In their systematic study of groups and lobbying, Schlozman and Tierney (1986, 150–55) found that 80 percent of their responding groups used grassroots lobbying techniques, that such tactics consumed substantial resources for many groups, and that the use of these methods was increasing for almost 60 percent of all groups. In the wake of the 1994 Republican Party capture of Congress, Gimpel (1998, 115) argues that grassroots lobbying can be understood in terms of cycles in which the "out-party status" plays a major role in bringing groups and parties together.

The single instance of grassroots lobbying that has received the most attention in recent scholarship is the intense contest over the nomination and rejection of U.S. Supreme Court nominee Robert Bork in 1987. John Wright concludes that:

> The mobilization efforts of the liberal groups ultimately proved more compelling, not because they generated more mail or phone calls—the conservatives probably won the mail battle—but because the political information of the liberal groups was more focused and informed. (Wright 1996, 102)

With technological advances in computing and communications, grassroots lobbying has grown more sophisticated, especially in terms of: (1) targeting the constituents of key legislators, (2) facilitating contacts between constituents and legislators, and (3) creating the appearance, for a price, of local support on national issues. This so-called *astroturf* support can affect what legislators hear from home. This involves organized interests and grassroots lobbying firms purchase cable television time to run issue-based advertisements in a few congressional districts in order to spur constituent communications. Grassroots specialists, such as Washington-based Jack Bonner, charge clients by the letter or phone call that they generate. The trade journal *Campaigns and Elections* routinely lists dozens of firms that specialize in grassroots lobbying. And they make it easy for citizens, who need not even place their own calls to members of Congress or the president. Rather, a grassroots firm or an in-house specialist will call constituents from a well-researched list, ascertain the position of the respondent on the major issue, and then offer to connect the constituent to his or her legislator, at no cost (A. Cigler and Loomis 1995a, 396; 1998a).

Stimulating the communication of public sentiments has various implications for decision making. First, there is the clear opportunity for fraud. A good example occurred in 1995 on telecommunications legislation when a grassroots lobbying firm sent thousands of telegrams from alleged supporters who in fact never approved such an action. Second, the sophistication of grassroots efforts may lead legislators to become aggressive in soliciting information from trusted confidants who represent alternative channels to those provided by either organized groups or constituents (Browne 1995a). Third, it may make little sense to differentiate between grassroots and insider lobbying. Increasingly, grassroots techniques simply reflect one more way for well-funded interests to make their case, dressed up to appear like constituent sentiments. While the distinction between inside and outside strategies has always been artificial, technology has rendered it almost meaningless. As it has grown in sophistication, grassroots lobbying has become one more technique for major interests to use when it suits their purposes.

7.14. USE OF THE MEDIA, PUBLIC RELATIONS, AND ADVERTISING

Burdett A. Loomis

Most organized interests attempt to use the media and public relations to their advantage, and some use advertising (Schlozman and Tierney 1986, 151). However, although in the 1980s, organized interests in Washington, D.C., reported that they increased their attention to the media more than any other tactic, still only 10 percent of groups stated that such media relations represented one of their three most important tactics (Schlozman and Tierney 1986, 155). Public relations is thus widely practiced but rarely relied upon. Rather, its use is frequently reactive, often by prospective policy losers who seek to expand the scope of the conflict. Nevertheless, this group tactic of using the media, as well as sophisticated public relations strategies and, increasingly, expensive advertising campaigns, has increased steadily, particularly in the 1990s among established interests like business (West and Loomis 1999).

Despite this increase, little research has been conducted on the subject and there is no comprehensive survey of these tactics for the post-1960s period. Furthermore, some general texts on interest groups give the subject cursory attention or none at all. For example, in his interest group text, Jeffrey Berry (1997) makes just one scholarly reference to this tactic; and in their examination of interest groups, Baumgartner and Leech (1998) do not mention public relations at all. Stanley Kelley's *Professional Public Relations and Political Power* (1956) offers an important mid-1950s baseline as well as some useful historical perspective. The research and writing since then has been fragmented, with work being conducted mainly by political scientists and students of public relations. Although some communications studies (see Ellwood 1995) do seek to bridge the disciplinary gap, no overall survey of public relations/media approaches to politics has been produced.

Public Relations

For the most part, public relations studies emphasize particular cases (J. White and Mazur 1994) and offer prescriptive advice to corporate executives (Gollner 1983). This scholarship often provides simplistic assessments of public relations and media campaigns, but these campaigns are frequently anything but simplistic. Rather, skilled lobbyists and group representatives may seamlessly weave public relations approaches into a broader campaign of influence (Birnbaum 1992). In the end, specific influences on policies are extremely difficult to pin down and differentiate from each other (see section 7.17.) although expensive and elaborate multistage polling may capture the capacity to move public opinion (Van Leuven and Slater 1991, 167). Most public relations and media efforts, however, are targeted at Washington, D.C.-based policy communities, either through capital-oriented publicity or highly focused campaigns designed to mobilize specific geographic (e.g., a few congressional districts) or interested (e.g., environmentalists, gun owners) constituencies (West, Heith, and Goodwin 1995).

Spending substantial sums to pursue sophisticated public relations strategies is no longer confined to U.S. politics. Studies of Great Britain (White and Mazur 1994) and Canada (Gollner, 1983) provide both analyses of public relations campaigns and prescriptions for corporate leadership. Indeed, White and Mazur (1994, xvi) emphasize the importance of shaping corporate images and messages across national boundaries, especially in Europe.

The Media

Central to understanding the development of lobbying through the media is the continuing struggle between public interest groups and business interests. Funded both by members and patrons, consumer groups and environmental organizations made great headway in shaping the policy agenda in the 1970s and '80s (Vogel 1989, 93ff). Although public interest groups employed a wide array of tactics, many of their efforts focused on educating both policy makers and the public and depended heavily on free media coverage of their conferences, reports, and findings (J. Berry 1989; Shaiko 1991). In particular, Ralph Nader and other activists attracted substantial media attention to their causes, and, during the 1960s and early 1970s, business interests were ineffective in voicing their concerns to either the public or to key decision makers (Vogel 1989; J. Berry 1989). Subsequently, corporate interests did find ways to shape and deliver their messages, as they employed public relations and advertising to communicate both to the public and to political elites (Birnbaum 1992; Vogel 1989, chap. 8).

Advertising

As of the early 1980s, Schlozman and Tierney (1986, 151, 155) reported neither much use of advertising by organized interests nor much of an increase. But Sethi (1977, 1987) noted that business interests often felt constrained by news reports and wished to present their messages in an undiluted form. Attempting to reach the public at large through advertising is prohibitively expensive (J. Berry 1989), but smaller audiences may well be addressed. The Mobil Oil company's path-breaking advocacy advertisements were "directed toward . . . the president . . . [or] the members of a congressional committee" (Schmertz 1986).

The potential of advocacy advertising was demonstrated, and perhaps mythologized, in the campaigns prompted by President Clinton's proposed health care reforms of 1993–94, especially in the so-called "Harry and Louise" ads purchased by the Health Insurance Association of America (M. A. Peterson 1995; West, Heith, and Goodwin 1995). The HIAA received tremendous free media coverage of its $14-million ad campaign, which ran mostly in Washington, D.C., on national cable (CNN), and in the home districts of key members of Congress. Despite modest, at best, evidence of the ads' effectiveness, the health insurers took credit for killing Clinton's plan. Subsequently, many other interests came to see advertising as a valuable tool of influence (West and Loomis 1999).

However, demonstrating the influence of public relations campaigns or advocacy advertising is most difficult. The evidence of impact is often gross—ultimate victory or defeat—or ephemeral—the repetition of a key phrase, here or there, mouthed by a legislator or top executive official (Loomis and Sexton 1995). In the end, public relations and advertising tactics are used when the stakes are high, when well-heel interests are involved, and when lots of information is available. In such a setting, the ability to create a powerful narrative (on health care costs or the evils of the North American Free Trade Agreement–NAFTA) may overwhelm the conventional lobbying efforts of other interests (A. Cigler and Loomis 1995a, 1998a; West and Loomis 1999).

7.15. PROTESTS, DEMONSTRATIONS, AND VIOLENCE

Ronald J. Hrebenar

Protests, demonstrations, and sometimes violence have been a part of interest group politics across the Western world since World War II. French farmers, the U.S. Civil Rights movement and the antinuclear movement around the world are just three well-known examples of groups that have used protests and demonstrations. Violence, too, has been a tactic used by certain elements of some groups such as the antiabortion movement in the United States in the 1990s and the so-called *eco-terrorists* such as the group Earth First!

However, while the use of protests, demonstrations, and violence have been widely publicized in the mass media and are imprinted in the public's mind throughout the Western world, systematic investigation has been largely absent. In fact, of all the tactics used by interest groups, these are probably the ones we know the least about. Although there is some understanding of the utility of these tactics—particularly violence—in

U.S. history, there is little systematic understanding of their efficacy since World War II in the United States or in any other country. Furthermore, the research that has been conducted focuses mainly on the United States.

However, there is some coverage of other countries, such as G. Jordan and Maloney's (1997) detailing of the British experience, particularly environmental and other public interest groups; Graeme Hayes's (2001) coverage on environmental protests in France; and David Meyer and Tarrow's (1998) coverage of protest tactics in a number of western countries. Probably the best known international interest group using the tactic of protest is the environmental organization Greenpeace, known world-wide for, among other actions, its protests against the killing of baby seals in the arctic region and against Shell Oil drilling in the North Sea (G. Jordan 2001).

The U.S. literature on protests, demonstrations, and violence received its major impetus from the riots in several U.S. cities during the 1960s (Graham and Gurr 1969; Hubbard 1968; R. Moss 1971).During this time, scholars were very concerned with the rising social disorder in U.S. cities and were trying to determine the utility of these tactics in furthering political objectives (Brill 1971; Feierabend et al. 1969; Garson 1969, 1970; Lipsky 1968, 1970). Some work on protests, demonstration, and violence has been conducted by political scientists (Costain and McFarland 1998; G. Jordan and Maloney 1997; Lowi 1971; Taft and Ross 1969; J. Walker 1963; J. Q. Wilson 1960, 1961); but most work is the province of sociologists. In part, this may be because these tactics are associated more with social movements rather than with interest groups as most political scientists define an interest group (see section 1.2.).

The seminal work on protests, demonstrations, and violence as interest group tactics is *The Strategy of Social Protest* by sociologist William Gamson. The first edition (Gamson 1975) examines 53 groups in pre-1945 U.S. politics. The second edition (Gamson 1990) adds three movements of the post-1945 era: the Civil Rights movement, the anti-Vietnam War, and the antinuclear power movements. Gamson's book was an important part of the resource mobilization approach to social movements (Chong 1991; Lipsky 1968; McCarthy and Zald 1977; Melucci 1980). Both editions are gold mines for generating hypotheses for future study of interest group strategies and tactics. The publication of the first edition in 1975 generated a cottage industry in studies on the efficacy of protests, demonstrations, and particularly violence in interest group politics.

Gamson argues that violence has been successful under certain circumstances, but not any more successful than normal lobbying tactics. Furthermore, he argues that violence was almost always incidental to other commonly used tactics and that it was almost always a decision of frustration with the pace of success and not simply the last tactic of a failed cause. He also offers various propositions on the role of group organization and the necessity of systemic crises as an impetus to generate challenges to established authority.

In the post–World War II era, Gamson notes that there have been two major changes in the political environment that altered the rules regarding the use of violence by interest groups. The first, which tends to constrain the actions of violent protest, is the rise of the national security state and the difficulties it poses for groups that challenge the establishment. The second factor is the media, in particular, television. The role of the media has helped reward unruly tactics for some groups under certain conditions while penalizing others. Groups with very selfish and low-profile goals appear to be less successful using these tactics. The framing and articulation of a group's goals must be done in the context of a broad public interest objective. One conclusion is that under these circumstances feistiness is rewarded in the interest group game. Another is that the tactic of embarrassment caused by violence is increasingly successful.

Some subsequent research produced similar conclusions to Gamson (Mirowsky and Ross 1981; Steedley and Foley 1979); others cast doubt on his central findings (Goldstone 1980) to which Gamson (1980) responded. Steedley and Foley concluded that strong alliances produce success and that small groups that are associated with violence are usually losers. Large powerful groups can use violence and ignore the adverse effects of the violent tactics. Mirowsky and Ross argue that third party support is essential for group success.

James Q. Wilson is the political scientist who has written the most on the efficacy of protests, demonstrations, and violence (J. Q. Wilson 1960, 1961, 1995). And J. Q. Wilson (1995) is also an excellent source of hypotheses on the role of violence in interest group politics. While other case studies have been conducted on protests, demonstrations, and violence (Barkan 1979), Wilson, together with J. Jordan and Maloney (1997) and Costain and McFarland (1998), is among the few political scientists attempting to draw generalizations on the utility of these tactics. Costain and McFarland (1998) provide valuable insights into the role of social movements in U.S. politics and the variety of tactics that they employ.

7.16. IRON TRIANGLES, POLICY NETWORKS, AND OTHER SUBGOVERNMENTAL SYSTEMS OF INTEREST GROUP ACTIVITY

William P. Browne

Iron triangles, cozy triangles, policy networks, policy niches, issue networks, triple alliances, and whirlpools of activity are all metaphors used by interest group scholars. These and related terms refer to subgovernmental systems, or arrangements—semiautonomous groupings of policy makers within a larger governmental system such as the United States,

France, and the Province of Alberta in Canada. These metaphors have been developed by scholars to reduce the complexities and numbers of participants in the policy process to a few key ones and bring some order to an otherwise confusing world of interest group activity. Most of the work in this subfield has been conducted on the U.S. political system; but an increasing amount is being produced on interest group systems in other Western democracies.

A Brief History

This search for order can be traced back to Bentley (1908), who merely observed that small groups of people make public policy. Crawford (1939) wrote of insider relationships between the pressurers and the pressured. He complained that the lobbying process was far from an open and democratic one. Business elites were the dominant players. Griffith (1939) explained generally what was going on within this insider, capturing style of politics. Those who regularly and routinely dealt with recurring public policy matters got commonly sucked into a vortex of interaction with one another. Each vortex, according to Griffith, was a whirlpool of activity. Members of Congress from appropriate committees, agency administrators, and the lobbyists who sought to influence them were the ones sucked in. Everyone else in government was but a passive participant in whirlpool matters. Generations of scholars escalated the whirlpool metaphor into a full-blown theory of public policy making as they looked for better labels (Browne 1998). Cater (1964) wrote of subgovernments; however, the terms iron or cozy triangles were metaphors favored by the majority of scholars.

The Emergence and Decline of Triangle Theory

By far the major subgovernment explanation of interest group activity over the years has been triangle theory. Although this theory was assembled piece by piece, one study at a time, it came to encapsulate the following comprehensive explanation. Each triangle was successful because either conflict or cooperation within it sorted out solutions (J. L. Freeman 1965). The tight relationships within the triangles rewarded each of the participants, with organized interests winning their policy goals (Maass 1951). Reciprocity between triangles allowed governing of the whole to continue, as cooperation ensued and one triangle left each of the others alone (R. Davidson 1977). This was government by specialists. Leaders of the executive and legislative branches exercised poor oversight (Dodd and Schott 1979). The public and the media were too overwhelmed and confused by all the action to provide scrutiny (Lowi 1969). Public policy proliferated but, as study after study showed (Ferejohn 1974; Fritschler 1969; Lawrence 1966; Redford 1960), it was all very narrow in intent and purpose. This was constituent politics, as in the organized interest constituents of Crawford's insiders.

Over time, however, triangle theory came to be seen as too simple an explanation—too tidy a metaphor—of the reality of interest group involvement in policy making. In looking for the triangle's main players, other important players were ignored (J. Berry 1997, 194–205). Furthermore, the triangle metaphor was becoming increasingly misleading as politics became more open and an increasing number of emerging interests were making demands within the process. Triangles of closeness and comfort, through interest expansion, were giving way to Heclo's (1978) shifting cloud-like shapes and large sloppy hexagons (C. Jones 1979). The overlap of both issues and institutional jurisdictions also had an effect (Bosso 1987) in undermining triangle theory.

Several extensive empirical projects cast serious doubt on triangle theory. John Mark Hansen (1991), in studying transitions in agricultural politics and policy in the 1920s and 1930s, found that insider relationships explained very little of what had taken place. Gais, Peterson, and Walker (1984) using a survey of lobbyists, also found little supportive evidence. In a survey of lobbyists and other policy players, Heinz and his associates (1993) found numerous and complex relationships but only one obscure example that fit the triangle metaphor. See also Hamm (1983b) and Salisbury et al. (1992).

Using two large data sets with hundreds of lobbyist and public official respondents, Browne (1988, 1995a) concluded that contemporary triangles are largely a myth; Hadwiger (1982) and Cook (1998) concluded the same. So many and such diverse interests now make demands and win access to public officials that perhaps even the network metaphor is unsatisfactory. Diana Evans (1991), by examining modern congressional committee politics in transportation, offers similar evidence. Thus, the triangle explanation that many scholars still use seems, at best, part of an earlier political era and may have been a too simplistic and too tidy a metaphor, even in Bentley's time.

A More Realistic Explanation

Theories of issue niches—where interests develop a particular identity and pattern of activity—may offer a more realistic explanation. Niche theory abandons the metaphor of shapes in patterns of interest relationships in policy making. It starts with James Q. Wilson's (1973, 263) observation that interests are risk averse. Add to this the observation that risk-averse interests develop strategies for being safe. Both the issues that they pursue and the styles of lobbying they follow are recurring, or repetitive (Browne 1990). The combination of the two brings a political identity, and an organized interest tends to stick with it.

Within those repetitions, however, interests in the early twenty-first century lobby whomever they feel the need to contact within a very broad political environment. They follow issues from one policy arena, or domain, to another as governing jurisdictions shift. Although their research was based on group activity in the U.S. states, work by Gray and Lowery (1996a, 1996c) has general relevance for niche theory in U.S. politics in general. Their work has considerably expanded knowledge of niche activity and explains a great deal about this in regard to particular interest groups as well as the collective behavior of large populations of interests.

The predominant view of interest politics research in the early 2000s follows the niche explanation of political relationships being based on strategic and often short-term choices about whom to contact. Groups are seen as single and individual entities rather than contained segments of larger and broader units such as triangles. Two excellent examples of such research are Kollman (1997) and Hojnacki and Kimball (1998) in which both find that friends, but not permanent allies, are the best choices to lobby.

Comparative Research and Work on Parliamentary Democracies

Because of the relative lack of power of parliaments in comparison with the U.S. Congress and U.S. state legislatures, the iron triangle has not been relevant to interest group activity in most parliamentary democracies. However, policy networks, issue networks, and other subgovernmental arrangements (primarily between interest groups and the executive branch where power is concentrated in parliamentary systems) have to some extent always existed. And in the past 20 years, there has been increasing interest in the role of subgovernments by scholars in these systems. Much of the work on these subgovernmental arrangements and the role of interest groups in them has been conducted within the neocorporatist theoretical framework. Therefore, those readers not familiar with neocorporatism should first review section 3.4. In addition, chapter 10, on comparative interest group studies, considers both the place of policy and issue networks and a critique of them. That chapter includes many references to the major work on policy networks and other subgovernmental arrangements.

As regards to specific books and articles, a volume by Martin Smith (1993) provides a comparative analysis of policy networks in Britain and the United States. His emphasis is on the role of the state in policy networks and how this is affected by pluralist, neocorporatist and, to a lesser extent, neo-Marxist paradigms. A useful collection of articles on policy networks in European politics, with an emphasis on transnational networks, is a special issue of the *European Journal of Political Research* (1992). The three most useful articles in this issue for those studying European and comparative policy networks for the first time are: G. Jordan and Schubert (1992) on the various terms used in the study of policy networks; Van

Waarden (1992a) on the nature and types of policy networks; and another article by Van Waarden (1992b) on the comparison of policy networks in the United States and the Netherlands.

New Research Directions

There is much work yet to be done in studying lobbying relationships with policy makers. However, three areas stand out. First, more historical analysis, such as John Mark Hansen's (1991), should be conducted. It should focus mainly on explaining what relationships led to specific public policies and how these worked. Were there ever more than a few triangles? If so, where and why? Was politics really dominated only by insiders?

Second, following Gray and Lowery (1996a, 1996c), more study of interactive and interfacing interest populations needs to be done. Do networks always develop? That seems obviously true. But how and why? Are these risk-aversive adaptive strategies?

Third, the entire concept of interest behavior and possible networking within interest populations should be studied on a more internationally comparative basis. And it should be done from some common conceptual framework, perhaps by a team of scholars each being familiar with their own unique environments. Marin and Mayntz (1991) and Martin Smith (1993) have shown the way in this regard.

7.17. INTEREST GROUP POWER AND INFLUENCE

Clive S. Thomas

Egged on by the press, the public often see interest groups as synonymous with political power (Benedict, Thomas, and Hrebenar 1996), which we can initially define as the ability of a group to achieve its political objectives. While there is some truth in this perception, the exercise of power by interest groups is a much more complex phenomenon than the public, the press, and many politicians would have us believe. Although group power and influence is one of the most investigated aspects of interest group activity, scholarly studies are largely inconclusive as to any definitive explanation of group power (Baumgartner and Leech 1998, 13–14). This may be largely because group power is a dynamic phenomenon involving many variables and it is difficult to identify all of them in each situation. This seriously inhibits the development of a general theory of group power. Nevertheless, the extensive literature on the subject enables us to make many observations about group power.

As the vast majority of studies on group power have been conducted on the U.S. political system, this entry is confined to such studies at the national and state levels. However, these studies and the general literature on political power have much relevance to group power beyond the United States.

Several scholars have attempted to differentiate between the degree of pressure exerted in achieving public policy goals and the levels of group effectiveness by distinguishing between *power* and *influence* (Richardson 1993b, 57). Yet, while some scholars see influence as less extensive and decisive than power, others see it as more extensive and more subtle in its operation. Thus, the exact difference between influence and power has yet to be satisfactorily operationalized. Consequently, in this entry the terms power and influence are used synonymously and interchangeably.

Although space does not permit a review of the general literature on political power, as background it is useful to consult the classic work by Dahl (1957) and his critics (e.g., Bachrach and Baratz 1962, 1963; Baldwin 1978; Clegg 1989; Wrong 1988). Also useful is the post-1970s local community power literature (e.g., Abney and Lauth 1985; C. Stone, Whelan, and Murin 1986; see section 6.5.), which has been drawn upon by scholars concerned with state interest group power.

Studies on U.S. National Politics

Studies of interest group power at the national level in U.S. politics, or studies that treat power as part of a broader topic, fall into seven broad categories. First, there are general impact studies assessing the overall effect of interest groups on the political system. Petracca (1992a, 350–53) shows that this literature has gone through four phases. The first, down to the mid-1940s, saw interest groups as very influential (e.g., Childs 1938; Goodnow 1900). The second phase, down to the late 1950s, reversed this judgement seeing interest group as less powerful (e.g., Chamberlain 1946; Penniman 1952). The third phase saw a debate between pluralists and their critics with pluralists such as Dahl (1961) arguing the influential importance and benefit to democracy of interest groups, and critics arguing that they had little influence (e.g., Bauer, Pool, and Dexter 1972; Milbrath 1963; see section 3.2.). Other critics like Schattschneider (1960), M. Olson (1965, 1982), and Lowi (1969, 1979) recognized the power of groups but saw them as often acting against the public interest. The fourth phase, since the advocacy explosion of the late 1970s, has come to no clear conclusion about the effects of group power on the political system in regard to both public policy making or democracy (e.g., Baumgartner and Leech 1998, chaps. 5 and 6; P. Peterson 1992).

The second category includes studies that theorize about the nature of interest group power and its limitations, particularly the concept of countervailing power, such as those by McConnell (1966) and McFarland (1987, 1992). Third, are sector-level studies that attempt to assess the power of a lobby as a whole. Most of these focus on business, such as the studies of Bauer, Pool, and Dexter (1972), Vogel (1989), and Mitchell (1997), but some have focused on other sectors or interests such as agriculture (Browne 1988) and the women's lobby (Costain 1992b). Fourth, are studies focusing on the affect of interest group power on particular institutions such as Congress or state legislatures (e.g., Tierney 1992; see section 7.10.), the presidency (e.g., Petracca 1992d), and the courts (e.g., L. Epstein 1991). This category also includes literature on the affect of PACs on the policy process, particularly on congressional voting (see section 7.4.); other studies on PACs fall into the next category. The fifth category, and by far the largest body of literature on group power, are case studies of individual groups and their influence on policy making. These cover a very broad range from Garceau's (1941) study of the American Medical Association to McFarland's (1984a) study of Common Cause to numerous studies on the political effect of the environmental movement (e.g., Lester 1995). Sixth, are studies of interest group power (and its limitations) gleaned, in whole or in part, from the activities of lobbyists. It includes Milbrath (1970), M. Hayes (1981), and Heinz et al. (1993). Finally, as part of one of the above categories (or separately), there are studies on group power in a policy area or areas. Some such studies are narrowly focused as in a policy niche (like tobacco subsidies). Others are broadly conceived (such as health policy). And some cut across several policy areas, such as those on budgetary policy (e.g., see sections 9.12. and 9.18.). Section 17.16. (Iron Triangles and Subgovernments) explores this policy area aspect of interest group power.

Shortcomings in the Literature

As extensive as it is, this literature has several shortcomings. A review and critique of the group power and influence literature is provided by Baumgartner and Leech (1998, 13–14, 129–33). They argue that the weaknesses stem, in part, from the inconclusive and heated debate about the nature of group power in the 1950s and 1960s. As a result, in recent years scholars have avoided many important general questions about power and instead conducted narrow case studies and more scientific studies, many of which are too specific to have general application. Several new problems have arisen with this recent literature such as its inconclusiveness in many areas, particularly on whether or not lobbying has an affect on policy, and that of the role of PACs on decision making. It can be argued that another reason for the disparate and questionable value of this literature is the lack of a core analysis of the elements of group power, which is one problem with Dahl's work and that of his critics in the study of political power in general.

Viewing interest group power less as a game—who wins and who loses—and more in terms of its relation to the political system as a whole, is one recommendation that Salisbury (1994, 18) makes in regard to the important questions awaiting to be asked and answered. He sees the game metaphor as very misleading as there is often no definite conclusion to the political process, no permanent winners or losers. Rather than linking group activity to influence, Salisbury suggests a focus on the relationship between various groups and between groups and officials. He might also have suggested another dimension—the relationship between groups and institutions such as political parties and legislatures.

Extending the critiques of Baumgartner and Leech and of Salisbury, three additional criticisms of the existing literature can be made. First, few studies can or do relate their findings to the broader context of the political system. This may be, in part, because of the second concern, which is that no general framework for understanding group power at its various levels of the political system—individual group power, power at the group sector level, and that of groups at the system level—exists. And third, while they often recognize the elusive nature and the difficulties of assessing group power, most studies, explicitly or implicitly, conceive of group power as one phenomenon with one definition. Such is the case in Dahl's classic definition, "'A' has power over 'B' to the extent that he can get 'B' to do something 'B' would not otherwise do" (Dahl 1957, 203); or as defined at the beginning of this entry, "the ability of a group to achieve its political objectives."

The State Politics Literature on Group Power

Although the U.S. state politics literature on group power is far less extensive than that on national politics and has its own shortcomings, it has added to our understanding. Besides producing a small category of case studies of groups and interests and their affects on state politics and policy (e.g., De Soto 1995a on state chambers of commerce; Hunter 1999 on interest groups and state economic development), state interest group scholars have also attempted to deal with some of the criticisms of the national group power literature. In particular, these scholars have differentiated between types of interest group power and from it, attempted to assess elements and develop theoretical frameworks to explain the relationship of group power to state politics (Morehouse 1981, chap. 3; Morehouse and Jewell 2003, chap. 3; Thomas and Hrebenar 1996b, 1999b, 2003; Zeller 1954, chap. 13). Three categories of power have been identified.

First, *single group power*, which is the ability of a group or coalition to achieve its goals as it defines them. Some groups can be very successful in achieving their goals but keep a very low profile in a state and are not singled out as powerful by public officials and political observers. Single group power is easy to define and is the only assessment of power that counts to a group, its leaders, and its lobbyists. However, developing a method to assess the relative power of groups based on their own assessment of success is virtually impossible. The major contribution to interest group studies and to understanding state politics that the concept of single group power offers is insight into the elements that constitute an effective group or lobby. Among the two most important of these elements are the extent of a government's need of a group and the skill of its lobbyists (see Thomas and Hrebenar 1996b, 1999b, 2003).

Second, *overall individual interest group and interest power,* which is defined as those groups and interests having the most influence on politics and policy making in a state as a whole. This aspect of group power interests the press and the public the most (see section 6.7.). This perspective not only involves the ability of a group to achieve its goals, but the added dimension of its significance and influence in state politics because of their high profile. It is, in essence, an identification and assessment of the influence of the big players in a state past and present. Such groups may not always win. In fact, they may often lose or get only a portion of what they seek; but they are seen as major forces in state politics. Over the years, several scholars have attempted to identify the most powerful groups across the states (Abney and Lauth 1986; Francis 1967; Hrebenar and Thomas 2003, table A; Morehouse 1981; Thomas and Hrebenar 1990, 1996b, 1999a, 1999b, 1999c, 2003, table 4.3).

Third is *interest group system power.* The interest group system is an array of groups and organizations, both formal and informal, and the lobbyists who represent them, working to affect public policy within a state or other political jurisdiction (see section 1.2. for a fuller explanation). Beginning with Zeller (1954), scholars have attempted to assess this group system power (see also, Morehouse 1981; Thomas and Hrebenar 1990, 1996b, 1999a, 1999b, 2003). A more specific study by Gray and Lowery (1996a, 236–40, 245–46) examines the relationship between group system power and the density and diversity of the group system.

Since the 1940s, scholars of state politics have recognized the importance of the relationship of political parties and interest groups. Accordingly, several studies have made observations on the party-group connection and developed explanations of its effect on significant aspects of state politics, such as access to policy makers, policy outcomes, the location of power in state politics, and the relative strength of parties and groups (e.g., Key 1964, 154–65; Morehouse 1981, 1997; Morehouse and Jewell 2003, chap. 3; Thomas 2001b; Zeller 1954, 190–93).

A General Assessment of the Literature

In combination, this literature on national and state interest group power offers many insights. It tells much about the strategies and tactics that are most successful in achieving influence and in what circumstances. It has contributed to an understanding of the dynamics of the policy process in general and specific policy areas in particular. It facilitates comparisons of the role and importance of particular interest groups and interests over time. It offers assessments of the overall effect of groups on U.S. national and state politics and by extrapolation on the politics of other political systems. However, the fragmented nature of the literature and the gaps in the understanding of interest group power offers one of the major opportunities for further research in interest group studies.

Chapter 8

Interests and Interest Groups in the Public Policy Process: (II) The Traditional Interests— Business, Labor, Agriculture, Education, and Government

8.1. CLASSIFYING INTERESTS AND INTEREST GROUPS: PROBLEMS AND APPROACHES

Clive S. Thomas

This chapter is the second of three consecutive chapters focusing on interest groups and interests in the public policy-making process. Section 7.1. provides an introduction to all three chapters and explains how they are integrated. As a prerequisite for understanding the division of the material in this and the next chapter, this first entry provides an overview of the ways in which interests and interest groups are often classified and the problems involved in classification. Two entries that will be useful to consult before reading this one and this chapter is the one explaining the development of interest group systems in general (see section 4.2.) and the one dealing with the development and present composition of the U.S. group universe (see section 6.2.).

Problems of Classifying Interest Groups

Although scholars have suggested several ways of classifying or categorizing interests and interest groups (see, for example, the discussion in Warhurst 1986) including dividing them by area of policy focus, there is no general consensus on any one scheme or method of classification. This is not only the case with regard to interest groups in general—across all types of political systems—but also there is no agreed upon classification for any one type of system, such as liberal democracies or, indeed, individual systems like the United States or Taiwan. In general this problem of classification stems from a combination of factors including varying ways of defining the terms *interest* and *interest group* (see section 1.2.), that there are no water-tight categories and always the potential for overlap between categories of classification, and that most classification systems focus on the situation in liberal democracies. More specifically, the problem can be illustrated by posing and giving short answers to three sets of interrelated questions that face anyone attempting to classify interest groups.

First, what definition of *interest group* should be used? Should broad, informal interests be included as well as formal interest groups? A narrow definition, for example, one that excludes government agencies or tribal groups, will produce a different classification system than one that embraces these. Furthermore, scholars look at interest groups in different ways in different political systems (see sections 11.1. and 12.1.). In fact, many scholars studying nonpluralist, transitional, and developing societies do not recognize interest groups in the way that they are viewed by most scholars of pluralist societies. This means that any attempt at classifying interest groups across types of political systems runs into serious problems of definition that preclude anything but a very broad classification system.

Second, if we confine our classification to one type of political system, say liberal democracies, would a broad classification system deal with problems of categorization? For example, what if a distinction were made between groups composed of individual members, such as unions, and organizations composed of groups or institutions, such as school boards or businesses? Or perhaps a categorization method distinguishing groups by policy area such as business, labor, agriculture, the environment, health, and so on might lend itself to a more clearly delineated classification system? Alternatively, what if an even broader categorization were used, distinguishing interests by whether they are economic or noneconomic?

Whichever of these three or other broad systems of classification are used, there will be inevitable overlap—groups and interests will often fit into more that one category. For example, some groups, like many professional associations, have both individual and institutional members. And in regard to classification by broad policy areas, should Tyson Foods (a major food-processing corporation in the United States) be classed as a business interest or an agricultural or agribusiness interest? Obviously, it is all three. Similarly, while many trade unions are primarily concerned with economic issues, they may also have a keen interest in such policy areas as reform of the political system, human rights issues, and even certain aspects of foreign policy.

Third, would a narrow definition of *interest* or *interest group*, such as breaking business down into various sectors or types of business, such as transportation, high-tech, auto manufacturers, and so on, or dividing labor into blue-collar and white-collar unions, solve the classification problem? Again, this would not avoid groups or interests falling into more than one category such as companies like Philip Morris and the Disney Corporation, which have interests across several business sectors.

These issues of classification are compounded by three additional problems. The first is that groups may broaden their representational or policy interests over time, such as businesses getting involved in health care cost issues and other issues beyond the specifics of their major economic activity. This makes it difficult to standardize classification systems over time. The second problem is that many useful terms like *economic group*, *social group*, and *single issue group* cut across boundary lines such as those between membership and nonmembership interests. The third problem is the issue of definition. There is a lack of consensus among scholars on the terminology used in interest group studies as related in section 1.4. For example, while some scholars include all occupational groups under the category of *labor*, others distinguish between *traditional labor* (mainly blue-collar occupations) and *the professions* (teachers, physicians, accountants, and so on). Similar problems of terminology and definition exist in attempting to distinguish between such labels as *public interest group* and *citizen group* among many other ambiguous and overlapping designations (see sections 9.5. and 9.6.). As McFarland (see section 9.5.) so aptly expresses it: "there exists no professional referee nor language court to deal with problems resulting from definitions."

Problems of categorization of groups and interests are never likely to be satisfactorily resolved. However, while to some extent they inhibit the study of interest groups, particularly comparisons between group systems and developing a general or "grand theory" of interest groups, they have not been a major problem for the individual researcher or team of researchers. With no consensus on classification, researchers investigating some element of the so-called group universe generally use the categorization system or develop one that is most appropriate to their research objectives.

Moreover, although there is no complete agreement on classification, over the past twenty years there has been increasing consensus among scholars on broad types of classification and approaches to viewing the group universe both within advanced individual political systems and comparatively across various types of systems—pluralist and nonpluralist, transitional, and developed and developing societies. The next two subsections set out these two approaches; then we briefly explain the classification system used in this and the next chapter in examining groups and interests in the public policy-making process. All three systems of classification are a useful starting point for new and seasoned researchers as all three provide broad categories that can be broken down into various subcategories as needed for a particular research project.

A Classification System for Advanced Pluralist Interest Group Systems

Largely based on research on the U.S. interest group system, one useful classification typology sees individual pluralist interest group systems as being made up of three broad categories of interests: (1) traditional membership groups, (2) organizational interests, and (3) institutional interests. While this classification may best fit highly pluralist societies like the United States, Canada, and Britain, it also has much relevance for neo-corporatist societies such as those in Scandinavia, Austria, and Germany.

Traditional membership groups are made up of individuals promoting a host of economic, social, and political concerns. Such individuals include senior citizens, environmentalists, schoolteachers, farmers, consumers, antitax advocates, and so on. Organizational interests are composed not of individuals but of organizations, such as businesses or trade unions—they are organizations of organizations. The third category of institutional interests is not really composed of groups at all. As Salisbury (1984) points out for Washington, D.C., and Gray and Lowery for the U.S. states (1995, 1996a, 2001), a large percentage of the organized interests represented before government are those of various private and public entities—businesses, think tanks, universities, state and federal agencies, and local governments. Today, institutions constitute the largest category of organized interests operating in U.S. state capitals (Gray and Lowery 2001, Fig. 3) and most likely in Washington, D.C., and many national capitals around the world, though no empirical evidence is available to verify this.

A Classification System for Comparative Analysis

As indicated above, most classifications of types of interest groups reflect the situation in advanced pluralist democracies. The following five-part classification system uses standard terminology and embraces the major groups and interests in all types of political systems.

1. Economic Interests or Producer Groups. These exist in every society, democratic and authoritarian, developed and underdeveloped. There are literally thousands of them with offices in national capitals from London to Ottawa to New Delhi to Canberra. As indicated above, some economic groups are made up of individual members while in other instances they are composed of other organizations. These latter types of organizations are often called *peak associations* (see section 4.10.) as they are, in effect, the major organizations in their economic sector in a country.

2. Special Interest Cause Groups. These are groups that represent a segment of society but have a primary purpose that is noneconomic and usually attempt to promote a cause or cherished value. This category is wide-ranging, from churches and religious organizations, like Catholic

Action in Italy, to ex-servicepersons (veterans) groups (such as the French Union of Veteran's and Victim's Groups–UFAC), groups supporting or opposing issues like gay rights, the rights of the handicapped (for example, the National Organization of the Spanish Blind), and profeminist and antifeminist groups (for example, Women Who Want to be Women, an Australian group opposed to many of the positions of the women's rights movement in that country). In recent years the term *single issue group* has increasingly been applied to cause groups that focus on one narrow issue such as pro-life (right-to-life) groups.

3. Public Interest Groups. As also indicated above, there is often a fine line and overlap between many cause and public interest groups. Whereas economic interest and most cause groups tend to benefit a narrow constituency, public interest groups promote issues of general public concern such as protecting the environment or promoting human rights (see section 9.5.). Many public interest groups operate in one country only, such as the Federal Association of Citizen-Action Groups for Environmental Protection (BBU) in Germany. Increasingly, however, many have an international presence, such as the environmental group Greenpeace and the human rights group Amnesty International, which monitors activities and publishes reports on the criminal justice systems of individual countries, including the treatment of prisoners.

4. Private and Public Institutional Interests—Particularly Government. Private institutional interests include think tanks like the Brookings Institution in Washington, D.C., the numerous private universities in the United States, and various forms of news media, particularly newspapers, that take up causes from time to time. But by far the largest component of this category is government in its many forms. At the national level, an example is the British Department of the Environment; at the provincial level in Canada the University of Alberta, a public university, lobbying the provincial government for its budget; at the local level the School Board in Fairbanks, Alaska, lobbying the Borough Assembly for money for a new high school gymnasium; and at the international level, the United Nations lobbying the U.S. Congress and the president to pay the United States' overdue financial contributions to that organization.

Governmental institutional interests are often the most important interests in authoritarian regimes where private interest groups are restricted or banned. The military, particularly the senior officer corps, has usually been the dominant force in Latin American dictatorships, as was the case in Chile, Argentina, and Paraguay. In past and present communist societies, government entities, like economic planning and agricultural agencies and the secret police, particularly if they are included in the top policy-making body, such as the Politburo in the former Soviet Union, are the major interests. And in some authoritarian regimes, such as Iran under the Ayatollah Khomeini and today in Saudi Arabia and many Muslim nations, religious institutions are prominent interests.

5. Nonassociational Groups—Interests. These can be groups with a more or less permanent and on-going existence, or they can be *anomic* groups—short-lived, often spontaneous groups, such as those organized to demonstrate against unpopular policies.

Examples of more permanent, informal groups and interests would include an ad hoc group of influential Turkish business leaders travelling to Brussels to promote Turkey's entry into the European Union; liberal Catholic bishops in many Latin American countries working to promote human rights in their respective countries; a group of Ebo tribal leaders from eastern Nigeria going to Abuja, the national capital, to represent their region of Biafra to government officials; the network of merchants and small businessmen in the Tehran bazaar that coalesced during the 1970s against the economic reforms of the Shah of Iran; and large landowners in India working through the personal ties they have in local politics and in state and national political party organizations to protect themselves against major land reforms.

Besides French farmers, renowned for their spontaneous demonstrations in Paris and other French cities, examples of anomic groups are the mainly indigenous poor of the southern Mexican state of Chiapas who rose up in 1994 in protest against social, economic, and political injustice and protesters who vented their opposition to the World Trade Organization (WTO) policies during a meeting of the organization in Seattle in November 2000.

Political systems at different levels of development and within different types of regimes manifest different combinations and varying ranges of these five types of interest groups (see section 4.2.). So-called advanced or "post-industrial" democracies—those of Western Europe, Japan, the United States, and Canada, for example—have all five types in large numbers, in a wide variety, and with an increasing number of public interest and cause groups. Less-developed countries, like those of most of Africa, and those with authoritarian regimes, like Cuba and Burma, have a narrower range of economic groups with very few—if any—public interest and cause groups plus some government interests. In these regimes informal interests are generally the most important and most numerous.

The Classification System Used in this Chapter and Chapter 9

Many classification systems could have been used in this and the next chapter, none of which would have been ideal because of the inherent problems of categorization explained above. The broad classification system used here is based on a historical perspective, and one that is associated most with scholars of U.S. politics (Zeigler 1983). Nevertheless, the classification system has relevance to other political systems, particularly those within developed countries. It divides interests broadly and based on their length of existence and prominence in politics. This chapter reviews research on the so-called traditional interests, those that have existed as prominent forces in political systems for several generations—business, labor, agriculture, education, and various governmental interests, including the foreign lobby in Washington, D.C. As a category, these are both the most numerous interests in most political systems plus the most active and influential. Then, chapter 9 examines the so-called new interests—those that, while they may have existed for many decades, have come to political prominence in the last thirty years or so—such as environmentalists, racial and ethnic groups, public interest groups, and so on.

This classification system based on historical prominence strikes a balance between the broad categorizations explained in the last two subsections and a highly specific system that breaks interests down into individual groups within narrowly defined categories. This particular classification was chosen because it best serves the users of this *Guide*—particularly students, teachers, and researchers in the United States—who need specific information on particular groups and interests—and particularly those in the U.S.—set in the context of the overall organization of this *Guide*.

8.2. BUSINESS INTERESTS AND POLITICS: AN OVERVIEW

Neil J. Mitchell

How does business (almost invariably big business) fit into the political system? This is a central question for social scientists—economists and sociologists, as well as political scientists—and opens inquiry into a profusion of issues from the nature of political power and democracy to the components of national economic competitiveness.

Since World War II, the theoretical focus has largely been on how business shares significant common characteristics, perhaps purpose, structure, and modes of participation, with other groups. Challenging this perspective are those who argue that business has a special place in the political system and a distinct advantage in securing political influence. Business, they argue, approaches politics as a class, from a position of privilege, through modes of participation not open to other groups, or with the benefit of a particular incentive structure, and achieves a qualitatively different level of success in the policy struggle. Related to these opposing viewpoints is the central question of the extent to which business is united or fragmented politically and how this affects its success in the political arena.

In the 1950s and early 1960s, the thesis of a self-regulating system of countervailing power, popular among economists, and the development of pluralist theory by political scientists provided the conceptual environment in which Bauer, Pool, and Dexter (1963, 1972) researched business political activity. These authors were struck by the complexity of the political process, the divisions among business interests, the growth of interests constraining the political influence of business, and the "self-denial" exercised by those, like DuPont or Detroit car companies that appear to have power. The Bauer, Pool, and Dexter book delineates some of the major themes for those who currently make the argument that the power of business is not in a class by itself but on a par with other interests.

The major critical work on business political power in the 1970s was Lindblom (1977). He argued that business interests, through their influence on public preferences and ideology, their advantages in the representational process, and the importance to governments of maintaining business confidence, had a privileged position. This work stimulated considerable scholarly interest and sharp criticism (for example, Hessen 1982) focusing on the issues of whether business has ideological influence and whether business resources translate into political influence. Neil Mitchell (1997) returned to these themes and investigated why, despite its considerable political resources, business can still lose in the policy process.

The use of pluralist theory to explain business power reemerged in the 1980s in the idea of a "cycle" in the policy influence of business groups and the interest in issue networks and policy communities (see section 7.16.). Arguing that business power to influence policy changes over time and based on an analysis of the win-loss legislative record of American business in the areas of environmental, health and safety, energy, and tax policy since 1960, Vogel (1989) identifies a policy cycle driven by public perceptions of the performance of the economy and the amount of business political activity, resulting in fluctuations in business policy success (see also McFarland 1991). How this cycle fits other periods and to what degree it fits the policy experience in other countries remains to be investigated. The 1980s also saw renewed interest in capitalists as a "class." Corporate interlocks, including business association and club memberships, its advocates argue, give businesspeople a collective, business-wide outlook that has an important impact on their political and social activities (Useem 1984).

Neocorporatist theory (see section 3.4.) has provided the major alternative to pluralism in the analysis of European politics, encouraging attention to the structure and efficacy of business representation and business associations and to the impact on economic performance (Streeck 1984; G. Wilson 1985; W. Coleman and Grant 1988). During the 1980s there was a shift of focus from whole political systems to sectoral (industry) analysis, permitting detailed accounts and suggestive cross-national comparisons weighing the relative importance of sector and political system characteristics. Differences among countries and political systems persist (Hollingsworth, Schmitter, and Streeck 1994a). Lehne (1993) provides a cross-national overview with a focus on the United States; and Wyn Grant (1993) provides the most comprehensive and authoritative account for the United Kingdom, including a good bibliography. For the United States, Baumgartner and Leech (1998) include a useful critique of the literature on business interest group activity.

The issue of the degree of unity among business interests remains a critical one for research. Business countervails itself to such a degree that it becomes more difficult to claim that business interests are overrepresented in the policy process, although one must consider whether business divisions adequately compensate for the poorer representation of other interests. Cathie Martin (1991) focuses on the divisions among U.S. business interests that produced the 1986 Tax Reform Act (see also, Mucciaroni 1995); and Ferguson (1995) examines the divisions that characterized the New Deal. Also at issue, in questions of unity (or lack thereof) and of the role of business in the political system is the challenge facing bureaucrats and politicians of how to properly conceive the incentives to aid or stymie business interests (J. Q. Wilson 1980).

The development of the global economy forces political scientists to examine business political activities beyond domestic national arenas. This includes not only semisovereign entities like the European Union but also cross-border political activity. The activities of Japanese corporations in the United States have attracted particular attention, though given the stakes there is reason to think that any business, whatever its "nationality," will seek to influence policies wherever the policy arena is located. So far, analysis of the global polity and the advantages that international mobility provides business interests in the policy process lags behind research on the global economy.

8.3. CHAMBERS OF COMMERCE

William De Soto

Chambers of commerce are highly visible representatives of the general interests of employers. The U.S. Chamber of Commerce (USCC) represents the collective interests of business at the federal level in Washington, D.C. Its policy goals include reduced corporate and personal taxation, less stringent environmental regulation, less worker safety regulation, protection from frivolous lawsuits, and increased respect for business interests. In addition, most states and all but the smallest communities have chambers of commerce that organize their business communities. However, academic analysis of these organizations at all three levels of government and in other countries is rather limited.

Scholars have given little attention to the USCC. However, four sources are useful for acquiring some basic information. One by Donald

Hall (1969) is a rather outdated study but useful for historical background. Hall uses the USCC and its cooperation with other business groups to explain about lobbying as a political activity. A second, Green and Buchsbaum (1980), covers the Business Roundtable as well as the USCC. A third is Mundo's (1992) textbook on interest groups. Mundo includes a chapter on the Chamber in which he describes its organizational structure, its history, and its policy issues. The fourth source is a profile of the USCC in Ness (2000, 117–20).

Many other writers briefly discuss the USCC in their work on the political position of business. Vogel (1989, 199) writes that the chamber's "stature and membership increased dramatically during the 1970s." Other useful books include Useem (1984), Graham Wilson (1981), and McQuaid (1982). These provide surveys of the recent history of business-government relations, including reference to the USCC. On the state level, there is a study of the role and effectiveness of chambers in three states (Pennsylvania, South Carolina, and Wisconsin) by De Soto (1995a).

One challenge chambers of commerce face in organizing the millions of U.S. businesses is reconciling disagreements among different types of business interests. For example, some types of industries welcome free trade with foreign companies while others oppose it. Cathie Martin (1991) uses recent corporate tax history to show how capital-intensive manufacturing interests favored the tax incentives contained in the Economic Recovery Tax Act of 1981, while small business interests wanted to reduce tax rates and were willing to eliminate the incentives. The latter interests benefited from the Tax Reform Act of 1986. Martin refers frequently to the chamber in her analysis of disputes within the business community over tax issues.

There is little work on the political strategies the chamber employs to achieve its goals, although many of the studies mentioned above make some reference to the chamber's lobbying activities. One of the chamber's greatest political strengths is its ability to organize a coalition of diverse business interests through its state and local chamber affiliates. A time-series study of interest groups in the fifty states conducted over the past twenty years (Thomas and Hrebenar 2003; see also Hrebenar and Thomas 2003, table A) has consistently ranked state chambers together with schoolteachers as one of the two most powerful interests in the states overall.

8.4. THE ENERGY LOBBY

Andrew S. McFarland

When the Organization of Petroleum Producing Countries (OPEC) succeeded in raising oil prices in 1973 and 1977, the resultant public attention and concern was dubbed "the energy crisis," and more scholarly attention was paid to lobbying by energy groups than at any other time, including in recent years. Accordingly, research conducted in the early and mid-1980s serves as a frame of reference for later studies. The best introduction to energy politics and lobbying is David Davis (1993); and Rosenbaum (1987) is another useful introduction. President Reagan's first term witnessed the end of "the energy crisis," cutbacks in federal support for alternative sources, and the decreasing influence of the lobby for nuclear electric power whose influence has further declined since then.

A good starting point for information on individual energy interest groups is Wenner (1990). This reference work includes profiles of over sixty energy interest groups with each profile describing the group's organization, resources, membership, and policy positions. Entries range across the entire field of energy from the American Gas Association to the American Council for an Energy Efficient Economy to the American Petroleum Institute to the American Wind Energy Association. The data was compiled by a survey conducted in 1988 and 1989, but most of the information is still applicable.

Energy was one of the four sectors studied in the largest empirical studies of lobbying ever conducted (Heinz et al. 1993; Laumann and Knoke 1987). The emphatic finding of these studies, which included about 200 interviews with energy lobbyists and the targets of their lobbying, is that the energy sector consists of several discrete subsectors: oil and gas, coal, nuclear power, alternative sources (e.g., solar), and electric power. Environmental issues overlap with energy policy, and thus environmental lobbies are also participants in this area but normally do not closely interact with energy corporations (Laumann and Knoke 1987; McFarland 1993). Heinz et al. (1993) reports a wealth of data about the personal characteristics of energy lobbyists. In comparison with lobbyists for other sectors, energy lobbyists are more likely to be men, have technical rather than legal backgrounds, and come from the Southwest. McFarland (1984b) lists the basic characteristics of several dozen energy lobbies in 1984 and shows that the structure of influence varies by subsector and by time.

There are several scholarly studies of energy policy that do not emphasize interest groups but do contain considerable reference to the activities of energy groups. Sanders (1981), on the regulation of natural gas, contains general information about producers' lobbies. On the oil industry, Engler (1961) is a standard work from a left-wing perspective; Krasner (1978) contains analyses of the role of oil companies in American foreign policy decisions; and Uslaner (1989) examines congressional politics of subsidizing the development of oil trapped in shale rock. On coal, Ackerman and Hassler (1981) is an analysis of the politics of regulating the burning of coal; and Harris (1985) focuses on strip-mining regulation. Nivola (1986) deals with the politics of deregulation of oil and natural gas in the early 1980s. A study by Chubb (1983) shows that public interest groups had almost no influence on the federal energy bureaucracy in the

1970s, while energy producers did. Price (1990) contains considerable information about antinuclear interest groups.

In general, after 1990 the study of energy interest groups lapsed due to a decline of social concern about energy policy. This may be one reason why the most extensive reference guide to interest groups in the United States (Ness 2000) includes virtually no energy groups.

8.5. UTILITY INTERESTS

Paul Teske

Utilities have long been viewed as major players and powerful interests in American national, state, and local politics (Wildavsky 1962; Sanders 1981). Thomas and Hrebenar (1990, 1996b, 1999a, 2003; Hrebenar and Thomas 2003, table A) found that utilities are ranked among the most effective of all groups in the U.S. states.

Since the early twentieth century, U.S. governments have regulated public utilities, restricting prices in return for a monopoly-supply position with assured profits. The technical nature of policy making led to a subgovernment structure characterized mostly by iron triangles and capture (see section 7.16.), which limited access by other affected parties. Utilities provide considerable input into policy evaluation, legislation, administrative implementation, and judicial challenges. Public utilities regulated today as quasi-monopolies include electricity and gas, telecommunications, cable TV, and some water and sewer firms. Previously, this list also included railroads, truckers, and airlines, but these are now largely deregulated, arguably because the regulated interests lost their favored political position (see Derthick and Quirk 1985).

Utilities are regulated by somewhat insulated independent commissions at both the federal and state levels. According to some theories, the regulators themselves can largely be ignored (Stigler 1971; Peltzman 1976) as powerful interests battle over critical issues. In other theories, the regulators are seen as playing a critical role in mediating interest group input (J. Q. Wilson 1980, 1985; Derthick and Quirk 1985; Teske 1990).

Today, the key utility interest groups include (1) the regulated public utilities, (2) their new competitors, (3) large business users of these services, and (4) dispersed small consumers. As might be expected, the utility interest group environment is more pluralist in Washington, D.C., than in most states; but it is highly complex at both levels, especially in telecommunications (J. Berry 1989, 191). The political environment is no longer well described by the iron triangle metaphor; the increased salience of existing issues and the emergence of new issues together with the emergence of new groups has transformed it into something better described by "issue networks" (Heclo 1978; section 7.16.) or "advocacy coalitions" (Sabatier and Jenkins-Smith 1993). Yet, no comprehensive bibliography of utility interest groups is available, although some related areas have been profiled (see Wenner 1990). A profile of several utility interest groups can be found in Ness (2000).

Studies of utilities include both quantitative analyses and qualitative case studies. Utilities are well-funded repeat players with large numbers of employees and have been shown to be strategic in their choices of political levels (Douglas Anderson 1981; J. Cohen 1992) and venues (e.g., legislative versus regulatory body, see Teske 1991), as well as in their specific policy requests (see H. Campbell 1996). In energy regulation, Gormley (1983) and Peter Navarro (1985) found strong evidence of utility influence over policy. In telecommunications, Teske (1990) found strong influence particularly by one aggressive firm, U.S. West (now Qwest Communications). While individual utilities are large enough to lobby on their own, utilities also have powerful trade associations, including the U.S. Telephone Association and state telephone and energy associations.

Utilities have several groups often opposing their policy proposals. Their new competitors are sometimes small operators, but more often are backed by other large firms in related industries. MCI helped transform telecommunications, and Stigler (1971) and Hacker (1962) found that competitor railroads influenced state trucking regulatory policies. Large business users of utility services are well organized and powerful; if they depend upon utility services, they may mobilize. Shipper groups were influential in state railroad regulation in the 1880s (McCraw 1984; Gilligan, Marshall, and Weingast 1989), as well as in state trucking regulation in the 1980s (Teske, Best, and Mintrom 1995). Douglas Anderson (1981) found that large electricity users played an important role in energy policy changes in the 1970s. Teske (1990) found that large business telecommunications users were influential. Finally, small consumers are represented by grassroots and proxy advocates that have been shown to influence energy regulation (Gormley 1983; W. Berry 1984), as well as telecommunications (Teske 1990).

8.6. INDUSTRIAL AND MANUFACTURING INTERESTS

Maria Green Cowles

While scholars debate the extent of the political influence of business groups, including industrial and manufacturing interests (see sections 7.17. and 8.2.), there can be no doubt that these interests are among the most important and influential forces in all societies, pluralist and nonpluralist alike. However, despite the importance of industrial and manufacturing groups in the policy-making process across the Western world, there is little recent work on them and many gaps in the literature. For example, one of the last important books on American industrial interests, Vogel (1989), is well over a decade old. And there are few in-depth English-language works on national European industrial groups, although comparative business-government texts provide overviews. A number of these comparative texts contain good bibliographies of industrial and manufacturing interests in North America and Europe (Audretsch 1989; Richardson 1993a; Wilks and Wright 1987; G. Wilson 1990b).

The general literature on U.S. business interests, detailed in section 8.2., includes many references to industrial and manufacturing groups. Works specifically examining key industry groups in Washington, D.C., include Gable (1953) and Burch (1973) on the National Association of Manufacturers (NAM); Green and Buchsbaum (1980) on the U.S. Chamber of Commerce (they also cover the Business Roundtable); and Slavin (1975–76), McQuaid (1981), and Plotke (1992) on the Business Roundtable. A profile of several U.S. industrial and manufacturing interests can be found in Ness (2000, Vol. I). The Canadian literature includes important works by Stanbury (1986), William Carroll (1986), and William Coleman (1988); the later being the most extensive treatment of Canadian business groups to date. An article by Jacek (1994) on the role of major companies and industry groups in promoting the North American Free Trade Agreement (NAFTA) points to the growing importance of transnational industry groups. A study by W. Coleman and Grant (1984) provides an interesting comparison of business associations and public policy in the United Kingdom and Canada, and one by Useem (1984) compares the United States and the United Kingdom.

The European literature focuses on national peak associations, the primary industrial and manufacturing interest groups. On the United Kingdom, W. Grant and Marsh (1977) on the Confederation of British Industry (CBI), although quite dated, remains the classic. Other important United Kingdom works include A. Jordan and Richardson (1987) and W. Grant (1989b). English-language sources on the role of French and German business groups in the policy-making process are very limited. Ehrmann (1957), on the French peak organization, provides an important historical overview while other helpful texts include Hayward (1975), Zysman (1977), and Frank Wilson (1987). More recently, Vivien Schmidt (1996a) has explored the growing influence of the French industrial elite on French policy making. On Germany, Braunthal (1965) is another very dated but comprehensive overview while Bulmer and Paterson (1987) and Glouchevitch (1992) bring the material more up-to-date.

The European Union (EU) provides an important new area of research on industrial and manufacturing interests, although much of the literature is highly descriptive. Early English-language studies examining the historical role of business groups in the EU include Feld (1966), Sidjanski (1967), and Robinson (1983). Van Tulder and Junne (1988) and Sandholtz and Zysman (1989) relaunched the study of EU industrial groups. Van Schendelen (1993) and Bulmer and Paterson (1987) provide overviews of how national industry groups have attempted to address EU policy making; and Cowles (1996a, 1996b) considers political coalition-building among EU industrial groups with a focus on the activities of French and German industrial elites. Cowles (1995) also provides a detailed account of the European Round Table of Industrialists' role behind the 1992 program of further EU integration as well as the influence of American firms in shaping lobbying practices in Brussels (Cowles 1996c). Coen (1997) analyzes the strategies of large firms in EU policy making, while Sandholtz (1992) and John Peterson (1993) focus specifically on the high-tech industry. More recently, research has begun to focus on the influence of EU policy-making and lobbying activities on national business-government relations (Kassim and Menon 1996; Cowles 2001a; Greenwood 2002b, 2003b).

One area of future study will likely be that of multinationals and transnational industrial interests. First launched with the studies by Vernon (1971, 1974, 1977), new work has been conducted by Ostry (1990), Strange and Stopford (1991), Strange (1988, 1996), and Cowles (2001b) that contributes to a growing research agenda on transnational interests and multinational firms.

8.7. BANKING AND FINANCE INTERESTS

Andrew Skalaban

In the United States, the most contentious banking policy questions were settled before and during the New Deal of the 1930s. Moreover, although banking institutions and regulations underwent reform in the 1980s and 1990s, the politics of banking and financial deregulation has generally been confined to a narrow range of political players and has not resulted in significant mass mobilization of groups or shifts in electoral coalitions. Partly for this reason, banking and finance interest group politics have not been a major concern of political science.

However, political scientists have not totally ignored this area. Furthermore, work has been done on this subject by legal, economics, and finance scholars who consider banking and finance politics to be major concerns of their disciplines. This includes work on international banking and financial interests and their influence. There is also a profile of several U.S. national banking and finance interest groups in Ness (2000, Vol. I, 3–61). Overall, however, there is little work on individual banking and finance interest groups: one must glean such information from the broader literature on banking and financial politics.

One area that has received considerable attention is monetary politics and the role of interests in monetary policy decisions. The two primary research questions addressed by this literature are: (1) what is the extent of short-term political control over monetary policy, and (2) is monetary and other bank regulatory policy made primarily for the benefit of the financial services industry? Works by Beck (1984), Chappell, Havrilesky, and McGregor (1993), Lombra and Witte (1982), Havrilesky (1993), Stein (1994), and Woolley (1984) address one or both of these issues. Works by Frieden (1991b) and Cerney (1993) evaluate monetary policy manipulation within the international financial system with its ever-increasing cross-border capital flows. Other useful sources on interest activity in monetary and banking policy, including the international dimension, are Peter Hall (1986), Moran (1984, 1991, 1994), Reinicke (1995), and Stein (1994).

In addition, the following sources are useful as introductory guides to the politics of the securities markets and include references to various interest groups: Phillips and Zecher (1981), Sobel (1994), Stonham (1987), and Walter (1985).

The financial services revolution since 1980 has been accompanied by a wide array of regulatory changes. In the United States, some of the most important specific changes have been the deregulation of savings and loan business operations and elimination of interstate banking restrictions. Works that address these and other closely related issues include Gart (1994), Hill (1990), Krause (1994), and Skalaban (1992, 1993).

Given the dearth of material on individual interest groups in the banking and finance areas in books and articles, researchers should consult *Congressional Quarterly Weekly Report, Federal Reserve Bulletin, The Economist, The Wall Street Journal,* and regular hearings by Congressional committees. These publications provide the best description of the political activities of organized interest groups on banking and financial services policy issues.

8.8. INSURANCE INTERESTS

Loree G. Bykerk

Insurance is often considered among the politically powerful industries in the United States at both the federal and state levels (Hrebenar and Thomas 2003, table A), but there is little political science research on the industry and almost none on its interest groups. Historian H. Roger Grant (1979) outlines the enhancement of insurance regulation at the state level and efforts to develop regulation at the federal level in the early twentieth century. He notes the involvement of the American Life Convention and large individual corporations in shaping regulation. Kenneth Meier's *The Political Economy of Regulation: The Case of Insurance* (1988) is the broadest political science study of the insurance business; it encompasses both state and federal regulatory relationships. The liability insurance crisis of the mid-1980s is its core case study, but it covers other issues as well in a framework of public law and regulatory politics. A few of the larger interest groups are considered in Meier's analysis, including the American Council of Life Insurance and the Independent Insurance

Agents of America; however, interest groups do not play a substantial role in his analysis. Among Meier's conclusions is that insurance companies are so divided internally that they should be considered multiple businesses rather than one. Profiles of several national insurance interest groups can be found in Ness (2000, Vol. I, 15–51).

Other scholarship touching on insurance interest groups are case studies of issues that have gotten on the national agenda during the late twentieth century. The Federal Trade Commission's unsuccessful attempt to investigate the industry during the 1970s is outlined in Pertschuk (1982) and Harris and Milkis (1989). The former is an exciting insider's account, the latter a more theoretical analysis of regime change in the administrative state.

The insurance case studies of the 1980s focused mainly on the liability insurance crisis and the unisex issue. A very readable account of the liability issue is found in *The Washington Lobby* (1987), which includes reference to the Insurance Services Office, although its focus is on the role of consumer advocates. Thorough accounts of the legal and economic perspectives are available in Walter Olson (1988).

The unisex issue was the insurance lobby's label for rates to be set without consideration of the gender of a person. It was a federal legislative proposal that the industry was able to defeat. The issue is treated by Meier (1988) from the political economy perspective and by Bykerk (1988, 1992) from an interest group perspective. Harry and Louise's killing of President Clinton's health care reform proposal is *the* insurance case study of the 1990s. The central role of the Health Insurance Association of America in this massive media campaign is portrayed in West and Loomis (1999). Other texts attest to the prominence of this case, including Hrebenar (1997) and Wolpe and Levine (1996).

The body of research on interest group influence at the state level in the United States includes the insurance industry. Its stature varies dramatically from state to state, but Connecticut is uniformly cited as having the most powerful insurance lobby (Hrebenar and Thomas 1993a, 2003, table A; Rosenthal 2001).

Consistent with the scant attention to insurance interest groups, interpretation of their role is relatively undeveloped. On the one hand, both Meier and Bykerk maintain that the industry is significantly divided. Bykerk points to lobbying efforts dissipated by dissension. By contrast, Pertschuk and West and Loomis characterize their cases as displays of impressive lobbying might.

8.9. AGRICULTURAL INTERESTS

William P. Browne

Although agricultural interests have been studied in many countries, the bulk of the literature focuses on those operating in the U.S. political system. Historians, economists, political scientists, and sociologists have all made major contributions to the research in this field. This has resulted in an extensive literature that is often used in generalizing about other types of interest groups.

In fact, work on agriculture has provided much of the general theory about U.S. interest groups. This stems, in part, from the fact that beginning in the period after the American Civil War, farmers were an important political force and were among the first prominent organized interests as Carl Taylor (1953) and Mooney and Majka (1995) illustrate in studying farmer movements. Thus, farmers set a sort of benchmark for those studying interest groups. Furthermore, even though the number of farmers decreased during the twentieth century, other interest groups became active in agricultural policy making from the late 1960s onward. These ranged from agribusiness to welfare advocates to environmental activists, among many others. Because of the involvement of these new interests, agricultural policy today is far more than just farm policy as it largely was until the 1970s. As to bibliographies on agricultural interests, the most recent and comprehensive can be found in John Mark Hansen (1991, 231–50) and Browne (1995a, 255–60, 271–75).

Studies of the Early Years and of Farm Protest

For several decades scholars paid the greatest attention to farm groups involved in protest politics. This research, mostly by historians, expanded on the tendency of rural farmers, as first observed by Tocqueville (1835/1840), to become active joiners in local organizations. Buck (1913) produced the seminal work on the early Grange. Decades later, others produced excellent books on southern farm protest groups (Saloutos 1960), the Southern Farmers Alliance (McMath 1975), the Greenback Party and their Free Silver movement (Weinstein 1970), Midwestern farm protests (Saloutos and Hicks 1951), and the Farmers Holiday Association (Shover 1965). And Clemens (1997, especially chapter 5), in her comprehensive study of the emergence of the modern interest group system in the United States (1890–1925), examines the development of new strategies and tactics by state farm groups—mainly those from California, Washington state, and Wisconsin—and their lobbying activities in Washington, D.C. This combined work, plus the classic work by Hofstadter (1955) on the reform era, thoroughly covers the diversity and influence (Saloutos 1982) of agrarian politics from 1867 to 1939.

Important findings came from these largely descriptive studies. First, it was clear that organized regional groups played the critical role in galvanizing farm social movements. Second, these groups depended on organizational entrepreneurs who personally marketed their associations and who used social benefits to attract supporters. Salisbury (1969) used these farm groups and this literature to develop much of his argument of an exchange theory of interest groups.

Third, groups of this era were primarily political in purpose and directed mostly toward public policy changes (Browne and Dinse 1985). Groups organized when farm prices were very low or when major price fluctuations threatened farmers. Group organizers/entrepreneurs depended greatly on ideological explanations of price problems to solidify their memberships, on political rhetoric and myths to keep members involved, and on disruptive protest as the strategic means for both pressuring government and maintaining group solidarity. As Moe (1980a) concluded, both political and social benefits were integral to member satisfaction.

Studies of Permanent Farm Organizations

Mancur Olson (1965, 148–49) also used farm protest groups, particularly their tendency to die quickly, in developing his theory of collective action. He contrasted these groups with two general farm organizations, the American Farm Bureau Federation (AFBF) and the National Farmers Union (NFU), that became full-service organizations, representing farmers as an interest and providing an array of selective benefits. This gave these general farm groups, which also came to include the Grange, a stability and permanence that other groups lacked. Two sociologists (Gilbert and Howe 1991) and a historian (Hamilton 1991) expanded significantly on Olson's theme of permanence. They looked at the institutional linkages between general farm groups, especially the AFBF and government. Farm groups thrived and found influence because of this relationship between farmers, their associations, and a government that encouraged their involvement.

These statist theories (so-called because of the active involvement of government) were augmented by an important work by a political scientist. John Mark Hansen (1991) produced an excellent analysis of how the AFBF, in competition with three other generalist farm groups of the 1920s, came to be the dominant and most influential agricultural interest. Congress accepted AFBF influence because legislators from both the South and the Midwest were convinced that issues of low farm prices would not go away without government intervention and because the group became a superior source of political information about farmers and their principal mobilizing force. Hansen and the statists brought a new sophistication and complexity to understanding the political relationships underlying agricultural policy and its processes, showing clearly that farm politics had for years been a hard and divisive business.

Prior to these studies, a number of less empirical and detailed works led to a widespread view that after the New Deal general farm interests controlled farm opinions and the policy process. McConnell (1953, 1966) portrayed permanent farm groups as stymieing diversity of farm values as they were articulated in the age of reform. Lowi (1969, 1979) and other scholars such as Zeigler (1964, 163–98) saw some continued diversity while Christiana Campbell (1962) saw none. Little or no diversity popularized the idea that agricultural policy making was dominated by iron triangles or subgovernments (see section 7.16.).

According to iron triangle theory, farm politics was largely noncontentious and well supported because a simple three-part, nonpartisan governing structure had emerged. Agriculture committees in Congress wrote policy, the U.S. Department of Agriculture supplied the technical expertise to let the committees proceed, and the Farm Bureau provided the political support necessary to insulate the triangle from other policy players. To Lowi (1964b) this was how farmers got their way. This secondary research was based mostly on descriptive and even muckraking accounts of general farm groups and their allies, such as Crampton (1965) on the NFU, Kile (1948) on the AFBF, and McCune (1956).

The iron triangle literature missed a key factor in the political economy of agriculture. This was the continuing conflict due to chronic commodity surpluses, low prices, and the resulting need for farms to adjust by either getting larger or closing. Only a few scholars, such as Hadwiger and Talbot (1968), noted the ferocity of partisan politics over policy because of these problems. And only Heinz (1962) picked up on the rising influence of commodity groups for major crops and the related decline in influence of general farm groups that could no longer speak credibly for all types of farmers. Hansen and the statists deserve recognition for explaining why agricultural politics was never as smooth as triangle theory implied and why those divisions needed greater attention.

Studies of the Expanding Range of Agricultural Interests

Agricultural politics became much more complex after the 1960s as policies became driven by more than just farm problems and as a larger and more diverse universe of interests entered the field of agricultural politics. A few scholars conducting empirical field research studied what was taking place and why.

An economist, Bonnen (1980), led the way observing a proliferation of both groups and organizations within government that influenced agricultural politics and policy. Hadwiger (1982) and Bosso (1987) examined conflict between farm and environmental groups and its effect on agricultural research and pesticide policy respectively. The complexities of the food stamp program and competing interests were documented by Jerry Berry (1984). Browne (1988) compiled an inventory of the over 200 groups active in omnibus farm bills and developed the niche theory (Browne 1990) of how these groups manage to coexist legislatively with nominal conflict and cooperation. Browne and Cigler (1990) produced an encyclopedia of these modern groups adding to one by Dyson (1986) on earlier farm groups. Both works show extensive group proliferation as does the survey by Guither (1980). Browne (1995a) also examined how entrepreneurism within Congress encouraged even greater proliferation of interests, especially among constituents. Heinz et al. (1993), in a comparison of four policy areas, found agriculture to be especially lacking in centralizing mechanism to bring diverse interests together.

These studies help to explain why agricultural policy making became so cumbersome, fragmented, and lacking in coherence in its efforts to accommodate the diversity of the sector's interests. The 1970s saw the emergence of further obstacles to enacting coordinated farm policy as fringe protest groups reemerged (Browne 1993; A. Cigler 1986, 1991c) and as assorted regional groups developed their own schemes for addressing surpluses and low prices (Amato 1993). The work on agricultural interests by these researchers not only reveals the expanding universe of U.S. interests but also demonstrates the often negative policy impact of these groups (Browne and Schweikhardt 1995; Bonnen, Browne, and Schweikhardt 1996; Browne, Allen, and Schweikhardt 1997). In particular, the plethora of groups and their rivalries have made comprehensive and lasting policy reform impossible.

The cumulative knowledge of research on agricultural interests in the United States provides a considerable understanding about how interest groups and governing institutions affect one another and public policy. While more attention needs to be given to the role of agribusiness, most other types of agricultural interests have been well studied. Only rarely do studies of agricultural interests in other nations provide such detail and relate it to policy decisions. Graham Wilson's (1977) comparison of Britain and the United States and Bates's (1981) analysis of ties between markets and interests in tropical Africa stand out as exceptions. Since so much is known of the United States, future agricultural interest research needs to collect information worldwide and make comparisons between countries.

8.10. LABOR INTEREST GROUPS

Eric S. Heberlig

The literature on labor and labor unions as interest groups is extensive. Unions have received considerable attention because they have been politically active in U.S. politics and politics in other Western democracies from the mid-nineteenth century onward. This entry focuses mainly on labor as an interest in U.S. politics with some reference to other Western countries.

Labor Interests in U.S. Politics

In the United States, studies have frequently focused on unions' legislative lobbying and their electoral involvement by mobilizing their members and providing contributions to candidates through political action committees (PACs). Union alliances with the Democratic Party are key sources of their political influence, and exploring the evolution of this relationship also has been a major theme of the literature (Dark 1999).

Masters and Delaney (1987) provide a thorough overview of the literature through the mid-1980s. They classify the literature into four topical areas: (1) union members' voting behavior, (2) unions' electoral activities, (3) union lobbying, and (4) the influence of unions on public policy. They detail the time period, principal research question, and source of data. And for each study they cover, they identify particular union internationals and locals that were studied.

Three books provide comprehensive discussions of the development of unions as political forces. Greenstone (1977) documents the development of the political aspects of union organization, particularly the American Federation of Labor-Congress of Industrial Organization's (AFL-CIO) Committee on Political Education (COPE), and examines union political mobilization in three cities in the 1950s. Bok and Dunlop (1970) review the electoral and lobbying activities of unions through the 1960s. Graham Wilson (1979) examines union lobbying activities through the 1970s. Like these books, most studies of union political action focus on the AFL-CIO. However, some studies document the political histories of particular internationals, such as the National Education Association (NEA) (A. West 1980; M. Berube 1988), the United Auto Workers (UAW), or the International Association of Machinists (Mundo 1992). And Ness (2000, 350–421, 671–75) reviews the political history and political activities of several unions as well as the major labor PACs. Finally, Clemens (1997, especially chapter 4), as part of her comprehensive study of the emergence of the modern U.S. interest group system (1890–1925), examines the development of new strategies and tactics by state labor groups—especially in California, Washington state, and Wisconsin—and the development of their lobbying activities in Washington, D.C.

Electoral Mobilization. The voting behavior and political participation of union members has received substantial attention because union members are major contributors to Democratic candidates. Yet, individuals join the union for workplace benefits and protections rather than to support the political positions of union leaders. Thus, there has been considerable interest in the extent to which members respond to leader's endorsements and attempts to mobilize members on behalf of Democratic candidates. Kornhauser, Sheppard, and Mayer (1956) and Lipset, Trow, and Coleman (1956) were early studies of the relationship between union leaders and members of the UAW and the International Typographical Union, respectively, and the implications of these relationships for political action. Both studies point out that union members are not monolithic politically.

David Sousa (1993) provides a comprehensive analysis of the effect of union membership on voting behavior and turnout from 1960 to 1988.

Asher et al. (2001) analyze the strategies used by union leaders to mobilize their members and how and why members respond. They discuss differences between traditional AFL-CIO unions and public employee and teacher unions. In addition, they document the ways in which unions changed their electoral strategies in the mid-1990s in response to changes both in the labor movement and in response to the Republican Party's electoral successes in 1994.

Campaign Finance. Sorauf (1992) and Sabato (1984) credit the predecessors of the AFL-CIO's COPE with developing the PAC as the major mechanism by which interest groups could provide political education to their members and simultaneously raise contributions to give to endorsed candidates. Gopoian (1984) and Grier and Munger (1993) examine the characteristics of candidates to whom labor PACs contribute. Delaney, Fiorito, and Masters (1988) analyze the characteristics of unions that explain the amount of their PAC contributions and expenditures on lobbying. Wilcox (1994) and Baer and Bailey (1994) examine the decision-making processes of COPE and the NEA's Educator's PAC as well as changes in their allocation decisions over time. Thomas Rudolph (1999) analyzes the effect of the Republican's takeover of majority status in Congress on union PAC contributions. All these studies consistently find that unions give overwhelmingly to Democrats and target more money to candidates in competitive races and to challengers than do many other PACs.

Lobbying. Similar to the rest of the lobbying literature, many studies of labor lobbying have focused on the relationship between PAC contributions and the votes of members of Congress. For example, the *Journal of Labor Research* (1999) published a special issue symposium on "Union Money, Political Action, and Government Regulation." Like the findings on the influence of PAC contributions in general (see section 7.4.), those on labor PAC contributions have been inconclusive. Some studies have found that substantial contributions from labor PACs increase the probability that members of Congress will vote the "pro-labor" position (Kau and Rubin 1981; Moore et al. 1995; Pohlmann and Crisci 1982–83; Saltzman 1987), while others have found no relationship (D. Evans 1986; Chappell 1982). Burns, Francia, and Herrnson (2000) expand their analysis beyond PAC contributions to assess whether campaign assistance with fundraising, communications, management, and grassroots mobilization affects legislators' votes. They find that all of these activities increase the recipient's prolabor voting and that most types of assistance influence both Democrats and Republicans. Studies of union influence on Congress as well as studies of union influence in the states (Hrebenar and Thomas 1987, 1992, 1993a, 1993b) find that the levels of union organization and membership correspond to union political power. A time-series analysis of the relative influence of the AFL-CIO and individual unions—both traditional and white collar—at the state level can be found in Thomas and Hrebenar (1990, 1996b, 1999a, 1999b, 2003; see also

Hrebenar and Thomas 2003, table A). These studies consistently find that the NEA (together with state chambers of commerce) is one of the two most influential interests across the fifty states.

Studies of union efforts to influence the executive and judicial branches are far fewer than those examining the legislative branch (though the Hrebenar and Thomas assessment in the states include the executive branch). Waltenberg (2002) finds that union decisions to influence policy through Congress, the National Labor Relations Boards (NLRB), and the courts depend on the political control of those institutions and labors' recent successes in each venue. Moe (1985) also finds that labor's success at the NLRB is constrained by influence of the president, Congress, the courts, and the state of the economy. Scholz and Wei (1986) find that labor activism is the strongest influence on the vigor of enforcement of the Occupational Safety and Health Administration (OSHA), trumping the influence of the president, Congress, and state-level players. Studies of unions advocating before the courts have been meager, perhaps because studies of group advocacy before the courts find that unions are no more active than other organizations (L. Epstein 1991; Scheppele and Walker 1991).

Research on Labor Interests in Other Liberal Democracies

There is an extensive literature on the role of labor interests in other liberal democracies. Since the mid-1970s much of this literature has been produced within a neocorporatist analytical framework as in many countries, particularly in continental Europe, labor, together with business and government, has been one of the three major partners in economic policy making. For those not familiar with neocorporatism and the role of labor in it, section 3.4. provides essential background. In addition, the entries in chapter 11 (on individual liberal democracies) and chapter 12 (on nonpluralist, transitional, and developing countries) include many references to labor interest groups and interests in these countries.

Three useful introductory sources to the types of labor organizations in various Western democracies and their role in politics are Richardson (1993a) and Thomas (1993a, 2001a). Together these volumes cover interest groups in twenty countries (including the transitional regimes of Poland and the Czech Republic and Argentina and Mexico in Latin America), identify the major labor organizations, and explain their role in politics. In depth treatments of individual countries include the following works: Australia (Rawson 1986), Germany (Thelen 1991), Italy (Regini and Regalia 1997), Japan (Pemple and Tsunekawa 1979), Mexico (Carr 1991), and Poland (Ost 1990).

Further Research

One weakness of the research on labor interest groups and interests is that much of it is dated. Although this entry has highlighted recent literature, many of the studies cited were conducted in the 1950s and 1960s, when unions organized a larger proportion of workers and represented a more blue-collar, less-educated constituency than today. Future research should address these changes over time and how they relate to the political activities of unions and their members.

More work should be done to document the effects of union political action. It is unclear whether union efforts make a difference in electing endorsed candidates or help to pass favored legislation, both of which are made more difficult to assess when the efforts of allied and opposing organizations are considered. It does appear, however, that unions are more likely to succeed both electorally and legislatively when they form alliances with other key members of the Democratic Party's coalition—especially civil rights and women's organizations, environmentalists, and student activists. Much work has been done on unions' relationships with the party, but little on the dynamics of its relationships with other allied interest groups.

Finally, interest group involvement with executive branch agencies is generally a neglected area of study, and this is also true for the study of labor. Yet, on a daily basis union operations are affected to a greater extent by the NLRB, OSHA, and many state and local executive agencies (particularly since many union members now work in the public sector) than by legislative bodies. Greater attention should be paid to how unions attempt to influence the rule-making and enforcement processes.

8.11. EDUCATION INTEREST GROUPS

Michael C. MacLeod and Frank R. Baumgartner

Because of the decentralization of education policy making in the United States, education interest groups are active at all levels of government. However, while many studies of education policy include the activities, strategies, and impacts of interest groups, few studies focus specifically on education interest groups. Furthermore, there is little systematic empirical research or theoretical work on the role of interest groups in American education policy at the national, state, and local levels. This entry combines work on K–12 education groups and post-secondary interests and lobbies.

Major Works on the National Level

Several major studies on education interest groups at the national level were conducted in the 1970s and 1980s. Based on interview data, Summerfield (1974) and Norman Thomas (1975) explain education policy making as relationships between interest groups, officials in the executive branch, and congressional committees. These authors describe distinct policy communities in elementary, secondary, and higher education.

However, they also point out that major initiatives within each of these policy areas often come from outsiders: the president, candidates for office, academics and think tanks, and executive branch task forces are often the sources of pressure for change. Professional associations are more likely to react to initiatives than to be the source of new proposals.

Several authors have categorized the great variety and diversity of education interest groups at the national level. These categories include: (1) umbrella organizations; (2) institutional associations; (3) teachers' unions; (4) professions, fields, and disciplines; (5) librarians, suppliers, and technologists; (6) religion, race, and gender-based groups; (7) ideology-based lobbies and labor unions; (8) institutions and institutional systems; (9) administrators and boards; and (10) miscellaneous (S. K. Bailey 1975, 9; Cook 1998; Bloland 1985, 14; Lauriston King 1975). Interests representing parents, students, and others not professionally involved in education are not as well organized as the professional interest groups (see Jack Walker 1991).

Two studies that focus specifically on the strategies and resources of education interest groups are Richard Smith (1984) and Baumgartner and Walker (1989). In his study of the debate surrounding the creation of the U.S. Department of Education during the Carter administration, Smith finds that congressional support for education-related legislation can be explained, in part, by the lobbying activities of the National Education Association (NEA), representing teachers, which is the largest education interest group at the national level (see also Ness 2000, 396–98). Based on a large survey of education interest groups in the United States and France, Baumgartner and Walker find that these groups receive substantial financial support from their respective national governments, that government agencies in both countries are more likely to consult the larger and richer interest groups, and that U.S. groups generally avoid the ideological and professional divisions that often characterize similar groups in other countries.

Several authors focus on educational policy making in specific institutions. For example, Brademas (1987) focuses on education policy making in Congress, Maurice Berube (1991) reviews major presidential initiatives in education, and Radin and Hawley (1988) discuss the politics surrounding the development of the U.S. Department of Education. Each of these authors notes that presidential initiatives have a major impact on governmental action in education policy.

Research in the 1990s focused on school reform, mainly the debate over school choice programs. Here the most important contribution is Chubb and Moe's *Politics, Markets, and America's Schools* (1990). Henig (1994) and K. B. Smith and Meier (1995) provide rebuttals to Chubb and Moe's contention that school choice initiatives are the solution for many of the problems facing American education. While the school choice issue has dominated much of the education policy debate since the early 1990s, this research is not primarily oriented toward interest group activities but includes the treatment of groups as a secondary focus.

Major Works Focusing on the State and Local Level

Governmental control of education policy is extremely fragmented at both the state and local levels, and as a consequence, the interest group community is also fragmented. While state education agencies are charged with coordinating the state's public schools, operational authority rests with the thousands of local school boards. In many urban school districts, power is further decentralized among district administrators, school principals, teachers' unions, and parent groups (for a review, see Cibulka, Reed, and Wong 1992). Based on interview data with education officials and education interest groups, Abrams (1993) provides detailed examples of the many political forces involved in education politics in Utah. He concludes that the artificial separation of elementary and secondary education from higher education has created greater fragmentation and increased conflict in this policy area. Education policy making is fragmented, not only by geography and levels of government, but also by grade level and substantive topic. This fragmentation may be a partial explanation for the relative dearth of systematic research into education interest group activity—both K–12 and higher education—at the state level.

Scholars consistently find that large education interest groups, particularly state teachers' associations and especially the NEA, are among the most powerful interest groups in each state (Hrebenar and Thomas 1987, 1992, 1993a, 1993b, 2003; Thomas and Hrebenar 1990, 1996b, 1999a, 2003; Rosenthal 1993). These authors note that among education interest groups, professional, labor, and administrative associations are dominant. They are very influential in state and local politics because of their expertise; their large, geographically dispersed and articulate memberships; and their financial resources (often wielded during political campaigns). For example, the New Jersey Education Association has developed a grass-roots campaign support system that provides funds to committees of educators in the state who campaign on behalf of endorsed candidates (Rosenthal 1993, 144).

Another important area of interest group activity in the education sector is the ongoing battle between Christian fundamentalist groups and more liberal groups over school prayer and textbook choices in public schools. Provenzo (1990) provides a good review of the strategies employed by Christian fundamentalist groups to promote their agenda and his bibliography is a good reference source to other works in the area.

8.12. SELECTED ASPECTS OF THE GOVERNMENT LOBBY IN THE UNITED STATES

8.12.1. U.S. States Lobbying in Washington, D.C.

Dennis O. Grady

Scholarly attention to the role of the U.S. states in national policy making has largely been subsumed within the literature on intergovernmental relations (e.g., Deil Wright 1988, especially chapter 1; Nice and Fredericksen 1995, especially chapter 2). However, there is a small amount of work specifically examining state activity from an interest group perspective. Most of this work can be organized around three themes: state governments as a collective interest, institutional/administrative arrangements facilitating individual state lobbying activity, and the role of the governor as a state interest representative.

Three books have focused on state governments as a collective interest group and provide a rich history of the evolution of state efforts to assert themselves as players in intergovernmental policy debates. The first is Brooks (1961), which reviews the history of the development of the National Governors' Conference (NGC—since renamed the National Governors' Association). Although now quite dated, it includes useful case studies of the NGC's involvement in policy debates during the 1940s and 1950s. The second book and the most cited work is Haider (1974). While dealing with the role of mayors and county officials as lobbying forces, Haider gives extensive attention to governors and especially the National Governors' Conference involvement during the development of President Johnson's Great Society programs. A noteworthy aspect of the work is its examination of the tensions and competition among states, cities, and counties as their respective organizations (National League of Cities, U.S. Conference of Mayors, National Association of County Officials, and the NCC) attempted to affect national policy debates. The third and most recent work is Arnold and Plant (1994), which examines the history and purpose of dozens of national associations representing both general state and local interests as well as specialist associations (e.g., the Government Finance Officers Associations, the Federation of Tax Administrators). While this book focuses on the internal development and operation of these associations rather than on their impact in national policy debates, there is treatment of lobbying activity. Chapter 6, for example, discusses the separation of the National Governors' Association from the Council of State Governments and the creation of the Hall of the States on Capitol Hill as the nerve center for state lobbying efforts.

Studies on the administrative/institutional structures facilitating state government lobbying are few but informative. The Council of State Government's formerly biennial but since 2002 annual publication, *The Book of the States* (Council of State Governments 2003), has provided a series of chapters over the years on the issues that have prompted the most intense lobbying activity between the states and federal government. Bruce Carroll (1969) provided the first systematic survey data on formal interaction between federal and state officials. As this data was collected in the early 1960s, it precedes the explosion of intergovernmental lobbying contacts spawned during President Johnson's Great Society era. But the data provides a historical benchmark. Writing at the height of the federal grant explosion, Deil Wright (1972) outlines the difficulties governors experienced in attempting to deal with the cascade of grants and cross-cutting requirements overwhelming the administrative capacity of most states. In the same volume as Wright's piece, Williams (1972, 3) coined the term "federal-system-officer" to describe the institutional role of the states' chief executives in this era of creative federalism. Another insightful piece focusing specifically on the institutional dimension of state-federal lobbying is Pelissero and England (1987). This descriptive work examines the activities undertaken by individual state lobbyists in their attempts to influence federal policy makers, who they typically lobby, and the relative effectiveness of these efforts.

Like the other aspects of this topic, the literature on the role of the governor as a state lobbyist is also sparse. A chapter by Beyle and Muchmore (1983) examines both the institutional aspects of this gubernatorial responsibility and the attitudes of governors to this role during the transitional decade of the 1970s. Extending this work through the 1980s are two articles by Grady (1984, 1987). The first goes beyond description by including control variables such as party affiliation and the term of service to determine whether predictable patterns are identifiable in this role of governors. The second article posits that certain personal attributes of a governor and institutional features of the office help explain why some governors are more active than others as intergovernmental lobbyists.

8.12.2. U.S. State Agencies as a Lobbying Force

Dennis O. Grady

The vast majority of literature examining the involvement of state agencies in policy development views the agency as an inside or institutional player rather than as a lobbying force (e.g., Abney and Lauth 1986; Brudney and Hebert 1987; Elling 1999). There are, however, a few pieces of work exploring the role of state agencies as a lobbying entity. The most extensive is a conference paper by Thomas and Hrebenar (1992b) that explores the general role of state agencies as a lobby in state politics.

The only published journal length article on the topic is by Abney (1988). Relying on in-depth interviews with officials in 13 Georgia state agencies and survey data from 92 members of the Georgia legislature, he tests 10 propositions regarding the differences between private sector lobbyists and public agency lobbyists. For example, he finds that public lobbyists (i.e., legislative liaisons) have easier access to decision makers and possess more institutional legitimacy, but are more restricted in the range of issues on which they may lobby.

The only other major publications on the topic are four editions of a chapter by Thomas and Hrebenar (1990, 1996b, 1999a, 2003) that include state agencies in an in-depth, fifty-state study of interest group influence. Thomas and Hrebenar find that state agency legislative liaisons are mentioned frequently as continually active players across the states. In examining their reputed influence, state agencies have been ranked within the top 25 interests in state government on each of the four occasions that Thomas and Hrebenar have assessed state interest group power (see also Hrebenar and Thomas 2003, table A). In setting out a classification scheme of different types of state level lobbyists, one of the five categories identified in these studies is devoted to government lobbyists and legislative liaisons indicating how distinctive this form of lobbying is perceived to be by interest group scholars (Thomas and Hrebenar 2003, table 4.3).

State agency legislative liaisons can influence legislation as representatives of their executive department or agency. Their influence is often considerable within fairly narrow debates on substantive policy making. They enjoy institutional access, possess expertise available in few other places, and are considered legitimate actors in policy development by legislators. A major distinction between these lobbyists and those employed in the private sector is their inability to reward a sympathetic legislator with a campaign contribution or other tangible benefits. See sections 7.6., 7.7., and 7.8.

8.12.3. The Local Government Lobby in the United States

Virginia Gray and Wy Spano

In this entry the *local government lobby* means lobbying by, not of, local governments. Two sets of literature exist on the subject. The first, and by far the most extensive, examines local and state governments lobbying in Washington, D.C. A good bibliography on this subject can be found in Beverly Cigler (1995). A smaller body of work exists on the subject of local governments lobbying at the state level. Here a paper by Thomas and Hrebenar (1992b) provides the best discussion and bibliography to date.

The Local Government Lobby in Washington, D.C.

The tone and focus of much of the writing about local and state government lobbying in Washington can be traced to *When Governments Come to Washington* (Haider 1974). This book begins with a historical account of the seven major subnational governmental associations, then traces their activities through the early 1970s. Another book from the period by Hale and Palley (1981) describes the astonishing changes that grant chasing and acquiring wrought inside state and local governments; Washington used local units of government to change behaviors in the hinterlands.

Ironically, Republican Richard Nixon fueled the tremendous growth in subnational governmental associations, especially the "big seven," by funneling technical assistance and contract management through them. Nixon had made state and local government interest groups (SLIGS) part of a "cozy subsystem" (see section 7.16.). The election of Ronald Reagan changed the direction of local government lobbying at the federal level as Reagan defunded the programs and the SLIGS (Levine and Thurber 1986).

More recent literature about subnational lobbying at the federal level shows that SLIGS are no longer part of a cozy subsystem; they still advocate their positions but now provide more member services. Menzel (1990) notes that, after Reagan, SLIGS had to find different services to provide; information is one of those services. Berch analyzed grants to the states from 1985 to 1987 and regressed the rate of change against certain lobbying practices to see if the demand (lobbying) side could better explain change than the supply side, for example, seniority of the state's members. The conclusion was that "lobbying works" (Berch 1992, 375). Arnold and Plant (1994, 134–35) bring up to date the history of major "public official associations" in the United States. They stress a new era of cooperation between the "big seven" lobbying organizations that replaced the competition and disagreements among them during the Reagan years.

Local Governments Lobbying in the States

Local government lobbying at the state level is a topic in many of the state-by-state analyses organized by Thomas and Hrebenar. Prior to their surveys, state-level works about lobbying typically ignored government as a category, in part because government employees usually are not required to register as lobbyists. Thus, quantification of the practice was difficult. "General local government organizations" ranked eighth in Thomas and Hrebenar's list of "most effective interests" at the state level, compiled from the 2002 update of their regional studies; individual cities and towns, a separate category, ranked thirty-first (Thomas and Hrebenar 2003, table 4.3). Both interests have been ranked similarly over the past twenty years; though individual cities and towns have lost some power over the years (Hrebenar and Thomas 2003, table A). The authors (Thomas and Hrebenar 1992b) persuasively argue that local governments should not be ignored in studying interest groups since they are a large and powerful force in state capitals.

Despite their importance, however, Beverly Cigler estimated the prospects of financial success for local governments lobbying at the state level to be limited. She saw it as unlikely that states would be able, in the 1990s and the early 2000s, to increase aid to local governments (B. Cigler 1993, 183). Cigler also reported that some observers believed the clout of intergovernmental lobbies waned in the 1980s (B. Cigler 1995).

One of the few surveys of state-level lobbying by cities was conducted by De Soto in 1994. He found that 98 percent of the respondent cities of over 60,000 in population joined a municipal league and 52 percent had hired additional contract or in-house lobbyists. For cities with a population greater than 100,000, the number with additional lobbyists rose to 72 percent (De Soto 1995b, 192). Local officials were asked how they were regarded in the capitol: interestingly, they responded that the "special interest" label was used to describe them more often than the label of "valued governmental partner."

Most scholars agree that state-local relations will become more important in the future. Hanson (1998, 14) predicts:

> As the national government reduces its role in domestic politics, state governments will become the focal point of citizens' demands for public goods and services . . . any increase in the power of states necessarily means a larger role for local governments, too.

Consequently, we can expect more local government lobbying of state officials which will offer research opportunities for scholars interested in the role of local government as a lobbying force.

8.13. NONMEMBERSHIP LOBBIES

8.13.1. Private Foundations

Anthony J. Nownes

Interest group scholars are interested in private foundations for two reasons. First, some private foundations are themselves interest groups. Second, some private foundations provide financial support for interest groups.

A private foundation can be defined as:

> A nongovernmental, nonprofit organization having a principal fund of its own, managed by its own trustees and directors, and established to maintain or aid charitable, educational, religious, or other activities serving the public good, primarily by making grants to other nonprofit organizations. (Read 1986, 12)

Foundations are classed as operating or nonoperating. Operating foundations are, in essence, interest groups that lobby, while nonoperating foundations grant money to other groups but generally do not lobby. All foundations are tax-exempt organizations, which means that donors are given tax deductions and that foundation income is not taxed at the corporate rate. Therefore, to understand the role of foundations in interest group politics, we need to understand something about the U.S. Internal Revenue Code (IRC). The most important part of the IRC here is Section

501(c), covering tax-exempt organizations. There are many types of 501(c) organizations of which 501(c)(3) organizations are most important. These are allowed to lobby extensively (though there are limits, see Shaiko 1991), which makes them interest groups. In fact, most public interest groups, and virtually all charitable organizations and think tanks are 501(c)(3) operating foundations.

There are four major types of foundations, two of which are nonoperating and two operating entities: (1) private, nonoperating foundations (those set up mainly to distribute funds) established with capital donated by a wealthy individual or group of individuals, existing to make grants to nonprofit organizations; (2) nonoperating foundation attached to a corporation: (3) community foundations that generally support only grassroots groups in their community; and (4) operating foundations conducting research, social welfare, or charitable programs that seldom make grants (Kurzig 1981; Read 1986).

The IRC states that 501(c)(3) operating foundations are eligible to receive financial support from nonoperating foundations. Studies have shown that large numbers of politically active 501(c)(3) public interest groups, think tanks, and charities receive financial support from nonoperating foundations. For example, Jeffrey Berry's (1977) study of 83 nationally active public interest groups found that a third depended primarily on outside sources of support such as foundations. In a more extensive study Jack Walker (1983) found that interest groups of all kinds depend heavily upon foundations for "seed money" and continuing operating revenue (see also Haines 1984; Jenkins and Perrow 1977; Jenkins 1985; Zald and McCarthy 1980, 1986).

Not all public interest groups opt for 501(c)(3) tax status. Some opt for 501(c)(4) status. A group with 501(c)(4) status must forgo tax deductible contributions and grants from nonoperating foundations, but is allowed to lobby more extensively than a 501(c)(3) group. In recent years, many public interest groups have opted to have 501(c)(4) organizations and affiliated 501(c)(3) organizations. This type of "piggybacking" allows a group to remain eligible for foundation grants and tax deductible contributions, while avoiding lobbying limits (Shaiko 1991).

The best source of information on foundations and their activities is the Foundation Center, which focuses almost exclusively on nonoperating grant-making foundations. The Center, founded in 1956, is a nonprofit clearinghouse for grant-seeking information. It publishes a variety of useful indices, directories, and guidebooks, including the annual *Foundation Grants Index*, *The Foundation Directory*, *The National Data Book*, *Foundation Grants Quarterly*, *Source Book Profiles*, and *Corporate Foundation Profiles*. The Center maintains libraries in Washington, D.C., New York City, Cleveland, and San Francisco and has depositories all over the United States.

Other useful sources include those published by the Taft Group of Washington, D.C., such as *Corporate Giving Watch* and *Foundation Giving Watch*, both of which are periodic publications that provide tips for grantseekers, as well as selected grant listings. In addition, the *Taft Corporate Giving Directory* includes detailed information on over 500 of the largest corporate giving programs in the United States.

8.13.2. Think Tanks

Michael G. Bath

One type of nonmembership institution that often acts as an interest group is the public policy research institute, commonly known as the "think tank." While a number of studies on think tanks have been conducted, many are case studies and organizational histories, which makes generalizing about their activities difficult. In addition, there is no agreed upon definition of think tank, and certain topics of inquiry (such as think tank influence over the making of policy) are not easily operationalized. Thus, the study of these organizations from an analytical perspective and particularly their role as institutional interests in politics is still in its infancy. The main works on think tanks can be found in a bibliography in Diane Stone (1996, 301–24), which includes work on think tanks from both the British and American literatures.

Two early works are Dickson (1971) and Orlans (1972), which were descriptive studies setting out the organizational features of think tanks. Many of the ensuing works were case studies of particular research organizations. Notable examples include Schulzinger's (1984) study of the Council on Foreign Relations; Critchlow's (1985) and James Allen Smith's (1991a) work on the Brookings Institution; and Carol Weiss's (1991) edited volume, which includes an examination of several research institutes.

As the number of think tanks expanded in the 1970s and 1980s, the increasing number of studies seeking to explain how these organizations fit into the American political system has led some observers to speak of the "rediscovery" of think tanks (D. Stone 1991, 199). Polsby's (1983) piece, for example, after making a distinction between "true" think tanks and the more common public policy research institutes, attributes their success in the United States to the permeability and flexibility that characterize American government. James Allen Smith (1991b) concentrated on the role played by think tanks as research brokers. One of his conclusions is that think tanks refine academic research and render it intelligible to policy makers. Perhaps the most ambitious study of this type is Ricci (1993). He argues that think tanks rarely live up to the ideal of objectivity, as think tank personnel and policy makers use research to affirm previously held beliefs and values.

The perspective from which scholars have viewed the role of think tanks in the representative process has varied (Rich and Weaver 1998). Some scholars take a pluralist approach (Polsby 1983). Others are more guarded, yet still refer to the competitiveness inherent in the think tank business (McGann 1995; Ricci 1993; J. A. Smith 1991a, 1991b; D. Stone 1996, 1991; Weiss 1991). Running counter to these studies is a small body of literature that sees think tanks as participants in a process that represents class (Domhoff 1978) and elite-based interests (Dye 1990; Peschek 1987).

A small but increasing part of the literature on think tanks is comparative. Compared to think tanks in the United States, Diane Stone (1991) found research organizations in the parliamentary systems of Great Britain and Australia to be fewer in number and lacking in resources. However, recent changes in the British political environment in particular have resulted in increased access for think tank entrepreneurs (D. Stone 1996, 44). Think tank growth is a global phenomenon, and some effort has been made to explore the parameters of think tank influence within particular countries and internationally (Higgott and Stone 1994). Denham and Garnett (1995), however, raise a note of caution by questioning the assumption that conceptual definitions in their present form regarding think tanks and their goals can be used to bridge diverse political environments.

8.14. INTEREST GROUPS AND U.S. FOREIGN POLICY

Kevin Snider

In the body of literature on interest groups and U.S. foreign policy there is continuing dispute about three major questions: (1) whether interest groups have any influence on foreign policy, (2) whether it is better to lobby Congress or the executive branch, and (3) what exactly constitutes influence. The complex question of influence is beyond the scope of this short entry (see section 7.17.). However, we can make some observations on the first two questions, which will also provide a grounding in the literature on interest groups in U.S. foreign policy making.

Over forty years ago, Bernard Cohen (1959, 2) noted that knowledge of interest groups and foreign policy was based on "a legend of pressure group potency in foreign policy [that] appears to be accepted and passed on without evidence to new generations of students and researchers." Milbrath (1967), besides arguing that group efforts to influence foreign policy should be directed at the executive and contending that interest groups often serve as a communication tool for public officials, sees them as having little direct influence. Bauer, Pool, and Dexter's (1963) work on U.S. trade policy is the classic case study of this minimal influence thesis. Spanier and Uslaner (1982) explore the limits on interest group influence on foreign policy by explaining its formulation as occurring within a series of circles. The president is in the center, bureaucrats and advisors are in the second ring, and interest groups and parties are in a third outer circle. Interest groups have little impact on foreign policy because, in times of crisis, decisions have to be made quickly with little time for input from those outside the inner circles (see also Rourke 1972; Kumar and Grossman 1986; Orman 1988). The end of the Cold War has tempered this minimal influence thesis somewhat; but it is still prevalent among some scholars (see Uslaner 1995).

The increase in lobbying by ethnic groups on foreign policy has been reflected in increased scholarship and also offers insights into the debate on the influence or lack thereof of interest groups in foreign policy. Most of these studies are on one ethnic group, such as Jewish lobbying groups and their success in influencing policy toward Israel. As with the studies of other ethnic groups, the literature on Jewish groups is divided as to the extent of success of lobbying efforts. Those who argue Jewish lobbying is successful usually focus on Congress (Curtiss 1990; Trice 1976, 1977) and have found that ethnic groups are much more likely to succeed on issues, usually economic, which Congress can control (Bard 1988). Other scholars argue that the Jewish lobby is not successful (Organski 1990). A debate continues over the definition and measurement of influence as well as lack of power over the executive branch (see section 7.17.).

The lobbying role of other ethnic groups has also received some attention. Overview sources include Garrett (1978), Halley (1985), and DeConde (1992). Two edited texts provide lobbying case studies on a variety of American ethnic groups (Ahrari 1987; Said 1981). More recently, scholars of ethnic participation in foreign policy have begun to examine interest groups and the executive branch. Shain (1994–95) explores how the link between the ethnic homeland and U.S. politics is affected by the circumstance of the issue. Jonathan Smith (1998) examines the impact that presidential style and disposition to ethnic groups has on success in politics.

Turning to the body of literature claiming that interest groups are influential in foreign policy, Ogene's (1984) case studies of U.S. policy toward Africa are frequently cited as examples. However, his broad definitions of the terms *influence* and *interest group* raise questions about his conclusions. Perhaps the widest agreement on influence relates to that of business and particularly multinational corporations. Several studies argue that corporations have a significant impact on the formulation of foreign policy within both the executive branch and Congress (Bayes 1982; Brookstone 1976; Chittick 1970; Ogene 1984). Other studies indicate success in Congress depends on policy areas (G. Adams 1982).

The answers to the debates over whether or not interest groups matter in U.S. foreign policy and whether it is best to lobby Congress or the executive are not simple ones. As in most aspects of interest group studies, several factors come into play: the nature of the group, its past record of successes or failures, the issue, timing, and so on. These numerous variables mean that, in most instances, the reality likely lies somewhere in between. Consequently, it is misleading to frame the questions in terms of groups being either successful or not successful, or that the executive not Congress is the only branch for foreign policy interest groups to lobby or vice versa.

8.15. THE FOREIGN LOBBY IN THE UNITED STATES

Kevin Snider

Foreign lobbies are groups comprised of non-American nationals who participate in the U.S. political process in order to influence domestic elections or policy or both. Despite highly publicized cases of foreign lobbying, such as that by Libya in the late 1970s, by the People's Republic of China (PRC) in the 1990s, and Japan since the 1960s (Kujawa and Bob 1988; Levy 1987), few systematic studies have been conducted on foreign lobbies. However, information can be found in work on foreign direct investment (FDI), journalistic accounts of the impact of foreign money, case studies on the activities of selected groups, studies on ethnic lobbying on foreign policy, and attempts to determine the impact of the contributions of foreign-affiliated political action committees (PACs). In addition, profiles of the lobbying activities of several countries, including the PRC, Taiwan, Mexico, and Turkey, can be found in Ness (2000, 586–618).

Foreign direct investment (FDI) refers to the purchase of U.S. assets by foreign investors. Graham and Krugman (1991) and *The Annals* (1991, no. 516) are excellent resources for understanding FDI and gaining an initial understanding of its political ramifications. Between 1984 and 1988, FDI increased 378 percent, and more than doubled between 1987 and 1997 (Graham and Richardson 1997), producing a public outcry and resulting in several studies most notably those examining the spending patterns of foreign-affiliated PACs, or FAPACs (Rehbein 1995; N. Mitchell 1995; Snider 1994). These studies indicated that FAPAC activity varies by industry and by pending legislation and that countries whose cultures are similar to the United States were more likely to participate in the U.S. political process. A methodological problem regarding the political influence of FAPAC is that of distinguishing between what is foreign money and what is money contributed by U.S. domestic affiliates of foreign businesses and other organizations. Avery (1990) attempts to avoid this ambiguity by examining the characteristics of foreign firms that have established Washington, D.C., offices. However, his major finding that the presence of an office is linked to the home country's U.S. exports adds little to our understanding.

The increase in foreign direct investment also spurred a number of journalistic attempts to examine the role of foreign interests in American politics. During the late 1980s and early 1990s, several books were published with such sensational titles as *Selling Out* (Frantz and Collins 1989), the *New Competitors* (Glickman and Woodward 1989), and *Buying into America* (Tolchin and Tolchin 1989). If one can get past the sensationalist and anecdotal evidence, these examinations do offer some valuable insights into foreign lobbying in the United States, particularly *Buying into America*, which is the most comprehensive and provides cases of influence by foreign lobbies at all levels of American government.

One book in this vein that most directly focuses on foreign lobbying is *Agents of Influence* (Choate 1990). Choate's controversial examination portrays a unified Japanese foreign lobbying effort that takes advantage of a corrupt and ineffective American political process. At the heart of this corruption are foreign agents and American lobbyists hired by foreign nationals to lobby the U.S. political system. Although Choate's evidence is anecdotal, his book stimulated an extensive debate about foreign influence in American politics. For example, Hrebenar and Thomas (1995) examined Choate's work and concluded that, when compared to other countries with similar interests in the United States such as Britain and Canada or Israel, Japan's lobbying effort is commensurate with its interests in and links to the United States.

As to scholarly examinations of the lobbying efforts of a foreign nation, Moon (1988) examines South Korea's efforts to defend itself in U.S. debates on foreign policy. This treatment includes both direct and indirect lobbying: direct lobbying through foreign agents and indirect lobbying through members of the public and ethnic groups associated with South Korea. This case study is an excellent example of how scholars can examine the topic of foreign lobbying.

The influence of ethnic groups is perhaps the most studied area of foreign lobbying in U.S. politics, and many of the major sources are cited elsewhere in this *Guide* (e.g., see sections 8.14., 9.2.; see also 7.17. on the subject of group power). One methodological issue is difficulty in determining when lobbying by U.S. citizens of an ethnic group should be considered domestic politics and when it should be considered an extension of foreign influence on the U.S. political system.

Important questions about foreign lobbying remain unanswered by the existing literature. Which countries are most successful in lobbying efforts and why? Is lobbying by non-U.S. nationals isolated to a few issue areas? If so, which ones? When should foreign lobbying be considered an essential component of an increasingly interconnected world, and when should it be considered detrimental to national sovereignty? What is the effect of foreign lobbying on American democracy? Clearly there is a need for additional research into this area.

Chapter 9

Interests and Interest Groups in the Public Policy Process: (III) The New Interests and Groups

9.1. INTRODUCTION

Clive S. Thomas

Together with chapters 7 and 8, this chapter focuses on interest groups and interests in the public policy-making process. Chapter 7, which includes an introduction to all three chapters and explains how they are integrated (section 7.1.), is concerned with the strategies and tactics that groups use in attempting to influence public policy. Chapter 8 reviews research on the so-called traditional interests—business, labor, agriculture, education, and various governmental interests. This present chapter is concerned with the so-called new interests—those that have come to prominence in the last thirty years. Some entries are useful to consult as background before reading this chapter: section 8.1. explaining problems with the classification of interest groups and interests, section 4.2. outlining the development of interest group systems in general, and section 6.2. covering the development and present composition of the U.S. group universe.

The inclusion or exclusion of new interests and interest groups in this chapter is based on three major criteria. First, the new interests and groups considered are mainly those that have become prominent in U.S. politics at the national, state, and to a lesser extent at the local levels since the 1960s, such as minority, religious, environmental, and antitax groups. However, where material exists, reference is made to these interests in other countries as with the women's lobby (see section 9.4.) and the gun-control lobby (see section 9.17.). Some treatment—though often only a passing reference—on new interests in specific countries can also be found in the entries in chapters 6 and 11 (dealing with the United States and other individual pluralist systems respectively) and chapter 12 (focusing on individual nonpluralist and transitional political systems). Second, because space is limited, the focus is on groups that have been most politically active and visible (though not necessarily influential—see section 7.17.) in the United States and across the Western world and, therefore, are likely of most interest to students and scholars. For this reason, such interests as those representing the arts, the physically and mentally handicapped, and many social issue and ideological groups have not been included. However, in regard to the U.S. political system, many of the new interests not covered in this chapter are profiled in Ness (2000), for example, "Political, Religious and Ideological" (Ness 2000, vol. 2, sec. 10) and "Single Issue Groups" (Ness 2000, vol. 2, sec. 11). Third, new interest groups that have a presence in many countries but generally are considered as international interests, such as Amnesty International and Greenpeace, are considered in chapter 13 on international and transnational lobbying.

9.2. ETHNIC AND RACIAL MINORITY GROUPS

9.2.1. African Americans

Dianne M. Pinderhughes

Because electoral participation for the majority of African Americans is just four decades old, interest representation in conjunction with a mobilized electorate and with elected representatives is still in its early stages. Consequently, political science research on African American interests and the politics and policy issues related to these interests is sparse. Walton, Miller, and McCormick (1991) have noted both the reluctance of political science to approach the study of African Americans and the racially conservative philosophical orientation of the work published. Others have debated the extent to which African American interests are integrated into the American political system. In this vein, Dawson (1995) and Cathy Cohen (1999) explore the impact of class, gender, and sexuality in the activities of black organizations.

Fortunately, research on African American interest groups is not confined to political science and spreads across the disciplines of urban studies (including urban politics), history, sociology, and legal history and intersects with studies of civil rights groups. Scholars in these fields have tended to concentrate on protest-oriented civil rights organizations, social movements, and single organizations. The social movement literature includes debate about the origins of social protest and the importance and types of resources used for social mobilization. Another major focus of this literature explores the impact of public interest litigation on public policy and its positive consequences for African Americans.

Studies of Civil Rights Organizations and Civil Rights Protest

The National Association for the Advancement of Colored People (NAACP) and the National Urban League are the most frequently studied African American interest groups. Among these studies is a profile of the NAACP in Ness (2000, 578–80), Kluger (1975) on the history of the organization's legal attacks on educational segregation, and McNeil (1983) on the role of Charles Hamilton Houston in the founding of the NAACP Legal Defense Fund. On social movements and the protest activities of civil rights organizations, Ness (2000, 569–71) also provides a profile of the Congress of Racial Equality (CORE); Meier and Rudwick (1973) wrote a history of CORE; and Morris (1984) and Charles Payne (1995) developed broader conceptual and theoretical explorations of the conditions that supported civil rights protest in the South.

Policy Analyses of African American Interest Groups

These studies include Hamilton and Hamilton (1998), which examines the creation of two racially distinct policy tiers within social welfare policy; Pinderhughes (1995), which considers civil rights interest groups and voting rights policy; and Hine (1989), who studied the black nurses organization and its critical role in shaping a civil rights coalition to attack segregation in the military during World War II. There is much new work in urban politics including an examination by Orr (1999) of the development of social capital in Baltimore's educational policy arena.

James Q. Wilson (1973) analyzes the incentives that affect the behavior of civil rights organizations; Wilbur Rich (1996) and Morris and Williams (1989) consider options for coalition politics of African American interests. Robert G. Smith (1996) argues that African American organizations have forsaken their most important philosophical responsibilities as they have moved from protest to politics and into more institutionalized structures and relations. The debate on the applicability of pluralist theory to the study of African American interest group activity includes Perry and Parent (1995) and McClain and Garcia (1993). The latter includes a bibliography of African American, Latino, and minority groups.

9.2.2. Latinos

Christine Marie Sierra

The term *Latino* refers to those persons in the United States of Mexican, Puerto Rican, Cuban, Central and South American, or Spanish descent. Although the literature on Latinos includes studies on the various national-origin groups, work on the Mexican origin population dominates the literature. However, scholarly work on Latinos is meager in the political science literature on interest groups. Leading anthologies and textbooks on U.S. interest groups do not include Latino organizations and groups as subjects of analysis. Nevertheless, an important corpus of work on Latino interests can be found in other scholarly sources, including interdisciplinary journals, publications in related social science fields, and in works on Latino/Chicano Studies. Yet compared to scholarship on other topics in Latino politics, interest group behavior remains relatively understudied. This dearth of scholarship belies the importance of interest groups to Latino politics overall.

Barrera's overview (1985) of significant Mexican American organizations from the nineteenth century to the late twentieth century serves as an excellent introduction to the multiplicity of groups prominent in Mexican American politics over time. General anthologies and textbooks on Latino politics contain chapters on specific Latino organizations or brief overviews of the Latino interest group universe (F. Garcia 1997; Hero 1992, 71–79).

Predominant in the literature on Latino interest groups are case studies of specific groups, ranging from community-based organizations (Pardo 1998) to prominent national civil rights organizations (O'Connor and Epstein 1988; Marquez 1993). There are also studies focusing on specific policy areas, such as education (San Miguel 1987), immigration (Sierra 1991, 1999), and U.S. foreign policy (Haney and Vanderbush 1999), and the groups active within these policy domains. Less prevalent are works that provide a synthesis or comparative theoretical assessment of a number of Latino groups along specific organizational dimensions (e.g., Barrera 1985; Ortiz 1991).

Much of the literature on Latino interest groups consists of organizational histories that address internal group dynamics, such as goals, membership, ideology, and strategies for mobilization, and analyze stages in group development (that is, origin, maintenance, decline), taking into consideration the impact of the external political environment. Of special note are studies that delve into the politics of the first generation of U.S.-born Mexican Americans, the so-called Mexican American Generation (Allsup 1982; M. Garcia 1989), as well as political mobilization during the Chicano Movement of the 1960s and 1970s (Muñoz 1989; A. Navarro 1995). Organizational activity from these political eras greatly affected the subsequent emergence and development of a number of Latino interest groups.

Recent studies of Latino interest groups make several important observations: (1) an advocacy explosion has fostered the emergence of hundreds of new groups on the local, state, and national levels; (2) Latino groups are more diverse and geographically dispersed, representing the interests of an increasing number of Spanish-origin groups; and (3) through more formalized and sophisticated politics, Latino groups are penetrating previously inaccessible policy arenas.

9.2.3. Native Americans

Franke Wilmer

The Native American role in politics has taken the form of both formal interest groups utilizing the normal political processes—lobbying, fund raising, mobilizing and educating voters, joining in law suits, and so on—and also of social movements (see section 1.2.), which by contrast represent those excluded from, or marginalized by, normal political processes and institutions. While movements engage in some of the same activities as interest groups, their situation compels them to spend more time and resources on extraordinary political action like protests, boycotts, and lawsuits.

Native Americans were excluded from participating in normal mechanisms of politics from the time the United States was founded until well into the twentieth century. Viewed originally as alien, but domestic dependent nations, it was not until 1924 that U.S. citizenship was conferred on Native Americans. For some—certain constituencies of the Iroquois, for instance—exclusion is not regarded negatively, but rather as evidence of their continuing sovereignty. For most, however, exclusion, marginalization, and a long history of U.S. policies overtly directed at eliminating their distinct cultural existence have given rise to political action more characteristic of a movement aimed at restructuring their relationship with the U.S. government. This history is treated in several popular and academic sources. See Deloria (1969, 1985) and Weaver and Means (1996) for firsthand Native American accounts. Academic studies are found in Bahr, Chadwick, and Day (1972), Cornell (1988), Troy Johnson (1994), Nagel (1996), and Paul Smith and Warrior (1996).

The earliest groups—religious groups known as "Friends of the Indians"—that organized to influence U.S. policy regarding Native Americans in the nineteenth century were, not surprisingly, neither comprised of Native Americans nor interested in securing Native American cultural rights. They promoted the assimilation of Native Americans into Euro-American society. Native Americans themselves were preoccupied with physical survival until after World War II. The total Native American population reached its lowest point between 1890 and 1920.

The first major Pan-Indian Native American controlled organization was the National Congress of American Indians (NCAI) founded in 1944. Like the National Indian Youth Council, founded in 1961, the NCAI was a product of youth activism. In 2003 the NCAI represented some 250 tribes. Consciousness raising and political mobilization among American minorities and women in the 1960s and 1970s also spawned an increase in activism throughout Native American communities, both on reservations and in urban areas. This included the establishment of the American Indian Movement (AIM) in 1968 in Minneapolis (Ness 2000, 564–66).

AIM received major media coverage because of its demonstrations and protests. Since then there has been a mushrooming of organizations engaged in rights advocacy, legal defense, political action pertaining to environmental and energy issues, and a variety of policy concerns including repatriation of sacred and funeral objects, cultural and language revival, economic enterprise (including gaming), education, substance abuse, and mental health conditions in reservation and urban Native American communities. Although somewhat outdated, a good source on these groups is LaPotin (1987); see also Wells (1994) for a bibliography on Native Americans as a political force. These works can be supplemented by using the Internet where lists of organizations, Web sites, and chat groups on Native American politics and activism can be found.

Currently, Native American politics is somewhere between a highly engaged resistance movement and a set of normalized interest groups. Accounts of Native American political action during the 1960s and 1970s tended toward a sociological orientation, viewing Indian activism as a case of civil and minority rights. More recently published work has centered less on the phenomenon of Native American activism and more on the nature, content, and rationale for activism and advocacy (see Niezen 1997; Wilkins 1997; Troy Johnson 1999). Research on the systematic analysis of the mobilization and outcomes of Native American activist organizations has not yet been undertaken and would certainly be a fruitful area of study.

9.2.4. Asian Americans

Pei-te Lien

Excluded from the electoral process during most of their history in the United States, Asian Americans have relied heavily on interest groups to fight discriminatory legislation and judicial rulings, political party and labor union hostility, and other forms of racism (Parrillo 1982; S. Chan 1991). Despite this important role, research on Asian American interest groups is scanty. This is due partly to the small size of the population relative to the nation (3 percent in 2000) and the heterogeneity of Asian American subgroups; partly to the variety of existing organizations and the emergence of new ones, whose politics are often complicated by homeland political issues; and also to problems of defining the Asian American community and identifying its interests (Espiritu 1992).

To capture the range of Asian American interest group activities, one has to look beyond political science to other social sciences and to historical and ethnic studies. An excellent place to begin is Sucheng Chan (1991, chap. 4 and 5) and relevant sections in Nakanishi (1986, 1998). In addition, there are several specific categories of research. One focuses on traditional organizations in specific ethnic communities such as the Chinese Consolidated Benevolent Associations (Wong 1982; Kwong 1987), the Japanese Association (Ichioka 1988), and the Korean Association of

Southern California (Kim 1977). Although these organizations were instrumental in helping early immigrants adapt to America, they were also instrumental in perpetuating the old social order through coercive rule, corruption, and influence from the various homelands.

Following the civil rights movement and anti–Vietnam War protests, these traditional organizations were challenged by new leftist organizations. In the late 1960s and early 1970s, many native-born students and professionals of Chinese, Japanese, and Filipino origin adopted nonviolent direct action tactics to advocate for racial equality, workers' rights, and Pan-Asian community empowerment (Wei 1993). Although in the 1980s many members of these groups moved to focus on electoral politics, some remained committed to advocating for the disadvantaged members of their community (Omatsu 1994).

The largest number of Asian American political groups today are those related to elections and single issues. Typical of these are the Chinese American Democratic Club in San Francisco, the Korean American Coalition in Los Angeles, and the West San Gabriel Valley Asian Pacific Democratic Club (Saito and Horton 1994). There are also political action committees (PACs) for each of the major ethnic groups as well as for the Pan-Asian group (Erie and Brackman 1993). At the national level, major advocacy groups such as the National Asian Pacific American Legal Consortium, the Japanese American Citizens League, and the Organization of Chinese Americans often lobby Congress and the executive to address Pan-Asian concerns over immigration, civil rights, education, and employment opportunities.

Few studies address the question of the effectiveness of Asian American groups in influencing public policy. One exception is a study of the Japanese American redress and reparation movement and the role of community organizations and other parties in the passage of the Civil Liberties Act of 1988 (Hatamiya 1993). However, a more important concern than political effectiveness for groups in an expanding multiethnic community such as Asian America is the question: How are they able to fulfill the dual roles of community building and political and economic incorporation? In an excellent account of the formation of panethnicity, Espiritu (1992) affirms the possibility of such integration by describing situations when intracommunity division and strife can be overcome and Pan-Asian group consciousness forged through concerted cross-ethnic efforts to secure racial justice and more extensive social services.

9.3. INDIGENOUS PEOPLES' INTEREST GROUPS

Franke Wilmer

The term *indigenous* has become politically and legally relevant due largely to the international and local activism of aboriginal or native peoples living in postcolonial settler states, primarily the Americas, Australia, and New Zealand. The United Nations' definition of indigenous peoples highlights characteristics used to distinguish them as a global constituency: they are descended from aboriginal or precolonial occupants of the area in which they now reside; they have lost control over their own political destiny as a result of colonization; and they wish to assert political and cultural self-determination, or to evolve in continuity with their own cultures and traditions that differ from those of the settler societies in which they live. Indigenous peoples have asserted political resistance to colonization since its inception. For instance, in the late nineteenth century, indigenous representatives living in the settler states of the British Empire (now the British Commonwealth) took their grievances directly to the British monarch, though they were not granted an audience.

Three sources provide a good starting point. Wilmer (1993) traces indigenous international political activism from its inception to the proliferation of indigenous nongovernmental organizations (NGOs) since the 1970s. A booklet by Akwesasne Notes (1978), written by indigenous activists (though credited only to Akwesasne Notes), gives an excellent background including elaborating the philosophical arguments central to the international claims of indigenous activists. And Burger (1987) is an excellent documentary source for a summary of indigenous activism globally.

An important issue of the international indigenous movement is the cultural survival of indigenous peoples in the face of state policies aimed at the destruction of indigenous culture—albeit in the name of assimilation, modernization, or development. An association founded by eminent anthropologists, Cultural Survival, publishes a journal as well as a variety of reports and studies on the situations threatening the cultural and physical integrity of indigenous peoples worldwide. See, for example, Cultural Survival (1993) and a work by Cultural Survival's founder David Maybury-Lewis (1997), a monograph that provides an overview of the international issues.

Two publications specifically address the activities of indigenous peoples in international forums: van de Fliert (1987), while a little out-of-date, is still the only comprehensive work and the United Nations's (United Nations 1994) report on indigenous activities in the UN. Also, Ewen (1994) edited the testimonies of indigenous representatives at the UN. And the International Independent Commission for Humanitarian Affairs, an NGO, published its investigation of indigenous concerns (Aga Kahn and Talal 1987). Like Burger (1987), it is a poignant account of the contemporary battles between states and state systems and indigenous peoples.

Several authors have written books comparing the political status and activist strategies of indigenous peoples in different state settings. These include: Leger (1994) on Central and South America; Werther (1992) who examines self-determination in Western democracies; Fleras (1992) who compares aboriginal-state (governmental) relations in Canada, the

United States, and New Zealand; and Richard Perry (1996) who provides the most comprehensive and theoretical examination of indigenous peoples and state relations.

Finally, indigenous peoples have been very effective in using the Internet to mobilize, document, and educate others about indigenous concerns. The South and Meso American Indian Institute publishes its journal, archives, and other information on indigenous struggles in *Abya Yala News* online (http://www.nativeweb.org/abyayala). The Fourth World Documentation Project at the Center for World Indigenous Studies in Olympia, Washington, maintains an archive of documents, essays, and studies on indigenous issues (http://www.cwis.org/). The Indigenous Environmental Network (http://www.alphacdc.com/ien/) sponsors annual meetings and works with other indigenous organizations. The International Working Group for Indigenous Affairs (http://www.pip.dknet. dk/~pip1917/) publishes a newsletter and yearly reports on the conditions of indigenous peoples worldwide. And the Indian Law Resource Center (http://www.indianlaw.org/), founded and directed by Native Americans, advocates on behalf of indigenous peoples' rights in national and international legal arenas.

9.4. THE WOMEN'S LOBBY

Anne N. Costain

The many questions scholars have raised about women's interest groups include the following: How are social movements and interest groups linked? Have women's groups been co-opted by the Washington establishment, abandoning a vision of substantive change for merely symbolic change? Do rivalries between groups or policy disagreements within them consume resources that should be directed toward combating hostile groups? And, how much change in policy has resulted from organized lobbying on behalf of women's interests? Regarding bibliographies on women's organizations, some of the best are by Ferree and Martin (1995), Schlozman (1990), and Boles (1991).

Lobbying by women's groups in America dates back before winning the vote in 1920. Elisabeth Clemens (1993, 1997, especially chap. 6) and Kristi Anderson (1996) found that women, excluded as a group from suffrage, employed lobbying as a way to petition government on issues of concern. They pioneered a new style of applying congressional pressure, which combined "political education, public opinion, expert testimony, and the increasingly sophisticated legislative tactics of issue- or constituency-based organizations" (Clemens 1993, 774). These tactics still form the backbone of modern lobbying by numerous interest groups.

Many contemporary women's groups formed as part of the 1960s social movement supporting feminism, such as the National Organization for

Women (NOW), founded in 1966 (Ness 2000, 583–85), while many of the older groups began during or immediately after the women's suffrage movement (Costain 1981, 1992b). The women's lobby is highly diverse. It reflects splits within the broader social movements that energized it and mirrors female occupations in modern society. Groups organized themselves in different ways, some hierarchically, while others pioneered newer feminist styles of organization (C. Mueller 1995). Groups now advocate diverse issues, from controversial ones like abortion and gay rights to more mainstream issues such as equality and government support for child care (Costain 1992a).

These differences among groups reflect, not just historic experience, but a conflict inherent in social movement organizations. Ferree and Martin (1995, 8) have observed that "A movement organization is not a contradiction in terms, but it is, by definition, in tension. It is always a compromise between the ideals by which it judges itself and the realities of its daily practices." Women's groups are trying to balance political success and organizational growth against their commitment to the women's movement.

Scholarly work to the mid-1980s described the women's lobby as an effective, movement-linked cluster of varied and sometimes competing organizations. The literature was divided as to whether the lobby attained more by acting conventionally or behaving more like a social movement. Jo Freeman (1975), in a path-breaking book, raised the central issue of what it means to be a social movement lobby in America. She also critiqued existing academic analysis that separated the study of social movements from that of American politics and public policy. Movements generally were ignored by political scientists until they took shape as a political party or an interest group. This issue was taken up by Costain (1980, 1981) who examined the organizational factors that pushed social movements to lobby, as well as the advantages of scope, diffuseness, and ties to a mobilized constituency. Gelb and Palley (1982, 1987) examined the structure of lobbying by women as a movement-linked interest. They suggested that women achieve most as lobbyists when they ask for incremental change and avoid unconventional tactics.

A watershed year for the women's lobby was 1982 when the Equal Rights Amendment (ERA) failed ratification by the states. The fact that constitutionally guaranteed equality was no longer politically viable affected women's groups in two ways. First, antifeminist, conservative women's groups became empowered by their success in helping defeat the ERA. Second, liberal women's groups had to turn to issues that were less consensual than ERA for subsequent lobbying efforts (see Costain 1980, 1992a).

As a result, scholarship on the women's lobby took several new directions. There was renewed focus on links between feminist and antifeminist groups and the social movement to which each was tied. There was an overwhelming consensus that despite growing Republican strength, the women's lobby remained effective in preserving earlier legislative gains (Gelb and Palley 1987; Costain 1992a). Some of this scholarship emphasized the professionalism and institutionalization of the women's lobby as explanations for its success (Gelb 1995; Spalter-Roth and Schreiber 1995; Schlozman 1990). Others argued that the opening of the gender gap in voting and the partisan "gendering" of many political issues forced more attention to women's concerns (C. Mueller 1988; Costain 1992a). There is also work arguing that the most important political gains of the women's movement are embodied in grassroots activism, not national politics (Boles 1991; M. Katzenstein 1990, 1995; Woliver 1993).

The Clinton presidency provided new challenges to the women's lobby. Clinton's re-election in 1996 was the first time in U.S. history when the women's vote was crucial in electing the president. The alliance between Clinton, women, and the Democratic Party sustained the popularity of his presidency. Until the airing of the sex scandal that nearly cost Clinton his job, organized lobbying seemed both less central and less crucial to women's interests than at any time since suffrage. Given the Republican victories in the elections of 2000 and 2002, an unanswered question is whether the Republican Party will begin to seriously compete for women's support.

Representation of women's interests raises challenging questions about the nexus between social movements and interest groups. Scholars do not yet completely understand whether social movements enhance, diminish, or simply pose tactical and strategic challenges for interests linked to them (Costain and McFarland 1998).

For an overview of the activities of women's groups in international and transitional politics, see section 13.7.

9.5. PUBLIC INTEREST GROUPS

Andrew S. McFarland

Public interest group is a term widely used since the late 1960s to refer to interest groups representing environmentalist, consumer, and good government causes. Predecessors to these types of groups certainly existed, such as the Sierra Club, which was active in California as early as 1910, but 1966–71 were boom years in the formation of new groups for environmental, consumer, and government reform causes, while existing groups expanded and refocused their platforms (J. Walker 1991; J. Berry 1977). A term was needed to refer to this political phenomenon, and it became known as the presence of *public interest* lobbies. This term, however, is both ambiguous and controversial. Opponents of environmental, consumer, and government reform groups deny that they represent the public interest. Conversely, virtually all lobbies argue that they represent some public interest, no matter how seemingly oriented toward special interest their proposals might be.

The public interest label acquired some substance with the publication of Mancur Olson's *The Logic of Collective Action* (1965), which emphasized the difficulties of organizing widely shared but diffused interests. Following Olson, one might argue that a category of groups exists in which members do not lobby for policies selectively benefiting group members themselves, but which benefit some larger public as a whole (J. Berry 1989).

But there exists neither a professional referee nor a language court to deal with problems resulting from definitions such as Berry's. First, for instance, both pro-choice and pro-life groups are not lobbying to selectively benefit themselves but for a larger public; yet they are on directly opposing sides of the same issue (Yarnold 1995). Members of a group to feed the hungry are not seeking to benefit themselves, but the public that they seek to benefit is rather small (Meyer and Imig 1993). So should this group be called a "poverty group" but not a "public interest" group? Some might be reluctant to use *public interest* to refer to *conservative public interest groups,* such as the Rocky Mountain Legal Foundation, largely financed by conservative wealth, which seeks to defend the legal rights of property owners against land-use, endangered species, wetlands, and other environmental regulations (O'Connor and McFall 1992). But realizing that the term is ambiguous, it is nevertheless used widely. See section 8.1. for a more complete discussion of the problems of categorizing interest groups.

McFarland (1976) provides a short introduction to public interest groups. Rothenberg (1992) is an excellent study of why individuals join and continue to participate in these groups. Other useful introductory sources are chapters in readers (McFarland 1983; Shaiko 1991; A. Cigler and Nownes 1995) and profiles of various public interest groups in Ness (2000, vol. 2); but there is no scholarly bibliography of public interest groups.

The definitive work on American public interest groups is Jeffrey Berry (1977). This book contains a great deal of information about organizational structure, finances, membership, and lobbying strategy and tactics. It is based on extensive interviews of personnel at 83 Washington-based public interest lobbies during 1972 and 1973. There was little need for another general scholarly book on this topic for fifteen years, but now another such study is needed.

Both McFarland and Berry argued that public interest groups had the positive function of representing those diffused and widely shared interests that, according to Mancur Olson's collective action theory, are difficult to organize. McFarland also argued that one should avoid reference to the public interest because in a single political situation there might be several different public interests needing organization and representation. The arguments put forth by Berry and McFarland gained widespread acceptance among political scientists who had formerly concentrated on criticizing the idea of the public interest as well as arguing that reformers tended to be culturally biased or politically incompetent (Schubert 1960; J. Wilson 1962; Douglas and Wildavsky 1982).

However, disagreement continues to exist among scholars, such as that between McFarland (1993) and Amy (1987) regarding the need for public interest lobbies to negotiate with their business opponents. And Michael McCann (1986) has perhaps written the most persuasive critique of public interest lobbies. On the one hand, he praises their work as a serious effort to reform society, using conventional strategy and tactics to succeed within established political boundaries. On the other, he argues that, in the long run, such lobbying efforts will not accomplish a lot because public interest lobbyists have not created new forms of public participation, and without mass support society will change very little.

9.6. GOOD GOVERNMENT GROUPS

Andrew S. McFarland

Good government groups are lobbies seeking governmental reform in the tradition of the Progressive Era, 1901–14. Such groups are led and supported by highly educated members of high status professions, in contrast to short-lived groups aiming for reform, which arise in conjunction with populist or conservative social movements (e.g., term limit lobbies). Good government groups have been active at the local government level, particularly in larger cities, since the turn of the twentieth century and even earlier in New York City. However, except for Common Cause, such groups have received little scholarly attention and are mostly mentioned in passing in historical treatments of urban politics. A profile of some good government groups, including Common Cause and the League of Women Voters, can be found in Ness (2000, vol. 2, sec. 9 and 10). However, there is no bibliography of scholarly work on good government groups.

Common Cause is the outstanding example of this type of lobby. Founded in 1970 by former cabinet member John W. Gardner, it was the first large, and continues to be the most important, citizens' lobby for government reform at the national and state levels. Gardner (1973) wrote an early insider account of the organization.

The first major academic treatment was McFarland (1984a) who considers its history during the early years and its organizational structure, membership, platform, and internal political dynamics. The book emphasizes Common Cause's capacity of exercising significant influence on Congress in pursuit of reforms such as public financing of federal elections, stricter controls on lobbying practices, and open meetings laws (sunshine laws) for governmental boards and commissions. This perspective contrasts with the formerly widely held viewpoint that good government lobbies are by nature ineffective because their leadership prefers to take ideological postures rather than focus on the practice of exercising influence (J. Wilson 1960) and because of a lack of commitment to exercising influence in a sustained fashion (Riordan 1963).

Rothenberg's (1992) study of Common Cause focuses on theoretical questions concerning the representative nature of the leadership of citizen interest groups, but it also contains a great deal of information about Common Cause itself and is an excellent supplement and continuation of McFarland's earlier study. Rothenberg's main point is that, in order to understand Common Cause as well as other groups lobbying for noneconomic ideals, one must realize that the group's leadership tends to respond to the opinions of the group's active participants, even though this is probably less than five percent of the total membership. Such groups, therefore, should be analyzed in terms of the relationships among the three strata of leaders, activists, and ordinary members.

The League of Women Voters (LWV) was formed in the 1920s, incorporating a remnant of the woman's suffrage movement, and has devoted itself to the political education of its members and public advocacy of reform, especially government reform. A complete scholarly study does not exist, but significant references may be found in work by Bauer, Pool, and Dexter (1963), McFarland (1976, 1984a), and John Mark Hansen (1985). Ness (2000, 444–46) provides a succinct overview of the LWV.

To view earlier good government groups in context, it is useful to consult works on the Progressive Era (e.g., Wiebe 1967, 183). There are several schools of thought about early twentieth century progressive reformers. Wiebe considers government reform to be another aspect of the drive of a newly forming professional class to modernize institutions. On the other hand, Hofstadter (1955) considers such reformers to be defending a middle-class position against challenge by urban immigrant elements. Samuel P. Hays (1964) considers municipal reformers to be controlled by upper-class wealth; while David Thelen (1972) viewed small-town municipal reformers of the Progressive Era to be expressing a community-wide viewpoint.

9.7. CRIMINAL JUSTICE INTEREST GROUPS

Michael C. MacLeod and Frank R. Baumgartner

Researchers have identified distinct policy communities within criminal justice at the national, state, and local levels based on function. The three primary communities are police and prosecutors, courts, and corrections; with bar associations, prosecuting and defense attorneys, law enforcement officers, corrections officials, and judges the most important criminal justice interest groups (Berk 1977; Berk, Brackman, and Lesser 1977; Stolz 1984). Heinz and Manikas (1992) provide a bibliography of research on criminal justice interest groups, and Fairchild (1981) provides a critique of several studies conducted before 1980.

Interest groups are organized mainly by profession (Berk, Brackman, and Lesser 1977; Berk 1977; Melone and Slagter 1983; Stolz 1984). Heinz and Manikas's (1992) main finding is that while groups contact each other, there is no single coordinating authority in criminal justice policy (see also Jacob 1984). In fact, this policy area is fragmented. The law enforcement community is divided between prosecution and defense groups, including civil liberty lobbies such as the American Civil Liberties Union, the ACLU (Ness 2000, 433–34). In addition, many outside interest groups get involved when criminal justice matters affect their interests, often exacerbating fragmentation and conflict. For example, the Association of American Publishers and the Moral Majority conflict over obscenity provisions in crime legislation. Political conflict also stems from the high public salience of many crime-related issues (John Hagan 1983; Jacob 1984; Scheingold 1984; J. Wilson 1983, 1990).

Several studies of criminal justice agencies illustrate the role of interest groups. These include Lindesmith (1965) who traced the Federal Narcotics Bureau's lobbying efforts to increase its role in determining drug offenses; Gray and Williams (1980); Feeley (1980); and Heinz, Jacob, and Lineberry (1983) who studied the role of groups in the operation and politics of the Law Enforcement Assistance Administration (LEAA), formerly the most important federal agency in criminal justice policy.

Other scholars have studied interest groups involved in criminal justice policy. G. Downs (1976) includes various interest groups as factors affecting state criminal justice policy making. Heinz and Laumann (1982) studied the Chicago Bar Foundation, while R. Nelson and Heinz (1988) assess the influence of Washington, D.C., lawyers on national politics. O'Connor and Epstein (1988) conducted research on the activities of lawyers for the Mexican-American Legal Defense Fund. Barbara Nelson (1984) examines the agenda status of child abuse, and Osha Davidson (1998) provides an account of the National Rifle Association's (NRA) activities in handgun control legislation.

9.8. SOCIAL ISSUE AND IDENTITY INTERESTS

9.8.1. Gay, Lesbian, and Bisexual Interests

Steven H. Haeberle

Gay, lesbian, and bisexual (GLB)—or the catchall "queer" that is gaining popularity—are labels for a diverse group of sexual identities. Many differences exist among those who use one of those labels to describe themselves. This diversity is reflected in the GLB political movement, which defies generalization. However, several works stand out as useful for guiding interest group research on the GLB movement. The bulk of the literature is recent, and some of the conclusions are tentative; and empirical political science has only recently begun to explore the politics of sexual orientation. Much of the foundation for this research was laid by interdisciplinary social theorists who analyzed sexual identity. A central identity issue has been whether sexuality is an essential characteristic consistent across time and cultures or a socially constructed variable dependent on contemporary values. Boswell (1980) defended the essentialist argument. D'Emilio (1983, 1992) supported constructionism.

The roots of the modern GLB movement stem from World War II and the postwar resettlement patterns of those dislocated by defense mobilization (A. Berube 1990). Under those circumstances, many first discovered that others shared their sense of same-sex eroticism. After World War II many homosexuals chose to stay in larger cities instead of returning to small towns and farms. In the early 1950s urban-based seminal organizations coalesced into what was labeled the "homophile" movement (D'Emilio 1983; Marcus 1992).

A watershed event occurred in June 1969. New York police raided the Stonewall Bar intending to arrest its gay customers, but the patrons trapped the police inside the building and the two-day Stonewall Riot ensued. Symbolically, it was the beginning of the Gay Liberation movement. The National Gay and Lesbian Task Force, the oldest gay and lesbian national interest group, was founded in 1973 (Ness 2000, 581–82). Politically, the main target of the GLB movement remained local government and especially urban government. Large cities have been especially receptive to adopting ordinances banning discrimination based on sexual orientation (Button, Rienzo, and Wald 1997). Robert Bailey (1999) has carefully documented the impact of gay and lesbian voters in helping to secure the election of several big city mayors. Hertzog (1996) studied GLB voting patterns in different types of elections. Rayside (1998) and Yeager (1999) examined the dual roles of gay office holders. Serious differences persist within the GLB community, however. Men and women hold different attitudes and like much of the rest of America, racism remains a problem.

GLB issues rarely entered the national policy agenda until about 1990 when "outing" became a controversy. In 1993 "gays in the military" became a controversy (Rimmerman 1996). During the Clinton administration, other GLB issues to gain public attention included: the 1996 Defense of Marriage Act, which would allow states to refuse to accept gay partnerships recognized by the laws of other states; the 1996 Employment Nondiscrimination Act, which would have banned discrimination against homosexuals in the workplace; and Clinton's appointment of openly gay and lesbian individuals to government service. Riggle and Tadlock (1999) offer a thorough account of GLB politics during this period.

The backlash against GLB political successes came largely from conservative Christians. Button, Rienzo, and Wald (1997) conclude that gay and lesbian rights activists have encountered greater opposition in the United States than in other Western democracies because of the strong strain of Evangelical Christianity in America. National opinion polls confirm that Evangelical Christians are among the staunchest adversaries of civil rights for gay men and lesbians. Tolerance toward gay men and lesbians is related to a number of factors with partisanship and ideology among the most important (Riggle and Tadlock 1999).

Nothing has touched the contemporary GLB community as profoundly as HIV/AIDS. Because AIDS first struck marginalized groups, it initially received not a medical interpretation but a social construction that seemed to spin out of control (Rushing 1995). Mass public opinion linked homosexuals to AIDS, and the perception was slow to change (Seltzer 1993). See also section 9.20. for an international perspective on the GLB lobby in the broader context of human rights interest groups.

9.8.2. The Poverty, Welfare, and Hunger Lobby

Jeffrey M. Berry

The irony of the literature on interest groups and poverty is that very little work has been done, but we know a great deal. This is because broader theories of interest groups are relevant to poverty groups, and because the problems facing poverty-related groups are so serious and so enduring that they are easy to discern. The broader literature on interest groups suggests that the poor will be difficult to organize because they lack both the means of overcoming the collective action problem (M. Olson 1965) and the institutional bases to acquire the resources they lack (Salisbury 1984). Political participation is highly correlated with social class, and those with the lowest levels of education and income are less inclined to join groups or engage in other political activities.

Even though the obstacles are great, there have been efforts to organize the poor to press for more economic opportunities and for greater welfare, nutrition, and social service benefits. Most groups, however, such as the National Welfare Rights Organization, have foundered even when they have had energetic and impassioned leadership (Bailis 1974; Kotz and Kotz 1977). Most successes in organizing the poor come from ad hoc local groups that rally around a specific issue and use protest to lobby for some immediate objective. But protest groups fade away quickly, and building effective poor people's lobbies with influence over the long term remains difficult (Browning, Marshall, and Tabb 1984; Woliver 1993).

However, while the poor have not been effectively organized themselves, they have been represented by two other types of interests. First are public interest groups that act on behalf of the poor and hungry (J. Berry 1977; Imig 1995). In the area of nutrition, for example, the Community Nutrition Institute and the Food Research and Action Center have no poor people as members but developed into effective proponents of food stamps and other nutrition programs (J. Berry 1984). These groups exist because they tap sources of support other than the dues of a membership that could never be mobilized. As Jack Walker (1991) found, it is common for interest groups to obtain a significant portion of their resources from patrons. These patrons, such as wealthy individuals, foundations, and corporations, make large gifts and grants to fund causes they care about. The public interest groups working on poverty and nutrition issues would not exist without these patrons.

The second source of proxy representation for the poor comes from organizations with related interests or who have constituencies sympathetic to the poor. Two types of organizations stand out. One is organized labor, which although more interested in issues affecting the working poor than the chronic nonworking poor, has been a staunch advocate of programs for low-income Americans. The other is civil rights groups, which see discrimination as one of the causes of poverty, and they have worked assiduously on behalf of programs providing income support, job training, and educational opportunities. Other interest groups that have worked on behalf of the poor include churches and women's lobbies. Unfortunately, liberal interest groups concerned with the problems of the poor have become less influential with policy makers as amply illustrated by the 1996 welfare reform law. The law abolished Aid to Families with Dependent Children (AFDC) and turned responsibility for welfare over to the states.

Scholars have also examined the policy consequences of the general failure of the poor to organize. Many assume that if the poor were well organized politically, American social policy would be much more supportive of low-income citizens. Conceivably, America would look more like the welfare states of Western Europe. Verba et al. (1993, 311) show that when the poor do participate, their communications to government focus on issues of "basic human needs, such as poverty, jobs, housing, and health." In short, the poor send the right message, but few send messages to those making the policies relevant to their lives.

Thus, there is a need for research on questions concerning the involvement of the poor in the political process. First, the "poor" do not form one homogeneous sector of the population. Too often the poor are equated with the "underclass," but there are many subgroups of poor people and such a stereotype misses the potential for political activism by the poor (J. Berry, Portney, and Thomson 1991). Second, the workplace is important for imparting skills to employees that are transferable to the political arena (Verba et al. 1995). Are there ways through schools, churches, and other institutions that comparable skills may be taught to those whose work tends to be intermittent and whose jobs may nurture little personal growth? Third, is there a way that proxy organizations can effectively mobilize the poor rather than just speaking on their behalf?

9.8.3. Animal Rights Interest Groups

Christopher J. Bosso

There is little work on animal rights groups as distinct organizations. Most of the literature focuses on the more philosophical, ethical, and legal questions that mark the lines of dispute over the issue of animal rights (see, for example, Regan 1983; Hargrove 1992; and Andrew et al. 1998). However, Singer (1985), Jasper (1992), Finsen (1994), and Guither (1998) examine the evolution of the animal rights movement. And there are good annotated bibliographies on the movement by Nordquist (1991) and Manzo (1994).

Groups with an animal rights agenda can be divided into two categories. The first are biocentric or "deep ecology" groups like Earth First! or the Sea Shepherds, for whom animal rights extends logically from their broader environmental values. On these groups see Watson and Rogers (1981), D. Day (1987, 1989), Manes (1990), Scarce (1990), Devall (1992), and Zakin (1993).

The second kind of group is one devoted exclusively to animal rights. These run the gamut from traditional anticruelty groups like the American Society for the Prevention of Cruelty to Animals and the American Anti-Vivisection Society to "radical" groups such as People for the Ethical Treatment of Animals (PETA) (Ness 2000, 539–41). The older groups promote issues such as caring for pets or preserving endangered species but do not necessarily oppose hunting or meat eating. By contrast, PETA promotes vegetarianism as a logical extension of its value system. However, both kinds of groups criticize research on animals, with PETA in particular aggressively attacking animal research as unnecessary and immoral.

Beyond PETA are "fringe" groups with names like the Animal Liberation Front. These groups are usually small and loosely organized cliques of activists, whose tactics, including the "liberation" of research animals from laboratories, have put the issue of animal rights on the public agenda. See, especially, Blum (1994), Newkirk (1992), Luther and Simon (1992), Garner (1997), Guither (1998), and, for a very radical perspective, Marquarat (1993).

9.9. PRO-LIFE AND PRO-CHOICE INTEREST GROUPS

Glen A. Halva-Neubauer

Much of the work on abortion politics has been conducted by sociologists and anthropologists. Thus, little is known about the impact of pro-life and pro-choice groups on policy processes or about long-term effects of electioneering efforts by mainstream pro-life groups. Existing literature on these groups falls into three categories: (1) works discussing the motivations of abortion activists; (2) scholarship analyzing pro-life and pro-choice organizations; and (3) research on abortion interest groups within the context of broader political science questions. A comprehensive reference that was issued annually until 1991 is *Abortion Bibliography*. A profile of three major pro-life/pro-choice national interest groups (the

National Abortion and Reproductive Rights League [NARAL], Planned Parenthood of America, and the National Right to Life Committee) can be found in Ness (2000, vol. 2, sec. 11).

Studies Focusing on Abortion Activists

Kristin Luker (1984) argues that the abortion debate is contentious because activists come from divergent social spheres and hold opposing views rooted in contrasting perspectives on sexuality, gender roles, contraception, and morality. For pro-life activists, legalized abortion symbolizes the degradation of motherhood—the most ennobling role for women. In contrast, pro-choice activists see motherhood as one part of womanhood; therefore, legalized abortion is central to enabling women to make choices about their lives.

While Luker's work remains standard, several studies challenge her findings. After studying the conflict surrounding the opening of a Midwestern abortion clinic, Ginsburg (1989) roots pro-choice and pro-life activism in reactions to a market-based economic system that devalues the nurturing of dependents. In addition to defending motherhood, Cuneo (1989) identified Canadians who were drawn to antiabortion activism by their desire to preserve all life or to revive the Catholic church.

Violence as a tactic in the pro-life movement has been studied by Blanchard and Prewitt (1993) who base their study on the 1984 abortion clinic bombings in Pensacola, Florida. They conclude that social movement activists given to violence tend to be working-class males below age 35 who hold fundamentalist Christian beliefs and who live in relative isolation from the larger community. However, the most comprehensive work to date covering the militant antiabortion movement is Risen and Thomas (1998).

Studies Focusing on Pro-Life and Pro-Choice Organizations

In the most systematic examination of the abortion rights movement, Staggenborg (1991) challenges the conventional wisdom that pro-choice organizations languished after the 1973 U.S. Supreme Court decision in *Roe v. Wade*. Her study shows that the pro-choice movement remained viable after *Roe* by developing formal organizational structures, hiring professional leaders, and employing conventional political strategies. Becoming an insider, however, did not quell the movement's grassroots organizing efforts. Later, Meyer and Staggenborg (1996) examined how the mobilization and countermobilization of pro-life and pro-choice movements shaped governmental abortion policy.

Blanchard's (1994) comprehensive analysis of the pro-life movement contains an excellent description of the diversity of pro-life organizations. He argues that cultural fundamentalism—support for traditional family values—is essential to linking the divergent religious traditions involved in the pro-life movement. Moreover, it is the most significant factor motivating membership in Operation Rescue-like organizations. In addition, Blanchard (1996) is an excellent reference to the antiabortion movement.

Other Studies of Pro-Life and Pro-Choice Groups

General discussions of abortion interest groups appear in Tatalovich and Daynes (1981). The role interest groups play in abortion litigation is analyzed by L. Epstein and Kobylka (1992), O'Connor (1996), Craig and O'Brien (1993), and Garrow (1994). Byrnes and Segers (1992) examine the Catholic church's role in the pro-life movement. Interest group influence of pro-life and pro-choice organizations in the United States has been studied by Segers and Byrnes (1995).

9.10. ENVIRONMENTAL INTEREST GROUPS

Christopher J. Bosso

Scholarship on environmental interest groups mirrors the growth in the movement itself. There was little of it before 1970 since groups such as the Environmental Defense Fund did not exist and older "conservation" groups like the National Audubon Society were not the professionalized environmental lobbying giants of today (but see Lacey 1991). Today, however, the literature is massive. Moreover, environmental groups are perfect for studying the kinds of questions that relate to all public interests. And as environmental values and the groups representing them challenge social, economic, and political orthodoxy (Paehlke 1989; G. Jordan and Maloney 1997), studying them also provides a window into competing value systems.

Start any examination of environmental groups with reference works (Wenner 1990; Paehlke 1995; Ness 2000, 256–90). Then move to studies of the evolution of the environmental movement (S. Hays 1958; Nicholas 1970; Donald Baldwin 1972) and the struggles between environmentalists and their adversaries (Milbrath 1984; S. Hays 1987; Dunlap and Mertig 1992; Shaiko 1999).

Another category of works addresses recent dynamics within the environmental community. There are studies by academics (R. Gottleib 1993; Bosso 1991, 1999; Shaiko 1999) that apply interest group literature and theory to environmental group mobilization, organizational maintenance, agendas, tactics, and resources. There are some works by activists (Borrelli 1988; Snow 1992) that aim to foster change within these organizations. And there are critiques by the hostile (A. Gottlieb 1989), the skeptical (Bramwell 1994), and the disappointed faithful (Brower 1990; Shabecoff 1993; Sale 1993; Dowie 1995).

Next move to group-specific works. The Sierra Club gets a lot of ink, but see Schrepfer (1983), Michael Cohen (1988), Werbach (1997), and certainly Brower (1990). On the Audubon Society see Frank Graham (1990); on the Environmental Defense Fund, Roe (1984) and Rogers (1990); and on the National Wildlife Federation, Allen (1987) and Tober (1989).

Among the "radicals" are groups such as Earth First!, the Sea Shepherds Society, and, to some degree, Greenpeace. For general assessments of the "radical" wing, see D. Day (1987, 1989), Manes (1990), and Scarce (1990). On Earth First! see Zakin (1993) and Martha Lee (1995); on the Sea Shepherds, Watson and Rogers (1981); on Greenpeace, Robert Hunter (1979) and Brown and May (1989).

At the grassroots are groups that tend to mobilize around specific hazards, such as toxic waste. Above all, such grassroots groups try to mobilize citizens not known traditionally as environmentalists, the working class and racial minorities in particular (see Bullard 1990; Freidenberg 1984; Gibbs 1991; Zisk 1992).

For a review of environmental interest group activity in international and transitional politics, see section 13.7.

9.11. CONSUMER GROUPS

Loree G. Bykerk

Although we are all consumers, research focusing on consumer groups is surprisingly scarce. Nadel (1971) documented the rise of the movement, its utility as an issue to a few members of Congress, and its ties to the executive branch. Colorful insider accounts of the Carter years' "golden age" and its demise under powerful business lobbying are found in Pertschuk (1982, 1986). Lucco (1992) details how consumers have been represented on White House staffs from presidents Kennedy to George Bush Sr.

Other early works treating consumer groups from various critical perspectives are Vogel and Nadel (1977) and Creighton (1976). Michael McCann (1986) and Harris and Milkis (1989) include consumer groups among others in analyses of the public interest reform movement. Studies of Ralph Nader abound but tend to be either uncritical, such as that by Bollier (1989), or exclusively critical. Nader himself and many of his allies are also fruitful authors, and their works (Nader 1965, 1973; Nader and Taylor 1986; Nader and Smith 1996; Green 1983) portray the breadth and depth of the consumer movement's critique of business behavior.

An extensive body of more recent research on consumer groups and their influence on public policy through lobbying Congress is Bykerk and Maney (1991, 1995a, 1995b) and Maney and Bykerk (1994). References listed in these publications provide a good initial bibliography on the subject. These works analyze which organizations are active in national policy making on consumer issues, describe their resources such as staff size and budget, and include case studies of specific issues on which they lobby. Organizations range from long-standing generalist groups such as the Consumers Union, the Consumer Federation of America, and Public Citizen to newer, more specialized groups such as Bankcard Holders of America, the National Insurance Consumer Organization, and the Center for Science in the Public Interest.

Organized consumer access to presidential decision makers is more symbolic than influential as Lucco (1992) points out; congressional access is a much more important tool for these organizations. They frequently work in coalitions. Organized labor, particularly the AFL-CIO, and groups representing the elderly, particularly the American Association of Retired Persons (AARP), often ally with consumer groups. Among policy makers, Democrats tend to be more receptive to their demands than Republicans. Data from congressional hearing testimony shows consumer groups to be outnumbered by two or three to one by producer organizations such as trade associations and corporations.

More recent scholarship on consumer groups (M. McCann 1986; Harris and Milkis 1989; Maney and Bykerk 1994) interprets their activity as being of broader significance than did earlier works. Today both more organizations and more issues are included within the scope of consumer politics. This broader interpretation allows the use of consumer issues to test various theories of how private and public influences interact within the U.S. political system. McCann and Harris and Milkis attribute the failure of consumer groups to inherent weaknesses in their beliefs. Bykerk and Maney argue that consumer groups face daunting market biases and thereby challenge pluralist interpretations of U.S. politics.

9.12. HEALTH-CARE INTEREST GROUPS

Jeffery C. Talbert and Frank R. Baumgartner

The health-care interest group system has been transformed since the 1960s by the creation and growth of new specialized health-care groups, by the involvement of many groups from other policy areas, and by the breakdown of an American Medical Association (AMA)-centered consensus that once dominated all of healthcare policy making in America. A useful bibliography highlighting changes in the health-care group system is Mark Peterson (1994). Several health-care groups—including the AMA, the American Nurses Association, and the Blue Cross and Blue Shield Association—are detailed in Ness (2000, 159–208).

The Watershed Years of the 1960s

Before the 1960s the health-care lobby was defined by the actions of the powerful AMA (Garceau 1941; Alford 1975; Campion 1984). Historical treatments describing changes in the health system and the AMA's role in it include Paul Starr (1982), Laham (1993), and Keith Mueller (1993). The AMA continued to influence the focus of the health lobby down to the 1960s, but new types of groups organized as the medical profession expanded. As a consequence, the AMA struggled in vein to retain its position as the dominant voice in health care.

Many of these new groups, such as the American Lung Association and the Muscular Dystrophy Association, focused on fundraising to promote research, awareness, and treatment of specific diseases (Baumgartner and Talbert 1995b). Other interests, such as those representing insurance providers, hospitals, and specialized physicians, became increasingly active, but most worked with the AMA to promote a common goal—opposition to government involvement in health care (M. Peterson 1994; Wilsford 1991). Marmor's (1973) study of the passage of Medicare details how AMA opposition was responsible for derailing national health-care proposals from the 1930s to the 1960s. Studies attribute the early success of the AMA to the closely united group system and the shared goals between physicians, insurers, and health-care facilities. As the group system in health care grew more diverse, however, this unity of action would prove impossible to maintain.

Fragmentation of the Health-Care Lobby

Since the 1960s, health groups have multiplied at a much faster rate than the group system as a whole, the types of groups involved in the health-care lobby have diversified, there are more groups from other policy areas interested in health-care issues than ever before, and the health-care lobby has been transformed from a close-knit iron triangle to a more open issue network (Baumgartner and Talbert 1995a; M. Peterson 1994). Baumgartner and Talbert (1995b, 105) find that health groups have produced particularly strong growth in professionalization, nearly doubling their staff sizes in each decade from 1960 to 1990. By 1990, the largest groups active in Washington, D.C., health-care debates (those with over 100 staff) had a combined staff exceeding 11,000. This does not include many insurance groups, private businesses, and health groups with fewer than 100 staff members. Laumann and Knoke (1987) and Heinz et al. (1993) provide detailed analyses of the diversity of interests represented in the health-care area. And health groups are well financed. During the effort to enact a national health policy in 1993 and 1994, health groups spent $60 million in advertising and lobbying (Steinmo and Watts 1995).

Other influential organizations have recently entered the health-care policy arena, most notably business associations. Sapolsky et al. (1981) found that business groups delayed responding to health-care cost inflation since their health costs were small compared with overall expenses. But, as health costs increased, businesses were forced to become involved in health-care policy to control runaway inflation. Bergthold (1987, 1990) details the strategy of the Business Roundtable and the Washington Business Group on Health, noting their increasing involvement in planning a strategy to contain health expenses. Small business, as represented by the National Federation of Independent Businesses (NFIB), supports any reform that does not include a mandate. Then there are citizen groups, like the American Association of Retired Persons (AARP), that demand better access and higher quality care, including their support in 2003 of adding drug benefits to Medicare.

This increasing diversity reduced policy cohesion and began to fragment the health-care policy community. First, the power of the AMA declined as new physician associations (such as the Group Health Association of America) mobilized in opposition to AMA positions on managed care. Other specialty physician groups (such as the American Society of Internal Medicine) broke from traditional AMA positions and focused on their particular interests rather than on the general viewpoint that was more characteristic of the AMA (M. Peterson 1994).

Medical insurers faced a similar fragmentation, as the one-time position of opposing all government intervention fractured into several divisions. Large insurers such as Blue Cross favored arrangements that benefited their large multistate operations, while small insurers, such as those represented by the Health Insurance Association of America, fought for their survival. Even business associations were plagued with conflict, as internal division prevented business groups from reaching consensus on reform efforts in 1994 (C. Martin 1995).

9.13. RELIGIOUS INTERESTS

Daniel Hofrenning

Gathering data about religious interest groups is difficult. While political scientists have produced major surveys of interest groups in the United States and elsewhere, none of these has developed a separate category for religious interest groups. Usually religious groups are placed within the broader category of public interest groups, which in many ways is an unsatisfactory classification (see sections 8.1. and 9.5. for problems of group classification). Four other factors inhibit the collection of data. First, most religious lobbies do not register officially as lobby groups because they wish to preserve the preferred 501c(3) federal tax status of their organization. Federal law allows these types of tax exempt organizations to do a minor amount of lobbying (see section 8.13.1.). Second, only a handful of religious organizations make financial contributions to candidates and political parties, thus making this source of data of limited value. Third, media coverage of religious organizations is wildly variable. And fourth, the internal records of religious organizations are inconsistent.

Existing literature on religious lobbying focuses either exclusively on the Religious Right or on a broader spectrum of groups. In addition, Weber and Stanley (1984) and Weber and Jones (1994) provide useful descriptions of individual religious interest groups in the United States. A profile of some major national religious interests groups, including the Christian Coalition and the United States Catholic Conference, can be found in Ness (2000, vol. 2, sec. 10). Overall, the number of religious interest groups grew from sixteen in the 1950s to over one hundred in the 1990s.

Studying the Religious Right, Moen (1989) argues that it had considerable success in altering the political agenda, but less success in achieving actual policy victories. More recently (Moen 1992), he argues that the Religious Right has become increasingly secular as it has become more political. Steve Bruce (1988) argued that the Religious Right, after failing to achieve majority status, has shrunk to assume the role of a legitimate minority in the national policy debate. Wilcox (1992) provides a broader historical context by assessing the role of the Religious Right throughout the twentieth century.

Several studies have assessed the broader purview of religious lobbying. Ebersole (1951) identifies sixteen active organizations representing Catholic, Jewish, and the major Protestant churches in the 1950s, while James Adams (1970) details the political activity of organized religion during the 1960s. Whereas Ebersole and Adams take a journalist's approach, two recent books by Hertzke and Hofrenning use political science theories and approaches to explain the behavior of religious interest groups.

Hertzke's *Representing God in Washington* (1988) uses the analytical concept of representation to illuminate the politics of religious lobbies. He argues that, unlike other interest groups, religious lobbies simultaneously represent their membership, their theological tradition, institutional interests, and international concerns. This multidimensional representation distinguishes religious lobbyists and produces unique forms of lobbying. Often, religious lobbyists see a conflict between these four types of representation. For example, a conflict between membership opinion and theological tradition may lead religious lobbyists to ignore member opinion or institutional interests. Hertzke concludes that religious lobbies enjoy "episodic effectiveness."

Hofrenning's *In Washington but Not of It* (1995) covers a similar range of groups as Hertzke but provides a more intensive use of interest group theories. Hofrenning utilizes the pluralist model (see section 3.2.) and exchange theory (see sections 5.2. and 5.3.) to explain the behavior of religious interest groups. He broadens the pluralist model to account for religious lobbies that eschew compromise. Like Hertzke and others, he finds conflict between member views and the lobbying behavior of religious leaders. Modifying exchange theory, he contends that religious lobbyists only ignore contrasting member opinion on low-salience issues. On other issues, there is more congruence between members and lobbyists.

Hofrenning also argues that religious lobbyists adopt a prophetic perspective. Similar to many ideologically motivated political activists, they resist compromise. Religious lobbyists avoid insider lobbying, refuse to hire former government officials as other lobbies do, fail to narrow their legislative agenda, and express profound disillusionment with the Washington elite. All these choices lessen the possibility of legislative success; however, religious lobbyists usually value political loyalty over political success.

While liberal religious lobbies were preeminent in the 1960s, religious conservatives were most prominent in the 1990s and in the early 2000s. Among conservatives, the Christian Coalition and the Family Research Council are the most influential. Unlike other religious lobbyists, both organizations have hired leaders with considerable political experience outside of religious political activism (for example, Gary Bauer of the Family Research Council and Ralph Reed of the Christian Coalition). This may change these groups' strategies, tactics, and rate of success.

Future research should look at the Religious Right more thoroughly. Following Moen (1992), conservative religious behavior should be compared to that of nonreligious or secular conservatives. The relationship between leaders and members should be studied more intensively across all religious interest groups. Finally, the literature on issue networks and iron triangles could be used to determine the role and significance of religious lobbyists in Washington, D.C., and in the U.S. states and communities.

9.14. THE SENIOR CITIZENS' LOBBY

Janie S. Steckenrider

Interest groups representing the elderly are thriving and their membership is expanding with over 1,000 age-based groups at the national, state, and local levels in the United States with over 5,000 local chapters. Yet the research on the "gray lobby" (Pratt 1976) is a small body of literature dominated by a few major works (Pratt 1976; C. Day 1990). Much of the research on senior interest groups is encompassed within the literature on the broader senior movement and on specific aspects, such as Social Security (Lubove 1986) or the Townsend Movement for old age pensions of the early 1930s (Holtzman 1963). A comprehensive annotated bibliography of over 800 books and articles on the senior movement and age-based organizations is S. Wallace and Williamson (1992), which also includes an appendix listing names and addresses of senior advocacy interest groups.

Seniors' interest groups first emerged during the 1930s pension movement as loosely organized groups centered on a charismatic leader, such as Upton Sinclair's EPIC (End Poverty in California), but these groups dissolved in the years following the enactment of Social Security (1935). New groups with varying organizational structures and political agendas such as the American Association of Retired Persons (AARP), the National Council for Senior Citizens (NCSC), and the Gray Panthers formed from the late 1940s to the early 1970s. By 1980, a senior citizen lobbying network of stable bureaucratic, institutionalized mass membership groups and organizations run by professionals had developed. Paralleling these developments, literature began to appear on the role and influence of elderly interest groups. Binstock (1972) was one of the first to pay scholarly attention to seniors' interest groups, which he examined within the context of interest group liberalism.

The seminal and most cited work on seniors' interest groups is Pratt's *The Gray Lobby* (1976), which explores the rise of seniors' organizations from the 1920s through the 1970s. He gives particular attention to the structure and function of the Senior Citizens for Kennedy for their importance in bringing seniors' issues into electoral politics. John Williamson, Evans, and Powell (1982) also provide a historical overview of seniors' interest groups, but their focus is on the political power of the elderly and the conditions determining their power or lack thereof.

A significant contribution, *What Older Americans Think: Interest Groups and Aging Policy*, by Christine Day (1990) combines an examination of the evolution and current status of age-related interest groups with an emphasis on political attitudes and behavior of the elderly. She discusses seniors' interest groups within the broader interest group literature and focuses on the three themes of group origin and maintenance, group power and influence, and what constitutes representation by interest groups for the elderly. She contends that seniors' advocacy groups were the political success stories of the later twentieth century given their burgeoning number, size, visibility, and political activity. However, she also points out their limitations in representing such a vast and diverse membership and that many seniors join for material rewards of travel or for discounts on medicine, not for purposive goals based on political beliefs. Much of this study's strength comes from information gleaned in interviews with individuals in the senior citizen political network including executive agencies, congressional staff, and the personnel of senior citizen interest groups.

An important reference source is Van Tassel and Meyer (1992). It is a collection of 83 sketches of advocacy groups for the elderly outlining their mission, development, funding, policy concerns, and activities. Ness (2000, 561–63) provides a good overview of AARP. Powell, Williamson, and Branco (1998) provide a historical overview and an emphasis on the rhetoric of symbolic senior citizen interest group politics. Steckenrider and Parrott (1998) and Robert Hudson (1997) devote chapters to senior citizen interest groups.

Public policies regarding seniors have changed because of budget deficits and fiscal constraints forcing senior citizen interest groups to defend against program cutbacks instead of pushing for program expansion. Generational conflict is also increasing as "greedy" seniors are being accused of draining resources from the young and needy. In response, interest groups for the elderly are expected to shift more toward both horizontal coalitions such as the Leadership Council of Aging Organizations (C. Day 1990) and vertical alliances like Generations United (Torres-Gil 1992).

The enormous baby boom of the late 1940s will, of course, slowly become a senior boom and will certainly change the complexion and activities of senior citizen interest groups. The extent of this change will be a fruitful subject of future study. Another subject for study is whether senior citizen interest groups actually influence policy or merely defend current benefits and secure minor changes. Without question, senior interest groups are Washington insiders and are increasingly becoming insiders in many states like Florida and Arizona; but unresolved is whether this status translates into significant policy consequences.

9.15. NONGOVERNMENTAL ORGANIZATIONS (NGOs)

David Lewis

Nongovernmental Organizations (NGOs) are "self-governing, private, not-for-profit organizations that are geared to improving the quality of life for disadvantaged people" (Vakil 1997, 2060). The term NGO appeared after World War II when Article 71 of the United Nations Charter provided for nongovernmental involvement in UN activities. NGO has now become a common acronym and refers to third sector organizations from both industrialized countries and the Third World that are active in international development, human rights, and environmentalism. NGOs usually deliver services or undertake campaigning work; many combine both.

The number of development NGOs registered in the Organization for Economic Development and Cooperation (OECD) countries increased from 1,600 in 1980 to nearly 3,000 by 1993, and their expenditure increased from \$2.8 to \$5.7 billion (Hulme and Edwards 1997). This growth has been due partly to their increasing share of foreign aid and that they are seen as more administratively flexible, close to the poor, innovative in problem-solving, and cost-effective than government (Cernea 1988). Renewed interest in civil society, generated by popular resistance to Eastern European and Latin American totalitarian and authoritarian regimes, also helped focused attention on NGOs and created a policy climate in which they have increased their profile and voice (Keck and Sikkink 1998).

NGOs range from small informal grassroots groups to large multinational organizations—such as CARE or Oxfam—and are active at international, national, and local levels and have diverse origins and influences. In Latin America, some NGOs have been influenced by liberation theology and the ideas of Brazilian educator Paolo Freire, while in the Indian subcontinent Gandhian values and philosophical ideas have often been important (D. Lewis 2001). A distinction is usually made between grassroots membership organizations (GROs) and grassroots support organizations (GRSOs), the latter being a form of intermediary organization (Fisher 1997). In some cases, NGO identities can be ambiguous, such as when established by governments or by commercial organizations (Clarke 1998).

The research literature on NGOs reflects their high level of diversity. There are two main aspects of this literature. The first is found within the discipline of international relations. This traces the evolution of NGO roles in international affairs from emergence between 1775 and 1918 (the abolition of the slave trade, the peace movement, and support for labor rights) to the current period of empowerment dating from the 1992 UN Earth Summit in Rio de Janeiro. NGOs are now directly involved in important areas of international policy formulation and campaigning (Charnovitz 1997).

The second aspect of the literature focuses on the roles of NGOs within development projects and programs and on the role of NGOs in organizing and promoting community participation. One element of this literature is its domination by the two central questions of accountability and performance (Edwards and Hulme 1995; D. Lewis and Wallace 2000). Like most third sector organizations, NGOs face the challenge of multiple accountability—to users, funders, staff, supporters, local governments, and governing bodies. NGOs may focus on their responsibilities to patrons—because of the threat of withdrawal of funding—far more than those to clients or to their own values. Unbalanced accountability leads to goal displacement and unplanned growth, and successful NGOs can easily evolve into unwieldy hierarchical organizations.

A second key element of the development literature is the debate about NGO roles and effectiveness. Efforts to evaluate NGO performance have produced mixed findings. For example, in comparing four local NGOs in South Asia, Edwards (1999) found vastly differing levels of impact and suggests that the most effective NGO is characterized by independent thinking, clear goals, personal qualities of commitment among staff and volunteers, and close community working relationships built over time. With regard to political advocacy and lobbying, Covey's (1995) assessment of NGO outcomes separates out policy effectiveness from civil society impact. Thus, even if the desired policy outcome was not achieved, NGOs might still raise awareness and increase community participation.

For the researcher, the subject of NGOs remains complex and ambiguous. It is unwise to generalize about NGOs, not least because of the diversity of the NGO sector and a lack of accurate, detailed data. Najam (1996) shows the limitations of much NGO literature as narrowly focused and parochial but presents a useful guide through key concepts for future research.

9.16. GOVERNANCE INTERESTS: ANTITAX AND TERM LIMIT GROUPS

Richard Braunstein

Governance groups can be distinguished from good government groups in two main ways. First, the latter are largely an outgrowth of progressive politics oriented toward procedural fairness in election finance, voter registration, lobbying practices, and so on, while governance groups are principally concerned with conservative priorities of governmental efficiency and effectiveness and are an outgrowth of public dissatisfaction with representative institutions.

Second, whereas good government groups are typically concerned with a range of issues, governance groups usually focus on a single issue such as term limits (Benjamin and Malbin 1992; Donovan and Snipp 1994), tax and spending limitations (Berkman 1993), and the introduction of supermajority qualifications for tax increases (Tolbert 1998). Together, these reforms can be labeled "governance policy" (Tolbert 1998). Like good government groups, however, governance groups seek public goods that provide widely distributed benefits, even though, in contrast to good government groups, they have a conservative agenda (Tolbert 1996).

Little research has been conducted that explicitly studies the role of governance groups in the political process and there are no bibliographies on governance groups; however, bibliographies on direct democracy (see section 7.5.) are helpful for studying governance groups. Also, a profile of many governance groups and think tanks that focus in whole or in part on governance issues can be found in Ness (2000, vol. 2, sec. 10 and 11).

Strategically, governance groups have followed the lead of the proponents of California's Proposition 13 enacted in 1978, using referendum and initiative elections to bypass institutional resistance to changes in governance policies (Berkman 1993). The success of these efforts has made the ballot campaign the primary tactic of governance groups. However, this strategy is limited to states and localities with the constitutional provisions for direct democracy; thus it is not the only method that these groups adopt. They are also active in the direct lobbying of legislatures in states both with and without the initiative and referendum processes. Governance groups also attempt to influence national governance policies by pushing for amendments to the U.S. Constitution. To date, they have pursued amendments for English as an official language, a balanced budget, and congressional term limits. The effort to influence national governance policies is often coordinated with state and local efforts and vice versa.

As a new phenomenon in American politics, there is a need to understand what variables have contributed to the rise and success of governance groups. This might include a study of their membership—their racial, economic, and educational characteristics—as well as the social, economic, and political environments that create opportunity for governance groups to acquire popular support and political strength. In addition, while there is speculation on the relationship between governance groups and the Republican Party and conservative social movements, little has been done to empirically test this relationship. Knowledge of this relationship might be uncovered by studying how governance groups are linked to and shaped by candidate elections. It may be the case that there is a symbiotic relationship between the parties, their candidates, and governance groups wherein political parties use governance groups to pursue their issue agenda through the support of particular ballot campaigns. Finally, there is a need to better understand the relationship between state, local, and national governance organizations. There is evidence to support the fact that state and local governance groups rely on the support and direction of national organizations (Magleby 1984; Cronin 1989), as well as evidence that national politics can be directed by state and local priorities (Berkman 1993).

9.17. PRO– AND ANTI–GUN CONTROL INTEREST GROUPS

Michael L. Boyer

Because issues involving gun control have long occupied a prominent place in America's public policy debates, there is a considerable body of writing on pro– and anti–gun control interest groups. However, much of this is polemical and journalistic commentary and only a small body of academic work exists.

However, some of the popular articles are useful sources. For example, Birnbaum (1999) examines the National Rifle Association (NRA), its funding, and its political power; and David Anderson (1999) profiles the trend toward the use of litigation by gun control groups. In addition, general background work, such as the diverse collection by Dizard, Muth, and Andrews (1999), provides an instructive orientation to the many facets of the gun control debate and the lobbies involved.

Scholarly work focusing directly on anti–gun control and gun control interest groups is much more narrow in focus, with the majority of attention devoted to the perennial big player—the NRA. It is by far the dominant anti–gun control interest group and widely regarded as one of the most powerful groups in the United States. Ness (2000, 532–35) provides an overview of the organization; Leddy (1985, 1987) traces the evolution of the NRA from a sports organization to a powerful lobby group; Beauchamp (1992) focuses on the NRA's structure, leadership, and resource base; Osha Davidson (1998) analyzes the NRA's lobbying tactics and efforts; Daigon (2000b) provides an overview of the organization as well as its financial data; and Patterson and Singer (2002) examine recent challenges to the NRA's power. Handgun Control, Inc., a major gun control group, has received minimal scholarly attention (Daigon 2000a). The group is outlined in Ness (2000, 521–23). There are other less prominent groups, such as Second Amendment Sisters, but no major research has been conducted on minor gun control groups.

Also useful are works that take a broader look at gun control interest groups. Spitzer (1995) covers gun control groups in his examination of the politics of gun control, as do Bruce and Wilcox (1998); Brennan (1997) looks at the gun control lobby in the 1990s; and Vizzard (2000) devotes a chapter to gun control interest groups. While based on the situation in Australia, Crook (1997), *Understanding the Gun Lobby*, offers a comparison with other Western democracies and insights into gun lobby ideology.

Likely future trends in gun control group activity may be foreshadowed in events such as the unprecedented Million Mom March in 2000 in Washington, D.C., and the use of the courts as a forum for future policy skirmishes. These developments—judicial lobbying and mass demonstrations—will likely complement gun control interest group tactics in the next decade.

9.18. THE TOBACCO AND ANTISMOKING LOBBIES

Laura C. Savatgy and Clive S. Thomas

Tobacco and antismoking lobbies have been prominent in U.S. national politics since the late 1950s and, more recently, have become active in state and local politics. While there is limited academic research on the specific interest groups involved, there are numerous sources, both academic and popular, in books, journals, and on the Internet on the politics of smoking, from which information on these lobbies can be gleaned. Information can also be found in treatments of health groups and in material on smoking and antismoking organizations. Because the antismoking issue came to Western Europe much later than to North America, most work focuses on U.S. groups, but there is some work on groups in other countries.

In U.S. politics the tobacco and antismoking issues came to the forefront in 1956 when the American Heart Association issued the first warning of the dangers of tobacco products. This precipitated the emergence of an organized tobacco lobby consisting of businesses such as Philip

Morris, R. J. Reynolds, and other tobacco companies, and organizations such as the Smokeless Tobacco Council and the Tobacco Institute.

Over the years, these and other interests have contributed large amounts of money to prosmoking political action committees (PACs). Originally, the antismoking lobby consisted mainly of health organizations such as the American Heart Association (Ness 2000, 184–85) and the American Cancer Society (Ness 2000, 167–68); but it was later augmented by organizations like Action on Smoking and Health (ASH), the Campaign to Curb Youth Smoking, the Council for Tobacco Research, and The Smokers Lounge. In addition, the U.S. Food and Drug Administration (FDA) became a major antismoking advocate.

A few articles, such as those by Peter Stone (1993), Godshall (1993), and Douglas and Wilbur (1993), deal directly with tobacco and anti-smoking lobby groups. However, most research on this lobby focuses on the policies advocated by particular groups and only incidentally deals with the groups themselves. For instance, Studlar (2002) compares tobacco politics in the United States and Canada, while Pollock (1999) traces the political history of smoking and health. There are sources on tobacco regulation in Rabin and Sugarman (2001) and in Samuels and Glantz (1991); and on smoking policy in Fritschler (1989), Fritschler and Hoefler (1996), and Rabin and Sugarman (1993). Nannie Tilly (1985) examines one of the prosmoking PACs' largest contributors, R. J. Reynolds. In Glantz (1996), a chapter considers the role of the tobacco lobby in stalling antismoking legislation through public relations. MacSween (1999) cites a case for the Canadian Dental Association having a strong antitobacco lobby. Galen Ellis, Hobart, and Reed (1996) approach the tobacco lobby from a local government perspective. And a report by *Congressional Quarterly* (1997) examines the smoking lobby and the difficulties it faces when lobbying government.

Other useful sources on these lobbies are publications by interest groups and individuals involved on both sides of the smoking issue. David Kessler (2001) was the head of the FDA and offers a governmental perspective. Sullum (1998) provides a historical look at smoking as well as the governmental obligation to stop any activities that harm "public health." Derthick (2001) examines litigation and legislation in tobacco politics. Glantz and Balbach (2000) detail political battles in the tobacco industry in California. And Peter Taylor (1984) and Stephen Moore (1993) offer insights into the influence of tobacco money on politics including international politics.

On the Internet, sites such as Smoking Lobby (www.smoking lobby.com) give smokers and nonsmokers the opportunity to look at both sides of the issues. And groups such as The Truth (www.thetruth.com) may affect future legislation as they campaign against big tobacco. The R. J. Reynolds site (http://www.rjrt.com/index.asp) has links to sites dealing with tobacco issues and tobacco laws and legislation. The site www.infact.org/health.html contains useful links to documents that provide research material on various aspects of the tobacco lobby and the antismoking issue.

9.19. CIVIL LIBERTIES INTEREST GROUPS AND LOBBIES IN THE UNITED STATES

John H. Culver

The terms *civil liberties* and *civil rights* are often used interchangeably, but they are not synonymous. An important distinction lies in the role of government in honoring these rights. With civil rights the government assumes a protective role, one to ensure that rights will not be abridged by others. Usually civil rights are associated with discrimination based upon gender, race, ethnicity, and religion. By contrast, civil liberties involve fundamental freedoms that the government itself cannot infringe upon. In the United States these rights are mainly those enumerated in the Constitution in the First Amendment of the Bill of Rights—freedom of speech, religion, press, assembly, and to petition government (often to protest its actions), in addition to procedural guarantees in criminal justice matters (Domino 2003, 1–2). A more recent term with universal application is *human rights.* This umbrella term is used primarily in reference to developing countries, referring to basic civil and political rights that governments should not violate (see section 9.20.). Each of these three terms is evolving as courts and legislative bodies give them additional meaning.

Characteristics of the Activities of Civil Liberties Interests

There are five particularly notable characteristics of the political activities of civil liberties organizations in the United States that, to a large extent, have shaped or are in the process of shaping the research agenda and literature on civil liberties interests.

First, there is some overlap of the activities of civil liberties interests with those of ethnic and racial minority groups, women's organizations, criminal justice interest groups, and those identified with specific social issues and identity politics. For example, the NAACP (most closely associated with African Americans and the fight for civil rights) has joined with anti-death penalty organizations in challenging capital punishment on the grounds that it is racially discriminatory. Similarly, some liberal women's organizations join with abortion-rights organizations to ensure that abortion rights are not further eroded. See sections 9.2., 9.4., 9.8.1., and 9.9.

Second, conservative and liberal civil liberties interest groups devote most of their energies to the following issues: freedom of expression; drug policies; capital punishment; the rights of prisoners, women, students,

269

immigrants and gays; the flag salute and school prayer; religious toler-ance; reproductive freedom; and a vast array of privacy matters, including the right to be left alone.

Third, while much lobbying by these organizations occurs at the national and subnational levels of government in the executive, legislative, and administrative arenas, a disproportionate amount of the literature addresses their efforts in state and federal courts.

Fourth, liberal and conservative civil liberties groups often find them-selves in odd coalitions in civil liberties disputes. The hate speech case involving a 1990 St. Paul, Minnesota, ordinance prohibiting certain actions that could be construed as offensive to people because of their color, race, religion, and gender illustrates this. In *R.A.V. v. St. Paul, Minnesota* (1992), a unanimous U.S. Supreme Court overturned the ordi-nance. Lobbies that filed amicus curiae briefs in opposition to the ordinance included the Center for Individual Rights, the Association of American Publishers, the American Civil Liberties Union and its Min-nesota affiliate, and the American Jewish Congress. Lobbies in support of the ordinance included the National Black Women's Health Project, the Anti-Defamation League of B'nai B'rith, the Asian American Legal Defense and Education Fund, the National Asian Pacific American Bar Association, and the NAACP (L. Epstein and Walker 1996).

Fifth, civil liberties interest groups have long been concerned about pri-vacy issues. The sophistication and increased use of computers in both the private and public sectors has added to their concerns. More recently, their apprehension has increased because of government efforts to com-bat terrorism. This is an emerging area that will be fruitful for interest group scholars to examine as the consequences of these developments on privacy, nationally and internationally, become more clearly evident.

Studies of Civil Liberties Interest Groups

There is probably more information available on the American Civil Liberties Union (ACLU) than any other civil liberties lobby. The ACLU is usually associated with a liberal position, one that calls for minimal gov-ernment interference with individual rights. However, it is officially non-partisan and has sided with groups such as the Ku Klux Klan over free speech and association controversies. Founded in 1920, the ACLU's early focus was on First Amendment issues, but this has expanded into privacy and criminal justice issues. It has a national office in Washington, D.C., and chapters in all 50 states, which are allowed considerable autonomy (Ness 2000, 433–34). Books on the ACLU include Samuel Walker (1992, 1999), Donohue (1985), and Markmann (1965). The ACLU's controver-sial defense of American Nazis from the National Socialist Party of Amer-ica to demonstrate in Skokie, Illinois, in 1977, is documented by J. Gibson and Bingham (1985) and Hamlin (1980).

Other prominent liberal civil liberties groups include: People for the American Way, the American Jewish Congress, Americans United for Separation of Church and State (Ness 2000, 513–15), and the National Organization for Women (Ness 2000, 583–85; section 9.4.). People for the American Way was established by Hollywood producer Norman Lear in 1980. Its main focus is to counter the influence of the "Religious Right," the common term used to connote the religious advocacy of televangelists like Jerry Falwell and Pat Robertson, who call for prayer in public schools and government policies that affirm the United States is a Christian nation.

Civil liberties interest groups with a conservative posture include the National Right to Life Committee (Ness 2000, 536–38), the American Center for Law and Justice, the Center for Individual Rights, the Eagle Forum, the Pacific Legal Foundation, and the Rocky Mountain Legal Foundation. These lobbies argue for government restrictions on certain individual freedoms (abortion, free speech, sexual orientation, and dissemination of pornography) and fewer freedoms for those accused or convicted of breaking the law, and they support efforts to make Christian religious practices more widespread in public places. The increase in conservative interest group litigation is analyzed by Lee Epstein (1985), while Hertzke (1988) examines conservative religious lobbies.

Other studies that address both conservative and liberal civil liberties organizations primarily in a legal context include: O'Connor and Epstein (1983), Caldeira and Wright (1990), McGuire and Caldeira (1993), and Kobylka (1987). Two works focusing on civil liberties and women are Gelb and Palley (1979) and Haider-Markel and Meier (1996).

Much work remains to be done on civil liberties interests. In particular, there is a need for more studies of individual civil liberties groups, factors determining cooperation and coalition building among the lobby and related interests, and on the internal operations, dynamics, and strategies of civil liberties interest groups.

9.20. HUMAN RIGHTS INTERESTS: DEFINITIONAL PROBLEMS, CROSS-REFERENCES, AND SUPPLEMENTARY SOURCES

Laura C. Savatgy and Clive S. Thomas

The designations *human rights interests* and *human rights interest groups* are among the vaguest categorizations in interest group studies. They suffer from all the delineation problems and more set out in section 8.1. These umbrella terms are used primarily in reference to authoritarian and developing countries, referring to basic civil and political rights that governments should not violate. However, the use of the terms can be narrow or broad.

Some scholars use the term human rights narrowly to refer to what in developed countries would be seen as civil liberties and civil rights. Civil rights include those based upon gender, ethnicity, and skin color, which are often the basis of discrimination. Major civil rights include: those to participate in governmental activities such as voting; to be able to speak out—particularly to be critical of the government—without fear of recriminations; to enjoy religious freedom; and to ensure criminal justice safeguards—particularly those of the accused and of prisoners.

Other scholars use a broader catch-all definition to include groups that promote some philosophical, value-based definition of "basic human rights." This can include a gamut of causes among which are freedom from poverty and hunger, the rights of indigenous peoples, the rights of refugees and displaced persons, opposition to Third World sweat-shop labor, the rights of gays and lesbians, various children's rights, and the rights of women, particularly in societies where women have minimal legal protections.

The problem of definition does not end here, however. The vague boundary lines of what is and is not a human rights group becomes even vaguer because some interest groups that do not primarily focus on human rights—narrowly or broadly defined—may have a human rights advocacy element to their activities, such as the Catholic Church, many Jewish organizations, and various national trade union federations.

Given these definitional problems and the great potential for overlap in examining various interests, this entry first identifies cross references in this *Guide* where treatment of groups and interests promoting human rights—broadly defined—as part of their mission can be found. This is then supplemented by some major sources on human rights interests, including Web sites.

Related Sources in this *Guide*

The entries in this *Guide* that treat some aspect of human rights, broadly defined, are mostly found in the first part of this chapter and in chapter 13 on international and transnational interests. The four entries under section 9.2. deal with ethnic and racial minority interests, section 9.3. covers indigenous peoples, section 9.4. deals with the women's lobby, section 9.8.1. covers gay and lesbian interests, and section 9.8.2. deals with the poverty, hunger, and welfare lobby. Entry 9.15. dealing with nongovernmental lobbies (NGOs) will also be useful as many NGOs are human rights organizations. And in chapter 13, sections 13.7. and 13.8. deal with several international human rights interests including Amnesty International, the international women's lobby, and cultural interests.

Supplementary Sources on Human Rights Interests

In addition to the cross-references listed above, the following major sources are a useful starting point for exploring human rights interests in general and with regard to specific organizations.

General Sources. Two books provide useful background information. Keck and Sikkink, *Activists Beyond Borders* (1998), approach various human rights issues, such as those of women and antislavery campaigns, from a transnational perspective. A more general review of the politics of human rights, including the role of various interests, is an edited volume by Wheeler and Dunne (1999). The leading academic journal in the human rights field, *Human Rights Quarterly*, has published many articles on various human rights interest groups since its founding in 1978. On the Internet, Human Rights Internet (www.hri.ca/welcome.asp), Human Rights Web (www.hrweb.org), and Amnesty International (http://web.amnesty.org/web/aboutai.nsf) are sites with many general sources of information on human rights interests.

Human Rights Watch (HRW). In regard to particular interest groups, HRW is probably the most prominent and well-known general human rights organization. The group is covered in overview in Ness (2000, 441–43). The HRW Internet address is www.hrw.org. Founded in 1978 (when it was known as Helsinki Watch), HRW is dedicated to protecting the human rights of people around the world: to prevent discrimination, to uphold political freedom, to protect people from inhumane conduct in wartime, and to bring offenders to justice. HRW challenges governments and those who hold power to end abusive practices and respect international human rights laws.

Women's Rights. On women's rights in an international context, two books that focus, in part, on the political and lobbying aspects of the struggle are worthy of note even though they are written from an advocacy as opposed to an academic perspective. Joanna Kerr, *Ours by Right: Women's Rights as Human Rights*, explores current approaches to advancing the rights of women and outlines the tasks ahead, including lobbying policy makers, legal reform, and altering social attitudes. Katarina Tomasevski, *Women and Human Rights* (1991), describes the lack of adequate attention to the rights of women. She draws attention to categories of women who are most at risk, including women refugees, the disabled, indigenous women, and women in prison. The book concludes with proposals for a plan of action, involving educating women as to their rights, community-level mobilization, and international networking and litigation.

Refugees and Displaced Persons. One valuable source of information on groups and organizations working in this field is the Norwegian Refugee Council/Advisory Functions and Lobbying. Its Internet address is www.nrc.no/NRC/advisory_functions.htm. The Council is a prime mover in the work of defending and strengthening the rights of refugees and displaced persons by means of improving their protection from persecution and violation of fundamental human rights. Its work is oriented towards Norwegian authorities, the UN system, and other organizations.

Gay and Lesbian Human Rights. A useful source regarding the organization promoting this cause is the International Gay and Lesbian Human

Rights Commission (IGLHRC) at www.iglhrc.org/site/iglhrc/ on the Internet. The mission of IGLHRC is to secure the full enjoyment of the human rights of all people and communities subject to discrimination or abuse on the basis of sexual orientation, gender identity or expression, and/or HIV/AIDS status. A U.S.-based NGO, IGLHRC works to achieve this mission through advocacy, documentation, coalition building, public education, and technical assistance.

Children's Rights. The sources on this aspect of human rights are extensive. The following are useful starting points on both children's rights groups and policies in the United States and internationally.

John Pardeck, *Children's Rights: Policy and Practice* (2002), which encompasses legal, psychological, sociological, policy, and child advocacy aspects, is an introductory source. It considers the tension between a child's right to self-determination and the same child's need to be protected and how this plays out in policy and political advocacy. A concise history of the children's liberation and child protection movements is covered, with an emphasis on the legislation and legal decisions they produced.

There are also organizations that provide comprehensive information including reference to children's rights interests and interest groups on the Internet: Child Rights Information Network (CRIN) at www.crin.org/index/asp; the National Association for Prevention of Child Abuse and Neglect (NAPCAN) established in 1987, a nongovernment, not for profit, volunteer-based organization, which can be found at www.napcan.org.au/Policies/Childrens%20Rights.shtml; and Defense for Children International Australia, which is the Australian section of Defense for Children International and provides a link to a global network of children's rights agencies recognized by the United Nations (its Web address is www.dci-au.org/index.html).

Chapter 10

Comparative Interest Group Studies

Bert Pijnenburg and Clive S. Thomas

10.1. COMPARATIVE ANALYSIS AND INTEREST GROUP STUDIES

In political science, comparative analysis generally refers to the comparing of national political systems—examining and attempting to explain both their similarities and their differences. This is often labeled as *cross-national research*. Comparisons can be made of political systems as a whole or their components, such as electoral systems and the structure and role of political parties.

There are alternative conceptions, however. Apart from the tradition of labeling in political science, there is no reason why comparative analysis should restrict itself to a cross-national perspective. After all, the distinctive characteristic of this type of analysis is that it makes comparisons. In fact, it can be argued that the term *comparative analysis* is a redundancy as any kind of *analysis* involves some sort of *comparison*. Thus, a strong case can be made that several types of comparative analysis are possible. Within the same national political system—the United States, for example—comparisons of interest groups and parties have been made between states and between large cities. But comparisons within a country are usually not included within comparative analysis in political science. The deeper meaning and nuances of the term *comparative* will not be pursued here, however; the issue has been raised to further illustrate the problems of terminology mentioned in several places in this *Guide* (see section 1.4.) and to make readers aware of other types of comparative analysis. This chapter uses the traditional political science definition of *comparative* and focuses only on cross-national comparative research on interest groups and, for the reason explained in the next section, focuses specifically on liberal democracies.

Much has been written on both the advantages and pitfalls of cross-national comparative research, and the discussion continues. Useful texts in this regard, which are relevant to comparing interest groups, are by Almond, Powell, and Mundt (1993), Chilcote (1994), and Keman (1993). An illustration of the continuing debate over the methodology of comparative analysis is available in the *British Journal of Political Science*. The debate centers around how to best conceptualize and operationalize neo-corporatism (see section 3.4.) with Lijphart and Crepaz (1991) and Crepaz and Lijphart (1995) arguing one position, and Keman and Pennings (1995) arguing another position.

While there are selected bibliographies in general texts on comparative interest groups (such as Ball and Millard 1987; Richardson 1993a; C. Thomas 1993a), a comprehensive bibliographical guide covering the field of cross-national research on interest group politics is still lacking. There are some detailed bibliographies, but they are not available as separate publications, and they only mention literature on a specific part of the research field, such as on pluralism (e.g., Garson 1978) and on neo-corporatism (e.g., P. Williamson 1989).

Turning to the specifics of this chapter, it is structured as follows: First, we briefly outline the development of the study of comparative interest groups. The following section examines variations in research with regard to the differences in approach, focus, and scope. The longest section of this chapter provides a critical analysis of existing research. The conclusion suggests some possible directions for future research, including lessons from the growing body of work on social movements. The analysis in this chapter assumes that the reader is familiar with the concept of pluralism (see section 3.2.), neocorporatism (see section 3.4.), new institutionalism (see section 3.9.), and policy networks and niches (see section 7.16.). Those not familiar with these concepts or those who need an overview should consult these entries mentioned before reading on.

10.2. THE EVOLUTION OF COMPARATIVE INTEREST GROUP STUDIES: THE DOMINANCE AND RESILIENCE OF THE NEOCORPORATIST APPROACH

The vast majority of research on comparative interest groups has been conducted on liberal democracies as well as those nations transitioning to liberal democracy. This is largely due to the accessibility of information, but there are other reasons for this (see section 12.1.). Accordingly, this chapter focuses on the research produced on liberal democracies. As to the theoretical foundations of cross-national comparative research on interest groups, until the mid-1970s, the small body of research that existed was based primarily on a pluralist perspective (see for example, Almond 1958; Durverger 1972; and G. Wilson 1977). Until that time, studies of interest group politics were influenced by the experience in the United States with its quintessential (in comparison with other liberal democracies) but aberrant pluralist associational system (C. Thomas 1993b). However, interest group studies were rarely at the forefront of political science in parliamentary democracies (see section 11.1.).

It was not until the 1970s that political scientists began empirical research on cross-national interest group studies, particularly on groups in Western Europe. Many scholars began questioning the utility of pluralism as a theoretical framework for analyzing and understanding interest group politics in a number of Western European countries. The major theoretical approach developed to supplement pluralism (and for some writers to replace it) was neocorporatism; and from the mid-1970s on, research on cross-national interest group expanded considerably. Much of this research has been devoted to how countries compare in the pluralist/neocorporatist characteristics of their group system at the macro (or national) level and at the meso (or sectoral) level.

From the mid-1980s, there has been a growing dissatisfaction with the exclusively pluralist and neocorporatist approaches to interest group politics, as well as the approaches that combine the two. This has resulted in the development of two new perspectives: policy networks and neo-institutionalism (or new institutionalism). The policy networks perspective has a number of components and dimensions upon which distinctions can be made between various types of policy networks. Van Waarden (1992a) has developed one such typology. In it he systematically describes the characteristics of statism (see section 3.7.), clientelism (a close relationship between government and certain groups), *parentela* (an Italian term referring to close ties between certain groups and the dominant political party in a country), iron triangles and issue networks (section 17.16.), as well as several categories of pluralism (sections 3.2. and 3.3.) and neocorporatism (section 3.4.).

According to Immergut the major tenets of neoinstitutionalism are:

> While we can acknowledge the general trend toward a growth in organized interest groups and the role they play in policy decisions, these groups have not replaced traditional forms of democratic representation. Rather, interest group activities are embedded within these political institutions and the scope of interest group influence depends upon the logic of these political institutions. Political decisions taken in representative institutions set boundaries and create opportunities for the more hidden policy processes that occur within administrative agencies and interest-group associations. (Immergut 1992, 5)

Initially, when these two perspectives emerged among some scholars of Western European politics, they were seen as heralding the decline, if not the complete disappearance, of neocorporatism. Among the reasons given at the time for macro and meso forms of interest group systems becoming less neocorporatist were: the impact of the worldwide economic crisis in the 1980s, economic and political globalization, and the center of gravity of governmental decision making and policy making increasingly shifting from the national to the European Union (EU) level.

Since the mid-1990s there has been a reappraisal of this diagnosis as the neocorporatist perspective has gone through modifications, but it is still alive and well. Neocorporatism proved strong enough to resist and adapt to the various trends affecting advanced capitalist countries during the 1980s that should have spelled its demise (except, possibly, in Sweden). The country that is presented in the literature as the example *par excellence* of this tenacity and flexibility of neocorporatist interest group politics is the Netherlands. That the developments of the late 1980s and 1990s in the Netherlands, with respect to the consolidation and expansion of neocorporatism, are not only highly significant, but have also been contrary to almost every academic prognosis is expressed in the title of a book on the subject, *A Dutch Miracle* (Visser and Hemerijck 1997).

Schmitter and Grote (1997, 1) sum up the way that the neocorporatist perspective had evolved over the years: " . . . just as many observers had announced its demise corporatism has risen again and now seems to be carrying its twin burdens of interest associability and policy-making to new heights during the 1990s." By the mid-1990s there were several single-country as well as cross-national studies substantiating this view, such as the comparative research findings of Compston (1998), Crepaz (1992), C. Crouch (1993), Dermot McCann (1995), M. Rhodes (1997), and Traxler (1995a).

Whether the neocorporatist perspective will reassert and consolidate its position as the major paradigm in comparative interest group studies in the long term remains to be seen. Certainly, the resilience of neocorporatism through all these challenges has resulted in an adaptation and refinement of its conceptual frameworks. For example, Martin Rhodes (1997) makes the distinction between previous kinds of neocorporatism and a current *competitive* type. Visser and Hemerijck (1997) propose a four-fold typology to describe and explain postwar evolutions: *immobile*, *responsive*, and *innovative* corporatism, as well as *corporatist disengagement*. C. Crouch and Menon (1997, 154) have introduced the concept of *consociationism*, which might be regarded as a special type of corporatism in that it is not concerned exclusively with specific, economic, producer interests, but embraces wider social and cultural identities.

10.3. VARIATIONS IN RESEARCH: DIFFERENCES IN APPROACH, FOCUS, AND SCOPE

The purpose of this section is to provide a systematic overview of the field of cross-national interest group research by classifying studies according to three categories: their approach, their scope, and their focus. This is done with the aid of two tables. In Table 10.1, publications are divided into categories of approach and scope. Then, in Table 10.2, the same publications are ordered according to their focus.

Before turning to this analysis some words of caution are in order. The categorizations in the tables are to some extent subjective. A number of publications do not fall neatly into one category. One possible solution to this is to take only the publication's primary subject into account and classify it accordingly. This, however, does not eliminate the risk of arbitrary classification and may obscure other enlightening elements about the work. Therefore, in both tables, studies for which the primary subject criterion appears too narrow are listed with an additional specification as to whether they can be classified *mainly* or *partly* in one category. The inventory of cross-national studies listed in these tables does not claim to be exhaustive. It is, however, a representative sample covering the major books and articles written in English in this field.

Varying Approaches

A distinction can be made as to the approach studies have taken (see the vertical list on the left of Table 10.1). Here there are two categories. One consists of studies that are pure and atheoretical descriptions of interest group politics in various countries (see the last category of Table 10.1). A good example is the volume on employers' associations edited by Windmuller and Gladstone (1984). The second and the largest category is theoretically inspired analyses. As indicated above, the theoretical framework of these studies varies.

Of the studies completed since the early 1970s, several fit neatly into a single paradigm theoretical framework. Most of these take a neocorporatist approach with a slightly lesser number taking a policy-network approach. In contrast, only one example of cross-national interest group research (Wilson 1977) limited itself to an exclusively pluralist approach and the only one using a purely neo-Marxist approach (Useen 1984).

However, a great majority of the studies combine elements of different perspectives. A considerable number of them (listed in Table 10.1 under "Theoretical Mix") use the conceptual framework of which the neocorporatist approach is either the main element or at least an important one. The combination of different theories also often includes the pluralist perspective but not as frequently. And when pluralism is combined with neocorporatism, pluralism is usually employed as the subordinate theory. However, from the mid-1980s onward, the development of policy-network analysis in cross-national interest group research has also meant a gain of terrain in approach for pluralism. This is because pluralist patterns of interest group politics are then presented as one form of

TABLE 10.1 The Approach and Scope of Cross-National Interest Group Studies

		SCOPE	
APPROACH	**Macrolevel**	**Mesolevel**	**Microlevel**
THEORETICAL STUDIES		G. Wilson (1977)	
Pluralism			
Neocorporatism	Berger (1981a)*	Cawson (1985)	
	Cox and O'Sullivan (1988)	Compston (1994)	
	Goldthorpe (1984)**	Compston (1995a)	
	Katzenstein (1985)	Compston (1995b)	
	Lehmbruch and Schmitter (1982)	Compston (1997)	
	Nyang'oro and Shaw (1989)	Compston (1998)	
	Schmitter (1995)*	Crepaz (1992)	
		C. Crouch (1995)	
		Goldthorpe (1984)**	
		M. Rhodes (1997)	
		Schmitter and Grote (1997)*	
		Scruggs (1999)	
		Streeck and Schmitter (1985)	
		Treu (1992)	
Neo-Marxism			Useem (1984)
Policy Networks	Van Waarden (1992b)	Appleby and Bessant (1987)	
		Atkinson and Coleman (1989a)	

280

TABLE 10.1 (continued)

	Bressers, O'Toole, and Richardson (1995)		W. Coleman (1990)
	Cavanagh (1998)		Lane and Bachmann (1997)*
	Daugbjerg (1998a)		Pratt (1993)
	Daugbjerg (1998b)		
	Dunn and Perl (1994)		
	W. Grant (1992)		
	W. Grant, Paterson, and Whitston (1987)		
	W. Grant, Paterson, and Whitston (1988)		
	Knoke et al. (1996)		
	MacMillan and Turner (1987)		
	Schenkel (1998)		
	M. J. Smith (1993)		
	Wilks and Wright (1987)		
Neoinstitutionalism	Baumgartner (1996)		Haverland (1998)
	Greenwood and Thomas (1998)		Immergut (1992)
	Yishai (1998b)		Vogel (1993)
Theoretical Mix	Ball and Millard (1987)*	Ball and Millard (1987)**	W. Coleman and Grant (1988)
	Crepaz and Lijphart (1995)	Baumgartner and Walker (1989)	Collier and Mahoney (1997)
	Czada (1987)	Chiesi (1991)	Frenkel (1993)
	Hausner, Pederson, and Ronit (1995)*	W. Coleman (1994)	Heilbrunn (1997)
	Keman and Pennings (1995)	W. Coleman and Jacek (1989)	D. McCann (1995)**
	Lehmbruch (1998)**	C. Crouch (1993)	Misra and Hicks (1994)
	Lehner (1987)	C. Crouch and Menon (1997)	Van Waarden (1995)
	Lijphart and Crepaz (1991)	W. Grant (1991a)	
	M. Olson (1982)	W. Grant (1991b)	

TABLE 10.1 (continued)

APPROACH	Macrolevel	Mesolevel	Microlevel
THEORETICAL STUDIES			
Theoretical Mix	Richardson (1982)**	W. Grant (1991c)	
	Richardson (1993a)	W. Grant and Paterson (1994)	
	Shambayati (1994)	Hicks and Kenworthy (1998)	
	C. Thomas (1993a)	Hollingsworth, Schmitter, and	
	C. Thomas (2001a)	Streeck (1994a)	
	Van Schendelen (1993)	Jacek (1991)	
	G. Wilson (1990a)	Lehmbruch (1998)**	
	G. Wilson (1992)	Lehner (1998)	
	Zeigler (1988)	D. McCann (1995)**	
		Paterson (1991)	
		Richardson (1982)**	
		Streeck (1998)	
		Traxler (1993)	
		Traxler (1995a)	
		Traxler (1995b)	
		Traxler and Unger (1994)	
		Whitston (1991)	
		Wilsford (1991)	
		G. Wilson (1990b)*	
ATHEORETICAL STUDIES	Ehrmann (1958)		Windmuller and Gladstone (1984)
	Presthus (1974b)		

* The scope is *mainly* in this catagory.
** The scope is *partly* in this catagory.
Source: Compiled by the authors.

TABLE 10.2 The Focus of Cross-National Interest Group Studies

Interest Group Creation and Maintenance

Berger (1981a)**
W. Coleman (1990)**
W. Coleman and Jacek (1989)**
Crepaz and Lijphart (1995)**
C. Crouch (1993)**
Frenkel (1993)**
Hausner, Pedersen, and Ronit (1995)**
Heilbrunn (1997)**
Keman and Pennings (1995)**
Lijphart and Crepaz (1991)**

Misra and Hicks (1994)
Pratt (1993)*
Shambayati (1994)**
Streeck (1998)**
C. Thomas (2001a)**
Traxler (1993)**
Useem (1984)**
Whitston (1991)**
Windmuller and Gladstone (1984)**
Zeigler (1988)**

Interest Group Membership

Baumgartner (1996)**
Berger (1981a)**
Chiesi (1991)
W. Coleman (1990)**
W. Coleman and Grant (1988)**
W. Coleman and Jacek (1989)**
C. Crouch (1993)**
C. Crouch and Menon (1997)**
Frenkel (1993)**
W. Grant (1991a)
Hausner, Pedersen, and Ronit (1995)**
Haverland (1998)**
Heilbrunn (1997)**
Lane and Bachmann (1997)

D. McCann (1995)**
Schmitter (1995)*
Shambayati (1994)**
Streeck (1998)**
C. Thomas (2001a)**
Traxler (1993)**
Traxler (1995a)**
Traxler (1995b)*
Useem (1984)**
Van Waarden (1995)*
Windmuller and Gladstone (1984)**
Yishai (1998b)**
Zeigler (1988)**

Interest Groups in the Public Policy Process

Appleby and Bessant (1987)
Atkinson and Coleman (1989a)
Ball and Millard (1987)
Baumgartner (1996)**
Baumgartner and Walker (1989)
Berger (1981a)**
Cavanagh (1998)
Cawson (1985)*
W. Coleman (1994)
W. Coleman and Grant (1988)**
W. Coleman and Jacek (1989)**
Collier and Mahoney (1997)
Compston (1994)
Compston (1995a)
Compston (1995b)

Jacek (1991)
Katzenstein (1985)
Keman and Pennings (1995)**
Knoke, et al. (1996)
Lehmbruch (1998)
Lehmbruch and Schmitter (1982)*
Lehner (1987)
Lehner (1998)
MacMillan and Turner (1987)
D. McCann (1995)**
Nyang'oro and Shaw (1989)*
M. Olson (1982)
Paterson (1991)
Presthus (1974b)
M. Rhodes (1997)

(continued)

TABLE 10.2 (continued)

Compston (1997)	Richardson (1982)
Compston (1998)	Richardson (1993a)
Cox and O'Sullivan (1988)*	Schenkel (1998)
Crepaz (1992)	Schmitter and Grote (1997)*
Crepaz and Lijphart (1995)**	Scruggs (1999)
C. Crouch (1993)**	Shambayati (1994)**
C. Crouch (1995)	M. J. Smith (1993)
C. Crouch and Menon (1997)**	Streeck and Schmitter (1985)
Czada (1987)	C. Thomas (1993a)
Daugbjerg (1998a)	C. Thomas (2001a)**
Daugbjerg (1998b)	Traxler (1995a)**
Dunn and Perl (1994)	Traxler and Unger (1994)
Frenkel (1993)**	Treu (1992)*
Goldthorpe (1984)*	Van Schendelen (1993)
W. Grant (1991b)	Van Waarden (1992b)
W. Grant (1991c)	Vogel (1993)
W. Grant (1992)	Whitston (1991)**
W. Grant and Paterson (1994)	Wilks and Wright (1987)
W. Grant, Paterson, and Whitston (1987)	Wilsford (1991)
W. Grant, Paterson, and Whitston (1988)	G. Wilson (1977)*
Greenwood and Thomas (1998)	G. Wilson (1990a)*
Hausner, Pedersen, and Ronit (1995)**	G. Wilson (1990b)*
Haverland (1998)**	G. Wilson (1992)*
Hicks and Kenworthy (1998)	Windmuller and Gladstone (1984)**
Hollingsworth, Schmitter, and Streeck (1994a)	Yishai (1998b)**
Immergut (1992)	Zeigler (1988)**
Lijphart and Crepaz (1991)**	

* The scope is *mainly* in this category.
** The scope is *partly* in this category.

Source: Compiled by the authors.

policy network such as issue networks, policy communities, and various other categories of neocorporatism.

As mentioned before, in the late 1980s and early 1990s it looked as if the neocorporatist paradigm would be replaced as the mainstream conceptual framework for cross-national research by the policy-network approach and, to a lesser extent, by neoinstitutionalism. However, this has not yet occurred. Daugbjerg (1998b, 78–79) notes that "cross-national studies of policy networks are the exception rather than the rule" and this is borne out in Table 10.1. According to the classification list in Table 10.1, there have also been only a handful of neoinstitutionalism studies since the late 1980s.

Thus, the introduction of policy-network analysis and neoinstitutionalism has not meant a marginalization of the two established perspectives of pluralism and neocorporatism. On the contrary, as the previous section makes clear, the neocorporatist perspective in particular still appears to be very vibrant. In fact, at present there is no single paradigm or conceptual framework setting the tone for cross-national comparisons of interest groups. In the early 2000s theoretical eclecticism is increasingly becoming the most attractive approach.

The Scope of Analysis

There is no existing *comprehensive* cross-national study of interest group politics. In fact, the existing *scope* of analyses in this field is very limited. Such a limited scope is, of course, inevitable. Covering every example of an interest group or even interest group system on this globe is simply impossible and therefore cross-national research has to be selective. Selectivity will depend, in part, on the theoretical approach and the focus of a study (see Table 10.2). The combination of approach and focus leave many options open for the inevitable narrowing of a study's scope. Narrowing the scope involves a selection of countries to be compared.

There are cross-national studies of 10 countries or more, such as those by Compston (1997), W. Grant (1991c), Martinelli (1991), M. Rhodes (1997), Richardson (1993a), Schmitter and Grote (1997), and C. Thomas (1993a and 2001a). There are also comparative studies of no more than two countries, for instance, studies by Appleby and Bessant (1987), Baumgartner (1996), Cavanagh (1998), C. Crouch (1995), Daugbjerg (1998a and 1998b), Dunn and Perl (1994), Heilbrunn (1997), Lane and Bachmann (1997), MacMillan and Turner (1987), Schenkel (1998), Shambayati (1994), M. J. Smith (1993), Useem (1984), Wilsford (1991), and G. Wilson (1977).

Besides selecting which countries to compare, deciding on the scope of the research is a function of the level of interest group politics to be analyzed. It is on these level-related differences (macro, meso, and micro) between studies that the second, the horizontal (left to right), classification in Table 10.1 is based. Some studies are macro-level analyses that examine the whole population (system) of interest groups in each country. Others are meso-level studies and limit themselves to the comparison of interest groups in a particular sector, such as the chemical or the dairy industry, or in a one-policy domain, such as health care. Micro-level studies compare examples of a specific type of interest group in two or more countries, for instance, environmentalist organizations, unions, or employers' associations.

Finally, to date studies have been narrow in scope, concentrating overwhelmingly on producer interests—mainly various types of business associations and trade unions. Public interest or cause groups seem to constitute some sort of blind spot in research. Again, this can be attributed to the exclusively or partially neocorporatist orientation of much comparative research. Whether alternative approaches, such as neoinstitutionalism and policy-network analysis, may lend themselves more to studying public interest or cause groups cross-nationally (and stimulate a widening of the scope of studies) remains to be seen. Scholars who have taken the first step toward that direction are Baumgartner (1996), Pratt

285

(1993), and Vogel (1993), in addition to (albeit more modestly) Bressers, O'Toole, and Richardson (1995), Haverland (1998), Schenkel (1998), and M. J. Smith (1993). However, for the moment cross-national studies on public interest groups still seem largely the preserve of social movement research (see section 10.6.).

The Focus of Studies

Not only has the approach and scope varied in comparative interest group studies, but so has the *focus*. First, some studies concentrate on origin, organization, and maintenance of groups (see section 1.6.). Second, and to a certain extent within this first category, but large enough to warrant being mentioned separately, several studies examine the relationship between established interest groups and their members and nonaffiliated supporters. Then there are studies focusing on the role of interest groups in the public policy process (see section 1.6.). Thus, using neocorporatist terminology, there are logic-of-organization, logic-of-membership, and logic-of-influence studies. To these a fourth category should be added: studies that examine interest groups from two of these or from all three angles.

Since the early 1970s, however, studies devoted to various aspects of logic-of-influence constitute the bulk of cross-national comparisons of interest groups. This is likely due to the omnipresence, and for a time the predominance, of the neocorporatist approach. As Van Waarden (1992c, 523–24) points out, neocorporatism looks at interest groups primarily from a logic-of-influence angle, concentrating on: (1) their relations with other stakeholders in political arenas (the government always playing a leading part); and (2) directly linked to these arenas, how these organizations fulfil their top down control function and their capacity for self-discipline and for regulating the behavior of their members.

In this respect, the development of alternative approaches to comparative research since the late 1980s—mainly policy network and neoinstitutionalist research—have made few changes in the focus of studies. On the contrary, even more than the neocorporatist perspective, policy-network studies are inclined to a logic-of-influence bias. This is also the focus of many neoinstitutionalist analyses but less so overall. Some exceptions are the works of W. Coleman (1990), Lane and Bachmann (1997), and Pratt (1993), as well as Baumgartner (1996), Haverland (1998), and Yishai (1998b). While often including the logic-of-influence approach, these studies have mainly focused on a logic-of-organization or a logic-of-membership approach and sometimes the combination of the two.

There is one important study that is not classified in Table 10.1 or 10.2 because the study has not been published. But it needs to be mentioned because it is referenced frequently in bibliographies and publications of cross-national interest group studies. It is a discussion paper of more than 250 pages by Schmitter and Streeck (1981) setting out the research design and underlying conceptual framework of a large cross-national project on the organization of business interests (OBI). This study was conducted during the 1980s and involved 10 national research teams. Examples of publications reporting on the OBI project's findings are: W. Coleman and Grant (1988), W. Coleman and Jacek (1989), W. Grant (1987), W. Grant and Streeck (1985), Martinelli (1991), Sargent (1985b), and Van Waarden (1995).

10.4. A CRITICAL ASSESSMENT OF CROSS-NATIONAL INTEREST GROUP STUDIES

Undoubtedly, cross-national research has taught us much about interest group politics, both in general and with regard to the specific characteristics of what happens in one country or a group of countries. However, existing studies have their weaknesses and shortcomings. In this section we examine four of these: conceptual confusion; a dearth of comparisons in many comparative studies; a questionable selection of countries and topics; and a disconnect between empirical evidence and theory. In part, this critique serves as a charting of further directions for research. Then the concluding section of the chapter offers three other possible approaches and directions for future work on cross-national interest groups.

Conceptual Confusion

One of the major problems of cross-national interest group research is conceptual confusion and differences in the operationalization of concepts. The result is that the findings of many cross-national comparative studies are, ironically, not comparable. In particular, through the years this has been a trademark of studies on neocorporatism.

A major cause of this conceptual confusion is that definitions of neocorporatism vary widely. This definitional problem was acknowledged in the formative years of the neocorporatist approach by leading scholars such as Lehmbruch (1982) and Schmitter (1982). Since then, some of the confusion has been cleared up; but, as Peter Williamson (1989, 5) indicates, neocorporatism remains "a rather elastic concept with a somewhat uncertain core." Most definitions are vague and lend themselves to more than one interpretation. This leads to considerable differences in the operationalization of concepts. For example, the disagreement between Frank Wilson (1983) and Keeler (1985) over whether or not French interest group politics is neocorporatist is rooted in different definitions of neocorporatism.

Another example is provided by Peter Williamson (1989). He examined the findings of several researchers who have attempted to construct a sort of cross-national neocorporatist league table. Two of them, Schmitter and Lehmbruch, have ranked countries according to their degree of neocorporatism at the national level. Schmitter's operationalization of neocor-

TABLE 10.3 Cross-National Comparison of the Degree of Neocorporatism

Schmitter	Lehmbruch
Strong	
1. Austria	1. Austria
2. Norway	2. Sweden
3. Denmark	3. Norway
4. Finland	4. Netherlands
5. Sweden	
Medium	
6. Netherlands	5. Belgium
7. Belgium	6. West Germany
8. West Germany	7. Denmark
9. Switzerland	8. Finland
	9. Switzerland
Weak	
10. Canada	10. United Kingdom
11. Ireland*	11. Italy**
12. United States	
13. France*	
14. United Kingdom	
Pluralism	
None	12. United States
	13. Canada

* Listed by Schmitter only.
** Listed by Lehmbruch only.

Source: Adapted from Peter J. Williamson, *Corporatism in Perspective: An Introductory Guide to Corporatist Theory* (London: Sage Publications, 1989), 148–50.

poratism was based on two structural characteristics of trade unions: the degree of organizational centralization and the extent to which a single national association enjoyed a representational monopoly. Lehmbruch, on the other hand, measured neocorporatism as the degree of institutionalized participation of labor unions and organized business in governmental policy making. As shown in Table 10.3, the consequence is that Schmitter's ranking of countries and that of Lehmbruch differed. As Williamson also pointed out, Schmidt (1982) offers yet another variation in ranking (P. Williamson 1989, 148–50).

However, differences in definition and in the operationalization of core concepts have not only bedeviled neocorporatist writings. The policy-network approach is handicapped by similar problems. A series of assessments of work in this field (G. Jordan and Schubert 1992; R. Rhodes and Marsh 1992; Van Waarden 1992a) point out various elements of conceptualization and measurement on which there is no unanimity. Researchers disagree on central elements such as what constitutes a *policy network* and a *policy community*, and those who opt for a similar definition of the former concept often do not agree on its distinctive dimensions.

As indicated earlier, the policy-network perspective is a recent development and these disagreements might be considered as both its inevitable growing pains and a stimulating and fruitful diversity of views. In fact, Schmitter (1982, 259–62, 278) made a similar point about how the neocorporatist perspective had evolved during the previous decade. His optimism, however, proved to be a miscalculation. Even in the early 2000s it may still be too soon to cast a final verdict, but the omen for the policy-network analysis perspective is not encouraging: see, for instance, the views expressed by Börzel (1998) and Guy Peters (1998). As Peters points out, the risk of heading toward an impasse should not be underestimated:

> These are more than merely definitional questions. If this corpus of social theory [i.e., the network approach] is to be able to make meaningful statements about the differential impacts of different types of interest group structures then researchers need to be able to separate one from another. (Peters 1998, 24)

The neoinstitutionalist perspective has embarked on a similarly unsettled course. There are two distinctive aspects to this neoinstitutionalism (Bulmer 1998, 369). First is a shift away from formal constitutional-legal interpretations of what constitutes an institution, taking into account some of the less formalized arenas of politics. A second distinctive characteristic—particularly the sociological variant—is the importance attached to the way in which behavior of, for instance, interest groups is guided not only by cognitive elements but also by prescriptive, obligatory, interpretative, and identity-building dimensions of its context. Institutions form a major part of that context and they are the embodiment and dynamic carriers of values and norms, cultures, knowledge and routines, beliefs and meanings. Paraphrasing Bulmer: interest group politics proceeds in a web of all kinds of codes of conduct and it is difficult to isolate this institutional context of formal and informal rules from its normative elements (Bulmer 1998, 369).

These two distinctive aspects to neoinstitutionalism make it a very broad perspective; this besets it with problems of conceptual confusion and a similar scenario with regard to the problems of policy networks. As Peters notes, a fundamental issue appears to be how to know that an institution exists, or indeed what constitutes an institution. He writes: "All the various approaches to institutional analysis offer some form of definition, but all contain sufficient vagueness to make identification of an institution problematic" (G. Peters 1996, 214). Matters are not made any easier by the tendency of some authors to treat institutions as independent and dependent variables simultaneously. This considerably complicates—and in some cases precludes—separating endogenous and exogenous factors and distinguishing between institutions *per se* and surrounding social, economic, and political structures.

Another serious handicap of neoinstitutionalism is that it might easily get trapped in tautologies. As Peters also notes:

> If the rules that shape behavior are expanded to include implicit rules and vague understandings, in order to cover instances in which observed behaviors do not correspond to the formal rules of an institution, then the theory may not be falsifiable. If we observe behaviors that do not conform to the strictures of the formal rules then there must be other rules that were not identifiable. (G. Peters 1996, 215)

Adding to the confusion, as Peters (1996, 211) also points out: "some of the most important characterizations of the relationship between state and society (e.g., corporatism and networks), have many relevant features that could be classified as structural or institutional." This is borne out by the way in which a number of authors have combined neocorporatist, network-related, and neoinstitutionalist concepts as the following examples illustrate. Crepaz (1992, 146) considers neocorporatism to be "a structural institution." Schmitter and Grote (1997, 1) agree and start their analysis by the assertion that the neocorporatist approach "emerged as one subspecies of a much broader genus of theorizing in political economy that has been labeled 'institutionalist.'" For Lane and Bachmann industry associations are essential components of the institutional environment influencing the quality of inter-firm relations:

> Similar to legal regulation, they represent institutional forms of shared knowledge which provide members with orientations for action. Thus, they ensure the validity of commonly accepted technical standards and rules of business behaviour. (Lane and Bachmann 1997, 230)

The equation on which Hicks and Kenworthy (1998, 1660) build their cross-national comparison of determinants of political economic performance is neocorporatism as a "polity-centered" political institution. Lehmbruch (1998) argues that the neocorporatist, policy-network, and neoinstitutionalist approaches can be blended with each other. Yet another option is what Börzel (1998, 263) terms the governance variant of policy-network studies: focusing on the specific form of public-private interaction that is characterized by nonhierarchical coordination. Here networks are conceptualized as informal institutions.

Is all this an indication of a battle over turf between neoinstitutionalists, proponents of the policy-network perspective, and neocorporatists?

For instance, the latter may argue that taking institutional parameters into account when the position and role of interest groups are analyzed is really nothing new. Institutions have always figured prominently in neocorporatist analyses, particularly when they are concerned with how logic-of-influence processes work. From the beginning, neoinstitutionalists have more or less acknowledged this neocorporatist argument (Immergut 1992, 21–22). However, neoinstitutionalists claim that their analysis of institutions is wider and more thorough. The way they justify that claim, theoretically and by carrying out empirical research, will not convince everyone. And this may well herald a reenactment of the battle pluralists and neocorporatists have been fighting for many years.

A Dearth of Comparisons in Many Comparative Studies

Another major weakness of cross-national interest group research is that many studies that claim to be comparative are, in fact, very limited in their comparisons. Their contribution to knowledge on interest groups is often very valuable; but their contribution to comparative research is questionable.

Take, for instance, the volume on pressure groups edited by Richardson (1993a). It contains an excellent chapter devoted to France. However, its author tells us very little about how France compares with other countries. The same goes for the chapters on the United Kingdom, Germany, and Italy, among others. In fact, only the introductory chapter by the editor provides a genuinely comparative perspective. The remainder of the book, apart from four chapters discussing general elements of pressure group theory, is a series of country-by-country case studies. It is left up to the reader to compare the findings of these case studies. The edited volumes on EC-lobbying by Van Schendelen (1993), by Clive Thomas (1993a) on First World interest groups, and his (2001a) volume on the relationship between political parties and interest groups are in the same vein. However, the books by Thomas have introductory and concluding comparative chapters that attempt to integrate the individual country chapters and point to trends in cross-national interest group activity.

The problem is largely a matter of research format. A country-by-country approach is not the most appropriate way to thoroughly understand cross-national differences and similarities of interest group politics, or, indeed, any other political phenomena. This may be especially true when the study involves a team of researchers each working independently on one country.

A Questionable Selection of Countries and Topics

As indicated earlier, the limited scope of cross-national interest group studies is something that cannot be avoided. However, to date the resultant selectivity of countries and topics lacks systematic logic and shows little concern about a cumulative building of findings and knowledge. This is, to a large extent, inevitable given the fragmented, uncoordinated, and predominately individualistic nature of the scholarly community in this and many other academic fields in Western countries. The upshot is that the selection aspect of existing studies has produced a very mixed bag of information.

With regard to the general comparative studies of countries, there is a lack of comparative studies on southern and Eastern Europe, as well as South America and Asia. Cross-national research still overwhelmingly concentrates on interest groups in what Thomas (1993a) calls First World liberal democracies. These include: the United States; Canada; the northern countries in Western Europe, usually the United Kingdom, Germany, Austria, Belgium, the Netherlands, Denmark, Sweden, Norway, and sometimes France and Italy; and very occasionally Australia and New Zealand. Finland, Greece, Portugal, Spain, Switzerland, Turkey, and countries in Eastern Europe and on other continents, apart from Israel and Japan, remain largely uncharted territory.

Work by Thomas (1993a), which includes chapters on Italy, Switzerland, Australia, and New Zealand, and Thomas (2001a), which includes chapters on Italy, Spain, Poland, the Czech Republic, Argentina, and Mexico attempts to address this problem. The studies by Ball and Millard (1987) and Zeigler (1988), plus what Collier and Mahoney (1997), Schmitter (1995), and Yishai (1998b) have done, and the volumes edited by Frenkel (1993), Hausner, Pedersen, and Ranit (1995), and Nyang'oro and Shaw (1989), have also taken a broader country perspective. In addition, there are a few publications on very specific topics. For example, there is Shambayati's (1994) analysis of the rentier state type of interest groups and Heilbrunn's (1997) article on Togo's cloth retailers' cartel and Benin's merchants' association. However, these publications are the exceptions to this First World liberal democracy rule of the choice of countries.

Turning to the choice of sectors for comparative interest group analysis, many studies have been conducted on the position and role of business interest groups including business associations. These include the chemical construction, dairy, food processing, pharmaceutical, and steel industry sectors, as well as the labor-relations area. Other business sectors, however, such as the automobile industry, banking, tourism, and road transport, have been largely neglected.

Moreover, for those business sectors that have been compared cross-nationally, a limited number, but not of a consistent range, of countries have been used. Certainly, as mentioned above, this is understandable given that researchers are free to choose their topics and focus, but it does make cross-country comparisons difficult from the existing research. Leaving aside comprehensive studies covering 10 or more countries, the comparison of business most frequently found is between the former

West Germany (FRG) and the United Kingdom, for example, in Appleby and Bessant (1987), C. Crouch (1995), W. Grant, Paterson, and Whitston (1987, 1988), W. Grant and Streeck (1985), Lane and Bachmann (1997), MacMillan and Turner (1987), W. Coleman (1994; FRG versus UK versus U.S.), Haverland (1998; FRG versus Netherlands versus UK), and Traxler and Unger (1994; Austria versus FRG versus UK).

With regard to the countries chosen for comparison of specific business sectors, these also vary considerably. For the chemical sector there is V. Schneider (1985) comparing former West Germany and the United States. For the steel industry there is M. Rhodes (1985) comparing France, Germany, and Italy. For the pharmaceutical sector there are two of the series of country-by-country case studies in Streeck and Schmitter (1985), one discussing the United Kingdom (Sargent 1985) and the other, the Netherlands (De Vroom 1985). Four of that same series of country-by-country case studies analyze the dairy sector's interest group landscape in Austria (Traxler 1985), the Netherlands (Van Waarden 1985), Switzerland (Farago 1985) and the United Kingdom (W. Grant 1985b).

Not only do the selections of countries differ because comparisons of sectoral business associations are chosen by researchers independently of others working in a similar area, sometimes this problem is also found in a book where it would be expected that systematic choice is essential. One example is the edited volume by Hollingsworth, Schmitter, and Streeck (1994a) on modes of economic governance (sectoral regimes) from the point of view of their efficiency and performance in the 1970s and 1980s. Here, as in many other such single volumes, selectivity is less than systematic. The editors admit that in the series of case studies they present, the number and selection of countries compared for each sector differ widely because: "the choice of sectors was constrained by the need to connect with ongoing research . . . and to find participants who were sympathetic to the project's general approach." Their argument that this should be acceptable "since the project does not primarily aim either at understanding particular countries or at surveying the universe of sectors, but tries to shed light on the general relationship between institutional structures and economic performance" is disputable (Hollingsworth, Schmitter, and Streeck 1994b, 13–14).

The Failure of Empirical Studies to Draw Adequately upon the Theory

A fourth criticism of existing cross-national research is a disconnect between empirical work and theory. As Williamson expresses it in regard to the neocorporatist approach:

> It is not the case that such works can be characterized as a-theoretical. There is, nonetheless, a general looseness with which the theory is applied.

> Usually the theoretical stance is outlined and the evidence is held to fit with it, but it is doubtful whether it is properly, and certainly fully, tested. . . . It should be added straight away that there are exceptions to this. . . . Overall, however, one has to scour reasonably enthusiastically the pages of these empirically based studies to find evidence in support, or indeed against, the kind of general propositions raised in the theoretical discussions. (P. Williamson 1989, 198)

This empirical-theoretical disconnect is even greater with regard to the policy-network and the neoinstitutionalist perspectives. Indeed, one objection often raised against both perspectives is that to date there is no policy-network or neoinstitutionalism theory that facilitates meaningful empirical analysis.

With regard to the policy network approach, according to Börzel (1998, 266) one of its fundamental problems is a lack of explanatory power. She argues that studies are unable to formulate hypotheses that systematically link the nature and structure of networks with the character and outcome of policy processes. Hence, the judgement that policy-network analysis has not moved beyond the stage of being merely a useful toolbox for describing mechanisms of interest intermediation. In fact, in terms of measurement methods and techniques that requires precise, valid, and reliable descriptive analysis, the policy-network perspective may turn out to be much less of an adequate toolbox than is commonly supposed. Sociological and anthropological network research is much more sophisticated in this respect. However, there seems to be a widespread reluctance among political scientists to employ the methods and techniques developed in these fields of study (see section 10.5.).

Like Börzel, Peters questions the insights and knowledge that can be gained through policy-network analyses:

> . . . it is not clear if the implicit causal analysis contained within the network approach to policy can be falsified. When there are policy outcomes of whatever sort, they can always be attributed *ex post* to the actions and interactions of the network. While that may well be true, it does not advance the process of explaining and predicting the outcomes unless the nature of the effects can be predicted *ex ante*. (G. Peters 1998, 23)

Peters also criticizes the lack of any substantial theory on why and how policy networks make a difference, such as for interest intermediation. As indicated above, this is in large part due to the problems in defining what constitutes a network and to what are appropriate criteria for operationalizing and measuring the different forms it can take. In this regard, Peters writes:

> As it is, in few if any of the available network conceptualizations do the networks have sufficient articulation and elaboration to be used as explanatory

factors. . . . The only hypothesis available is the fundamental one—networks matter—but that alone is almost certainly insufficient as the starting point for a serious theoretical investigation. (G. Peters 1998, 25)

Indeed, at present not much that goes beyond the metaphorical level is to be expected from the policy-network approach; " . . . theoretical meat must be added to these strong metaphorical bones" (G. Peters 1998, 26) to reach the level of models capable of explaining outcomes in a systematic manner.

Turing to neoinstitutionalism, some skeptics are very outspoken. For instance, Rothstein considers that this approach is synonymous with theoretical emptiness. He writes:

To say that "institutions matter" does not tell us anything about *which institutions* are more important than others and *for what issues*. The value of the institutional approach may only emerge when it is combined with a more substantial theory from which we can draw hypotheses about why some agents, resources and institutions are more important than others. (Rothstein 1996, 154)

It is clear that the neoinstitutionalists' theory building is seriously hampered by the definition and conceptualization-related problems mentioned above. Also problematic is that they are often overambitious and want to reduce all politics to institutional variables. By attempting to explain, or perhaps even claiming to explain everything, neoinstitutional analysis may end up explaining nothing (G. Peters 1996, 217).

10.5. ADDITIONAL FUTURE DIRECTIONS FOR COMPARATIVE INTEREST GROUP RESEARCH

In critiquing existing comparative interest group research, the previous section of the chapter implicitly provided directions for future research. In this final section we offer three additional suggestions that would improve both the methodology and the range of research addressed by comparative interest group studies.

The Value of Research on Social Movements

So far this chapter has discussed only cross-national research that falls explicitly under the heading "interest group studies." There is, however, a closely connected field of research of social movement studies. This is situated in a no-man's land between political science and sociology but if tapped can be of considerable value in enhancing comparative interest group research.

Historically, a borderline has developed separating the research fields of interest groups and social movements. This is partly because most interest group studies have been conducted by political scientists, whereas social movement research has been mainly the province of sociologists. Whether or not this distinction can be justified will not be discussed here. However, some researchers (for example, J. Walker 1991; Knoke et al. 1996) have crossed the borders between both fields of research with some enlightening results. Therefore, the argument here is that it may be very worthwhile for comparative interest group scholars to review the methods, findings, and insights cross-national social movement studies have to offer.

The value of tapping these studies becomes clearer by taking into account the common ground they share with interest group research. First, the research agendas in both areas are very similar in terms of the kind of phenomena and processes to be analyzed—organization, membership, extent of influence, and so on. Second, many interest groups began as social movements or as off-shoots of social movements. An obvious example is trade unions in Western European countries. Third, a distinction is often made between social movements in general and the specific organizations that form their core. The latter are called social movement organizations (SMOs) and many have most of the characteristics of an interest group.

Indeed, many established interest groups can still be considered SMOs. This is particularly true of many so-called public interest or cause groups. The number of these organizations has significantly risen since the 1970s in Western countries and they have had a major effect on interest group politics. However, a difficult question often arises as to whether political phenomena such as environmentalism and the promotion of women's rights are primarily SMOs or conventional interest groups. Obviously, the answer varies depending on the country and, often even more so, on the specific organization being considered. For instance, there may be a world of difference between Greenpeace, the Sierra Club (a U.S. environmental group), and the British Society for the Protection of Birds. Furthermore, an organization such as Greenpeace may switch from an SMO to an interest group, or vice versa, depending on the type of issue as well as the characteristics of the political arena involved.

To draw up a list of recent cross-national social movement studies is beyond the boundaries of this chapter. However, three very good examples of what this field has to offer are Dalton and Kuechler (1990), Jenkins and Klandermans (1995), and Meyer and Tarrow (1998).

The Internal Dynamics of Groups

It was noted earlier that most subjects regarding the creation and formation of interest groups and group membership (in neocorporatist terms their logic-of-organization and logic-of-membership) are relatively under-studied. In particular, the internal structures and dynamics of interest groups have been almost completely neglected. The analysis of interest groups and associations in the United States developed by Knoke

(1990), what he calls the internal political economy of these organizations, does not seem to have interested researchers in the area of cross-national studies.

The conceptual framework developed by Clive Thomas (1993a, 15–22) as a basis for comparisons illustrates this. It sets out a series of factors influencing the makeup, operating techniques, and effect on public policy of interest groups. This framework will prove very useful for further research. However, Thomas leaves us empty-handed when it comes to analyzing the internal dynamics of the interest groups in regard to group organization and internal operating techniques, how variations in these might affect the operation of groups in the public policy process, and how the interaction of the internal and external role of interest groups can be compared cross-nationally. But Thomas's volume is not alone in these shortcomings: it is illustrative of the great majority of cross-national interest group studies. In contrast, in cross-national social movement research, placing emphasis or focus on explaining the origins and genesis of collective action appears to be an enduring concern.

Subnational Studies

Finally, also missing in the field of cross-national interest group studies are studies on subnational politics. So far, barely any attention has been paid to cross-national variations in the morphology, position, and role of interest groups at the regional or local level. The edited volume by W. Coleman and Jacek (1989) is the exception that confirms the rule.

Comparative political research has invariably concentrated on phenomena at the national level. To what extent this reflects the view that politics at a regional or local level matters less and can therefore be neglected is difficult to say. If that view was ever held and possibly defended (although this is very doubtful), it can no longer be justified today.

Regardless of whether or not regional and local politics carries less weight than what happens at the national level in a country, a number of recent studies have demonstrated that it provides an excellent terrain for cross-national research: see, for example, Mellors and Pijnenburg (1989). Moreover, particularly in Western Europe, the indications are that local communities, and even more so, regions have actually become and are further developing into major political entities. For instance, trends towards decentralization, regionalization, and, in some cases, even federalization can be observed in Britain, Belgium, and Italy, to name only the major examples. For cross-national interest group research to ignore these significant changes will leave a major gap in the literature.

Chapter 11

Interest Groups in Selected Western European and Other Advanced Pluralist Democracies

11.1. THE "RECENT DISCOVERY" OF INTEREST GROUPS

Clive S. Thomas

With the exception of the United States, the study of interest groups as a force in public policy making in pluralist democracies has developed in a significant way only since the mid-1970s. Until then, other than the work of a few scholars, interest groups were believed to be uniquely American and not seen as existing in the parliamentary democracies of Western Europe and the rest of the world. Interest groups had, of course, always existed in these systems and some interests—particularly business and labor—had long been influential (Thomas 2001a). With regard to British politics, for instance, Wootton (1972) clearly shows that organized interests were prominent in the late eighteenth century and, indeed, in the middle ages in the form of craft and merchant guilds (see also Wootton 1963; and Rush 1990).

However, the strong political party system and the concentration of power in the cabinet in pluralist parliamentary systems focused scholarly work away from interest groups for two major reasons. First, scholars concentrated their investigations on parties, cabinets, and bureaucracies as these appeared to be the powerhouses of parliamentary systems. Second, interest group activity was (and to a large extent remains) much less visible than in the United States, operating behind the scenes in parties and the executive, and was virtually nonexistent in parliaments and there was no corps of lobbyists in the American sense. The upshot was the belief that interest groups were of little if any significance with a consequent lack of scholarly work on them. As a result, as recently as the early 1970s, no text on politics in Britain, Canada, or Japan, among other countries, included a separate chapter on interest groups and few included the terms *interest group* (or *pressure group* as was the term used outside the United States), *lobbying*, or *lobbyist* in their index.

By 1980, however, there was substantial work on the interest group systems of several parliamentary democracies, and a coterie of interest group scholars developed in most of these countries and has gradually expanded in number. In addition, several scholars began to study interest groups in the European Union (EU) policy process. The impetus for the increasing focus on interest groups in parliamentary systems was twofold.

First, in the 1950s and 1960s, some scholars who took a pluralist approach began to examine interest groups as significant political organizations. This included a project directed by Almond (1958), which examined several countries; work by Beer (1956) and Finer (1958) on Britain; and by LaPalombara (1964) on Italy. Second, a seminal article by Philippe Schmitter (1974), "Still the Century of Corporatism?", while not originating the subfield of corporatist studies (see section 3.4.), in effect, initiated the neocorporatist approach to the study of public policy making in liberal democracies, particularly those of continental Europe. Schmitter gave a great boost to the study of interest groups in pluralist systems outside the United States (which is generally considered to lack the elements necessary for neocorporatist policy making). The result has been an extensive literature on the neocorporatist approach to interest groups.

Thus, since the mid-1970s, there have been three broad categories of literature on interest groups and public policy making in liberal democracies: (1) pluralist studies, (2) neocorporatist studies, and (3) some combination of the two. The degree to which the work on a particular country is dominated by one or the other categories depends, as might be expected, on the extent to which pluralist or neocorporatist arrangements reflect its actual policy-making process. The literature on countries such as Austria, Switzerland, and particularly the Scandinavian countries where neocorporatism is seen as a major factor in policy making is dominated by neocorporatist studies. In contrast, work on Canada and Japan and even Australia and New Zealand, where pluralism appears to be more dominant in policy making, have a literature emphasizing the pluralist approach. Falling in between is the literature on countries such as Britain, France, and Italy and work on the EU. As the countries selected for this chapter include all the major Western democracies (plus the EU) and many smaller ones, it provides a spectrum of the pluralist and neocorporatist approach and combinations of the two.

In combination, these various categories of literature have shown that interest groups are indeed a central part of policy making in parliamentary democracies. In fact, some groups, such as the Schweizereische Handels- und Industries-Verein (VORORT), the peak association for Swiss business, and the Landsorganisationen (LO), the Confederation of Swedish Trade Unions, are dominant forces and are likely relatively more influential in the policy process in their respective countries than any groups in the United States, the country where interest groups *were* seen to be most dominant. Furthermore, the gradual erosion of social democracy and neocorporatism and the consequent increase in pluralism in many parliamentary democracies, have increased the options open to interest groups. Thus, in effect (though likely not by intent) an Americanization of interest group activity has taken place with increased visibility of groups, an expansion in their points of access, and in strategies and tactics available to them. Expansion in the range of the strategies and tactics includes an increase in the use of lobbyists, public relations campaigns, the emergence of grassroots lobbying, and even the lobbying of parliaments (P. Norton 1999). However, the trend toward homogenization of lobbying activity across Western democracies is restrained by the particular political history and political development of each country, by their political cultures, and by their particular governmental institutional structures among other factors, as the following entries on individual countries illustrate.

11.2. THE UNITED KINGDOM

Grant Jordan

As in most parliamentary democracies, interest groups were not seen to exist in Britain until the work of Beer (1956) and Finer (1958). It was particularly Finer who "discovered" them in his ground-breaking work *Anonymous Empire* (1958). Interest groups have, of course, always existed in Britain in large numbers. One study, which did not include campaign groups, recorded 5,766 organizations active in 1993 (CBD 1994). Of these, 1,179 appear to engage in major lobbying activity. The data allowed analysis by date of creation showing that current groups are more likely to have been formed in the past 30 years than earlier: 698 were created from 1900 to 1929, 1,146 between 1930 and 1959, but 2,798 from 1960 to 1989. In the brief period from 1990 to 1993 the total number created was 304.

Stimulated by Beer and Finer, the major expansion in interest groups and the decreasing appeal of parties, considerable scholarship has been conducted on groups in the United Kingdom since the late 1970s. Major general works include Richardson and Jordan (1979), Marsh and Chambers (1983), A. Jordan and Richardson (1987), W. Grant (1995), and Baggott (1995). On lobbyists and lobbying there is work by Greer (1985), G. Jordan (1991), and C. Miller (1990, 2000); and G. Jordan (1998) examines the issue of lobby regulation. The juncture between interest groups and political parties is considered in G. Jordan and Maloney (2001).

Two major and interrelated discussions in the British interest group literature center on the role of groups and the extent of their power. The classic account of policy making in the pre-1980s—the Thatcher years—stressing the integration of groups, was by Finer (1958, 21) who wrote: "When a group wants something, it will try to go to the ministry first. . . . The relationship between some lobbies and the ministry may be very close, with each side having something to give the other." Finer's work and that of others underpinned the policy community interpretation of British politics explored by A. Jordan and Richardson (1987), Richardson and Jordan (1979), and D. Marsh and Rhodes (1992), among others. This echoes the group subgovernment concept developed in the United States, which sees policy making as a product of sectoral relationships between niche and sectoral groups and specialist civil servants. However, work by A. G. Jordan, Maloney, and McLaughlin (1994) challenges the view that policy-making influence is restricted to peak associations in a sector. While the list of influential groups in a sector, for example, in agriculture, is restricted, the list appears to include agribusinesses, narrow specialist associations, and retailing and other interests, not just the National Farmers Union (NFU).

Given the scale of interest group numbers and memberships, the "decline of parties" and their replacement by group participation, interest groups are now taken seriously in Britain (W. Grant 1995). Thus, the policy about face by Shell Oil over the deep sea disposal of the Brent Spar oil facility in 1995 after an occupation by Greenpeace was seen as a triumph of single-issue politics (G. Jordan 2001).

In contrast, other academic work on the role and power of interest groups in the United Kingdom over the past two decades suggests a reduction in their influence (for example, G. Wilson 1990a, 84, 99). Comments about reduced influence, however, tend to be about the more established and insider groups. One interpretation is that Mrs. Thatcher disliked groups and was determined to reduce corporatist arrangements. There was certainly a conscious attempt to reduce trade union influence. But it would be a mistake to confuse a (perhaps) marginal decrease in group influence with a position of no influence. After noting the Thatcher challenge to practice, Richardson (1993a, 99) concluded: "Thus despite attempts to radically change Britain's policy style during the 1980s, interest groups retained their key role." Similarly, Coxall, Robins, and Coxall (1998, 174) summarized the Conservative government years (1979–97) as follows: "It should not be assumed that relations between the executive and pressure groups broke down. . . . Even where relations with Ministers [ended] groups often retained contacts with civil servants."

Further evidence of this continued importance of groups in the Thatcher years is a study by the Hansard Society (1993) showing an increase in the 1980s in the number of consultation and policy papers produced by government departments, from 72 in 1979 to 232 in 1991.

Less formally, most policy proposals were routinely circulated among a wide constituency.

Under the New Labour Government, the role of groups has not markedly changed. There is still elaborate formal consultation, intense informal negotiation with interests with policy relevance, and, separately, a considerable degree of media-based campaigning by cause and single issue groups on topics such as roads, genetically modified food, and country pursuits (especially fox hunting). In 1956 Beer claimed, "If we had a way of measuring political power, we could possibly demonstrate that at the present time pressure groups are more powerful in Britain than in the United States" (Beer 1956, 3). We still cannot measure power but Beer's is still a reasonable hunch about the significance of British interest groups.

11.3. CONTINENTAL EUROPE

11.3.1. Germany, Austria, Switzerland, and the Benelux Countries

Pamela G. Camerra-Rowe

Germany

Because of Germany's large population and its post-war economic success, interest groups in Germany have received considerable scholarly attention in English. Good overviews of Germany's system of interest representation are Von Beyme (1993), Edinger (1993), and Gellner and Robertson (2001). There is a short essay on attempts to regulate lobbying and lobbyists by Ronit and Schneider (1998). Peter Katzenstein (1987) provides an extensive bibliography, and Clive Thomas (2001a) provides a shorter but more current list of key sources.

Germany's economic success in the 1970s was attributed to its system of corporatist intermediation between peak business and labor groups (Paterson and Smith 1981; Markovits 1982). Some analysts have suggested that elements of the traditional patterns of corporatism are breaking down, in part, because of increasing competition from the global economy (P. Katzenstein 1989). However, interest group representation remains more comprehensive and structured in Germany than in most large, advanced industrialized democracies. The integration of interest groups into the policy process has led to an incremental consensus style of policy making that works against radical change and innovation (P. Katzenstein 1987; Dyson 1982).

Organizations representing labor and business interests are the most studied groups in Germany. Much of the interaction between these groups and government officials occurs at the sectoral level, and there are substantial variations across sectors (P. Katzenstein 1989). Sectoral studies of business groups include W. Grant, Paterson, and Whitston (1988) and W. Grant and Streeck (1985). Streeck (1983) discusses the more general relationship of business associations with the state. Although rather outdated, the most comprehensive work on business associations is Braunthal (1965) on the Federation of German Industry. Among the most extensive studies of German labor unions are Markovits (1986) and Thelen (1991).

The 1970s and 1980s saw the rise of new social movements in Germany, including environmental, feminist, and peace movements (Nelkin and Pollak 1981; Kolinsky 1984; Kitschelt 1986). Unlike traditional interest associations, these new groups tend to work at the grassroots level. Some have been quite effective at influencing policy (Edinger 1993). Environmental movements have received the most attention because of the formation and success of the Green Party (Papadakis 1984).

Austria

Austria has received attention in the interest group literature because it is considered the premier example of neocorporatism. It has a highly institutionalized and centralized system of consultation and bargaining among peak economic groups known as the social partnership. A bibliography on Austrian interest groups can be found in Luther and Müller (1992a). A brief overview of the group system is provided by Gerlich (1987). Peter Katzenstein (1984) provides a comprehensive analysis of economic policy making in Austria.

Labor, business, and agriculture are organized into three compulsory chambers. These three groups, along with Austria's voluntary Trade Union Federation, include almost all working citizens and they participate in all economic and social policy making (Farnleiter and Schmidt 1982; Marin 1985). While this system has been credited for Austria's economic success, it has also been criticized for stifling innovation and limiting flexibility (Pelinka 1987; Crepaz 1995). Some scholars suggest that the social partnership is weakening (Gerlich 1992; Luther and Müller 1992b; Crepaz 1995). The extent of this change and the effects of European integration on Austria's system of interest representation requires further research.

Switzerland

Switzerland's political stability has been attributed to its system of institutionalized, consensus decision making among the leaders of its linguistic and religious subcultures. This is known as consociational (Lijphart 1969) or "amicable agreement" politics (Steiner 1974). General descriptions of Swiss interest group relations can be found in Sidjanski (1974), Kriesi (1982), and Zeigler (1993). Peter Katzenstein (1984) and Armingeon (1997) discuss the organization of economic interests.

There has been controversy over whether Switzerland really fits the consociational model (B. Barry 1975; Bohn 1980). Even if consociationalism described Swiss politics in the past, some scholars suggest that new groups and issues do not fit the consociational pattern (Church 1989). More research needs to be done on how new issues and groups are incorporated into the Swiss interest group system.

The Benelux Countries

Most of the literature on interest groups in the Benelux countries (Belgium, the Netherlands, and Luxembourg) stems from the consociational and corporatist literature, with the Netherlands receiving the most attention. Daalder and Irwin (1989) provide a bibliography on the Netherlands. Overviews of Dutch interest group politics can be found in Daalder and Irwin (1974), Gladdish (1991), and Andeweg and Irwin (1993).

The Netherlands is divided into distinct subcultures, each with its own political parties, labor unions, and employer organizations. Elites from these subcultures engage in formalized and centralized bargaining (Daalder 1966; Lijphart 1975). Peak economic interest groups engage in tripartite negotiations on economic and social policy. There is controversy in the literature about whether the Netherlands is moving away from centralized, consensus policy making and towards a more adversarial style of politics (Scholten 1987b; Lijphart 1989; Wolinetz 1989; Mair 1994).

Belgium is often considered a model case of consociational democracy (Lijphart 1969, 1981). Policy negotiations occur among the leaders of the country's two linguistic subcultures, French and Flemish, in a centralized and formalized system (Lorwin 1971, 1975). A bibliography of interest group relations can be found in Lijphart (1981) and DeWachter (1987), and general overviews of the interest group system are in Fitzmaurice (1983) and DeWachter (1987). A discussion of Belgium's neocorporatist decision making can be found in Van den Bulck (1992).

There are few English-language studies of interest groups in Luxembourg and what exists is quite dated. Luxembourg is mentioned in the consociational literature (Lorwin 1971; Lijphart 1977) and has experimented with neocorporatist policy making (Hirsch 1986). A general description of its policy process can be found in Weil (1970).

11.3.2. France, Italy, Spain, Portugal, and Greece

John Constantelos

Although there is a large body of literature on interest group politics in France, Italy, and southern Europe, most of it is not in English. Nonetheless, the English-language literature on French and Italian interest groups is substantial and its theoretical contribution is significant. There is also a small, but growing, body of English-language literature on Spanish groups, but little on Portugal and Greece. Works on Portugal include studies of corporatism (Schmitter 1975; Wiarda 1977); and on Greece there are case studies of interest groups involved in European Union-related issues (Close 1998; Lavdas 1997). Morlino's (1998) comparative study of southern European countries examines party and interest group politics during democratic transitions in Portugal and Greece as well as in Italy and Spain. And Warner (2000) examines the important role of the Catholic church as an interest group in several southern European countries. The rest of this entry focuses on France, Italy, and Spain.

France

While slightly outdated, the most comprehensive book on French interest groups is Frank Wilson (1987). Useful chapter-length overviews are Frank Wilson (1993) and P. A. Hall (1993). The relationship of French political parties and interest groups is treated by Appleton (2001) who includes an excellent overview of the French interest group community and its operating techniques at the turn of the twenty-first century. Bibliographies can be found in V. Schmidt (1996a), Frank Wilson (1987), and C. Thomas (1993a, 2001a).

After the establishment of the French Fifth Republic in 1958, researchers focused on the relationships between interest groups and the executive. Suleiman's (1974) study of the high civil service examines interest group relations with the central administration. Others have studied the labor movement (Chapman, Kesselman, and Schain 1998; Howell 1992; Touraine 1987), and the policy-making role of interest groups in various sectors, including banking (W. Coleman 1993), education (Baumgartner 1989), and health (Immergut 1992; Wilsford 1991).

Frank Wilson (1987) found that, although the central administration is a prime target of lobbying, interest groups use a variety of strategies to influence public policy, including participating in government committees and lobbying parliament. Strategies depend on the type of issue and the political context. Respondents to his survey rated contacts with ministers and civil servants as the most effective strategy, but this assessment varied by interest group type. Groups less favored by the government used alternative strategies. Labor unions, for example, emphasized the importance of a *rapport de force*, the ability to demonstrate mass support.

John Keeler (1985, 1987), Frank Wilson (1983, 1987) and others have engaged in a lengthy debate over the nature of interest intermediation in France. The issue is whether interest group politics in France should be characterized as pluralist, neocorporatist, something in-between, or something altogether different.

On the one hand, Frank Wilson (1987) finds that corporatist structures exist in a few sectors, such as agriculture, but their powers are insignificant and they depend on state prerogatives. A strong state and fragmented groups have meant that interest group influence in France is limited. This has often led to the politics of the streets. He concludes that the coexistence of corporatist and pluralist patterns can be explained largely by the strength of the state and its ability to "exercise choice over the level of group involvement and the forms of influence groups can use" (F. Wilson 1987, 280).

In contrast, Keeler (1985) criticizes Wilson's pluralist characterization of France and provides evidence of corporatist patterns of interest intermediation, not only in the agricultural sector, but also in business and even in the labor sector. Keeler's 1987 study shows the depth and range of institutionalized relationships between the state and the Fédération Nationale des Syndicats d'Exploitants Agricoles (FNSEA), France's largest agricultural interest group. Culpepper (1993) argues that Keeler understates the degree of interest group competition within the agricultural sector. Vivien Schmidt (1996a) rejects both "limited pluralist" and "moderate corporatist" labels for France. Her historical analysis places France firmly in the tradition of state-dominated *dirigisme* (strong management by the bureaucracy), at least until the late 1980s when the European Union began to have a profound impact on state-business relations.

Italy

No recent book-length treatment of Italian interest groups is available in English. There are, however, three chapter-length overviews that are very useful: Zariski (1993), Lanzalaco (1993) and Constantelos (2001). The Constantelos study, although focusing on the party-group relationship, provides the most recent account of the structure and dynamics of the Italian interest group system. Lange and Regini (1989) include articles that directly or indirectly analyze the political role of key economic interest groups. Useful bibliographies include Golden (1988), Locke (1995) and Clive Thomas (1993a, 2001a).

The classic study is LaPalombara (1964) which still provides a good introduction to interest group politics in Italy. LaPalombara provides data on interest group goals, membership, internal structure and patterns of communications and interaction, especially with the legislature and the bureaucracy. He also explains that the Christian Democrats' dominance of the legislature allowed them to develop many income sources and reduce their financial dependence on industrial and other groups. More valuable than money was the mass membership of organized interests such as Catholic Action and the Direct Cultivators.

One of LaPalombara's contributions was to identify two major patterns of bureaucratic intervention on behalf of interest groups in Italy which has sometimes been applied to other systems such as Japan. The first is *clientela* which:

> ... exists when an interest group ... succeeds in becoming, in the eyes of a given administrative agency, the natural expression and representative of a given social sector which, in turn, constitutes the natural target or reference point for the activity of the administrative agency. (LaPalombara 1964, 262)

The Ministry of Industry and Commerce's relations with Italy's leading business association, Confindustria, is the archetypal model of *clientela*. The second type of relationship is *parentela*. It occurs when an agency intervenes on behalf of an interest group because of the latter's close ties to the governing party such as that between Catholic Action and the Christian Democrats.

Some of the most important literature examines the role of trade unions in the Italian political economy (Bedani 1995; Franzosi 1995). Lange, Ross, and Vannicelli (1982) analyze trade union responses to the economic crisis of the mid-1970s. They argue that union strategies are mediated by political, economic, and union organizational factors. Golden (1988) also examines the strategic choices of Italian trade unions. Locke (1995) explores the crisis national unions face as they attempt to adjust to industrial reorganization resulting from the globalization and segmentation of markets.

Spain

No book length manuscript in English exists on Spanish interest groups. However, Hamann's (2001) chapter on the party-group connection in Spain provides a succinct overview of the development of interest group activity, the current scene, the strategy and tactics of groups, and the strengths and weaknesses of the group system. Most English language research on Spanish groups is usually part of broader political economic studies, especially of the transition to democracy (Encarnación 1997; R. Gunther 1993; Wiarda 1989; Morlino 1998). This is explained partly by the marginal importance of interest groups during the Spanish dictatorships. Some scholars, however, dispute the prevalent characterization of an anemic civil society in Franco's Spain (Pérez-Díaz 1993). Linz (1981) provides a valuable historical analysis of politics and interests in Spain; Molins and Casademunt (1998) is a more recent overview, while Brassloff (1998) examines the political role of the Church.

Two important studies examine the role of business associations (Martínez 1993) and trade unions (Fishman 1990) during Spain's transition to democracy. Martínez maps the formal and informal channels of interest representation in the Spanish Confederation of Business Organizations and finds that employers are motivated to join business associations primarily for collective goods rather than for selective incentives. He also finds that organized business played an important role in legitimizing democratic consolidation in Spain. Fishman examines how organized labor in Spain, long repressed under Franco, responded to the dual tasks of consolidating democracy and developing the organizational growth and strength necessary to defend workers' interests. The democratic transition succeeded but the organizational development of labor foundered. He concludes that labor's organizational weakness is the result of authoritarian rule and the economic crisis that limited workers' material gains.

11.4. INTEREST REPRESENTATION IN THE EUROPEAN UNION

Justin Greenwood

The literature on European level interest groups has expanded considerably since the late 1980s as the European Union (EU) has become increasingly important as a policy making entity. This literature now includes: two texts on Euro groups (Greenwood 1997, 2003a), one on interpretations of interest group mediation (Gorges 1996), several edited collections (e.g., Greenwood, Grote, and Ronit 1992a; Mazey and Richardson 1993a; Pedler and Van Schendelen 1994; Pedler 2002; Van Schendelen 1993), some practical guides to lobbying the EU (Gardner 1991; Van Schendelen 2002), books on specific organizations and alliances (e.g., Greenwood 2002a, 2002b, 2003b), some chapters in books, such as Shephard (1999) on lobbying the European parliament, and several articles including one on attempts to regulate lobbying in the EU (Greenwood 1998; see section 14.5.). Extensive bibliographies on Euro groups can be found in Greenwood (1997, 2003a).

The study of EU interest representation has been linked to the popularity of institutionalist based accounts of European integration. The neofunctionalist account of integration by Haas (1958, 1964) saw groups as crucial mechanisms to encourage the transfer of authority (often referred to in Europe as *competency*) and loyalties from member states to the European level, manipulated by a European Commission lacking a natural democratic constituency. As European integration faltered in the 1970s, and accounts of integration based upon the self-interest of member states became popular, the study of interest group activity waned. When integration quickened again in the 1980s, the study of interest representation regained momentum as the focus switched to forces other than member states for explaining integration. Since the early 1990s, the response of groups to the single market project, their demands for integration, and their relationship with the European institutions, have rekindled interest in institutionalist based accounts (e.g., Gorges 1996).

In its early days, the Commission sought to develop Euro groups by a policy of dealing only with European level groups. This proved impossible, not least because of unevenness in the development of such groups. Caporaso (1974) noted the lack of development of Euro groups, pointing instead to the importance of the relationship between national groups and member states in European policy making; while Averyt (1977) suggested that the "orthodox strategy" was for groups to access the European level through national organizations, often aided by their member states. This issue of channels of access has been prominent in the literature ever since. Wyn Grant (1995) noted the continued weakness of many European level groups, particularly EU federations of national federations, and the importance of the "national route" of influence.

This debate expanded to include the relevance of pluralism and neocorporatism at the European level following work by Streeck and Schmitter (1991). These authors argued that the multi-level EU structure, with its multiple points of access, lacked the institutional centralization for neocorporatist style associational governance. Multiple points of access resulted in a lack of dependency by business interests upon a peak association for political representation. If firms and national associations could easily bypass their EU associations and go directly to the European institutions, the conditions were laid for pluralist type interest representation. The importance of business in shaping this pluralist situation become clear when it is realized that in 2003, of the estimated 800–850 EU lobbying groups, two thirds to three quarters were business groups.

While the Streeck and Schmitter argument is widely accepted, Greenwood, Grote, and Ronit (1992a), found "islands of corporatism" in certain sectoral governance arrangements. Later work (Pedler and Van Schendelen 1994; Greenwood 1995, 2002a, 2002b; Gorges 1996) found evidence of a number of strong business interest groups whose relationships with the European institutions seemed to explain public policy outputs during the completion of the Single European Market. In part, this strength comes from the dependence by the Commission, a relatively small bureaucracy, on the resources which outside interests bring. On the subject of EU business associations see Greenwood (2002a, 2002b, 2003b).

Public interest groups, on the other hand, have focused on politicizing issues of concern to them to remove these issues from exclusive, producer dominated policy communities, into public arenas in which they have equality of access. Where they are able to achieve this, public interests have often triumphed over business in some key legislative areas, particularly involving the European Parliament, where public interests have found a sympathetic ear (see Shephard 1999). Trade Union, territorial, consumer, and other public interest (particularly environmental) groups, have become increasingly effective in recent years, not least in agenda setting within a climate increasingly welcoming to citizens as the EU attempts to address its problems of democratic deficit (Greenwood 1997, 2003). Most of these groups are funded by the Commission, which has a key interest in expanding its competencies in the functional areas represented by trade union and public interest groups.

Much of what is known about the general conditions in which interest groups thrive or struggle can therefore be applied to the EU. Yet there are also ways in which the unique environment of the EU exerts specific influences upon the organization and maintenance of groups and upon group strategies and tactics. Because most Euro groups are based around national associations, collective action is often relatively easy because it is built upon organizations already politically active. Among firms, which have various choices in representing themselves to government, their basis of membership in Euro groups is a form of insurance policy. Here the potential costs of nonmembership arising from a relatively uncertain EU operating environment (compared to the tried and tested national level) seem to drive membership decisions more than do analysis of the cost/benefits of membership (Greenwood and Aspinwall 1997).

11.5. THE NORDIC COUNTRIES

Brent F. Nelsen

The Nordic societies of Denmark, Finland, Iceland, Norway and Sweden are among the world's most politically organized societies. Sweden, as the leading nation in the region, has attracted much attention from interest group scholars writing in English. There is also extensive work on Norwegian and Danish groups, but Finnish and especially Icelandic groups are little discussed in the English-language literature.

An initial understanding of Nordic interest groups can be found in general texts on Nordic politics and in various edited collections. Eliassen (1981) provides a general introduction to interest groups in all five Nordic countries. Einhorn and Logue (1989, 99–108) describe the interest group systems in Denmark, Norway and Sweden. Kenneth Miller (1991, 81–98) explains the Danish system and Rechtman and Larsen-Ledet (1998) review lobbying regulation in Denmark. On Sweden, Elvander (1974) describes the system in its most organized form in the 1970s; Micheletti (1993) depicts the system under pressure in the 1990s; and Widfeldt (2001) examines the relationship of parties and groups and provides an overview of the group system at the turn of the twenty-first century as well as explaining the development of Swedish interest groups.

Interest Groups and Neocorporatism in the Nordic Region

Attention to interest groups in Nordic countries grew in the 1960s and 1970s as it was recognized that group theories used to explain American

311

politics did not fit the Nordic experience. Nordic interest representation had developed along clearly defined social cleavages that pitted peripheral regions against the economic center, rural against urban areas, and owners against workers (Rokkan 1967; Valen and Rokkan 1974). Scholars also recognized that in the twentieth century Nordic states had encouraged the formation of peak associations that held a monopoly of representation for a particular economic interest (such as labor) and had invited these interests to take part in making and implementing government decisions through institutionalized consultation and bargaining processes. This corporatist policy-making system, built on cooperation, appeared in stark contrast to the competitive pluralism of the United States.

Early examinations of Nordic corporatism include: Laux (1963) on Danish interest groups; Kvavik's (1974, 1976) studies on Norwegian organizations; Elvander (1974) on Swedish groups; and Helander and Anckar (1983) on Finland. These studies demonstrated how thoroughly integrated the economic organizations were in making and implementing government policy. At the heart of the governing process was not interest group competition but cooperation with each other and the state. Further studies in the mid-1980s strengthened the case for corporatism by confirming that: (1) groups sometimes implement policy for the state (Anckar and Helander 1985); and (2) corporatism extends, at least in Norway, to the local level (T. Hansen and Newton 1985).

However, questions about the democratic legitimacy, effectiveness and true extent of corporatist structures were raised as early as the 1970s. Marvin E. Olsen (1977) concluded that the Swedish government, far from being influenced by the incorporated interests, used corporatist structures as a means of control. Furthermore, Ruin (1974) argued that corporatism led to a national elite disconnected from the rank-and-file it represented and spawned new demands for representation. Johan P. Olsen (1983) and Micheletti (1990b) looked at the new social movements alluded to by Ruin and came to different conclusions. Micheletti, observing Swedish interests, argued that the demands of keeping very large organizations together have kept corporate interests from representing their members' special interests satisfactorily. Such interest "inarticulation" has led to group fragmentation and new protest movements that threaten the legitimacy and effectiveness of the neocorporatist system. Lewin (1994) uses similar arguments in considering the rise and decline of Swedish corporatism. On the other hand, Johan Olsen, in his wide-ranging examination of Norwegian politics, refused to view protest groups as threats. He prefers to ask why some Norwegian groups participate in governing and others do not. He argues that the corporatist model is far too simple. In practice, the model applies only to "some organizations, for some policies, in some situations" (J. Olsen 1983, 187). Damgaard and Eliassen (1978) came to similar conclusions in examining Denmark. Thus, today scholars of Nordic politics, as do scholars of other political systems, tend to view neocorporatism as part of a wider system employing many forms of interest group strategy and tactics.

Case Studies of Nordic Interest Groups

Most case studies on Nordic interests focus on economic interests involved in neocorporatist policy making (labor, business and agriculture) or examine noneconomic groups that are generally outside of the corporatist network.

The importance of labor in Nordic policy making, especially in Sweden, has inspired a host of studies. Korpi (1981) looks at labor movements throughout the region through the 1970s. Pontusson (1993) focuses on successful and unsuccessful labor-initiated reforms in Sweden since the 1920s. Micheletti (1985) examines the problems of interest representation in the Swedish Central Organization of Salaried Employees (TCO). The most recent studies on Nordic unions have explored the crisis facing the labor movement in the new international environment. Amoroso (1990) describes the changes taking place in Denmark, Geyer (1997) those in Norway, and Thelen (1993) those in Sweden. Jørgen Andersen (1990) and Jahn (1993) explore the impact that environmentalism and the "new politics" in Europe has had on labor in Denmark and Sweden respectively. As a counter to the gloomy views of most labor scholars, Galenson (1998) argues that Danish, Norwegian and Swedish unions are remarkably successful by European standards.

Scholars have paid relatively little attention to the other two major economic interests—business and agriculture. Pierre (1992) examines the role of local business associations in local government in Sweden, and Nelsen (1991) discusses the role of industry associations in Norwegian oil policy making. Regarding agriculture, Stolpe's (1981) study of the cooperative moment in all five Nordic countries includes information on agricultural cooperatives, while Steen (1985) explores the influence of farmers on agricultural policy in Norway and Sweden. Micheletti's (1990a) study of the Federation of Swedish Farmers (LRF) also looks at farmers' influence on agricultural policy but emphasizes the growing influence of consumer groups and the resulting policy changes.

Scholars have recently begun to study new social movements and noneconomic interests in Nordic countries. Several works examine national movements for and against membership in the European Union (EU) in Norway (Aardal 1983; Nelsen 1993), Denmark (Aardal 1983; Svensson 1994), Sweden (Miles 1997), and the Nordic region in general (Miles 1996; Redmond 1997; Ingebritsen 1998). Other groups studied include revival movements in all five Nordic countries (Suolinna 1981), antinuclear movements in Sweden (Kitschelt 1986), Swedish consumer groups (Pestoff 1988), protest movements in Finland (Siisiäinen 1992), and the link between voluntary organizations and political parties in Norway (Selle 1997).

The study of Nordic women's groups has grown rapidly since the mid-1980s. Lovenduski (1986) covers Sweden extensively in her classic work on European feminist movements. Haavio-Mannila (1981) and Dahlerup and Gulli (1985) describe women's organizations in all five Nordic countries, while Bystydzienski (1988, 1992) examines Norway and Gelb (1989, 137–78) Sweden. Two books on Nordic women in politics by Kelber (1994) and Karvonen and Selle (1995) include valuable information on women's groups throughout the region. Klausen (1996) focuses on women in Scandinavian sports associations.

11.6. CANADA

Henry J. Jacek

Until the late 1960s the traditional view was that interest associations were relatively unimportant in Canadian politics; the conventional wisdom was that they were an American phenomenon only. The first major challenge to this view came from Englemann and Schwartz (1967, 114) who wrote: "observers of Canadian political life hesitate to face up to the realities of interest-party relations and tend to maintain that these are illegitimate, or non-existent." The first textbook to include a chapter on Canadian interest groups was Van Loon and Whittington (1971).

Despite a counter attack by scholars such as Glyn Berry (1974), interest groups became a new subject in Canadian political science. The traditional view was further attacked as inaccurate by left-wing political scientists (Hunnius 1972), specialists in Canadian labor unions (R. Adams 1995), American academics in Canada (Presthus 1971, 1974a), and extensive work by Pross (1975, 1989, 1992). The latter reference contains the best bibliography on Canadian interest groups (Pross 1992, 309–31). The traditional view was finally put to rest by a major project conducted at McMaster University begun in 1980 which focused on public economic policy.

The major finding of the new interest group literature in Canada is that organizations matter in influencing public policy. This is particularly true of business, the largest segment of Canadian interests (Jacek 1986) which are much more important in public policy terms than labor unions. Business, especially large business, is better organized as a political force than any other segment of Canadian society and business interest associations have a much longer life than other types of associations (W. Coleman and Jacek 1983). Within business itself, large corporations are the best organized as in the Business Council of National Issues (BCNI) although the comprehensive Canadian Chamber of Commerce system is very important (W. Coleman 1988). Other economic interest groups representing agriculture and the professions are important in some areas. The least influential interest groups are environmental, ethnic, religious, linguistic and social issue organizations; but at times they can have an impact especially in the period leading up to elections.

Research demonstrates that in Canada a careful cultivation of non-elected bureaucrats is best for long-term policy results (Englemann and Schwartz 1967). Canadian policy-making is highly technical and thus relies on a great deal of specific expertise that interest groups give to civil servants (J. Anderson 1977). Astute interest group leaders recognize that bureaucratic memoranda shape cabinet decisions (Kernaghan 1985) and surveys of interest group leaders show that these groups target bureaucrats before contacting the legislature and its committees, cabinets and their staff or the courts (Presthus 1974a).

Among other important research findings are the enduring importance of sectoral corporatism in the guise of private interest government (Jacek 1991; Tuohy 1976). The importance of regional interest groups and their influence on public policy in such a decentralized country as Canada as noted by W. Coleman and Jacek (1989), Schultz (1980), and Pross (1989) also stands out. And while Canadian interest groups are relatively unimportant in foreign policy (D. Barry 1975) and in negotiating large international trade agreements (Winham 1986), they are very important in smaller-scale trade agreements (Jacek 1994). An emerging explanation of how Canada maintains its autonomy from the United States centers on the close connection between interest groups and government officials in Canada (Jacek 1987–88; von Riekhoff and Neuhold 1993). Finally, the regulation of lobbying in Canada is treated by Rush (1994, 1998).

11.7. AUSTRALIA AND NEW ZEALAND

John Warhurst

Australia

The study of interest groups in Australia lacks a comprehensive, recent study. There are, however, a number of summary chapters and articles as well as studies of interest groups in established sectors. Most studies focus on the national level but there is one on state groups (R. Scott 1980). The bulk of studies are descriptive with few attempts to grapple with interest group theories and only a few studies are based on comprehensive data gathering. The methodology is generally in the pluralist tradition. However, neo-Marxist scholars have recently been attracted to the subject by theories of corporatism and the popularity of business-government relations as a field of study.

The first study of Australian interest groups was by Townsley (1958). But the major modern work begins with Trevor Matthews (1967, 1980; Matthews and Warhurst 1993) who wrote a series of general accounts of the Australian interest group system. He also mapped the interaction of groups with the national government revealing the dominance of producer groups (T. Matthews 1976), as well as writing case studies of business interest groups (T. Matthews 1983, 1990). Others have also written general accounts of Australian interest groups (Loveday 1970; Harman 1980; Warhurst 1985). The Australian experience with the regulation of interest groups and lobbyists is considered by Warhurst (1998).

Case studies include a path-breaking account of the national veterans' association, the Returned Services League (Kristianson 1966), a study of Catholic pressure groups (Hogan 1978), and several studies of the trade union movement (R. Martin 1975; Rawson 1978, 1986) including a history of the peak association, the Australian Council of Trade Unions—ACTU—(Hagan 1981). Analysis of business associations developed in the early 1980s, first in connection with accounts of tariff politics and industry assistance (Warhurst 1982; Tsokhas 1984). Later, as the Labour government, elected in 1983, developed a tripartite arrangement, known as the Accord, with business and labor, academics concentrated on the particular characteristics of this era (e.g., Galligan and Singleton 1991; Bell and Wanna 1992). Far less work exists on farmer organizations but there are some brief accounts including discussion of the peak association, the National Farmers Federation (Trebeck 1990).

Academic analysis of new social movements include one general account of the environmental, women's, gay and lesbian, and Aboriginal movements, but it lacks details of group organization and is written from a movement rather than an interest group perspective (Burgmann 1993). Providing further details are studies of the environmental movement (Papadakis 1993), the women's movement (Sawer and Simms 1993; Sawer and Groves 1994), Aboriginal interests (Bennett 1989), and immigrant organizations (Jupp and Kabala 1993). Few case studies exist of individual organizations, with one exception being the Australian Conservation Foundation (Warhurst 1994). There are also studies which measure the impact of these groups, and their rivals such as the Right to Life Association, on electoral outcomes (Warhurst 1983).

The direction of research on Australian interest groups is promising in terms of both more innovative methodologies and more comprehensive data gathering. Sawer and Groves' (1994) study of women's groups uses social network analysis, Bell's (1995) study of business associations is based on a comprehensive survey; I. Marsh's (1995) compilation of information; and Abbott's (1996) survey of groups which interact with the national parliament provide more information on individual Australian interest groups than previously available.

New Zealand

Unlike Australia, there is a book-length study of interest groups in New Zealand, but it is quite dated (Cleveland 1972). Its successors are a chapter in an international comparative volume (Vowles 1993) and chapters in textbooks on New Zealand politics (Mulgan 1994; Wood 1988) as well as work by Cleveland (1985) himself on ideological groups.

In regard to in-depth studies of particular groups and group sectors, there are even fewer than on Australia. What studies there are concentrate on producer group activism, especially by business associations (Deeks and Perry 1992). The general conclusion is that business captures or controls the state: the evidence being the direction of New Zealand governments in recent years.

There are a few studies of social movement interest groups. One is of the suffrage movement, focusing in particular on the key organization, the Women's Christian Temperance Union (Grimshaw 1987). But there is no equivalent study of modern feminist organizations.

11.8. JAPAN

Ronald J. Hrebenar

Despite the fact that Japan has a large and healthy group sector, with an array of interest groups similar to that in the United States, the study of interest groups in Japan has been largely ignored. The reason for this lack of interest is twofold. First, few Japanese believe groups, other than a few powerful business peak associations, are important influences in the public policy making process. Second, most Japanese universities have political science faculties dominated by political theorists. Thus, while there are hundreds of books in Japanese on Japanese party politics and politicians, there are only a few on Japanese interest groups. Even among books written on Japanese politics in English, the majority focus on parties and just a few on group politics.

The majority of scholarly work on Japanese interest groups are case studies of interest sectors such as business and labor. One of the most well-known is Curtis' (1975) study of big business and political influence. Yanaga (1968) also studied the political roles of Japanese business associations. Steslicke (1973) examined the politics of the Japanese Medical Association; and Thurston (1973) studied the role that militant school teachers' associations played in Japanese politics in the 1960s. Recently, studies covering Japanese health politics as well as construction policies have included extensive interest group analyzes (J. C. Campbell 1992; Woodall 1995). Hrebenar (1992) summarizes the political links of various religious groups in Japan such as the Nichirin Buddhist lay sect, the Soka Gakkai. And Hrebenar, Nakamara, and Nakamara (1998) address the issue of interest group regulation (or lack thereof) in Japan.

There are, however, three comprehensive attempts to analyze Japanese interest groups. Aurelia George (1988) used an institutional approach to study Japanese interest group behavior. Hrebenar (2001) examines the relationship between political parties and interest groups and covers the major interests in some detail. And Hrebenar and Nakamura (1993) provide short descriptions of the major interest sectors, examine strategies and tactics, and explain the role the Japanese bureaucracy and party system play in interest group politics. Hrebenar and Nakamura also explain that Japanese and foreign political scientists have engaged in a spirited debate concerning which of three competing models—tripartite, pluralist and modified corporatist—best describes interest group politics in Japan.

The argument that a tripartite model existed enjoyed wide support among scholars from 1955 to the early 1980s (Okimoto 1988; van Wolferen 1989). It argued that power in Japan is exercised by a triumvirate of the ruling Liberal Democratic Party, big business, and the governmental bureaucracy. While the tripartite model continues to command strong support from both Japanese and Western scholars, some began to challenge the exclusivity of this model by suggesting that the 1970s and 1980s had greatly increased the range of interest group participation in policy making beyond the business world (Curtis 1975; Inoguchi 1985). The third major line of analysis argues that Japan better fits into the corporatist model, developed in Western Europe, than the pluralist model of the United States (A. George 1988; Pemple and Tsunekawa 1979). As these competing models suggest, there is controversy over the nature of interest group politics in Japan.

Zeigler (1988) writes of the special category of Confucian tradition nations which have two fundamental principles: groups are more important than individuals and society is organized on a hierarchical basis. He argued that a form of corporatism has emerged in neo-Confucian nations such as Japan. These nations also have traditions of elite bureaucracies which dominate the determination and administration of public policies. Asian Confucian nations also share a preference for single, ruling party governments.

These Confucian nations have also developed a form of corporatism, societal corporatism—a system with interest groups sanctioned by government and with all but a few peak associations excluded from the decision making processes. According to Zeigler, labor is the key element in the success of a corporatist system. In Western Europe, labor is made docile by involving it in the policy making process. In quasi-authoritarian Asian nations such as Taiwan, South Korea and Japan, a "corporatism without labor" has emerged in which organized labor has been repressed and is not directly involved in governmental decision making. In Japan, for example, labor unions are legal but the more radical private sector unions were crushed soon after World War II. Docile company unions became the norm, and labor was largely excluded from the policy making process. Among the Asian nations which Zeigler (1988, 164) studied, only Japan had developed the formal institutions of corporatism common to the European style of corporatism.

Japan, as categorized by Manfred Schmidt (1982), has one of the highest levels of corporatism and is dominated by business interests. Pemple and Tsunekawa (1979) also conclude that Japan is a corporatist nation with the additional distinguishing feature of labor being excluded. They see in both pre– and post–World War II Japan the key elements of corporatism. The pre-war version is that of state corporatism with almost all the peak interest represented in the Imperial Rule Assistance Association formed in 1940. In the post-war era, Japan's version of liberal corporatism has almost all major interests organized into powerful trade associations or powerful peak associations. Pemple and Tsunekawa correctly note that labor had not been represented by such an organization nor was it included in the regular policy making decision making processes of Japan. However, with the rise of Rengo, the new moderate labor confederation, in the late 1980s and the disappearance of ideological politics with the end of international communism, organized labor has gradually become more and more of a player in mainstream interest group politics in Japan.

11.9. ISRAEL

Yael Yishai

Until the mid-1980s, interest groups in Israel attracted little specific attention from political scientists (one exception was Yishai 1979). This dearth of attention was mainly because political parties, probably the most important Israeli political actors, were the focus of research. Research on interest groups was also overshadowed by a preoccupation with the major issue dominating Israeli politics—the Arab-Israeli conflict. Most references to interest groups prior to 1985 lacked an empirical foundation and were made within the broader context of Israeli politics. In the early 1990s, however, two books (Drezon-Tepler 1990; Yishai 1991) and one book chapter (Arian 1993) were published focusing specifically on Israeli interest politics.

Works on interest groups in Israeli can be divided into three categories, broadly associated with chronological development: (1) interest groups as party extensions; (2) interest groups as challengers; and (3) interest groups as legitimate actors.

Interest Groups as Party Extensions

The publication of many scholarly works during the 1980s enhanced the understanding of Israeli politics (for example, Shimshoni 1982; Galnoor 1982; Arian 1989). Yet, only perfunctory reference was made to interest groups. Galnoor and particularly Arian devote part of their discussion to voluntary associations, using a systems perspective. Both were reluctant to admit, however, that interest groups are autonomous actors exerting influence on public policy. According to Galnoor, the role of interest groups in the political process, although on the rise, was still very limited. Likewise, Arian asserts that the primacy of parties precludes effective influence of interest groups. Analysis of the largest labor federation in the country (Histadrut) also places it within this category (Shalev 1990). Most recently, Yishai (2001) has shown how the dominance of interest groups by parties has waned over the past 20 years and groups have become more independent. She has also shown that a fine line exists between certain groups and parties and she has used the term *interest parties* for these organizations (Yishai 1994).

Interest Groups as Challengers

Until 1967 Israeli society was highly consensual with only a few civic activities challenging political authorities. This harmony was breached after the Six Day War with the occupation of the "territories" (see Beilin 1992; Smooha 1978). Some interest groups organized to challenge accepted values and offered policy alternatives. These were active mainly in foreign and security policy and, to a lesser extent, welfare policy. In the first category are Peace Now and Gush Emunim. Most scholarly works devoted to these movements emphasize their role in shaping Israel's ideological positions on the occupied territories. Several scholars note the "deviant" aspects of these associations, and the effect of their challenge on both the structure of political institutions and the discourse of political ideology (Newman 1985; Schnall 1979).

Scholarly attention (particularly among sociologists) has also been devoted to protest movements, particularly among immigrants from Asia and Africa. The emergence of the Black Panthers (a protest movement consisting of residents of distressed neighborhoods of Moroccan descent) in the 1970s shattered the image of Israel as an egalitarian society whose resources were devoted to the absorption of immigrants (see Jansen 1987; Sprinzak 1991). Challenge, however, did not generate legitimization of "interest politics." Political culture, backed by strong state institutions, was still hostile to the exertion of associational pressures, even though they were cloaked in broad national images.

Interest Groups as Legitimate Actors

The two major works of the 1990s (Drezon-Tepler 1990; Yishai 1991) regard interest groups not as adjacent to political parties, or as minor challengers, but as legitimate actors using a variety of strategies, targeting their influence at various policy makers, and seeking multiple channels to achieve their legitimate goals. Both studies place their analysis within interest group theory, using concepts such as pluralism and corporatism. Drezon-Tepler (1990) presents a historical analysis of three important interest groups in Israel: The Manufacturers' Association, a settlement movement, and Gush Emunim. Yishai (1991) bases her discussion on an empirical analysis of all interest groups operating on the Israeli scene, divided by specific categories. Both authors reach similar conclusions regarding the mix of various groups and tactics in the Israeli polity. Yishai (1998a) also examined attempts to regulate interest groups and lobbying in Israel.

Chapter 12

Interest Groups in Selected Nonpluralist Regimes, Transitional Democracies, and Developing Societies

12.1. THE CHARACTERISTICS OF INTERESTS AND INTEREST GROUP ACTIVITY AND APPROACHES TO STUDYING INTERESTS

Clive S. Thomas

Compared with scholarship on pluralist and developed societies, the study of interest groups in nonpluralist regimes, those in transition to pluralism, and in developing societies has been far less extensive. This is not because interest groups and interests do not exist in these societies as they were defined in chapter 1 (see section 1.2.). It is due, in large part, to the nature of these political systems that has resulted in scholarship focusing on topics other than interest groups. And where interest groups are studied it is usually not as interest groups per se; information on them usually has to be gleaned from studies of other aspects of these systems.

The category of *nonpluralist, transitional democracies*, and *developing countries* is, indeed, a broad one. It includes totalitarian and authoritarian regimes from those of the former Soviet Union and contemporary Cuba to religious authoritarian regimes such as Iran and Afghanistan in recent years to the military dictatorships of Latin America and the authoritarian systems of both Saharan and sub-Saharan Africa. The category also includes countries that are in various stages of transition to pluralist democracy, like those of Eastern Europe. And it includes underdeveloped countries such as those of Africa and parts of Asia, some of which are at various stages of pluralism like Bangladesh, as well as strict authoritarian regimes such as Burma. Although this broad category of political systems embraces a wide range of interest group activity in terms of levels of development, types of systems, and operating techniques, it has much more in common than simply a catch-all category to include all those countries and types of systems that are not advanced pluralist democracies.

The Characteristics of Interests and Interest Group Activity

Nonpluralist, transitional, and developing societies share one or more, and usually several, of five elements concerning interest group activity. These elements are interrelated and one may influence others. In combination they determine the general characteristics of interest group activity, or lack thereof, in a particular political system; the level of development of the political system; the extent of legitimization of group activity; the types of groups or interests operating; the techniques of influence; and so on. These five characteristics are as follows:

1. Restricted Autonomy of Interest Groups. The right of freedom of association and the existence of private voluntary interest groups—particularly their role in lobbying government—may be legally restricted, curtailed by the official ideology, and in some cases banned. Restrictions imposed by authoritarian regimes range from outright banning in totalitarian and extremely repressive systems to restrictions on freedom of assembly and group activities as well as groups being co-opted or functioning as puppets of the government. What Schmitter (1974) calls *state corporatism*—the forerunner of neocorporatism—as practiced in Nazi Germany, Vichy France, and pre–World War II Austria, is a form of co-opted interest group activity where the state determines the role of groups (see section 3.4.). The various organizations set up by Communist countries, usually as part of the party apparatus, such as youth and labor organizations, are also co-opted interests that must tow the line of the party and the regime, which are usually one and the same (Best, Rai, and Walsh 1986, 231–37).

2. Special Interests are Often Viewed as Illegitimate. Although interest groups are viewed with skepticism and distrust in many developed pluralist societies, they are still seen as necessary to the functioning of the political system. In contrast, in many nonpluralist, transitional, and developing societies the political culture views them as detrimental to the functioning of society, and consequently they are often viewed as illegitimate as they place special or sectoral interests above that of the nation. This is not only true as manifested in the official ideology of Communist countries but also unofficially in many authoritarian and developing countries as expressed in the attitudes of elites (see section 12.2. on South Asia). Even in transitional regimes where the development of formal interest group activity is essential to establishing liberal democracy, interest groups can be viewed as antithetical to the success of the society. This is, for example, the case in the Czech Republic (Evanson and Magstadt 2001).

3. Associational versus Informal Groups and Interests. In contrast to developed societies where the major form of interest group is the associational group based on formal membership, informal groups, such as political and professional elites, and broad-based interests, such as the bureaucracy and the military, are more characteristic of nonpluralist, transitional, and developing societies. Thus, in these societies *interests* as opposed to *interest groups* are more significant politically, as these terms were defined in chapter 1 (see section 1.2.). In developing societies the major type of interest is the primordial group based on kinship, tribe, lineage, neighborhood, religion, and so on. One characteristic of transitional regimes is the increase in the number of associational groups.

4. Less-Formalized Strategies and Tactics. Fewer associational and more informal groups plus the generally underdeveloped nature of interest group systems in these types of political systems also means that group strategies and tactics are less formalized compared with those of advanced pluralist democracies. To be sure, informal contacts and personal relationships are important in all societies for interests to achieve their goal of influencing public policy. However, in advanced pluralist systems a combination of the legality and minimal restrictions on interest group activity, the political power of many groups, the need to involve them in policy making, and often the regulation of lobbying activity have produced a set of formalized means and institutional channels by which groups work to affect public policy. These include: the use of lobbyists or their equivalent; committee hearings involving groups; formal channels of access to the executive branch; and group involvement in court action, political campaigns, political party organizations, and so on.

Such formalized and institutional channels are minimal or nonexistent in nonpluralist, transitional, and developing societies. In these systems informal personal contacts and power plays within and between government entities and related organizations, such as the ruling party or the court circle around a monarch, are the most significant. Thus, even more pressure politics is conducted behind closed doors and far from public scrutiny in these systems than in pluralist democracies.

5. Less-Significant Vehicles of Representation. An important role of interest groups in advanced pluralist societies is that they act as a major link between citizens and government by aggregating numbers of people with similar views and articulating their views to government. This is particularly the case with mass-membership organizations such as trade unions and public interest groups like environmental interests. Because large percentages of the population belong to interest groups, these may even be more important than political parties in performing a mass-representational function (C. Thomas 2001a, chaps. 1 and 15). In contrast, and due to a combination of the four elements just explained, interest groups in nonpluralist, transitional, and developing societies rarely perform the role of mass representation, as they represent a very small segment of the population and then only in an informal way. Interest groups and interests in these societies perform other functions similar to those in advanced pluralist democracies—such as providing information, aiding in policy implementation, and providing political training—but this lack of a mass-representational role gives them a much less significant place in the overall politics of their societies. This includes the mass organizations in one party and totalitarian regimes (such as some Communist systems) whose representative role is perfunctory and tightly controlled by the party and/or the regime.

The entries in this chapter provide more details on each of these five characteristics and on the nature of interest groups and interest activity in nonpluralist, transitional, and developing societies in general and specifics on particular countries and regions.

Approaches to Studying Interests and Interest Groups and the Various Sources of Literature

In regard to the extent and type of research, the above explanation of commonalties of interests and interest group activity throws light on why scholars have often not studied interest groups in these societies in the same way that these organizations are examined in advanced pluralist societies. Three related reasons are most important in this regard.

First, until very recently, because it was less formalized and often far from view, interest group activity appeared to be minimal or nonexistent and thus was not seen as important to study. Even in the 1970s and 1980s when scholars began to revise their views on this, especially on Communist countries and authoritarian regimes, interest groups still seemed less relevant than such entities as dominant, sometimes single political parties, strong leaders, or government institutions for controlling the economy.

Second, particularly in developing societies but also in authoritarian and transitional regimes, scholars saw issues of social class, religion, problems of economic development and poverty, the role of the military, ethnic and racial conflict, the aftermath of colonialism, and so on, as the forces driving the politics of these societies. In this environment, interest groups and interest activity in the way it is viewed and studied in advanced countries seemed much less relevant.

Third, the study of interest groups originated and flourished in pluralist liberal democracies where interest groups are legal, highly institutionalized, generally accepted as legitimate, and provide a major vehicle for political representation. As we saw above, these elements are either very rudimentary or nonexistent in many authoritarian, transitional, and developing societies. Consequently, not only did the lack of these elements make the study of interest groups seem less relevant, but when they were studied the reasons and approach were usually different than those of scholars of pluralist democracies.

As to the sources of literature and research on interest groups and interests in these regimes, there are some studies that take a similar approach to studies of interest groups in advanced pluralist societies. Most notable among these is work by Skilling (1966, 1983) and Skilling and Griffiths (1971) on Communist systems, particularly the Soviet regime. Others include Bianchi (1984, 1986a, 1986b, 1989) on the Third World, Turkey, and Egypt; and Ogden (2000) on the Peoples Republic of China. Generally, however, and as the entries in this chapter clearly show, information on interest groups and interests in nonpluralist, transitional, and developing societies is found in a broad range of sources; the major focus of which is not interest groups or interests per se, even though these studies may be dealing, in whole or in part, with groups and interests as defined in this *Guide*. For example, literature on democratization and economic development is a major source of information on groups and interests in the literature on Saharan and sub-Saharan Africa and on Latin America. Work on the emerging civil society is an increasingly important source on political organizations in North Africa and the Middle East. And work on various political, professional, and religious elites, on the bureaucracy, and on the military are important sources on groups and interests in most authoritarian, transitional, and developing systems.

12.2. INDIA AND SOUTH ASIA

Stanley A. Kochanek

Although the states of South Asia—India, Pakistan, Bangladesh, Sri Lanka (formerly Ceylon), Nepal, Bhutan, and the Maldives—have been influenced by the British pluralist tradition, the study of interest groups in the region has received little attention. There are a number of reasons for this.

First, interest groups have tended to be seen by South Asian elites as illegitimate and most intellectuals have been more preoccupied with social class than interest as a basic motivating force of group action. Second, governments in South Asia enjoy a considerable degree of autonomy, decision making is highly centralized, and interest groups have a minimal impact. Third, the most dominant interest articulators have not been social and economic interest but their still-pervasive caste, community, religious, tribal, and language antecedents. Fourth, except for business, most social and economic groups are controlled by political parties, lack autonomy, are poorly organized, are transitory, and have limited influence. Finally, the political systems of South Asia are highly personalized, and the keys to access and influence are often family networks, friends, and connections based on a mutual exchange of benefits. However, given the social and economic development of the past half-century of independence, rapid urbanization, and the growing size of the middle class in the region, interest groups have begun to grow and proliferate.

The only bibliography on interest groups in India is Sirsikar (1979). There are no separate bibliographies on interest groups for the other countries in the region except brief references in textbooks that deal with the individual countries of South Asia.

India

Given its size and importance, the study of interest groups in India has received the most attention of the countries in the region. The pioneering work was done by Weiner (1962) who was primarily concerned with the impact of interest groups on democracy and development in India. He found that government efforts to control, restrain, ignore, and repress organized demands had largely negative consequences. Weiner's study was followed by Fadia (1980) who provided a survey of the traditional interest group literature, an overview of the role of interest groups in India, and case studies of the impact of business and the caste system on Indian politics.

Although written from a political economy perspective, the study by Lloyd Rudolph and Susanne Rudolph (1987) represents a major contribution to the field. The interest group system in India, they argue, is characterized by state-dominated pluralism in which an all-pervasive and all-powerful state constrains and manipulates interest group activity. The most important form of interest representation in India, they also argue, is not formally organized interest groups but expressions of movement and issue politics called demand groups. Major demand groups include student, trade union, and agrarian movements.

The most detailed studies of interest groups in India have focused on the role of business and labor. The earliest studies of business were by Lamb (1959), Bernard Brown (1962), and Kochanek (1970, 1971). The first book was by Kochanek (1974), which dealt with the impact of environmental and organizational factors on the ability of business to influence the political process. Overall, studies of the impact of business on public policy demonstrate the limited influence business can have in a highly controlled and regulated economy. More recent work by Kochanek (1995–96, 1996b) outlines the impact of economic liberalization on business, a relative increase in the ability of business to influence economic policy, and the changing character of business associations.

Unlike business, which is the only autonomous interest in India, studies of trade unions by Harold Crouch (1966), Raman (1967), and Ramaswamy (1995) note the very limited influence of labor on government and the weakness of trade unions due to control by political parties, the domination by outside leadership, and the low status of workers in a labor-surplus country.

Other Countries in South Asia

The literature on interest groups in the smaller states of South Asia is much more limited. The earliest studies of interest groups in Pakistan were by Maniruzzaman (1966) and Burki (1971). The most comprehensive interest group studies of Pakistan, Bangladesh, and Sri Lanka are Kochanek (1983, 1993, 1995, 1996a) and Kearney (1971). They demonstrate the limits of business, labor, and other organized interests in highly personalized political systems.

12.3. THE PEOPLE'S REPUBLIC OF CHINA (PRC)

Patricia M. Thornton

The relative dearth of literature on interest groups in the People's Republic of China (PRC) is partly due to the historical evolution of the field and partly due to definitional and theoretical difficulties. As a study of interest groups in the Soviet Union observed, the "totalitarian" paradigm of the 1950s and 1960s exaggerated the role of state power in Communist systems, and minimized the importance of social forces (Skilling and Griffiths 1971). Studies of Chinese politics during this period followed suit, with the notable exception of Townsend's (1968) study of political participation.

The upheavals of the Cultural Revolution beginning in 1966 forced a reversal of this trend. Work by Oksenberg (1968) on China's principal occupational groups was followed by studies of both mass and elite groups (H. Lee 1978; Rosen 1982), an extensive literature on the nature and operation of factions (Bridgham 1970; Y. Chang 1976; Dittmer 1978; Tsou 1976), and informal politics and group formation (Burns 1979; Whyte 1974). Political and economic decentralization in the 1970s produced a wave of studies that stressed the fragmented nature of governmental authority and the roles of bargaining and lobbying between central leaders and subordinate groups (see, for example, Goodman 1984; Lampton 1987; Lieberthal and Lampton 1992; Lieberthal and Oksenberg 1988). Rising social unrest, culminating in the protests of 1989 focused scholarly attention onto the social sphere and its relative autonomy from state control. Historical and contemporary evidence for the existence of a civil society and/or public sphere was widely debated; and studies of social movements assessed the ability of previously state- and party-controlled corporatist entities to exert pressure on central authorities (C-B. Francis 1989; E. Perry and Fuller 1991; L. Sullivan 1990; Whyte 1992).

Since 1989 Western scholars have sought increasingly fine instruments for analyzing group formation and interest articulation (Findlay and Shu 1992; Goodman 1994; White 1993). The most interesting contributions seek to move beyond the state/society distinction by questioning the necessary opposition between these two terms (Pearson 1997; E. Perry 1994; Shue 1988; Solinger 1993; Waller 1984), including the observation "that participation can be *both* constrained *and* effective" (Falkenheim 1987, 5, emphasis added). Recent studies of public associations in urban China have highlighted the blurred boundaries between private ties, public organizations, and state institutions among workers, intellectuals, and students (Deborah Davis et al. 1995). In one study of Chinese labor associations, Anita Chan (1994, 171) proposes that "social corporatism entails a form of interest group politics." Minxin Pei's (1998, 315) empirical analysis of rapidly multiplying "civic associations" concludes that these "do not yet constitute a full-fledged civil society." Others point out that deepening economic reforms have gradually increased associational pluralism over time and will surely continue to do so in the future (Ogden 2000; Parris 1999).

12.4 TAIWAN—REPUBLIC OF CHINA (ROC)

Patricia M. Thornton

Coverage of political events in the PRC has often eclipsed important changes in Taiwan, with the result that less has been written on the recent political evolution of the Republic of China (ROC). Furthermore, interest groups are relatively new to Taiwan and the available literature is primarily descriptive; analytical frameworks remain in early stages of development. As a starting point, Tien (1993) includes a chapter on interest groups in Taiwan, and Hsiao (1990) documents social movement and group formation in the ROC from 1970 to 1990. Lerman (1978) analyzed the role of interest groups in lobbying the municipal councils of Taiwan's two largest cities, Taipei and Kaohsiung.

Taiwan's dominant party, the Kuomintang (KMT), was founded on the Chinese mainland in the 1920s under the tutelage of Soviet advisors. The KMT established an authoritarian regime in Taiwan after losing control of the mainland to the Chinese Communist Party in the late 1940s. The KMT built a web of state- and party-controlled corporatist organizations that penetrated virtually every level of society (Gold 1986; C. Johnson 1987; Tai 1970). However, some scholars have noted that even in the politically repressive 1950s and 1960s, autonomous social groups existed in Taiwan and influenced the policy-making process (Cole 1967; Moody 1977).

Increasing social unrest in the late 1970s coupled with rapid economic growth led to the increasing politicization of the citizenry and increased social mobilization (Hsiao 1990; Nathan and Chou 1987; Ngo 1993). The KMT responded by gradually implementing democratic reforms. However, as one scholar noted in 1993, most Taiwanese interest groups remained predominantly corporatist in structure, operating under a system of "limited pluralism" (Tien 1993, 44–45).

Interest groups have proliferated in Taiwan since 1990 and include agricultural and industrial interests (Tien 1993), consumer protection groups (Hsiao 1990), local and provincial interests (Lerman 1977, 1978), and environmental conservation organizations (K. Chang 1989; Sigwalt 1989). Yet as Hsiao (1990, 70) has noted, such groups avoided association with political parties and instead lobbied the state individually. Zeigler (1988) suggested that conflict avoidance between such groups and the state stems in part from Confucian influences on Taiwanese political culture. Nonetheless, an empirical analysis comparing "civic associations" in Taiwan and the PRC found a greater diversity of such groups in Taiwan, as well as better access to economic resources (Pei 1998). The most recent assessments of democratic consolidation in Taiwan have been positive (Gold 2000; Tien 2000).

12.5. THE MIDDLE EAST AND NORTH AFRICA (Excluding Israel)

Ali Abdullatif Ahmida

Material on interest group activity in the Middle East and North Africa is very limited. This paucity is the result of political and methodological factors. Until the 1970s, the persistence of authoritarian, one-party states and traditional monarchies in the region was interpreted by Western scholars to mean that interest groups were insignificant or nonexistent. The transition to pluralism in Egypt in 1974 spawned the study of Egyptian interest groups (e.g., Bianchi 1989; Kandil 1994; D. Sullivan 1994). There is also work on Turkish interest groups mainly by Bianchi (1984, 1985); and Yishai (1998b) includes Turkey in her comparative review of interest group regulation. Nevertheless, interest group studies of the region are still in their infancy. There is no extensive bibliography; though Bianchi's (1984, 247–60) list of references is useful, if rather outdated.

The interest group literature on the region falls into four categories. The first category is the study of informal groups associated with Middle Eastern political culture, such as those by Clement Moore (1974), Springborg (1975, 1978), and Bill and Springborg (1993). These so-called modernization theorists argue that informal interests—those based upon kinship, friendship, religious, and regional affiliations—are more important than formal groups in the region. They contend that, unlike the situation in Western democracies, formal interest groups are very weak due to a lack of an independent clergy and Roman law traditions, and the impact of the traditional political culture, especially Islam and the patrimonial repressive nature of the state.

The second category is historical research on the origins of modern professional groups, mainly by Donald Reid (1974, 1981). Reid focuses less on informal groups and the role of Islamic political culture and more on the modern development of the professions and professionalism in Egypt. His specialty is the lawyers' syndicate, which was formed in 1912 as the first modern profession in Egypt. He argues that in Egypt between 1912 and 1980 lawyers adapted well to changes in the political system. They became active in political parties during the monarchical period (1922–52); and when political parties were banned in 1954 they shifted their activities to the state bureaucracy under Abdul Nasser.

The third category is a body of literature by Bianchi—the first scholar to focus specifically on interest groups in the Middle East and North Africa—examining the relevance of the corporatist model to group activity in Turkey and Egypt (Bianchi 1984, 1985, 1986a, 1986b, 1990). Bianchi suggests that the authoritarian nature of the state in the region restricts the autonomy of formal and corporatist-type interest groups, but at the same time allows them to organize as was the case in Turkey and Egypt after 1974. Therefore, unlike the pluralistic model of the industrial Western countries and the corporatist model of Latin America, the major characteristic of this state-interest group relationship in Egypt falls neither into pluralism nor corporatism but a combination of the two.

The fourth category is the study of interest groups as a component of the study of the new emerging civil society. Although the Middle East and North Africa have been moving from authoritarianism to democratization since the early 1970s, the transition has been slower than in Eastern Europe and Latin America. Even so, in Egypt, Turkey, Jordan, Yemen, and Morocco a plethora of political parties, associational, religious, human rights, and feminist organizations has emerged. Consequently, many scholars have become interested in studying civil society in the region. Major works are A. R. Norton (1995, 1996), Schwedler (1995), and Ahmida (1994a, 1994b, 1994c, 1997). The two volumes edited by Norton examine the rise of new interest groups and their increasing autonomy from state control and the relationship between Islam and democracy. There is no agreement among the contributors to these volumes on whether Islam is compatible with liberal democracy and whether to include autonomous religious organizations in the study of civil society. Furthermore, most of the contributors assume that this modern civil society developed only since the early 1970s. Other scholars such as Gran (1977), Abou-El-Haj (1991), Goldberg (1993), and Ahmida (1994b) suggest an earlier existence of civil society dating back before the twentieth century.

12.6. SOUTH AFRICA

Howard P. Lehman

Research on interest groups in South Africa falls into two main categories: (1) groups involved in the antiapartheid struggle and (2) group activity during the transition to democratic rule. Two bibliographies provide sources on the two categories. Robert Davies et al. (1984) is a two-volume bibliography and directory with a politically radical perspective. The first volume lists and discusses the economic organizations that supported apartheid. The second focuses on antiapartheid groups, including political movements, trade unions, local associations, and other societal interest groups. An excellent bibliography and directory of postapartheid societal groups is Geoffrey Davis (1994).

Black political organizations received widespread attention from scholars during the apartheid era. Gerhart (1978) and Tom Lodge (1983) trace the rise of mass Black movements from 1945 until the Soweto riots of the mid-1970s. Another important study considers the economic context within which Black groups and white interests interacted (Lipton 1985). Since apartheid was supported and maintained by an extensive military, Grundy (1988) examines the military as a societal group. Two books focus on the role of churches in South Africa during the transition from apartheid (Borer 1998; Elphick and Davenport 1997).

When the downfall of apartheid became evident, scholars shifted their focus to societal groups that would lead the country to democracy under Black majority rule. Sisk (1995) provides an excellent study and bibliography focusing on political leaders, their parties, and civil society organizations during the negotiations to establish democracy. Gastrow (1995) describes the roles of professional groups, religious organizations, business associations, and labor unions during the period of constitutional negotiations. Deegan (1999) examines political parties, women, youth, and civil society in general.

Another category of recent studies focuses on particular groups during the transition to democracy. Examples include: Lanegran (1995) on the Civil Association Movement in South Africa; Kotze and Du Toit (1995) on elite attitudes; Griffiths (1995) on civil-military relations; Cock (1994) on women and the military; Adler and Webster (1995) on trade unions; an annotated bibliography by Limb (1993) on the African National Congress and Black workers; Szeftel (1994) on ethnicity and democratization; Desai and Habib (1997) on labor relations; and a case study by Maseko (1997) on the Cape Areas Housing Action Committee.

12.7. SUB-SAHARAN AFRICA

Howard P. Lehman

Interest groups as they are studied in liberal democracies have not been a major focus of African studies because of the scarcity of pluralist and democratic societies on the continent. However, this does not mean that African societal groups have not been active or influential. Throughout

Africa's colonial and postcolonial history, formal and informal groups have played a variety of roles in society and in relation to government.

This essay divides the literature review into three periods: colonialism, the independence period, and postcolonialism. There are many bibliographies on African societal groups. An early one listing standard works is Markovitz (1977, 350–77). A more recent general bibliography is Widner (1994, 273–95). An excellent bibliography and directory of organizations in Africa is McIlwaine (1993).

The Colonial Period

Three scholars are noted for their research on societal groups during the colonial period. Hodgkin (1956) studied the rise of groups within the context of nationalism during the 1950s. He focused on the relationship between colonial administration and the emergence of nationalist associations in towns and villages. James Coleman (1960) used functionalism as a theoretical framework to analyze African political groups, their functions, and their articulation and aggregation of interests. While these scholars wrote at a general level, Wallerstein (1966) analyzed the specific group formation of voluntary associations in Africa. A common theme in these studies is the break up of traditional associations and the dislocation of individuals as they were confronted with colonialism, urbanization, Western values, and new forms of association. A. L. Epstein (1958), Little (1965), and Abner Cohen (1969) conducted research on the relationships between urbanization and the development of trade unions and between urbanization and voluntary associations consisting of rural migrants and younger men and women. The peasantry as a political, social, and economic group was also a focus of study (see Klein 1980; Rosberg and Nottingham 1966).

Nationalist Movements

Many of these societal groups and voluntary associations provided a political base for nationalist leaders and their followers during the period leading up to independence. Markovitz (1977) uses an analytical framework to explore the social base of African nationalism. In particular, he examines the development of an "organizational bourgeoisie," or an indigenous administrative elite. This study illustrates how information, resources, values, ideas, and experience began to institutionalize the relationship between society and the African state.

The Postcolonial Period

Research since the 1980s has focused on two major areas: (1) expansion of informal participation and (2) the emergence of groups that actively seek to implement and institutionalize democracy in Africa. Hyden (1983) and Chazan (1982) are typical of the first set of studies. Their research suggests that as state structures and formal political institutions decay, informal political participation increases. Participation is channeled either into functional interest groups (such as trade unions, women's organizations, youth and student groups) or into ascriptive associations (such as ethnic and local improvement groups). In Villalon and Huxtable (1998) there is an examination of the linkages between the withdrawal of state power and the rise of nonstate actors in African society.

Much of this recent research focuses on specific groups as defined by occupation, gender, religion, and ethnicity. The military has been analyzed by Conteh-Morgan (1994) and Luckham (1994). Business associations have been studied by Heilbrunn (1997), labor in Nigeria by Ihovbere (1997), and farmers in Zimbabwe by Burgess (1997). African women have been studied by several scholars including Hay and Stichter (1995), Tripp (1994), and Mikell (1997).

Gifford (1995) considers the relationship between Christian churches and the democratic movement in Africa. His more recent book examines the public role of African Christianity (Gifford 1998). Regional studies include H. Hansen and Twaddle (1995) on religion and politics in East Africa and Callaway and Creevey (1994) on the relationship between Islam, women, and politics in West Africa. Political elites have been studied as a crucial intervening group between state policies and societal interests (Schraeder 1994; and Clark Gibson 1999). The politics of ethnic groups have been considered by many scholars, including Crawford Young (1976) who developed an influential "cultural pluralism" framework. More recent studies include Uvin (1999) who examines mass violence in Central Africa; and an interesting constructivist focus on ethnic politics is found in Yeros (1999).

Recent studies suggest that democratization will emerge not from the state but from more active and participatory societal groups within civil society. Bratton (1989) and Bratton and Van de Walle (1997) have argued that civil society can act as the cutting edge of a new democratic system in Africa. Richard Joseph (1997) provides an interesting survey of the recent democratization process in Africa. Other studies that address the relationship between civil society and political change include Ndegwa (1994), Fatton (1995), Rothchild (1994), Harbeson et al. (1994), and Peter Lewis (1998).

12.8. EASTERN EUROPE: COMMUNIST AND TRANSITIONAL SYSTEMS

David M. Olson

Under Communism, private voluntary associations were permitted neither by ideology nor by law. However, Western scholarship considered potential or latent groups in Communist societies as interests or interest groups. These included categories of the population or economy, and especially sectors as well as employees of state enterprises (Janos 1979). Most of this Western literature concentrated on the USSR; only minor attention was paid to Eastern Europe. The leading works (Skilling 1966, 1983) summarized their diverse approaches. The major studies of groups in both Eastern Europe and the Soviet Union were collected in anthologies (Skilling and Griffiths 1971; Fleron 1969).

The slow development of opposition and dissident groups, especially in Poland after 1956, provided the subject matter and the opportunity for research on nonstate and dissident groups, especially Solidarity and the Roman Catholic Church (Bielasiak and Simon 1984; Kolankiewicz 1988). A wide range of interest groups were described in Communist East Europe (Skilling 1973; F. Starr 1991), particularly Poland (Morrison 1968; Siemienska 1986), and especially Solidarity in relationship to the Communist Parliament (Mason 1991). One anthology examined religion and nationality issues and groups in the whole region (Ramet 1984). The pressure for freedom of thought and expression in Poland generated the concept of "civil society" (Staniszkis 1984), as opposed to state-sanctioned groups. An overview of the development of pressure groups in the latter years of Soviet rule and the early years of transition to Russian democracy is provided by Terry Cox (1993).

After 15 years of post-Communist transformation, no comprehensive bibliography or review of group formation or activity is available. However, Padgett's (1999) work on interest groups in post-Communist East Germany makes comparisons with other Eastern European countries. An inventory of groups in Hungary is available based on registration records (Vass 1993). The only studies of groups in relation to parliaments are on Poland (Fuszara 1993) and Hungary (Kovacs 1995). Most of the literature on interest groups now focuses on specific populations and issues: women (Siklova 1993; Wolchik 1993), youth (Tymowski 1994), and the environment (Hajba 1994) have received the most attention.

The experience of Communism has given not only political parties but all organizations an unsavory reputation. Most groups, as illustrated by women's and labor groups, seem to consist of a few activists (Siklova 1993; Kramer 1995; Zaborowski 1993; Rychard 1998). Participation by interest groups in elections and with political parties tends to be avoided, with the exceptions of labor unions in Poland and Hungary (Waller and Myant 1994; Ost 2001; Evanson and Magstadt 2001). Based upon a corporatist model, tripartite negotiation bodies (of employers, labor, and government) consider not only wage levels but also incomes policy (Malova 1997). Solidarity is by far the single most studied labor union (Ost 1990; Kennedy 1991), some business and other labor groups are also discussed (Agh and Ilonszki 1996; Hethy 1994). We may anticipate a rapid development of private associations in the new Eastern European democracies during the second decade of post-Communism.

12.9. RUSSIA: POST-COMMUNIST INTEREST GROUP ACTIVITY

Sergei P. Peregudov and Irina S. Semenenko

Part of the last entry (12.8.) identified the major texts on interest groups during the existence of the USSR. This entry concentrates on work on interest groups, and the broader category of *interests*, since the end of Communist rule. While there is an increasing output of work on the new interests in Russia, as with Eastern European countries, because of the newness of the system there is little in books or articles. Most work is found in conference papers and in in-house publications of research institutes; and the major work is in Russian not in English.

Currently, there is no general text in English on Russian interest groups. The work that is in English falls into three categories: (1) general treatments; (2) work on specific groups, mainly business groups; and (3) the broader categories of emerging elite interests in national and local politics. Three general works are of particular interest. Terry Cox (1993) examines the relationship between democratization and the emergence of pressure groups in both Soviet and post-Soviet Russia. Mancur Olson (1995) analyzes the connections between elitist interest groups dominating the Russian economy and politics and the corruption practices in centers of political power. He argues that the powerful lobbies and lobbyists, striving to achieve monopolistic positions, are the main architects of the criminally penetrated Russian economy. And Peregudov (1997) analyzes the activities of interest groups in Russia and other Russian federation countries and their influence on the process of economic integration.

On business groups, Rutland (1997a) provides an overview of these in contemporary Russia. Stykow (1996) analyzes the structures and activities of business associations and unions and their relations with the state. She offers answers to key questions concerning corporatist arrangements that are being formed in Russia. Schmitter (1996) and Schmitter and Grote (1997) have also examined Russian business associations, their intermediation with the state, and their role in the formation of a liberal democracy.

The third category deals with elite interests in government and the economy. Rutland (1997b) provides an overview of these groups and their mutual relations. He emphasizes the negative influence of the split of the ruling oligarchy on political stability in Russia and on the process of democratization. The origin of the main elite groupings has also been traced by Eberhard Schneider (1997). And David Lane (1997) describes the political attitudes and behavior of three main elite groupings—executive, parliament, and party leaderships—and stresses that they are working mainly in their own interests. Local interests have been studied by Brie (1998) who builds a model of the urban machine as a specific local political regime emerging in a situation of rapid social change. He sees the main forces in the Moscow machine as big business and the municipal administration as consolidated by Moscow Mayor J. Luzkov. Work dealing with the so-called financial oligarchy and its main groupings, clans and cliques, including criminal ones, has been conducted by Kryshtanovskaja (1996).

Finally, two major works in Russian should be mentioned. Peregudov, Lapina, and Semenenko (1999) have produced the first general text on Russian interest groups in the post-Communist period focusing on relations between various interest representatives (corporations, regional polities, trade unions, voluntary organizations, etc.) and the structures of the state. The authors are affiliated with the Institute of World Economy and International Relations (IMEMO) in Moscow where major recent research has been conducted on Russian interests. Scholars at the Institute (Kholodkovsky 1998) produced an edited volume covering a broad range of interest sectors and their lobbying activities.

12.10. LATIN AMERICA

Jonathan Rosenberg

Although there is an extensive literature on political organizations, interests, behavior, and the efficacy of groups in Latin America, Latin Americanists have not typically concerned themselves with interest groups per se, or empirical tests of interest group theory. The reasons are both empirical and ideological. First, there is the region's political volatility, resulting in few cases of long-lived pluralist systems. Second, there are Marxist and social democratic contentions that interest group theory is ethnocentric, imperialistic, and prescriptive. Consequently, early structural-functional approaches (e.g., McDonald 1971; Needler 1968) were quickly overtaken by events and attacked with class analysis and studies of extra-systemic behavior and revolutionary movements.

To understand political change, John Johnson et al. (1958) applied sectoral analysis to middle sectors, and later to peasants, rural laborers, writers, artists, the military, industrialists, and university students (J. Johnson 1964). Lipset and Solari (1967) and Horowitz (1970) followed with volumes on elites and the masses respectively. Militaries have been studied for their sociopolitical attributes (Nun 1968; Lieuwen 1961, 1964) and regarding their motivations for taking and relinquishing state power (Hagopian 1990; Karl 1991; Stepan 1988; Rouquie 1987). Organized labor has been studied as a source of support for populism, revolution, and democracy (Collier and Collier 1991; Keck 1989; Valenzuela 1989;

Conniff 1982). The Church, religious movements (D. Levine 1980; Berryman 1987), and peasants (Grindle 1977; Sharpe 1977) have been analyzed as sources of both conservatism and grassroots activism.

Dependency theory's (Furtado 1970) loose form of Marxian class analysis inspired debates on the political roles of capital and the revolutionary potential of workers and peasants, and later, sectoral differences within classes (Cardoso and Faletto 1979; P. Evans 1979). O'Donnell (1973) added complex propositions about the sectoral bases of authoritarianism and the political economy of military rule. Works on postrevolutionary states revealed interest-based politics behind authoritarian facades (e.g., Becker 1981; J. Rosenberg 1992). By the early 1970s, corporatism dominated non-Marxian analyses of groups. Studies influenced by Schmitter (1971) argued that Latin American groups are shaped by state institutions that intermediate at points of potential class conflict (Purcell 1975; Malloy 1977).

Booth and Seligson (1978, 1979) helped introduce political scientists to the expanded notion of group participation found in anthropological and sociological studies of new social movements (Safa and Nash 1976; Perlman 1976). Other political scientists eventually followed suit (Mainwaring 1989; Foweraker and Craig 1990).

The debt crisis of the 1980s introduced new methodologies, such as rational choice and modern political economy analysis, to study the interactions of groups and policy (Stallings and Kaufman 1989; Przeworski 1991; Frieden 1991a; J. Nelson 1994). Democratization has renewed interest in the formation of civil society and pluralist notions of state-society relations (O'Donnell, Schmitter, and Whitehead 1986).

Chapter 13

Interest Groups in International and Transnational Politics

Polly J. Diven

13.1. INTERNATIONAL AND TRANSNATIONAL LOBBYING DEFINED

This chapter reviews literature on both transnational and international interest group activity. What differentiates the two is their focus on state versus nonstate actors. *International lobbying* focuses on states as sources and/or as targets of lobbying activity. In contrast, *transnational lobbying* is characterized by interest group activity that occurs across state boundaries but is not rooted in or targeted at governments directly. Willetts (1982, 1) defines *transnationalism* as "relations between different societies across country boundaries, which bypass governments." Morss (1991, 55) identifies transnational organizations as having weak or nonexistent primary country allegiance. He describes three categories of transnational organizations, which he calls "the new global players": (1) private economic organizations (including transnational corporations, business associations and trade unions); (2) international nonprofit organizations (including humanitarian, issue-specific, professional, and scientific groups); and (3) transnational special interest groups (from a multitude of churches, such as the Catholic Church, to pro-choice and pro-life groups to groups opposing the repatriation of artifacts).

Of these three categories, the literature on private economic actors is the most developed and abundant (for example, Barnet and Muller 1974; Gilpin 1975; Helleiner 1987; Friman 1993). There is also a substantial literature on private economic interests and nongovernment organizations (NGOs) active in the European Union (EU—see sections 9.15. and 11.4.). This chapter focuses on international nonprofit, NGOs, and transnational interest groups.

Traditionally, however, transnational and international lobbying have not been a part of mainstream research in either the international relations or interest groups subfields of political science. Yet several recent developments have led to increased interest in these topics, including the growth of multinational corporations and transnational banks, the evolution of international economic integration, the expansion of transnational religious and indigenous movements, and the internationalization of many nonprofit organizations. In addition, the end of the Cold War has fueled the decline of neorealism and other state-centered theories as the dominant paradigms in the field of international relations. In sum, the transnational level of analysis has become more important as the emphasis on the state has declined and as transnational actors have increased in number, scope, and impact.

13.2. EARLY LITERATURE ON TRANSNATIONALISM AND REGIME THEORY

Current research on international and transnational lobbying builds upon and reflects the literature on transnationalism and the role of nonstate actors in international politics. Classic works on transnational actors and transnationalism include Wolfers (1962) and Rosenau (1969). In *Transnational Relations and World Politics*, Keohane and Nye (1970) introduce an alternative "world politics paradigm" as a substitute for the traditional state-centered approach. In the introduction, they note that their world politics paradigm "attempts to transcend the 'level of analysis problem' both by broadening the conception of actors to include transnational actors and by conceptually breaking down the 'hard shell' of the nation-state." The edited volume includes case studies of multinational corporations and transnational pressure groups.

The first systematic study of NGOs was conducted by Feld (1972) based on data from the 1960s. He presents descriptive data and finds little evidence that expanding numbers of nonstate actors either seriously challenge national sovereignty or contribute to a more peaceful world. Despite the major increase in the number of NGOs, he argues that their impact has been "undramatic, diffuse, slow, and does not suggest any single direction" (Feld 1972, 5). He notes that international pressure groups could both reduce and aggravate hostilities among states and argues that the impact of nonstate actors is most pronounced at the regional level.

Willetts examines several transnational interests in *Pressure Groups in the Global System* (1982). Like Keohane and Nye (1970), Willetts rejects the realist emphasis on state security in favor of a more complex view of international politics. He (Willetts 1982, 8) divides international pressure groups into (1) "sectional" groups that seek to protect the interests of a particular sector of society (for example, professional organizations or labor organizations); and (2) "promotional" groups that "come together solely for the purpose of promoting social change on a particular issue, usually by seeking a change in government policy." He argues that both types of pressure groups could play significant roles in the international system.

Despite these early efforts, the movement toward analysis of transnational actors in international relations was overshadowed by the more amorphous regime theory, which focused less on particular interests and more on " . . . principles, norms, rules and decision-making procedures" (Krasner 1982, 186). Major literature on regime theory includes: Haggard and Simmons (1987), Krasner (1983), Kratochwil and Ruggie (1986), Strange (1982), and Young (1986). Peter Haas (1992) later gave the name "epistemic communities" to informal multinational communities of experts that organize the way states and international organizations approach specific international issues. Debate over the existence and definition of regimes and epistemic communities dominated attempts to move away from state-centered analysis during this period. During this time, theoretically driven and empirically grounded research into transnational lobbying was neglected.

13.3. REVIVING TRANSNATIONALISM

M. J. Peterson (1992) traces the waning scholarly interest in transnationalism during the late 1970s and 1980s and its resurgence in the wake of the Cold War (see also Jackie Smith, Chatfield, and Pagnucco 1997). Despite the scant literature during the Cold War, Ghils (1992) emphasizes the consistent, long-standing influence of transnational groups, citing such diverse transnational phenomena as the Benedictines in the Middle Ages and the Puritans in Colonial New England.

Three books heralded the revival of transnationalism in the academic literature. The first response to the call for empirically grounded analysis of transnational influence in the post–Cold War period was an edited volume by Risse-Kappen, aptly titled *Bringing Transnational Relations Back In* (1995). Contributors examine cross-national links between domestic and international institutions for a variety of profit and nonprofit international organizations. The editor contends that a mix of instrumental and communicative rationales govern the formation of international issue networks. He notes the failure of both realist and Marxist approaches, each of which focus on material structures as defining interests and that transnational movements influence state decision making by linking national groups into a transnational organization that aids in their struggle and eventually shapes domestic policy making. Building, in part, on the work of Gourevitch (1978) and Putnam (1988), he stresses the importance of domestic structures as an explanatory variable for predicting the ability of transnational pressures to influence state policy (Risse-Kappen 1995, 187).

A second reader by Jackie Smith, Chatfield, and Pagnucco, *Transnational Social Movements and Global Politics: Solidarity Beyond the State* (1997), assembles a variety of recent literature in order to document and assess the impact of transnational interest group activity. The editors provide a theoretical framework that explains the impact of transnational interests based on three factors: mobilizing structures, political opportunities, and strategies to mobilize resources. Contributors document nine case studies of international interest group activities, including Earth Action, the Neptune Group, and the Peace Brigades in Sri Lanka. This volume and Risse-Kappen's work attempt to go beyond description of transnational activities and to identify the conditions under which issue networks will influence domestic and international politics. Defining *influence* in these cases is critical since it can be construed as anything from agenda setting to actual policy change.

The third noteworthy work on transnational interest groups is Keck and Sikkink's *Activists Beyond Borders: Advocacy Networks in International Politics* (1998). The authors present case studies of transnational advocacy networks that are able to define global issues and win commitments from policy makers. These networks are dominated by nonstate actors who rely on transnational influence. Keck and Sikkink apply their model to cases that emphasize improving human rights, reducing tropical deforestation, and focusing international attention on violence against women. In one case, the authors document how Latin American human rights activists supplied information to international NGOs who in turn pressured the United States and European governments to link economic aid and human rights reforms.

Like Risse-Kappen, Keck and Sikkink in *Activists Beyond Borders* refute realist theory and emphasize the power of ideas in world politics. They also cite the importance of international issue networks in promoting change in international relations. This emphasis on the power of ideas in international relations is based on Goldstein and Keohane's *Ideas and Foreign Policy* (1993) and Sikkink's *Ideas and Institutions* (1991). However, Keck and Sikkink's model for transnational influence still relies heavily on the state as the target of nonstate interest group activity.

Although the dominant trend has been to cite the growth in transnational lobbying, other scholars caution that this phenomenon is exaggerated and subject to cyclical changes. Tarrow (1994) contends that the most successful movements build upon indigenous social networks in domestic societies. This is a result of the fact that the "transaction costs" of building a movement are much higher among people who have no prior connections with one another. Perhaps because his focus is primarily on national social movements, Tarrow raises concerns that the importance of national social movements has been overshadowed by global economic and communication networks. He contends that the state uses transnational organizations to combat domestic social movements. Webber (1994) also identifies a number of difficulties that transnational interest groups confront, including the need to move beyond Western cultural confines, to attract and incorporate Third World membership, and to sustain membership and organization beyond cyclical trends.

13.4. SOURCES AND TARGETS OF TRANSNATIONAL LOBBYING

To help comprehend the wide range of literature on international and transnational lobbying, it is useful to divide this literature into sources of lobbying activity—who or what is doing the lobbying—and targets of lobbying activity—who or what is being lobbied. Both lobbing sources and targets, can be further divided into four levels: (1) international, (2) national, (3) subnational, and (4) businesses or firms. Interest groups at the transnational, national, subnational, and firm levels may target policy making at any of these levels. Some groups may focus on more than one level and even all four levels at the same time. The literature focusing on the sources of transnational lobbying tends to be issue specific rather than target specific: their focal point is more likely to be the desired policies than the organizations or institutions involved. The more theoretical literature examines the implications of transnational lobbying for states, international organizations, the international system, and the academic study of international relations.

In other cases, the central focus of the research is the policy-making body being targeted by international or transnational lobby groups. This literature discusses the variety and impact of lobbying efforts at one of the many international or regional organizations such as the United Nations (UN), UN specialized agencies, and other international organizations. In these cases, the research may compare the impact of different levels and/or types of transnational lobbying.

Whether organization specific or issue specific, much of this literature is case study analysis of transnational lobbying and transnationalism. The extent to which authors relate these case studies to a body of theory varies widely. The following sections present several studies of transnational lobbying. In the next section (13.5.), the focus is on lobbying targeted at the state level, followed by lobbying directed at global and regional international organizations (see section 13.6.). Then, two sections examine the sources of lobbying: first the literature on transnational issue areas, including the environment, human rights, and the international women's movement (see section 13.7.), followed by the impact of transnational religious and cultural movements (see section 13.8.).

13.5. TARGETS OF TRANSNATIONAL LOBBYING: (I) THE STATE

The primary theme connecting much of the literature on international lobbying is the relationship between states and transnational interests. To the extent that transnational organizations acquire power in the international system, they may be a threat to the sovereignty and primacy of states. Clearly, Tarrow (1994) believes that the impact of transnational organizations is limited by the state. Phillip Taylor (1984) presents a similar hypothesis. He completely dismisses the potential impact of nonstate actors, writing: "The primary actors in world politics are nation-states; any attempt to suggest otherwise is completely erroneous" (Phillip Taylor 1984, 3).

By contrast, Morss (1991, 55) argues that the impact of transnational organizations is frequently underestimated:

> The era in which nations ruled the world is over. With the information revolution and the demise of the United States as the dominant world power, three groups have joined nations as important global players: transnational corporations, international organizations, and special interest groups.

Morss argues that the focus on nation-states within the discipline of international relations does not provide a broad enough theoretical framework to adequately consider the impact of emerging transnational actors on world politics. He contends that the new global players are shedding their national identities and that national borders are becoming less consequential. He cites large-scale human migration, the spread of environmental pollutants, and new informational technologies as evidence of this trend.

Work by William Coleman (1997) examines the impact of internationalization on interest group governance at the national level. He contrasts sectors in decline with sectors at "full maturity" and argues that increased supranational governing agreements among states may lead to an increasing role for national-level interest associations. He writes, "In short, on balance, any increase in influence for supranational associative action has been countermanded, if not superseded, by increased governing powers for national level associations" (W. Coleman 1997, 25). One of the themes of a volume by Jane Bayes (1982) is how the international political economy has affected the operation of interest groups in the United States and their relations with government. She argues that the international activity of U.S. multinational interests, such as oil companies and other businesses, strengthens their domestic influence.

Many domestic lobby groups, not only those representing business, have been strengthened through their contact or association with transnational groups. Ayres (1997) documents the evolution of the anti-NAFTA (North American Free Trade Agreement) protest movement in Canada during a 15-year period. Although the original Canadian movement was weak, it was strengthened by its evolution into a transnational movement. Ayres notes that Canada is particularly vulnerable to the effects of globalization as a result of its proximity to the United States and its increasingly decentralized government. Hogenboom (1996) is less convinced of the long-term impact of transnational interest groups that influenced Mexican environmental policy making during the NAFTA negotiations. She concedes that the pressure from transnational environmental groups outweighed the ineffective activities of national environmental groups and led to temporary successes. However, Hogenboom predicts that the effects of NAFTA's environmental provisions and the impact of transnational environmental groups may be transitory, especially in light of Mexico's economic and political difficulties.

13.6. TARGETS OF TRANSNATIONAL LOBBYING: (II) INTERNATIONAL ORGANIZATIONS

International organizations and their various institutions and agencies are a key target for international interest groups. Private firms, nonprofit organizations, and governments all lobby global organizations such as the UN and regional organizations such as the EU. NGOs are a major, if not the major, source of interest group pressure on international organizations. Although the records of the organizing meeting of the UN made no mention of NGOs, about 1,200 of them attended the San Francisco conference that finalized the UN Charter in 1945. Since then, growing numbers of NGOs have played an increasing role in the UN and its affiliated organizations (Ritchie 1996).

An example of an early case study of an international agency as a target of lobbying is Harvey Silverstein (1978), which examines the transnational politics of the Intergovernmental Maritime Consultative Organization (IMCO). The author considers participation in decision making at the IMCO by a wide range of actors, including individual private interest groups and NGOs.

With the exception of the EU (see section 11.4.), very little academic literature exists on lobbying of regional international organizations. One exception is Woods (1993), focusing on the importance of NGOs in fostering the Pacific economic cooperation movement. He claims that economic interdependence in the region supports and is supported by the Association of Southeast Asian Nations (ASEAN). The book describes how prominent transnational organizations in the region (such as the Pacific Basin Economic Council and the Pacific Economic Cooperation Council) have contributed to the region's contemporary diplomatic framework. He uses this regional case study to argue that other transnational pressure groups "often carry out functions that governments are unable to perform or unable to agree on how to perform" (Woods 1993, 6).

Two recent works highlight the impact of NGOs on international organizations in Central America. Macdonald (1994) documents the new forms of transnational links among NGOs that occurred in the 1980s in Central America. She argues that these NGO movements were not part of a trend toward global civil society but were rooted in one of two larger movements—the neoconservative U.S. government counter-insurgency strategy or the network of alternative popular organizations opposed to U.S. intervention in Central America. Macdonald effectively argues that relations between these two groups of transnational NGOs were highly conflictual; therefore, "idealistic and abstract approaches to the concept of global civil society . . . are inadequate" (Macdonald 1994, 269).

Sollis (1996) is more sanguine about the role of NGOs in Central America. He notes that their ability to "weather the conflicts of the 1980s as a robust and growing sector is a display of versatility and durability" (Sollis 1996, 203). He also believes that if NGOs make careful decisions about strategies and partners, they may continue to play a key role in Central American governance. In addition, he notes the critical roles of the UN and the UNDP (United Nations Development Program) in linking NGO pressure groups to governments.

In an edited volume, Weiss and Gordenker (1996) assemble several case studies of NGO influence on UN agencies. These cases include causes such as HIV/AIDS, the environment, the women's movement, and human rights. In the introductory and concluding chapters, the editors identify NGOs as a significant challenge to state sovereignty and argue that many NGOs provide "more ordered and more reliable responses to problems that go beyond the individual and even the collective capacities of states." The relationship between NGOs and UN agencies is not limited to the former pressuring the latter. Rather, NGOs are involved, to varying degrees, in "conflict, competition, cooperation, and co-optation" in their relationship with UN agencies. The editors recommend increased transparency, accountability, and participation for NGO pressure groups working with UN agencies (Weiss and Gordenker 1996, 217, 221). They also note that their volume, and the literature on transnational lobbying in general, suffers from a lack of data and empirical rigor.

13.7. SOURCES OF TRANSNATIONAL LOBBYING: (I) ISSUE-SPECIFIC INTEREST GROUPS

Several studies on transnational lobbying approach the growing phenomenon from the perspective of the interest groups themselves. Of these, the largest number of books and articles focus on international lobbying by environmental and human rights organizations. Some issue areas lend themselves to greater international pressures than do others. For example, decision making on security issues is traditionally state centered and highly centralized, whereas: "On such issues as human rights and the environment, by contrast, NGOs have the capacity to act directly and independently" (Spiro 1994, 48).

Environmental Lobbying Groups

Environmental pollutants are not easily contained within national borders—pollution problems are by nature transnational. The long-standing conflict between the United States and Canada over acid rain resulting from U.S. pollutants drifting across the Canadian border is a good example. Using mass media appeals and other outsider interest group strategies, watchdog groups such as Greenpeace can influence policy making when governments fail to respond to environmental concerns. Although its roots go back a century or more, the current environmental movement began in the United States and Western Europe in the late 1960s and early 1970s. Today there are multitudes of domestic, regional, international, and transnational environmental agencies (see section 9.10.). The focus of these organizations ranges from pollution control and the anti-nuclear movement to efforts to reverse population trends and income inequities. What is the influence of these organizations? And what channels do they use to influence policy makers at the state and international levels?

Although most authors agree that the international environmental movement has enjoyed success in recent years, there is substantial disagreement about the root of this success. Some observers argue that international environmental institutions are the key to reform, others credit civil society, public opinion, and local environmental organizations. Princen and Finger (1994) present both approaches. In Part I of their book, they set out and critique both the political bargaining and social movement theoretical perspectives on international environmental activism. In Part II, they use four case studies to demonstrate the ambiguity and uncertainty of NGO success. One important theme in this volume is that international environmental groups provide critical links between the "essential knowledge base" and world politics. NGOs confront state-centered attitudes that emphasize borders and industrial development (Princen and Finger 1994, 223). The authors argue that the international environmental movement is most effective in translating information about the global ecological crisis into political change at the local and global levels.

In general, however, the literature on international environmental lobbying tends to be strong on polemic and weak on theoretical and empirical grounding. For example, Bruce Rich (1994, xii) takes stock of "the profound human and ecological damage" caused by World Bank lending. He focuses on the 1992 Earth Summit in Rio de Janeiro, contrasting this type of global centralized environmental management with the countervailing forces of "emerging global civil society" (Rich 1994, xii). He favors a more bottom-up approach. Similarly, Tobin (1990) and Lerner (1991) critique the current international environmental management organizations and highlight the activities of several communities promoting sustainable development in the Third World.

Other authors are more favorably disposed toward international management of the environment. They note that transnational interest groups have been able to set the agenda and promote reform within a number of international organizations. Hurrell (1991) provides strong evidence of the pressure that transnational groups of ecologists brought to bear in reforming Brazil's rainforest policy. Recalling the debate about epistemic communities and regimes, Hjorth (1994) cites Baltic Sea environmental cooperation as a case in which expert knowledge and influence produced a shift in the existing regime, first in attitudes and then in policy.

In some cases, the transnational interest group has eclipsed the role of the state in international organizations. Spiro (1994) cites the phenomenon whereby state influence is "captured" by transnational interest groups, indirectly and directly. An example of a direct capture is the case of small states, like those in Micronesia, ceding their representation to NGOs in international government forums (Spiro 1994, 50).

Clearly, the environmental movement has also enjoyed success outside the realm of institutional policy making. Wapner (1996) argues that environmental groups such as Greenpeace and Earth First! are best thought of as transnational interest groups that work to disseminate "environmental sensibility" through civil society. In turn, either directly or indirectly, these grassroots citizen groups influence multinational corporations and government policy makers. In *Environmental Activism and World Civic Politics* (1996), Wapner presents a framework in which states are not the dominant target of transnational activity. He evaluates the strategies of three environmental pressure groups—Greenpeace, the World Wildlife Fund, and Friends of the Earth—and their impact on international institutions. Greenpeace's strategy of "political globalism" is particularly notable since this is evidence of a transnational interest group that is able to influence policy making outside the context of public institutions. In essence, Wapner's argument is directed toward augmenting, not replacing, state-centered conceptions of international relations.

Also emphasizing the global environmental movement, Caldwell (1990) argues that international pressure and public opinion have successfully changed the attitudes of world leaders toward environmental protection. He writes, "The politicians have at last caught up with the opinion polls. Effective publicity by NGOs played an indispensable role in mobilizing and focusing public attention on environmental matters" (Caldwell 1990, 304).

By contrast, Vig and Kraft (1990a) emphasize the role of economic incentives in promoting the transnational environmental agenda. They contend that enactment of stricter environmental legislation will be the result of market forces and changing economic incentives to encourage more regulation of industry.

A few authors offer insights into the successes and failures of the environmental agenda within a variety of state cases. For example, Sprinz and Vaahtoranta (1994) provide a theoretical framework for analyzing why some countries are more likely than others to allocate scarce resources to improving the international environment. The authors present an interest-based explanation for an individual country's susceptibility to the efforts of the transnational environmental movement. They classify countries in one of four categories ("pushers," "draggers," "intermediaries," and "bystanders") on the basis of the country's ecological vulnerability and the costs to that country of pollution abatement. Roger Payne (1995) also examines the conditions under which transnational environmental pressures will influence state behavior. He contends that transnational actors are more likely to achieve their goals in centralized, society-dominated countries and less likely to achieve influence in decentralized, state-dominated countries. Similarly, Shams (1994) argues that the economic structure of the target country is key to the success of the international pressure group. Environmental movements tend to be dominated by urban intellectuals, and anxiety over economic growth and welfare naturally overshadows environmental concerns among policy makers and ordinary citizens. Environmental reforms also are likely to run counter to domestic interest group coalitions such as loggers, miners, some trade unions, and major industrialists.

Human Rights Lobbying Groups

Amnesty International is probably the most well known international pressure group working to improve human rights. Since the 1970s, however, the number of international and regional interest groups concerned with human rights has increased considerably. The number of groups and the scope of activity are particularly extensive in Latin America (Scoble and Wiseberg 1981). What is the impact of these transnational interest groups, and how successful are they in influencing state and international organization policy? Literature in this field is inconsistent, and the findings are often based on single case studies rather than comparative analysis.

One perspective is offered by Gubin (1995) and Hovey (1997) both of whom provide case studies of transnational human rights groups having a significant influence on policy outcomes. Gubin argues that Soviet compliance with Jewish immigration policy within the framework of the Conference on Security and Cooperation in Europe (CSCE) was partly the result of pressure exerted by transnational human rights interest groups. In a study documenting the impact of the international Quaker organization on UN conscientious objector policy, Hovey contends that the group had an enormous effect. This transnational group was educating policy makers, working the system, and facilitating consensus in order to establish a new norm at the international level. Similarly, Sikkink (1993) emphasizes the impact of "principled issue networks" in creating and enforcing human rights policy in Latin America. Keck and Sikkink (1998) build upon this work, adding case studies and issue areas.

In contrast, Farer (1988), Tolley (1989), and Gaer (1996) present more guarded evaluations of the influence of transnational human rights interest groups on state and international institutions. Farer (1988) recognizes the important impact of transnational human rights groups in recent years, but notes that right-wing groups in the Western Hemisphere have absorbed and exploited the rhetoric of human rights organizations. This presents important political challenges for U.S. policy makers and how they respond to governments in the Americas. Gaer (1996) provides a "reality check" on the role of human rights NGOs at the UN. She notes that the UN is dependent on these transnational organizations and attributes almost all advances in human rights there to the work of human rights interest groups. However, she also notes that the UN is careful to distance itself from activist organizations such as Amnesty International. In addition, member governments under fire from transnational interest groups want to limit the access of human rights groups to the UN and will consistently challenge the legitimacy of negative findings.

According to Tolley (1989, 361), without political parties and elections to voice concerns at the international level, nongovernmental pressure groups are even more vital in world politics than they are at the domestic level. However, he notes that there are several obstacles to NGO influence in international human rights policy making. The most important include the tendency of Third World governments to question the dominance of NGOs by First World and particularly Western interests and the simple fact that " . . . private groups cannot press diplomats negotiating a treaty with the type of inducements, threats, and promises that influence domestic legislators" (Tolley 1989, 362). Tolley goes on to contend that whereas multinational corporations and terrorist groups have acquired power in global politics, human rights activists lack the economic and paramilitary instruments of these groups (Tolley 1989, 362).

Women's International Lobby Groups

Women's international interest groups played key roles in influencing policy making made by states and international institutions during the twentieth century. Chatfield (1997) notes that groups such as the Women's International League for Peace and Freedom (established in 1915) have generated constituencies for international programs and mobilized transnational pressures on national policy. However, there is only a small body of literature on international pressure groups that focuses on women's issues, and almost all of it is descriptive. This literature encompasses a variety of causes, including population policy, abortion rights, the role of women in socioeconomic and political development, and women workers' rights. Women's groups have also sprung up around issues that are not strictly speaking women's issues, such as disarmament, human rights, and alcohol abuse. In fact, the international women's movement has suffered as a result of disagreements over its primary objectives. Sienstra (1994) questions whether the women's movement is one coherent movement at all. Chen (1996, 142) notes that much of the UN Decade of the Woman (1975–1985) was spent debating differences in approaches to feminism and differences between women who come from diverse social and cultural perspectives. She contends that the transnational women's movement became more coherent over time. By the time of the 1992 Conference on the Environment in Rio de Janeiro, women's issues had been effectively incorporated into the global agenda.

In an edited volume that is largely descriptive and historical, J. Peters and Wolper (1994) gathered accounts of the transnational movement for improving the human rights of women around the world. Lubin and Winslow (1990) focus exclusively on women and labor law. This is also mainly a historical work in which the authors describe the gradual shift from demands for physical safety in the workplace to lobbying for equal remuneration and freedom from discrimination. The authors detail efforts by interest groups to enact international labor laws for women and they assess the International Labor Organization's (ILO) role in reflecting and influencing the transnational movement for greater equality. They also explore the growing dichotomy between the demands of women in industrialized societies and their counterparts in developing regions. The impact of international women's interest groups on the UN is considered in Pietila and Vickers (1994). The authors argue that transnational women's groups have enjoyed success at the UN exceeding all expectations.

Martha Madison Campbell (1998) examines the impact of international pressure groups on population policy making. She uses epistemic community theory as a framework for understanding the configuration of five competing interest groups: women's groups promoting reproductive rights, population control groups, the Vatican, private enterprise groups, and developing country actors who prefer to focus on poverty and inequitable resource distribution. Of all the literature cited here on women's groups, Campbell's is the only article that is analytical.

13.8. SOURCES OF TRANSNATIONAL LOBBYING: (II) RELIGIOUS AND CULTURAL MOVEMENTS

One measure of the renewed interest in transnational movements can be attributed to the rise of international religious and cultural movements. In some areas of the world, ethnic identity and religious loyalty are major challenges to the sovereignty of the state. In an edited volume,

Stack (1981) demonstrates the importance of transnational ethnic groups in international politics based on the argument that increasing interdependence has allowed these groups to play an expanding role in world politics. He views the traditional interstate system as significantly altered by the increasing "complex interdependence" first identified by Keohane and Nye (1970). The book includes selections on the emerging ethnic movements among Saudi people in the Middle East and African populations in South America, among others.

The growing importance of transnational religious movements in relation to a more state-centered approach is highlighted by Ghils: "In Islam. . . . The community of believers (umma) derives its legitimacy from God, whereas political power is merely a practical necessity" (Ghils 1992, 429). In fact, as Marset (1987, 190) points out, one of the major sins (min alkabair) for a Muslim is to live under an illegitimate government. Marset contends that the use of religion to legitimize political opposition or to counter existing regimes is not limited to the Arab world.

Indeed, leaders of the radical antiabortion movement in the United States argue that their allegiance is to God's laws first. In the case of the Roman Catholic Church, there is debate over whether the activities of the Vatican make it more akin to an international pressure group or a sovereign state. In an edited volume, Hoeber Rudolph and Piscatori (1997) compile a number of cases in which both Muslim and Christian religious movements have overshadowed the constraints of state power. One chapter in Casanova (1997) documents the globalization of the Catholic church and its return to a "universal" church.

13.9. QUESTIONS FOR FUTURE RESEARCH

Researchers are only beginning to tackle questions that will help estimate the effects of international lobbying and the impact of transnational interest groups across borders. Currently, most of the literature on transnational pressure groups is descriptive or polemic. Existing case studies set the stage for more systematic analysis, but they need to be organized to enable researchers to draw more general conclusions about the impact of transnational lobbies on policy outcomes. The following are three of the most important research questions:

1. What strategies and channels do international interest groups use to influence policy? Are some types of interest groups and some strategies more likely to be successful than others?
2. Do transnational lobby groups pose a serious threat to national sovereignty? To what extent and how have governments suffered from a loss of control as a result of transnational interest group activity?
3. Are the sources and effects of international lobbying symmetrical across states? Are weaker states disproportionately affected?

These are just three issue areas attention to which can help structure the evolving literature on transnational and international lobbying. Although the debate over the relative influence of state and nonstate actors will continue, the general movement away from state-centered research in international relations bodes well for the development of scholarship on transnational lobbying. Many scholars studying transnational lobbying appear to be unaware of much of the valuable literature on domestic lobbying that has relevance to their work. Thus, researchers would be wise to consider applying some of this theory and methodology. Comparative analysis of pressure group success and failure across a carefully selected range of countries and issues is critical. Of course, controlling for conditions across countries and measuring "success" is complex. Nonetheless, researchers need to more rigorously analyze and assess the strategies, importance, and effects of transnational lobbying.

Chapter 14

Concerns about Interest Groups: Questions of Democracy, Representation, Bias, and Regulation

14.1. THE CONCERNS AND THE MAJOR APPROACH FOR ADDRESSING THEM: AN OVERVIEW

Clive S. Thomas

All political institutions can have both positive and negative effects on a political system and on the society at large. Nowhere is this more evident than with interest groups. Given this situation, this chapter focuses on the concerns about interest groups and the attempts by various societies to address these problems. The crux of the problems stems from the fact that although interest groups are indispensable to all political systems, pluralist and nonpluralist alike, they have the potential to undermine and, in some cases, destroy the fundamental goals of a society and to promote the benefit of some segments of society over others.

However, the concerns about the detrimental effects of interest groups and some of the ways of attempting to deal with them are different in liberal democracies and authoritarian systems. Moreover, both because the bulk of academic work on this subject has focused on liberal democracies and because nonpluralist societies are wide-ranging in their approach to dealing with the detrimental effects of interest groups, this chapter focuses mainly on the situation in liberal democracies.

The concern about interest groups is reflected in an ambivalent attitude toward them among the public and many politicians and political leaders in liberal democracies and authoritarian regimes alike (see section 4.8.). For example, Americans, who join interest groups by the tens of millions, are particularly skeptical of the detrimental effects of what they derogatorily refer to as "special interests" (see section 6.7.); Israelis long saw interest groups as signifying particularistic sentiments and not the communal values needed to build a new nation after World War II (Yishai 2001); and corporatist regimes like Franco's Spain and pre–World War II Austria viewed interest groups with great suspicion (see section. 3.4.).

In regard to liberal democracies, James Madison set out the classic explanation of this potential antithetical role of interest groups, or "factions" as he called them, way back in 1787 in *The Federalist* No. 10 (Brock 1965). In general, Madison's concerns, and those of a host of scholars and observers since him, focus mainly on the extent to which interest groups are representationally biased and, therefore, may undermine the public interest and democracy and promote the benefit of one, often a very small, segment of society at the expense of the society as a whole. The following entry (see section 14.2.) explores the concerns in liberal democracies about the democratic nature, representativeness, and biases of interest group activity. As in many aspects of interest group studies, most of the research on these concerns has been conducted on the U.S. political system. However, the problems and the debate about them has relevance for all liberal democracies.

In nonpluralist systems, concerns about interest groups arise mainly from the ability of groups and interests to undermine the national interest or major societal goals, which are often expressed in the official ideology (as in Communism) or as articulated by the leader or leadership as in Chile under General Pinochet in the 1970s and 1980s where the military junta running the country sought to protect itself from Communism and other radical elements. Together with a free press and political parties, independently formed interest groups are potentially a major source of opposition to any authoritarian government. Thus, the level of concern about interest groups and the approach to dealing with it varies with the degree of authoritarianism and the extent to which a regime sees independent interest groups as a threat to its goals.

Regulation of group activity in some form is the major public policy approach used to deal with concerns about interest groups in most liberal democracies and in virtually all authoritarian regimes (though *control* is a more appropriate term for this action than is *regulation* in most authoritarian systems). In all political systems, the general goal of regulation is to promote the public or national interest, however defined, over that of the narrow segments of society represented by various interest groups. In authoritarian regimes the dictator and perhaps the political elite will likely define this public or national interest; or, in part, it may be defined by the political ideology that in some societies, such as parts of the Muslim world, may include major religious principles. In its particular form, however, regulation varies considerably in scope and extent and in specific focus between democratic and authoritarian regimes. Furthermore, at least as far as liberal democracies are concerned, there is inconclusive evidence as to the effects of regulation in dealing with the representational biases of interest groups and the potential inequalities of political power that result from these biases. The complex questions regarding the extent of the representativeness and biases in democratic group systems is considered in section 14.2.

A consideration of the research and literature on interest group regulation constitutes most of the sections in this chapter. Section 14.3. provides an overview of the major approaches to regulation in both pluralist and nonpluralist political systems and points out that the analytical literature on regulation is very small, with only a few major works. Because it is in the United States that regulation has been most extensive, sections 14.4.1. and 14.4.2. detail regulation at the federal level and at the state and local levels respectively. Then an example of regulation in a liberal democratic system outside the United States is considered (see section 14.5). This section examines the European Union (EU) since it is one of the most recent attempts at regulation and epitomizes many of the political and administrative problems involved in enacting regulation in parliamentary systems. The final entry in the chapter (see section 14.6.) provides a review of the lessons to be learned from lobby and interest group regulation in the United States and in other liberal democracies.

14.2. REPRESENTATIVENESS AND BIAS IN INTEREST GROUP ACTIVITY IN LIBERAL DEMOCRACIES: AN INCONCLUSIVE DEBATE

Grant Jordan and Clive S. Thomas

The extent to which interest groups as they operate in the public policy process are representative of society as a whole or bias in favor of certain segments of a society is a subject on which public opinion and the evidence from academic research differ. Particularly in the United States (see section 6.7.), but also in other countries (see section 4.8.), there is a strong public belief (albeit often based on minimal information) that interest groups are not representative of society as a whole and promote the interest of certain groups, particularly "moneyed and business interests" at the expense of the general interest. Certainly, academic research has found many *individual* instances, some extremely blatant, of interests promoting very narrow, selfish goals and benefiting themselves at the expense of the society. In general, however, despite a host of studies focusing on the question of representation and bias, the overall academic evidence is inconclusive.

This inconclusiveness is largely a product of scholars using different points of reference for assessing the extent of representation and bias. For example, they use varying definitions of representation, the public interest, and what constitutes bias. Additionally, scholars often focus on a particular issue or issues, on a specific policy area or areas, or on one point in time. Each of these factors, or two or more in combination, may produce different, often contradictory results (Baumgartner and Leech 1998, 83). In short, while the research on questions of representation and bias is not as inconclusive as that on interest group power (see section 7.17.), it leaves many unanswered questions and offers a fruitful area for future research.

There is no bibliography that deals specifically with this topic. However, there are four sources that provide a useful initial exploration of the subject. The first two can be found in Jeffrey Berry (1997). Chapter 1 explores the general advantages and disadvantages of interest group activity, and Chapter 10 more specifically examines questions of bias and representation. The third and fourth sources are more in-depth considerations of the question of bias that contain many useful references for advanced study. One is Baumgartner and Leech (1998, chap. 5). This chapter is particularly useful for gaining an understanding of the inconclusive nature of research on the subject of interest group bias. The other source is Graziano (2001) who makes concerns about interest groups a major theme of his book and devotes the final section (chaps. 9 and 10) to an historical consideration (1960–90) of the question of group representation and bias.

With these preliminaries in mind, this section provides an overview of the major problems, questions, and complexities involved in making an assessment of the extent of representativeness and bias of interest group systems in the policy process in liberal democracies and, of necessity, involves a consideration of concepts of democracy. It should be emphasized that this section is concerned with democracy, representation, and bias in the public policy process and not with the internal organization and operation of groups. Questions regarding these internal aspects of group dynamics are considered in section 5.3.

Democracy, Representation, and Bias Defined

Because the extent and form of representation, the role of interest groups, and the views of bias in group systems are shaped by varying views of liberal or pluralist democracy, the essence of democracy as a foundation for understanding the differing perceptions of democracy and their consequences for representation and bias is presented first.

Liberal or pluralist democracy is representative, responsible, and limited government. It has four fundamental and interrelated elements. First, government actions are subject to the rule of law buttressed by an independent judiciary. Second, there is adult suffrage to elect lawmakers through periodic elections where various political persuasions (usually in the form of political parties) compete for power. Thus, the power of government emanates from the people, and the government is responsible to the electorate through elections and other legal and political devices. Third, is the institutionalization (official recognition in a constitution and statutes) of the legitimacy of political opposition to government manifested in various points of view on public issues and policies, bolstered by the freedom to organize political parties and the existence of a free press. Fourth is the right of citizens to organize groups based upon their interests—economic, social, political, religious and so on—and to represent these interests to government in an effort to affect public policy to their advantage.

Representation as generally defined in liberal democratic theory involves the second and fourth fundamental elements of democracy: the right to participate in choosing those who will govern and the right to have a voice, either directly oneself or indirectly through a representative, in the public policy decisions made by government officials. Some democratic systems go further and attempt to incorporate other elements, such as proportional representation in voting, equal representation for some subdivisions of a country in one house of the legislature or parliament as in many federal systems like the United States, representation of various interests in a legislature body as with Life Peers in the British House of Lords, and so on, into representation.

Bias, as used by scholars in this aspect of interest group studies, refers to two interrelated elements. The first is bias in representation. That is, the extent (or lack thereof) to which the group system is representative of the society as a whole in regard to the degree that various interests are organized and can articulate their views to government. The second element is the extent to which the group system may be skewed in favor of certain segments of society and some specific interests, such as business, exerting more influence than others. While the two aspects of bias are closely linked in that reducing representational bias may produce conditions more conducive to influence by hitherto underrepresented interests, the situation is far more complex than this. Dealing with the influence aspect of bias in a liberal democratic society is at best very difficult and at worst likely impossible. The reasons for this and the relationship between representation and group influence are explored later in this section.

Varying Views of Liberal Democracy and the Issue of Representation

While liberal democracy has common elements (explained above), it is a continually evolving form of government that has changed over time from the ancient Greek form to contemporary forms in so-called post-industrial democracies like the United States and Germany. There are also variations in the operation of specific elements of liberal democracy from country to country at the same time. For example some systems, such as many in continental Europe, use a proportional representation system in voting, whereas the United States and Britain use a plurality, a first-past-the-post system. And in regard to the specific activity of interest groups, particularly their strategies and tactics, it is shaped by the governmental structure (see sections 4.3. and 11.1.), the political culture (see section 4.4.), and to some extent, the relationship of interest groups with political parties (see section 4.5.). Thus, while interest groups are important in all societies, their representational role in a particular democracy will vary according to the political and governmental environment of that country. This makes it very difficult to generalize about the representational role of group systems and the extent of their bias across western democracies. An accurate assessment of this role and its biases is really only possible on a country-by-country basis.

Nevertheless, since interest groups together with political parties are the two major forms of political participation and representation between elections, the role of groups has featured prominently in theories of liberal democracy. Even though most of these perspectives on democracy and the role of groups in them have been developed with the U.S. political systems foremost in mind, they do have relevance to other democracies, especially because the important role of political parties is undergoing major changes both in the social democracies of Western Europe and in the new democracies developing in Eastern Europe. These constantly evolving views of democracy have varying interpretations of representation and the role of interest groups. Thus, the concerns about interest groups, including the extent of bias in the group system, have also changed over time.

The forerunner to modern liberal democracy is the *direct democracy* of ancient Greece and Rome. According to Held (1992, 12) two of their major principles were direct participation, where individual citizens held office; and attended and contributed to meetings in which decisions were made and the idea that participation was not intended as a means to pursue self-interest, but as a means to promote the common interest. However as Dahl (1989, 21) points out, in this early form of democracy there were no rights for women, slaves, freedmen, nor long-term resident aliens and their families. So various groups were excluded from participation even though those participating in governmental decision making had an obligation to consider the interest of these nonparticipants. Thus, the biases of this system, although apparent, are difficult to assess empirically.

By the late eighteenth century, largely as a result of the growing size of political units, direct democracy was reinterpreted as participation via the selection of representatives—*representative democracy*. This became and remains the dominant notion of democracy with Schumpeter (1944) presenting perhaps the strongest case for it among modern scholars. However, the defects of this method as a democratic form are often noted. These range from concerns about the precise rules of the selection of elected officials (for example, the case for and against proportional representation) to a more fundamental debate about the relationship between the public interest and the ability of special interests with privileged access, particularly business, to shape public preferences (see Lindblom 1977). It has also been pointed out that "one person, one vote" neglects the "intensity issue"—the minority with vital concerns on an issue might be overridden by the majority with only a casual interest in that issue.

As a consequence, the *realist* view of democracy that emerged in the 1950s was that electoral participation was low and poorly informed. Empirical studies of voting behavior confirmed this low turnout and that voting did not reflect the careful consideration of alternatives. Thus, even as early as the 1950s, there was a loss of confidence in the idea of representative democracy among some scholars. In this regard, Hudson (1995, 145) refers to the phenomenon of "trivialized elections."

Added to these concerns, questions began to be raised among scholars about the representational value of political parties versus that of interest groups. To many scholars there was a period from the 1930s to 1960s in the United States and for 40 years after World War II in Western Europe when parties as a means of representation appeared to be superior to interest groups. The champion of this view was E. E. Schattschneider who wrote, "By every democratic principle the parties, as mobilizers of majorities, have claims on the public more valid and superior to those asserted by pressure groups which merely mobilize minorities" (Schattschneider 1942, 193; see also section 3.6.). Part of this argument was based on the belief that there was an inverse relationship between the power of parties and of interest groups; that is, strong parties meant weak interest groups, and weak parties resulted in strong interest groups (Schlozman and Tierney 1986, 201). Therefore, strong parties would curb the worst effects of special interest groups and promote a more general public interest.

However, since the early 1970s in the United States, the early 1990s in Western Europe and other liberal democracies, and 1989 in Eastern Europe with the development of emerging democracies, two trends in party development have appeared to undermine the superiority of the representational role of parties. One trend is that parties have survived by becoming more catchall and by professionalizing, rather than mobilizing, the public (Dalton and Wattenberg 2000, 269, 282; W. Grant 1995, 1; C. Thomas 2001a, chap. 15). A second trend, as evidenced in Eastern Europe and Israel, is the development of *interest parties* where parties are so narrow in policy focus—such as several of the religious parties in Israel—that they are almost indistinguishable from interest groups (Evanson and Magstadt 2001; Ost 2001; Yishai 2001).

Furthermore, research at the state level in the United States (Thomas and Hrebenar 1999a) and on the party-group relationship across the western world (C. Thomas 2001a) shows that strong parties do not necessarily mean weak interest groups. In fact, strong interest groups can operate within strong parties, and likely this has always been the case. Therefore, at times, this situation may skew the representational role of a party, or coalition of parties, in government away from the public interest and in favor of the powerful interest or interests within the party or coalition.

By the 1970s, as a result of these concerns about democracy and representation, interest groups, rather than parties and elected party representatives, became central to the interpretation of pluralist democracy in the United States (Dahl 1982). Parties began to decline as more and more Americans joined interest groups, seeing them as the most effective means for achieving their political goals. A burgeoning of interest groups occurred in national, state, and local politics across America and across the western world in general. A new model of democracy emerged. As Dahl (1984) explained it, a polyarchy developed with many organized centers of power (mainly interest groups) in society that had a major influence on policy making. The new model contrasted with the previous era in which a few controlling entities, such as parties or strong centralized government (including a professionalized bureaucracy), had the major influence (see also McFarland 1987, 129). Such an approach saw politics as about self-interest; saw meaningful citizen participation as coming through support for interest groups rather than voting; and saw the consent of affected interests as a valid test of policy. It was an empirical approach to political theory that devised a definition of democracy (or at least polyarchy) from the practices of systems that were thought to be democratic.

There appears to be an empirical link between large-scale democracy and this type of group intermediation (Dahl 1984, 34). In this reinterpretation, individual apathy is no longer crucial—the indicator of a healthy democracy is group activity. As Dunleavy and O'Leary (1987, 23) observe, " . . . pluralists know that citizens do not and cannot directly control policy making in polyarchies." An interest group is more likely to be in a position to make a well-argued case on behalf of the members than members could individually. In this interpretation, democracy is seen as a more continuous process of governmental-group relations rather than as an accountability that is only effective at elections.

It is clear from this brief review of changing interpretations of democracy and its key element of representation that interest groups have been viewed across the gamut in terms of their detriment or value to the democratic process. These changing views of the legitimacy and necessity of interest groups together with the extent to which groups represent the various economic, social, political, religious, and other interests within a particular society (what neocorporatists call the encompassing nature of the interest groups system (see section 3.4.), shape perspectives on the extent of bias in the interest group system.

Factors Producing Bias and the Question of the Extent and Consequences of Bias

Even though perspectives on representation and the role of interest groups in democracy are wide-ranging, producing varying benchmarks for assessing bias, most scholars see some inherent bias in the U.S. interest group system (see Zeigler 1983; J. Berry 1997; Hrebenar 1997; Baum-gartner and Leech 1998). These general biases are likely common to all liberal democracies.

First, as vehicles of representation, interest groups are far from ideal since they do not represent all segments of the population equally. This bias is toward the better-educated, higher-income, majority culture (whites in most western democracies), and male segments of the population. Minori-ties (including women) and the less-well-educated and lower-income seg-ments of society are underrepresented by interest groups (see section 4.6.).

Second, resources—mainly money—do matter, and those groups, par-ticularly business and the professions, that have the most resources tend to be more successful in gaining the all-important access as a prerequisite to influence than those groups with fewer resources. Third, extensive resources—including money, good lobbyists, and perhaps, favored status with government officials—mean that some groups exert power out of all proportion to the number of their members, and in some instances, that they can thwart the will of a much larger number of people favoring a cause. Fourth, there is often concern about the activities of foreign lob-bies influencing policy that might be considered against a country's national interest, particularly on issues of national security.

In terms of specific aspects of the group system that produce bias, one of the most common is the so-called bias to business because of its exten-sive resources and importance to government. Another is that certain kinds of interests are inherently easier to organize and finance than oth-ers. This was a major point of Mancur Olson's work (1965, 1971) whose concern over the bias in group mobilization was based on the proposition that consumer and public interest groups are congenitally weak as a con-sequence of free riding (see section 5.2.). Even though free riding may not stop public interest groups from developing as Olson implied, it may con-strain them from prospering. Such groups suffer from instability of mem-bership and from the fact that the participatory role available for individuals through large-scale public interest groups is shallow. Godwin (1988, 78) has noted that "participation through [financial] contribution" may be a substitute form of participation, albeit a less effective one.

Other specific arguments regarding bias have also been advanced. One is that the shift from a vote-based to a group-based democracy might exacerbate political inequality since it is generally accepted that the rel-atively small class-based differences in participation in voting are exag-gerated in the group sphere (Dalton and Wattenberg 2000, 283). This was captured by Schattschneider's (1960, 35) observation that "the flaw in the pluralist heaven is that the heavenly chorus sings with a strong upper–class accent." And critics of insider politics (for example, Lowi 1979) argue that the fairly stable arrangements, captured in metaphors like the iron triangle, that link cliental agencies and interest groups serves to advantage the easily organized interests over the public interest.

There are arguments that question the extent of these biases. In practice, public interest groups have flourished; though by any definition, business groups seem numerically more important (Graziano 2001, chap. 10). It can be argued, however, that the increase in business group mobilization is not so much a sign of business strength as weakness: business has organized because it has been affected by taxation, trade, safety, and other policies (J. Walker 1991, 28; J. Berry 1993, 38). Salisbury (1990, 229) says groups "come to Washington out of need and dependence rather than because they have influence." The large number of business groups leads to a fragmentation and weakening of the business view. Rarely, if ever, is there a united business lobby on an issue. The business community is riddled with division such as those between big and small business over issues like unionization. Furthermore as many observers, including Salisbury (1990), have pointed out so-called hyperpluralism (a major increase in groups trying to influence public policy) has made political outcomes less certain even for the most organized and well-financed interests. With regard to the iron triangle argument, many writers have shown that the rigidity once seen in these arrangements is now much more fluid and outcomes far less certain (see section 7.16.). And for a well-argued case that the interest group systems at the U.S. state level are more representative and less biased than many scholars have contended, see Lowery and Gray (2001).

Finally, the strength of the public in a pluralist democracy is not the sum of the strengths of public interest organizations. Many pluralists and most neocorporatists would argue that government itself often stands as a surrogate consumer or public interest force (see section 3.7.). This is, for example, the case in Sweden where the government works to organize groups that would otherwise not be organized, such as immigrant workers, to seek their input on policies that affect them (Micheletti 1993).

Thus while biases undoubtedly exist in all interest group systems, determining their extent is extremely problematic. Biases vary due to many factors including interpretations of the meaning of democracy and representation, the particular time and phase of political development in a political system, the sector and issue, and likely, the country.

Representation and Political Influence: Not a Simple Relationship

Rarely if ever stated, but often implied in the public's and some reformers' belief that interest group systems are biased, is that reductions in bias (meaning some form of equal representation for all groups and interests) will lead to increased influence of presently underrepresented groups. In other words, there is some implicit belief that a simple causal relationship exists between representation of a group and its political influence. Certainly, representation is an essential step for exercising influence; but representation is one thing, influence is quite another. No theory of democracy or representation advocates equal power for all groups and interests. Even if such a theory were advocated, it could not be made to work in practice.

Formal representation as defined earlier in this section is easily included in a constitution or a statute. But turning representation into power involves several factors that cannot be guaranteed by any legal means. These include the possession of resources (money, time, status, personal contacts, and so on), political knowledge and skill, the current political environment (including the extent of support and opposition on an issue), and many other, often intangible, factors (section 7.17.). Some groups and interests have what it takes to turn representation into influence, while others do not. Thus, the relationship between representation of interests and influence is not a simple one. So it should not be assumed that the representation or the visibility of a group or interest means that it will be effective in the political process.

In fact, at least as far as the 50 states in the U.S. are concerned, evidence from a 20-year study clearly shows that, even with the major expansion of the number of groups in the states, those groups considered effective have not changed that much over these years. Business, the professions, and government are consistently those ranked near the top of the list, and the new interests like senior citizens, environmentalists, and minorities (including women), while much more visible than in the 1960s, enjoy much less success (Hrebenar and Thomas 2003, table A). This is likely also the situation in Washington, D.C. and other western capitals (though no empirical evidence is available on this). Furthermore, the hyperpluralism that has occurred since 1970, where political outcomes are less certain for all groups, puts many of the new interests at a disadvantage in competing for influence if they do not have the resources needed to be effective. In contrast such resources can be mustered relatively easily by many business, professional, and government groups.

Academic Findings and Public Policy Regarding Interest Group Activity

There are numerous examples across the western world (see *Parliamentary Affairs* 1998) of legitimate concerns about the activities of interest groups. These range from blatant abuses, such as the illegal activities of some groups in Arizona and South Carolina in the early 1990s, to concerns in many western European countries about members of parliament who have strong ties to, or are even employed by, an interest group to a range of more subtle concerns about the issues of group system representation and bias considered in this section. Beginning in the United States around 1900, these concerns became issues that government attempted to address, mainly through regulation. Then, after a 50-year lull in interest in the United States, the 1970s saw a major increase in attempts to deal with concerns about interest groups. The 1970s also marked the beginning of regulation in other western democracies. These efforts have been very broad-ranging but have had mixed success. The inconclusiveness of academic research on the question of the representativeness and bias of interest group systems provides some insights into why public policy attempts to deal with various concerns about interest groups are so varied and why such attempts often fail to deal with the problems that they seek to solve.

As discussed, the issues involved in interest group system representation and bias are very wide-ranging, complex, and dynamic in nature. On the other hand, public policies regarding interest groups are usually the result of a specific incident, or a series of incidents, involving abuses (or perceived abuses) by interest groups and/or their lobbyists. These incidents are usually well-publicized by the press and demand action by government. Thus, the resultant policies are often ad hoc solutions that may not take into account many other factors—several of which may not be known—that affect the situation. For example, if the abuse is associated with a parliament, the resultant policy may not address lobbying the executive administrative branch, which may be a much more important target of lobbying as is the case in parliamentary democracies. Furthermore, policy makers recognize the need to develop regulations that reduce abuses and biases; but at the same time, they do not want to stifle the democratic right of representation as defined by any particular society. This combination of the likely unknown factors affecting the situation plus the challenge of striking a democratic balance in a dynamic situation often leads to problems in the effectiveness of particular regulatory policies.

The complexities of the relationship between political representation and political influence is a good illustration of the difficult challenges facing policy makers and of where academic research offers some insights. Research tells us that the best policy makers can hope for is to attempt to set some equal rules of access, such as restricting financial contributions by groups or requiring public disclosure of lobbying activity to reveal who is lobbying—who has access to whom? But to what extent should policy makers go to regulate the access—and political advantage—of established interests such as business, the professions, and labor? Whatever its success in equalizing access and publicizing its extent by established interests, public policy cannot substantially increase the financial resources of a group—a major factor in turning access into influence. It cannot reduce the advantages inherent in long-term economic, political, and social connections that are also so often the foundation of political influence. Nor can public policy enhance another crucial element of effective lobbying, that of political skill, for those who do not have it.

The variety of practical public policy attempts to deal with the concerns about interest group activity in general is treated in the next section

(14.3.). and specifics on individual western democracies are covered in Greenwood and Thomas (1998). As with many aspects of interest group studies, most of the research on this subject focuses on the U.S. political system. However, as section 14.6. suggests, the experience of the United States likely has wide relevance for other liberal democracies. The evidence from combining research on the United States and on other western countries indicates that there is no one, ideal approach to dealing with these concerns—including that of representation and bias—and likely there never will be. Thus, this area of public policy in liberal democracies is often revisited as circumstances change.

14.3. APPROACHES TO REGULATING INTEREST GROUP ACTIVITY

Yael Yishai

As discussed in section 14.1., concerns about interest groups are usually different in liberal democracies than they are in authoritarian regimes. The concerns in democracies mainly focus around the fact that groups and interests may undermine the democratic process. Often this concern includes ethical questions regarding the relationship of groups and their lobbyists with public officials. In authoritarian systems, the concerns center on the potential threats of interest groups to the government, often to the dominance of its ideology, and to the monopoly on power of its political leaders—the dictator and, perhaps, the ruling elite. In some instances as in Turkey and Israel for reasons explained below, the concerns about interest groups combine threats to democracy and to the stability of government.

In democracies and authoritarian systems alike, these concerns are dealt with by some form of regulation of interest groups and their activities. The common definition of regulation refers to state (governmental) constraints on private activity in order to promote the public interest. Different concerns about interest groups in democracies and authoritarian regimes lead to different approaches to regulation. In authoritarian systems, where independent interest groups are viewed with great suspicion, the scope of control is often wide ranging, and the major focus is to control group formation and channel group access and influence. The form of control varies from the banning of some interest groups and the co-option of others in state corporatist systems, as in Nazi Germany, to the outright banning of all private interests in extreme communist regimes, like that of communist Albania and the early years of the People's Republic of China (PRC). In contrast in liberal democracies, where the pursuance of private interests is regarded as a legitimate means of political interaction and where there are often constitutional or statutory protections of the right of representation and free speech, regulation tends to be far less extensive and targets different aspects of group activity.

The Academic Literature and What It Reveals about Approaches to Regulation

The research and literature on government regulation of interest groups is scant. This is particularly the case for authoritarian political systems, although there was a surge of academic interest in regulation in liberal democracies during the latter 1990s. Surprisingly, considering how important interest group regulation has been in U.S. politics, there is only a small body of literature available (see sections 14.4.1. and 14.4.2.). Only recently has a general overview of U.S. group regulation at the federal, state, and local levels been produced (C. Thomas 1998a).

Work on individual countries includes: on Britain, Berrington (1995); on Canada, Pross (1991; 1992, 260–66), Stark (1992), and Atkinson (1995); and on Australia, Warhurst (1987, 1990). Three publications provide a more comprehensive examination. One is a comparative perspective, on interest group regulation and its rationale covering both liberal democracies and authoritarian systems (Yishai 1998b). A second is Rush (1994) who, although focusing mainly on Canada to explain the pros and cons of a British proposal for registration, summarizes the experience of lobbying in Germany, Australia, Britain (as proposed), as well as the United States. He also considers lobby regulation under various headings including the targets, the information required, the frequency of updating, access to the register, privileges, and codes of conduct (Rush 1994, 632, table 1). The third, and most extensive treatment on liberal democracies, is found in a special issue of *Parliamentary Affairs* (1998). Despite the fact that this volume focuses mainly on regulation of the legislative activities of groups and their representatives and pays much less attention to executive branch lobbying, it marks a major advance in knowledge. It includes articles on the United States, Britain, Australia, Canada, Germany, Israel, Japan, Scandinavia (using the example of Denmark), and the European Union. An introductory article explores the various rationales behind regulation in western democracies and the different approaches to regulation and identifies similarities and differences in regulation across the case studies presented in the volume.

A major conclusion that can be drawn from this literature is that not only does the extent and form of regulation vary between democracies and authoritarian regimes, but there is also a wide range of approaches to regulation within both types of systems. The scope of these regulations or constraints reveals values and attitudes regarding both state authority and interest group activity. Political culture, political ideology, historical experience, governmental structure, the strength and role of political parties, the extent of pluralism versus neocorporatism, all appear to have an influence on the form and extent of regulation in liberal democracies. Compare, for example, the wide range of regulation in the United States, particularly across the states (see sections 14.4.1. and 14.4.2.). Similar factors, plus the type of regime (fascist, communist, religion-based, and so on) and, particularly, the attitude of the dictator and, perhaps, the political elite, produce variations in constraints on interest groups in authoritarian systems.

Nevertheless, based on the literature, some generalizations can be made about the targets of regulation in both democracies and authoritarian systems. Regulation varies not only in scope but also in object. The following analysis briefly elaborates on the different targets of regulation that also affects the scope of regulation. However, this section does not evaluate the extent of the success of these approaches. An evaluation, particularly in regard to the United States and other liberal democracies, is provided in the last section of this chapter (see section 14.6.).

Regulation of Interest Group Formation

In nondemocratic regimes (and often in many systems in transition to democracy), interest groups are under strict government control. In 1966 in Bangladesh (then East Pakistan), for example, the government introduced a system of compulsory membership in an official business association for certain categories of business (Kochanek 1993). In the overwhelming majority of democratic societies, the state does not interfere with the establishment and operation of interest groups. Even in centralized states such as France, interest groups are not subject to state regulation (F. Wilson 1987; Appleton 2001). Textbooks on associational politics in many democracies do not even mention the option of formal regulation of interest groups by the state. In Germany, an attempt to enact an interest group law, which like the party law would subject associations to state regulation, did not materialize. There are, however, a few exceptions to this rule, particularly in states undergoing rapid economic development or facing domestic and/or external threats. Two prominent examples are Turkey and Israel.

In Turkey, a Law of Associations enacted in 1946 required only the presentation of a copy of the group's constitution to the Interior Ministry and the publication of a notice in the press. However, a 1972 law grants broad government authority regarding surveillance and inspection of the internal organization and operations of associations. Local officials are authorized to appoint government commissioners to act as observers at association meetings (Bianchi 1984; Yishai 1998b).

In Israel, an Associations' Law of 1980 requires voluntary associations to register. The law specifies that the official existence of an association is recognized only on registration by the registrar, an appointed official. The registrar has far-reaching powers to determine the eligibility of an interest group to register, and is authorized to supervise the internal affairs of associations, which are obliged by law to adopt democratic procedures. The government can dismantle an association under one of five options specified by the law. The major impetus behind this legislation was fear of subversive activity (Yishai 1991, 1998a, 1998b).

In Turkey and Israel regulation of interest groups reflects internal and external tensions. In both countries regulation mirrors the dual role of the state—serving as the custodian of liberty and the protector of national interests. Regulation imposes internal democracy on interest groups, while at the same time precluding from politics groups deemed to undermine the foundations of society.

Regulating Access—Regulating Lobbyists

In liberal democracies regulation of lobbyists grew out of two concerns. One was the unfair advantage of professional lobbyists in the policy-making process over those who could not hire their services. The other concern was the perception of unethical conduct by lobbyists in their attempts to influence public officials.

Generally, this regulation is achieved not by restricting access and attempting to blunt influence directly, but through public exposure or *monitoring* of interest group activity. This requires that interest groups and their lobbyists register with public authorities and declare their targets (the government entities and sometimes the issue areas) of lobbying and their expenditures. The theory behind monitoring is that other interest groups, public officials, and the public at large will be more informed about group activity and thus able to plan political action, including lobbying and voting, based on this increased knowledge.

However, largely because apprehensions regarding government involvement in interest group activities are so strong, the extent of regulation varies widely across democracies. Regulatory efforts range from the United States, which has the longest history and the most extensive regulations, to western European countries, which have far less extensive regulation (*Parliamentary Affairs* 1998), to Australia, which enacted regulation in 1983 and then abandoned it in 1996 in favor of self-regulation by interest groups and lobbyists (Warhurst 1998). Even in Japan, subject to recurring scandals of corruption linked with business associations, there are no laws requiring the registration of lobbyists or the reporting of expenditures except for money formally given to candidates for public office (Hrebenar and Nakamura 1993; Hrebenar, Nakamura, and Nakamura 1998).

Attempts to Regulate Influence—Campaign Contributions

As section 14.2. points out, even though attempting to promote the influence of certain groups and restrict that of others is fraught with difficulties, and may well be impossible, governments continue to attempt to affect group influence. One of the major means governments use is to impose limits on campaign contributions or other forms of financial remittance from interest groups to candidates for office, and sometimes, to political parties. For example, as related below, in the United States restrictions exist on the amount of money that interest groups can give to candidates, and in some states, certain interests are prohibited from donating money to candidates. In Israel and France the sums interest groups (and corporations) may donate to political parties is limited. Very little information is available on government regulation to affect influence, although studies on political money usually include some reference to the issue.

The Case of the United States

Like virtually all democracies, the United States does not restrict group formation. And while it restricts certain activities in the interests of attempting to promote access, curb undue influence, and prevent ethical violations, monitoring is the primary means of attempting to deal with the concerns about interest groups. This situation, in large part, is likely a product of the free speech and right to "petition government" provisions of the First Amendment to the U.S. Constitution. Laws dealing with interest group regulation and monitoring in the United States are of five types.

1. Lobby Laws. These provide for the registration of lobbyists and usually their employers, the reporting of expenditures, and sometimes, prohibit certain types of activities, such as lobbying for a contingency fee (a percentage of the amount of money that the lobbyist secures or saves the group he or she represents).

2. Conflict of Interest and Personal Financial Disclosure Provisions. These are sometimes generically referred to as ethics codes or laws. They are intended to make public the financial connections that legislators, elected executive officials, and senior civil servants have with individuals, groups, organizations, and businesses. Sometimes they prohibit certain types of financial relations or dealings. In an attempt to reduce corruption, public ethics laws at the federal, state, and local levels of government often prohibit top level civil servants, particularly political appointees, from being employed by an interest group within a period of time (usually a year) of their being involved in governmental decisions that directly affected that interest.

3. Campaign Finance Regulations. These, to a varying extent, provide for public disclosure of contributions from individuals and interest groups to candidates for public office. They often impose limits or prohibitions on contributions. Restrictions are sometimes placed on the period in which contributions can be made. For example, in some of the states contributions are prohibited during legislative sessions. Some states also limit or prohibit contributions from certain organizations, particularly unions and regulated industries (especially public utilities).

4. Regulation of Political Action Committees (PACs). These regulations are another aspect of campaign finance. PACs are formed primarily for the purpose of channeling money to political campaigns, often to circumvent campaign contribution limits. The federal government, all states, and some larger cities have laws relating to PACs. As is the case with campaign finance regulations, some of these laws impose limits and prohibitions on contributions from PACs.

5. Tax Laws. These can affect interest group activity, particularly that of nonprofit organizations and foundations. The status of an organization under the U.S. Internal Revenue Code (IRC) affects the extent to which nonprofits—many of which are public interest groups—can lobby. The details of these laws are explained in section 8.13.1.

Sections 14.4.1. and 14.4.2. examine the details of the various laws and provisions of interest group regulation at the federal, state, and local level in the United States.

Further Research

As many questions remain unanswered, to understand how governments regulate interest groups much more research needs to be conducted. Examples of those questions follow.

How effective is lobby regulation in controlling political corruption (on Australia see Warhurst 1990).

Where it exists, what is the extent of self-regulation of interest groups and their lobbyists both on a voluntary basis and by self-regulation authorized by government?

How active are various governments in setting up institutional frameworks for regulating interest group activity, and what motivates this governmental interest?

How does regulation affect the organization and behavior of interest groups?

What is the affect of regulation on the strength of democratic institutions on the one hand and on the influence of interest groups on the other?

When and why do governments regulate certain areas of interest group activity, such as donating money to political parties for electoral purposes, but ignore other areas, such as regulating contacts with civil servants?

In short, why, when, how, and with what consequences does the state interfere, through regulation, in the autonomy of interest groups?

14.4. REGULATION OF INTEREST GROUPS IN THE UNITED STATES

14.4.1. Federal Regulation

Loree G. Bykerk

As explained in section 14.3. due to the protections to free speech and the right to "petition government" in the First Amendment to the U.S.

Constitution, the American approach to lobby regulation—including that at the federal level—has been as much monitoring (providing information for the public and other groups about group activities) as it has been regulation (restricting what groups can do). However, as it is the commonly understood term, in this section the term *regulation*, will be used rather than the term *monitoring*. As summarized in section 14.3., federal laws that deal with the regulation of lobbying activity are of five types: (1) lobby laws; (2) conflict of interest and personal financial disclosure provisions; (3) campaign finance regulations; (4) the regulation of PACs; and (5) tax laws (see section 14.3. for an explanation of each).

The bulk of the research on lobby regulation at the federal level relates to campaign finance laws, particularly the candidate contributions of PACs. By contrast, relatively little research has focused on the 1946 Federal Regulation of Lobbying Act, the Lobbying Disclosure Act of 1995, the Foreign Agents Registration Act of 1938, ethics laws governing gifts, honoraria, financial disclosure, and subsequent employment, or the tax status of organizations. However, there are two unsigned articles that deal with the serious drafting problems of the 1946 act (*Columbia Law Review* 1947; *Yale Law Journal* 1947). No comprehensive bibliography on regulation of interest groups at the federal or any other level of U.S. government is available.

The best general introduction to the American approach to lobby regulation, its rationale, development, and consequences, is Clive Thomas (1998a). He clearly shows that the major impetus for lobby regulation came from the states and not from the federal level and that monitoring rather than regulation is the major thrust of American lobby regulation even at the federal level. Thomas' thesis, which would be generally accepted by most scholars of U.S. interest groups, is that the effect of lobby regulation in the United States has been to change the modus operandi of some interest groups, some lobbyists, and in particular, politicians. He goes on to argue that while lobbying is much more open as a result of regulation than it use to be, this openness apparently has not reduced the power of many insider groups (such as business and the professions) or increased the power of outsider groups (such as peace activists). In this regard, regulation has, in fact, fallen short of many of the hopes of its proponents (Thomas 1998a, 500). A weakness of Thomas's article is that he ignores the role of the tax code as a means of lobby regulation.

Informative textbook accounts of the statutes and judicial interpretations intended to regulate lobbying are Hrebenar (1997), J. Berry (1997), Schlozman and Tierney (1986), and Nownes (2001). Like Thomas' (1998a) analysis, a theme common to these accounts is that lobbying laws rely on disclosure of lobbyists' identity and expenditures but that these disclosures do not necessarily effectively regulate group behavior. Many who lobby for organized interests, foreign governments, and corporations do not register even their identity let alone their specific interest or their lobbying expenditures as required by law.

While not qualifying as research in the academic sense, another source of general information on lobby regulation is journalistic accounts. Prominent among these are Birnbaum (1992), Drew (1983), Stern (1992), and Jackson (1990).

In regard to specific academic studies, as mentioned above, the main focus has been on PAC contributions and whether these funds influence the behavior of policy makers. Prominent in this subfield are works by Sabato (1984), Malbin (1984), Sorauf (1992), Conway and Green (1995, 1998), and Diana Evans (1986). The Federal Election Campaign Act of 1971 and subsequent amendments require campaign contributions and expenditures to be disclosed and reported. Research concludes that the law has successfully brought this money to light with relatively minor exceptions.

Analyses differ on whether the contributions of either PACs or individuals buy influence. Journalistic accounts strongly conclude that they do and that such contributions are grossly incompatible with democratic standards. However, academic researchers who control for other variables such as party affiliation, ideology, and constituency preferences conclude that contributions influence congressional voting under only limited circumstances. Correlation of PAC funds and other kinds of decision-maker behavior, such as introducing and promoting legislation in committee, may prove to be more fruitful research strategies (R. Hall and Wayman 1990). See section 7.4. on PACs and the debate over their influence.

Conflict of interest and personal disclosure provisions (often referred to as ethics laws) aim to restrict gifts, travel, honoraria, and to impose a period of time before members of Congress and executive branch personnel may accept employment offers from interest groups after leaving government positions. Here again the general wisdom is that the loopholes are much larger than the constraints on the favors that pass between organizations and decision makers (Tierney 1992). Investigations of lobbying improprieties over the years and attempts to reform the laws are included in *The Washington Lobby* (1987), Hrebenar (1997), and Rozell and Wilcox (1999).

Perhaps the most effective regulators of interest group behavior are the tax laws and Internal Revenue Service (IRS) rulings under which public interest organizations qualify for tax exempt [501(c)(3)] status. Research suggests that groups often piggyback a tax exempt arm to do research, education, and fund-raising onto a lobbying organization that does not have tax exempt status (Shaiko 1991).

There is considerable disagreement about the effectiveness of regulation of interest group behavior at all levels of American government, including the federal level, and a debate about whether further reform is needed. The spectrum ranges from arguing that organizations disclose no more under regulation than what was always available through various sources to the positivist argument that there are now so many legal avenues of influence that little illegal activity goes on to the argument that matters now are much worse because evidence documents why the public regard for the system is so low as to threaten its legitimacy (see sections 4.8. and 6.7.). Concern over the role of private resources in attempting to influence public policy are as old as representative government. As indicated earlier, a major problem facing regulation in the United States and attempts to extend it are First Amendment guarantees of freedom of expression and freedom to assemble and petition government for redress of grievances.

Future research could focus on the impact of ethics laws and tax status regulations and their enforcement by the IRS. Repeated efforts to reform lobbying, ethics, and campaign finance laws have met with limited success, and more research could usefully focus on why this has been so. Finally, a broad effort to reconcile the common wisdom among journalists and other observers with that of political science research on what campaign contributions yield would be beneficial in connecting political science with genuine concerns about the legitimacy of representative government as presently constituted in the United States.

14.4.2. State and Local Regulation

Virginia Gray and Wy Spano

Since the early 1990s the body of academic literature on the regulation of interest groups at the state level in the United States has been growing; plus several reference sources are now available. However, there is very little available on regulation at the local level, and so this section focuses mainly on the states. A good general introduction to the approach to lobby regulation in the United States, including the state and local levels, is Clive Thomas (1998a). The specific types of laws that are used to regulate interest groups at all three levels of government in the United States, including the focus on monitoring group activity rather than regulating it, are set out in section 14.3. As Thomas (1998a, 500) points out, the states rather than the federal government took the lead in lobby regulation. They have been the laboratories in which various approaches to regulation have been tested and refined.

State Regulation

There are three types of information sources available on state-level lobbying regulations. One is primarily descriptive—a cataloging of what laws exist state-by-state. For many years the most extensive compilation was the annually published *Blue Book: Campaign Finance, Ethics, and Lobby Laws* (COGEL 1995) by the Council on Governmental Ethics Laws (COGEL). Today this information is only available on COGEL's Web site at www.cogel.org by annual subscription. Less extensive information can be found in tables of the annually published *Book of the States* or in its occasional chapter highlighting changes in lobby laws (e.g., Ensign 1996). Further information is available from the two editions of the *Public Integrity Annual* (1996, 1997). A successor to this publication is the journal, *Public Integrity* (1999) published quarterly. A comprehensive legal summary of state laws regarding lobbying and campaign finance rules is *Lobbying, PACs, and Campaign Finance* (2002).

The second kind of research is, in essence, informed description. Some of the best of this research is found in the Hrebenar and Thomas series (1987, 1992, 1993a, 1993b) on interest group politics in the American states. These are state-by-state analyses of interest group systems gathered into four regional books (see section 6.4.). Also in this category are two works by Rosenthal. His *The Third House* (2001) contains colorful descriptions of lobbying ethics and response to regulation from the perspective of the lobbyists themselves. His *Drawing the Line* (1996) puts ethics reforms into a political context.

The third type of information available on lobbying regulation can be classified as theory building—attempts to find causality. There are two principal strands in this research. One focuses on how and why states differ in their extent of lobby regulation. The other asks whether lobbying regulations make a difference in either the number or the impact of groups.

Regarding how and why states differ in the extent of lobbying regulation, Morehouse (1981, 130–31) argues that states with the most stringently enforced lobby laws tend to have weaker interest group systems. This hypothesis was tested by Opheim (1991, 417) who found that political culture and legislative professionalism are the best predictors of the stringency of state lobby regulation. Thomas and Hrebenar note the increase in stringency of lobbying regulations since Morehouse's work. They agree that a state's political culture probably has more to do with that stringency than do other factors (Thomas and Hrebenar 1991b, 1996a).

As to whether the stringency of lobbying regulation has any effect on the numbers and range of groups registered in a state or on their influence, one rational choice article suggests that lobby laws lower the numbers of groups by creating barriers to entry (Brinig, Holcombe, and Schwartzstein 1993). Another perspective asserts that stricter lobbying laws have raised the number of registered groups by casting a wider net (Hamm, Weber, and Anderson 1994). However, other scholars are persuasive in their rebuttal of the concept that stringency of lobby laws is related to lobbyists' registrations in a state (Hunter, Wilson, and Brunk 1991; Lowery and Gray 1994, 1997; Brasher, Lowery, and Gray 1999). Gray and Lowery (1998) present evidence showing that it is unlikely that lobby regulations influence the diversity of state interest communities.

The question of the extent to which specific provisions—increased monitoring and regulation—change the behavior of lobbyists and elected and appointed officials has not been systematically studied. However, assessments of these effects based upon extrapolation from studies on other aspects of regulation do exist. With regard to the nation as a whole, Thomas (1998a, 511–14) concludes that the effects of increased monitoring and regulation have altered the behavior of elected and appointed officials and lobbyists rather than reduced the power of insider interests such as business and the professions. Specific to the states, Thomas and Hrebenar (1999a) argue that stricter rules have resulted in increased professionalism among lobbyists and fewer wheeler-dealers (see also section 14.6.). For greater precision, a single-state longitudinal study detailing lobbying practices and legislative outputs before and after significant strengthening of lobby laws is needed.

Local Regulation

The regulation of lobbying activity at the local level in the United States is in its early stages, originating in the 1980s and gathering some momentum in the 1990s. However even by the early 2000s, such regulation was confined to large cities such as New York and Los Angeles.

As Clive Thomas (1998a) points out, the small number of local governments that have regulations tends to emphasize public disclosure—monitoring—and not restriction on lobbying activity. Local governments (along with many state governments) have been concerned with writing lobby regulations that only include professional lobbyists and that do not inhibit the activities of civic and community groups or individual members of the public. This, for example, was a major concern in the drafting of the Orange County (greater Orlando area) ordinance in Florida. Most local governments have similar provisions to those of Los Angeles that require lobbyists and their clients to register if they spend over a specified amount of money in a specified period of time. In Los Angeles, lobbyists must register if they spend over $4,000 in a calendar quarter. Such provisions aim to identify professionals without restricting citizens. In New York, similar provisions resulted in 75 lobbyists and 200 of their clients registering in 1995.

Because local lobby regulations are in their infancy, their effects, both positive and negative, are yet to be assessed. In most local governments, often including those with lobby regulations, more information about the activities of lobbyists can be obtained from related provisions such as conflict of interest statements and campaign finance disclosure. Obviously, the academic study of local lobby laws and their effects is a wide-open field.

14.5. REGULATION OF INTEREST REPRESENTATION IN THE EUROPEAN UNION (EU)

Justin Greenwood

Only one major article (Greenwood 1998) exists on the regulation of lobbying in the European Union (EU). This dearth is, in part, a reflection of the youth of the EU; but it is also an indication of the low priority Western countries outside the United States give to lobbying regulation. These translate into a lack of interest by scholars in the subject. However, attempts to regulate lobbying in the EU provide an instructive case study both in the difficulties of establishing lobby regulation and the various approaches to regulation. Efforts to regulate lobbying in the EU reflect Kingdon's (1984) model of agenda setting, where various circumstances are linked by a policy entrepreneur to several broader issues to offer a workable regulatory solution.

Several socialist Members of the European Parliament (MEPs) had been seeking ways to regulate lobbying since 1989. This effort was precipitated by a combination of circumstances including tales of lobbyists trespassing on EU premises, intercepting or exhausting supplies of documents meant for MEPs, selling confidential information, proffering minor free gifts and hospitality, and bothering MEPs during meal times. However, a major obstacle in getting such legislation to a vote was the failure to provide a working definition of what constituted a lobbyist.

Regulatory efforts by MEPs galvanized the EU Commission (the EU's executive branch) to take up the issue because of its concern that regulation might infringe on the supply of information from interest groups on which it depended. Consequently, the Commission began to work on a directory that listed both producer and nonproducer interests engaged in European-level interest representation. The Commission also encouraged the Brussels lobbying community to respond with self-regulation. Besides damage limitation, the Commission was responding to a much wider range of concerns surrounding democratic legitimacy following the near rejection of the Maastricht Treaty on European Union in a number of ratification votes held in member states in 1992 and 1993.

Although commercial public affairs practitioners developed a code of self-regulation, issued in September 1994, that code did little to deter a new MEP, Glynn Ford, from seizing the issue and presenting a new proposal in May 1995. The code in itself went little beyond stating rather obvious canons of good practice. However, the regulatory device proposed by Ford was politically masterful in that it did not attempt to define a lobbyist, but relied upon self-definition through the incentive of applying for a pass. All those lobbyists wishing to visit the Parliament would find it much easier to obtain a regular pass, available in return for signing a code of conduct, than to stand in line for a day pass.

Political circumstances led to the Ford proposal being linked with a package aimed at regulating the behavior of MEPs in their dealings with lobbyists. The linking of the two issues meant that the Ford proposal was unlikely to survive unadulterated not least because it produced such controversy, particularly in regard to regulating MEP's behavior. The dual package was only passed the second time it was presented to the Parliament in July 1996, and then only after significant amendment. The result was that the code which public affairs practitioners had to sign in exchange for a pass was based very closely upon the one produced two years earlier by commercial lobbyists. An agenda of other issues for further consideration relating to lobbyists was set, but never really addressed since the issue has receded. Most of the attention surrounding the issue has focused upon MEPs and their eligibility to receive, and requirements upon them to declare, any gifts or favors that might influence their behavior. What vestiges of the issue remain can be found among attempts by public affairs practitioners to turn the agenda of openness and transparency to their own advantage.

14.6. AN EVALUATION OF LOBBY REGULATION AND ITS LESSONS: THE UNITED STATES AND OTHER LIBERAL DEMOCRACIES

Justin Greenwood and Clive S. Thomas

Based on academic research, what has the regulation of interest group activity and lobbyists achieved across liberal democracies? To what extent has it dealt with the concerns about interest groups including representational bias, the potential for unethical behavior by lobbyists and those they lobby? And to what extent has it affected inequalities of influence? By drawing on the experience in the United States and parliamentary democracies, this final section of the chapter evaluates the experience with regulation and the lessons to be learned from it. Then it makes some brief comments on what these experiences and lessons from academic research might mean for the role of regulation and interest group activity in the future. The material in this section is drawn from two main sources, Clive Thomas (1998a) and Greenwood and Thomas (1998).

The Lessons of Regulation from the United States

Research explained in sections 14.4.1. and 14.4.2. enable us to make some observations about the lessons of interest group regulation in the United States. To do this, we first make some general points about the U.S. experience with regulation. This is followed by an assessment of the apparent specific effects of regulation on U.S. politics.

Ten general observations can be made about group regulation.

1. Like most public policies in the United States, lobby regulations develop largely by an incremental process, usually in response to a specific "scandal."
2. The development of lobby regulation has been a highly contentious political issue and continues to be so. Like many public policy issues, the public's and politicians' interest in regulation recedes rapidly after policy has been enacted to deal with a particular scandal.

3. The U.S. public policy approach to concerns about interest groups combines restrictions on group activity with monitoring of that activity, with the emphasis on the latter.

4. These regulations to date are ineffective at the federal level, vary widely across the states, and are so new at the local level that, as yet, no meaningful assessment of them can be made.

5. Largely as a result of this fourth point, lobby registration records are an inadequate indication of the extent and type of lobbying being conducted in the United States. This means that even the monitoring role of regulations may be inadequate.

6. At least as far as lobby laws are concerned, comprehensiveness of regulations in a particular state does not mean stringent enforcement of them. Conversely, the lack of comprehensive lobby laws in a state does not necessarily indicate a lax attitude toward public disclosure or toward unsavory and corrupt politics.

7. Because of different levels of commitment to these laws in various states, the state agencies charged with administering lobby regulation and related regulations, are often underfunded and have other impediments imposed on them.

8. The extent to which these laws deal with representational bias of the group system as a whole is far from clear.

9. While regulation may have increased the effectiveness of some previously ineffective groups, so-called outsider interests, it has likely not undermined, in any significant way, the influence of so-called insider, or established, groups and interests.

10. However, indications are that these regulations have made U.S. politics much more open and probably have reduced corruption (or at least the potential for corruption).

What, then, have been the specific effects of lobby regulation on American politics? There are three aspects to be briefly commented on: (1) who has benefited from regulation and public disclosure of lobbying; (2) the effect of lobby regulations on the conduct of business by established interest groups and lobbyists; and (3) how public officials, particularly elected officials, have been affected by these regulations.

Who Has Benefited? The public has certainly benefited. At least at the state level, and probably at the federal level too, the growth of lobby regulations and other disclosure provisions has had a positive affect on the conduct of public policy making. Even though the political playing field will never be completely level, these laws have helped to identify the players and their relationships. In providing information on who is lobbying for whom, on what public officials have what relationships with what groups and lobbyists, and on who is contributing to whose campaign, the states have ushered in a more open and professional era in politics and government. In fact, as indicated above, it has not been the control or the channeling of interest group activity that has been the major contribution of lobby regulation to the democratic process in the United States. Rather, as a former clerk of the Florida state house observed, it has been the provision of public information in the form of the identification of the players (Kelley and Taylor 1992). Increased public information has probably been the element of lobby regulation that has had the major impact on state politics and government and appears to be having a similar effect at the local level. The 1995 reforms should also strengthen this element at the federal level (see section 14.4.1.).

Yet, according to lobby agency officials at both the state and local levels, the press, candidates seeking election or re-election, and interest group personnel and lobbyists, not the public, make the most use of lobby registration and related information, as might be expected. The bulk of the information about lobbyist expenditures and activities is disseminated by the press. So while the public has benefited from these provisions, the extent of these benefits is largely determined by the press.

This, of course, raises questions about the selectivity of press coverage, filtered as it is through the hands of reporters and editors. To overcome this potential problem, several states make this information more readily available through unedited newspapers listings and other public information forums, most recently the Internet. But such attempts are highly sensitive politically and meet with varying degrees of success. What are often called outsider interests may also benefit from lobby regulations. Public information makes the activities of their entrenched opponents more visible and, as a result, more restrained in many instances.

The Effect on Established Interests and Their Lobbyists. Restraint in dealing with public officials, a greater concern for their group's public image, and the increased professionalism of lobbyists appear to be the three major effects of regulation. Lobbyists, especially those representing powerful interests, are much less likely to use blatant, strong-arm tactics. Even dominant interests like the Mormon Church in Utah and the coal companies in West Virginia prefer to use low-key approaches buttressed by public relations campaigns. Though the relationship is far from simple, the more public disclosure of lobbying that exists in a state and the more stringently these laws are enforced, the more transparent are interest group attempts to influence public policy.

Public exposure and disclosure of lobbying and lobbyists' activities is also partly the reason for the apparent disappearance of the old wheeler-dealer lobbyist from the state and, to some extent, from the federal political scene. Though in actual fact what has happened is that the modern big-time lobbyist is a wheeler-dealer under a different guise. Like the old wheeler-dealers, they realize the need for a multifaceted approach to establishing and maintaining good relations with public officials. This approach includes everything from participating in election campaigns to helping officials with their personal needs. In addition, these modern wheeler-dealers are very aware of the increased importance of technical information, the increased professionalism and changing needs of public officials, and the increased public visibility of lobbying.

The Effect on the Conduct of Public Officials. Evidence also suggests that public disclosure of lobbying activity, including campaign contributions and PAC activities, have changed the way that elected officials deal with interest groups and lobbyists. Much more cognizant of their public image than in the past, legislators and elected executive officials alike are much less likely to deal with or tolerate unsavory practices by interest groups and their representatives.

Perhaps a less noticeable, but nevertheless important, impact of lobby regulation on some elected officials is that it often increases antagonism between them and the press. In addition, as mentioned above, regulation has provided a new source of antagonism between elected officials and the regulating agency or agencies that results from disagreements about the application and enforcement of lobby disclosure information, especially when it affects a public official directly. This may appear to be of little consequence until one realizes that, in most states, legislators and senior executive officials are the ones who must approve the funding of these regulatory agencies. Severe, or even slightly reduced, funding can drastically impair an agency's ability to perform its tasks. Hence the idea of *capture* of this regulatory process by those being regulated.

Lessons from Parliamentary Democracies

Regulation of interest groups in liberal democracies outside the United States has largely developed since 1980. Despite this short history, there are some common patterns of development of regulation and some similar experiences among parliamentary systems that offer insights into dealing with concerns about interest groups and their representatives. Here 10 of these major experiences and insights are identified. These 10 encapsulate those identified in the introductory essay (Greenwood and Thomas 1998) and in the country contributions of a special issue of *Parliamentary Affairs* (1998) on lobby regulation mentioned above. Be aware, however, that the essays in this special issue focus primarily on lobby regulation affecting legislative bodies and are much less concerned with executive branch lobbying.

1. Regulatory Schemes Are the Exception, Not the Rule, and Minimal Where They Exist. Partly to avoid inhibiting citizen participation but also for other reasons set out below, regulatory schemes are the exception and not the rule. There is also the legitimate issue of whether the cost of establishing and administering regulations can be justified in increased public awareness or other benefits. In the face of little evidence in support of regulation, whether to establish or extend it becomes a political decision. As a consequence of these concerns, where regulatory schemes do exist, with the exception of Israel, they tend to be minimal in their coverage. In Australia, lobby regulation was tried, found wanting, and then abandoned (Warhurst 1998).

An argument can be made that regulation is more suited to pluralist than neocorporatist systems. Pluralism, with its emphasis on individualism and a market-type competition between interests for the attention of policy makers, stands in contrast to corporatism, where economic interests are formally incorporated into government policy making (though often at the expense of other types of interests). In corporatist systems, the boundary lines between government and society are often blurred. In this situation, lobby regulation may undermine the principles of interest intermediation on which corporatism is based and stymie the major goal of corporatism—promoting the public interest.

2. Problems in Defining Lobbying. Many countries, and particularly the European Union (see section 14.5.), have grappled with the problem of defining lobbying. Generally, the intention is to include professional lobbyists within the purview of regulatory schemes without inhibiting members of the general public from exercising their right to represent their views to government. The definitional difficulties surrounding lobbying have very much influenced the character of systems designed to regulate concerns about interest groups, particularly in regard to the extensiveness, or lack thereof, of regulation.

3. The Impetus for Regulation. Impetus has come from three major sources: (1) scandals involving lobbyists and government officials; (2) the need seen by parliamentarians and/or civil servants to control the flow of information to public officials; and (3) much less often, a general concern arising from questions of undue influence, ranging from ethical standards in public life to the desire to promote equal access to government. The impetus in Britain and Canada is an example of the first source, in the EU an example of the second, and in Germany an example of the third. The case of Israel and national security is perhaps a fourth category, but a rare one among liberal democracies.

4. Political Motivations Often Drive Regulation. Particularly when the impetus for regulation is scandal, the drive for dealing with the issue often becomes a highly political, usually a partisan, issue. While, at least in theory, this is a public interest issue, in reality it is subject to all the conflicts inherent in the public policy-making process. In the end it is politics, not some ideal theory of the public interest, that determines the extent and enforcement of lobby regulations. As Greenwood and Thomas (1998, 495) have noted:

> The debate on lobby regulation may proceed under the irresistible language and banners of "democracy," "public interest," "open government," "equal opportunities," "ethics," and "standards," but may be motivated more by factionalism and vested interests.

The situations in Canada and the United Kingdom (UK) provide examples of such motivations. This is not to say that there are not some well-intentioned schemes developed by politicians and reformers to deal with the problems of interest groups; but often these intentions are turned to someone's, or some group's, political advantage.

Another aspect of the politics of regulation is that the development of regulatory schemes has often involved the regulated—interest groups and lobbyists. While from a participatory and democratic perspective it is laudable to involve those affected, this has often resulted in watering down regulations or in self-regulatory schemes that prove ineffective.

5. The Rise and Decline of the Salience of the Regulatory Issue. Perhaps largely because of the political motivations behind regulation in most countries, the regulatory issue tends to recede rapidly once the issue that brought reform to the fore has been dealt with. Furthermore, when the political pressure is past, even self-regulatory arrangements often lapse into a dormant state.

6. Types of Regulatory Schemes. The form—the scope and target or targets—that regulation takes varies considerably. Typically regulation involves schemes designed to regulate the activities of legislators and/or of lobbyists. Most are schemes directly aimed at the regulation of lobbying, such as those in Australia, Canada, Scandinavia, and the EU. Others, such as in Germany, Israel, Japan, and the UK, are schemes aimed either at governing the relationship between parliamentarians and outside interests or those based around the regulation of interest groups, or their role, within governmental structures. In many cases, self-regulatory arrangements exist alongside these statutory schemes. Where corporatism exists, regulation is aimed more at formalizing and structuring the input of interests into government affairs.

Several regulatory schemes target particular sections of the lobbying community. Some countries regulate direct lobbying, such as attempts to influence policy makers, whereas others regulate indirect lobbying, such as access strategies and financing candidates and political parties. Canada, Germany, and Israel all have schemes aimed at interest groups, including requirements for their registration. In the UK and the EU, provisions aimed at regulating commercial lobbyists are undertaken by lobbyists themselves.

7. Self-regulation of Lobbying. The examples of the UK and the EU illustrate both the advantages and disadvantages of self-regulation of lobbying. Self-regulatory schemes are popular among those seeking regulation and often among those who are the targets of regulation. This is because of a number of features of self-regulatory instruments, some benefiting all parties, some benefiting the regulator, and some benefiting the regulated.

First, self-regulatory schemes are more flexible instruments than formal legislation. They regulate according to the spirit, rather than the letter, of the law. They are able to embrace conduct, such as courtesy in contacting officials (such as not bothering them in private settings, etc.), which are difficult to define in law. Plus, as the EU example illustrates (section 14.5.), self-regulation can circumvent the thorny issue of defining lobbying. Second, self-regulation involves the exercise of self-discipline rather than reliance on imposed authority. It also shifts regulatory costs and a certain degree of responsibility to the regulated. It may also reduce difficult and unnecessary conflicts with powerful and vested interests, and can provide a quick form of redress of grievances. Third, for the regulated, it permits the retention of control over their activities, and may forestall or delay legal controls.

The big disadvantage of self-regulation, especially where it exists independently of legal provisions, is that it may be weak and lack effectiveness in tackling the problem it is designed to address. This is particularly the case when the issue of regulation wanes in importance.

8. Problems of Administration and Enforcement. The fact that controls on interest group activity sometimes contradict tenets of democracy often shapes the institutional capacities for regulation. In many cases, arrangements for the implementation of rules are halfhearted. Enforcement always seems problematic when agencies have little chance of effectively managing their duties, such as when definitional problems arise over the scope of administration. Often registration and regulatory units are subsumed within multipurpose administrative units that are often overloaded for the range of functions they are asked to undertake. These units often evidence reluctance about becoming involved in unnecessary resource-sapping conflicts, particularly with powerful private or public interests.

9. Difficulty in Assessing the Effectiveness of Regulation. Determining the effectiveness of a regulatory scheme in a particular country or jurisdiction is fraught with difficulty. Since most schemes involve some type of monitoring, it may be that they increase public knowledge of group activity and may curb some abuses by lobbyists and legislators. However, the general conclusion conveyed by the scholars contributing to the special issue of *Parliamentary Affairs* (1998) on lobby regulation is that regulatory and monitoring schemes have, for the most part, not been very effective in reducing system bias or improving access. The difficulty in assessing the effects of regulation leads many countries to question whether the costs of regulation are worth it. This, together with the likely negative effects of regulation on democracy, makes countries reluctant to extend these schemes.

10. Who Has Benefited? If the benefit to the public of these various schemes is likely positive but its extent questionable, who else has benefited? Three categories of interests appear to have benefited more directly. One is political parties and politicians who use this issue to their advantage to gain power or to attack their opponents. A second is that of other interests who benefit from the registration and public information provided by regulation. In Canada, for example, the greatest use of registered information is made not by public sources, but by private lobby firms interested in monitoring the activities of competitors and in seeking potential clients. And third, while few lobbyists welcome regulation, the legal regulation or the chance to establish self-regulatory schemes may be used by them as an opportunity to enhance their image with the public. For example, in the EU and the UK, interest groups and lobbyists have called for certain types of regulation, such as registration, so as to provide themselves a form of quasi-official status and to limit new entrants to their profession.

Implications for the Future of Interest Group Activity

Despite differences in the length of time regulation has been in existence and in the structures of government and practice of politics, similarities in experiences with lobby regulation are discernable across liberal democracies. These similarities include: most regulation results from a particular incident or series of incidents; regulation is often driven by political and partisan considerations; a definition of lobbying is difficult to articulate; concerns about restricting democratic rights exist; administrative constraints hamper enforcement of regulations; and assessing the success of regulatory provisions is difficult. Based on these common experiences and their lessons, the following comments consider the likely future course of regulation and how it might affect interest group activity.

Developments across the Western world in the first quarter of the twenty-first century are likely to lead to increased demands for regulation. There are many reasons for this, but three are particularly important. First, the major expansion of interests that has characterized liberal democracies since the early 1970s is likely to continue, even if at a slower rate. As economies become more complex and the interests associated with post-industrial societies (such as public interest groups of all types) increase in numbers, so too does interest group activity, which contributes to the density of public life. In this atmosphere of increased group competition, the conditions exist for suspect political practices that will likely lead to demands for increased regulation. Second, as corporatist systems break down, increased regulation may be sought in these societies to substitute for the controlling influence once wielded by government. Third, the increased complexities of societies, including the political fragmentation in corporatist systems, is likely to lead to an increased need for professionals—consultants and lobbyists—to handle the needs of various interests in their dealings with government. Since the activities of these professionals have often precipitated regulation in the past, it is likely that their activities will remain a source of calls for new regulations or the reform of existing ones.

In this expanding world of interest group activity, reformers and politicians will likely seize events such as scandals to push public policies to deal with these problems. But judging by past experience, although regulation may produce a more open political process, it is unlikely to have a fundamental effect on the nature of any interest group system in a liberal democracy. Experience has shown that there is no ideal form of regulation and that although regulation may affect access, it can do very little to affect influence. Interest group systems will continue to favor those interests with major resources at their disposal. But lobby regulations, and particularly public disclosure provisions, can provide information for those who care to use it to make more informed political decisions. Increasing public awareness and the exposure of scandals are the most likely influences to produce a more open—if not equal—lobbying process. In this regard, monitoring of interest group activity, perhaps in conjunction with some form of self-regulation, may be the best that can be hoped for given the representational imperatives in a liberal democracy.

From a practical perspective, however, dealing with the concerns about interest groups will be shaped by individual circumstances and views of democracy in a particular country plus, as in the case of a country like Israel, other national imperatives. A particular country's political culture including its views of interest groups and lobbyists, pressure, or lack thereof, from the public and the press on politicians, and political maneuvering, among other factors will be the determinants of future attempts to deal with problems concerning interest groups in any particular liberal democracy.

Chapter 15

Conducting Research on Interest Groups

Michael J. Gorges

15.1. INTRODUCTION

How do you conduct research on interest groups? A review of the literature shows that scholars have used many techniques in their work. In fact, the research strategies available are numerous. How do you choose? With a focus on academic research, in this chapter, we review the *research methodologies* scholars have employed when conducting research on interest groups. For the most part, we will limit this discussion to *empirical* research. It is assumed that the reader has little to no familiarity with methodological issues; those readers who do may skip these discussions when they occur.

The chapter first explains the context within which scholars conduct research on interest groups focusing on the nature of academic research. The focus then moves to the importance and components of a research design—the blueprint for a research project. This section discusses finding a topic, types of scholarly interest-group studies, literature reviews, theory and theoretical frameworks, and the research methodology.

15.2. ACADEMIC RESEARCH ON INTEREST GROUPS

As in other areas of political and social science, there are various types of writing on interest groups. These types of writing range from those intended for a general readership, such as newspapers, magazines, and popular books, to textbooks, to works for academic specialists, including scholarly articles, books, and research reports of the type referred to in this *Guide*. The authors of these various writings employ a range of research techniques, from the least systematic or rigorous, often (but not always) associated with popular writing, to the most systematic or rigorous, as should be the goal of scholarly writing. For a review of these various sources of information on interest groups and an overview of the research methods used in them, the reader should refer back to chapter 2. Here we focus on academic research on interest groups.

Unlike popular writing, scholarly writing is based upon a systematic research method which includes certain key elements, discussed below. Scholarly writing may have one or a combination of three purposes: (1) exploration, (2) description, and (3) explanation.

1. Scholars undertake *exploratory* studies of topics that are new to them or that are themselves new. Exploratory studies may test the waters for further research or develop the methods scholars will use in further studies of the same topic.

2. Descriptive studies, on the other hand, report on a phenomenon based on *systematic and deliberate* observation.

3. Explanatory studies tell us *why* something occurred. Why, for example, do interest groups form? In the language of social scientists, you need to present *dependent* and *independent variables*, linked in some kind of causal argument. The dependent variable is the outcome being explained. In this example, the dependent variable would be the formation of interest groups. Independent variables are those variables which give rise to the dependent variable. In our example, a more sophisticated division of labor in society might be one independent variable that could account for the formation of interest groups.

Most scholarly studies of interest groups aim to describe and explain. Indeed, it is hard not to describe on the way to explaining. Whatever your goals, however, it is important to be as methodologically rigorous as possible.

15.3. THE IMPORTANCE AND ELEMENTS OF A RESEARCH DESIGN

Methodological rigor depends, in part, on the strength of your research design. In this section, we discuss the components of an ideal research design: (1) finding a topic, (2) the contribution of the study, (3) the type of study, (4) the literature review, (5) the theory, and (6) the evidence. Then, in the next section (15.4.), we go into various types of research methodologies and their appropriateness for providing types of evidence. More detailed guides to developing a research design can be found in Babbie (1995) and Gary King et al. (1994).

1. Finding a Topic

The first task is to come up with a topic and an argument. To do this, you must answer two questions: (1) What exactly are you studying? and (2) What do you want to say about interest groups? In other words, why are you undertaking the study? At some point near the beginning of a piece of writing, the reader should know what it is you are trying to accomplish, whatever your goal, exploration, description, or explanation.

2. Contribution of the Study

The researcher should also explain the intellectual contribution he or she hopes to make with the study. This contribution may take one or more of several forms. You can test a preexisting hypothesis that has not been systematically examined or that you suspect is false. McLaughlin and Jordan (1993) in their study of automobile manufacturers' interest associations in the European Community (EC) test Olson's claim that "rational, self-interested individuals will not act to achieve their common or group interests" (McLaughlin and Jordan 1993, 123). While their study confirms Olson's stress on the need for selective benefits, they dissent from his conclusion that lobbying for collective goals is as irrational as he claims.

You may also attempt to contribute to an ongoing debate in the literature. Greenwood, Grote, and Ronit (1992b) in their introductory chapter to a collection on organized interests in the EC, attempt to refute claims by scholars such as Sargent (1985a) and Streeck and Schmitter (1991) that interest intermediation in the EC is predominantly pluralist in nature. You might also argue that a topic that no one has explored is important and worthy of study. Browne points to "scholarly neglect of geographically fragmented interests" as justification for his study of agricultural interest groups (Browne 1995b, 281). Loomis and Sexton (1995) pose a new question when they ask, "How do organized interests make decisions on how to employ their resources?" In the wake of the European Union's (EU) plans to complete the Internal Market and establish an Economic and Monetary Union (EMU), scholars have focused on the impact of interest groups on European integration and the effects of these momentous changes on interest groups themselves (Streeck and Schmitter 1991; Greenwood, Grote, and Ronit 1992a; Mazey and Richardson 1993a; Gorges 1993, 1996).

One can also apply theories or concepts used elsewhere to a new area. Streeck and Schmitter's (1991) analysis of interest intermediation in the EC uses concepts developed by theorists of neocorporatism (see section 3.4.) to analyze the organization of interests in the EC and their role in policy making. Others have applied the neocorporatist perspective to interest intermediation at the sector level. Here, we can cite work by W.

Grant, Paterson, and Whitston (1988) on the chemical industry, Cawson (1992) on consumer electronics, and Grunert's (1987) study of the EC's response to the steel crisis of the 1980s.

3. The Type of Study

Studies of interest groups usually focus on one of four areas: (1) what we can call "grand theory," or works that attempt to devise general explanations for interest-group behavior or systems of interest intermediation (for example, Truman 1951; Lowi 1979; M. Olson 1965, 1971, 1982; Schmitter 1974, 1982); (2) the organization of interest groups (for example, the essays in Berger 1981a; and part 1 of A. Cigler and Loomis 2002); (3) the ways in which interest groups seek to influence elections (see the essays in part 2 of Cigler and Loomis 2002); and (4) interest-group participation in the policy-making process (see the essays in part 3 of Cigler and Loomis 2002; Mazey and Richardson 1993a; Greenwood, Grote, and Ronit 1992a; and Berger 1981a). The writing of "grand theory" is a task best left to senior scholars. Nevertheless, junior scholars, graduate students, and undergraduates, should be well-versed in the classics before undertaking empirical research, so that they may know where they can make a contribution.

As chapter 1 (see section 1.7.) pointed out, most studies of interest groups are case studies—research on one or a few groups.[1] Though the focus of a case study may also be the circumstances surrounding a particular incident in a group's history, such as a major rise or decline in its membership or the examination of a particular policy issue and the groups involved in it, such as the fight over the North American Free Trade Agreement (NAFTA) in the early 1990s in the United States. Sometimes, researchers conduct comparative case studies of a small number of cases. Collier (1993) reviews the strategies a researcher with a small number of cases may use in conducting research and the evolution of the "comparative method" since the publication of Lijphart's (1971) seminal piece on the comparative research method.[2]

4. The Literature Review

It is in the literature review that you demonstrate why previous research has not answered the crucial question you are posing and why your research is necessary and important. Again, whatever your topic, you must always justify the value of your study. The literature review allows you to place your study in relation to previous research and to show how your own research will contribute to advancing knowledge in the field. As in other areas of the social sciences, new research on interest groups should seek to make a contribution to the literature.

Most scholars devote a substantial part of an introductory chapter of a book, or several introductory paragraphs of an article or paper, to an evaluation of previous research. The introductory chapter to an important collection of essays on interest groups in Western Europe published in 1981, for example, discusses problems the pluralist and Marxist paradigms encounter in trying to explain the operation and evolution of industrial societies, especially the role of organized interests in those societies (Berger 1981b). Likewise, the first chapter of a collection of essays on U.S. interest groups published in 1992 analyzes how American political scientists have studied interest groups (Petracca 1992b). Petracca (1992c) also concludes his collection of essays with an appendix entitled "The Changing State of Interest Group Research: A Review and Commentary." Literature reviews, however, need not be lengthy. Foreman (1995), for example, succinctly summarizes the literature on voluntary group formation in approximately five paragraphs of his study of victims' grassroots organizations.

5. The Theory

Social science theories attempt to develop general explanations for social phenomena. In writing about interest groups, one may either attempt to write "grand theory" or to test or modify existing theories. Most undergraduates, graduate students, and junior scholars will undertake the latter task. One can do so by situating an argument about a specific case or cases within a general theoretical framework and show that the framework requires modification in light of the new evidence unearthed.[3]

A theoretical framework generates hypotheses—statements that propose relationships between the dependent and independent variables—and structures the search for independent variables in order to test the hypothesis. We can illustrate this as follows.

As explained in chapter 3, much writing on U.S. interest groups has been strongly influenced by pluralist theory, which views political power as divided among competing groups, with many groups working to counteract the power of other groups. There is no hierarchy of interests, and crosscutting cleavages prevent the establishment of relationships of domination and subordination. Groups form as "spontaneous emanations of society" (Berger 1981b, 5). In contrast, neocorporatist analysts tend to focus on the role of the state (government) in shaping interest intermediation and argue from a perspective that "socio-economic structures, history, politics and organizational transformation provide complementary accounts of the process of interest formation" (Berger 1981b, 11). Thus, a hypothesis derived from a neocorporatist framework might focus on the relationship between changes in state capacity and changes in patterns of interest intermediation. If, on the other hand, the goal is to explain the presence of several trade unions in a given country, a pluralist framework might be more appropriate. It could be hypothesized that ideological differences lead to the establishment of competing trade-union organizations. You would then try to find links between the development of a particular ideology and splits in the trade-union movement.

6. The Evidence to Support the Argument

Finally, it is necessary to present empirical information to substantiate the argument. If one is conducting an empirical study of one or more interest groups, the questions immediately arise: What information constitutes proof? What information should one seek? How should one seek it? The answers to these questions depend on the argument, and the research methodology chosen should be based on the information needed to prove the argument. In the next section, we provide a guide to methods of information gathering which assumes one is seeking empirical data in order to answer questions on some aspect of interest-group activity.

The Argument. Once you have gathered your evidence, you will write up your findings. Now you need to put together your evidence in order to make an argument. A word of caution: *causality*—the link between the dependent and independent variables—is not easy to prove. Most explanations are *probabilistic:* this is, we can only argue that certain outcomes are more likely than others in the presence of certain variables (or the opposite). The wise researcher will remember the fundamental problem of causal inference: we will never know a causal inference for certain. This uncertainty arises because most outcomes are *overdetermined:* there are so many possible independent variables and so few dependent variables, especially in cases where one has few outcomes to explain, that it is impossible to state with total certainty that our independent variables are indeed responsible for the outcome we are explaining.

15.4. RESEARCH METHODOLOGIES

How do we find evidence? Many research techniques discussed in methodology textbooks are designed to provide data appropriate for statistical analysis. If you have the capability to generate large amounts of data, statistical analyses may be useful. As a rule, however, quantitative studies are best suited to a team of researchers and lots of data. It may be difficult for a single, underfunded researcher to obtain the information necessary for large-scale quantitative studies. In this case, if you decide that statistics are necessary or useful, you can either use existing data provided by the government, secondary sources (perhaps from interest groups), or you can try and acquire your own data if you have the resources. You may also quantify qualitative information, but the utility of doing so will depend on the amount of information at your disposal.

Extensive quantification may not be useful to many students of interest groups, because studying small groups generates limited quantitative information.

Qualitative research "has tended to focus on one or a small number of cases, to use intensive interviews or depth analysis of historical materials, . . . and to be concerned with a rounded or comprehensive account of some event or unit" (King et al. 1994, 4). Qualitative research methodologies are not only a useful option when we lack quantitative data, they are often desirable in their own right, because some questions simply cannot be answered using quantitative data and statistical analyses. Why did a certain person win a leadership struggle in a particular interest group? What influence did a specific interest group have on a given policy outcome? Nevertheless, quantitative and qualitative studies should both adhere to the same rigorous standards of scientific inquiry. Moreover, a given study may include statistical analyses of large amounts of data *and* detailed case studies (for examples of these, see King et al. 1994, 5).

Survey Research

Survey research is designed to generate large amounts of data that can be analyzed using certain statistical techniques. Surveys allow researchers to collect data on populations that are "too large to be observed directly" (Babbie 1995, 257). Guth et al. (1995), for example, were able to survey 5,002 religious activists in eight religious interest groups. One may survey in person, by mail, or by telephone. One advantage of mail surveys is that you are not limited to contacting only those people you can interview in person or by telephone. On the other hand, you are still dependent on the good will or patience of the recipients of the survey. You must also be wary of certain pitfalls of survey research—writing questions that produce meaningful answers, studying a topic that can usefully be studied with surveys, reliability, if not truthfulness, of the respondents, and so on.

The first stage of survey research involves designing a set of questions. The second task is to choose the sample. It is important to explain how the sample was chosen, who was surveyed, the response rate, and when the research was conducted, either in the body of your writing or in an explanatory footnote, as Allan Cigler and Nownes do quite succinctly (1995, 98). What is striking about research on interest groups, however, is that even studies using surveys with large numbers of respondents do not contain elaborate or complicated quantitative analyses. Although Guth et al. (1995) surveyed 5,002 religious activists, every table in their article reports on their findings in simple percentages. There is nothing wrong with this; what it seems to demonstrate is that elaborate quantitative analyses (regressions, etc.) may be unnecessary for most interest group studies.

Content Analysis

Content analysis records "who says what, to whom, why, how, and to what effect" (Babbie 1995, 307). In the study of interest groups, this could include examining past and current interest-group documents—position papers, reports, internally generated research, memos, circulars, brochures, advertisements, presentations to legislators, letters to politicians—by using some type of content analysis. Loomis and Sexton (1995), for example, in their study of how interest groups decide where to use their resources, examined interest-group advertising in Washington, D.C., sorting through and categorizing various types of advertisements and appeals.

One advantage of content analysis is that it can be applied to any form of communication. The researcher only needs to develop a systematic procedure or conceptual framework (Bernstein and Dyer 1992, 75) for coding the documents. One also needs access to a sufficient number of documents in order to have enough information to code.

Participant-Observers

A participant-observer is a researcher who examines a phenomenon from the inside. The researcher may or may not choose to inform his or her colleagues that they are being observed. Babbie (1995, 283–85) discusses the choices available to participant-observers. In the case of interest groups, one might try to obtain a position at a group's headquarters, either as a paid staff member or as a paid or volunteer intern. If you were studying trade unions, for example, you could get a job and join the relevant union. Few academic researchers, graduate students, or undergraduates, however, can take the time off necessary to join an organization, learn its ins and outs, perform the tasks they are expected to perform, and conduct research.

Interviews

Interviews are another way of gaining information about interest groups. Although researchers may conduct interviews for survey research, they usually do so with the help of a team of interviewers in order to survey a lot of people. Survey research is, after all, designed to provide lots of data. Questions are structured, and the same questions are asked of a representative sample of a given population.

The type of interview referred to in this section is much less formal. In this type of interviewing, the number of interviewees is much more limited than in survey research; the researcher is not attempting to replicate the scope of survey-research interviewing. But this type of interviewing is also much more flexible: the interviewer can, if desired, ask follow-up questions or pursue topics raised by a particular response, which is not possible in standard survey research. On the other hand, as an interviewer you must remain on your toes, because you must not only listen to and record the response to your question, but interpret the response, and either pose follow-up questions to elicit more information, or, if your informant goes off the track, ask questions that will bring the interview back to what you want to discuss. Many studies of particular interest groups, or of patterns of interest intermediation for a given sector, are based on interviews (see Mazey and Richardson 1993b; Gorges 1993, 1996; A. Cigler and Nownes 1995).

As a researcher, you must make some important decisions before undertaking a program of interviews. First, you must decide on the purpose of the interviews. Are you seeking basic information or looking for more in-depth details? It is important to decide this *before* the interview. Many informants will resent the interviewer who wastes their time trying to ferret out information that is readily available elsewhere. Second, will the interview be structured or not? In other words, will the interviewer pose specific questions in a specific order, or will he or she "go with the flow" as the interview develops? Both kinds of interviews have their purpose, and what begins as a structured interview may become unstructured as the conversation wanders, or as follow-up questions are posed.

Whom should you interview? Babbie, following McCall and Simmons (Babbie 1995, 287) suggests three types of sampling methods: the quota sample, the snowball sample, and deviant cases. In the first case, one tries to interview various kinds of participants in the group one is studying, for example, leaders and the rank and file, radicals and moderates. In the snowball sample, one begins with a few informants and expands the list through referrals. For example, in my own research on the European Trade Union Confederation (ETUC), I began with interviews of ETUC staff, but expanded my initial set of contacts to include representatives of ETUC member-federations, representatives of trade unions that are not members of the ETUC, staff of the EU and the Economic and Social Committee of the EU, national-level bureaucrats, and various consultants and think-tank experts (Gorges 1996).

Finally, you should always try to find a dissenting opinion, or a deviant case. If you hear nothing but praise for the functioning of a particular interest group, for example, you should be sure to try to interview critics of the group or to pose questions that might elicit a critical response. Thus, although interviews are an important tool of field research, you must always be wary of the information you obtain. You have to cross-check information with other informants and seek other evidence to assess the quality of the information obtained through interviews.

Process Tracing

Process tracing examines the role of different factors in explaining the process leading to a particular outcome (Aggarwal 1985, 39). This technique focuses on "the decision process by which various initial conditions are translated into outcomes" (George and McKeown 1985, 35). In interest-group studies, process tracing is useful in determining the role played by an interest group in the elaboration of a particular policy. Gorges (1996), for example, traces the role played by EU-level interest groups representing business and trade unions in the attempts to establish an EU-wide system of tripartite bargaining.

Combining Techniques and Their Relations to the Research Design

As indicated in the introduction to this chapter, scholars may employ many techniques to gather the information they seek. No technique is more or less appropriate. The utility of any given methodology depends on its ability to generate the information needed to prove an argument as set out in the research design. If the method does not do so, either the argument is unprovable, or the information will have to be sought in other ways. That is why a combination of methods—survey research, content analysis, interviews, and so on—is probably the best way to generate the kinds of information sought and will ensure that the information produced is both reliable and replicable. To help bring together the elements discussed in this chapter, the following list sets out the components of a sample research design.

A Sample Research Design

1. *The Topic:* Interest Intermediation in the European Union (EU).
2. *Type of Study and Its Contribution:* This study applies neoinstitutional theories[4] directly to the analysis of interest intermediation in the EU. It provides a coherent framework to account for the variety of patterns of interest intermediation in the EU and the role of EU institutions in shaping the response of interest groups to European integration.
3. *The Literature Review:* A review of the literature on interest intermediation in the EU. Main claim: The literature is deficient in that it fails to account for the variety of patterns of interest intermediation observed in the EU.
4. *The Theoretical Framework:* A revised neoinstitutionalist theoretical framework that takes into account the intraorganizational factors that work against institutional determinism is employed to characterize patterns of interest intermediation and to explain the variety of forms of interest intermediation in the EU. The framework sees the choices of political actors as sharply constrained by institutional norms and rules. These institutional variables constitute the context within which interest groups formulate their responses to the development of the EU. Cost-benefit calculations, membership preferences, and cohesion, the ability or desire to overcome intraorganizational conflicts based on national, regional, sectoral, ideological, cultural, and policy differences, all shape the response of interest groups to EU policy and increased integration.
5. *The Evidence:* Chapters on the role of EU institutions (policy-making authority, voting rules, and decision-making styles) and EU organs (the Commis-

sion, Council of Ministers, European Parliament, and Economic and Social Committee); EU-level interest groups at the macro and sectoral levels, and attempts to establish EU-level tripartite bargaining.

6. *Research Methodology:* Interviews with members of EU-level and national-level interest groups, national governments, think tanks, and representatives of EU institutions; analysis of interest group and EU publications and other documentation; and process tracing of attempts to establish EU-level tripartite bargaining (Gorges 1996).

15.5. KEYS TO COMPLETING A SUCCESSFUL STUDY

Everyone who conducts empirical research knows that preparing a research design before going out into the field to execute it is one thing and that actually following the design is another. Nevertheless, following the steps outlined here should allow you to justify your work to the larger scholarly community and to complete your research without too many unnecessary delays. Moreover, beginning your research with a clear idea of what you are trying to describe or explain, and arriving in the field with at least some tentative hypotheses and an idea of how you should proceed in order to find the information you need, is vitally important, if only to save time and to avoid casting too wide a net.

Everyone who conducts empirical research will also tell the aspiring researcher that you will be deluged with information once you leave the confines of a campus. You are usually on a firmer intellectual and methodological footing if you begin your information gathering with some idea of what you are trying to do and of how you want to go about doing it. Thinking through the methodological issues discussed here will facilitate that task and enable you to produce a more useful, interesting, and sophisticated analysis.

NOTES

1. Useful guides to case studies include Yin (1994) and Ragin and Becker (1992).

2. The literature on the comparative method is quite extensive. For an excellent brief introduction, see Lawrence Mayer (1989, 28–59).

3. See Gary King et al. (1994, 19–23) for more on theory building.

4. For a review of neoinstitutionalism, see section 3.9.

References

ABBREVIATIONS USED IN THESE REFERENCES

AEI	American Enterprise Institute
AJPS	*American Journal of Political Science*
AJS	*American Journal of Sociology*
Annals	*Annals of the American Academy of Political and Social Science*
APQ	*American Politics Quarterly*
APSR	*American Political Science Review*
BJPS	*British Journal of Political Science*
CQP	Congressional Quarterly Press
CUP	Cambridge University Press
HUP	Harvard University Press
IPSR	*International Political Science Review*
JHUP	Johns Hopkins University Press
JOP	*Journal of Politics*
LSQ	*Legislative Studies Quarterly*
MJPS	*Midwest Journal of Political Science*
OUP	Oxford University Press
PRQ	*Political Research Quarterly*
PSQ	*Political Science Quarterly*
PUP	Princeton University Press
SMP	St. Martin's Press
SPS	*Scandinavian Political Studies*

REFERENCES

SSQ	*Social Science Quarterly*
SUNY	State University of New York
UCAP	University of California Press
UCP	University of Chicago Press
UPA	University Press of America
WPQ	*Western Political Quarterly*
YUP	Yale University Press

Aardal, Bernt Olav. 1983. "Economics, Ideology and Strategy: An Analysis of the EC-Debate in Norwegian and Danish Organizations 1961–72." *SPS* 6: 27–49.

Abbott, K. 1996. *Pressure Groups and the Australian Federal Parliament.* Canberra: Australian Government Publishing Service.

Abel, Richard L. 1995. *Politics by Other Means: Law in the Struggle Against Apartheid, 1980–1994.* New York: Routledge.

Abney, Glenn, and Thomas P. Lauth. 1985. "Interest Group Influence in City Policy-Making." *WPQ* 38: 148–61.

———. 1986. "Interest Group Influence in the States: A View of Subsystem Politics." Paper presented at the annual meeting of the American Political Science Association.

Abney, Glenn. 1988. "Lobbying by the Insiders: Parallels of State Agencies and Interest Groups." *Public Administration Review* 48: 911–17.

Abortion Bibliography. 1991. Troy, N.Y.: Whitston.

Abou-El-Haj, Rifa'at Ali. 1991. *Formation of the Modern State.* Albany, N.Y.: SUNY Press.

Abrams, Douglas. 1993. *Conflict, Competition or Cooperation?: Dilemmas of State Education Policymaking.* Albany, N.Y.: SUNY Press.

Abramson, Paul R. 1983. *Political Attitudes in America.* San Francisco: Freeman.

Ackerman, Bruce A., and William T. Hassler. 1981. *Clean Coal/Dirty Air.* New Haven, Conn.: YUP.

Adams, Gordon. 1981. *The Iron Triangle.* New York: Council on Economic Priorities.

———. 1982. *The Politics of Defense Contracting: The Iron Triangle.* New Brunswick, N.J.: Transaction Books.

Adams, James Luther. 1970. *The Growing Church Lobby in Washington.* Grand Rapids, Mich.: Eerdmans.

Adams, Roy. 1995. *Industrial Relations Under Liberal Democracy: North America in Comparative Perspective.* Columbia, S.C.: University of South Carolina Press.

Adler, Glenn, and Eddie Webster. 1995. "Challenging Transition Theory: The Labor Movement, Radical Reform, and Transition to Democracy in South Africa." *Politics and Society* 23: 75–106.

Aga Kahn, Sadruddin, and Hassan bin Talal. 1987. *Indigenous Peoples: A Global Quest for Justice.* Geneva: International Independent Commission for Humanitarian Affairs.

Aggarwal, Vinod K. 1985. *Liberal Protectionism: The International Politics of the Organized Textile Trade.* Berkeley: UCAP.

Agh, Attila, and Gabriella Ilonszki, eds. 1996. *The Second Steps: Parliaments and Organized Interests.* Budapest: Hungarian Center for Democracy Studies.

Ahmida, Ali Abdullatif. 1994a. "Colonialism, State Formation and Civil Society in North Africa: Theoretical and Analytical Problems." *International Journal of Islamic and Arabic Studies* XI: 1–22.

———. 1994b. *The Making of Modern Libya: State Formation, Colonialization, and Resistance, 1830–1932.* Albany, N.Y.: SUNY Press.

———. 1994c. "Explaining Islam, the State and Modernity," *Humboldt Journal of Social Relations* 20: 177–85.

———. 1997. "Inventing or Recovering Civil Society in the Middle East." *Critique* 10 (Spring): 127–34.

Ahrari, Mohammed E., ed. 1987. *Ethnic Groups and U.S. Foreign Policy.* New York: Greenwood.

Ainsworth, Scott. 1993. "Regulating Lobbyists and Interest Group Influence." *JOP* 55: 41–56.

———. 2002. *Analyzing Interest Groups: Group Influence on People and Politics.* New York: Norton.

Ainsworth, Scott, and Itai Sened. 1993. "The Role of Lobbyists: Entrepreneurs with Two Audiences." *AJPS* 37: 834–66.

Akwesasne Notes. 1978. *Basic Call to Consciousness.* Rooseveltown, N.Y.: Akwesasne Notes.

Aldrich, John H., and David W. Rohde. 1997–98. "The Transition to Republican Rule in the House: Implications for Theories of Congressional Politics." *PSQ* 112: 541–67.

Alexander, Herbert E. 1983. *The Case For PACs.* Washington, D.C.: Public Affairs Council.

———. 1984. *Financing Politics.* 3rd ed. Washington, D.C.: CQP.

———. 1992. *Financing Politics: Money, Elections and Political Reform.* Washington, D.C.: CQP.

———. 1995. *Financing the 1992 Election.* Armonk, N.Y.: M. E. Sharpe.

Alexander, Herbert E., and Brian Haggerty. 1984. *PACs and Parties: Relationships and Interrelationships.* Los Angeles: Citizens Research Foundation.

Alford, Robert R. 1975. *Health Care Politics: Ideological and Interest Group Barriers to Reform.* Chicago: UCP.

Allardt, Erik, et al., eds. 1981. *Nordic Democracy: Ideas, Issues and Institutions in Politics, Economy, Education, Social and Cultural Affairs of Denmark, Finland, Iceland, Norway and Sweden.* Copenhagen: Det Danske Selskab.

Allen, Thomas B. 1987. *Guardian of the Wild: The Story of the National Wildlife Federation, 1936–1986.* Bloomington: Indiana University Press.

Allsup, Carl. 1982. *The American G. I. Forum: Origins and Evolution.* Austin: Center for Mexican American Studies, The University of Texas at Austin.

Almond, Gabriel A. 1958. "A Comparative Study of Interest Groups and the Political Process." *APSR* 52: 270–82.

———. 1983. "Corporatism, Pluralism, and Professional Memory." *World Politics* 35: 245–60.

———. 1988. "Return to the State." *APSR* 82: 853–74.

Almond, Gabriel A., G. Bingham Powell and R. J. Mundt. 1993. *Comparative Politics: A Theoretical Framework.* New York: HarperCollins.

Almond, Gabriel, and Sidney Verba. 1963. *The Civic Culture.* Princeton, N.J.: PUP.

REFERENCES

———. 1980. *The Civic Culture Revisited.* Boston: Little, Brown.

Amato, Joseph A. 1993. *The Great Jerusalem Artichoke Circus: The Buying and Selling of the Rural American Dream.* Minneapolis: University of Minnesota Press.

Ambrosius, Margery M. 1989. "The Role of Occupational Interests in State Economic Development Policies." *WPQ* 42: 283–300.

American Talk Issues Foundation. 1993. *Americans Talk Issues 22: Improving Democracy in America,* April 30.

Amoroso, Bruno. 1990. "Development and Crisis of the Scandinavian Model of Labour Relations in Denmark." In, *European Industrial Relations: The Challenge of Flexibility,* eds. Guido Baglioni and Colin Crouch, London: Sage.

Amy, Douglas. 1987. *The Politics of Environmental Mediation.* New York: Columbia University Press.

Anckar, Dag, and Voitto Helander. 1985. "Public Allocation by Private Organizations: The Case of Finland." *SPS* 8: 283–94.

Andersen, Jørgen Goul. 1990. "Denmark: Environmental Conflict and the 'Greening' of the Labour Movement." *SPS* 13: 185–210.

Andersen, Kristi. 1996. *After Suffrage.* Chicago: UCP.

Anderson, Brian B. 1997. "Interest Group Federations: A View from the States." Ph.D. Dissertation, The Pennsylvania State University.

Anderson, David C. 1999. "Smoking Guns," *American Prospect,* (September/ October): 27–33.

Anderson, Douglas. 1981. *Regulatory Politics and Electric Utilities: A Case Study in Political Economy.* Boston: Auburn House.

Anderson, J. E. 1977. "Pressure Groups and the Canadian Bureaucracy." In *Public Administration in Canada,* 3rd ed., ed. Kenneth Kernaghan. Toronto: Methuen.

Anderson, S. S., and K. A. Eliassen. 1991. "European Community Lobbying." *European Journal of Political Research* 20: 173–87.

Andeweg, R. B., and Galen A. Irwin. 1993. *Dutch Government and Politics.* London: MacMillan.

Andrew, Linzey, et al., eds. 1998. *Animals on the Agenda: Questions About Animals for Theology and Ethics.* Urbana: University of Illinois Press.

Andsager, Julie. 2000. "How Interest Groups Attempt to Shape Public Opinion with Competing News Frames." *Journalism and Mass Communication Quarterly* 77: 577–93.

Annals. 1991. Number 516.

Annual U.S. Union Sourcebook. 2001. 16th ed. West Orange, N.J.: Industrial Relations and Information Services.

Appleby, Colin, and John Bessant. 1987. "Adapting to Decline: Organizational Structures and Government Policy in the UK and West German Foundry Sectors." In *Comparative Government-Industry Relations,* S. Wilks and M. Wright, cited below.

Appleton, Andrew. 2001. "France: Party-Group Relations in the Shadow of the State." In *Political Parties and Interest Groups.* C. Thomas, cited below.

APSA [American Political Science Association]. 1950. American Political Science Association Committee on Political Parties. "Toward A More Responsible Two Party System." *APSR* 44 (supplement).

Arian, Asher. 1989. *Politics in Israel: The Second Generation.* rev. ed. Chatham, N.J.: Chatham House.

———. 1993. "Israel: Interest Group Pluralism Constrained." In *First World Interest Groups*. C. Thomas, cited below.

Armingeon, Klaus. 1997. "Swiss Corporatism in Comparative Perspective." *West European Politics* 20: 164–79.

Arnold, David S., and Jeremy F. Plant. 1994. *Public Official Associations and State and Local Government.* Fairfax, Va.: George Mason University Press.

Arrington, Karen McGill, and William L. Taylor. 1993. *Voting Rights in America: Continuing the Quest for Full Participation.* Lanham, Md.: UPA.

Asher, Herbert B., Eric S. Heberlig, Randall B. Ripley, and Karen C. Snyder. 2001. *American Labor Unions in the Electoral Arena.* Lanham, Md.: Rowman & Littlefield.

Atkinson, M. M. 1995. "The Integrity Agenda: Lead Us Not into Temptation." In *How Ottawa Spends 1995–96: Mid-Life Crises*, ed. S. D. Phillips. Ottawa: Carleton University Press.

Atkinson, M. M., and W. Coleman. 1989a. *The State, Business and Industrial Change in Canada.* Toronto: University of Toronto Press.

———. 1989b. "Strong States and Weak States: Sectoral Policy Networks in Advanced Capitalist Economies." *BJPS* 19: 47–67.

Audretsch, David B. 1989. *The Market and the State: Government Policy Towards Business in Europe, Japan, and the U.S.A.: A Comparative Analysis.* New York: New York University Press.

Austin-Smith, David. 1993. "Information and Influence: Lobbying for Agendas and Votes." *AJPS* 37: 799–833.

Austin-Smith, David, and John R. Wright. 1994. "Counter-Active Lobbying for Legislative Votes." *AJPS* 38: 25–44.

Avery, W. F. 1990. "Managing Public Policy Abroad: The Case of Foreign Corporate Representation in Washington." *The Columbia Journal of World Business* 25: 32–41.

Averyt, W. 1977. *Agro Politics in the European Community: Interest Groups and the Common Agricultural Policy.* New York: Praeger.

Axelrod, Robert. 1984. *The Evolution of Cooperation.* New York: Basic Books.

Ayres, Jeffrey M. 1997. "From National to Popular Sovereignty: The Evolving Globalization of Protest Activity in Canada." *International Review of Canadian Studies* 16 (Fall): 107–23.

Babbie, Earl. 1995. *The Practice of Social Research.* 7th ed. Belmont, Calif.: Wadsworth.

Bachrach, Peter, and Morton S. Baratz. 1962. "Two Faces of Power." *APSR* 56: 947–52.

———. 1963. "Decisions and Nondecisions: An Analytical Framework." *APSR* 57: 632–42.

———. 1970. *Power and Poverty.* New York: OUP.

Baer, Denise L., and Martha Bailey. 1994. "The Nationalization of Education Politics." In *Risky Business?* Robert Biersack, et al., cited below.

Baer, Denise L., and David A. Bositis. 1988. *Elite Cadres and Party Coalitions: Representing the Public in Party Politics.* Westport, Conn.: Greenwood.

———. 1993. *Politics and Linkage in a Democratic Society.* Englewood Cliffs, N. J.: Prentice-Hall.

REFERENCES

Baer, Denise L., and Julie A. Dolan. 1994. "Intimate Connections: Political Interests and Group Activity in State and Local Parties." *American Review of Politics* 15: 257–89.

Baggott, Rob. 1995. *Pressure Groups Today.* Manchester, U.K.: Manchester University Press.

Bahr, Howard M., Bruce A. Chadwick, and Robert C. Day, eds. 1972. *Native Americans Today: Sociological Perspectives.* New York: Harper & Row.

Bailey, Robert W. 1999. *Gay Politics / Urban Politics: Economics and Identity in the Urban Setting.* New York: Columbia University Press.

Bailey, Stephen K. 1975. *Education Interest Groups in the Nations Capital.* Washington, D.C.: American Council on Education.

Bailis, Lawrence Neil. 1974. *Bread or Justice?* Lexington, Mass.: Lexington Books.

Baker, Tod A., Robert P. Steed, and Laurence W. Moreland, eds. 1983. *Religion and Politics in the South: Mass and Elite Perspectives.* New York: Praeger.

Baldwin, David A. 1978. "Power and Social Exchange." *APSR* 72: 1229–42.

Baldwin, Donald N. 1972. *The Quiet Revolution: Grass Roots of Today's Wilderness Preservation Movement.* Boulder, Colo.: Pruett Publishing.

Ball, Alan R., and Francis Millard. 1987. *Pressure Politics in Industrial Societies: A Comparative Introduction.* Highland Heights, N.J.: Humanities Press International.

Balme, Richard, Jean Becquart-LeClercq, and Terry Nichols Clark. 1987. "New Mayors: France and the United States." *The Tocqueville Review* 8: 263–78.

Bard, Mitchell. 1988. "The Influence of Ethnic Interest Groups on American Middle Eastern Policy." In *The Domestic Sources of American Foreign Policy*, eds. Charles Kegley and Eugene Wittkopf. New York: SMP.

Barkan, Steven E. 1979. "Strategic, Tactical and Organizational Dilemmas of the Protest Movement Against Nuclear Power." *Social Problems* 27: 19–37.

Barnet, Richard J., and Ronald E. Muller. 1974. *Global Reach: The Power of the Multinational Corporations.* New York: Simon & Schuster.

Barrera, Mario. 1985. "The Historical Evolution of Chicano Ethnic Goals: A Bibliographic Essay." *Sage Race Relations Abstracts* 10: 1–48.

Barry, Brian. 1975. "Political Accommodation and Consociational Democracy." *BJPS* 5: 477–505.

Barry, Donald. 1975. "Interest Groups and the Foreign Policy Process: The Case of Biafra." In *Pressure Group Behaviour in Canadian Politics.* P. Pross. cited below.

Bass, Jack, and Walter DeVries. 1976. *The Transformation of Southern Politics: Social Change and Political Consequences Since 1945.* New York: Basic Books.

Bates, Robert H. 1981. *Markets and States in Tropical Africa.* Berkeley: UCAP.

Bauer, Raymond A., Ithiel de Sola Pool, and Lewis A. Dexter. 1963. *American Business and Public Policy: The Politics of Foreign Trade.* Chicago: Aldine Atherton.

———. 1972. *American Business and Public Policy.* 2nd ed. Chicago: Aldine Atherton.

Baumgartner, Frank R. 1989. *Conflict and Rhetoric in French Policymaking.* Pittsburgh: University of Pittsburgh Press.

———. 1996. "Public Interest Groups in France and the United States." *Governance: An International Journal of Policy and Administration* 9: 1–22.

References

Baumgartner, Frank R., and Bryan D. Jones. 1993. *Agendas and Instability in American Politics.* Chicago: UCP.

Baumgartner, Frank R., and Beth L. Leech. 1998. *Basic Interests: The Importance of Groups in Politics and in Political Science.* Princeton, N.J.: PUP.

Baumgartner, Frank R., and Jeffery C. Talbert. 1995a. "From Setting a National Agenda on Health Care to Making Decisions in Congress." *Journal of Health Politics, Policy and Law* 20: 437–45.

———. 1995b. "Interest Groups and Political Change." In *New Directions in American Politics,* ed. Bryan D. Jones. Boulder, Colo.: Westview.

Baumgartner, Frank R., and Jack L. Walker, Jr. 1988. "Survey Research and Membership in Voluntary Associations." *AJPS* 32: 908–28.

———. 1989. "Education Policymaking and the Interest Group Structure in France and the United States." *Comparative Politics* 21: 273–88.

Bayes, Jane H. 1982. *Ideologies and Interest-Group Politics: The United States as a Special Interest State in the Global Economy.* Navato, Calif.: Chandler & Sharp.

Beauchamp, Clive. 1992. "The National Rifle Association of America (NRA): Lobbying Against Federal Gun Controls 1970–1986," Ph.D. Dissertation, University of New South Wales.

Beck, Nathaniel. 1984. "Domestic Political Sources of Monetary Policy: 1955–1982." *JOP* 46: 786–817.

Becker, David G. 1981. *The New Bourgeoisie in Peru.* Princeton, N.J.: PUP.

Becker, Gary S. 1985. "Public Policies, Pressure Groups and Deadweight Costs." *Journal of Public Economics* 28: 329–47.

Bedani, Gino. 1995. *Politics and Ideology in the Italian Workers' Movement: Union Development and the Changing Role of the Catholic and Communist Subcultures in Postwar Italy.* Oxford: Berg.

Beer, Samuel H. 1956. "Pressure Groups and Parties in Britain." *APSR* 50: 1–23.

Beilin, Yossi. 1992. *Israel: A Concise Political History.* London: Weidenfeld & Nicolson.

Bell, Charles G., Keith E. Hamm, and Charles W. Wiggins. 1985. "The Pluralistic Model Reconsidered: A Comparative Analysis of Interest Group Policy Involvement in Three States." Paper delivered at the annual meeting of the American Political Science Association.

Bell, S. 1995. "Between Market and the State: The Role of Business Associations in Public Policy." *Comparative Politics* 28: 25–53.

Bell, S., and J. Wanna, eds. 1992. *Business-Government Relations in Australia.* Sydney: Harcourt Brace Jovanovich.

Bell, S., and John Warhurst. 1993. "Business Political Activism and Government Relations in Large Companies in Australia." *Australian Journal of Political Science* 28: 201–20.

Bendor, Jonathon, and Terry M. Moe. 1985. "An Adaptive Model of Bureaucratic Politics." *APSR* 79: 755–74.

Benedict, Robert C., Clive S. Thomas, and Ronald J. Hrebenar. 1996 "Public Perceptions of Interest Groups: Varying Attitudes to Business, Labor and Public Interests." Paper presented at the annual meeting of the Western Political Science Association.

Benjamin, Gerald, and Michael Malbin, eds. 1992. *Limiting Legislative Terms.* Washington, D.C.: CQP

Bennett, S. 1989. *Aborigines and Political Power.* Sydney: Allen & Unwin.

Bentley, Arthur F. 1908. *The Process of Government: A Study of Social Pressures.* Chicago: UCP.

Berch, Neil. 1992. "Why Do Some States Play the Federal Aid Game Better Than Others?" *APQ* 20: 366–77.

Berg, Larry, and C. B. Holman. 1987. "Losing the Initiative: The Impact of Rising Costs on the Initiative Process," *Western City,* (29 June).

Berger, Suzanne D., ed. 1981a. *Organizing Interests in Western Europe: Pluralism, Corporatism and the Transformation of Politics.* Cambridge, Mass.: CUP.

———. 1981b. "Introduction." In *Organizing Interests in Western Europe,* S. Berger, cited above.

Bergthold, Linda A. 1987. "Business and Pushcart Vendors in an Age of Supermarkets." *International Journal of Health Services* 17: 7–26.

———. 1990. *Purchasing Power in Health.* New Brunswick, N.J.: Rutgers University Press.

Berk, Richard A. 1977. *Prison Reform and State Elites.* Cambridge, Mass.: Ballinger.

Berk, Richard A., Harold Brackman, and Selma L. Lesser. 1977. *A Measure of Justice: An Empirical Study of Changes in the California Penal Code, 1955–1971.* New York: Academic Press.

Berkman, Michael. 1993. *The State Roots of National Politics: Congress and the Tax Agenda.* Pittsburgh: University of Pittsburgh Press.

Bernstein, Robert A., and James A. Dyer. 1992. *An Introduction to Political Science Methods.* 3rd ed. Englewood Cliffs, N.J.: Prentice-Hall.

Berrington, H. 1995. "Political Ethics: The Nolan Report." *Government and Opposition* 30: 431–51.

Berry, Glyn. 1974. "The Oil Lobby and the Energy Crisis." *Canadian Public Administration* 17: 600–35.

Berry, Jeffrey M. 1977. *Lobbying for the People: The Political Behavior of Public Interest Groups.* Princeton, N.J.: PUP.

———. 1984. *Feeding Hungry People.* New Brunswick, N.J.: Rutgers University Press.

———. 1988. "Subgovernments, Issue Networks, and Political Conflict." In *Remaking American Politics,* eds. Richard A. Harris and Sidney M. Milkis. Boulder, Colo.: Westview.

———. 1989. *The Interest Group Society.* 2nd ed. Glenview, Ill.: Scott Foresman / Little, Brown.

———. 1993. "Citizen Groups and the Changing Nature of Interest Group Politics in America." *The Annals* Vol. 528: 30–41.

———. 1997. *The Interest Group Society.* 3rd ed. New York: Addison Wesley Longman.

———. 1999. *The New Liberalism: The Rising Power of Citizen Groups.* Washington, D.C.: Brookings.

Berry, Jeffrey M., and Kent E. Portney. 1994. "Centralizing Regulatory Control and Interest Group Access: The Quayle Council on Competitiveness." In *Interest Group Politics,* 4th ed., A. Cigler and B. Loomis, cited below.

Berry, Jeffrey M., Kent E. Portney, and Kenneth Thomson. 1991. "The Political Behavior of Poor People." In *The Urban Underclass,* eds. Christopher Juncos and Paul E. Peterson. Washington, D.C.: Brookings.

————. 1993. *The Rebirth of Urban Democracy.* Washington, D.C.: Brookings.

Berryman, Phillip. 1987. *Liberation Theology: The Essential Fact About the Revolutionary Movement in Latin America and Beyond.* New York: Pantheon.

Berube, Allan. 1990. *Coming Out Under Fire: The History of Gay Men and Women in World War Two.* New York: Free Press.

Berube, Maurice R. 1988. *Teacher Politics.* New York: Greenwood.

————. 1991. *American Presidents and Education.* Westport, Conn.: Greenwood.

Best, Paul J., Kul B. Rai, and David F. Walsh. 1986. *Politics in Three Worlds.* New York: Wiley.

Beyle, Thad L., and Lynn R. Muchmore. 1983. "Governors and Intergovernmental Relations: Middlemen in the Federal System." In *Being Governor: The View from the Office*, eds. T. Beyle and L. Muchmore. Durham, N.C.: Duke University Press.

Bianchi, Robert. 1984. *Interest Groups and Political Development in Turkey.* Princeton, N.J.: PUP.

————. 1985. "Business Associations in Egypt and Turkey." *Annals* 482: 147–59.

————. 1986a. "The Corporatization of the Egyptian Labor Movement," *The Middle East Journal* 40: 429–44.

————. 1986b. "Interest Group Politics in the Third World." *Third World Quarterly* 8: 507–39.

————. 1989. *Unruly Corporatism: Associational Life in Twentieth-Century Egypt.* New York: OUP.

————. 1990. "Interest Groups and Politics in Mubarak's Egypt." In *The Political Economy of Contemporary Egypt*, ed. Ibrahim Oweiss. Washington, D.C.: Georgetown University Press.

Bielasiak, Jack, and Maurice D. Simon, eds. 1984. *Polish Politics: Edge of the Abyss.* New York: Praeger.

Biersack, Robert, Paul S. Herrnson, and Clyde Wilcox, eds. 1994. *Risky Business: PAC Decisionmaking in Congressional Elections.* New York: M. E. Sharpe.

————, eds. 1999. *After the Revolution: PACs and Lobbies in the New Republican Congress.* Boston: Allyn & Bacon.

Bill, James, and Robert Springborg. 1993. *Politics of The Middle East.* 4th ed. New York: HarperCollins.

Binstock, Robert H. 1972. "Interest Group Liberalism and the Politics of Aging." *Gerontologist* 12: 265–80.

Birnbaum, Jeffrey H. 1992. *The Lobbyists: How Influence Peddlers Get Their Way in Washington.* New York: Times Books.

————. 1999. "Under the Gun," *Fortune*, (December): 211–12.

Birnbaum, Jeffrey H., and Alan S. Murray. 1987. *Showdown at Gucci Gulch: Lawmakers, Lobbyists and the Unlikely Triumph of Tax Reform.* New York: Random House.

Black, Earl, and Merle Black. 1987. *Politics and Society in the South.* Cambridge, Mass.: HUP.

Blanchard, Dallas A. 1994. *The Anti-Abortion Movement and the Rise of the Religious Right: From Polite to Fiery Protest.* New York: Twayne.

————. 1996. *The Anti-Abortion Movement: References and Resources.* New York: G. K. Hall.

REFERENCES

Blanchard, Dallas A., and Terry J. Prewitt. 1993. *Religious Violence and Abortion: The Gideon Project.* Gainesville: University Press of Florida.

Block, Fred. 1977. "The Ruling Class Does Not Rule." *Socialist Revolution* 7: 6–28.

Bloland, Harland G. 1985. *Associations in Action: The Washington, DC, Higher Education Community.* ASHE-ERIC Higher Education Report No. 2. Washington, D.C.: Association for the Study of Higher Education.

Blum, Deborah. 1994. *The Monkey Wars.* New York: OUP.

Bohn, David E. 1980. "Consociational Democracy and the Case of Switzerland." *JOP* 42: 165–79.

Bok, Derek C., and John T. Dunlop. 1970. *Labor and the American Community.* New York: Simon & Schuster.

Boles, Janet. 1991. "Form Follows Function." *Annals* 515: 38–49.

Bollier, David. 1989. *Citizen Action and Other Big Ideas: A History of Ralph Nader and the Modern Consumer Movement.* Washington, D.C.: Center for Study of Responsive Law.

Bonnen, James T. 1980. "Observations on the Changing Nature of National Agricultural Policy Decision Processes, 1946–1976." In *Farmers, Bureaucrats and Middlemen: Historical Perspectives on American Agriculture*, ed. Trudy H. Peterson. Washington, D.C.: Howard University Press.

Bonnen, James T., William P. Browne, and David B. Schweikhardt. 1996. "Further Observations on the Changing Nature of National Agricultural Policy Decision Processes, 1946–1995." *Agricultural History* 70: 130–52.

Booth, John A., and Mitchell A. Seligson, eds. 1978. *Political Participation in Latin America, Volume 1: Citizen and State.* New York: Holmes and Meier.

———. 1979. *Political Participation in Latin America, Volume 2: Politics and the Poor.* New York: Holmes and Meier.

Borer, Tristan Anne. 1998. *Challenging the State: Churches as Political Actors in South Africa, 1980–1994.* Notre Dame, Ind.: University of Notre Dame Press.

Borrelli, Peter, ed. 1988. *Crossroads: Environmental Priorities for the Future.* Washington, D.C.: Island Press.

Börzel, Tanja. A. 1998. "Organizing Babylon: On the Different Conceptions of Policy Networks." *Public Administration* 76: 253–73.

Bosso, Christopher J. 1987. *Pesticides and Politics: The Life Cycle of a Public Issue.* Pittsburgh: University of Pittsburgh Press.

———. 1991. "Adaptation and Change in the Environmental Movement." In *Interest Group Politics*, 3rd ed., A. Cigler and B. Loomis, cited below.

———. 1999. "Environmental Groups and the New Political Landscape." In *Environmental Policy in the 1990s*, 4th ed., eds. Norman J. Vig and Michael E. Kraft. Washington, D.C.: CQP.

Boswell, John. 1980. *Christianity, Social Tolerance and Homosexuality.* Chicago: UCP.

Bowler, Sean, Todd Donovan, and Caroline Tolbert. 1998. *Citizens as Legislators: Direct Democracy in the United States.* Columbus: Ohio State University Press.

Boyte, Harry. 1980. *The Backyard Revolution.* Philadelphia: Temple University Press.

Brace, Paul. 1988. "The Political Economy of Collective Action: The Case of the American States." *Polity* 20: 648–64.

References

Brace, Paul, and Youssef Cohen. 1989. "How Much Do Interest Groups Influence Economic Growth?" *APSR* 83: 1297–1308.

Brademas, John. 1987. *The Politics of Education: Conflict and Consensus on Capitol Hill*. Norman: University of Oklahoma Press.

Bradley, Robert B. 1980. "Motivations in Legislative Information Use." *LSQ* 5: 393–406.

Bramwell, Anna. 1994. *The Fading of the Greens: The Decline of Environmental Politics in the West*. New Haven, Conn.: YUP.

Brasher, Holly, David Lowery, and Virginia Gray. 1999. "The Validity of State Lobby Registration Data: The Anomalous Case of Florida (and Minnesota too!)." *LSQ* XXIV: 303–14.

Brassloff, Audrey. 1998. *Religion and Politics in Spain: The Spanish Church in Transition, 1962–96*. Basingstoke, U.K.: Macmillan.

Bratton, Michael. 1989. "Beyond the State: Civil Society and Associational Life in Africa." *World Politics* 41: 407–30.

Bratton, Michael, and Nicolas Van de Walle. 1997. *Democratic Experiments in Africa*. Cambridge, U.K.: CUP.

Braunstein, Richard. 1999. "Practicing Democracy: Initiative and Referendum Voting in the Late 20th Century." Ph.D. Dissertation, University of Colorado, Boulder.

Braunthal, Gerard. 1965. *The Federation of German Industry in Politics*. Ithaca, N.Y.: Cornell University Press.

Brennan, Jill W. 1997. *Gun Control in the 1990s: Gun Advocacy, the Gun Control Lobby and the Militia*. Kettering, Ohio: PPI Publishing.

Bressers, Hans, Laurence J. O'Toole, and Jeremy Richardson, eds. 1995. *Networks for Water Policy: A Comparative Perspective*. London: Frank Cass.

Bridgham, Philip. 1970. "Factionalism in the Chinese Communist Party." In *Party Leadership and Revolutionary Power in China*, ed. John W. Lewis. London: CUP.

Brie, Michael. 1998. *The Political Regime of Moscow: Creation of a New Urban Machine?* Berlin: WZB.

Brigham, John. 1996. *The Constitution of Interests: Beyond the Politics of Rights*. New York: New York University Press.

Bright, Stephen B. 1997. "Political Attacks on the Judiciary." *Judicature* 80: 165–73.

Brill, Harry. 1971. *Why Organizations Fail: The Story of a Rent Strike*. Berkeley: UCAP.

Brinig, Margaret, Randall G. Holcombe, and Linda Schwartzstein. 1993. "The Regulation of Lobbyists." *Public Choice* 77: 377–84.

Brock, W. A., ed. 1965. *The Federalist Papers*. London: Dent.

Brooks, Glenn E. 1961. *When Governors Convene*. Baltimore: JHUP.

Brookstone, Jeffrey M. 1976. *The Multinational Businessman and Foreign Policy: Entrepreneurial Politics in East-West Trade and Investment*. New York: Praeger.

Brower, David. 1990. *For Earth's Sake: The Life and Times of David Brower*. Salt Lake City: Peregrine Smith.

Brown, Bernard E. 1962. "Organized Business in Indian Politics," *The Indian Journal of Political Science* 12: 126–43.

REFERENCES

Brown, Michael, and John May. 1989. *The Greenpeace Story*. London: Dorling Kindersley.

Browne, William P. 1977. "Organizational Maintenance: The Internal Operation of Interest Groups." *Public Administration Review* 37: 48–57.

———. 1988. *Private Interests, Public Policy, and American Agriculture*. Lawrence, Kans.: University Press of Kansas.

———. 1990. "Organized Interests and Their Issue Niches: A Search for Pluralism in a Policy Domain." *JOP* 52: 477–509.

———. 1993. "Challenging Industrialization: The Rekindling of Agrarian Protest, 1977–1987." *Studies in American Political Development* 7: 1–34.

———. 1995a. *Cultivating Congress: Constituents, Issues, and Agricultural Policymaking*. Lawrence, Kans.: University Press of Kansas.

———. 1995b. "Organized Interests, Grassroots Confidants and Congress." In *Interest Group Politics*, 4th ed., A. Cigler and B. Loomis, cited below.

———. 1998. *Groups, Interests and U.S. Public Policy*. Washington, D.C.: Georgetown University Press.

Browne, William P., Kristen Allen, and David B. Schweikhardt. 1997. "Never Say Never Again: Why the Road to Agricultural Policy Reform Has a Long Way to Go." *Choices* 12 (Fourth Quarter): 4–9.

Browne, William P., and Allan J. Cigler. 1990. *U.S. Agricultural Groups: Institutional Profiles*. Westport, Conn.: Greenwood.

Browne, William P., and John Dinse. 1985. "The Emergence of the American Agriculture Movement, 1977–1979." *Great Plains Quarterly* 5: 221–35.

Browne, William P., and David B. Schweikhardt. 1995. "Demosclerosis: Implications for Agricultural Policy." *American Journal of Agricultural Economics* 77 (December): 1128–34.

Browning, Rufus P., Dale Rogers Marshall, and David H. Tabb. 1984. *Protest Is Not Enough*. Berkeley: UCAP.

Bruce, John, and Clyde Wilcox, eds. 1998. *The Changing Politics of Gun Control*. Lanham, Md.: Rowman & Littlefield.

Bruce, Steve. 1988. *The Rise and Fall of the New Christian Right: Conservative Protestant Politics in America 1978–1988*. New York: OUP.

Brudney, Jeffrey, and Ted Hebert. 1987. "State Agencies and Their Environments: Examining the Influence of Important External Actors." *JOP* 49: 186–206.

Bruer, Patrick. 1987. "Faction in Court: A Study of Interest Group Litigation." Ph.D. Dissertation. University of Wisconsin-Madison.

Brunk, Gregory, Kennith G. Hunter, and Laura A. Wilson. 1991. "Economic Innovation and Interest Groups: The Case of Patents Granted to Residents of the American States. *SSQ* 72: 601–7.

Buchanan, James, Robert D. Tollison, and Gordon Tullock, eds. 1980. *Towards a Theory of the Rent-Seeking Society*. College Station, Tex.: Texas A & M University Press.

Buchanan, James, and Gordon Tullock. 1962. *Calculus of Consent*. Ann Arbor: University of Michigan Press.

Buck, Solon J. 1913. *The Granger Movement*. Cambridge, Mass.: HUP.

Budge, Ian, and Richard I. Hofferbert. 1990. "Mandates and Policy Outputs: U.S. Party Platforms and Federal Expenditures." *APSR* 84: 111–31.

Buksti, Jacob. B. 1993. "Interest Groups in Denmark." In *Pressure Groups*. J. Richardson, cited below.

Bullard, Robert D. 1990. *Dumping in Dixie: Race, Class and Environmental Quality*. Boulder, Colo.: Westview.

Bulmer, Simon J. 1998. "New Institutionalism and the Governance of the Single European Market." *Journal of European Public Policy* 5: 365–86.

Bulmer, Simon, and William Paterson. 1987. *The Federal Republic of Germany and the European Community*. London: Allen & Unwin.

Burch, Philip H., Jr. 1973. "The NAM as an Interest Group." *Politics and Society* 4: 97–130.

Burdette, Franklin L. 1950. *Lobbyists in Action: How Strings Are Pulled*. Manassas, Va.: National Capitol Publishers.

Burger, Julian. 1987. *Report from the Frontier: The State of the World's Indigenous Peoples*. London: Zed Press.

Burgess, Stephen F. 1997. "Smallholder Voice and Rural Transformation: Zimbabwe and Kenya Compared," *Comparative Political Studies* 29: 127–49.

Burgmann, V. 1993. *Power and Protest: Movements for Change in Australian Society*. Sydney: Allen & Unwin.

Burki, Shahid Javed. 1971. *Social Groups and Development: A Case Study of Pakistan*. Cambridge, Mass.: Center for International Affairs, Harvard University.

Burns, John P. 1979. "China," *Studies in Comparative Communism*, Special Issues on Clientelism in Communist Systems: A Symposium, 12 (2 & 3): 190–94.

Burns, Peter F., Peter L. Francia, and Paul S. Herrnson. 2000. "Labor at Work: Union Campaign Activities and Legislative Payoffs in the U.S. House of Representatives." *SSQ* 81: 507–22.

Button, James W., Barbara A. Rienzo, and Kenneth D. Wald. 1997. *Private Lives, Public Conflicts*. Washington, D.C.: CQP.

Bykerk, Loree G. 1988. "Gender in Insurance: Organized Interests and the Displacement of Conflicts." *Policy Studies Journal* 17: 261–76.

———. 1992. "Business Power in Washington: The Insurance Exception," *Policy Studies Review* 11, 3 / 4: 259–79.

Bykerk, Loree, and Ardith Maney. 1991. "Where Have All the Consumers Gone?" *PSQ* 106: 677–94.

———. 1995a. "Consumer Groups and Coalition Politics on Capitol Hill." In *Interest Group Politics*, 4th ed. A. Cigler and B. Loomis, cited below.

———. 1995b. *U.S. Consumer Interest Groups: Institutional Profiles*. Westport, Conn.: Greenwood.

Byrnes, Timothy A., and Mary C. Segers, eds. 1992. *The Catholic Church and the Politics of Abortion: A View from the States*. Boulder, Colo.: Westview.

Bystydzienski, Jill M. 1988. "Women in Politics in Norway." *Women and Politics* 8: 73–95.

———. 1992. "Influence of Women's Culture on Public Politics in Norway." In *Women Transforming Politics: Worldwide Strategies for Empowerment*, ed. Jill M. Bystydzienski. Bloomington: Indiana University Press.

Caldeira, Gregory A., and John R. Wright. 1988. "Interest Groups and Agenda-setting in the Supreme Court of the United States." *APSR* 82: 1109–27.

———. 1990. "*Amici Curiae* before the Supreme Court: Who Participates, When, and How Much?" *JOP* 52: 782–806.

————. 1995. "Lobbying for Justice: The Rise of Organized Conflict in the Politics of Federal Judgeships." In *Contemplating Courts*, ed. Lee Epstein. Washington, D.C.: CQP.

Caldwell, Lynton K. 1990. "International Environmental Politics: America's Response to Global Imperatives." In *Environmental Policy in the 1990s*. N. Vig and M. Kraft, cited below.

Callaway, Barbara, and Lucy Creevey. 1994. *The Heritage of Islam: Women, Religion and Politics in West Africa*. Boulder, Colo.: Lynne Rienner.

Cammisa, Anne Marie. 1995. *Governments as Interest Groups: Intergovernmental Lobbying and the Federal System*. New York: Praeger.

Camp, Roderic A. 1995. *Political Recruitment Across Two Centuries: Mexico, 1884–1991*. Austin: University of Texas Press.

Campbell, Christiana M. 1962. *The Farm Bureau and the New Deal*. Urbana: University of Illinois Press.

Campbell, Colton C., and Roger H. Davidson. 1998. "Coalition Building in Congress: The Consequences of Partisan Change." In P. Herrnson, R. Shaiko and C. Wilcox, *The Interest Group Connection*, cited below.

Campbell, Heather. 1996. "The Politics of Requesting: Strategic Behavior and Public Utility Regulation." *Journal of Policy Analysis and Management* 15: 395–424.

Campbell, Joan. 1992. *European Labor Unions*. Westport, Conn.: Greenwood.

Campbell, John C. 1992. *How Policies Change: Japanese Government and the Aging Society*. Princeton, N.J.: PUP.

Campbell, Martha Madison. 1998. "Schools of Thought: An Analysis of Interest Groups Influential in International Population Policy." *Population and Environment: A Journal of Interdisciplinary Studies* 19: 487–512.

Campion, Frank D. 1984. *The AMA and U.S. Health Policy Since 1940*. Chicago: UCP.

Caporaso, J. 1974. *The Structure and Function of European Integration*. Pacific Pallisades, Calif.: Goodyear.

Cardoso, Fernando Henrique, and Enzo Faletto. 1979. *Dependency and Development in Latin America*. Berkeley: UCAP.

Carnoy, Martin. 1984. *The State and Political Theory*. Princeton, N.J.: PUP.

Carr, Barry. 1991. "Labor and the Political Left in Mexico." In *Unions, Workers and the State in Mexico*, U.S.-Mexico Contemporary Perspectives Series, 2, ed. Kevin J. Middlebrook. San Diego: Center for U.S.-Mexican Studies, University of California San Diego.

Carroll, R. Bruce. 1969. "Intergovernmental Administrative Relations." In *Cooperation and Conflict: Readings in American Federalism*, eds. Daniel J Elazar, et al., Itasca, Ill.: F. E. Peacock.

Carroll, William K. 1986. *Corporate Power and Canadian Capitalism*. Vancouver: University of British Columbia Press.

Casanova, Jose. 1997. "Globalizing Catholicism and the return to a 'universal church.'" In *Transnational Religion and Fading States*. S. Hoeber Rudolph and J. Piscatori, cited below.

Castells, Manuel. 1983. *City and the Grassroots*. Berkeley: UCAP.

Castles, Francis G. 1967. *Pressure groups and political culture: A comparative study*. London: Routledge & Kegan Paul.

Cater, Douglass. 1964. *Power in Washington*. New York: Vintage.

Cavanagh, Michael. 1998. "Offshore Health and Safety Policy in the North Sea: Policy Networks in Britain and Norway." In *Comparing Policy Networks*. D. Marsh, cited below.

Cawson, Alan. 1978. "Pluralism, Corporatism and the Role of the State." *Government and Opposition* 13: 178–98.

———, ed. 1985. *Organised Interests and the State: Studies in Meso-Corporatism*. London: Sage.

———. 1986. *Corporatism and Political Theory*. Oxford: Blackwell.

———. 1988. "Is There A Corporatist Theory of The State?" In *Democracy and the Capitalist State*, ed. G. Duncan. Cambridge, U.K.: CUP.

———. 1992. "Interests, Groups and Public Policy-Making: The Case of the European Consumer Electronics Industry." In *Organized Interests in the European Community*. J. Greenwood, cited below.

Cawson, Alan, K. Morgan, D. Webber, P. Holmes, and A. Stevens. 1990. *A Hostile Brothers: Competition and Closure in the European Electronics Industry*. Oxford: Clarendon.

CBD. 1994. *Directory of British Associations*. Beckenham: CBD Research.

CBS / *New York Times* Poll. 1984. (2 July).

Cernea, Michael. 1988. *Non-Governmental Organisations and Local Development*. Washington, D.C.: The World Bank.

Cerney, Philip G., ed. 1993. *Finance and World Politics*. Brookfield, Vt.: Edward Elgar.

Chamberlain, Lawrence. 1946. *The President, Congress and Legislation*. New York: Columbia University Press.

Chan, Anita. 1994. "Revolution or Corporatism? Workers and Trade Unions in Post-Mao China." In *China's Quiet Revolution*. D. Goodman, cited below.

Chan, Sucheng. 1991. *Asian Americans: An Interpretive History*. Boston: Twayne.

Chang, King-yuh, ed. 1989. *Political and Social Changes in Taiwan and Mainland China*. Institute of International Relations of National Chengchi University, Monograph No. 35.

Chang, Y. C. 1976. *Factional and Coalition Politics in China: The Cultural Revolution and Its Aftermath*. New York: Praeger.

Chapman, Herrick, Mark Kesselman, and Martin Schain, eds. 1998. *A Century of Organized Labor in France: A Union Movement for the Twenty-first Century?* New York: SMP.

Chappell, Harry W., Jr. 1982. "Campaign Contributions and Congressional Voting." *Review of Economics and Statistics* 64: 77–83.

Chappell, Henry, Thomas Havrilesky, and Rob McGregor. 1993. "Partisan Monetary Policies: Presidential Influence Through the Power of Presidential Appointments." *Quarterly Journal of Economics* 108: 185–218.

Charnovitz, Steven. 1997. "Two centuries of participation: NGOs and international governance." *Michigan Journal of International Law* 18: 183–286.

Chatfield, Charles. 1997. "Intergovernmental and Nongovernmental Associations to 1945." In *Transnational Social Movements and Global Politics*. Jackie Smith, et al., cited below.

Chazan, Naomi. 1982. "The New Politics of Participation in Tropical Africa," *Comparative Politics* 14: 169–90.

REFERENCES

Chen, Martha Alter. 1996. "Engendering World Conferences: The International Women's Movement and the UN." In *NGOs, the UN, and Global Governance.* T. Weiss and L. Gordenker, cited below.

Childs, Harwood L. 1938. "Pressure Groups and Propaganda." In *The American Political Scene,* rev. ed., ed. Edward B. Logan. New York: Harper & Brothers.

Chiesi, Antonio M. 1991. "The Logic of Membership in Chemical Business Interest Associations." In *International Markets and Global Firms.* A. Martinelli, cited below.

Chilcote, Ronald H. 1994. *Theories of Comparative Politics.* 2nd ed. Boulder, Colo.: Westview.

Chittick, William O. 1970. *State Department, Press and Pressure Groups: A Role Analysis.* New York: Wiley-Interscience.

Choate, Pat. 1990. *Agents of Influence: How Japan's Lobbyists in the United States Manipulate America's Political and Economic System.* New York, Knopf.

Chong, Dennis. 1991. *Collective Action and the Civil Rights Movement.* Chicago: UCP.

Christensen, Terry. 1995. *Local Politics: Governing at the Grassroots.* Belmont, Calif.: Wadsworth.

Chubb, John E. 1983. *Interest Groups and the Bureaucracy: The Politics of Energy.* Stanford, Calif.: Stanford University Press.

Chubb, John E., and Terry M. Moe. 1990. *Politics, Markets and America's Schools.* Washington, D.C.: Brookings.

Church, Clive H. 1989. "Behind the Consociational Screen: Politics in Contemporary Switzerland." *West European Politics* 12: 35–54.

Cibulka, James G., Rodney J. Reed, and Kenneth K. Wong, eds. 1992. *The Politics of Urban Education in the United States.* Washington, D.C.: Falmer Press.

Cigler, Allan J. 1986. "From Protest Group to Interest Group: The Making of American Agriculture Movement, Inc." In *Interest Group Politics,* 2nd ed. A. Cigler and B. Loomis, cited below.

———. 1991a. "Political Parties and Interest Groups: Competitors, Collaborators and Uneasy Allies." In *American Political Parties: A Reader,* ed. Eric Uslaner. Itasca, Ill.: F. E. Peacock.

———. 1991b. "Interest Groups: A Subfield in Search of an Identity." In *Political Science: Looking to the Future,* ed. William Crotty. Vol. 4. Evanston, Ill: Northwestern University Press.

———. 1991c. "Organizational Maintenance and Political Activity on the Cheap: The American Agriculture Movement." In *Interest Group Politics,* 3rd ed. A. Cigler and B. Loomis, cited below.

Cigler, Allan J., and Burdett A. Loomis. 1995a. "Contemporary Interest Group Politics: More Than 'More of the Same.'" In *Interest Group Politics,* 4th ed., A. Cigler and B. Loomis, cited below.

———. 1998a, "From Big Bird to Bill Gates: Organized Interests and the Emergence of Hyperpolitics." In *Interest Group Politics,* 5th ed. A. Cigler and B. Loomis, cited below.

Cigler, Allan J., and Burdett A. Loomis, eds. 1983. *Interest Group Politics.* Washington, D.C.: CQP.

———. 1986. *Interest Group Politics.* 2nd ed. Washington, D.C.: CQP.

———. 1991. *Interest Group Politics.* 3rd ed. Washington, D.C.: CQP.

———. 1995b. *Interest Group Politics.* 4th ed. Washington, D.C.: CQP.

————. 1998b. *Interest Group Politics*. 5th ed. Washington, D.C.: CQP.

————. 2002. *Interest Group Politics*. 6th ed. Washington, D.C.: CQP.

Cigler, Allan J., and Anthony J. Nownes. 1995. "Public Interest Entrepreneurs and Group Patrons." In *Interest Group Politics*, 4th ed. A. Cigler and B. Loomis, cited above.

Cigler, Beverly A. 1993. "Challenges Facing Fiscal Federalism in the 1990s." *PS: Political Science and Politics* 36: 181–86.

————. 1995. "Not Just Another Special Interest: Intergovernmental Representation." In *Interest Group Politics*, 4th ed. A. Cigler and B. Loomis, cited above.

Cingranelli, David L. 1983. "State Government Lobbies in the National Political Process." *State Government* 56: 22–27.

Clark, Peter B., and James Q. Wilson. 1961. "Incentive Systems: A Theory of Organizations." *Administrative Science Quarterly* 6: 129–66.

Clarke, G. 1998. "Nongovernmental organisations and politics in the developing world." *Political Studies* XLVI: 36–52.

Clegg, Stewart R. 1989. *Frameworks of Power*. London: Sage.

Clemens, Elisabeth S. 1993. "Organizational Repertoires and Institutional Change." *AJS* 98: 755–98.

————. 1997. *The People's Lobby: Organizational Innovation and the Rise of Interest Group Politics in the United States 1890–1925*. Chicago: UCP.

Cleveland, Les. 1972. *The Anatomy of Influence: Pressure Groups and Politics in New Zealand*. Wellington: Hicks Smith.

————. 1985. "The Sound and the Fury: Ideologically Motivated Pressure Groups." In *New Zealand Politics in Perspective*, ed. Hyam Gold. Auckland: Longman Paul.

Close, David H. 1998. "Environmental NGOs in Greece: The Acheloos Campaign as a Case Study of their Influence." *Environmental Politics* 7: 55–77.

Cock, Jacklyn. 1994. "Women and the Military: Implications for Demilitarization in the 1990s in South Africa." *Gender and Society* 8: 152–69.

Coen, David. 1997. "The Evolution of the Large Firm as a Political Actor in the European Union." *Journal of European Public Policy* 4: 91–108.

COGEL [Council on Governmental Ethics Laws]. 1995. *Blue Book: Campaign Finance, Ethics, and Lobby Laws*. Lexington, Ky.: Council of State Governments.

Cohen, Abner. 1969. *Custom and Politics in Urban Africa*. Berkeley: UCAP.

Cohen, Bernard C. 1959. "The Influence of Non-Governmental Groups on Foreign Policy-Making." Studies in Citizen Participation in International Relations. Boston: World Peace Foundation.

Cohen, Cathy. 1999. *The Boundaries of Blackness: AIDS and the Breakdown of Black Politics*. Chicago: UCP.

Cohen, Jeffrey. 1992. *The Politics of Telecommunications Regulation: The States and the Divestiture of AT & T*. Armonk, N.Y.: M. E. Sharpe.

Cohen, Michael P. 1988. *The History of the Sierra Club, 1892–1970*. San Francisco: Sierra Club Books.

Coker, F. W. 1924. "Pluralistic Theories and the Attack Upon State Sovereignty." In *A History of Political Theories: Recent Times*, eds. Charles E. Merriam and H. Barnes. New York: Macmillan.

Cole, Allan B. 1967. "Political Roles of Taiwanese Enterprises." *Asian Survey* 7: 645–54.

REFERENCES

Coleman, James S. 1960. "The Politics of Sub-Saharan Africa." In *The Politics of Developing Areas*, eds. Gabriel A. Almond and James S. Coleman. Princeton, N.J.: PUP.

Coleman, William D. 1988. *Business and Politics: A Study of Collective Action.* Kingston, Ontario: McGill-Queen's University Press.

———. 1990. "State Traditions and Comprehensive Business Associations: A Comparative Structural Analysis." *Political Studies* 38: 231–52.

———. 1993. "Reforming Corporatism: The French Banking Policy Community." *West European Politics* 16: 122–43.

———. 1994. "Keeping the Shotgun Behind the Door: Governing the Securities Industry in Canada, the United Kingdom and the United States." In *Governing Capitalist Economies.* J. Rogers Hollingsworth, P. Schmitter, and W. Streeck, cited below.

———. 1997. "Associational Governance in a Globalizing Era: Weathering the Storm." In *Contemporary Capitalism: The Embeddedness of Institutions*, eds. J. Rogers Hollingsworth and Robert Boyer. Cambridge, U.K.: CUP.

Coleman, William D., and Wyn Grant. 1984. "Business Associations and Public Policy: A Comparison of Organisational Development in Britain and Canada." *Journal of Public Policy* 4: 209–35.

———. 1988. "The Organizational Cohesion and Political Access of Business: A Study of Comprehensive Associations." *European Journal of Political Research* 16: 467–87.

Coleman, William, and Henry Jacek. 1983. "The Roles and Activities of Business Interest Associations in Canada." *Canadian Journal of Political Science* XVI: 257–80.

———, eds. 1989. *Regionalism, Business Interests and Public Policy.* London: Sage.

Collier, David. 1993. "The Comparative Method." In *Political Science: The State of the Discipline*, ed. Ada Finifter. Washington, D.C.: The American Political Science Association.

Collier, Ruth Berins, and David Collier. 1979. "Inducements Versus Constraints: Disaggregating Corporatism." *APSR* 73: 967–86.

———. 1991. *Shaping the Political Arena: Critical Junctures, the Labor Movement and Regime Dynamics in Latin America.* Princeton, N.J.: PUP.

Collier, Ruth Berins, and James Mahoney. 1997. "Adding Collective Actors to Collective Outcomes: Labor and Recent Democratization in South America and Southern Europe." *Comparative Politics* 29: 285–304.

Columbia Law Review. 1947. "Federal Lobbying Act of 1946." (Jan.): 98–109. [no author given].

Compston, Hugh. 1994. "Union Participation in Economic Policy-Making in Austria, Switzerland, the Netherlands, Belgium and Ireland, 1970–1993." *West European Politics* 17: 123–45.

———. 1995a. "Union Participation in Economic Policy-Making in Scandinavia, 1970–1993." *West European Politics* 18: 98–115.

———. 1995b. "Union Participation in Economic Policy-Making in France, Italy, Germany and Britain, 1970–1993." *West European Politics* 18: 314–39.

———. 1997. "Union Power, Policy Making, and Unemployment in Western Europe, 1972–1993." *Comparative Political Studies* 30: 723–51.

———. 1998. "The End of National Policy Concertation? Western Europe Since the Single European Act." *Journal of European Public Policy* 5: 507–26.

Congressional Quarterly, Inc. 1997. "Tobacco lobby faces a tougher road in an era in which smoking has lost cachet." *Congressional Quarterly Weekly Report* 55, No. 44 (8 November 1997).

Conniff, Michael L., ed. 1982. *Latin American Populism in Comparative Perspective.* Albuquerque: University of New Mexico Press.

Constantelos, John. 2001. "Italy: The Erosion and Demise of Party Dominance. In *Political Parties and Interest Groups.* C. Thomas, cited below.

Conteh-Morgan, Earl. 1994. "The Military and Human Rights in a Post-Cold War Africa." *Armed Forces and Society* 21: 69–87.

Conway, M. Margaret. 1991. "PACs in the Political Process." In *Interest Group Politics.* 3rd ed. A. Cigler and B. Loomis, cited above.

Conway, M. Margaret, and Joanne Connor Green. 1995. "Political Action Committees and the Political Process in the 1990s." In *Interest Group Politics,* 4th ed. A. Cigler and B. Loomis, cited above.

———. 1998. "Political Action Committees and Campaign Finance." In *Interest Group Politics,* 5th ed. A. Cigler and B. Loomis, cited above.

Cook, Constance Ewing. 1998. *Lobbying for Higher Education: How Universities and Colleges Influence Federal Higher Education Policy.* Nashville: Vanderbilt University Press.

Cornell, Stephen. 1988. *Return of the Native: American Indian Political Resurgence.* New York: OUP.

Cortner, Richard C. 1968. "Strategies and Tactics of Litigants in Constitutional Cases." *Journal of Public Law* 17: 287–307.

———. 1970. *The Reapportionment Cases.* Knoxville: University of Tennessee Press.

Costain, Anne N. 1980. "The Struggle for a National Women's Lobby." *WPQ* 33: 476–91.

———. 1981. "Representing Women." *WPQ* 34: 100–15.

———. 1992a. *Inviting Women's Rebellion.* Baltimore: JHUP.

———. 1992b. "Social Movements as Interest Groups: The Case of the Women's Movement." In *The Politics of Interests.* M. Petracca. cited below.

Costain, Anne N., and Andrew S. McFarland, eds. 1998. *Social Movements and American Political Institutions.* Lanham, Md.: Rowman & Littlefield.

Council of State Governments. 2003. *The Book of the States.* Vol. 35. Lexington, Ky.: Council of State Governments. Published biannually.

Covey, J. 1995. "Accountability and effectiveness in NGO policy alliances." *Journal of International Development* 7: 857–67.

Cowles, Maria Green. 1995. "Setting the Agenda for a New Europe: The ERT and EC 1992." *Journal of Common Market Studies* 33: 501–26.

———. 1996a. "German Big Business: Learning to Play the European Game." *German Politics and Society,* 14: 73–107.

———. 1996b. "Organising Industrial Coalitions." In *Participation and Policymaking in the European Union,* eds. Helen Wallace and Alasdair Young. London: OUP.

———. 1996c. "The EU Committee of AmCham: The Powerful Voice of American Firms in Brussels." *Journal of European Public Policy* 3: 339–58.

———. 2001a. "The TABD and Business-Government Relations: Challenge and Opportunity." In *Transforming Europe: Europeanization and Domestic Change,* eds. Maria Green Cowles, James Caporaso, and Thomas Risse. Ithaca, N.Y.: Cornell University Press.

———. 2001b. "The Transatlantic Business Dialogue: The Private Face of Transatlantic Relations." In *Ever Closer Partnership: Policy-Making in US-EU Relations*, eds. Eric Philippart and Pascaline Winand. Brussels: Peter Lange / Inter-University Press.

Cox, A., and N. O'Sullivan. 1988. *The Corporate State*. Brookfield, Vt.: Gower.

Cox, Terry. 1993. "Democratization and the Growth of Pressure Groups in Soviet and Post-Soviet Politics." In *Pressure Groups*. J. Richardson, cited below.

Coxall, Bill, Lynton Robins, and W. N. Coxall. 1998. *British Politics Since the War.* London: SMP.

Craig, Barbara Hinkson, and David M. O'Brien. 1993. *Abortion and American Politics.* Chatham, N.J.: Chatham House.

Crampton, John A. 1965. *The National Farmers Union: Ideology of a Pressure Group.* Lincoln: University of Nebraska Press.

Crawford, Alan. 1980. *Thunder on the Right.* New York: Pantheon.

Crawford, Kenneth G. 1939. *The Pressure Boys: The Inside Story of Lobbying in America.* New York: Julian Messner.

Creighton, Lucy Black. 1976. *Pretenders to the Throne: The Consumer Movement in the United States.* Lexington, Mass.: Lexington Books.

Crepaz, Markus M. L. 1992. "Corporatism in Decline? An Empirical Analysis of the Impact of Corporatism on Macroeconomic Performance and Industrial Disputes in 18 Industrialized Democracies." *Comparative Political Studies* 25: 139–68.

———. 1995. "An Institutional Dinosaur: Austrian Corporatism in the Post-industrial Age," *West European Politics* 18: 64–88.

Crepaz, Markus M. L., and Arend Lijphart. 1995, "Linking and Integrating Corporatism and Consensus Democracy: Theory, Concepts and Evidence." *BJPS* 25: 281–88.

Critchlow, Donald T. 1985. *The Brookings Institution, 1916–1952.* DeKalb: Northern Illinois University Press.

Cronin, Thomas E. 1989. *Direct Democracy: The Politics of Initiative, Referendum and Recall.* Cambridge, Mass.: HUP.

Crook, John. 1997. *Understanding the Gun Lobby.* Melbourne: GCA [Gun Control Australia].

Crotty, William J. 1984. *American Parties in Decline.* Boston: Little, Brown.

Crotty, William, Mildred A. Schwartz, and John C. Green, eds. 1994. *Representing Interests and Interest Group Representation.* Lanham, Md.: UPA.

Crouch, Colin. 1993. *Industrial Relations and European State Traditions.* Oxford: OUP.

———. 1995. "Organized Interests as Resources or as Constraint: Rival Logics of Vocational Training Policy." In *Organized Industrial Relations in Europe.* C. Crouch and F. Traxler, cited below.

Crouch, Colin, and R. Dore, eds. 1990. *Corporatism and Accountability.* Oxford: Clarendon.

Crouch, Colin, and Anand Menon. 1997. "Organised Interests and the State." In *Developments in West European Politics*, eds. Martin Rhodes, Paul Heywood, and Vincent Wright. London: Macmillan.

Crouch, Colin, and Franz Traxler, eds. 1995. *Organized Industrial Relations in Europe: What Future?* Aldershot: Avebury.

Crouch, Harold. 1966. *Trade Unions and Politics in India.* Bombay: Manaktalas.

Cullen, Peter, ed. 1990. *No is Not an Answer: Lobbying for Success.* Sydney: Allen & Unwin.

Culpepper, Pepper D. 1993. "Organisational Competition and the Neo-corporatist Fallacy in French Agriculture." *West European Politics* 16: 295–315.

Cultural Survival. 1993. *State of the Peoples.* Cambridge, U.K.: Cultural Survival.

Cuneo, Michael. 1989. *Catholics Against the Church: Anti-Abortion Protest in Toronto, 1969–1985.* Toronto: University of Toronto Press.

Curtis, Gerald L. 1975. "Big Business and Political Influence." In *Modern Japanese Organization and Decision-Making,* ed. Ezra F. Vogel. Berkeley: UCAP.

Curtiss, Richard H. 1990. *Stealth PACs: How Israel's American Lobby Seeks to Control U.S. Middle East Policy.* Washington, D.C.: American Educational Trust.

Czada, Roland. 1987. "The Impact of Interest Politics on Flexible Adjustment Policies." In *Coping with the Economic Crisis: Alternative Responses to Economic Recession in Advanced Industrial Societies,* eds. Hans Keman, Heikki Paloheimo, and Paul F. Whiteley. London: Sage.

Daalder, Hans. 1966. "The Netherlands: Opposition in a Segmented Society." In *Political Opposition in Western Democracies,* ed. Robert Dahl. New Haven, Conn.: YUP.

Daalder, Hans, and Galen Irwin. 1974. "Interests and Institutions in The Netherlands: An Assessment by the People and by Parliament." *Annals* 413 (May): 58–71.

———, eds. 1989. *Politics in the Netherlands: How Much Change?* Special Issue of *West European Politics* 12 (1).

Dahl, Robert A. 1956. *A Preface to Democratic Theory.* Chicago: UCP.

———. 1957. "The Concept of Power." *Behavioral Science* 2: 201–15.

———. 1961. *Who Governs?* New Haven, Conn.: YUP.

———. 1982. *Dilemmas of Pluralist Democracy.* New Haven, Conn.: YUP.

———. 1984. "Polyarchy, Pluralism and Scale." *SPS* 7 225–39.

———. 1989. *Democracy and Its Critics.* New Haven, Conn.: YUP.

Dahlerup, Drude, and Brita Gulli. 1985. "Women's Organizations in the Nordic Countries: Lack of Force or Counterforce?" In *Unfinished Democracy: Women in Nordic Politics,* eds. Elina Haavio-Mannila, et al. Oxford: Pergamon.

Daigon, Glenn. 2000a. "Handgun Control, Inc." In *Encyclopedia of Interest Groups and Lobbyists.* I. Ness, cited below.

———. 2000b. "The National Rifle Association." In *Encyclopedia of Interest Groups and Lobbyists.* I. Ness, cited below.

Dalton, Russell J., and Manfred Kuechler, eds. 1990. *Challenging the Political Order: New Social and Political Movements in Western Democracies.* Cambridge, Mass.: Polity Press.

Dalton, Russell J., and Martin P. Wattenberg, eds. 2000. *Parties Without Partisans: Political Change in Advanced Industrial Democracies.* New York: OUP.

Damgaard, Erik, and Kjell A. Eliassen. 1978. "Corporate Pluralism in Danish Law-Making." *SPS* 1: 285–313.

Dark, Taylor E. 1999. *The Unions and the Democrats.* Ithaca, N.Y.: ILR Press.

REFERENCES

Daugbjerg, Christian. 1998a. "Linking Policy Networks and Environmental Policies: Nitrate Policy Making in Denmark and Sweden, 1970–1995." *Public Administration* 76: 275–94.

———. 1998b. "Similar Problems, Different Policies: Policy Networks and Environmental Policy in Danish and Swedish Agriculture." In *Comparing Policy Networks*. D. Marsh, cited below.

Davidson, Chandler, and Bernard Grofman. 1994. *Quiet Revolution in the South: The Impact of the Voting Rights Act, 1965–1990*. Princeton, N.J.: PUP.

Davidson, Osha Gray. 1998. *Under Fire: The NRA and the Battle for Gun Control*. Iowa City, Iowa: University of Iowa Press.

Davidson, Roger H. 1977. "Breaking Up Those Cozy Triangles: An Impossible Dream?" In *Legislative Reform and Public Policy*, eds. Susan Welch and John G. Peters. New York: Praeger.

Davies, Robert, et al. 1984. *The Struggle for South Africa: A Reference Guide to Movements, Organizations and Institutions*, Vols. I and II. London: Zed Press.

Davis, David Howard. 1993. *Energy Politics*. 4th ed. New York: SMP.

Davis, Deborah, et al., eds. 1995. *Urban Spaces in Contemporary China*. New York: CUP.

Davis, Frank L., and Albert H. Wurth, Jr. 1993. "American Interest Group Research: Sorting Out Internal and External Perspectives." *Political Studies*, XLI: 435–52.

Davis, Geoffrey V. 1994. *South Africa*. rev. ed., World Bibliographical Series, Vol. 7. Oxford: Clio Press.

Davis, Steven M. 1996. "Environmental Politics and the Changing Context of Interest Groups Organization." *Social Science Journal* 33: 343–57.

Dawes, Robyn M., John M. Orbell, Randy T. Simmons, and Alphons J. C. van de Kragt. 1986. "Organizing Groups for Collective Action." *APSR* 80: 1171–85.

Dawson, Michael C. 1995. *Behind the Mule Race and Class in African-American Politics*. Princeton, N.J.: PUP.

Day, Christine L. 1990. *What Older Americans Think: Interest Groups and Aging Policy*. Princeton, N.J.: PUP.

Day, D. 1987. *The Whale War*. San Francisco: Sierra Club Books.

———. 1989. *The Environmental Wars: Reports from the Front Lines*. New York: SMP.

Deakin, James. 1966. *The Lobbyists*. Washington, D.C.: The Public Affairs Press.

DeConde, Alexander. 1992. *Ethnicity, Race and American Foreign Policy: A History*. Boston: Northeastern University Press.

Deegan, Heather. 1999. *South Africa Reborn: Building a New Democracy*. London: University College of London Press.

Deeks, J., and N. Perry, eds. 1992. *Controlling Interests: Business, the State and Society in New Zealand*. Auckland: Auckland University Press.

DeGregorio, Christine, and Jack E. Rossotti. 1995. "Campaigning for the Court: Interest Group Participation in the Bork and Thomas Confirmation Process." In *Interest Group Politics*, 4th ed. A. Cigler and B. Loomis, cited above.

deKieffer, Donald E. 1981. *How to Lobby Congress: A Guide for the Citizen Lobbyist*. New York: Dodd, Mead.

———. 1997. *The Citizen's Guide to Lobbying Congress*. Chicago: Chicago Review Press.

Delaney, John Thomas, Jack Fiorito, and Marick F. Masters. 1988. "The Effects of Union Organizational and Environmental Characteristics on Union Political Action." *AJPS* 42: 616–43.

DeLeon, Richard. 1992. *Left Coast City*. Lawrence: University Press of Kansas.

Deloria, Vine, Jr. 1969. *Custer Died for Your Sins: An Indian Manifesto*. New York: Macmillan.

———. 1985. *Behind the Trail of Broken Treaties: An Indian Declaration of Independence*. rev. ed. Austin: University of Texas Press.

D'Emilio, John. 1983. *Sexual Politics, Sexual Communities*. Chicago: UCP.

———. 1992. *Making Trouble: Essays on Gay History, Politics and the University*. New York: Routledge.

Demsetz, Harold. 1968. "Why Regulate Utilities?" *Journal of Law and Economics* 8: 55–65.

Denham, Andrew, and Mark Garnett. 1995. "Rethinking 'Think Tanks': A British Perspective." In *Contemporary Political Studies*, Vol. 1. eds. J. Louenduski and J. Stanyer. Great Britain: Political Studies Association.

Denzau, Arthur T., and Michael C. Munger. 1986. "Legislators and Interest Groups: How Unorganized Interests Get Represented." *APSR* 80: 89–106.

Derthick, Martha A., ed. 2001. *Up in Smoke: From Legislation to Litigation in Tobacco Politics*. Washington, D.C. CQP.

Derthick, Martha, and Paul Quirk. 1985. *The Politics of Deregulation*. Washington, D.C.: Brookings.

Desai, Ashwin, and Adam Habib. 1997. "Labour Relations in Transition: The Rise of Corporatism in South Africa's Automobile Industry." *Journal of Modern African Studies* 35: 495–518.

De Soto, William. 1995a. *The Politics of Business Organizations: Understanding the Role of State Chambers of Commerce*. Lanham, Md.: UPA.

———. 1995b. "Cities in State Politics: Views of Mayors and Managers." *State and Local Government Review* 27: 188–94.

Devall, Bill. 1992. "Deep Ecology and Radical Environmentalism." In *American Environmentalism: The U.S. Environmental Movement, 1970–1990*, eds. Riley E. Dunlap and Angela G. Mertig. Philadelphia: Taylor & Francis.

Devine, Donald. 1972. *The Political Culture of the United States*. Boston: Little, Brown.

De Vries, Walter. 1960. "The Michigan Lobbyist." Ph.D. Dissertation, Michigan State University.

De Vroom, Bert. 1985. "Quality Regulation in the Dutch Pharmaceutical Industry: Conditions for Private Regulation by Business Interest Associations." In *Private Interest Government*. W. Streeck and P. Schmitter, cited below.

DeWachter, Wilfried. 1987. "Changes in a Particratie: The Belgian Party System from 1944 to 1986." In *Party Systems in Denmark, Austria, Switzerland, The Netherlands and Belgium*, ed. Hans Daalder, London: Frances Pinter.

Dexter, Lewis Anthony. 1956. "What Congressmen Hear: The Mail." *Public Opinion Quarterly* 20: 16–57.

———. 1969. *How Organizations Are Represented in Washington*. Indianapolis: Bobbs-Merrill.

Dickson, Paul. 1971. *Think Tanks*. New York: Atheneum.

Dilger, Robert Jay. 1992. *Neighborhood Politics: Residential Community Associations in American Governance.* New York: New York University Press.

DiMaggio, Paul, and Walter Powell. 1983. "The Iron Cage Revisited: Institutional Isomorphism and Collective Rationality in Organizational Fields." *American Sociological Review* 48: 147–60.

———. 1991. *The New Institutionalism in Organizational Analysis.* Chicago: UCP.

Dittmer, Lowell. 1978. "Bases of Power in Chinese Politics." *World Politics* 3: 26–61.

Dizard, Jan E., Robert M. Muth, and Stephen P. Andrews, eds. 1999. *Guns in America: A Reader.* New York: New York University Press.

Dodd, Lawrence C., and Richard L. Schott. 1979. *Congress and the Administrative State.* New York: Wiley.

Doig, A. 1990. *Corruption and Misconduct in Contemporary British Politics.* Special Issue of *Corruption and Reform,* Vol. 5, No. 3.

Domhoff, William G. 1978. *The Powers That Be: Processes of Ruling-Class Domination in America.* New York: Random House.

Domino, John C. 2003. *Civil Rights & Liberties in the 21st Century.* New York: Longman.

Donnelly, Thomas C., ed. 1940. *Rocky Mountain Politics.* Albuquerque: University of New Mexico Press.

Donohue, William A. 1985. *The Politics of the American Civil Liberties Union.* New Brunswick, N.J.: Transaction Books.

Donovan, Todd, and Joseph Snipp. 1994. "Support for Legislative Term Limitations in California: Group Representation, Partisanship, and Campaign Information." *JOP* 56: 492–501.

Douglas, Clifford E., and Phillip Wilbur. 1993. "The Tobacco Lobby Buys Acquiescence." *World Smoking & Health: An American Cancer Society Journal* 18, No. 1: 17–20.

Douglas, Mary, and Aaron Wildavsky. 1982. *Risk and Culture.* Berkeley: UCAP.

Dowie, Mark. 1995. *Losing Ground: American Environmentalism at the Close of the Twentieth Century.* Cambridge, Mass.: MIT Press.

Downs, Anthony. 1957. *An Economic Theory of Democracy.* New York: Harper & Row.

Downs, G. 1976. *Bureaucracy, Innovation and Public Policy.* Lexington, Mass.: D.C. Heath.

Drew, Elizabeth. 1983. *Politics and Money.* New York: Collier.

Drezon-Tepler, Marcia. 1990. *Interest Groups and Political Change in Israel.* Albany, N.Y.: SUNY Press.

Dubs, Alf. 1988. *Lobbying: An Insider's Guide to the Parliamentary Process.* London: Pluto Press.

Dunlap, Riley E., and Angela G. Mertig, eds. 1992. *American Environmentalism: The U.S. Environmental Movement, 1970–1990.* Philadelphia: Taylor & Francis.

Dunleavy, Patrick, and Brendan O'Leary. 1987. *Theories of the State: The Politics of Liberal Democracy.* London: Macmillan.

Dunn, James A., Jr., and Anthony Perl. 1994. "Policy Networks and Industrial Revitalization: High Speed Rail Initiatives in France and Germany." *Journal of Public Policy* 14: 311–43.

Duverger, Maurice. 1972. *Party Politics and Pressure Groups: A Comparative Introduction.* New York: Thomas Y. Crowell.

Dye, Thomas R. 1990. *Power and Society.* 5th ed. Pacific Grove, Calif.: Brooks / Cole,

Dye, Thomas R., and Harmon Zeigler. 1970. *The Irony of Democracy.* Belmont, Calif.: Wadsworth.

Dyson, Kenneth. 1982. "West Germany: The Search for a Rationalist Consensus." In *Policy Styles in Western Europe,* ed. Jeremy J. Richardson. London: Allen & Unwin.

Dyson, Lowell K. 1986. *Farmers' Organizations.* Westport, Conn.: Greenwood.

Eastman, Hope. 1977. *Lobbying: A Constitutionally Protected Right.* Washington, D.C.: AEI.

Ebersole, Luke. 1951. *Church Lobbying in the Nation's Capitol.* New York: Macmillan.

Eckstein, Harry. 1960. *Pressure Group Politics: The Case of the British Medical Association.* London: Allen & Unwin.

Edelman, Murray. 1964. *The Symbolic Uses of Politics.* Urbana: University of Illinois Press.

Edinger, Lewis J. 1993. "Pressure Group Politics in West Germany." In *Pressure Groups.* J. Richardson, cited below.

Edwards, Michael. 1999. "NGO performance—what breeds success?" *World Development* 27: 361–74.

Edwards, Michael., and David Hulme, eds. 1995. *Beyond the Magic Bullet: NGO Performance and Accountability in the Post-Cold War World.* London: Macmillan.

Ehrmann, Henry W. 1957. *Organized Business in France.* Princeton, N.J.: PUP.

———, ed. 1958. *Interest Groups on Four Continents.* Pittsburgh: Pittsburgh University Press.

Einhorn, Eric S., and John Logue. 1989. *Modern Welfare States: Politics and Policies in Social Democratic Scandinavia.* New York: Praeger.

Eisenberg, Avigail I. 1995. *Reconstituting Political Pluralism.* Albany, N.Y.: SUNY Press.

Eismeier, Theodore J., and Phillip H. Pollock III. 1988. *Business, Money and the Rise of Corporate PACs in American Elections.* Westport, Conn.: Quorum.

Elazar, Daniel J. 1972. *American Federalism: A View from the States.* New York: Crowell.

———. 1975. *The Ecology of American Political Culture.* New York: Crowell.

———. 1994. *The American Mosaic: The Impact of Space, Time, and Culture on American Politics.* Boulder, Colo.: Westview.

Eliassen, Kjell A. 1981. "Organizations and Pressure Groups." In *Nordic Democracy.* E. Allardt, et al., cited above.

Elling, Richard C. 1999. "Administering State Programs: Performance and Politics." In *Politics in the American States: A Comparative Analysis,* 7th ed., eds. Virginia Gray, Russell L. Hanson, and Herbert Jacob. Washington, D.C.: CQP.

Ellis, Galen A., Robin L. Hobart, and Diane F. Reed. 1996. "Overcoming a Powerful Tobacco Lobby in Enacting Local Smoking Ordinances: The Contra Costa County Experience." *Journal of Public Health Policy* 17, No. 1: 28–46.

Ellis, Nigel. 1998. *Parliamentary Lobbying.* London: Heinemann.

Ellis, Richard. 1993. *American Political Cultures.* New York: OUP.

Ellwood, William N., ed. 1995. *Public Relations Inquiry as Rhetorical Criticism.* Westport, Conn.: Praeger.

Elphick, Richard, and Rodney Davenport, eds. 1997. *Christianity in South Africa.* Berkeley: UCAP.

Elvander, Nils. 1974. "Interest Groups in Sweden." *Annals* 413: 27–43.

Encarnacíon, Omar G. 1997. "Social Concertation in Democratic and Market Transitions: Comparative Lessons From Spain." *Comparative Political Studies* 30: 387–419.

Encyclopedia of Associations. 2003. 39th ed. Farmington Hills, Mich.: Gale Group.

Encyclopedia of Associations: Regional, State and Local Organizations. 2001. 12th ed. Detroit: Gale Research.

Englemann, Fred, and Mildred Schwartz. 1967. *Political Parties and the Canadian Social Structure.* Scarborough, Ontario: Prentice-Hall.

Engler, Robert. 1961. *The Politics of Oil.* Chicago: UCP.

Ensign, David. 1996. "Reforming Public Integrity Laws in an Era of Declining Trust." In *The Book of the States*, Vol. 31. Lexington, Ky.: Council of State Governments, 477–84.

Epp, Charles R. 1998. *The Rights Revolution: Lawyers, Activists, and Supreme Courts in Comparative Perspective.* Chicago: UCP.

Epstein, A. L. 1958. *Politics in an Urban African Community.* Manchester: Manchester University Press.

Epstein, Edwin. 1980. "Business and Labor Under the Federal Election Campaign Act of 1971." In *Parties, Interest Groups and Campaign Finance Laws*, ed. Michael J. Malbin. Washington, D.C.: AEI.

Epstein, Lee. 1985. *Conservatives in Court.* Knoxville: University of Tennessee Press.

———. 1991. "Courts and Interest Groups." In *The American Courts: A Critical Assessment*, eds. John B. Gates and Charles A. Johnson. Washington, D.C.: CQP.

———. 1994. "Exploring the Participation of Organized Interests in State Court Litigation." *PRQ* 47: 335–51.

Epstein, Lee, and Joseph F. Kobylka. 1992. *The Supreme Court and Legal Change: Abortion and the Death Penalty.* Chapel Hill: University of North Carolina Press.

Epstein, Lee, and C. K. Rowland. 1991. "Debunking the Myth of Interest Group Invincibility in the Courts." *APSR* 85: 205–17.

Epstein, Lee, and Thomas G. Walker. 1996. *Constitutional Law for a Changing America.* Washington, D.C.: CQP.

Epstein, Leon. 1980. "What Ever Happened to the British Party Model?" *APSR* 74: 9–22.

Erie, Steven P., and Harold Brackman. 1993. *Paths to Political Incorporation for Latinos and Asian Pacifics in California.* University of California: The California Policy Seminar.

Erikson, Robert S., Gerald C. Wright, Jr. and John P. McIver. 1989. "Political Parties, Public Opinion, and State Policy in the United States." *APSR* 83: 729–50.

———. 1993. *Statehouse Democracy: Public Opinion and Policy in the American States.* Cambridge, Mass.: CUP.

Espiritu, Yen L. 1992. *Asian American Panethnicity.* Philadelphia: Temple University Press.

Eulau, Heinz. 1964. "Lobbyists: The Wasted Profession." *Public Opinion Quarterly* 28: 27–38.

European Journal of Political Research. 1992. Special Issue: Policy Networks, Vol. 21, Nos. 1 & 2 (February).

Evans, Diana. 1986. "PAC Contributions and Roll-Call Voting: Conditional Power." In *Interest Group Politics*, 2nd ed. A. Cigler and B. Loomis, cited above.

———. 1991. "Lobbying the Committee: Interest Groups and the House Public Works and Transportation Committee." In *Interest Group Politics*, 3rd ed. A. Cigler and B. Loomis, cited above.

Evans, Peter. 1979. *Dependent Development: The Alliance of Multinational, State, and Local Capital in Brazil.* Princeton, N.J.: PUP.

Evanson, Robert K., and Thomas M. Magstadt. 2001. "The Czech Republic: Party Dominance in a Transitional System." In *Political Parties and Interest Groups.* C. Thomas, cited below.

Ewen, Alexander, ed. 1994. *Voice of Indigenous Peoples: Native People Address the United Nations.* Santa Fe, N. Mex.: Clear Light.

Fadia, Bahulal. 1980. *Pressure Groups in Indian Politics.* New Delhi: Radiant Publishers.

Fairchild, E. 1981. "Interest Groups in the Criminal Justice Process." *Journal of Criminal Justice* 9: 181–94.

Falkenheim, Victor C., ed. 1987. *Citizens and Groups in Contemporary China.* Ann Arbor: University of Michigan Center for Chinese Studies.

Farago, Peter. 1985. "Regulating Milk Markets: Corporatist Arrangements in the Swiss Dairy Industry." In *Private Interest Government.* W. Streeck and P. Schmitter, cited below.

Farer, Tom J. 1988. "The United States and Human Rights in Latin America: On the Eve of the Next Phase." *International Journal* 43: 473–98.

Farnleiter, Johann, and Erich Schmidt. 1982. "The Social Partnership." In *The Political Economy of Austria*, ed. Sven Arndt. Washington, D.C.: AEI.

Fatton, Robert, Jr. 1995. "Africa in the Age of Democratization: The Limitations of Civil Society." *African Studies Review* 38: 67–100.

Federal Election Commission. 1995. *1994 Congressional Fundraising Climbs to New High.* Washington, D.C.: Government Printing Office.

———. 1999. "FEC Issues Semi-Annual Federal PAC Count," (20 July).

Feeley, Malcolm. 1980. *The Policy Dilemma: Federal Crime Policy and the Law Enforcement Assistance Administration.* Minneapolis: University of Minnesota Press.

Feierabend, Ivo K., et. al. 1969. "Social Change and Political Violence: Cross National Patterns." In *Violence in America.* H. Graham and T. Gurr, cited below.

Feld, Werner J. 1966. "National Economic Interest Groups and Policy Formation in the EEC." *PSQ* 81: 392–411.

———. 1972. *Nongovernmental Forces and World Politics.* New York: Praeger.

Fenton, John H. 1957. *Politics in the Border States.* New Orleans: Houser Press.

———. 1966. *Midwest Politics.* New York: Holt, Rinehart and Winston.

Ferejohn, John A. 1974. *Pork Barrel Politics: Rivers and Harbors Legislation, 1947–1968.* Stanford, Calif.: Stanford University Press.

Ferguson, Thomas. 1995. *The Golden Rule: The Investment Theory of Party Competition and the Logic of Money-Driven Political Systems.* Chicago: UCP.

Ferree, Myra, and Patricia Martin, eds. 1995. *Feminist Organizations.* Philadelphia: Temple University Press.

Findlay, Christopher, and Jiang Shu. 1992 "Interest Group Conflicts in a Reforming Economy." In *Economic Reform and Social Change in China*, ed. Andrew Watson. London: Routledge.

Finer, Samuel. E. 1958. *Anonymous Empire.* London: Pall Mall.

Finsen, Lawrence. 1994. *The Animal Rights Movement in America.* New York: Twayne.

Fiorina, Morris P. 1980. "The Decline of Collective Responsibility in American Politics." *Daedalus* 109: 25–45.

Fisher, Julie. 1997. *Nongovernments: NGOs and the political development of the third world.* Hartford, Conn.: Kumarian.

Fishman, Robert M. 1990. *Working Class Organization and the Return to Democracy.* Ithaca, N.Y.: Cornell University Press.

Fitzmaurice, John. 1983. *The Politics of Belgium: Crisis and Compromise in a Plural Society.* New York: SMP.

Fleischer, Richard. 1993. "PAC Contributions and Congressional Voting on National Defense." *LSQ* 18: 391–409.

Flemming, Roy B., Michael MacLeod, and Jeffery Talbert. 1998. "Witnesses at the Confirmations? The Appearance of Organized Interests at Senate Hearings of Federal Judicial Appointments, 1945–92." *PRQ* 51: 617–31.

Fleras, Augies. 1992. *The Nations Within: Aboriginal-State Relations in Canada, the United States and New Zealand.* New York: OUP.

Fleron, F. J., ed. 1969. *Communist Studies and the Social Sciences: Essays on the Methodology and Empirical Theory.* Chicago: Rand McNally.

Foley, M. 1991. *American Political Ideas.* Manchester: Manchester University Press.

Foreman, Christopher H., Jr. 1995. "Grassroots Victim Organizations: Mobilizing for Personal and Public Health." In *Interest Group Politics*, 4th ed. A. Cigler and B. Loomis, cited above.

Foundation for Public Affairs. 1998. *Public Interest Profiles, 2001–2002.* Washington, D.C.: CQP.

Foweraker, Joe, and Ann L. Craig, eds. 1990. *Popular Movements and Political Change in Mexico.* Boulder, Colo.: Lynne Rienner.

Fowler, Linda L. 1982. "How Interest Groups Select Issues for Rating Voting Records of Members of the U.S. Congress." *LSQ* 7: 401–14.

———. 1993. *Candidates, Congress and the American Democracy.* Ann Arbor: University of Michigan Press.

Francis, Corinna-Barbara. 1989. "The Progress of Protest in China: The Spring of 1989." *Asian Survey*, 29: 898–915.

Francis, Wayne L. 1967. *Legislative Issues in the Fifty States: A Comparative Analysis.* Chicago: Rand McNally.

Frantz, Douglas, and Catherine Collins. 1989. *Selling Out: How We Are Letting Japan Buy Our Land, Our Industries, Our Financial Institutions, and Our Future.* Chicago: Contemporary Books.

Franzosi, Roberto. 1995. *The Puzzle of Strikes: Class and State Strategies in Postwar Italy.* Cambridge, U.K.: CUP.

Fraser Associates. *1980. The PAC Handbook: Political Action for Business.* Cambridge, Mass.: Ballinger.

Freeman, Jo. 1975. *The Politics of Women's Liberation.* New York: McKay.

Freeman, J. Leiper. 1965. *The Political Process: Executive Bureau-Committee Relations.* rev. ed. New York: Random House.

Freidenberg, Nicholas. 1984. *Not in Our Backyards! Community Action for Health and the Environment.* New York: Monthly Review Press.

Frenkel, Stephen, ed. 1993. *Organized Labor in the Asia-Pacific Region: A Comparative Study of Trade Unionism in Nine Countries.* Ithaca, N.Y.: ILR Press.

Frieden, Jeffry A. 1991a. *Debt, Development and Democracy: Modern Political Economy and Latin America, 1965–1985.* Princeton, N.J.: PUP.

———. 1991b. "Invested Interests: The Politics of National Economic Policies in a World of Global Finance." *International Organization* 45: 425–52.

Friman, H. Richard. 1993. "Side-Payments Versus Security Cards: Domestic Bargaining Tactics in International Economic Negotiations." *International Organization* 47: 387–410.

Fritschler, A. Lee. 1969. *Smoking and Politics: Policymaking and the Federal Bureaucracy.* Englewood Cliffs, N.J.: Prentice Hall.

———. 1975. *Smoking and Politics.* 2nd ed. Englewood Cliffs, N.J.: Prentice-Hall.

———. 1989. *Smoking and Politics.* 4th ed. Englewood Cliffs, N.J.: Prentice-Hall.

Fritschler, A. Lee, and James M. Hoefler. 1996. *Smoking and Politics: Policy Making and the Federal Bureaucracy.* Upper Saddle River, N.J.: Prentice-Hall.

Frohlich, Norman, and Joe Oppenheimer. 1978. *Modern Political Economy.* Englewood Cliffs, N.J.: Prentice-Hall.

Furtado, Celso. 1970. *Economic Development in Latin America.* New York: CUP.

Fuszara, Malgorzata. 1993. "Abortion and the Formation of the Public Sphere in Poland." In *Gender Politics and Post-Communism*, eds. Nanette Funk and Magda Mueller. New York: Routledge.

Gable, Richard. 1953. "NAM: Influential Lobby or Kiss of Death?" *JOP* 15: 254–73.

Gaer, Felice D. 1996. "Reality Check: Human Rights NGOs Confront Governments at the UN." In *NGOs, the UN and Global Governance.* T. Weiss and L. Gordenker, cited below.

Gais, Thomas L., Mark A. Peterson, and Jack L. Walker. 1984. "Interest Groups, Iron Triangles and Representative Institutions in American National Government." *BJPS* 14: 161–85.

Gais, Thomas L., and Jack L. Walker. 1991. "Pathways to Influence in American Politics." In *Mobilizing Interest Groups in America.* Jack Walker, cited below.

Galanter, Marc. 1974. "Why the 'Haves' Come Out Ahead: Speculations on the Limits of Legal Change." *Law & Society Review* 9: 95–160.

Galenson, Walter. 1998. *The World's Strongest Trade Unions: The Scandinavian Labor Movement.* Westport, Conn.: Quorum.

Galligan, B., and G. Singleton, eds. 1991. *Business and Government Under Labor.* Melbourne: Longman Cheshire.

Gallup Poll. 1949. Gallup / American Institute of Public Opinion (May).

———. 1989. (April).

———. 1993. (March).

———. 1995. (May).

Galnoor, Itzhak. 1982. *Steering the Policy: Communication and Politics in Israel.* Beverly Hills, Calif.: Sage.

Gamson, William. 1975. *The Strategy of Social Protest.* Belmont, Calif.: Wadsworth.

———. 1980. "Understanding the Careers of Challenging Groups: A Commentary on Goldstone," *AJS* 85: 1043–60.

———. 1990. *The Strategy of Social Protest.* 2nd ed. Belmont, Calif.: Wadsworth.

Garand, James C. 1992. "Changing Patterns of Relative State Economic Growth Over Time." *WPQ* 45: 469–84.

Garceau, Oliver. 1941. *The Political Life of the American Medical Association.* Cambridge, Mass.: HUP.

Garcia, F. Chris, ed. 1997. *Pursuing Power: Latinos and the Political System.* Notre Dame, Ind.: University of Notre Dame Press.

Garcia, Mario T. 1989. *Mexican Americans: Leadership, Ideology and Identity, 1930–1960.* New Haven, Conn.: YUP.

Gardner, James N. 1991. *Effective Lobbying in the European Community.* Deventer: Kluwer.

Gardner, John W. 1973. *In Common Cause.* rev. ed. New York: Norton.

Garner, Robert, ed. 1997. *Animals Rights: The Changing Debate.* New York: New York University Press.

Garrett, Stephen A. 1978. "Eastern European Ethnic Groups and American Foreign Policy." *PSQ* 93: 301–23.

Garrow, David J. 1994. *Liberty and Sexuality: The Right to Privacy and the Making of Roe v. Wade.* New York: Macmillan.

Garson, G. David. 1969. "Collective Violence in America: 1863–1963." Ph.D. Dissertation. Harvard University.

———. 1970. "Collective Violence Re-examined: Alternate Theories of American Labor Violence." *Politics* V (Nov.): 129–43.

———. 1974. "On the Origins of Interest-Group Theory: A Critique of a Process. *APSR* 68: 1505–19.

———. 1978. *Group Theories of Politics.* Beverly Hills, Calif.: Sage.

Gart, Allan. 1994. *Regulation, Deregulation, and Reregulation: The Future of Banking, Insurance and Securities Regulation.* New York: Wiley.

Gastrow, Peter. 1995. *Bargaining for Peace: South Africa and the National Peace Accord.* Washington, D.C.: United States Institute of Peace.

Gelb, Joyce. 1989. *Feminism and Politics: A Comparative Perspective.* Berkeley: UCAP.

———. 1995. "Feminist Organization Success and the Politics of Engagement." In *Feminist Organizations.* M. Ferree and P. Martin, cited above.

Gelb, Joyce, and Marian Lief Palley. 1979. "Women and Interest Group Politics: A Comparative Analysis of Federal Decision-Making." *JOP* 41: 362–92.

———. 1982. *Women and Public Policies.* Princeton, N.J.: PUP.

———. 1987. *Women and Public Policies.* rev. ed. Princeton, N.J.: PUP.

Gellner, Winand, and John D. Robertson. 2001. "Germany: The Continuing Dominance of Neo-Corporatism." In *Political Parties and Interest Groups.* C. Thomas, cited below.

George, Alexander. 1979. "Case Studies and Theory Development: The Method of Structured Focused Comparison." In *Diplomacy: New Approaches in History, Theory and Policy*, ed. Paul Gordon. New York: Free Press.

George, Alexander, and Timothy J. McKeown. 1985. "Case Studies and Theories of Organizational Decision Making." In *Advances in Information Processes in Organizations 2*. Greenwich, Conn.: JAI.

George, Aurelia. 1988. "Japanese Interest Group Behavior: An Institutional Approach" In *Dynamic and Immobilist Politics in Japan*, ed. J. A. A. Stockwin. London: MacMillan.

Gerber, Elizabeth F. 1999. *The Populist Paradox: Interest Group Influence and the Promise of Direct Legislation*. Princeton, N. J.: PUP.

Gerhart, Gail M. 1978. *Black Power in South Africa: The Evolution of an Ideology*. Berkeley: UCAP.

Gerlich, Peter. 1987. "Consociationalism to Competition: The Austrian Party System Since 1945." In *Party Systems in Denmark, Austria, Switzerland, the Netherlands and Belgium*, ed. Hans Daalder. London: Frances Pinter.

———. 1992. "A Farewell to Corporatism." *West European Politics* 15: 132–45.

Getter, Russell, and Paul Schumaker. 1983. "Structural Sources of Unequal Responsiveness to Group Demands in American Cities." *WPQ* 36: 7–29.

Geyer, Robert. 1997. *The Uncertain Union: British and Norwegian Social Democrats in an Integrating Europe*. Aldershot, U.K.: Avebury.

Ghils, Paul. 1992. "International Civil Society: International Non-Governmental Organizations in the International System." *International Social Science Journal* 44: 417–31.

Gibbs, Lois. 1991. *Love Canal: My Story*. Albany, N.Y.: SUNY Press.

Gibson, Clark C. 1999. "Bureaucrats and the Environment in Africa: The Politics of Structural Choice in a One Party State." *Comparative Politics* 31: 273–93.

Gibson, James L. and Richard D. Bingham. 1985. *Civil Liberties and Nazis: The Skokie Free Speech Controversy*. Urbana, Ill..: Praeger.

Gifford, Paul, ed. 1995. *The Christian Churches and the Democratization of Africa*. Leiden: E. J. Brill.

Gifford, Paul. 1998. *African Christianity*. Bloomington: Indiana University Press.

Gilbert, Jess, and Carolyn Howe. 1991. "Beyond 'State vs. Society': Theories of the State and New Deal Agricultural Policies." *American Sociological Review* 56: 204–20.

Giles, Michael W., and Kaenan Hertz. 1994. "Racial Threat and Partisan Identification." *APSR* 88: 317–26.

Gilligan, Thomas, William Marshall, and Barry Weingast. 1989. "Regulation and the Theory of Legislative Choice: The Interstate Commerce Act of 1887." *Journal of Law and Economics* 32: 35–61.

Gilpin, Robert. 1975. *U.S. Power and the Multinational Corporation*. New York: Basic Books.

Gimpel, James G. 1994. "The Demise of a Lead PAC: The Free Congress PAC." In *Risky Business?* R. Biersack, P. Herrnson, and C. Wilcox, cited above.

———. 1998. "Grassroots Organizations and Equilibrium Cycles in Group Mobilization and Access." In *The Interest Group Connection*. P. Herrnson, R. Shaiko, and C. Wilcox, cited below.

Ginsburg, Faye D. 1989. *Contested Lives: The Abortion Debate in an American Community.* Berkeley: UCAP.

Gladdish, Kenneth. 1991. *Governing from the Centre: Politics and Policy-Making in The Netherlands.* London: Hurst.

Glantz, Stanton A. 1996. *The Cigarette Papers.* Berkeley: UCAP.

Glantz, Stanton A., and Edith D. Balbach. 2000. *Tobacco War: Inside the California Battles.* Berkeley: UCAP.

Glasser, Susan B., and Juliet Eilperin. 1999. "Don't Ask—They Don't Have to Tell: New PACs Avoid Fund Raising Limits." *The Washington Post National Weekly Edition,* (May 24): 10–11.

Glickman, Norman J., and Douglas P. Woodward. 1989. *The New Competitors: How Foreign Investors are Changing the U.S. Economy.* New York: Basic Books.

Glouchevitch, Philip. 1992. *Juggernaut: The German Way of Business.* New York: Simon & Schuster.

Godshall, William. 1993. "Exposing the Tobacco Lobby." *World Smoking and Health: An American Cancer Society Journal* 18, No. 1: 10–11.

Godwin, R. Kennith. 1988. *One Million Dollars of Influence: The Direct Marketing of Politics.* Chatham, N.J.: Chatham House.

Godwin, R. Kenneth, and Robert Cameron Mitchell. 1982. "Rational Models, Collective Goods and Non-electoral Political Behavior." *WPQ* 35: 160–80.

Gold, Thomas B. 1986. *State and Society in the Taiwan Miracle.* New York: M. E. Sharpe.

———. 2000. "Taiwan: Still Defying the Odds." In *Consolidating the Third Wave Democracies,* eds. Larry Diamond, et al. Baltimore: JHUP.

Goldberg, Ellis. 1993. "Private Goods, Public Wrongs, and Civil Society in Some Medieval Arab Theory and Practice." In *Rules and Rights in the Middle East,* eds. Ellis Goldberg, et al. Seattle: University of Washington Press.

Golden, Miriam. 1988. *Labor Divided: Austerity and Working-Class Politics in Contemporary Italy.* Ithaca, N.Y.: Cornell University Press.

Goldman, Ralph. 1991. "The Nomination Process: Factionalism as a Force for Democratization." *Midsouth Political Science Journal* 12: 42–64.

Goldstein, Judith, and Robert Keohane. 1993. *Ideas and Foreign Policy: Beliefs, Institutions and Political Change.* Ithaca, N.Y.: Cornell University Press.

Goldstein, Kenneth M. 1998. *Interest Groups, Lobbying, and Participation in America.* New York: CUP.

Goldstone, Jack A. 1980. "The Weakness of Organization: A New Look at Gamson's *The Strategy of Social Protest.*" *AJS* 85 (March and May): 1017–42 and 1426–32.

Goldthorpe, J. ed. 1984. *Order and Conflict in Contemporary Capitalism.* Oxford: Clarendon.

Gollner, Andrew B. 1983. *Social Change and Corporate Strategy.* Stamford, Conn.: Issue Action Publications.

Goodman, David S. G., ed. 1984. *Groups and Politics in the People's Republic of China.* Armonk, N.Y.: M. E. Sharpe.

———. 1994. *China's Quiet Revolution: New Interactions Between State and Society.* New York: SMP.

Goodnow, Frank J. 1900. *Politics and Administration.* New York: Russell and Russell.

Gopoian, David J. 1984. "What Makes PACs Tick? An Analysis of Allocation Patterns of Economic Interest Groups." *AJPS* 28: 259–81.

Gorges, Michael J. 1993. "Interest Intermediation in the EC After Maastricht." In *The State of the European Community, Volume 2: The Maastricht Debates and Beyond*, eds. Alan W. Cafruny and Glenda G. Rosenthal, Boulder, Colo.: Lynne Rienner.

———. 1996. *Euro-Corporatism? Interest Intermediation in the European Community.* Lanham, Md.: UPA.

Gormley, William. 1983. *The Politics of Public Utility Regulation.* Pittsburgh: University of Pittsburgh Press.

Gottlieb, Arnold M., ed. 1989. *The Wise Use Agenda.* Bellevue, Wash.: Merrill Press.

Gottlieb, Robert. 1993. *Forcing the Spring: The Transformation of the American Environmental Movement.* Washington, D.C.: Island Press.

Gourevitch, Peter. 1978. "The Second Image Reversed: The International Sources of Domestic Politics." *International Organization* 32: 881–911.

Grady, Dennis O. 1984. "American Governors and State-Federal Relations: Attitudes and Activities, 1960–80." *State Government* 57 (3): 106–12.

———. 1987. "Gubernatorial Behavior in State-Federal Relations." *WPQ* 40: 305–38.

Graham, Edward, and Paul R. Krugman. 1991. *Foreign Direct Investment in the United States.* Washington, D.C.: Institute for International Economics.

Graham, Edward M., and David J. Richardson, eds. 1997. *Global Competition Policy.* Washington, D.C.: Institute for International Economics.

Graham, Frank, Jr. 1990. *The Audubon Ark: A History of the National Audubon Society.* New York: Knopf.

Graham, Hugh Davis, and Ted Gurr, eds. 1969. *Violence in America: Historical and Comparative Perspective.* Washington, D.C.: Government Printing Office.

Gran, Peter. 1977. *Islamic Roots of Capitalism.* Austin: University of Texas Press.

Grant, H. Roger. 1979. *Insurance Reform: Consumer Action in the Progressive Era.* Ames: Iowa State University Press.

Grant, Wyn L. 1984. "Large Firms and Public Policy in Britain." *Journal of Public Policy* 4: 1–18.

———, ed. 1985a. *The Political Economy of Corporatism.* London: Macmillan.

———. 1985b. "Private Organizations as Agents of Public Policy: The Case of Milk Marketing in Britain." In *Private Interest Government.* W. Streeck and P. Schmitter, cited below.

———, ed. 1987. *Business Interests, Organizational Development and Private Interest Government: An International Comparative Study of the Food Processing Industry.* Berlin: de Gruyter.

———. 1989a. *Government and Industry: A Comparative Analysis of the US, Canada and the UK.* Brookfield, Vt.: Gower.

———. 1989b. *Pressure Groups, Politics and Democracy in Britain.* London: Philip Allan.

———. 1991a. "Associational Systems in the Chemical Industry." In *International Markets and Global Firms.* A. Martinelli, cited below.

———. 1991b. "The Overcapacity Crisis in the West European Petro-chemicals Industry." In *International Markets and Global Firms.* A. Martinelli, cited below.

————. 1991c. *The Dairy Industry: An International Comparison*. Aldershot: Gower.

————. 1991d. "DIY: The Government Relations Functions of Large Companies." In *The Commercial Lobbyists*. A. G. Jordan, cited below.

————. 1992. "Models of Interest Intermediation and Policy Formation Applied to an Internationally Comparative Study of the Dairy Industry." *European Journal of Political Research* 21: 53–68.

————. 1993. *Business and Politics in Britain*. London: Macmillan.

————. 1995. *Pressure Groups, Politics and Democracy in Britain*. Hemel Hempstead: Harvester Wheatsheaf.

Grant, Wyn L., and David Marsh. 1977. *The Confederation of British Industry*. New York: Holmes and Meier.

Grant, Wyn L., and William Paterson. 1994. "The Chemical Industry: A Study in Internationalization." In *Governing Capitalist Economies*. J. R. Hollingsworth, P. Schmitter, and W. Streeck, cited below.

Grant, Wyn L., William Paterson, and Colin Whitston. 1987. "Government-Industry Relations in the Chemical Industry: An Anglo-German Comparison." In *Comparative Government-Industry Relations*. S. Wilks and M. Wright, cited below.

————. 1988. *Government and the Chemical Industry: A Comparative Study of Britain and West Germany*. Oxford: Clarendon.

Grant, Wyn L., and Wolfgang Streeck. 1985. "Large firms and representation of business interests in the UK and West German construction industry," In *Organized Interests and the State*. A. Cawson, cited above.

Gray, Virginia, and David Lowery. 1988. "Interest Group Politics and Economic Growth in the American States: Testing the Olson Construct." *APSR* 82: 109–31.

————. 1995. "The Demography of Interest Organization Communities: Institutions, Associations and Membership Groups." *APQ* 23: 3–33.

————. 1996a. *The Population Ecology of Interest Representation: Lobbying Communities in the American States*. Ann Arbor: University of Michigan Press.

————. 1996b. "The World of Contact Lobbyists." *Comparative State Politics* 17, No. 5: 31–40.

————. 1996c. "A Niche Theory of Interest Representation." *JOP* 58: 91–111.

————. 1998. "State Lobbying Regulations and Their Enforcement: Implications for the Diversity of Interest Communities." *State and Local Government Review* 30: 78–91.

————. 2001. "The Institutionalization of State Communities of Organized Interests." *PRQ* 54: 265–84.

————. 2002. "State Interest Group Research and the Mixed Legacy of Belle Zeller." *State Politics and Policy Quarterly* 2 (1): 388–410.

Gray, Virginia, and Bruce Williams. 1980. *The Organizational Politics of Criminal Justice: Policy in Context*. Lexington, Mass.: Lexington Books.

Graziano, Luigi. 2001. *Lobbying, Pluralism and Democracy*. London: Palgrave Macmillan.

Green, John C., and James L. Guth. 1986. "Big Bucks and Petty Cash: Party and Interest Group Activists in American Politics." In *Interest Group Politics*, 2nd ed. A. Cigler and B. Loomis, cited above.

Green, Mark, and Andrew Buchsbaum. 1980. *The Corporate Lobbies: Political Profiles of the Business Roundtable and the Chamber of Commerce*. Washington, D.C.: Public Citizen.

Green, Mark, ed. 1983. *The Big Business Reader: On Corporate America*. New York: Pilgrim Press.

Greenberg, Jack. 1994. *Crusaders in the Court: How a Dedicated Band of Lawyers Fought for the Civil Rights Revolution*. New York: Basic Books.

Greenstone, J. David. 1977. *Labor in American Politics*. Chicago: UCP

Greenwald, Carol S. 1977. *Group Power, Lobbying and Public Policy*. New York: Praeger.

Greenwood, Justin, ed. 1995. *European Casebook on Business Alliances*. Hemel Hempstead: Prentice-Hall.

———. 1997. *Representing Interests in the European Union*. London: Macmillan.

———. 1998. "Regulating Lobbying in the European Union." *Parliamentary Affairs*, 51: 587–99.

———. 2002a. *Inside the EU Business Associations*. Basingstoke: Palgrave Macmillan.

———, ed. 2002b. *The Effectiveness of EU Business Associations*. Basingstoke: Palgrave Macmillan.

———. 2003a. *Interest Representation in the European Union*. New York: Palgrave Macmillan.

———, ed. 2003b. *The Challenge of Change in EU Business Associations*. New York: Palgrave MacMillan.

Greenwood, Justin, and Mark Aspinwall. 1997. *Collective Action in the European Union: Interests and the New Politics of Associability*. London: Routledge.

Greenwood, Justin, Jurgen R. Grote, and Karsten Ronit, eds. 1992a. *Organized Interests and the European Community*. London: Sage.

———. 1992b. "Introduction: Organized Interests and the Transnational Dimension." In *Organized Interests in the European Community*. J. Greenwood, J. Grote, and K. Ronit, cited above.

Greenwood, Justin, and Clive S. Thomas. 1998. "Regulating Lobbying in the Western World." *Parliamentary Affairs*, Special Issue, 51: 487–99.

Greer, Ian. 1985. *Right to be Heard*. London: Ian Greer Associates.

Grenzke, Janet M. 1989. "Shopping in the Congressional Supermarket: The Currency is Complex." *AJPS* 33: 1–24.

Grier, Kevin, and Michael C. Munger. 1993. "Corporate, Labor and Trade Association Contributions to the U.S. House and Senate." *JOP* 55: 615–44.

Griffith, Ernest S. 1939. *The Impasse of Democracy*. New York: Harrison-Hilton.

Griffiths, Robert. J. 1995. "South African Civil-Military Relations in Transition: Issues and Influences." *Armed Forces and Society* 21: 395–410.

Grimshaw, P. 1987. *Women's Suffrage in New Zealand*. 2nd ed. Auckland: Auckland University Press.

Grindle, Merilee S. 1977. *Bureaucrats, Politicians and Peasants in Mexico: A Case Study in Public Policy*. Berkeley: UCAP.

Grossman, Gene M., and Elhanan Helpman. 2001. *Special Interest Politics*. Cambridge, Mass.: MIT Press.

Grundy, Kenneth W. 1988. *The Militarization of South African Politics*. Oxford: OUP.

Grunert, Thomas. 1987. "Decision-Making Processes in the Steel Crisis Policy of the EEC: Neocorporatist or Integrationist Tendencies?" In *The Politics of Steel: Western Europe and the Steel Industry in the Crisis Years, 1974–1984*, eds. Yves Mény and Vincent Wright. New York: Water de Gruyter.

Gubin, Sandra L. 1995. "Between Regimes and Realism. Transnational Agenda Setting: Soviet Compliance with CSCE Human Rights Norms." *Human Rights Quarterly* 17: 278–302.

Guither, Harold D. 1980. *The Food Lobbyists*. Lexington, Mass.: Lexington Books.

———. 1998. *Animal Rights: History and Scope of a Radical Social Movement*. Carbondale: Southern Illinois University Press.

Gunnell, John G. 1996. "The Genealogy of American Pluralism." *IPSR* 17: 253–65.

Gunther, John. 1951. *Inside USA*. New York: Harper.

Gunther, Richard, ed. 1993. *Politics, Society and Democracy: The Case of Spain*. Boulder, Colo.: Westview.

Gurr, Ted Robert, and Desmond S. King. 1987. *The State and the City*. Chicago: UCP.

Guth, James A., et al. 1995. "Onward Christian Soldiers: Religious Activist Groups in American Politics." In *Interest Group Politics*, 4th ed. A. Cigler and B. Loomis, cited above.

Guyer, Robert L., and Laura K. Guyer. 2000. *Guide to State Legislative Lobbying*. Gainesville, Fla.: Engineering The Law.

Haas, Ernst. 1958. *The Uniting of Europe: Political, Economic and Social Forces 1950–1957*. Stanford, Calif.: Stanford University Press.

———. 1964. *Beyond the Nation State: Functionalism and International Organization*. Stanford, Calif.: Stanford University Press.

Haas, Peter M. 1992. "Introduction: Epistemic Communities and International Policy Coordination." *International Organization* 46: 1–36.

Haavio-Mannila, Elina. 1981. "The Position of Women." In *Nordic Democracy*. E. Allardt, et al., cited above.

Hacker, Andrew. 1962. "Pressure Politics in Pennsylvania: The Truckers versus the Railroads." In *The Uses of Power: Seven Cases in American Politics*, ed. Alan Westin. New York: Harcourt, Brace, and World.

Hadwiger, Don F. 1982. *The Politics of Agricultural Research*. Lincoln: University of Nebraska Press.

Hadwiger, Don F., and Ross B. Talbot. 1968. *Pressures and Protests: The Kennedy Farm Program and the Wheat Referendum of 1963*. San Francisco: Chandler.

Hagan, J. 1981. *The History of the ACTU*. Melbourne: Longman Cheshire.

Hagan, John. 1983. "The Symbolic Politics of Criminal Sanctions." In *The Political Science of Criminal Justice*, eds. S. Nagel, E. Fairchild, and A. Champagne. Springfield, Ill.: Charles C. Thomas.

Haggard, Stephan, and Beth A. Simmons. 1987. "Theories of International Regimes." *International Organization* 41: 491–517.

Hagopian, Frances. 1990. "Democracy by Undemocratic Means? Elites, Political Pacts, and Regime Transition in Brazil." *Comparative Political Studies* 23: 147–70.

Haider, Donald H. 1974. *When Governments Come to Washington: Governors, Mayors and Intergovernmental Lobbying*. New York: Free Press.

Haider-Markel, Donald P., and Kenneth Meier. 1996. "The Politics of Gay and Lesbian Rights." *JOP* 58: 332–49.

Haines, Herbert. 1984. "Black Radicalization and the Funding of Civil Rights." *Social Problems* 32: 31–43.

Hajba, Eva. 1994. "The Green Line in the Hungarian Transition." In *The Emergence of East Central European Parliaments: The First Steps*, ed. Attila Agh. Budapest: Hungarian Center for Democracy Studies.

Hakman, Nathan. 1966. "Lobbying the Supreme Court—An Appraisal of 'Political Science Folklore'." *Fordham Law Review* 35: 15–50.

———. 1969. "The Supreme Court's Political Environment: The Processing of Non-commercial Litigation." In *Frontiers of Judicial Research*, eds. Joel Grossman and Joseph Tannenhaus. New York: Wiley.

Hale, George E., and Marian Lief Palley. 1981. *The Politics of Federal Grants*. Washington, D.C.: CQP.

Hall, Donald R. 1969. *Cooperative Lobbying—The Power of Pressure*. Tucson, Ariz.: University of Arizona Press.

Hall, Peter. 1986. *Governing the Economy*. New York: OUP.

Hall. Peter A. 1993. "Pluralism and Pressure Politics in France." In *Pressure Groups*. J. Richardson, cited below.

Hall, Richard L., and Frank W. Wayman. 1990. "Buying Time: Moneyed Interests and Mobilization of Bias in Congressional Committees." *APSR* 84: 797–820.

Halley, Laurence. 1985. *Ancient Affections: Ethnic Groups and Foreign Policy*. New York: Praeger.

Hamann, Kerstin. 2001. "Spain: Changing Party-Group Relations in a New Democracy." In *Political Parties and Interest Groups*. C. Thomas, cited below.

Hamilton, Charles V., and Dona C. Hamilton. 1998. *The Dual Agenda: The African American Struggle for Civil and Economic Equality*. New York: Columbia University Press.

Hamilton, David E. 1991. *From New Day to New Deal: American Farm Policy from Hoover to Roosevelt, 1928–1933*. Chapel Hill: University of North Carolina Press.

Hamlin, David. 1980. *The Nazi / Skokie Conflict: A Civil Liberties Battle*. Boston: Beacon Press.

Hamm, Keith E. 1983a. "Legislative Committees, Executive Agencies, and Interest Groups." In *Handbook of Legislative Research*, eds. Gerhard Loewenberg, Samuel C. Patterson, and Malcolm E. Jewell. Cambridge, Mass.: HUP.

———. 1983b. "Patterns of Influence Among Committees, Agencies, and Interest Groups." *LSQ* 8: 379–427.

Hamm, Keith E., Andrew R. Weber, and R. Bruce Anderson. 1994. "The Impact of Lobbying Laws and Their Enforcement: A Contrasting View." *SSQ* 75: 378–81.

Handler, Joel F. 1978. *Social Movements and the Legal System: A Theory of Law Reform and Social Change*. New York: Academic Press.

Haney, Patrick J., and Walt Vanderbush. 1999. "The Role of Ethnic Interest Groups in U.S. Foreign Policy: The Case of the Cuban American National Foundation." *International Studies Quarterly* 43: 341–61.

Hansard Society. 1993. *Making the Law: The Report of the Hansard Society Commission on the Legislative Process.* London: The Hansard Society.

Hansen, Holger Brent, and Michael Twaddle, eds. 1995. *Religion and Politics in East Africa.* London: James Currey.

Hansen, John Mark. 1985. "The Political Economy of Group Membership." *APSR* 79: 79–96.

———. 1991. *Gaining Access: Congress and the Farm Lobby.* Chicago: UCP.

Hansen, Tore, and K. Newton. 1985. "Voluntary Organisations and Community Politics: Norwegian and British Comparisons." *SPS* 8: 1–21.

Hanson, Russell L., ed. 1998. *Governing Partners: State-Local Relations in the United States.* Boulder, Colo.: Westview.

Harbeson, John W., et al., eds. 1994. *Civil Society and the State in Africa.* Boulder, Colo.: Lynne Rienner.

Hardin, Russell. 1982. *Collective Action.* Baltimore: JHUP.

Hargrove, Eugene E., ed. 1992. *The Animal Rights / Environmental Ethics Debate: The Environmental Perspective.* Albany, N.Y.: SUNY Press.

Harman, G. S. 1980. "Pressure Groups and the Australian Political System." In *Government, Politics and Power in Australia*, 2nd ed., eds. A. Parkin, J. Summers, and D. Woodward. Melbourne: Longman Cheshire.

Harmon, Robert B. 1978. *Interest Groups and Lobbying in American Politics: A Bibliographic Checklist.* New York: Council of Planning Librarians.

Harris, Richard A. 1985. *Coal Firms Under the New Social Regulation.* Durham, N.C.: Duke University Press.

———. 1989. "Political Management: The Changing Face of Business in American Politics." In *Remaking American Politics*, eds. Richard A. Harris and Sidney Milkis. Boulder, Colo.: Westview.

Harris, Richard A., and Sidney M. Milkis. 1989. *The Politics of Regulatory Change: A Tale of Two Agencies.* New York: OUP.

Hatamiya, Leslie T. 1993. *Righting a Wrong.* Stanford, Calif.: Stanford University Press.

Hattam, Victoria. 1993. *Labor Visions and State Power.* Princeton, N.J.: PUP.

Hausner, Jerzy, Ove K. Pedersen, and Karsten Ronit, eds. 1995. *Evolution of Interest Representation and Development of the Labour Market in Post-Socialist Countries.* Cracow: Cracow Academy of Economics.

Havard, William C., ed. 1972. *The Changing Politics of the South.* Baton Rouge: Louisiana State University Press.

Haverland, Markus. 1998. *National Autonomy, European Integration and the Politics of Packaging Waste.* Utrecht: Netherlands School for Social and Economic Policy Research.

Havrilesky, Thomas. 1993. *The Pressure on American Monetary Policy.* Norwell, Mass.: Kluwer.

Hay, Margaret Jean, and Sharon Stichter, eds. 1995. *African Women South of the Sahara.* 2nd ed. London: Longman.

Hayes, Graeme. 2001. *Environmental Protest and the State in France.* London: Palgrave.

Hayes, Michael T. 1981. *Lobbyists and Legislators: A Theory of Political Markets.* New Brunswick, N.J.: Rutgers University Press.

———. 1986. "The New Group Universe." In *Interest Group Politics*, 2nd ed. A. Cigler and B. Loomis, cited above.

Hays, R. Allen. 1991. "Intergovernmenatal Lobbying: Toward an Understanding of Priorities." *WPQ* 44: 1081–98.

Hays, Samuel P. 1958. *Conservation and the Gospel of Efficiency*. Cambridge, Mass.: HUP.

———. 1964. "The Politics of Reform in Municipal Government in the Progressive Era." *Pacific Northwest Quarterly* 55: 157–69.

———. 1987. *Beauty, Health and Permanence: Environmental Politics in the United States, 1955–1985*. New York: OUP.

Hayward, Jack. 1975. "Employers' Associations and the State in France and Britain." In *Industrial Policies in Western Europe*, eds. Steven J. Warnecke and Ezra N. Suleiman. New York: Praeger.

Heclo, Hugh. 1978. "Issue Networks and the Executive Establishment." In *The New American Political System*, ed. Anthony King. Washington, D.C.: AEI.

Hedlund, Ronald D., and Samuel C. Patterson. 1966. "Personal Attributes, Political Orientations and Occupational Perspectives of Lobbyists: The Case of Illinois." *Iowa Business Digest* 37: 3–11.

Heilbrunn, John R. 1997. "Commerce, Politics and Business Associations in Benin and Togo." *Comparative Politics* 29: 473–92.

Heinz, Anne M., Herbert Jacob, and Robert L. Lineberry. 1983. *Crime in City Politics*. New York: Longman.

Heinz, John P. 1962. "The Political Impasse in Farm Support Legislation." *Yale Law Journal* 71: 954–70.

Heinz, John P., and Edward O. Laumann. 1982. *Chicago Lawyers: The Structure of the Bar*. New York: Russell Sage Foundation; Chicago: American Bar Foundation.

Heinz, John P., and Peter M. Manikas. 1992. "Networks Among Elites in a Local Criminal Justice System." *Law and Society Review* 26: 831–61.

Heinz, John P., Edward O. Laumann, Robert L. Nelson, and Robert H. Salisbury. 1993. *The Hollow Core: Private Interests in National Policy Making*. Cambridge, Mass.: HUP.

Heisler, M., ed. 1974. *Politics In Europe*. New York: McKay.

———. 1979. "Corporate Pluralism Revisited: Where is the Theory?" *SPS* 2: 281–92.

Helander, Voitto, and Dag Anckar. 1983. *Consultation and Political Culture: Essays on the Case of Finland*. Helsinki: Finnish Society of Sciences and Letters.

Held, David. 1992. "Democracy: From City-State to a Cosmopolitan Order?" *Political Studies*, Special Issue. XL: 10–39.

Helleiner, G. K. 1987. "Transnational Enterprises and the New Political Economy of U.S. Trade Policy." In *International Political Economy: Perspectives on Global Power and Wealth*, eds. Jeffrey A. Frieden and David A. Lake. New York: SMP.

Henig, Jeffrey R. 1994. *Rethinking School Choice: Limits of the Market Metaphor*. Princeton, N.J.: PUP.

Herman, Edward S. 1981. *Corporate Control, Corporate Power*. New York: CUP.

Hermann, John R. 1997. "American Indian Interests and Supreme Court Agenda Setting, 1969–92." *APQ* 25: 241–60.

Hermann, John R., and Karen O'Connor. 1996. "American Indians and the Burger Court." *SSQ* 77: 127–44.

Herndon, James F. 1982. "Access, Record and Competition as Influences on Interest Group Contributions to Congressional Campaigns." *JOP* 44: 996–1019.

Hero, Rodney E. 1992. *Latinos and the U.S. Political System: Two-Tiered Pluralism.* Philadelphia: Temple University Press.

Herring, Pendleton. 1929. *Group Representation Before Congress.* Baltimore: JHUP.

Herrnson, Paul S. 1988. *Party Campaigning in the 1980s.* Cambridge, Mass.: HUP.

———. 1995. *Congressional Elections: Campaigning at Home and in Washington.* Washington, D.C.: CQP.

Herrnson, Paul S., Ronald G. Shaiko, and Clyde Wilcox, eds. 1998. *The Interest Group Connection: Electioneering, Lobbying and Policymaking in Washington.* Chatham, N.J.: Chatham House.

———. 2003. *The Interest Group Connection: Electioneering, Lobbying and Policymaking* . 2nd ed. Chatham, N.J.: Chatham House.

Hertzke, Allen D. 1988. *Representing God in Washington: The Role of Religious Lobbies in the American Polity.* Knoxville: University of Tennessee Press.

Hertzog, Mark W. 1996. *The Lavender Vote: Lesbians, Gay Men and Bisexuals in American Electoral Politics.* New York: New York University Press.

Hessen, Robert, ed. 1982. *Does Big Business Rule America?* Washington, D.C.: Ethics and Policy Center.

Hethy, L. 1994. "Tripartism—Its Changes and Limits in Eastern Europe." In *New Frontiers in European Industrial Relations*, eds. Anthony Ferner and Richard Hyman. Oxford: Blackwell.

Hicks, Alexander, and Lane Kenworthy. 1998. "Cooperation and Political Economic Performance in Affluent Democratic Capitalism." *AJS* 103: 1631–72.

Hicks, Robyn. 1994. "Grassroots Organization in Defense of Mother Nature." In *Risky Business?* R. Biersack, P. Herrnson, and C. Wilcox, cited above.

Higgott, Richard, and Diane Stone. 1994. "The Limits of Influence: Foreign Policy Think Tanks in Britain and the USA." *Review of International Studies* 20: 15–34.

Hill, Edward W. 1990. "Current Anti-Trust Policy: A Liability in Today's Deregulated Banking Industry." *Policy Studies Journal* 18: 591–626.

Hine, Darlene Clark. 1989. *Black Women in White: Racial Conflict and Cooperation in the Nursing Profession, 1890–1950.* Bloomington: Indiana University Press.

Hirsch, M. 1986. "Tripartism in Luxembourg: The Limits of Societal Concertation." *West European Politics* 9: 54–66.

Hjorth, Ronnie. 1994. "Baltic Sea Environmental Cooperation: The Role of Epistemic Communities and the Politics of Regime Change." *Cooperation and Conflict* 29: 11–31.

Hocking, Brian. 1990. "Bringing the 'Outside' In: The Role and Nature of Foreign Interest Lobbying." *Corruption and Reform* 5: 219–33.

———. 1991 "Japanese Lobbying in the United States: Foreign Threat or Domestic Politics." *World Today* 47 (7): 64–66.

———. 1993. *Localizing Foreign Policy: Non-Central Governments and Multilayered Diplomacy,* London: Macmillan / SMP.

Hodgkin, Thomas. 1956. *Nationalism in Colonial Africa.* London: Frederick Muller.

Hoeber Rudolph, Susanne, and James P. Piscatori, eds. 1997. *Transnational Religion and Fading States*. Boulder, Colo.: Westview.

Hoenack, Stephen A. 1989. "Group Behavior and Economic Growth." *SSQ* 70: 744–58.

Hofrenning, Daniel J. B. 1995. *In Washington But Not of It: The Prophetic Politics of Religious Lobbyists*. Philadelphia: Temple University Press.

Hofstadter, Richard. 1955. *The Age of Reform: From Bryan to F.D.R.* New York: Vintage.

Hogan, M. C. 1978. *The Catholic Campaign for State Aid*. Sydney: Catholic Theological Faculty.

Hogenboom, Barbara. 1996. "Cooperation and polarisation beyond borders: the transnationalisation of Mexican environmental issues during the NAFTA negotiations." *Third World Quarterly* 17 (5): 989–1005.

Hojnacki, Marie, and David C. Kimball. 1998. "Organized Interests and the Decision of Whom to Lobby in Congress." *APSR* 92: 775–90.

Hollingsworth, J. Rogers, Philippe C. Schmitter, and Wolfgang Streeck, eds. 1994a. *Governing Capitalist Economics: Performance and Control of Economic Sectors*. Oxford: OUP.

———. 1994b. "Capitalism, Sectors, Institutions, and Performance." In *Governing Capitalist Economies*. J. R. Hollingsworth, P. Schmitter, and W. Streeck, cited above.

Holtzman, Abraham. 1963. *The Townsend Movement: A Political Study*. New York: Bookman Associates.

Holyoke, Thomas T. 2003. "Choosing Battlegrounds: Interest Group Lobbying Over Multiple Venues." *PRQ* 56: 325–36.

Horowitz, Donald. 1977. *The Courts and Social Policy*. Washington, D.C.: Brookings.

Horowitz, Irving L., ed. 1970. *Masses in Latin America*. New York: OUP.

Hovey, Michael W. 1997. "Interceding at the United Nations: The Human Right of Conscientious Objection." In *Transnational Social Movements and Global Politics*, Jackie Smith, et al., cited below.

Howell, Chris. 1992. *Regulating Labor: The State and Industrial Relations Reform in Postwar France*. Princeton, N.J.: PUP.

Hrebenar, Ronald J. 1992. *The Japanese Party System*. Boulder, Colo.: Westview.

———. 1997. *Interest Group Politics in America*. 3rd. ed. Armonk, N.Y.: M. E. Sharpe.

———. 2001. "Japan: Strong State, Spectator Democracy, and Modified Corporatism." In *Political Parties and Interest Groups*. C. Thomas, cited below.

Hrebenar, Ronald J., and Akira Nakamura. 1993. "Japan: Associational Politics in a Group Oriented Society." In *First World Interest Groups*. C. Thomas, cited below.

Hrebenar, Ronald J., Akira Nakamura, and Akio Nakamura. 1998. "Lobby Regulations in the Japanese Diet." *Parliamentary Affairs* 51: 551–58.

Hrebenar, Ronald J., Matthew J. Burbank, and Robert C. Benedict. 1999. *Political Parties, Interest Groups and Political Campaigns*. Boulder, Colo.: Westview.

Hrebenar, Ronald J., and Clive S. Thomas, eds. 1987. *Interest Group Politics in the American West*. Salt Lake City: University of Utah Press.

————, eds. 1992. *Interest Group Politics in the Southern States.* Tuscaloosa: University of Alabama Press.

————, eds. 1993a. *Interest Group Politics in the Northeastern States.* University Park: Pennsylvania State University Press.

————, eds. 1993b. *Interest Group Politics in the Midwestern States.* Ames: Iowa State University Press.

————, 1995. "The Japanese Lobby in Washington: How Different Is It?" In *Interest Group Politics*, 4th ed. A. Cigler and B. Loomis, cited above.

————, 2003. "Trends in Interest Group Politics in the States." *The Book of the States.* Vol. 35. Lexington, Ky.: The Council of State Governments.

Hsiao, Michael Hsin-huang. 1990. "Emerging Social Movements and the Rise of a Demanding Civil Society in Taiwan." In *Political Change in Taiwan*, eds. Tun-Jen Cheng and Stephan Haggard. Boulder, Colo.: Lynne Rienner.

Hubbard, Howard. 1968. "Five Long Hot Summers and How They Grew." *The Public Interest* (Summer): 3–24.

Hudson, Robert B., ed. 1997. *The Future of Age-Based Public Policy.* Baltimore: JHUP.

Hudson, William E. 1995. *American Democracy in Peril: Seven Challenges to America's Future.* Chatham, N.J.: Chatham House.

Hula, Kevin W. 1995. "Rounding Up the Usual Suspects: Forging Interest Group Coalitions in Washington." In *Interest Group Politics*, 4th ed. A. Cigler and B. Loomis, cited above.

————. 1999. *Lobbying Together: Interest Group Coalitions in Legislative Politics.* Washington, D.C.: Georgetown University Press.

Hulme, D., and M. Edwards, eds. 1997. *Too Close for Comfort? NGOs, States and Donors.* London: Macmillan.

Hunnius, Gerry. 1972. "Democracy and Parliamentary Politics." *Our Generation* 3: Part 2.

Hunter, Floyd. 1953. *Community Power Structure.* Chapel Hill: University of North Carolina Press.

Hunter, Kennith G. 1999. *Interest Groups and State Economic Development Policies.* New York: Praeger.

————. 2001. "An Analysis of the Effect of Lobbying Efforts and Demand-Side Economic Development Policies on State Economic Health." *Public Administration Quarterly* 25: 49–78.

————. 2002. "An Application of Herd Theory to Interest Group Behavior." *Administration & Society* 34: 389–410.

Hunter, Kennith G., Gregory G. Brunk, and Laura A. Wilson. 2002. "Organizing for Public Policy Effect: Aggregate Affiliated Interests in the American States." *Public Organization Review* 2: 117–39.

Hunter, Kennith G., Laura Ann Wilson and Gregory G. Brunk. 1991. "Societal Complexity and Interest Group Lobbying in the American States." *JOP* 53: 488–502.

Hunter, Robert. 1979. *Warriors of the Rainbow: A Chronicle of the Greenpeace Movement.* New York: Holt, Rinehart and Winston.

Hurrell, Andrew. 1991. "The Politics of Amazonian Deforestation." *Journal of Latin American Studies* 23: 197–215.

Hurwitz, Jon. 1988. "Determinants of Legislative Cue Selection." *SSQ* 69: 212–23.

Hyden, Goran. 1983. *No Shortcuts to Progress: African Development Management in Perspective.* London: Heinemann.

Ichioka, Yuji. 1988. *The Issei: The World of the First Generation Japanese Immigrants, 1885–1924.* New York: Free Press.

Ihovbere, Julius O. 1997. "Organized Labor and the Struggle for Democracy in Nigeria." *African Studies Review* 40: 77–110.

Imig, Douglas. 1995. *Poverty and Power.* Lincoln: University of Nebraska Press.

Imig, Doug, and Sidney Tarrow. 2001. *Contentious Europeans: Protest and Politics in an Emerging Polity.* Lanham, Md.: Rowman & Littlefield.

Immergut, Ellen M. 1992. *Health Politics: Interests and Institutions in Western Europe.* New York: CUP.

———. 1998. "The Theoretical Core of the New Institutionalism." *Politics and Society* 26: 5–34.

Ingebritsen, Christine. 1998. *The Nordic States and European Unity.* Ithaca, N.Y.: Cornell University Press.

Inglehart, Ronald. 1977. *The Silent Revolution: Changing Values and Political Styles Among Western Publics.* Princeton, N.J.: PUP.

———. 1990. *Culture Shift in Advanced Industrial Society.* Princeton, N.J.: PUP.

———. 1997. *Modernization and Postmodernization: Cultural Economic, and Political Change in 43 Societies.* Princeton, N.J.: PUP.

Inoguchi, Takeshi. 1985. "Gendai Nihon ni okeru Seiji Kate e no Apurochi [An approach to the contemporary Japanese political process]. *Handai Hogaku.* 136. (September): 190.

Ippolito, Dennis S., and Thomas G. Walker. 1980. *Political Parties, Interest Groups, and Public Policy in America: Group Influence in American Politics.* Englewood Cliffs, N.J.: Prentice-Hall.

Isaac, R. Mark, James M. Walker, and Susan H. Thomas. 1984. "Divergent Evidence on Free Riding: An Experimental Examination of Possible Explanations." *Public Choice* 43: 113–49.

Ivers, Gregg. 1995. *To Build a Wall: American Jews and the Separation of Church and State.* Charlottesville: University Press of Virginia.

Jacek, Henry. 1986. "Pluralist and Corporatist Intermediation, Activities of Business Interest Associations and Corporate Profits: Some Evidence from Canada." *Comparative Politics* 18: 419–37.

———. 1987–88. "Large State / Small State Relations in the North American Political Economy: Are There Lessons From Europe?" *The American Review of Canadian Studies* XVII: 419–38.

———. 1991. "The Functions of Associations as Agents of Public Policy." In *International Markets and Global Firms.* A. Martinelli, cited below.

———. 1994. "Public Policy and NAFTA: The Role of Organized Business Interests and the Labour Movement." *Canadian-American Public Policy* 19: 1–33.

Jackson, Brooks. 1990. *Honest Graft: Big Money and the American Political Process.* rev. ed. Washington, D.C.: Farragut.

Jacob, Herbert. 1984. *The Frustration of Policy: Responses to Crime by American Cities.* Boston: Little, Brown.

Jacobson, Gary C., and Samuel Kernell. 1983. *Strategy and Choice in Congressional Elections.* 2nd ed. New Haven, Conn.: YUP.

Jahn, Detlef. 1993. *New Politics in Trade Unions: Applying Organizational Theory to the Ecological Discourse on Nuclear Energy in Sweden and Germany.* Brookfield, Vt.: Dartmouth.

Janos, Andrew. 1979. "Interest Groups and the Structure of Power," *Studies in Comparative Communism* 12: 6–20.

Jansen, Michael. 1987. *Dissonance in Zion.* London: Zed Press.

Jasper, James M. 1992. *The Animal Rights Crusade: The Growth of a Moral Protest.* New York: Free Press.

Jenkins, J. Craig. 1985. *The Politics of Insurgency.* New York: Columbia University Press.

Jenkins, J. Craig, and Bert Klandermans, eds. 1995. *The Politics of Social Protest: Comparative Perspectives on States and Social Movements.* London: UCL Press.

Jenkins, J. Craig., and Charles Perrow. 1977. "Insurgency of the Powerless: Farm Worker's Movements, 1946 -1972." *American Sociological Review* 42: 248–68.

Jessop, B. 1979. "Corporatism, Parliamentarism and Social Democracy." In *Trends Toward Corporatist Intermediation.* P. Schmitter and G. Lehmbruch, cited below.

———. 1982. *The Capitalist State.* New York: New York University Press.

Johnson, Chalmers. 1982. *MITI and the Japanese Miracle: The Growth of Industrial Policy, 1925–1975.* Stanford, Calif.: Stanford University Press.

———. 1987. "Political Institutions and Economic Performance: The Government-Business Relationship in Japan, South Korea and Taiwan." In *The Political Economy of the New Asian Industrialism,* ed. Frederic C. Deyo. Ithaca, N.Y.: Cornell University Press.

Johnson, Diane E. 2001. "Argentina: Parties and Interests Operating Separately by Design and in Practice." In *Political Parties and Interest Groups.* C. Thomas, cited below.

Johnson, John J., et al. 1958. *Political Change in Latin America: The Emergence of the Middle Sectors.* Stanford, Calif.: Stanford University Press.

———, ed. 1964. *Continuity and Change in Latin America.* Stanford, Calif.: Stanford University Press.

Johnson, Troy R. 1994. *Alcatraz: Indian Land Forever.* Los Angeles: American Indian Studies Center, University of California Los Angeles.

———, ed. 1999. *Contemporary Native American Political Issues.* Walnut Creek, Calif.: Alta Mira Press.

Jonas, Frank H., ed. 1961. *Western Politics.* Salt Lake City: University of Utah Press.

———. 1969. *Politics in the American West.* Salt Lake City: University of Utah Press.

Jones, Brian D. 1983. *Governing Urban America: A Policy Focus.* Boston: Little, Brown.

Jones, Charles O. 1961. "Representation in Congress: The Case of the House Agriculture Committee." *APSR* 55: 358–67.

———. 1979. "American Politics and the Organization of Energy Decision Making." *Annual Review of Energy* 4: 99–121.

Jordan, A. G. 1984. "Pluralistic Corporatism and Corporate Pluralism." *SPS* 7: 137–51.

———. 1989. "Insider Lobbying: The British Version." *Political Studies* 37: 107–13.

———. 1990. "The Pluralism of Pluralism: An Anti-theory?." *Political Studies* 38: 286–301.

Jordan, A. G., W. Maloney, and A. McLaughlin. 1994. "Characterizing Agricultural Policy Making," *Public Administration* 72: 505–26.

Jordan, A. G., and J. J. Richardson. 1987. *Government and Pressure Groups in Britain.* Oxford: Clarendon.

Jordan, Grant, ed. 1991. *The Commercial Lobbyists.* Aberdeen: University of Aberdeen Press.

———. 1998. "Towards Regulation in the UK: From 'General Good Sense' to 'Formal Rules.'" *Parliamentary Affairs* 51: 524–37.

———. 2001. *Shell, Greenpeace and Brent Spar.* London: Palgrave Macmillan.

Jordan, Grant, and Klaus Schubert. 1992. "A preliminary ordering of policy network labels." *European Journal of Political Research* 21: 7–28.

Jordan, Grant, and William A. Maloney. 1996. "How Bumble-Bees Fly: Accounting for Public Interest Participation." *Political Studies* 44: 668–85.

———. 1997. *The Protest Business? Mobilising Campaign Groups.* Manchester, U.K.: Manchester University Press.

———. 2001. "Britain: Change and Continuity Within the New Realities of British Politics." In *Political Parties and Interest Groups.* C. Thomas, cited below.

Joseph, Richard. 1997. "Democratization in Africa after 1989: Comparative and Theoretical Perspectives." *Comparative Politics* 29 (3): 363–82.

Journal of Labor Research. 1999. "Symposium: Union Money, Political Action, and Government Regulation." 20: 270–366.

Jupp, J., and M. Kabala, eds. 1993. *The Politics of Australian Immigration.* Canberra: Australian Government Publishing Service.

Kandil, Amani. 1994. "Socioeconomic Policies and Interest Groups in Egypt." In *Developmentalism and Beyond*, eds. Ayse Oncue, et al. Cairo: The American University in Cairo.

Karl, Terry L. 1991. "Dilemmas of Democratization." *Comparative Politics* 23: 1–21.

Karvonen, Lauri, and Per Selle, eds. 1995. *Women in Nordic Politics: Closing the Gap.* Brookfield, Vt.: Dartmouth.

Kassim, Hussein, and Anand Menon, eds. 1996. *The European Union and National Industrial Policy.* London: Routledge.

Katzenstein, Mary. 1990. "Feminism within American Institutions." *Signs* 16: 27–54.

———. 1995. "Discursive Politics and Feminist Activism in the Catholic Church." In, *Feminist Organizations.* M. Ferree and P. Martin, cited above.

Katzenstein, Peter. 1984. *Corporatism and Change: Austria, Switzerland and the Politics of Industry.* Ithaca, N.Y.: Cornell University Press.

———. 1985. *Small States in World Markets: Industrial Policy in Europe.* Ithaca, N.Y.: Cornell University Press.

———. 1987. *Policy and Politics in West Germany: The Growth of a Semisovereign State.* Philadelphia: Temple University Press.

———, ed. 1989. *Industry and Politics in West Germany: Toward the Third Republic.* Ithaca: Cornell University Press.

Kau, James, and Paul H. Rubin. 1981. "The Impact of Labor Unions on the Passage of Economic Legislation." *Journal of Labor Research* 2: 133–45.

Kay, Barry J., Ronald D. Lambert, and Steven D. Brown. 1991. "Single-Issue Interest Groups and the Canadian Electorate: The Case of Abortion in 1988." *Journal of Canadian Studies* 26: 142–54.

Kazee, Thomas A., and Mary C. Thornberry. 1990. "Where's the Party? Congressional Candidate Recruitment and American Party Organizations." *WPQ* 43: 61–80.

Kearney, Robert N. 1971. *Trade Unions and Politics in Ceylon.* Berkeley: UCAP.

Keck, Margaret E. 1989. "The New Unionism in the Brazilian Transition." In *Democratizing Brazil: Problems of Transition and Consolidation,* ed. A. Stepan. New York: OUP.

Keck, Margaret E., and Kathryn Sikkink. 1998. *Activists Beyond Borders: Advocacy Networks in International Politics.* Ithaca, N.Y.: Cornell University Press.

Keeler, John T. S. 1981. "Corporatism and official union hegemony: the case of French agricultural syndicalism." In *Organizing Interests in Western Europe.* S. Berger, cited above.

———. 1985. "Situating France on the Pluralism-Corporatism Continuum: A Critique of and Alternative to the Wilson Perspective." *Comparative Politics* 17: 229–49.

———. 1987. *The Politics of Neocorporatism in France.* New York: OUP.

Kelber, Mim, ed. 1994. *Women and Government: New Ways to Political Power.* Westport, Conn.: Praeger.

Kelley, Anne E., and Ella L. Taylor. 1992. "Florida: The Changing Patterns of Power." In *Interest Group Politics in the Southern States.* R. Hrebenar, and C. Thomas, cited above.

Kelley, Stanley, Jr. 1956. *Professional Public Relations and Political Power.* Baltimore: JHUP.

Keman, Hans, ed. 1993. *Comparative Politics: New Directions in Theory and Method.* Amsterdam: VU University Press.

Keman, H, and P. Pennings. 1995. "Managing Political and Societal Conflicts in Democracies: Does Consensus and Corporatism Matter? *BJPS* 25: 271–81.

Kennedy, Michael D. 1991. *Professionals, Power and Solidarity in Poland.* Cambridge, Mass.: CUP.

Keohane, Robert O., and Joseph S. Nye, Jr., eds. 1970. *Transnational Relations and World Politics.* Cambridge, Mass.: HUP.

Kernaghan, Kenneth. 1985. "Pressure Groups and Public Servants in Canada." In *Public Administration in Canada,* 5th ed., ed. K. Kernaghan. Toronto: Methuen.

Kerr, Joanna. 1993. *Ours by Right: Women's Rights as Human Rights.* London: Zed Books, for the North-South Institute.

Kerwin, Cornelius. 1994. *Rulemaking.* Washington, D.C.: CQP.

Kessler, David. 2001. *A Question of Intent: A Great American Battle with a Deadly Industry.* New York: Public Affairs.

Kessler, Mark. 1990. "Legal Mobilization for Social Reform: Power and the Politics of Agenda Setting." *Law & Society Review* 24: 121–43.

Key, V. O., Jr. 1949. *Southern Politics in State and Nation.* New York: Knopf.

———. 1964. *Politics, Parties & Pressure Groups.* 5th ed. New York: Crowell.

———. 1967. *Public Opinion and American Democracy.* New York: Knopf.

Kholodkovsky, K., ed. 1998. *Civil Society in Russia: Its Structures and Mass Consciousness*. Moscow: Institute of World Economy and International Relations [available only in Russian].

Kile, Orville M. 1948. *The Farm Bureau through Three Decades*. Baltimore: Waverly Press.

Kim, Hyung-chan. 1977. "Korean Community Organizations in America: Their Characteristics and Problems." In *Korean Diaspora*, ed. Hyung-Chan Kim. Santa Barbara, Calif.: ABC-Clio.

King, Gary, et al.1994. *Designing Social Inquiry: Scientific Inference in Qualitative Research*. Princeton, N.J.: PUP.

King, Lauriston. 1975. *The Washington Lobbyists for Higher Education*. Lexington, Mass.: Lexington Books.

Kingdon, John W. 1981. *Congressmen's Voting Decisions*. 2nd ed. New York: Harper & Row.

———. 1984. *Agendas, Alternatives and Public Policy*. Boston: Little, Brown.

Kirchner, E. J. 1981. *The Role of Interest Groups in the European Community*. Aldershot: Gower.

Kirkpatrick, Evron M. 1971. "Toward a More Responsible Two Party System: Political Science, Policy Science, or Pseudo-Science?" *APSR* 65: 965–90.

Kitschelt, Herbert. 1986. "Political Opportunity Structures and Political Protest: Anti-Nuclear Movements in Four Democracies." *BJPS* 16: 57–85.

Klausen, Kurt Klaudi. 1996. "Women and Sport in Scandinavia: Policy, Participation and Representation." *SPS* 19: 111–31.

Klein, Martin, ed. 1980. *Peasants in Africa*. Beverly Hills, Calif.: Sage.

Kluger, Richard. 1975. *Simple Justice: The History of Brown v. Board of Education and Black America's Struggle For Equality*. New York: Vintage.

Klyza, Christopher McGrory. 1996. *Who Controls Public Lands?* Chapel Hill: University of North Carolina Press.

Knoke, David. 1986. "Associations and Interest Groups." *American Review of Sociology* 12: 1–21.

———. 1990. *Organizing for Collective Action: The Political Economies of Associations*. Hawthorne, N.Y.: Aldine de Gruyter.

Knoke, David, Franz Urban Pappi, Jeffrey Broadbent, and Yutaka Tsujinaka. 1996. *Comparing Policy Networks: Labor Politics in the U.S., Germany and Japan*. Cambridge, Mass.: CUP.

Kobylka, Joseph F. 1987. "A Court-Created Context for Group Litigation: Libertarian Groups and Obscenity." *JOP* 49: 1061–78.

———. 1991. *The Politics of Obscenity: Group Litigation in a Time of Legal Change*. New York: Greenwood.

Kochanek, Stanley A. 1970. "Interest Groups and Interest Aggregation: The Changing Patterns of Oligarchy in the F.I.C.C.I." *Economic and Political Weekly*, Vol. V. (July): 1291–1308.

———. 1971. "The Federation of Indian Chambers of Commerce and Industry and Politics." *Asian Survey* XI: 866–85.

———. 1974. *Business and Politics in India*. Berkeley: UCAP.

———. 1983. *Interest Groups and Development: Business and Politics in Pakistan*. New Delhi: OUP.

———. 1993. *Patron Client Politics and Business in Bangladesh*. New Delhi: Sage.

———. 1995. "Ethnic Conflict and the Politicization of Pakistan Business." In *Pakistan 1995*, eds. Charles Kennedy and Rasul Bakhsh Rals. Boulder, Colo.: Westview.

———. 1995–96. "The Role of Conflict in the Transformation of Indian Business Associations." *Pacific Affairs* (Winter): 529–50.

———. 1996a. "The Rise of Interest Politics in Bangladesh." *Asian Survey* 36 (7): 704–23.

———. 1996b. "Liberalization and Business Lobbying in India." *The Journal of Commonwealth and Comparative Studies* 34: 155–74.

Koelble, Thomas A. 1995. "The New Institutionalism in Political Science and Sociology." *Comparative Politics* 27: 231–43.

Kolankiewicz, George. 1988, "Poland and the Politics of Permissible Pluralism." *Eastern European Politics and Societies* 2: 152–83.

Kolasa, Bernard D. 1971. "Lobbying in the Nonpartisan Environment: The Case of Nebraska." *WPQ* 24: 65–78.

Kolinsky, Eva. 1984. *Parties, Opposition and Society in West Germany*. New York: SMP.

Kollman, Ken. 1997. "Inviting Friends to Lobby: Interest Groups, Ideological Bias and Congressional Committees." *AJPS* 41: 519–44.

———. 1998. *Outside Lobbying: Public Opinion and Interest Group Strategies*. Princeton, N.J.: PUP.

Kornhauser, Arthur, Harold L. Sheppard, and Albert J. Mayer. 1956. *When Labor Votes*. New York: University Books.

Korpi, Walter. 1981. "Labor Movements and Industrial Relations." In *Nordic Democracy*. E. Allardt, et al., cited above.

Kotz, Nick, and Mary Lynn Kotz. 1977. *A Passion for Equality*. New York: Norton.

Kotze, Hennie, and Pierre Du Toit. 1995. "The State, Civil Society and Democratic Transition in South Africa: A Survey of Elite Attitudes." *Journal of Conflict Resolution* 39: 27–48.

Kovacs, Gyula. 1995. "The Involvement of Interest Organizations in Legislation and in Committee Work." In *The First Parliament, 1990–1994*, eds. Attila Agh and Sandor Kurtan. Budapest: Hungarian Center for Democracy Studies.

Kovenock, David M. 1973. "Influence in the U.S. House of Representatives: A Statistical Analysis of Communications." *APQ* 1: 407–64.

Kramer, Mark 1995. "Polish Workers and the Post-communist Transition, 1989–1993." *Communist and Post-Communist Studies* 28: 71–114.

Krasner, Stephen D. 1978. *Defending the National Interest: Raw Materials Investments and U.S. Foreign Policy*. Princeton, N.J.: PUP.

———. 1982. "Structural Causes and Regime Consequences." *International Organization* 36: 185–206.

———. 1983. *International Regimes*. Ithaca, N.Y.: Cornell University Press.

Kratochwil, Friedrich, and John Gerald Ruggie. 1986. "International Organization: A State of the Art on the Art of the State." *International Organization* 40: 753–75.

Krause, George A. 1994. "Economics, Politics and Policy Change: Examining the Consequences of Deregulation in the Banking Industry." *APQ* 22: 221–43.

Krehbiel, Keith. 1990. "Are Congressional Committees Composed of Preference Outliers?" *APSR* 84: 149–63.

Kriesi, Hanspeter. 1982. "The Structure of the Swiss Political System." In *Patterns of Corporatist Policy-Making*. G. Lehmbruch and P. Schmitter, cited below.

Krislov, Samuel. 1963. "The *Amicus Curiae* Brief: From Friendship to Advocacy." *Yale Law Journal* 72: 694–721.

Kristianson, G. 1966. *The Politics of Patriotism: The Pressure Group Activities of the Returned Servicemen's League*. Canberra: Australian National University Press.

Kryshtanovskaja, O. 1996. "Russia's illegal structure." In *Post-Soviet Puzzles*, Vol. 3., eds. K. Segbers and S. Spiegelere. Baden-Baden: Nomos.

Kujawa, Duane, and Daniel Bob. 1988. *American Opinion on Japanese Direct Investment*. New York: Japan Society.

Kumar, Martha Joynt, and Michael Baruch Grossman. 1986. "Political Communications from the White House: The Interest Group Connection." *Presidential Studies Quarterly* 16: 92–101.

Kurzig, Carol M. 1981. *Foundation Fundamentals: A Guide for Grantseekers*. Washington, D.C.: Foundation Center.

Kvavik, Robert B. 1974. "Interest Groups in a 'Cooptive' Political System: The Case of Norway." In *Politics in Europe: Structures and Processes in Some Postindustrial Democracies*, ed. Martin O. Heisler. New York: McKay.

———. 1976. *Interest Groups in Norwegian Politics*. Oslo: Universitetsforlaget.

Kwong, Peter. 1987. *The New Chinatown*. New York: Hill and Wang.

Lacey, Michael J., ed. 1991. *Government and Environmental Politics: Essays on Historical Developments Since World War II*. Baltimore: JHUP.

Laham, Nicholas. 1993. *Why the United States Lacks a National Health Insurance Program*. Westport, Conn.: Greenwood.

Lamb, Helen B. 1959. "Business Organization and Leadership in India Today." In *Leadership and Political Institutions in India*, eds. R. L. Park and I. Tinker. Princeton, N.J.: PUP.

Lampton, David A., ed. 1987. *Policy Implementation in Post-Mao China*. Berkeley: UCAP.

Landy, Marc K., and Martin A. Levin, eds. 1995. *The New Politics of Public Policy*. Baltimore: JHUP.

Lane, Christel, and Reinhard Bachmann. 1997. "Co-operation in inter-firm relations in Britain and Germany: the role of social institutions." *British Journal of Sociology* 48: 226–54.

Lane, David. 1997. "Transition under Eltzin: The Nomenklatura and Political Elite Consolidation." *Political Studies* XLV: 855–74.

Lanegran, Kimberly. 1995. "South Africa's Civic Association Movement: ANC's Ally or Society 'Watchdog'? Shifting Social Movement-Political Party Relations." *African Studies Review* 38: 101–26.

Langbein, Laura I. 1986. "Money and Access: Some Empirical Evidence." *JOP* 48: 1052–62.

Lange, Peter, and Geoffrey Garrett. 1985. "The Politics of Growth." *JOP* 47: 792–826.

Lange, Peter, and Marino Regini, eds. 1989. *State, Market and Social Regulation: New Perspectives on Italy*. New York: CUP.

Lange, Peter, George Ross and Maurizio Vannicelli. 1982. *Unions, Change and Crisis: French and Italian Union Strategy and the Political Economy, 1945–1980*. London: Allen & Unwin.

REFERENCES

Lanzalaco, Luca. 1992. "Coping with Heterogeneity: Peak Associations of Business Within and Across Western European Nations." In *Organized Interests and the European Community*. J. Greenwood, J. Grote, and R. Ronit, cited above.

———. 1993. "Interest Groups in Italy: From Pressure Activity to Policy Networks." In *Pressure Groups*. J. Richardson, cited below.

LaPalombara, Joseph. 1964. *Interest Groups in Italian Politics*. Princeton, N.J.: PUP.

LaPotin, Armand. 1987. *Native American Voluntary Organizations*. Westport, Conn.: Greenwood.

Latham, Earl. 1952. *The Group Basis of Politics: A Study in Basing Point Legislation*. Ithaca, N.Y.: Cornell University Press.

Latus, Margaret Ann. 1984. "Ideological PACs and Political Action." In *The New Christian Right*, eds. Robert R. Leibman and Robert Wuthnow. New York: Aldine.

Laumann, Edward O., and John P. Heinz. 1985. "Washington Lawyers and Others: The Structure of Washington Representation." *Stanford Law Review* 37: 465–502.

Laumann, Edward O., and David Knoke. 1987. *The Organizational State: Social Choice in National Policy Domains*. Madison: University of Wisconsin Press.

Laux, William Edward. 1963. "Interest Groups in Danish Politics" [Doctoral dissertation: University of Nebraska]. *Dissertation Abstracts International* 24: 3402–03.

Lavdas, Kostas A. 1997. *The Europeanization of Greece: Interest Politics and the Crises of Integration*. London: Macmillan.

Lawrence, Samuel A. 1966. *United States Merchant Shipping Policies and Politics*. Washington, D.C.: Brookings.

Lawrence, Susan E. 1990. *The Poor in Court: The Legal Services Program and Supreme Court Decision Making*. Princeton, N.J.: PUP.

Lawson, Kay, ed. 1980. *Political Parties and Linkage*. New Haven, Conn.: YUP.

Lawson, Kay, and Peter Merkl, eds. 1988. *When Parties Fail: Emerging Alternative Organizations*. Princeton, N.J.: PUP.

Leddy, Edward F. 1985. "The National Rifle Association: The Evolution of a Social Movement (Gun Control, Shooting, History, National Defense)." Ph.D. Dissertation, Fordham University.

———. 1987. *Magnum Force Lobby: The National Rifle Association Fights Gun Control*. London: UPA.

Lee, Hong Yong. 1978. *The Politics of the Chinese Cultural Revolution*. Berkeley: UCAP.

Lee, Martha F. 1995. *Earth First! Environmental Apocalypse*. Syracuse: Syracuse University Press.

Leger, Marie, ed. 1994. *Aboriginal Peoples: Towards Self-Government*. Translated by Arnold Bennett. Montreal: Black Rose Books.

Lehmbruch, Gerhard. 1979a. "Consociational Democracy, Class Conflict and the New Corporatism." In *Trends Toward Corporatist Intermediation*. P. Schmitter and G. Lehmbruch, cited below.

———. 1979b. "Liberal Corporatism and Party Government." In *Trends Toward Corporatist Intermediation*. P. Schmitter and G. Lehmbruch, cited below.

———. 1982. "Introduction; Neo-corporatism in Comparative Perspective." In *Patterns of Corporatist Policy Making.* G. Lehmbruch and P. Schmitter, cited below.

———. 1998. "The Organization of Society, Administrative Strategies and Policy Networks." In *Institutions and Political Choice: On the Limits of Rationality*, rev. ed., eds. Roland Czada, Adrienne Héritier, and Hans Keman. Amsterdam: VU University Press.

Lehmbruch, Gerhard, and Philippe C. Schmitter, eds. 1982. *Patterns of Corporatist Policy-Making.* Beverly Hills, Calif.: Sage.

Lehne, Richard. 1993. *Industry and Politics: The United States in Comparative Perspective.* Englewood Cliffs, N.J.: Prentice Hall.

Lehner, Franz. 1987. "Interest Intermediation, Institutional Structures and Public Policy." In *Coping with the Economic Crisis: Alternative Responses to Economic Recession in Advanced Industrial Societies*, eds. Hans Keman, Heikki Paloheimo, and Paul F. Whiteley. London: Sage.

———. 1998. "The Institutional Control of Interest Intermediation: A Political Perspective." In *Institutions and Political Choice: On the Limits of Rationality*, rev. ed., eds. Roland Czada, Adrienne Héritier, and Hans Keman. Amsterdam: VU University Press.

Lerman, Arthur J. 1977. "National Elite and Local Politicians in Taiwan." *APSR* 71: 1404–22.

———. 1978. *Taiwan's Politics: The Provincial Assemblyman's World.* Washington, D.C.: UPA.

Lerner, Steve, ed. 1991. *Earth Summit: Conversations with Architects of an Ecologically Sustainable Future.* Bolinas, Calif.: Common Knowledge Press.

Lester, James P., ed. 1995. *Environmental Politics and Policy: Theories and Evidence.* 2nd ed. Durham, N.C.: Duke University Press.

Levine, Charles H., and James A. Thurber. 1986. "Reagan and the Intergovernmental Lobby: Iron Triangles, Cozy Subsystems, and Political Conflict." In *Interest Group Politics*, 2nd ed., A. Cigler and B. Loomis, cited above.

Levine, Daniel, ed. 1980. *Churches and Politics in Latin America.* Beverly Hills, Calif.: Sage.

Levy, Deborah M. 1987. "Advice for Sale." *Foreign Policy* 67: 64–86.

Lewin, L. 1994. "The Rise and Decline of Corporatism: The Case of Sweden." *European Journal of Political Research* 26: 59–79.

Lewis, Charles. 1996. *The Buying of the President.* New York. Avon.

Lewis, David. 2001. *The Management of Nongovernmental Organisations: An Introduction.* London: Routledge.

Lewis, D., and T. Wallace, eds. 2000. *New Roles and Relevance: Development NGOs and the Challenge of Change.* Hartford, Conn.: Kumarian.

Lewis, Peter, ed. 1998. *Africa: Dilemmas of Development and Change.* Boulder, Colo.: Westview.

Libby, Ronald T. 1999. *Eco-Wars: Political Campaigns and Social Movements.* New York: Columbia University Press.

Lieberthal, Kenneth, and David S. Lampton, eds. 1992. *Bureaucracy, Politics and Decision-Making in Post-Mao China.* Berkeley: UCAP.

Lieberthal, Kenneth, and Michel Oksenberg. 1988. *Policy-Making in China: Leaders, Structures and Processes.* Princeton, N.J.: PUP.

Lieuwen, Edwin. 1961. *Arms and Politics in Latin America*. New York: Praeger.

———. 1964. *Generals vs. Presidents: Neo-militarism in Latin America*. New York: Praeger.

Lijphart, Arend. 1969. "Consociational Democracy." *World Politics* 21: 207–25.

———. 1971. "Comparative Politics and the Comparative Method." *APSR* 65: 682–93.

———. 1975. *The Politics of Accommodation: Pluralism and Democracy in the Netherlands*. 2nd ed. Berkeley: UCAP.

———. 1977. *Democracy in Plural Societies: A Comparative Exploration*. New Haven, Conn.: YUP.

———. 1981. *Conflict and Coexistence in Belgium: The Dynamics of a Culturally Divided Society*. Berkeley: Institute of International Studies, University of California.

———. 1989. "From the Politics of Accommodation to Adversarial Politics in the Netherlands: A Reassessment." *West European Politics*. 12: 139–53.

Lijphart, Arend, and Markus M. L.. Crepaz. 1991. "Corporatism and Consensus Democracy in Eighteen Countries: Conceptual and Empirical Linkages." *BJPS* 21: 235–56.

Limb, Peter. 1993. *The ANC and Black Workers in South Africa, 1912–1992: An Annotated Bibliography*. London: H. Zell.

Lindblom, Charles. E. 1977. *Politics and Markets: The World's Political-Economic Systems*. New York: Basic Books.

———. 1979. "Still Muddling, Not Yet Through." *Public Administration Review* 39: 517–26.

———. 1982. "The Market as Prison." *JOP* 44: 324–36.

Lindesmith, Alfred R. 1965. *The Addict and the Law*. New York: Vintage.

Linz, Juan. 1981. "A Century of Politics and Interests in Spain." In *Organizing Interests in Western Europe*. S. Berger, cited above.

Lipset, Seymour Martin. 1990. *Continental Divide: The Values and Institutions of the United States and Canada*. New York: Routledge.

———. 1996. *American Exceptionalism: A Double-Edged Sword*. New York: Norton.

Lipset, Seymour Martin, and Aldo Solari, eds. 1967. *Elites in Latin America*. New York: OUP.

Lipset, Seymour Martin, Martin Trow, and James Coleman. 1956. *Union Democracy*. Garden City, N.Y.: Anchor.

Lipsky, Michael. 1968. "Protest as a Political Resource." *APSR* 62: 1144–58.

———. 1970. *Protest in City Politics: Rent Strikes, Housing and the Power of the Poor*. Chicago: Rand McNally.

Lipton, Merle. 1985. *Capitalism and Apartheid*. Totowa, N.J.: Rowman and Allanheld.

Little, Kenneth. 1965. *West African Urbanization: A Study of Voluntary Associations in Social Change*. Cambridge, Mass.: CUP.

Litvak, I. A. 1981. "Government Intervention and Government Corporate Relations." *Business Quarterly* 46 (3): 47–54.

Lloyd, C. 1991. "Political Lobbying: Dynamiting or Gentle Persuasion?" In *No is Not an Answer*. P. Cullen, cited above.

Lobbying, PACs, and Campaign Finance 50 State Handbook. 2002. Minneapolis, Minn.: West Publishing, compiled by the State Capital Global Law Firm Group.

Lockard, Duane. 1959. *New England State Politics.* Princeton, N.J.: PUP.

Locke, Richard M. 1995. *Remaking the Italian Economy.* Ithaca, N.Y.: Cornell University Press.

Lodge, J., ed. 1983. *Institutions and Policies of the European Community.* London: Pinter.

———. 1989. *The European Community and the Challenge of the Future.* London: Pinter.

Lodge, Tom. 1983. *Black Politics in South Africa Since 1945.* London: Longman.

Logan, John, and Harvey Molotch. 1987. *Urban Fortunes.* Berkeley: UCAP.

Lombra, Raymond, and Willard Witte, eds. 1982. *Political Economy of Domestic and International Monetary Relations.* Ames: Iowa State University Press.

Longoria, Thomas, Jr., Robert D. Wrinkle and J. L. Polinard. 1990. "Mexican American Voter Registration and Turnout: Another Look." *SSQ* 71: 356–61.

Loomis, Burdett A. 1983. "A New Era: Groups and the Grass Roots." In *Interest Group Politics.* A. Cigler and B. Loomis, cited above.

Loomis, Burdett A., and Eric Sexton. 1995. "Choosing to Advertise: How Interests Decide." In *Interest Group Politics,* 4th ed. A. Cigler and B. Loomis, cited above.

Lorwin, Val R. 1971. "Segmented Pluralism: Ideological Cleavages and Political Cohesion in the Smaller European Democracies." *Comparative Politics* 3: 141–75.

———. 1975. "Labor Unions and Political Parties in Belgium." *Industrial and Labor Relations Review* 28: 243–63.

Loveday, P. 1970. "Pressure Groups." In *Australia: A Survey,* ed. V. G. Venturini. Weisbaden: Otto Harrasovitz.

Lovenduski, Joni. 1986. *Women and European Politics: Contemporary Feminism and Public Policy.* Amherst.: University of Massachusetts Press.

Low, Kathleen. 1991. *Initiative and Referendum, the Process, Its Use, and Potential Problems: A Bibliography.* Public Administration Series Bibliography. Monticello, Ill.: Vance Bibliographies.

Lowery, David, and Holly Brasher. 2004. *Organized Interests and American Government.* Boston: McGraw Hill.

Lowery, David, and Virginia Gray. 1993a. "The Density of Interest Group Systems." *JOP* 55: 191–206.

———. 1993b. "State Interest Group Diversity." *PRQ* 46: 81–97.

———. 1994. "The Nationalization of State Interest Group System Density and Diversity." *SSQ* 75: 368–77.

———. 1995. "The Population Ecology of Gucci Gulch, or the Natural Regulation of Interest Group Numbers in the American States." *AJPS* 39: 1–29.

———. 1997. "How Some Rules Just Don't Matter: The Regulation of Lobbyists." *Public Choice* 91: 139–47.

———. 1998. "The Dominance of Institutions in Interest Representation: A Test of Seven Explanations." *AJPS* 42: 231–55.

———. 2001. "Bias in the Heavenly Chorus: Interests in Society and Before Government." Paper presented at the annual meeting of the American Political Science Association.

———. 2002. "Sisyphus Meets the Borg: Understanding the Diversity of Interest Communities." Paper presented at the annual meeting of the American Political Science Association.

Lowi, Theodore J. 1964a. "American Business, Public Policy, Case Studies and Political Theory." *World Politics* 16: 677–715.

———. 1964b. "How the Farmers Get What They Want." *Reporter* (May 21): 34–37.

———. 1969. *The End of Liberalism*. New York: Norton.

———. 1971. *The Politics of Disorder*. New York: Basic Books.

———. 1979. *The End of Liberalism*. rev. ed. New York: Norton.

Lubin, Carol Riegelman, and Anne Winslow. 1990. *Social Justice for Women: The International Labor Organization and Women*. Durham, N.C.: Duke University Press.

Lubove, Roy. 1986. *The Struggle for Social Security. 1900–1935*. 2nd ed. Pittsburgh: University of Pittsburgh Press.

Lucco, Joan. 1992. "Representing the Public Interest: Consumer Groups and the Presidency." In *The Politics of Interests*. M. Petracca, cited below.

Luckham, Robin. 1994. "The Military, Militarization and Democratization in Africa: A Survey of Literature and Issues." *African Studies Review* 37: 13–76.

Luker, Kristin. 1984. *Abortion and the Politics of Motherhood*. Berkeley: UCAP.

Lupia, Arthur. 1992. "Busy Voters, Agenda Control and the Power of Information." *APSR* 86: 390–403.

Luther, Kurt Richard, and Wolfgang Müller, eds. 1992a. *Politics in Austria: Still a Case of Consociationalism?* Special issue of *West European Politics* 15 (1).

———. 1992b. "Consociationalism and the Austrian Political System." *West European Politics* 15: 1–15.

Luther, Lorenz, and Margaret Simon. 1992. *Targeted: The Anatomy of an Animal Rights Attack*. Norman: University of Oklahoma Press.

Luttbeg, Norman R. 1992. *Comparing the States and Communities: Politics, Government and Policy in the United States*. New York: HarperCollins.

Maass, Arthur. 1951. *Muddy Waters: Army Engineers and the Nation's Rivers*. Cambridge, Mass.: HUP.

Macdonald, Laura. 1994. "Globalising Civil Society: Interpreting International NGOs in Central America." *Millennium: Journal of International Studies* 23: 267–85.

MacKenzie, G. Galvin, ed. 1987. *The In and Outers: Presidential Appointees and Transient Government in Washington*. Baltimore: JHUP.

MacMillan, Keith, and Ian Turner. 1987. "The Cost-Containment Issue: A Study of Government-Industry Relations in the Pharmaceutical Sectors of the United Kingdom and West Germany." In *Government-Industry Relations*. S. Wilks and M. Wright, cited below.

MacSween, Elizabeth. 1999. "The Case for a Strong Anti-Tobacco Lobby by the CDA—If Not Now, When, and If Not Us, Who?" *Journal of the Canadian Dental Association* 65, No. 1: 40–41.

Magleby, David. 1984. *Direct Legislation: Voting on Ballot Proposition in the United States*. Baltimore: JHUP.

————. 2000. *Outside Money.* Boulder, Colo.: Rowman & Littlefield.

Magleby, David B., and Candice J. Nelson. 1990. *The Money Chase: Congressional Campaign Finance Reform.* Washington, D.C.: Brookings.

Mahood, H. R. 1990. *Interest Group Politics in America: A New Intensity.* Englewood Cliffs, N.J.: Prentice-Hall.

————. 2000. *Interest Group Politics in American National Politics: An Overview.* Upper Saddle River, N.J.: Prentice-Hall.

Mainwaring, Scott. 1989. "Grassroots Popular Movements and the Struggle for Democracy: Nova Iguacu." In *Democratizing Brazil*, ed. A. Stepan. New York: OUP.

Mair, Peter. 1994. "The Correlates of Consensus Democracy and the Puzzle of Dutch Politics." *West European Politics* 17: 97–123.

Makielski, S. J., Jr. 1980. *Pressure Politics in America.* Washington, D.C.: UPA.

Malbin, Michael J. 1984. *Money and Politics in the United States: Financing Elections in the 1980s.* Washington, D.C.: AEI.

Malloy, J., ed. 1977. *Authoritarianism and Corporatism in Latin America.* Pittsburgh, Pa.: University of Pittsburgh Press.

Malova, Darina. 1997. "The Development of Interest Representation in Slovakia After 1989: From 'Transmission Belts' to 'Party-State Corporatism'?" In *Slovakia: Problems of Democratic Consolidation*, eds. Sona Szomolanyi and John A. Gould. Bratislava: Slovak Political Science Association, and Friedrich Ebert Stiftung.

Maltese, John Anthony. 1995. *The Selling of Supreme Court Nominees.* Baltimore: JHUP.

Manes, Christopher. 1990. *Green Rage: Radical Environmentalism and the Unmaking of Civilization.* Boston: Little, Brown.

Maney, Ardith, and Loree Bykerk. 1994. *Consumer Politics: Protecting Public Interests on Capitol Hill.* Westport, Conn.: Greenwood.

Maniruzzaman, Talukder. 1966. "Group Interests in Pakistan Politics: 1947–1958." *Pacific Affairs* 39: 83–93.

Mansbridge, Jane J. 1986. *Why We Lost the ERA.* Chicago: UCP.

Manzo, Bettina. 1994. *The Animal Rights Movement in the United States, 1975–1990: An Annotated Bibliography.* Metuchen, N.J.: Scarecrow Press.

March, James G., and Johan P. Olsen. 1984. "The New Institutionalism: Organizational Factors in Political Life." *APSR* 78: 734–48.

Marcus, Eric. 1992. *Making History: The Struggle for Gay and Lesbian Equal Rights, 1945–1990.* New York: Harper Perennial.

Marin, Bernd. 1985. "Austria—The Paradigm Case of Liberal Corporatism? In *The Political Economy of Corporatism.* W. Grant, cited above.

Marin, Bernd, and Renate Mayntz, eds. 1991. *Policy Networks: Empirical Evidence and Theoretical Considerations.* Frankfurt an Main and Boulder, Colo.: Campus Verlag and Westview Press.

Markmann, Charles L. 1965. *The Noblest Cry: A History of the American Civil Liberties Union.* New York: SMP.

Markovits, Andrei S., ed. 1982. *The Political Economy of West Germany: Modell Deutschland.* New York: Praeger.

————. 1986. *The Politics of the West German Trade Unions: Strategies of Class and Interest Representation in Growth and Crisis.* Cambridge, U.K.: CUP.

Markovitz, Irving Leonard. 1977. *Power and Class in Africa.* Englewood Cliffs, N.J.: Prentice-Hall.

Marks, G, F. Scharpf, P. Schmitter, and W. Streeck. 1996. *Governance in the European Union.* London: Sage.

Marmor, Theodore R. 1973. *The Politics of Medicare.* Chicago: Aldine.

Marquarat, Kathleen. 1993. *Animal Scam: The Beastly Abuse of Human Rights.* Lanham, Md.: Regnery Gateway.

Marquez, Benjamin. 1993. *LULAC: The Evolution of a Mexican American Political Organization.* Austin: University of Texas Press.

Marset, Afat Lutfi al-Sayyid. 1987. "Revolutionaries, Fundamentalists and Housewives: Alternative Groups in the Arab World." *Journal of Arab Affairs* 6: 178–97.

Marsh, David, ed. 1998. *Comparing Policy Networks.* Buckingham, U.K.: Open University Press.

Marsh, D., and J. Chambers. 1983. *Pressure Politics: Interest Groups in Britain.* London: Junction Books.

Marsh, D., and R. A. W. Rhodes. 1992. *Policy Networks in British Government.* Oxford: OUP.

Marsh, I. 1995. *Beyond the Two Party System: Political Representation, Economic Competitiveness and Australian Politics.* Melbourne: CUP.

Martin, Cathie J. 1991. *Shifting the Burden: The Struggle Over Growth and Corporate Taxation.* Chicago: UCP.

———. 1995. "Stuck in Neutral: Big Business and the Politics of National Health Reform." *Journal of Health Politics, Policy and Law* 20: 431–36.

Martin, R. 1975. *Trade Unions in Australia.* Ringwood: Penguin.

Martinelli, Alberto, ed. 1991. *International Markets and Global Firms: A Comparative Study of Organized Business in the Chemical Industry.* London: Sage.

Martínez, Robert E. 1993. *Business and Democracy in Spain.* Westport, Conn.: Praeger.

Marwell, Gerald, and Ruth E. Ames. 1979. "Experiments on the Provision of Public Goods, I: Resources, Interest, Group Size, and the Free Rider Problem." *AJS* 84: 1335–60.

———. 1980. "Experiments on the Provision of Public Goods, II: Provision Points, Stakes, Experiences, and the Free Rider Problem." *AJS* 85: 926–37.

———. 1981. "Economists Free Ride, Does Anyone Else?: Experiments on the Provision of Public Goods IV." *Journal of Public Economics* 15: 295–310.

Maseko, Sipoho S. 1997. "Civic Movement and Non-Violent Action: The Case of the Cape Areas Housing Action Committee." *African Affairs* 96: 353–69.

Mason, David. 1991. "The Polish Parliament and Labor Legislation During Solidarity." In *Legislatures in the Policy Process*, eds. David M. Olson and Michael L. Mezey. Cambridge, Mass.: CUP.

Masters, Marick F, and John Thomas Delaney. 1987. "Union Political Activities: A Review of the Empirical Literature." *Industrial and Labor Relations Review* 10: 336–53.

Matthews, Donald R. 1960. *U.S. Senators and Their World.* Chapel Hill: University of North Carolina Press.

Matthews, Trevor. 1967. "Pressure Groups in Australia." In *Australian Politics: A Reader,* 2nd ed., ed. H. Mayer. Melbourne: F. W. Cheshire.

———. 1973. "Australian Pressure Groups." In *Australian Politics: A Third Reader*, eds. H. Mayer and H. Nelson. Melbourne: Cheshire.

———. 1976. "Interest Group Access to the Australian Government Bureaucracy." In Royal Commission on Australian Government Administration. *Appendixes to Report, Volume Two*. Canberra: Australian Government Publishing Service.

———. 1980. "Pressure Groups." In *Australian Politics: A Fifth Reader*, eds. H. Mayer and H. Nelson. Melbourne: Longman Cheshire.

———. 1983. "Business Associations and the State, 1850–1979." In *State and Economy in Australia*, ed. B. W. Head. Melbourne: OUP.

———. 1990. "Federalism and Interest Group Cohesion: The Case of Australian Business Groups." *Publius* 20: 105–128.

Matthews, Trevor, and John Warhurst. 1993. "Australia: Interest Groups in the Shadow of Strong Political Parties." In *First World Interest Groups*. C. Thomas, cited below.

Maybury-Lewis, David. 1997. *Indigenous Peoples, Ethnic Groups and the State*. Boston: Allyn & Bacon.

Mayer, Lawrence C. 1989. *Redefining Comparative Politics: Promise versus Performance*. Newbury Park, Calif.: Sage.

Mayer, William G. 1992. *The Changing American Mind: How and Why American Public Opinion Changed Between 1960 and 1988*. Ann Arbor: University of Michigan Press.

Mazey, Sonia, and Jeremy J. Richardson, eds. 1993a. *Lobbying in the European Community*. Oxford: OUP.

———. 1993b. "Introduction: Transference of Power, Decision Rules, and Rules of the Game." In *Lobbying in the European Community*. S. Mazey and J. Richardson, cited above.

McAdam, Doug. 1985. *Political Process and the Development of Black Insurgency, 1930–1970*. Chicago: UCP.

McAneny, Leslie, and David W. Moore. 1995. "American Confidence in Public Institutions Rises." *The Gallup Poll Monthly* (May): 11–13.

McCann, Dermot. 1995. *Small States, Open Markets and the Organization of Business Interests*. Aldershot: Dartmouth.

McCann, Michael. 1986. *Taking Reform Seriously: Perspectives on Public Interest Liberalism*. Ithaca, N.Y.: Cornell University Press.

———. 1994. *Rights At Work: Pay Equity Reform and the Politics of Legal Mobilization*. Chicago: UCP.

McCarthy, John D., and Mayer N. Zald. 1977. "Resource Mobilization and Social Movements." *AJS* 82: 1212–41.

McClain, Paula D., and John A. Garcia. 1993. "Expanding Disciplinary Boundaries: Black, Latino and Racial Minority Group Politics in Political Science." In *Political Science: The State of the Discipline II*, ed. Ada W. Finifter. Washington, D.C.: The American Political Science Association.

McCloskey, Herbert, and Alida Brill. 1983. *Dimensions of Tolerance*. New York: Russell Sage Foundation.

McClure, K. 1992. "Pluralism and Political identity." In *Dimensions of Radical Democracy*, ed. C. Moufee. London: Verso.

REFERENCES

McConnell, Grant. 1953. *The Decline of Agrarian Democracy*. New York: Atheneum.

———. 1966. *Private Power and American Democracy*. New York: Knopf.

McCraw, Thomas. 1984. *Prophets of Regulation*. Cambridge, Mass.: HUP.

McCune, Wesley. 1956. *Who's Behind Our Farm Policy?* New York: Praeger.

McDonald, Ronald H. 1971. *Party Systems and Elections in Latin America*. Chicago: Markham.

McFarland, Andrew S. 1976. *Public Interest Lobbies: Decision Making on Energy*. Washington, D.C.: AEI.

———. 1983. "Public Interest Lobbies Versus Minority Faction." In *Interest Group Politics*. A. Cigler and B. Loomis, cited above.

———. 1984a. *Common Cause*. Chatham, N.J.: Chatham House.

———. 1984b. "Energy Lobbies." In *Annual Review of Energy, 1984*. Palo Alto, Calif.: Annual Reviews.

———. 1987. "Interest Groups and Theories of Power in America." *British Journal of Political Research* 17: 129–47.

———. 1991. "Interest Groups and Political Time: Cycles in America," *BJPS*, 21 (3): 257–84.

———. 1992. "Interest Groups and the Policy Making Process: Sources of Countervailing Power in America." In *The Politics of Interests*. M. Petracca, cited below.

———. 1993. *Cooperative Pluralism: The National Coal Policy Experiment*. Lawrence: University Press of Kansas.

McGann, James G. 1995. *The Competition for Dollars, Scholars and Influence in the Public Policy Research Industry*. Lanham, Md.: UPA.

McGrath, Conor. 2002. "Comparative Lobbying Practices: Washington, London, Brussels." Paper presented at the annual meeting of the American Political Science Association.

McGuire, Kevin T., and Gregory A. Caldeira. 1993. "Lawyers, Organized Interests and the Law of Obscenity: Agenda Setting in the Supreme Court." *APSR* 87: 717–26.

McIlwaine, John. 1993. *Africa: A Guide to Reference Material*. London: Hans Zell.

McLaughlin, Andrew, and Grant Jordan. 1993. "The Rationality of Lobbying in Europe: Why Are Euro-Groups So Numerous and So Weak? Some Evidence from the Car Industry." In *Lobbying in the European Community*. S. Mazey and J. Richardson, cited above.

McLennan, G. 1995. *Pluralism*. London: Open University Press.

McMath, Robert C., Jr. 1975. *Populist Vanguard: A History of the Southern Farmers' Alliance*. Chapel Hill: University of North Carolina Press.

McNeil, Genna Rae. 1983. *Groundwork: Charles Hamilton Houston and the Struggle for Civil Rights*. Philadelphia: University of Pennsylvania Press.

McQuaid, Kim. 1981. "The Roundtable: Getting Results in Washington," *Harvard Business Review* (May–June): 114–23.

———. 1982. *Big Business and Presidential Power*. New York: Morrow.

Meier, August, and Elliott Rudwick. 1973. *CORE: A Study in the Civil Rights Movement: 1942–1968*. New York: OUP.

Meier, Kenneth J. 1988. *The Political Economy of Regulation: The Case of Insurance*. Albany, N.Y.: SUNY Press.

Mellors, Colin, and Bert Pijnenburg. 1989. *Political Parties and Coalitions in European Local Government*. London: Routledge.

Melone, Albert P., and Robert Slagter. 1983. "Interest Group Politics and the Reform of the Federal Criminal Code." In *The Political Science of Criminal Justice*, eds. S. Nagel, E. Fairchild, and A. Champagne. Springfield, Ill.: Charles C. Thomas.

Melucci, Alberto. 1980. "The New Social Movements: A Theoretical Approach." *Social Science Information* 19: 199–226.

Menzel, Donald C. 1990. "Collecting, Conveying and Convincing: The Three C's of Local Government Interest Groups." *Public Administration Review* 50: 401–05.

Meyer, David S., and Douglas R. Imig. 1993. "Political Opportunity and the Rise and Decline of Interest Group Sectors." *Social Science Journal*, 30: 253–70.

Meyer, David S., and Suzanne Staggenborg. 1996. "Movements, Countermovements, and the Structure of Political Opportunity." *AJS* 101: 1628–60.

Meyer, David S., and Sidney Tarrow, eds. 1998. *The Social Movement Society: Contentious Politics for a New Century*. Lanham, Md.: Rowman & Littlefield.

Meyer, J. W., and B. Rowan. 1977. "Institutionalized Organizations: Formal Structure as Myth and Ceremony." *AJS* 83: 340–63.

Michael, Jay, Dan Walters with Dan Weintraub. 2001. *The Third House: Lobbyists, Money and Power in California*. Berkeley: Institute of Governmental Studies, University of California, Berkeley.

Micheletti, Michele. 1985. *Organizing Interest and Organized Protest: Difficulties of Member Representation for the Swedish Central Organization of Salaried Employees (TCO)*. Stockholm: University of Stockholm.

———. 1990a. *The Swedish Farmers' Movement and Government Agricultural Policy*. Westport, Conn.: Praeger.

———. 1990b. "Toward Interest Inarticulation: A Major Consequence of Corporatism for Interest Organizations." *SPS* 13: 255–76.

———. 1993. "Sweden: Interest Groups in Transition and Crisis." In *First World Interest Groups*. C. Thomas, cited below.

Michels, Robert. 1958. *Political Parties*. New York: Free Press. Originally published in 1915.

Mikell, Gwendolyn, ed. 1997. *African Feminism: The Politics of Survival in Sub-Saharan Africa*. Philadelphia: University of Pennsylvania Press.

Milbrath, Lester W. 1963. *The Washington Lobbyists*. Chicago: Rand McNally.

———. 1967. "Interest Groups and Foreign Policy." In *Domestic Sources of Foreign Policy*, ed. James Rosenau. New York: Free Press.

———. 1970. "Lobbyists Approach Government." In *Interest Group Politics in America*, ed. R. Salisbury. cited below.

———. 1984. *Environmentalists: Vanguard for a New Society*. Albany, N.Y.: SUNY Press.

Milburn, Josephine F., and Victoria Schuck, eds. 1981. *New England Politics*. Cambridge, Mass.: Schenkman Books.

Miles, Lee, ed. 1996. *The European Union and the Nordic Countries*. London: Routledge.

———. 1997. *Sweden and European Integration*. Aldershot, U.K.: Ashgate.

Miliband, Ralph. 1969. *The State in Capitalist Society*. London: Winfield & Nicholson.

———. 1977. *Marxism and Politics*. London: OUP.

Miller, Charles. 1990. *Lobbying Government: Understanding and Influencing the Corridors of Power*. 2nd ed. Oxford: Blackwell.

———. 2000. *Politico's Guide to Political Lobbying*. London: Politico's.

Miller, Kenneth E. 1991. *Denmark: A Troubled Welfare State*. Boulder, Colo.: Westview.

Miller, Stephen. 1983. *Special Interest Groups in American Politics*. New Brunswick, N.J.: Transaction Books.

Mirowsky, John, and Catherine E. Ross. 1981. "Protest Group Success: The Impact of Group Characteristics, Social Control and Context." *Sociological Focus* 14: 177–92.

Misra, Joya, and Alexander Hicks. 1994. "Catholicism and Unionization in Affluent Postwar Democracies: Catholicism, Culture, Party, and Unionization." *American Sociological Review* 59: 304–26.

Mitchell, Neil J. 1995. "The Global Polity: Foreign Firms' Political Activity in the United States." *Polity* 27: 447–63.

———. 1997. *The Conspicuous Corporation*. Ann Arbor: University of Michigan Press.

Mitchell, William C., and Michael C. Munger. 1991. "Economic Models of Interest Groups." *AJPS* 35: 512–46.

Moe, Terry M. 1980a. *The Organization of Interests: Incentives and the Internal Dynamics of Political Interest Groups*. Chicago: UCP.

———. 1980b. "A Calculus of Group Membership." *AJPS* 24: 593–632.

———. 1981. "Toward a Broader View of Interest Groups." *JOP* 43: 531–43.

———. 1985. "Control and Feedback in Economic Regulation: The Case of the NLRB." *APSR* 79: 1094–1116.

Moen, Matthew. 1989. *The Christian Right and Congress*. Tuscaloosa: University of Alabama Press.

———. 1992. *The Transformation of the Christian Right*. Tuscaloosa: University of Alabama Press.

Molins, Joaquim M., and Alex Casademunt. 1998. "Pressure Groups and the Articulation of Interests." *West European Politics* 21: 124–46.

Monroe. Alan D. 1983. "American Party Platforms and Public Opinion." *AJPS* 27: 27–42.

Moody, Peter. 1977. *Opposition and Dissent in Contemporary China*. Stanford, Calif.: Hoover Institution Press.

Moon, Chung-in. 1988. "Complex Interdependence and Transnational Lobbying: South Korea in the United States." *International Studies Quarterly* 32: 67–89.

Mooney, Patrick H., and Theo J. Majka. 1995. *Farmers' and Farm Workers' Movements: Social Protest in American Agriculture*. New York: Twayne.

Moore, Clement Henry. 1974. "Authoritarian Politics in Unincorporated Society," *Comparative Politics* 6: 193–218.

Moore, Stephen. 1993. *Contributing to Death: The Influence of Tobacco Money in the U.S. Congress*. Washington, D.C.: Public Citizen's Health Research Group.

References

Moore, William J., Denise R. Chadrere, Thomas D. Curtis, and David Gordon. 1995. "The Political Influence of Unions and Corporations on COPE Votes in the U.S. Senate, 1979–1988." *Journal of Labor Research* 16: 203–19.

Moran, Michael. 1984. *The Politics of Banking: The Strange Case of Competition and Credit Control.* New York: SMP.

———. 1991. *The Politics of the Financial Services Revolution.* London: Macmillan

———. 1994. "The State and the Financial Services Revolution: A Comparative Analysis." *West European Politics* 17: 158–77.

Morehouse, Sarah McCally. 1981. *State Politics, Parties and Policy.* New York: Holt, Rinehart and Winston.

———. 1997. "Interest Groups, Parties and Policies in the American States." Paper presented at the annual meeting of the American Political Science Association.

Morehouse, Sarah McCally, and Malcolm E. Jewell. 2003. *State Politics, Parties and Policy.* Latham, Md.: Rowman & Littlefield.

Morlino, Leonardo. 1998. *Democracy Between Consolidation and Crisis: Parties, Groups and Citizens in Southern Europe.* Oxford: OUP.

Morris, Aldon. 1984. *The Origins of the Civil Rights Movement: Black Communities Organizing for Change.* New York: Free Press.

Morris, Lorenzo, and Linda F. Williams. 1989. "The Coalition at the End of the Rainbow." In *Jesse Jackson's 1984 Presidential Campaign: Challenge and Change in American Politics*, eds. Lucius Barker and Ronald Walters. Urbana: University of Illinois Press.

Morrison, James F. 1968. *Polish People's Republic.* Baltimore: JHUP.

Morss, Elliott R. 1991. "The New Global Players: How They Compete and Collaborate?" *World Development* 19: 55–64.

Moss, Jordan. 1993. "Motor Voter: From Movement to Legislation." *Social Policy* 24: 21–31.

Moss, Robert. 1971. "Urban Guerilla Violence." Adelphi Papers, No. 79. London: International Institute for Strategic Studies.

Mucciaroni, Gary. 1995. *Reversals of Fortune: Public Policy and Private Interests.* Washington D.C.: Brookings.

Mueller, Carol. 1988. *The Politics of the Gender Gap.* Newbury Park, Calif.: Sage.

———. 1995. "The Organizational Basis of Conflict in Contemporary Feminism." In *Feminist Organizations.* M. Ferree and P. Martin, cited above.

Mueller, Keith J. 1993. *Health Care Policy in the United States.* Lincoln: University of Nebraska Press.

Muir, William K., Jr. 1982. *Legislature: California's School for Politics.* Chicago: UCP.

Mulgan, R. 1994. *Politics in New Zealand.* Auckland: Auckland University Press.

Mundo, Phillip. 1992. *Interest Groups: Cases and Characteristics.* Chicago: Nelson Hall.

Muñoz, Carlos, Jr. 1989. *Youth, Identity, Power: The Chicano Movement.* New York: Verso Press.

Nadel, Mark V. 1971. *The Politics of Consumer Protection.* Indianapolis: Bobbs-Merrill.

Nader, Ralph. 1965. *Unsafe at Any Speed.* New York: Grossman.

———. 1973. *The Consumer and Corporate Accountability.* New York: Harcourt Brace Jovanovich.

Nader, Ralph, and William Taylor. 1986. *The Big Boys: Power and Position in American Business.* New York: Pantheon.

Nader, Ralph, and Wesley J. Smith. 1996. *No Contest: Corporate Lawyers and the Perversion of Justice in America.* New York: Random House.

Nagel, Joane. 1996. *American Indian Ethnic Renewal.* New York: OUP.

Najam, A. 1996. "Understanding the third sector: revisiting the Prince, the Merchant and the Citizen." *Nonprofit Management and Leadership* 7: 203–19.

Nakanishi, Don T. 1986. "Asian American Politics: An Agenda for Research." *Amerasia Journal* 12: 1–27.

———. 1998. "When Numbers do Not Add Up: Asian Pacific Americans and California Politics." In *Racial and Ethnic Politics in California: Volume Two*, eds. Michael Preston, Bruce Cain, and Sandra Bass. Berkeley, Calif.: Institute of Governmental Studies.

Nathan, Andrew, and Chou Yangsun. 1987. "Democratizing Transition in Taiwan." *Asian Survey* 27 (3): 277–99.

National Opinion Research Center. 1993. "Confidence in Institutions." *The American Enterprise,* (November and December): 94–96.

National Trade and Professional Associations of the United States, 2001, 36th ed. Washington, D.C.: Columbia Books.

Navarro, Armando. 1995. *Mexican American Youth Organization: Avant-Garde of the Chicano Movement in Texas.* Austin: The University of Texas Press.

Navarro, Peter. 1985. *The Dimming of America: The Real Costs of Electric Utility Regulatory Failure.* Cambridge, Mass.: Ballinger.

Ndegwa, Stephen N. 1994. "Civil Society and Political Change in Africa: The Case of Non-Governmental Organizations in Kenya." *International Journal of Comparative Sociology* 35: (1/2): 19–37.

Needler, Martin C. 1968. *Political Development in Latin America: Instability, Violence and Evolutionary Change.* New York: Van Nostrand Rheinhold.

Nelkin, Dorothy, and Michael Pollak. 1981. *The Atom Besieged: Extra-Parliamentary Dissent in France and Germany.* Cambridge, Mass.: MIT Press.

Nelsen, Brent F. 1991. *The State Offshore: Petroleum, Politics and State Intervention on the British and Norwegian Continental Shelves.* New York: Praeger.

———. 1993. "The European Community Debate in Norway: The Periphery Revolts, Again." In *Norway and the European Community: The Political Economy of Integration*, eds. Brent F. Nelsen. Westport, Conn.: Praeger.

Nelson, Barbara J. 1984. *Making an Issue of Child Abuse: Political Agenda Setting for Social Problems.* Chicago: UCP.

Nelson, Joan M., ed. 1994. *A Precarious Balance: Democracy and Economic Reforms in Latin America, Volume II.* San Francisco: International Center for Economic Growth and Overseas Development Council.

Nelson, Robert L., John P. Heinz, Edward O. Laumann, and Robert H. Salisbury. 1987. "Private Representation in Washington: Surveying the Structure of Influence." *American Bar Foundation Research Journal,* (Winter): 141–200.

Nelson, Robert L., and John P. Heinz. 1988. "Lawyers and the Structure of Influence in Washington." *Law & Society Review* 22: 237–300.

Ness, Immanuel. 2000. *Encyclopedia of Interest Groups and Lobbyists in the United States.* 2 vols. Armonk, N.Y.: M. E. Sharpe.

Neuman, W. Russell. 1986. *The Paradox of Mass Politics: Knowledge and Opinion in the American Electorate.* Cambridge, Mass.: HUP.

Newkirk, Ingrid. 1992. *Free the Animals! The Untold Story of the U.S. Animal Liberation Front and Its Founder, "Valerie."* Chicago: Noble House.

Newman, David, ed. 1985. *The Impact of Gush Emunim.* London: Croom Helm.

Ngo, Tak-wing. 1993. "Civil Society and Political Liberalization in Taiwan." *Bulletin of Concerned Asian Scholars* 25 (1): 3–15.

Nice, David C. 1984. "Interest Groups and Policymaking in the American States." *Political Behavior* 6: 183–96.

Nice, David C., and Patricia Fredericksen 1995. *The Politics of Intergovernmental Relations.* 2nd ed. Chicago: Nelson-Hall.

Nicholas, E. M. 1970. *The Environmental Revolution.* New York: McGraw Hill.

Nicoll, W., and T. C. Salmon. 1994. *Understanding the New European Community.* New York: Harvester Wheatsheaf.

Niezen, Ronald. 1997. *Defending the Land.* Boston: Allyn & Bacon.

Nivola, Pietro S. 1986. *The Politics of Energy Conservation.* Washington, D.C.: Brookings.

Nordlinger, Eric. 1981. *The Autonomy of the Democratic State.* Cambridge, Mass.: HUP.

Nordquist, Joan. 1991. *Animal Rights: A Bibliography.* Santa Cruz, Calif.: Reference and National Services.

Norris, Pippa, and Joni Lovenduski. 1995. *Political Recruitment: Gender, Race and Class in the British Parliament.* Cambridge, U.K.: CUP.

North, Douglass C. 1990. *Institutions, Institutional Change and Economic Performance.* Cambridge, Mass.: CUP.

Norton, Augustus Richard, ed. 1995. *Civil Society in the Middle East.* Vol. I. Leiden: E. J Brill.

———, ed. 1996. *Civil Society in the Middle East.* Vol. II. Leiden: E. J Brill.

Norton, Philip, ed. 1999. *Parliaments and Pressure Groups in Western Europe.* London: Frank Cass.

Nownes, Anthony J. 2001. *Pressure and Power: Organized Interests in American Politics.* Boston: Houghton Mifflin.

Nownes, Anthony J., Christopher A, Cooper and Jacqueline Giles. 2002. "Citizen Groups in Big City Politics." Paper presented at the annual meeting of the Western Political Science Association.

Nownes, Anthony J., and Patricia Freeman. 1998a. "Interest Group Activity in the States." *JOP* 60: 86–112.

———. 1998b. "Female Lobbyists: Women in the World of 'Good ol' Boys'." *JOP* 60: 1181–1201.

Nownes, Anthony J., and Jacqueline Giles. 2001. "Lobbying in the Metropolis." Paper presented at the annual meeting of the Western Political Science Association.

Nugent, Neill. 1994. *The Government and Politics of the European Union.* London: MacMillan.

Nun, Jose. 1968. "A Latin American Phenomenon: The Middle-Class Military Coup." In *Latin America: Reform or Revolution?*, eds. J. Petras and M. Zeitlin. New York: Fawcett.

465

Nyang'oro, Julius E., and Timothy M. Shaw, eds. 1989. *Corporatism in Africa: Comparative Analysis and Practice.* Boulder, Colo.: Westview.

O'Connor, Karen. 1980. *Women's Organizations' Use of the Court.* Lexington, Mass.: Lexington Books.

———. 1996. *No Neutral Ground: Abortion Politics in an Age of Absolutes.* Boulder, Colo.: Westview.

O'Connor, Karen, and Lee Epstein. 1981–82. "Amicus Curiae Participation in U.S. Supreme Court Litigation: An Appraisal of Hakman's 'Folklore'." *Law & Society Review* 16: 311–20.

———. 1983. "The Rise of Interest Group Litigation." *JOP* 45: 479–89.

———. 1988. "A Legal Voice for the Chicano Community: The Activities of the Mexican American Legal Defense and Educational Fund, 1968–1982." In *Pursing Power.* F. C. Garcia, cited above.

O'Connor, Karen, and Bryant Scott McFall. 1992. "Conservative Interest Group Litigation in the Reagan Era and Beyond." In *The Politics of Interests.* M. Petracca, cited below.

Odegard, Peter. 1928. *Pressure Politics: The Story of the Anti-Saloon League.* New York: Columbia University Press.

O'Donnell, Guillermo. 1973. *Modernization and Bureaucratic-Authoritarianism: Studies in South American Politics.* Berkeley: University of California Institute of International Studies, Politics of Modernization Series, No. 9.

O'Donnell, Guillermo, Philippe C. Schmitter, and Lawrence Whitehead, eds. 1986. *Transitions from Authoritarian Rule: Latin America.* Baltimore: JHUP.

Offe, Claus. 1981. "The Attribution of Public Status to Interest Groups: Observations on the West German Case." In *Organizing Interests in Western Europe.* S. Berger, cited above.

———. 1984. *Contradictions of the Welfare State.* London: Hutchison.

Ogden, Suzanne. 2000. "China's Developing Civil Society: Interest Groups, Trade Unions and Associational Pluralism." In *Changing Workplace Relations in the Chinese Economy,* ed. Malcolm Warner. New York: SMP.

Ogene, Chidozie F. 1984. *Interest Groups and the Shaping of Foreign Policy: Four Case Studies of United States-African Policy.* New York: SMP.

Okimoto, Daniel K. 1988. "Political Inclusivity: The Domestic Structure of Trade." In *The Political Economy of Japan: Vol. 2.,* eds. Takeshi Inoguchi and Daniel I. Okimoto. Stanford, Calif.: Stanford University Press.

Oksenberg, Michel, 1968. "Occupational Groups in Chinese Society and the Cultural Revolution." In *The Cultural Revolution: 1967 in Review,* eds. Michel Oksenberg, et al. Ann Arbor: University of Michigan Center for Chinese Studies.

Oliver, Pamela, Gerald Marwell, and Ruy Teixeira. 1985. "A Theory of Critical Mass, I: Interdependence, Group Heterogeneity and the Production of Collective Goods." *AJS* 91: 522–56.

Olsen, Johan P. 1983. *Organized Democracy: Political Institutions in a Welfare State: The Case of Norway.* Bergen: Universitetsforlaget.

Olsen, Marvin E. 1977. "Influence Linkages Between Interest Organizations and the Government in Sweden." *Journal of Political and Military Sociology* 5: 35–51.

Olson, David. 1992. "Term Limits Fail in Washington: The 1991 Battleground." In *Limiting Legislative Terms,* eds. Gerald Benjamin and Michael Malbin. Washington, D.C.: CQP.

Olson, Mancur. 1965 and 1971. *The Logic of Collective Action: Public Goods and the Theory of Groups.* Cambridge, Mass.: HUP.

———. 1979. "Group Size and Contribution to Collective Action: A Response." *Research in Social Movements, Conflict and Change* 2: 149–50.

———. 1982. *The Rise and Decline of Nations: Economic Growth, Stagflation and Economic Rigidities.* New Haven, Conn.: YUP.

———. 1995. Report to the Conference on *Reforms in Russia: Established Interests and Practical Alternatives.* Moscow. Published by IRIS Publications, University of Maryland, 1999.

Olson, Susan M. 1981. "The Political Evolution of Interest Group Litigation." In *Governing Through Courts,* eds. Richard A. L. Gambitta, Marlynn L. May, and James C. Foster. Beverly Hills, Calif.: Sage.

———. 1990. "Interest Group Litigation in Federal District Court: Beyond the Political Disadvantage Theory." *JOP* 52: 854–82.

———. 1995. "Comparing Women's Rights Litigation in The Netherlands and the United States." *Polity* 28: 189–215.

Olson, Walter, ed. 1988. *New Directions in Liability Law.* New York: Proceedings of the Academy of Political Science, Vol. 37.

Omatsu, Glenn. 1994. "The 'Four Prisons' and the Movements of Liberation: Asian American Activism from the 1960s to the 1990s." In *The State of Asian America: Activism and Resistance in the 1990s,* ed. Karin Aguilar-San Juan. Boston: South End Press.

Opheim, Cynthia. 1991. "Explaining the Differences in State Lobby Regulation." *WPQ* 44: 405–21.

Organski, A. F. K. 1990. *The $36 Billion Bargain: Strategy and Politics in U.S. Assistance to Israel.* New York: Columbia University Press.

Orlans, H. 1972. *Contracting for Knowledge.* San Francisco: Jossey Bass.

Orman, John. 1988. "The President and Interest Group Access," *PSQ* 18: 787–91.

Ornstein, Norman, J., and Shirley Elder. 1978. *Interest Groups, Lobbying and Policy Making.* Washington, D.C.: CQP.

Orr, Marion. 1999. *Black Social Capital: The Politics of School Reform in Baltimore 1986–1998.* Lawrence: University Press of Kansas.

Ortiz, Isidro D. 1991. "Latino Organizational Leadership Strategies in the Era of Reaganomics." In *Latinos and Political Coalitions: Political Empowerment for the 1990s,* ed. Roberto E. Villarreal and Norma G. Hernandez. Westport, Conn.: Greenwood.

Ost, David. 1990. *Solidarity and the Politics of Anti-Politics.* Philadelphia: Temple University Press.

———. 2001. "Poland: Parties, Movements, Groups and Ambiguity." In *Political Parties and Interest Groups.* C. Thomas, cited below.

Ostry, Sylvia. 1990. *Governments and Corporations in a Shrinking World: Trade and Innovation Policies in the United States, Europe and Japan.* New York: Council on Foreign Relations Press.

O'Toole, Laurence J. Jr., ed. 2000. *American Intergovernmental Relations.* 3rd ed. Washington, D.C.. CQP.

Padgett, Stephen. 1999. *Organizing Democracy in Eastern Germany: Interest Groups in Post-Communist Society.* Cambridge, U.K.: CUP.

REFERENCES

Paehlke, Robert. 1989. *Environmentalism and the Future of Progressive Politics.* New Haven, Conn.: YUP.

———. 1995. *Conservation and Environmentalism: An Encyclopedia.* New York: Garland.

Panitch, L. 1979. "The Development of Corporatism in Liberal Democracies." In *Trends Toward Corporatist Intermediation.* P. Schmitter and G. Lehmbruch, cited below.

———. 1980. "Recent Theorizations of Corporatism: Reflections on a Growth Industry." *British Journal of Sociology* 31: 161–87.

Papadakis, Elim. 1984. *The Green Movement in West Germany.* New York: SMP.

———. 1993. *Politics and the Environment: The Australian Experience.* Sydney: Allen & Unwin.

Pardeck, John T. 2002. *Children's Rights: Policy and Practice.* New York: Haworth Social Work Practice Press.

Pardo, Mary. 1998. *Mexican American Women Activists: Identity and Resistance in Two Los Angeles Communities.* Philadelphia: Temple University Press.

Parliamentary Affairs. 1998. Special Issue, "The Regulation of Lobbying" Vol. 51, No. 4.

Parrillo, Vincent N. 1982. "Asian Americans in American Politics." In *America's Ethnic Politics,* eds. Joseph Roucek and Bernard Eisenberg. Westport, Conn.: Greenwood.

Parris, Kristen. 1999. "The Rise of Private Business Interests." In *The Paradox of China's Post-Mao Reforms,* eds. Merle Goldman and Roderick Mac Farquhar. Cambridge, Mass.: HUP.

Paterson, William E. 1991. "Self-regulation Under Pressure: Environmental Protection Policy and the Industry's Response." In *International Markets and Global Firms.* A. Martinelli, cited above.

Paterson, William, and Gordon Smith, eds., 1981. *The West German Model: Perspectives on a Stable State.* London: Frank Cass.

Patterson, Kelly D., and Matthew M. Singer. 2002. "The National Rifle Association in the Face of the Clinton Challenge." In *Interest Group Politics,* 6th ed. A. Cigler and B. Loomis, cited above.

Patterson, Samuel C. 1963. "The Role of the Lobbyist: The Case of Oklahoma." *JOP* 25: 75–92.

Payne, Charles M. 1995. *I've Got the Light of Freedom: The Organizing Tradition and the Mississippi Freedom Struggle.* Berkeley: UCAP.

Payne, Roger A. 1995. "Nonprofit Environmental Organizations in World Politics: Domestic Structure and Transnational Relations." *Policy Studies Review* 14 (1/2): 171–82.

Pearson, Margaret. 1997. *China's New Business Elite: The Political Consequences of Economic Reform.* Berkeley: UCAP.

Pedler, Robin, ed. 2002. *European Union Lobbying: Changes in the Arena.* Basingstoke: Palgrave.

Pedler, Robin, and M. P. C. M. Van Schendelen, eds. 1994. *Lobbying the European Union: Companies, Trade Associations and Issue Groups.* Aldershot: Dartmouth.

Pei, Minxin. 1998. "Chinese Civic Associations: An Empirical Analysis." *Modern China* 24: 285–319.

Peirce, Neal R. 1972a. *The Megastates of America: People, Politics and Power in the Ten Great States.* New York: Norton.

———. 1972b. *The Mountain States of America: People, Politics and Power in the Eight Rocky Mountain States.* New York: Norton.

———. 1972c. *The Pacific States of America: People, Politics and Power in the Five Pacific Basin States.* New York: Norton.

———. 1973. *The Great Plains States of America: People, Politics and Power in the Nine Great Plains States.* New York: Norton.

———. 1974. *The Deep South States of America: People, Politics and Power in the Seven Deep South States.* New York: Norton.

———. 1975. *The Border South States of America: People, Politics and Power in the Five Border South States.* New York: Norton.

———. 1976. *The New England States of America: People, Politics and Power in the Six New England States.* New York: Norton.

———. 1980. *The Great Lakes States of America: People, Politics and Power in the Five Great Lakes States.* New York: Norton.

Peirce, Neal R., with Michael Barone. 1977. *The Mid-Atlantic States of America: People, Politics and Power in the Five Mid-Atlantic States and the Nation.* New York: Norton.

Peirce, Neal R., and Jerry Hagstrom. 1983. *The Book of America: Inside Fifty States Today.* New York: Warner Books.

Pelinka, Anton. 1987. "Austrian Social Partnership: Stability versus Innovation." *West European Politics* 10: 63–75.

Pelissero, John P., and Robert E. England. 1987. "State and Local Governments' Washington "Reps": Lobbying Strategies and President Reagan's New Federalism." *State and Local Government Review* 19 (2): 68–72.

Peltzman, Sam. 1976. "Toward a More General Theory of Regulation." *Journal of Law and Economics* 19 (2): 211–40.

Pemple, T. J., and Keiichi Tsunekawa. 1979. "Corporatism Without Labor? The Japanese Anomaly." In *Trends Toward Corporatist Intermediation*, P. Schmitter and G. Lehmbruch, cited below.

Penniman, Howard R. 1952. *Sait's American Political Parties and Elections.* 5th ed. New York: Appleton-Century-Croft.

Peregudov, Sergei. 1997. "Business Interest Groups and State in the CIS." Paper presented at the XVIIth International Political Science Association meeting.

Peregudov, Sergei, N. Lapina, and Irina Semenenko. 1999. *Interest Groups and the Russian State.* Moscow: Institute of World Economy and International Relations [available only in Russian].

Pérez-Díaz, Víctor M. 1993. *The Return of Civil Society: The Emergence of Democratic Spain.* Cambridge, Mass.: HUP.

Perlman, Janice E. 1976. *The Myth of Marginality: Urban Poverty and Politics in Rio de Janeiro.* Berkeley: UCAP.

Perry, Elizabeth J. 1994. "Trends in the Study of Chinese Politics: State-Society Relations." *China Quarterly* 139: 704–13.

Perry, Elizabeth J., and Ellen V. Fuller. 1991. "China's Long March to Democracy." *World Policy Journal* 8: 663–85.

Perry, Huey L., and Wayne Parent, eds. 1995. *Blacks and the American Political System.* Gainesville: University Press of Florida.

Perry, Richard J. 1996. *From Time Immemorial: Indigenous Peoples and State Systems.* Austin: University of Texas Press.

Pertschuk, Michael. 1982. *Revolt Against Regulation: The Rise and Pause of the Consumer Movement.* Berkeley: UCAP.

———. 1986. *Giant Killers.* New York: Norton.

Peschek, Joseph G. 1987. *Policy Planning Organizations: Elite Agendas and America's Rightward Turn.* Philadelphia: Temple University Press.

Pestoff, Victor A. 1988. "Exit, Voice and Collective Action in Swedish Consumer Policy." *Journal of Consumer Policy* 11: 1–27.

Peters, Guy. 1996. "Political Institutions, Old and New." In *A New Handbook of Political Science*, eds. Robert E. Goodin and Hans-Dieter Klingemann, Oxford: OUP.

———. 1998. "Policy Networks: Myth, Metaphor and Reality." In *Comparing Policy Networks.* D. Marsh, cited above.

Peters, Julie, and Andrea Wolper, eds. 1994. *Women and Human Rights: An Agenda for Change.* London: Routledge.

Peterson, John. 1993. *High Technology and the Competitive State.* London: Routledge.

Peterson, Mark A. 1992. "The Presidency and Organized Interests: White House Patterns of Interest Group Liaison." *APSR* 86: 612–25.

———. 1994. "Congress in the 1990s: From Iron Triangles to Policy Networks." In *The Politics of Health Care Reform: Lessons From the Past, Prospects for the Future*, eds. James Morone and Gary Belkin. Durham, N.C.: Duke University Press.

———. 1995. "How Health Policy Information is Used in Congress." In *Intensive Care: How Congress Shapes Health Policy*, eds. Thomas E. Mann and Norman J. Ornstein. Washington, D.C.: Brookings.

Peterson , Mark A., and Jack L. Walker. 1986. "Interest Groups and the Reagan White House." In *Interest Group Politics*, 2nd ed. A. Cigler and B. Loomis, cited above.

Peterson, M. J. 1992. "Transnational Activity, International Society and World Politics." *Millennium: Journal of International Studies* 21: 371–88.

Peterson, Paul. 1981. *City Limits.* Chicago: UCP.

———. 1992. "The Rise and Fall of Special Interest Politics." In *The Politics of Interests.* M. Petracca, cited below.

Petracca, Mark P. 1992a. *The Politics of Interests: Interest Groups Transformed.* Boulder, Colo.: Westview.

———. 1992b. "The Rediscovery of Interest Group Politics." In *The Politics of Interests.* M. Petracca, cited above.

———. 1992c. "The Changing State of Interest Group Research: A Review and Commentary." In *The Politics of Interests.* M. Petracca, cited above.

———. 1992d. "Interest Mobilizations and the Presidency." In *The Politics of Interests.* M. Petracca, cited above.

Phillips, Kevin. 1994. *Arrogant Capital: Washington, Wall Street and the Frustration of American Politics.* New York: Little, Brown.

Phillips, Susan, and J. Richard Zecher. 1981. *The SEC and the Public Interest.* Cambridge, Mass.: MIT Press.

Pierce, John C., Mary Ann E. Steger, Brent S. Steel, and Nicholas P. Lovrich. 1992. *Citizens, Political Communication and Interest Groups: Environmental Organizations in Canada and the United States.* Westport, Conn.: Praeger.

Pierre, Jon. 1992. "Organized Capital and Local Politics: Local Business Organizations, Public-Private Committees and Local Government in Sweden." *Urban Affairs Quarterly* 28: 236–57.

References

Pietila, Hillka, and Jenne Vickers. 1994. *Making Women Matter: The Role of the United Nations*. London: Zed Press.

Pika, Joseph A. 1991. "Opening Doors for Kindred Souls: The White House Office of Public Liaison." In *Interest Group Politics*, 3rd ed. A. Cigler and B. Loomis, cited above.

———. 1993. "Reaching Out to Organized Interests: Public Liaison in the Modern White House." In *The Presidency Reconsidered*, ed. Richard W. Waterman. Itasca, Ill.: F. E. Peacock.

Pike, Frederick B., and Thomas Stritch, eds. 1974. *The New Corporatism: Social-Political Structures in the Iberian World*. South Bend, Ind.: University of Notre Dame Press.

Pinderhughes, Diane M. 1987. *Race and Ethnicity in Chicago Politics*. Urbana: University of Illinois Press.

———. 1995. "Interest Groups and the 1982 Voting Rights Extension: How the Lobby Shaped the Law, How the Law Shaped the Lobby." In *Blacks and the American Political System*. H. Perry and W. Parent, cited above.

Plotke, David. 1992. "The Political Mobilization of Business." In *The Politics of Interests*. M. Petracca, cited above.

Pohlmann, Marcus D., and George S. Crisci. 1982–3. "Support For Organized Labor in the House of Representatives: The 89th and 95th Congresses." *PSQ* 97: 639–52.

Pollock, David. 1999. *Denial & delay: the political history of smoking and health, 1951–1964: scientists, government and industry as seen in the papers at the Public Records Office*. London: Action on Smoking and Health.

Polsby, Nelson. 1980. *Community Power and Political Theory*. New Haven, Conn.. YUP.

———. 1983. "Tanks But No Tanks." *Public Opinion* 6 (April-May): 14–16.

Pontusson, Jonas. 1993. "The Comparative Politics of Labor-Initiated Reforms: Swedish Cases of Success and Failure." *Comparative Political Studies* 25: 548–78.

Poole, Keith T. 1981. "Dimensions of Interest Group Evaluation of the U.S. Senate, 1969–1978." *AJPS* 25: 49–67.

Poole, Keith T. and Howard Rosenthal. 1991. "Patterns of Congressional Voting." *AJPS* 35: 228–78.

Posner, Richard A. 1974. "Theories of Economic Regulation." *Bell Journal of Economics and Management Science* 52: 335–58.

Poulantzas, Nicos. 1969. "The Problem of the Capitalist State." *New Left Review* 58: 67–78.

———. 1974. *Political Power and Social Classes*. London: New Left Books.

———. 1975. *Classes in Contemporary Capitalism*. London: New Left Books.

Powell, Lawrence, John Williamson, and Kenneth Branco. 1998. *The Senior Rights Movement: Framing the Policy Debate in America*. New York: Twayne.

Pratt, Henry J. 1976. *The Gray Lobby*. Chicago: UCP.

———. 1993. *Gray Agendas: Interest Groups and Public Pensions in Canada, Britain and the United States*. Ann Arbor: University of Michigan Press.

Presthus, Robert. 1971. "Interest Groups and the Canadian Parliament: Activities, Interaction, Legitimacy and Influence." *Canadian Journal of Political Science* IV: 444–60.

———. 1974a. *Elites in the Policy Process.* London: CUP.

———, ed. 1974b. "Interest Groups in International Perspective." *Annals* 413 (May).

Price, Jerome. 1990. *The Antinuclear Movement.* rev. ed. Boston: Twayne.

Princen, Thomas, and Matthias Finger. 1994. *Environmental NGOs in World Politics: Linking the Local and the Global.* London: Routledge.

Pross, A. Paul, ed. 1975. *Pressure Group Behaviour in Canadian Politics.* Toronto: McGraw-Hill Ryerson.

———. 1989. "Mobilizing Regional Concern: Freight Rates and Political Learning in the Canadian Maritimes." In *Regionalism, Business Interests and Public Policy.* W. Coleman and H. Jacek, cited above.

———. 1991. "The Business Card Bill." In *The Commercial Lobbyists.* A. G. Jordan, cited above.

———. 1992. *Group Politics and Public Policy.* 2nd ed. Toronto: OUP.

Prothro, James W., and Charles M. Grigg. 1988. "Fundamental Principles of Democracy: The Bases of Agreement and Disagreement." *JOP* 22: 276–94.

Provenzo, Eugene. 1990. *Religious Fundamentalism and American Education: The Battle for Public Schools.* Albany, N.Y.: SUNY Press.

Przeworski, Adam. 1991. *Democracy and the Market: Political and Economic Reforms in Eastern Europe and Latin America.* New York: CUP.

Przeworski, Adam, and Michael Wallerstein. 1988. "The Structural Dependence of the State on Capital." *APSR* 82: 11–30.

Public Integrity. 1999. Published by ASPA [American Society of Public Administration] Ethics Section, and Westview Press.

Public Integrity Annual. 1996, 1997. Lexington, Ky.: Council of State Governments.

Purcell, Susan Kaufman. 1975. *The Mexican Profit-Sharing Decision: Politics in an Authoritarian Regime.* Berkeley: UCAP.

Puro, Stephen. 1971. "The Role of *Amicus Curiae* in the United States Supreme Court: 1920–1966." Ph.D. Dissertation. SUNY-Buffalo.

Putnam, Robert D. 1988. "Diplomacy and Domestic Politics: The Logic of Two-Level Games." *International Organization* 42: 427–60.

———. 1993. *Making Democracy Work: Civic Traditions in Modern Italy.* Princeton, N.J.: PUP.

Quirk, Paul J. 1980. "Food and Drug Administration." In *Politics of Regulation.* J. Wilson, cited below.

———. 1981. *Industry Influence in Federal Regulatory Agencies.* Princeton, N.J.: PUP.

Rabin, Robert L., and Stephen D. Sugarman. 1993. *Smoking Policy: Law, Politics & Culture.* New York: OUP.

———. 2001. *Regulating Tobacco.* New York: OUP.

Radin, Beryl A., and Willis D. Hawley. 1988. *The Politics of Federal Reorganization: Creating the U.S. Department of Education.* New York: Pergamon.

Ragin, Charles C., and Howard S. Becker, eds. 1992. *What is a Case? Exploring the Foundations of Social Inquiry.* Cambridge, Mass.: CUP.

Raman, N. Pattabhi. 1967. *Political Involvement of India's Trade Unions.* Bombay: Asia Publishing House.

Ramaswamy, E. A. 1995. "Organized Labor and Economic Reform." In *India Briefing: Staying the Course.* Armonk, N.Y.: M. E. Sharpe.

Ramet, Pedro, ed. 1984. *Religion and Nationalism in Soviet and East European Politics.* Durham, N.C.: Duke Univeristy Press Policy Studies.

Rauch, Jonathan. 1994. *Demosclerosis: The Silent Killer of American Government.* New York: Times Books.

Rawson, D. 1978. *Unions and Unionists in Australia.* Sydney: Allen & Unwin.

———. 1986. *Unions and Unionists in Australia.* 2nd ed. Sydney: Allen & Unwin.

Ray, David. 1982. "The Sources of Voting Cues in Three State Legislatures." *JOP* 44: 1074–87.

Rayside, David M. 1998. *On the Fringe: Gays and Lesbians in Politics.* Ithaca, N.Y.: Cornell University Press.

Read, Patricia. 1986. *Foundation Fundamentals.* 3rd ed. Washington, D.C.: Foundation Center.

Rechtman, René E., with Jasper Panum Larsen-Ledet. 1998. "Regulation of Lobbyists in Scandinavia: A Danish Perspective." *Parliamentary Affairs* 51: 579–86.

Redford, Emmette S. 1960. "Case Analysis of Congressional Activity: Civil Aviation, 1957–1958." *JOP* 22: 228–58.

Redmond, John, ed. 1997. *The 1995 Enlargement of the European Union.* Aldershot, U.K.: Ashgate.

Regan, Tom. 1983. *The Case for Animal Rights.* Berkeley: UCAP.

Regini, Marino, and Ida Regalia. 1997. "Employers, Unions and the State: The Resurgence of Concertation in Italy?" In *Crisis and Transition in Italian Politics,* eds. Martin Bull and Martin Rhodes. London: Frank Cass.

Rehbein, Kathleen A. 1995. "Foreign-owned Firms' Campaign Contributions in the United States: An Exploratory Study." *Policy Studies Journal* 23: 41–61.

Reid, Donald. 1974. "The Rise of Professions and Professional Organizations in Modern Egypt." *Comparative Studies in Society and History.* 16: 24–57.

———. 1981. *Lawyers and Politics in the Arab World.* Minneapolis: Bibliotheca Islam.

Reid, Traciel V. 1996. "PAC Participation in North Carolina Supreme Court Elections." *Judicature* 80: 21–29.

Reinicke, Wolfgang. 1995. *Banking, Politics and Global Finance.* Brookfield, Vt.: Edward Elgar.

Reisner, Marc. 1986. *Cadillac Desert: The American West and Its Disappearing Water.* New York: Penguin.

Rhodes, Martin. 1985. "Organized Interests and Industrial Crisis Management: Restructuring the Steel Industry in West Germany, Italy and France." In *Organized Interests and the State.* A. Cawson, cited above.

———. 1997. "Globalisation, Labour Markets and Welfare States: A Future of 'Competitive Corporatism'?" *EUI Working Paper RSC No. 97/36.* San Domenico (Florence): European University Institute.

Rhodes, R. A. W., and David Marsh. 1992. "New Directions in the Study of Policy Networks." *European Journal of Political Research* 21: 181–205.

Ricci, David M. 1993. *The Transformation of American Politics: The New Washington and the Rise of Think Tanks.* New Haven, Conn.: YUP.

Rich, Andrew, and R. Kent Weaver. 1998. "Advocates and Analysts: Think Tanks and the Politicization of Expertise." In *Interest Group Politics,* 5th ed. A. Cigler and B. Loomis, cited above.

REFERENCES

Rich, Bruce. 1994. *Mortgaging the Earth: The World Bank, Environmental Impoverishment and the Crisis of Development.* Boston: Beacon Press.

Rich, Wilbur C., ed. 1996. *The Politics of Minority Coalitions: Race, Ethnicity and Shared Uncertainties.* Westport, Conn.: Praeger.

Richardson, Jeremy J., ed. 1982. *Policy Styles in Western Europe.* London: Allen & Unwin.

———, ed. 1993a. *Pressure Groups.* Oxford: OUP.

———. 1993b. "Government and Groups in Britain: Changing Styles." In *First World Interest Groups.* C. Thomas, cited below.

Richardson, J. J., and A. G. Jordan. 1979. *Governing Under Pressure.* Oxford: Martin Robertson.

Riggle, Ellen D. B., and Barry L. Tadlock, eds. 1999. *Gays and Lesbians in the Democratic Process: Public Policy, Public Opinion, and Political Representation.* New York: Columbia University Press.

Rimmerman, Craig. 1996. *Gay Rights, Military Wrongs: Political Perspectives on Lesbians and Gays in the Military.* New York: Garland Publishing.

Riordan, William. 1963. *Plunkitt of Tammany Hall.* New York: Dutton.

Risen, James, and Judy L. Thomas. 1998. *Wrath of Angels: The American Abortion War.* New York: Basic Books.

Risse-Kappen, Thomas. 1994. "Ideas Do Not Float Freely: Transnational Coalitions, Domestic Structures, and the End of the Cold War." *International Organization* 48: 185–214.

———, ed. 1995. *Bringing Transnational Relations Back in: Non-State Actors, Domestic Structures and International Institutions.* London: CUP.

Ritchie, Cyril. 1996. "Coordinate? Cooperate? Harmonise? NGO Policy and Operational Coalitions." In *NGOs, the UN and Global Governance.* T. Weiss, and L. Gordenker, cited below.

Roberts, Michael, Peggy Hite, and Cassie F. Bradley. 1994. "Understanding Attitudes Toward Progressive Taxation." *Public Opinion Quarterly* 58: 165–90.

Robinson, John. 1983. *Multinationals and Political Control.* New York: SMP.

Roe, David. 1984. *Dynamos and Virgins.* New York: Random House.

Roeder, Edward. 1982. *PACs Americana: A Directory of PACs and Their Interests.* Washington, D.C.: Sunshine Services.

Rogers, Marion L. 1990. *Acorn Days: The Environmental Defense Fund and How it Grew.* New York: Environmental Defense Fund.

Rohde, David 1991. *Parties and Leaders in the Post-Reform House of Representatives.* Chicago: UCP.

Rokkan, Stein. 1965. "Norway: Numerical Democracy and Corporate Pluralism." In *Political Oppositions in Western Democracies,* ed. Robert A. Dahl, New Haven, Conn.: YUP.

———. 1967. "Geography, Religion and Social Class: Crosscutting Cleavages in Norwegian Politics." In *Party Systems and Voter Alignments: Cross-National Perspectives,* eds. Seymour M. Lipset and Stein Rokkan. New York: Free Press.

Ronit, Karsten, and Volker Schneider. 1998. "The Strange Case of Regulating Lobbying in Germany." *Parliamentary Affairs.* 51: 559–67.

Roper Poll. 1978. Public Broadcast System Poll, "Elections 1978," (October 22).

———. 1984. *The Roper Report 84–87* (September).

———. 1987. (April).

Rosberg, Carl G., and John Nottingham. 1966. *The Myth of "Mau Mau:" Nationalism in Kenya*. New York: Praeger.

Rosen, Stanley. 1982. *Red Guard Factionalism and the Cultural Revolution in Guangzhou*. Boulder, Colo.: Westview.

Rosenau, James N. 1969. *Linkage Politics: Essays on the Convergence of National and International Systems*. New York: Free Press.

Rosenbaum, Walter A. 1987. *Energy, Politics and Public Policy*. 2nd ed. Washington, D.C.: CQP.

Rosenberg, Gerald N. 1991. *The Hollow Hope: Can Courts Bring About Social Change?* Chicago: UCP.

Rosenberg, Jonathan. 1992. "Cuba's Free Market Experiment: Los Mercados Libres Campesinos, 1980–1986." *Latin American Research Review* 27: 51–89.

Rosenstone, Steven J., and John Mark Hansen. 1993. *Mobilization, Participation and Democracy in America*. New York: Macmillan.

Rosenthal, Alan. 1993. *The Third House: Lobbyists and Lobbying in the States*. Washington, D.C.: CQP.

———. 1996. *Drawing the Line*. Lincoln: University of Nebraska Press.

———. 2001. *The Third House: Lobbyists and Lobbying in the States*. 2nd ed. Washington, D.C.: CQP.

Rosenthal, Glenda G. 1975, *The Men Behind the Decisions*. Lexington, Mass.: Lexington.

Rossotti, Jack E., Laura Natelson, and Raymond Tatalovich. 1997. "Nonlegal Advice: The Amicus Briefs in *Webster v. Reproductive Health Services*." *Judicature* 81: 118–21.

Rothchild, Donald. 1994. "Structuring State-Society Relations in Africa: Toward an Enabling Political Environment." In *Economic Change and Political Liberalization in Sub-Saharan Africa*, ed. Jennifer A. Widner. Baltimore: JHUP.

Rothenberg, Lawrence S. 1988. "Organizational Maintenance and the Retention Decision in Groups." *APSR* 82: 1129–52.

———. 1992. *Linking Citizens to Government: Interest Group Politics at Common Cause*. Cambridge, U.K.: CUP.

———. 1994. *Regulation, Organizations and Politics: Motor Freight Policy at the Interstate Commerce Commission*. Ann Arbor: University of Michigan Press.

Rothstein, Bo. 1996. "Political Institutions: An Overview." In *A New Handbook of Political Science*, eds. Robert E. Goodin and Hans-Dieter Klingemann. Oxford: OUP.

Rouquie, Alain. 1987. *The Military and the State in Latin America*. Berkeley: UCAP.

Rourke, Francis E. 1972. *Bureaucracy and Foreign Policy*. Baltimore: JHUP.

Rozell, Mark, and Clyde Wilcox, eds. 1997. *God at the Grassroots, 1996: The Christian Right in the American Elections*. Lanham, Md.: Rowman & Littlefield.

———. 1999. *Interest Groups in American Campaigns: The New Face of Electioneering*. Washington, D.C.: CQP.

Rudolph, Lloyd I., and Susanne Rudolph. 1987. *In Pursuit of Lakshmi: The Political Economy of the Indian State*. Chicago: UCP.

Rudolph, Thomas J. 1999. "Corporate and Labor PAC Contributions in House Elections: Measuring the Effects of Majority Party Status." *JOP* 61: 195–206.

Ruin, Olof. 1974. "Participatory Democracy and Corporatism: The Case of Sweden." *SPS* 9: 171–84.

Rush, Michael, ed. 1990. *Parliament and Pressure Politics.* Oxford: Clarendon.

———. 1994. "Registering the Lobbyists: Lessons from Canada." *Political Studies* 42: 630–45.

———. 1998. "The Canadian Experience: The Lobbyists Registration Act." *Parliamentary Affairs* 51: 516–23.

Rushing, William A. 1995. *The AIDS Epidemic.* Boulder, Colo.: Westview.

Rutland, Peter. 1997a. "Business lobbies in contemporary Russia. *International Spectator* [Rome] 32 (1): 1–15.

———. 1997b. "Elite consolidation and political stability in Russia." Paper presented at the XVIIth International Political Science Association meeting.

Ryan, Mike H., Carl L. Swanson, and Rogene A. Bucholz. 1987. *Corporate Strategy, Public Policy and the Fortune 500.* New York: Blackwell.

Rychard, Andrej. 1998. "Institutions and Actors in a New Democracy: The Vanishing Legacy of Communist and Solidarity Types of Participation in Poland." In *Participation and Democracy East and West*, eds. Dietrich Rueschemeyer, Marilyn Rueschemeyer, and Bjoern Wittrock. Armonk, N.Y.: M. E. Sharpe.

Sabatier, Paul A. 1992. Interest Group Membership and Organization: Multiple Theories. In *The Politics of Interests.* M. Petracca, cited above.

Sabatier, Paul A., and Hank Jenkins-Smith, eds. 1993. *Policy Change and Learning: An Advocacy Coalitions Approach.* Boulder, Colo.: Westview.

Sabatier, Paul A., and Susan McLaughlin. 1990. "Belief Congruence Between Interest Group Leaders and Members: An Empirical Analysis of Three Theories and a Suggested Synthesis." *JOP* 52: 914–35.

Sabatier, Paul A., and David Whiteman. 1985. "Legislative Decision Making and Substantive Policy Information: Models of Information Flow." *LSQ* 10: 395–421.

Sabato, Larry J. 1984. *PAC Power: Inside the World of Political Action Committees.* New York: Norton.

———. 1989. *Paying for Elections: The Campaign Finance Thicket.* New York: Priority Press.

———. 1990. "PACs and Parties." In *Money, Elections and Democracy*, eds. Margaret Latus Nugent and John R. Johannes. Boulder, Colo.: Westview.

Sachs, Richard, with Joseph Cantor, and Thomas Neale. 1986. *Congress and Pressure Groups: Lobbying in a Modern Democracy.* U.S. Senate, Subcommittee on Intergovernmental Relations of the Committee on Governmental Affairs. Report prepared by Congressional Research Service, Library of Congress.

Safa, Helen I., and June Nash, eds. 1976. *Sex and Class in Latin America.* New York: Praeger.

Said, Abdul Aziz, ed. 1981. *Ethnicity and U.S. Foreign Policy.* New York: Praeger.

Saito, Leland T., and John Horton. 1994. "The New Chinese Immigration and the Rise of Asian American Politics in Monterey Park, California." In *The New Asian Immigration in Los Angeles and Global Restructuring*, eds. Paul Ong, Edna Bonacich, and Lucie Cheng. Philadelphia: Temple University Press.

Sale, Kirkpatrick. 1993. *Green Revolution: The American Environmental Movement, 1962–1992.* New York: Hill and Wang.

References

Salisbury, Robert H. 1969. "An Exchange Theory of Interest Groups." *MJPS* 13: 1–32. This article is reprinted in R. Salisbury (1992), *Interests and Institutions*, cited below.

———, ed. 1970. *Interest Group Politics in America.* New York: Harper & Row.

———. 1975. "Interest Groups." In *Handbook of Political Science*, ed. Fred I. Greenstein and Nelson W. Polsby. Vol. 4. Reading, Mass.: Addison-Wesley.

———. 1979. "Why No Corporatism in America?" In *Trends Toward Corporatist Intermediation.* P. Schmitter and G. Lehmbruch, cited below.

———. 1984. "Interest Representation: The Dominance of Institutions." *APSR* 78: 64–76.

———. 1986. "Washington Lobbyists: A Collective Portrait." In *Interest Group Politics*, 2nd ed. A. Cigler and B. Loomis, cited above.

———. 1990. "The Paradox of Interest Groups in Washington, D.C.: More Groups, Less Clout." In *The New American Political System*, ed. Anthony King. Washington, D.C.: AEI.

———. 1992. *Interests and Institutions: Substance and Structure in American Politics.* Pittsburgh: University of Pittsburgh Press.

———. 1994. "Interest Structures and Policy Domains: A Focus for Research." In *Representing Interests and Interest Group Representation.* W. Crotty, et al., cited above.

Salisbury, Robert H., John P. Heinz, Edward O. Laumann, and Robert L. Nelson. 1987. "Who Works with Whom? Interest Group Alliances and Opposition." *APSR* 81: 1217–34.

Salisbury, Robert H., Paul Johnson, John P. Heinz, Edward O. Laumann, and Robert L. Nelson. 1989. "Who You Know Versus What You Know: The Uses of Governmental Experience for Washington Lobbyists." *AJPS* 33: 175–95.

Salisbury, Robert H., et al. 1992. "Triangles, Networks and Hollow Cores." In *The Politics of Interests.* M. Petracca, cited above.

Saloutos, Theodore. 1960. *Farmer Movements in the South, 1865–1933.* Berkeley: UCAP.

———. 1982. *The American Farmer and the New Deal.* Ames: Iowa State University Press.

Saloutos, Theodore, and John D. Hicks. 1951. *Agricultural Discontent in the Middle West, 1900–1939.* Madison: University of Wisconsin Press.

Saltzman, Gregory M. 1987. "Congressional Voting on Labor Issues: The Role of PACs." *Industrial and Labor Relations Review* 40: 163–79.

Samish, Arthur H., and Bob Thomas. 1971. *The Secret Boss of California: The Life and High Times of Artie Samish.* New York: Crown Publishers.

Samuels, Bruce, and Stanton A. Glantz. 1991. *The Politics of Local Tobacco Control.* San Francisco: Department of Medicine, Institute for Health Policy Studies, University of California.

Sanders, M. Elizabeth. 1981. *The Regulation of Natural Gas: Policy and Politics, 1938–1978.* Philadelphia: Temple University Press.

Sandholtz, Wayne. 1992. *High-Tech Europe: The Politics of International Cooperation.* Berkeley: UCAP.

Sandholtz, Wayne, and John Zysman. 1989. "1992: Recasting the European Bargain." *World Politics* 42: 95–128.

REFERENCES

San Miguel, Guadalupe, Jr. 1987. *"Let All of Them Take Heed": Mexican Americans and the Campaign for Educational Equity in Texas, 1910–1981.* Austin: The Center for Mexican American Studies, University of Texas at Austin.

Sapolsky, Harvey, Drew Altman, Richard Greene, and Judith Moore. 1981. "Corporate Attitudes Toward Health Care Costs." *Health and Society* 59: 561–85.

Sargent, Jane A. 1985a. "Corporatism and the European Community." In *The Political Economy of Corporatism.* W. Grant, cited above.

———. 1985b. "The Politics of the Pharmaceutical Price Regulation Scheme." In *Private Interest Government.* W. Streeck and P. Schmitter, cited below.

Sartori, Giovanni. 1976. *Parties and Party Systems.* New York: CUP.

———. 1994. "The Background of 'Pluralism.'" Paper presented at the International Political Science Association meeting.

Sawatsky, John. 1987. *The Insiders: Government, Business and the Lobbyists.* Toronto: McLelland & Stewart.

Sawer, M., and A. Groves. 1994. "'The Women's Lobby': Networks, Coalition Building and the Women of Middle Australia." *Australian Journal of Political Science* 29: 435–59.

Sawer, M., and M. Simms. 1993. *A Woman's Place: Women and Politics in Australia.* 2nd ed., Sydney: Allen & Unwin.

Scarce, Ric. 1990. *Eco-warriors: Understanding the Radical Environmental Movement.* Chicago: Noble Press.

Schattschneider, E. E. 1935. *Politics, Pressures and the Tariff.* New York: Prentice-Hall.

———. 1942. *Party Government.* New York: Holt, Rinehart and Winston.

———. 1960. *The Semisovereign People.* New York: Holt, Rinehart and Winston.

Scheingold, Stuart A. 1974. *The Politics of Rights: Lawyers, Public Policy and Political Change.* New Haven, Conn.: YUP.

———. 1984. *The Politics of Law and Order: Street Crime and Public Policy.* New York: Longman.

———. 1994. "The Contradictions of Radical Law Practice." In *Lawyers in a Postmodern World*, eds. Maureen Cain and Christine B. Harrington. New York: New York University Press.

Schenkel, Walter. 1998. *From Clean Air to Climate Policy in the Netherlands and Switzerland: Same Problems, Different Strategies?* Bern: Peter Lang.

Scheppele, Kim Lane, and Jack L. Walker, Jr. 1991. "The Litigation Strategies of Interest Groups." In *Mobilizing Interest Groups in America*, J. Walker, cited below.

Schlosberg, David. 1998. "Resurrecting the Pluralist Universe." *PRQ* 51: 583–616.

Schlozman, Kay. 1990. "Representing Women in Washington." In *Women, Politics and Change*, eds. Louise Tilly and Patricia Gurin. New York: Russell Sage.

Schlozman, Kay Lehman, and John T. Tierney. 1983. "More of the Same: Washington Pressure Group Activity in a Decade of Change." *JOP* 45: 351–77.

———. 1986. *Organized Interests and American Democracy.* New York: Harper & Row.

Schlozman, Kay Lehman, Sidney Verba, and Henry E. Brady. 1995. "Participation's Not a Paradox: The View from American Activists." *BJPS* 25: 1–36.

Schmertz, Herbert. 1986. *Good-Bye to the Low Profile.* Boston: Little, Brown.

Schmidt, Manfred G. 1982. "Does Corporatism Matter? Economic Crisis, Politics and Rates of Unemployment in Capitalist Democracies in the 1970s." In *Patterns of Corporatist Policy-Making.* G. Lehmbruch and P. Schmitter. cited above.

Schmidt, Vivien A. 1996a. *From State to Market? The Transformation of French Business and Government.* Cambridge, Mass.: CUP.

———. 1996b. "Loosening the Ties that Bind: The Impact of European Integration on French Government and its Relationship to Business," *Journal of Common Market Studies* 34: 223–54.

Schmitter, Philippe. C. 1971 *Interest Conflict and Political Change in Brazil.* Stanford, Calif.: Stanford University Press.

———. 1974. "Still the Century of Corporatism?" *Review of Politics* 36: 85–131. This article can also be found in P. Schmitter and G. Lehmbruch (1979), *Trends Toward Corporatist Intermediation,* cited below.

———. 1975. *Corporatism and Public Policy in Authoritarian Portugal.* Beverly Hills, Calif.: Sage.

———. 1979. "Models of Interest Intermediation and Models of Societal Change in Western Europe." In *Trends Toward Corporatist Intermediation.* P. Schmitter and G. Lehmbruch, cited below.

———. 1981. "Interest Intermediation and Regime Governability in Contemporary Western Europe and North America." In *Organizing Interests in Western Europe.* S. Berger, cited above.

———. 1982. "Reflections on Where the Theory of Neo-Corporatism Has Gone and Where the Praxis of Neo-Corporatism May be Going." In *Patterns of Corporatist Policy-Making.* G. Lehmbruch and P. Schmitter, cited above.

———. 1985. "Neo-corporatism and the State." In *The Political Economy of Corporatism.* W. Grant, cited above.

———. 1989. "Corporatism is Dead! Long Live Corporatism!" *Government and Opposition* 24: 54–73.

———. 1995. "Organized Interests and Democratic Consolidation in Southern Europe." In *The Politics of Democratic Consolidation: Southern Europe in Comparative Perspective,* eds. Richard Gunther, P. Nikiforos Diamandouros, and Hans-Jürgen Puhle. Baltimore: JHUP.

———. 1996. "Neo-corporatism and the consolidation of democracy." Paper presented at the Challenges of Theory Symposium, Moscow.

Schmitter, Philippe C., and Gerhard Lehmbruch, eds. 1979. *Trends Toward Corporatist Intermediation.* Beverly Hills, Calif.: Sage.

Schmitter, Philippe C., and Jurgen R. Grote. 1997. "The Corporatist Sisyphus: Past, Present and Future." *EUI Working Paper SPS No. 97 / 4.* San Domenico (Florence): European University Institute.

Schmitter, Philippe C., and Wolfgang Streeck. 1981. "The Organization of Business Interests: A Research Design to Study the Associative Action of Business in the Advanced Industrial Societies of Western Europe." Discussion Paper IIM / LMP 81 / 13. Berlin: International Institute of Management.

Schnall, David S. 1979. *Radical Dissent in Contemporary Israeli Politics: Cracks in the Wall.* New York: Praeger.

Schneider, Eberhard. 1997. "The formation of the new Russian political elite." Paper presented at the XVIIth International Political Science Association meeting.

Schneider, Volker. 1985. "Corporatist and Pluralist Patterns of Policy-Making for Chemicals Control: A Comparison between West Germany and the USA." In *Organized Interests and the State*. A. Cawson, cited above.

Scholten, I. ed. 1987a. *Political Stability and Neo-Corporatism: Corporatist Integration and Societal Cleavages in Western Europe*. London: Sage.

———. 1987b. "Corporatism and the Neo-Liberal Backlash in the Netherlands." In *Political Stability and Neo-Corporatism*. I. Scholten, cited above.

Scholz, John T., and Feng Heng Wei. 1986. "Regulatory Enforcement in a Federalist System." *APSR* 80: 1249–70.

Schraeder, Peter. J. 1994. "Elites as Facilitators or Impediments to Political Development? Some Lessons from the 'Third Wave' of Democratization in Africa." *Journal of Developing Areas* 29 (1): 69–89.

Schrepfer, Susan R. 1983. *The Fight to Save the Redwoods: A History of Environmental Reform, 1917–1978*. Madison: University of Wisconsin Press.

Schriftgiesser, Karl. 1951. *The Lobbyists: The Art and Business of Influencing Lawmakers*. Boston: Little, Brown.

Schubert, Glendon. 1960. *The Public Interest*. Glencoe, Ill.: Free Press.

Schultz, Richard. 1980. *Federalism, Bureaucracy and Public Policy*. Montreal: McGill-Queen's University Press.

Schulzinger, Robert D. 1984. *The Wise Men of Foreign Affairs*. New York: Columbia University Press.

Schumaker, Paul. 1991. *Critical Pluralism, Democratic Performance and Community Power*. Lawrence: University Press of Kansas.

Schumpeter, Joseph A. 1944. *Capitalism, Socialism and Democracy*. London: Allen & Unwin.

Schwedler, Jillian, ed. 1995. *Toward Civil Society in the Middle East?* Boulder, Colo.: Lynne Rienner.

Scoble, Harry M., and Laurie S. Wiseberg, eds. 1981. *Human Rights Directory: Latin America, Africa, and Asia*. Washington, D.C.: Human Rights Internet.

Scott, Roger, ed. 1980. *Interest Groups and Public Policy: Case Studies from the Australian States*. South Melbourne: Macmillan.

Scott, W. Richard. 1987. "The Adolescence of Institutional Theory." *Administrative Science Quarterly* 32: 493–511.

Scruggs, Lyle A. 1999. "Institutions and Environmental Performance in Seventeen Western Democracies." *BJPS* 29: 1–31.

Segers, Mary C., and Timothy A. Byrnes, eds. 1995. *Abortion Politics in American States*. Armonk, N.Y.: M. E. Sharpe.

Sekuless, Peter. 1991. *Lobbying Canberra in the Nineties*. Sydney: Allen & Unwin.

Selle, Per. 1997. "Parties and Voluntary Organizations: Strong or Weak Ties?" In *Challenges to Political Parties: The Case of Norway*, eds. Karre Strøm and Lars Svåsand. Ann Arbor: University of Michigan Press.

Seltzer, Richard. 1993. "AIDS, Homosexuality, Public Opinion and Changing Correlates Over Time." *Journal of Homosexuality* 26: 85–97.

Sethi, S. Prakash. 1977. *Advocacy Advertising and Large Corporations*. Lexington, Mass.: Lexington.

———. 1987. *Handbook of Advocacy Advertising*. Cambridge, Mass.: Ballinger.

Shabecoff, Philip. 1993. *A Fierce Green Fire: The American Environmental Movement.* New York: Hill & Wang.

Shaiko, Ronald G. 1991. "More Bang for the Buck: The New Era of Full-Service Public Interest Organizations." In *Interest Group Politics*, 3rd ed. A. Cigler and B. Loomis, cited above.

———. 1998. "Reverse Lobbying: Interest Group Mobilization from the White House and the Hill." In *Interest Group Politics*, 5th ed. A. Cigler and B. Loomis, cited above.

———. 1999. *Voices and Echoes for the Environment: Public Interest Representation in the 1990s and Beyond.* New York: Columbia University Press.

Shaiko, Ronald G., and Marc A. Wallace. 1998. "Going Hunting Where the Ducks Are: The National Rifle Association and the Grassroots." In *The Changing Politics of Gun Control.* J. Bruce and C. Wilcox, cited above.

———. 1999. "From Wall Street to Main Street: The National Federation of Independent Business and the New Republican Majority." In *After the Revolution.* R. Biersack, P. Herrnson, and C. Wilcox, cited above.

Shain, Yossi. 1994–95. "Ethnic Diasporas and U.S. Foreign Policy," *PSQ* 109: 811–41.

Shalev, Michael. 1990. *Labour and the Political Economy in Israel.* Oxford: OUP.

Shambayati, Hootan. 1994. "The Rentier State, Interest Groups, and the Paradox of Autonomy: State and Business in Turkey and Iran." *Comparative Politics* 26: 307–32.

Shams, Rasul. 1994. "Environmental Policy and Interest Groups in Developing Countries." *Intereconomics*, (January / February): 16–24.

Shapiro, Martin. 1990. "Interest Groups and Supreme Court Appointments." *Northwestern University Law Review* 84: 935–61.

Sharpe, Kenneth Evan. 1977. *Peasant Politics: Struggle in a Dominican Village.* Baltimore: JHUP.

Sheldon, Charles H. 1994. "The Role of State Bar Associations in Judicial Selection." *Judicature* 77: 300–05.

Shelley, Mack., II, William F. Woodman, Brian J. Reichel, and William J. Kinney. 1990. "State Legislators and Economic Development." *Policy Studies Review* 9: 455–70.

Shephard, Mark P. 1999. "The European Parliament: Getting the House in Order." In *Parliaments and Pressure Groups in Western Europe.* P. Norton, cited above.

Shepsle, Kenneth A. 1978. *The Giant Jigsaw Puzzle: Democratic Committee Assignments in the Modern House.* Chicago: UCP.

Shimshoni, Daniel. 1982. *Israeli Democracy.* New York: Free Press.

Shover, John L. 1965. *Cornbelt Rebellion: The Farmer's Holiday Association.* Urbana: University of Illinois Press.

Shue, Vivienne. 1988. *The Reach of the State: Sketches of the Chinese Body Politic.* Stanford, Calif.: Stanford University Press.

Sidjanski, Dusan. 1967. "Pressure Groups and the European Community." *Government and Opposition* 3: 397–416.

———. 1974. "Interest Groups in Switzerland." *Annals* 413 (May): 101–23.

Siemienska, Renata. 1986. "Women and Social Movements in Poland." *Women & Politics* 6: 5–35.

Sienstra, Deborah. 1994. *Women's Movements and International Organizations.* New York: SMP.

Sierra, Christine Marie. 1991. "Latino Organizational Strategies on Immigration Reform: Success and Limits in Public Policymaking." In *Latinos and Political Coalitions: Political Empowerment for the 1990s*, eds. Roberto E. Villarreal and Norma G. Hernandez. Westport, Conn.: Greenwood.

———. 1999. "In Search of National Power: Chicanos Working the System on Immigration Reform, 1976–1986." In *Chicano Politics and Society in the Late Twentieth Century*, ed. David Montejano. Austin: University of Texas Press.

Sigwalt, Pierre. 1989. "Environmental Problems and Policies in Social Change in Taiwan." In *Political and Social Changes in Taiwan and Mainland China*, ed. King-yuh Chang. cited above.

Siisiäinen, Martti. 1992. "Social Movements, Voluntary Associations and Cycles of Protest in Finland 1905–91." *SPS* 15: 21–40.

Sikkink, Kathryn. 1991. *Ideas and Institutions: Developmentalism in Brazil and Argentina*. Ithaca, N.Y.: Cornell University Press.

———. 1993. "Human Rights, Principled Issue-Networks and Sovereignty in Latin America." *International Organization* 47 (3): 411–41.

Siklova, Jirina. 1993. "Are Women in Eastern Europe Conservative?" *Gender Politics and Post Communism*, eds. Nanette Funk and Magda Mueller. New York: Routledge.

Silverstein, Harvey B. 1978. *Superships and Nation-States: The Transnational Politics of the Intergovernmental Maritime Consultative Organization*. Boulder, Colo.: Westview.

Silverstein, Kenneth. 1999. *Washington on $10 million a Day*. New York: Common Courage Press.

Silverstein, Mark. 1994. *Judicious Choices: The New Politics of Supreme Court Nominations*. New York: Norton.

Simpson, Glenn R., and Larry J. Sabato. 1996. *Dirty Little Secrets: The Persistence of Corruption in American Politics*. New York: Times Books.

Singer, Peter. 1985. *In Defense of Animals*. London: Basil Blackwell.

Sirsikar, V. M. 1979. "Studies of Political Parties and Pressure Groups." In *Survey of Research in Political Science: Political Systems, Vol. 1*. New Delhi: Allied Publishers, 87–98. Sponsored by the Indian Council of Social Science Research.

Sisk, Timothy D. 1995. *Democratization in South Africa: The Elusive Social Contract*. Princeton, N.J.: PUP.

Skalaban, Andrew. 1992. "Interstate Competition and State Strategies to Deregulate Interstate Banking, 1982–1988." *JOP* 54: 793–809.

———. 1993. "Policy Cooperation Among the States: The Case of Interstate Banking Reform." *AJPS* 37: 415–28.

Skilling, H. Gordon. 1966. "Interest Groups and Communist Politics." *World Politics* 18: 435–51.

———. 1973. "Opposition in Communist East Europe." In *Regimes and Oppositions*, ed. Robert A. Dahl. New Haven, Conn.: YUP.

———. 1983. "Interest Groups and Communist Politics Revisited," *World Politics* 36: 1–27.

Skilling, H. Gordon, and Franklyn Griffiths, eds. 1971. *Interest Groups in Soviet Politics*. Princeton, N.J.: PUP.

Skocpol, Theda. 1979. *States and Social Revolution*. Cambridge, U.K.: CUP.

———. 1981. "Political Response to Capitalist Crisis: Neo-Marxist Theories of the State and the Case of the New Deal." *Politics and Society* 10: 155–201.

Skocpol, Theda, and Kenneth Finegold. 1982. "State Capacity and Economic Intervention in the Early New Deal." *PSQ* 97: 255–78.

Skowronek, Stephen. 1981. "National Railroad Regulation and the Problem of State-Building: Interests and Institutions in Late Nineteenth Century America." *Politics and Society* 10: 225–50.

———. 1982. *Building a New American State: The Expansion of National Administrative Capacities, 1877–1920.* Cambridge, U.K.: CUP.

Slavin, Peter. 1975–76. "The Business Roundtable: New Lobbying Arm of Big Business." *Business and Society Review* 16: 28–32.

Smith, Daniel A., and Robert J. Herrington. 1997. "The Process of Direct Democracy: The Case of Colorado's 1996 Parental Rights Amendment." Paper presented at the annual meeting of the American Political Science Association.

Smith, Dorothy. 1979. *In Our Own Interest: A Handbook for the Citizen Lobbyist in State Legislatures.* Seattle: Madrona.

Smith, Hedrick. 1988. *The Power Game: How Washington Works.* New York: Random House.

Smith, Jackie, Charles Chatfield, and Ron Pagnucco, eds. 1997. *Transnational Social Movements and Global Politics: Solidarity Beyond the State.* Syracuse, N.Y.: Syracuse University Press.

Smith, James Allen. 1991a. *Brookings at Seventy-Five.* Washington, D.C.: Brookings.

———. 1991b. *The Idea Brokers.* New York: Free Press.

Smith, Jonathan C. 1998. "Foreign Policy for Sale? Interest Group Influence on President Clinton's Cuba Policy." *Presidential Studies Quarterly* 28 (4); 207–20.

Smith, Kerry. 1985. "A Theoretical Analysis of the Green Lobby." *APSR* 79: 132–47.

Smith, Kevin B., and Ken Meier. 1995. *The Case Against School Choice: Politics, Markets and Fools.* Armonk, N.Y.: M. E. Sharpe.

Smith, Larry David. 1989. "A Narrative Analysis of the Party Platforms: The Democrats and Republicans in 1984." *Communication Quarterly* 37: 91–99.

———. 1992. "The Party Platforms as Institutional Discourse: The Democrats and Republicans in 1988." *Presidential Studies Quarterly* 22: 531–43.

Smith, M. 1990. "Pluralism, Reformed Pluralism and Neopluralism." *Political Studies* XXXVIII: 302–22.

Smith, Martin J. 1993. *Pressure, Power and Policy: State Autonomy and Policy Networks in Britain and the United States.* New York: Harvester Wheatsheaf and Pittsburgh: University of Pittsburgh Press.

Smith, Paul Chaat, and Robert Allen Warrior. 1996. *Like a Hurricane: The Indian Movement from Alcatraz to Wounded Knee.* New York: New Press.

Smith, Richard A. 1984. "Advocacy, Interpretation and Influence in the US Congress." *APSR* 78: 44–63.

———. 1995. "Interest Group Influence in the U.S. Congress." *LSQ* 20: 89–139.

Smith, Robert G. 1996. *We Have No Leaders: African Americans in the Post-Civil Rights Era.* Albany, N.Y.: SUNY Press.

Smith, Steven Rathgeb, and Michael Lipsky. 1993. *Nonprofits for Hire: The Welfare State in the Age of Contracting.* Cambridge, U. K.: HUP.

Smith, Zachary, ed. 1992. *Environmental Politics and Policy in the American West.* College Station: Texas A & M University Press.

Smooha, Sammy. 1978. *Israel: Pluralism and Conflict*. London: Routledge & Kegan Paul.

Snider, Kevin J. G. 1994. "Foreign Money in American Politics: The Influence of Foreign-Affiliated Political Action Committees." Ph.D. Dissertation, The American University.

Snow, Donald. 1992. *Inside the Environmental Movement: Meeting the Leadership Challenge*. Washington, D.C.: Island Press.

Sobel, Andrew C. 1994. *Domestic Choices, International Markets*. Ann Arbor: University of Michigan Press.

Solinger, Dorothy J. 1993. *China's Transition from Socialism: Statist Legacies and Marketing Reforms, 1980–1990*. Armonk, N.Y.: M. E. Sharpe.

Sollis, Peter. 1996. "Partners in Development? The State, NGOs and the UN in Central America." In *NGOs, the UN and Global Governance*. T. Weiss and L. Gordenker, cited below.

Songer, Donald R., et al. 1986. "The Influence of Issues on Choice of Voting Cues Utilized by State Legislators." *WPQ* 39: 118–25.

Songer, Donald R., and Ashlyn Kuersten. 1995. "The Success of *Amici* in State Supreme Courts." *PRQ* 48: 31–42.

Songer, Donald R., and Reginald S. Sheehan. 1993. "Interest Group Success in the Courts: Amicus Participants in the Supreme Court." *PRQ* 46: 339–54.

Sorauf, Frank J. 1980. "Political Parties and Political Action Committees: Two Life Cycles." *Arizona Law Review* 22: 445–63.

———. 1984. *What Price PACs?* New York: Twentieth Century Fund.

———. 1988a. "Parties and Political Action Committees in American Politics." In *When Parties Fail*. K. Lawson and P. Merkl, cited above.

———. 1988b. *Money in American Elections*. Glenview, Ill.: Scott Foresman / Little, Brown.

———. 1991. "PACs and Parties in American Politics." In *Interest Group Politics*, 3rd ed. A. Cigler and B. Loomis, cited above.

———. 1992. *Inside Campaign Finance: Myths and Realities*. New Haven, Conn.: YUP.

Sousa, David J. 1993. "Organized Labor in the Electorate, 1960–1988." *PRQ* 46: 741–58.

Spalter-Roth, Roberta, and Ronnee Schreiber. 1995. "Outsider Issues and Insider Tactics." In *Feminist Organizations*. M. Ferree and P. Martin, cited above.

Spanier, John, and Eric M. Uslaner. 1982. *Foreign Policy and the Democratic Dilemmas*. New York: Holt, Rinehart and Winston.

Spinelli, Altiero. 1966. *The Eurocrats*. Baltimore: JHUP.

Spiro, Peter J. 1994. "New Global Communities: Nongovernmental Organizations in International Decision-Making Institutions." *The Washington Quarterly* 18: 45–56.

Spitzer, Robert J. 1995. *The Politics of Gun Control*. Chatham, N.J.: Chatham House.

Spriggs, James F., II, and Paul J. Wahlbeck. 1997. "Amicus Curiae and the Role of Information at the Supreme Court." *PRQ* 50: 365–86.

Springborg, Robert. 1975. "Patterns of Association in the Egyptian Political Elite." In *Political Elites in The Middle East*, ed. George Lenczowski. Washington, D.C.: AEI.

———. 1978. "Professional Syndicates in Egyptian Politics, 1952–1970." *International Journal of Middle East Studies* 9: 275–95.

Sprinz, Detlef, and Tapani Vaahtoranta. 1994. "The Interest-based Explanation of International Environmental Policy." *International Organization* 48: 77–105.

Sprinzak, Ehud. 1991. *The Ascendance of Israel's Radical Right.* New York: OUP.

Stack, John F., Jr., ed. 1981. *Ethnic Identities in a Transnational World.* Westport, Conn.: Greenwood.

Staggenborg, Suzanne. 1991. *The Pro-Choice Movement: Organization and Activism in the Abortion Conflict.* New York: OUP.

Stallings, Barbara, and Robert Kaufman, eds. 1989. *Debt and Democracy in Latin America.* Boulder, Colo.: Westview.

Stanbury, W. T. 1978. "Lobbying and Interest Group Representation in the Legislative Process." In *The Legislative Process in Canada*, eds. W. A. W. Neilson and J. C. MacPherson. Montreal: Institute for Research on Public Policy.

———. 1986. *Business-Government Relations in Canada.* Toronto: Methuen.

Staniszkis, Jadwiga. 1984. *Poland's Self-Limiting Revolution.* Princeton, N.J.: PUP.

Stark, Andrew. 1992. "'Political Discourse' Analysis and the Debate over Canada's Lobbying Legislation." *Canadian Journal of Political Science* 25: 513–34.

Starr, Frederick. 1991. "The Third Sector in the Second World." *World Development* 19 (January): 65–71.

Starr, Paul. 1982. *The Social Transformation of American Medicine: The Rise of a Sovereign Profession and the Making of a Vast Industry.* New York: Basic Books.

Steckenrider, Janie, and Tonya Parrott. 1998. *New Directions in Old Age Politics.* Albany, N.Y.: SUNY Press.

Steedley, Homer R., and John F. Foley. 1979. "The Success of Protest Groups: Multivariate Analysis." *Social Science Research* 8: 1–15.

Steele, J. Valerie. 2001. *2001 National Directory of Corporate Public Affairs.* 19th ed. Washington, D.C.: Columbia Books.

Steen, Anton. 1985. "The Farmers, the State and the Social Democrats." *SPS* 8: 45–63.

Stein, Herbert. 1994. *Presidential Economics.* Washington D.C.: AEI.

Steiner, Jürg. 1974. *Amicable Agreement versus Majority Rule: Conflict Resolution in Switzerland.* Chapel Hill: University of North Carolina Press.

Steinmo, Sven, and Jon Watts. 1995. "It's the Institutions, Stupid! Why Comprehensive National Health Insurance Always Fails in America." *Journal of Health Politics, Policy and Law* 20: 329–72.

Stepan, Alfred. 1988. *Rethinking Military Politics: Brazil and the Southern Cone.* Princeton, N.J.: PUP.

Stern, Philip M. 1992. *Still the Best Congress Money Can Buy.* Washington, D.C.: Regnery Gateway.

Steslicke, William. 1973. *Doctors in Politics: The Political Life of the Japan Medical Association.* New York: Praeger.

Stewart, J. D. 1958. *British Pressure Groups: Their Role in Relation to the House of Commons.* Oxford: Clarendon Press.

Stewart, Joseph, Jr., and Edward V. Heck. 1983. "The Day-to-Day Activities of Interest Group Lawyers." *SSQ* 64: 173–82.

Stewart, Joseph, Jr., and James F. Sheffield, Jr. 1987. "Does Interest Group Litigation Matter? The Case of Black Political Mobilization in Mississippi." *JOP* 49: 780–98.

Stigler, George J. 1971. "The Theory of Economic Regulation." *Bell Journal of Economics and Management Science* 2: 3–21.

———. 1974. "Free Riders and Collective Action." *Bell Journal of Economics and Management Science* 5: 359–65.

———. 1975. *The Citizen and the State: Essays on Regulation.* Chicago: UCP.

Stigler, George, and Claire Freidland. 1962. "What Can Regulators Regulate? The Case of Electricity." *Journal of Law and Economics* 5: 1–16.

Stimson, James A. 1991. *Public Opinion in America: Moods, Cycles and Swings.* Boulder, Colo.: Westview.

Stolpe, Herman. 1981. "The Cooperative Movements." In *Nordic Democracy*, E. Allardt, et al., cited above.

Stolz, Barbara Ann. 1984. "Interest Groups and Criminal Law: The Case of Federal Criminal Code Revision." *Crime and Delinquency* 30: 91–106.

Stone, Clarence. 1989. *Regime Politics.* Lawrence: University Press of Kansas.

———. 1998. *Changing Urban Education.* Lawrence: University Press of Kansas.

Stone, Clarence N., Robert K. Whelan, and William J. Murin. 1986. *Urban Policy and Politics in a Bureaucratic Age.* 2nd ed. Englewood Cliffs, N.J.: Prentice-Hall.

Stone, Diane. 1991. "Old Guard Versus New Partisans: Think Tanks in Transition." *Australian Journal of Political Science* 26: 197–215.

———. 1996. *Capturing the Political Imagination: Think Tanks and the Policy Process.* London: Frank Cass.

Stone, Peter H. 1993. "Smoke Signals." *National Journal* 25, No. 4, p. 221.

Stonham, Paul. 1987. *Global Stock Market Reforms.* Cambridge, U.K.: Gower.

Strange, Susan. 1982 "Cave! Hic Dragones: A Critique of Regime Analysis." *International Organization* 36: 479–96.

———. 1988. *Politics and Markets.* London: Pinter.

———. 1996. *The Retreat of the State: The Diffusion of Power in the World Economy.* Cambridge, U.K.: CUP.

Strange, Susan, and John Stopford. 1991. *Rival States and Rival Firms.* Cambridge, U.K.: CUP.

Streeck, Wolfgang. 1983. "Between Pluralism and Corporatism: German Business Associations and the State." *Journal of Public Policy* 3: 265–84.

———. 1984. *Industrial Relations in West Germany.* London: Heinemann Educational.

———. 1998. "Interest Heterogeneity and Organizing Capacity: Two Logics of Collective Action?" *Institutions and Political Choice: On the Limits of Rationality*, rev. ed., eds. Roland Czada, Adrienne Héritier, and Hans Keman. Amsterdam: VU University Press.

Streeck, Wolfgang, and Philippe C. Schmitter, eds. 1985. *Private Interest Government.* London: Sage.

Streeck, Wolfgang, and Philippe C. Schmitter. 1991. "From National Corporatism to Transnational Pluralism: Organized Interests in the Single European Market." *Politics and Society* 19: 133–55.

Studlar, Donley T. 2002. *Tobacco Control: Comparative Politics in the United States and Canada.* Peterborough, Ontario: Broadview.

Stykow, Petra. 1996. "Organized Business in the Transformation Process, Eastern Europe and Russia: Toward Corporatism?" Arbeits Papiere AY TR AP N.96 / 11. Cologne: Max-Plank Gesellschaft.

Suleiman, Ezra. 1974. *Politics, Power and Bureaucracy in France: The Administrative Elite*. Princeton, N.J.: PUP.

Sullivan, Dennis Joseph. 1994. *Private Voluntary Organizations in Egypt: Islamic Development, Private Initiative and State Control*. Gainesville: University Press of Florida.

Sullivan, John. 1973. "Political Correlates of Social, Economic and Religious Diversity in the American States." *JOP* 35: 70–84.

Sullivan, Lawrence. 1990. "The Emergence of Civil Society in China, Spring 1989." In *The Chinese People's Movement: Perspectives on Spring 1989*, ed. Tony Saich. Armonk, N.Y.: M. E. Sharpe.

Sullum, Jacob. 1998. *For Your Own Good: The Anti Smoking Crusade and the Tyranny of Public Health*. New York: Free Press.

Summerfield, Harry L. 1974. *Power and Process: The Formulation and Limits of Federal Education Policy*. Berkeley: McCutchan Publishing.

Suolinna, Kirsti. 1981. "The Popular Revival Movements." In *Nordic Democracy*. E. Allardt, et al., cited above.

Svensson, Palle. 1994. "The Danish Yes to Maastricht and Edinburgh: The EC Referendum of May 1993." *SPS* 17: 69–82.

Sward, Ellen, and Burton A. Weisbrod. 1978. "Public Interest Law Activities Outside the U.S.A." In *Public Interest Law: An Economic and Institutional Analysis*, ed. Burton A. Weisbrod. Berkeley: UCAP.

Syer, John C. 1987. "California: Political Giants in a Megastate." In *Interest Group Politics in the American West*. R. Hrebenar and C. Thomas, cited above.

Szeftel, Morris. 1994. "Ethnicity and Democratization in South Africa." *Review of African Political Economy* 21: 185–99.

Taft, Phillip, and Phillip Ross. 1969. "American Labor Violence: Its Causes, Character and Outcome." In *Violence in America*. H. Graham and T. Gurr, cited above.

Tai Hung-ch'ao. 1970. "The Kuomintang and Modernization in Taiwan." In *Authoritarian Politics in Modern Society*, eds. Samuel P. Huntington and Clement H. Moore. New York: Basic Books.

Tarrow, Sydney. 1994. *Power in Movement: Social Movements, Collective Action and Politics*. Cambridge, U.K.: CUP.

Tatalovich, Raymond, and Byron Daynes. 1981. *The Politics of Abortion: A Study of Community Conflict in Public Policy Making*. New York: Praeger.

Taylor, Carl C. 1953. *The Farmers' Movement, 1620–1920*. Westport, Conn.: Greenwood.

Taylor, Peter. 1984. *The Smoke Ring: Tobacco, Money and Multinational Politics*. New York: Pantheon.

Taylor, Phillip. 1984. *Nonstate Actors in International Politics: From Transregional to Substate Organizations*. Boulder, Colo.: Westview.

Teske, Paul. 1990. *After Divestiture: The Political Economy of State Telecommunications Regulation*. Albany, N.Y.: SUNY Press.

———. 1991. "Rent-Seeking in the Deregulatory Environment: State Telecommunications." *Public Choice* 68: 235–43.

REFERENCES

Teske, Paul, Samuel Best, and Michael Mintrom. 1995. *Deregulating Freight Transportation: Delivering the Goods.* Washington, D.C.: AEI.

Teune, Henry. 1967. "Legislative Attitudes Toward Interest Groups." *MJPS* 11: 489–504.

Thelen, David P. 1972. *The New Citizenship.* Columbia: University of Missouri Press.

Thelen, Kathleen. 1991. *Union of Parts: Labor Politics in Postwar Germany.* Ithaca, N.Y.: Cornell University Press.

———. 1993. "West European Labor in Transition: Sweden and Germany Compared." *World Politics* 46: 23–49.

Thelen, Kathleen, and Sven Steinmo. 1992. "Historical Institutionalism in Comparative Politics." In *Structuring Politics: Historical Institutionalism in Comparative Analysis,* eds. Sven Steinmo, et al. New York: CUP.

Thomas, Clive S., ed. 1991. *Politics and Public Policy in the Contemporary American West.* Albuquerque: University of New Mexico Press.

———, ed. 1993a. *First World Interest Groups: A Comparative Perspective.* Westport, Conn.: Greenwood.

———. 1993b. "The American Interest Group System: Typical Model or Aberration." In *First World Interest Groups.* C. Thomas, cited above.

———. 1998a. "Interest Group Regulation Across the United States: Rationale, Development and Consequences." *Parliamentary Affairs* 51: 500–15.

———. 1998b. "American Interest Groups Operating in the European Union: How Appropriate are American Techniques of Lobbying?" Paper presented at the annual meeting of the American Politics Group, Manchester, England.

———, ed. 2001a. *Political Parties and Interest Groups: Shaping Democratic Governance.* Boulder, Colo.: Lynne Rienner.

———. 2001b. "The United States: The Paradox of Loose Party-Group Ties in the Context of American Political Development." In *Political Parties and Interest Group.* C. Thomas, cited above.

Thomas, Clive S., and Ronald J. Hrebenar. 1990. "Interest Groups in the States." In *Politics in the American States: A Comparative Analysis,* 5th ed., eds. Virginia Gray, Herbert Jacob, and Robert B. Albritton. Glenview, Ill: Scott Foresman / Little, Brown.

———. 1991a. "Nationalization of Interest Groups and Lobbying in the States." In *Interest Group Politics.* 3rd ed. A. Cigler and B. Loomis, cited above.

———. 1991b. "The Regulation of Interest Groups and Lobbying in the Fifty States: Some Preliminary Findings." Paper presented at the annual meeting of the Midwest Political Science Association.

———. 1991c. "A New Look at Lobbyists and the Lobbying Community in the American States." *American Review* 11: 2–16.

———. 1992a. "Changing Patterns of Interest Group Activity: A Regional Perspective." In *The Politics of Interests.* M. Petracca, cited above.

———. 1992b. "The Role of Government as a Lobbying Force in the American States." Paper presented at the annual meeting of the Western Political Science Association.

———. 1992c. "The Integration of Interest Group Activity at the National, State and Local Level in the United States: Causes and Consequences." Paper presented at the annual meeting of the American Political Science Association.

————. 1995. "Public Perceptions of Interest Groups and their Implications for Public Policymaking." Paper presented at annual meeting of the Western Political Science Association.

————. 1996a. "Regulating Interest Groups in the United States: National, State, and Local Experiences." Paper presented at the annual meeting of the American Political Science Association.

————. 1996b. "Interest Groups in the States." In *Politics in the American States: A Comparative Analysis*, 6th ed., eds. Virginia Gray and Herbert Jacob. Washington, D.C.: CQP.

————. 1999a. "Interest Groups in the States." In *Politics in the American States: A Comparative Analysis*, 7th ed., eds. Virginia Gray, Russell L. Hanson, and Herbert Jacob. Washington, D.C.: CQP.

————. 1999b. "A Reappraisal of Interest Group Power in the American States." Paper presented at the annual meeting of the American Political Science Association.

————. 1999c. "Who's Got Clout?: Interest Group Power in the States." *State Legislatures* 25: 30–34

————. 2003. "Interest Groups in the States." In *Politics in the American States: A Comparative Analysis*, 8th ed., eds. Virginia Gray and Russell L. Hanson. Washington, D.C.: CQP.

Thomas, Clive S., Ronald J. Hrebenar and Michael L. Boyer. 2001. "American Interest Groups Operating in the European Union: A Study in Transnational Lobbying." Paper presented at the annual meeting of the American Political Science Association.

Thomas, Clive S., Michael L. Boyer, and Ronald J. Hrebenar. 2003. "Interest Groups and State Court Elections: A New Era and Its Challenges." *Judicature* 87 (November and December): 135–44, 149.

Thomas, John Clayton. 1986. *Between Citizens and City: Neighborhood Organizations and Urban Politics in Cincinnati*. Lawrence: University Press of Kansas.

Thomas, Norman C. 1975. *Education in National Politics*. New York: McKay.

Thomas, Sue. 1994. "The National Abortion Rights Action League PAC: Reproductive Choice in the Spotlight." In *Risky Business?* R. Biersack, P. Herrnson, and C. Wilcox, cited above.

Thurston, Donald. 1973. *Teachers and Politics in Japan*. Princeton, N.J.: PUP.

Tichenor, Daniel J., and Richard A. Harris. 2002. "The Lost Years: Interest Group Formation, Attrition and Influence Over Time." Paper presented at the annual meeting of the American Political Science Association

Tien, Hung-mao. 1993. *The Great Transition: Political and Social Change in the Republic of China*. 6th ed. Taipei: SMC.

————. 2000. "Taiwan's Transition." In *Consolidating the Third Wave Democracies*, eds. Larry Diamond, et al. Baltimore: JHUP.

Tierney, John T. 1992. "Organized Interests and the Nation's Capital." In *The Politics of Interests*. M. Petracca, cited above.

Tillock, Harriet, and Denton E. Morrison. 1979. "Group Size and Contributions to Collective Action: An Examination of Olson's Theory Using Data from Zero Population Growth, Inc." In *Research in Social Movements, Conflicts and Change: A Research Annual*. Vol. 2, ed. Louis Kriesberg. Greenwich, Conn.: JAI Press.

REFERENCES

Tilly, Charles. 1978. *From Mobilization to Revolution*. Reading, Mass.: Addison-Wesley.

Tilly, Nannie M. 1985. *The R. J. Reynolds Tobacco Company*. Chapel Hill: University of North Carolina Press.

Time Yankelovich Poll. 1985. "Groups." (7 November).

Timmermann, Rieneke. 1996. "Lobbying in the European Parliament." Master's Thesis. University of Utrecht, the Netherlands.

Timpone, Richard J. 1995. "Mass Mobilization or Government Intervention? The Growth of Black Registration in the South." *JOP* 57: 425–42.

Tober, James A. 1989. *Wildlife and the Public Interest: Nonprofit Organizations and Federal Wildlife Policy*. New York: Praeger.

Tobin, Richard J. 1990. "Environment, Population and Development in the Third World." In *Environmental Policy in the 1990s*. N. Vig and M. Kraft, cited below.

Tocqueville, Alexis de. 1835 / 1840. *Democracy in America*, 2 vols. Notes and Translation by Phillips Bradley. New York: Knopf 1944.

Tolbert, Caroline. 1996. "Dismantling the Administrative State? Direct Democracy and State Governance Policies." Doctoral Dissertation. University of Colorado, Boulder.

———. 1998. "Changing Rules for State Legislatures: Direct Democracy and Governance Policies." In *Citizens as Legislators*. S. Bowler, T. Donovan, and C. Tolbert, cited above.

Tolchin, Martin, and Susan J. Tolchin. 1989. *Buying Into America: How Foreign Money is Changing the Face of Our Nation*. New York: Times Books.

Tolley, Howard. 1989. "Popular Sovereignty and International Law: ICJ Strategies for Human Rights Standard Setting." *Human Rights Quarterly* 11: 561–85.

Tollison, Robert D., and Robert E. McCormick. 1980. "Wealth Transfers in a Representative Democracy: Theory and Evidence." In *Towards a Theory of the Rent-Seeking Society*. J. Buchanan, R. Tollison, and G. Tullock, cited above.

———. 1981. *Politicians, Legislation and the Economy: An Inquiry into the Interest-Group Theory of Government*. Boston: Martinus Nijhoff.

Tomasevski, Katarina. 1991. *Women and Human Rights*. London: Zed Books.

Torres-Gil, Fernando. 1992. *The New Aging: Politics and Change in America*. New York: Auburn House.

Touraine, Alain. 1987. *The Workers' Movement*. New York: CUP.

Townsend, James, 1968. *Political Participation in Communist China*. 2nd ed. Berkeley: UCAP.

Townsley, W. A. 1958. "Pressure Groups in Australia." In *Interest Groups on Four Continents*. H. Ehrmann, cited above.

Traxler, Franz. 1985. "Prerequisites, Problem-Solving Capacity and Limits of Neo-Corporatist Regulation: A Case Study of Private Interest Governance and Economic Performance in Austria." In *Private Interest Government*. W. Streeck and P. Schmitter, cited above.

———. 1993. "Business Associations and Labor Unions in Comparison: Theoretical Perspectives and Empirical Findings on Social Class, Collective Action and Associational Organizability." *British Journal of Sociology* 44: 673–91.

———. 1995a. "Farewell to Labour Market Associations? Organized Versus Disorganized Decentralization as a Map for Industrial Relations." In *Organized Industrial Relations in Europe*. C. Crouch and F. Traxler, cited above.

———. 1995b. "Two Logics of Collective Action in Industrial Relations?" In *Organized Industrial Relations in Europe*. C. Crouch and F. Traxler, cited above.

Traxler, Franz, and Brigitte Unger. 1994. "Industry or Infrastructure? A Cross-National Comparison of Governance: Its Determinants and Economic Consequences in the Dairy Sector." In *Governing Capitalist Economies*. J. R. Hollingsworth, P. Schmitter, and W. Streeck, cited above.

Trebeck, D. 1990. "Farmer Organisations." In *Agriculture in the Australian Economy*, 3rd ed., ed. D. B. Williams. Sydney: Sydney University Press.

Treu, Tiziano, ed. 1992. *Participation in Public Policy-Making: The Role of Trade Unions and Employers' Associations*. Berlin: Walter de Gruyter.

Trice, Robert H. 1976. *Interest Groups and the Foreign Policy Process*. Beverly Hills, Calif.: Sage.

———. 1977. "Congress and the Arab-Israeli Conflict: Support for Israel in the U.S. Senate, 1970–1973." *PSQ* 92: 443–63.

Tripp, Aili Mari. 1994. "Gender, Political Participation and the Transformation of Associational Life in Uganda and Tanzania." *African Studies Review* 37: 107–31.

Truman, David B. 1951. *The Governmental Process: Political Interests and Public Opinion*. New York: Knopf.

Tsokhas, K. 1984. *A Class Apart? Businessmen and Australian Politics 1960–1980*. Melbourne: OUP.

Tsou, Tang. 1976. "Prolegomenon to the Study of Informal Groups in CCP Politics." *China Quarterly* 65 (January): 98–113.

Tuohy, Carolyn. 1976. "Private Government, Property and Professionalism." *Canadian Journal of Political Science* IX: 668–81.

Tymowski, Andrej W., ed. 1994. "Special Feature: Youth Activism in the East European Transformation." *Communist and Post-Communist Studies* 27 (1): 115–76.

United Nations. 1994. *Seeds of Partnership: Indigenous Peoples and the United Nations*. New York: The United Nations.

Useem, Michael. 1984. *The Inner Circle: Large Corporations and the Rise of Business Political Activity in the U.S. and the U.K.* New York: OUP.

Uslaner, Eric M. 1989. *Shale Barrel Politics: Energy Politics and Legislative Leadership*. Stanford, Calif.: Stanford University Press.

———. 1995. "All Politics are Global: Interest Groups and the Making of Foreign Policy." In *Interest Group Politics*, 4th ed., A. Cigler and B. Loomis, cited above.

Uvin, Peter. 1999. "Ethnicity and Power in Burundi and Rwanda: Different Paths to Mass Violence." *Comparative Politics* 31: 253–71.

Vakil, A. 1997. "Confronting the classification problem: towards a taxonomy of NGOs." *World Development* 25: 2057–71.

Valen, Henry, and Stein Rokkan. 1974. "Norway: Conflict Structure and Mass Politics in a European Periphery." In *Electoral Behavior: A Comparative Handbook*, ed. Richard Rose. New York: Free Press.

Valenzuela, J. Samuel. 1989. "Labor Movements in Transitions to Democracy: A Framework for Analysis." *Comparative Politics* 21: 445–72.

van de Fliert, Lydia, ed. 1987. *Indigenous Peoples and International Organizations*. Nottingham, U.K.: Russell Press.

Van den Bulck, Jan. 1992. "Pillars and Politics: Neocorporatism and Policy Networks in Belgium." *West European Politics* 15: 35–55.

Van Leuven, James K., and Michael D. Slater. 1991. "How Publics, Public Relations and the Media Shape the Public Opinion Process." In *Public Relations Research Annual.* Vol. 3, eds. Larissa A. Grunig and James E. Grunig. Hillsdale, N.J.: Lawrence Erlbaum.

Van Loon, Richard, and Michael Whittington. 1971. *The Canadian Political System.* Toronto: McGraw-Hill.

Van Schendelen, M. P. C. M., ed. 1993. *National Public and Private EC Lobbying.* Aldershot, U.K.: Dartmouth.

Van Schendelen, Rinus. 2002. *Machiavelli in Brussels: The Art of Lobbying the EU.* Amsterdam: University of Amsterdam Press.

Van Tassel, David D., and Jimmy Elaine Wilkinson Meyer, eds. 1992. *U.S. Aging Policy Interest Groups: Institutional Profiles.* Westport, Conn.: Greenwood.

Van Tulder, Rob, and Gerd Junne. 1988. *European Multinationals in Core Technologies.* Chichester, U.K.: Wiley.

Van Waarden, Frans. 1985. "Varieties of collective self-regulation of business: the example of the Dutch diary industry. In *Private Interest Government.* W. Streeck and P. Schmitter, cited above.

———. 1992a. "Dimensions and Types of Policy Networks." *European Journal of Political Research* 21: 29–52.

———. 1992b. "The Historical Institutionalization of Typical National Patterns of Policy Networks between State and Industry: A Comparison of the USA and the Netherlands." *European Journal of Political Research* 21: 131–62.

———. 1992c. "Emergence and Development of Business Interest Associations: An Example from the Netherlands." *Organization Studies* 13: 521–62.

———. 1995. "The Organizational Power of Employers' Associations: Cohesion, Comprehensiveness and Organizational Development." In *Organized Industrial Relations in Europe.* C. Crouch and F. Traxler, cited above.

van Wolferen, Karel. 1989. *The Enigma of Japanese Power.* New York: Knopf.

Vass, Laszlo. 1993. "Europeanization and Interest Groups in the New Hungarian Political System." *Suedost Europa* 42 (5): 301–17.

Verba, Sidney. 1965. "Comparative Political Culture." In *Political Culture and Political Development*, eds. Lucian W. Pye and Sidney Verba. Princeton, N.J.: PUP.

Verba, Sidney, and Norman H. Nie. 1972. *Participation in America.* New York: Harper & Row.

Verba, Sidney, Kay Lehman Schlozman, Henry Brady and Norman H. Nie. 1993. "Citizen Activity: Who Participates? What Do They Say?" *APSR* 87: 303–18.

———. 1995. *Voice and Equality.* Cambridge, Mass.: HUP.

Vernon, Raymond. 1971. *Sovereignty at Bay.* New York: Basic Books.

———, ed. 1974. *Big Business and the State: Changing Relations in Western Europe.* Cambridge, Mass.: HUP.

———. 1977. *Storm over the Multinationals: The Real Issues.* Cambridge, Mass.: HUP.

Vig, Norman J., and Michael E. Kraft, eds. 1990a. *Environmental Policy in the 1990s: Toward a New Agenda.* Washington, D.C.: CQP.

Vig, Norman J., and Michael E. Kraft. 1990b. "Conclusion: Toward a New Environmental Agenda." In N. Vig and M. Kraft, *Environmental Policy in the 1990s*, cited above.

Villalon, Leonardo A., and Phillip A Huxtable, eds. 1998. *The African State at a Critical Juncture: Between Disintegration and Reconfiguration.* Boulder, Colo.: Lynne Rienner.

Visser, Jelle, and Anton Hemerijck. 1997. *A Dutch Miracle: Job Growth, Welfare Reform and Corporatism in the Netherlands.* Amsterdam: Amsterdam University Press.

Vizzard, William J. 2000. *Shots in the Dark: The Policy, Politics and Symbolism of Gun Control.* Lanham, Md.: Rowman & Littlefield.

Vogel, David. 1978. *Lobbying the Corporation.* New York: Basic Books.

———. 1989. *Fluctuating Fortunes: The Political Power of Business in America.* New York: Basic Books.

———. 1993. "Representing Diffuse Interests in Environmental Policymaking." In *Do Institutions Matter? Government Capabilities in the United States and Abroad*, eds. R. Kent Weaver and Bert A. Rockman. Washington, D.C.: Brookings.

———. 1996. *Kindred Strangers.* Princeton, N.J.: PUP.

Vogel, David, and Mark Nadel. 1977. "Who Is a Consumer: An Analysis of the Politics of Consumer Conflict." *APQ* 5: 27–56.

von Beyme, Klaus. 1993. "West Germany and the New Germany: Centralization, Expanding Pluralism and New Challenges." In *First World Interest Groups.* C. Thomas, cited above.

von Riekhoff, Harold, and Hanspeter Neuhold, eds. 1993. *Unequal Partners.* Boulder, Colo.: Westview.

Vose, Clement E. 1957. "National Consumers' League and the Brandeis Brief." *MJPS* 1: 178–90.

———. 1958. "Litigation as a Form of Pressure Group Activity." *Annals* 319 (September): 20–31.

———. 1959. *Caucasians Only: The Supreme Court, the NAACP, and the Restrictive Covenant Cases.* Berkeley: UCAP.

———. 1966. "Interest Groups, Judicial Review and Local Government." *WPQ* 19: 85–100.

———. 1972. *Constitutional Change: Amendment Politics and Supreme Court Litigation Since 1900.* Lexington, Mass.: Lexington Books.

Vowles, Jack. 1993. "New Zealand: Capture the State?" In *First World Interest Groups.* C. Thomas, cited above.

Wahlke, John C., Heinz Eulau, William Buchanan, and Leroy C. Ferguson. 1962. *The Legislative System.* New York: Wiley.

Walker, Jack L. 1963. "Protest and Negotiation: A Case Study of Negro Leadership in Atlanta, Georgia." *MJPS* VII: 99–124.

———. 1983. "The Origins and Maintenance of Interest Groups in America." *APSR* 77: 390–406.

———. 1991. *Mobilizing Interest Groups in America: Patrons, Professions and Social Movements.* Ann Arbor: University of Michigan Press.

Walker, Samuel. 1992. *The American Civil Liberties Union: An Annotated Bibliography.* New York: Garland.

REFERENCES

———. 1999. *In Defense of American Liberties: A History of the ACLU.* Carbondale, Ill.: Southern Illinois University Press.

Wallace, H., et al. 1989. *Policymaking in the European Community.* Chichester, U.K.: Wiley.

Wallace, Steven P., and John B. Williamson. 1992. *The Senior Movement: References and Resources.* New York: G. K. Hall.

Waller, Michael. 1984. "Communist Politics and the Group Process: Some Comparative Conclusions." In *Groups and Politics in the People's Republic of China.* D. Goodman, cited above.

Waller, Michael, and Martin Myant, eds. 1994. *Parties, Trade Unions and Society in East-Central Europe.* London: Frank Cass.

Wallerstein, Immanuel. 1966. "Voluntary Associations." In *Political Parties and National Integration in Tropical Africa,* eds. James S. Coleman and Carl G. Rosberg, Jr. Berkeley: UCAP.

Walsh, Edward J., and Rex H. Warland. 1983. "Social Movement Involvement in the Wake of a Nuclear Accident: Activists and Free Riders in the TMI Area." *American Sociological Review* 48: 764–80.

Waltenberg, Eric. 2002. *Choosing Where to Fight.* Albany, N.Y.: SUNY Press.

Walter, Ingo, ed. 1985. *Deregulating Wall Street.* New York: Wiley.

Walters, Jonathan. 2000. "Lobbying for the Good Old Days." In *American Intergovernmental Relations.* L. J. O'Toole, cited above.

Walters, Ronald W. 1990. "Party Platforms as Political Process." *PS: Political Science and Politics* 23: 436–38.

Walton, Hanes, Jr., Cheryl M. Miller, and Joseph P. McCormick II. 1991. "Race and Political Science: The Dual Traditions of Race Relations Politics and African American Politics." In *Political Science in History, Research Programs and Political Traditions,* eds. James Farr, John S. Dryzek, and Stephen T. Leonard, New York: CUP.

Wapner, Paul. 1996. *Environmental Activism and World Civic Politics.* Albany, N.Y.: SUNY Press.

Warhurst, John. 1982. *Jobs or Dogma? The Industries Assistance Commission and Australian Politics.* St Lucia: University of Queensland Press.

———. 1983. "Minor Parties and Pressure Groups" In *Australia at the Polls: The National Elections of 1980 and 1983,* ed. H. R. Penniman. Washington, D.C.: AEI.

———. 1985. "Interest Groups." In *Government, Politics and Power in Australia,* 3rd ed., eds. D. Woodward, A. Parkin, and J. Summers. Melbourne: Longman Cheshire.

———. 1986. "The Classification of Interest Groups." Paper presented at the annual meeting of the Australasian Political Studies Association.

———. 1987. "Lobbyists and Policy-Making in Canberra." *Current Affairs Bulletin* 64 (3): 13–19.

———. 1990. "Political Lobbying in Australia." *Corruption and Reform* 5 (3): 173–87.

———. 1994. "The Australian Conservation Foundation: The Development of a Modern Environmental Interest Group." *Environmental Politics* 3 (Spring): 68–90.

———. 1998. "Locating the Target: Regulating Lobbying in Australia." *Parliamentary Affairs* 51: 538–50.

References

Warner, Carolyn M. 2000. *Confessions of an Interest Group: The Catholic Church and Political Parties in Europe*. Princeton, N.J.: PUP.

Wasby, Stephen L. 1995. *Race Relations Litigation in an Age of Complexity*. Charlottesville: University Press of Virginia.

The Washington Lobby, 5th ed. 1987. Washington, D.C.: CQP.

Washington Representatives, 2001, 25th ed. Washington, D.C.: Columbia Books.

———. 2003, 27th ed. Washington, D.C.: Columbia Books.

Wassenberg, A. 1982. "Neo-corporatism and the quest for control: the cuckoo game. In *Patterns of Corporatist Policy Making*. G. Lehmbruch and P. Schmitter, cited above.

Waste, Robert J. 1986. "Community Power and Pluralist Theory." In *Community Power: Directions for Future Research*, ed. Robert J. Waste. Beverly Hills, Calif.: Sage.

Watson, George, and John A. Stookey. 1995. *Shaping America: The Politics of Supreme Court Appointments*. New York: HarperCollins.

Watson, Paul, and Warren Rogers. 1981. *Sea Shepherd: One Man's Crusade for Whales and Seals*. New York: Norton.

Weaver, Jace, and Russell Means. 1996. *Defending Mother Earth*. Maryknoll, N.Y.: Orbis.

Webber, Michael J. 1994. "Challenges to Transnational Social Movements." *Peace Review* 6: 395–401.

Weber, Paul, and T. L. Stanley. 1984. "The Power and Performance of Religious Interest Groups." *Quarterly Review* 4: 28–43.

Weber, Paul, and W. Landis Jones. 1994. *U.S. Religious Interest Groups: Institutional Profiles*. Westport, Conn.: Greenwood.

Wei, William. 1993. *The Asian American Movement*. Philadelphia: Temple University Press.

Weil, Gordon L. 1970. *The Benelux Nations: The Politics of Small-Country Democracies*. New York: Holt, Rinehart and Winston.

Weiner, Myron. 1962. *The Politics of Scarcity: Public Pressure and Political Response in India*. Chicago: UCP.

Weinstein, Allen. 1970. *Prelude to Populism: Origins of the Silver Issue, 1867–1878*. New Haven, Conn.: YUP.

Weir, Margaret. 1992. *Politics and Jobs: The Boundaries of Employment Policy in the United States*. Princeton, N.J.: PUP.

Weiss, Carol H., ed. 1991. *Organizations for Policy Analysis: Helping Government Think*. Newbury Park, Calif.: Sage.

Weiss, Thomas G., and Leon Gordenker, eds. 1996. *NGOs, the UN and Global Governance*. Boulder, Colo.: Lynne Rienner.

Welch, Michael, David Leege, and Robert Woodberry. 1998. "Pro-life Catholics and Support for Political Lobbying by Religious Organizations." *SSQ* 79: 649–63.

Welch, Stephen. 1993. *The Concept of Political Culture*. New York: SMP.

Welch, William P. 1982. "Campaign Contributions and Legislative Voting: Milk Money and Dairy Price Supports." *WPQ* 35: 478–95.

Wells, Robert N., Jr., ed. 1994. *Native American Resurgence and Renewal: A Reader and Bibliography*. Metuchen, N.J.: The Scarecrow Press.

Wenner, Lettie. 1984. *The Environmental Decade in Court*. Bloomington: Indiana University Press.

REFERENCES

Wenner, Lettie McSpadden. 1990. *U.S. Energy and Environmental Interest Groups.* New York: Greenwood.

Werbach, Adam. 1997. *Act Now, Apologize Later.* New York: HarperCollins.

Werther, Guntram. 1992. *Self-Determination in Western Democracies.* Westport, Conn.: Greenwood.

West, Allan M. 1980. *The National Education Association.* New York: Free Press.

West, Darrell M., Diane J. Heith, and Chris Goodwin. 1995. "Political Advertising and Health Care Reform." Paper presented at the annual meeting of the Midwest Political Science Association.

West, Darrell M., and Burdett A. Loomis. 1999. *The Sound of Money: How Political Interests Get What They Want.* New York: Norton.

Wheeler, Tim, and Nicholas J. Dunne, eds. 1999. *Human Rights in Global Politics.* Cambridge, U.K.: CUP.

White, Gordon. 1993. *Riding the Tiger: The Politics of Economic Reform in Post-Mao China.* Stanford, Calif.: Stanford University Press.

White, Jon, and Laura Mazur. 1994. *Strategic Communications Management.* Wokingham, U.K.: Addison-Wesley.

Whitston, Colin. 1991. "Chemical Unions in the United Kingdom and Germany." In *International Markets and Global Firms.* A. Martinelli, cited above.

Whyte, Martin K. 1974. *Small Groups and Political Rituals in China.* Berkeley: UCAP.

———. 1992. "Urban China: A Civil Society in the Making?" In *State and Society in China: The Consequences of Reform,* ed. Arthur Rosenbaum. Boulder, Colo.: Westview.

Wiarda, Howard J. 1977. *Corporatism and Development: The Portuguese Experience.* Amherst: University of Massachusetts Press.

———. 1989. *The Transition to Democracy in Spain and Portugal.* Washington, D.C.: AEI.

Widfeldt, Anders. 2001. "Sweden: Weakening Links Between Political Parties and Interest Organizations." In *Political Parties and Interest Groups.* C. Thomas, cited above.

Widner, Jennifer A., ed. 1994. *Economic Change and Political Liberalization in Sub-Saharan Africa.* Baltimore: JHUP.

Wiebe, Robert H. 1967. *The Search for Order.* New York: Hill & Wang.

Wilcox, Clyde. 1992. *God's Warriors: The Christian Right in the Twentieth Century.* Baltimore: JHUP.

———. 1994. "Coping with Increasing Business Influence: The AFL-CIO's Committee on Political Education." In *Risky Business?* R. Biersack, P. Herrnson, and C. Wilcox, cited above.

———. 1996. *Onward Christian Soldiers?: The Religious Right in American Politics.* Boulder, Colo.: Westview.

Wildavsky, Aaron. 1962. *Dixon-Yates: A Study in Power Politics.* New Haven, Conn.: YUP.

Wilkins, David. 1997. *American Indian Sovereignty and the Supreme Court.* Austin: University of Texas Press.

Wilks, Stephen, and Maurice Wright. 1987. *Comparative Government-Industry Relations: Western Europe, the United States, and Japan.* Oxford: Clarendon.

Willetts, Peter, ed. 1982. *Pressure Groups in the Global System: The Transnational Relations of Issue-Orientated Non-Governmental Organizations.* London: Pinter.

Williams, Oliver J. 1972. "Changing Perspectives on the American Governor." In *The American Governor in Behavioral Perspective*, eds. Thad L. Beyle and J. Oliver Williams. New York: Harper & Row.

Williamson, John B., Linda Evans, and Lawrence A. Powell. 1982. *The Politics of Aging: Power and Policy.* Springfield, Ill.: Charles C. Thomas.

Williamson, Peter J. 1985. *Varieties of Corporatism.* Cambridge, U.K.: CUP.

———. 1989. *Corporatism in Perspective: An Introductory Guide to Corporatist Theory.* London: Sage.

Willis, Derek. 1999. "PAC Plays: How Political Action Committees, Large and Small, are Coping with Shifts in the Electoral Environment." *Campaigns and Elections* (April): 24–29.

Wilmer, Franke. 1993. *The Indigenous Voice in World Politics: Since Time Immemorial.* Newbury Park, Calif.: Sage.

Wilsford, David. 1991. *Doctors and the State: The Politics of Health Care in France and the United States.* Durham, N.C.: Duke University Press.

Wilson, Frank L. 1983. "French Interest Group Politics: Pluralist or Neocorporatist?" *APSR* 77: 895–910.

———. 1987. *Interest-Group Politics in France.* Cambridge, U.K.: CUP.

———. 1993. "France: Group Politics in a Strong State." In *First World Interest Groups.* C. Thomas, cited above.

Wilson, Graham K. 1977. *Special Interests and Policymaking: Agricultural Politics and Policies in Britain and the United States.* London: Wiley.

———. 1979. *Unions in American National Politics.* London: MacMillan.

———. 1981. *Interest Groups in the United States.* New York: OUP.

———. 1982. "Why is There No Corporatism in the United States?" In *Patterns of Corporatist Policy Making.* G. Lehmbruch and P. Schmitter, cited above.

———. 1985. *Business and Politics: A Comparative Introduction.* Chatham, N.J.: Chatham House.

———. 1986. "American Business and Politics." In *Interest Group Politics*, 2nd ed., A. Cigler and B. Loomis, cited above.

———. 1990a. *Interest Groups.* Oxford: Basil Blackwell.

———. 1990b. *Business and Politics: A Comparative Introduction.* 2nd ed. Chatham, N.J.: Chatham House.

———. 1992. "American Interest Groups in Comparative Perspective." In *The Politics of Interests.* M. Petracca, cited above.

Wilson, James Q. 1960. *Negro Politics.* New York: Free Press.

———. 1961. "The Strategy of Protest: Problems of the Negro Civic Action." *Journal of Conflict Resolution* III: 291–303.

———. 1962. *The Amateur Democrat.* Chicago: UCP.

———. 1973. *Political Organizations.* New York: Basic Books.

———, ed. 1980. *The Politics of Regulation.* New York: Basic Books.

———. 1983. *Crime and Public Policy.* San Francisco: ICS Press.

———. 1989. *Bureaucracy: What Government Agencies Do And Why They Do It.* New York: Basic Books.

———. 1990. *Drugs and Crime.* Chicago: UCP.

———. 1995. *Political Organizations.* rev. ed. Princeton, N.J.: PUP.

Windmuller, John P., and Alan Gladstone, eds. 1984. *Employers' Associations and Industrial Relations: A Comparative Study.* Oxford: Clarendon.

Winham, Gilbert. 1986. *International Trade and The Tokyo Round Negotiation.* Princeton, N.J.: PUP.

Wissel, Peter, Robert O'Connor, and Michael King. 1976. "The Hunting of the Legislative Shark: Information Searches and Reforms in U.S. State Legislatures." *LSQ* 1: 251–67.

Wolak, Jennifer, Adam Newmark, Todd McNoldy, David Lowery, and Virginia Gray. 2002. "Much of Politics is Still Local: Multi-State Lobbying in State Interest Group Communities. *LSQ* 27: 527–55.

Wolchik, Sharon L. 1993. "Women and the Politics of Transition in Central and Eastern Europe." In *Democratic Reform and the Position of Women in Transitional Economies,* ed. Valentine M. Moghadam. Oxford: Clarendon.

Wold, John T., and John H. Culver. 1987. "The Defeat of the California Justices: The Campaign, the Electorate, and the Issue of Judicial Accountability." *Judicature* 70: 348–55.

Wolfers, Arnold. 1962. *Discord and Collaboration: Essays on International Politics.* Baltimore: JHUP.

Wolinetz, Steven B. 1989. "Socio-economic Bargaining in the Netherlands: Redefining the Post-war Policy Coalition." *West European Politics* 12: 80–98.

Woliver, Laura R. 1993. *From Outrage to Action.* Urbana: University of Illinois Press.

Wolpe, Bruce. 1990. *Lobbying Congress.* Washington, D.C.: CQP.

Wolpe, Bruce C., and Bertram J. Levine. 1996. *Lobbying Congress: How the System Works.* 2nd ed. Washington, D.C.: CQP.

Wong, Bernard P. 1982. *Chinatown: Economic Adaptation and Ethnic Identity of the Chinese.* Fort Worth, Tex.: Holt, Rinehart and Winston.

Wood, G. A. 1988. *Governing New Zealand.* Auckland: Longman Paul.

Woodall, Brian. 1995. *Construction in Japan.* Berkeley: UCAP.

Woods, Lawrence T. 1993. *Asia-Pacific Diplomacy: Nongovernmental Organizations and International Relations.* Vancouver: University of British Columbia Press.

Woolley, John T. 1984. *Monetary Politics.* Cambridge, Mass.: CUP.

Wootton, Graham. 1963. *The Politics of Influence.* Cambridge, U.K.: HUP.

———. 1970. *Interest-Groups.* Englewood Cliffs, N.J.: Prentice-Hall.

———. 1972. *Pressure Groups in Britain, 1720–1970: An Essay in Interpretation with Original Documents.* London: Allen Lane.

———. 1985. *Interest Groups, Policy and Politics in America.* Englewood Cliffs, N.J.: Prentice-Hall.

Wright, Deil S. 1972. "Governors, Grants and the Intergovernmental System. In *The American Governor in Behavioral Perspective,* eds. Thad L. Beyle and J. Oliver Williams. New York: Harper & Row.

———. 1988. *Understanding Intergovernmental Relations.* 3rd ed. Pacific Grove, Calif.: Brooks / Cole.

Wright, John R. 1990. "Contributions, Lobbying, and Committee Voting in the U.S. House of Representatives." *APSR* 84: 417–38.

———. 1996. *Interest Groups and Congress: Lobbying, Contributions and Influence.* Boston: Allyn & Bacon.

Wrong, Dennis H. 1988. *Power: Its Forms, Bases and Uses.* Chicago: UCP.

Yale Law Journal. 1947. "Improving the Legislative Process: Federal Regulation of Lobbying." (January): 304–42. [no author given].

Yanaga, Chitoshi. 1968. *Big Business in Japanese Politics.* New Haven, Conn.: YUP.

Yarnold, Barbara M. 1995. *Abortion Politics in the Federal Courts: Right Versus Right.* Westport, Conn.: Praeger.

Yeager, Kenneth E. 1999. *Trailblazers: Profiles of America's Gay and Lesbian Elected Officials.* New York: Haworth.

Yeros, Paris, ed. 1999. *Ethnicity and Nationalism in Africa: Constructivist Reflections and Contemporary Politics.* New York: SMP.

Yin, Robert K. 1994. *Case Study Research: Design and Methods.* 2nd ed. Thousand Oaks, Calif.: Sage.

Yishai, Yael. 1979. "Interest Groups in Israel." *Jerusalem Quarterly* (Spring): 128–44.

———. 1991. *Land of Paradoxes: Interest Politics in Israel.* Albany, N.Y.: SUNY Press.

———. 1994. "Interest Parties: The Thin Line Between Groups and Parties in the Israeli Electoral Process." In *How Political Parties Work: Perspectives from Within,* ed. Kay Lawson. New York: Praeger.

———. 1998a. "Regulation of Interest Groups in Israel." *Parliamentary Affairs* 51: 568–78.

———. 1998b. "The Guardian State: A Comparative Analysis of Interest Group Regulation." *Governance: An International Journal of Policy and Administration* 11: 152–76.

———. 2001. "Israel: The End of Integration." In *Political Parties and Interest Groups: Shaping Democratic Governance.* C. Thomas, cited above.

Young, Crawford. 1976. *The Politics of Cultural Pluralism.* Madison: University of Wisconsin Press.

Young, Oran. 1986. "International Regimes: Toward a New Theory of Institutions." *World Politics* 39: 104–22.

Zaborowski, Wojciech. 1993. "Social Structure and Political Participation." In *Societal Conflict and Systemic Change: The Case of Poland 1980–1992,* ed. Wladyslaw W. Adamski, Warsaw: IFIS.

Zakin, Susan. 1993. *Coyotes and Town Dogs: Earth First! and the Environmental Movement.* New York: Viking.

Zald, Mayer N., and John D. McCarthy. 1980. "Social Movement Industries: Competition and Cooperation Among Movement Organizations." *Research in Social Movements, Conflicts, and Change* 3: 1–20.

———, eds. 1986. *Social Movements in an Organizational Society: Collected Essays.* New Brunswick, N.J.: Transaction Books.

Zaller, John R. 1992. *The Nature and Origin of Mass Opinion.* New York: CUP.

Zariski, Raphael. 1993. "Italy: The Fragmentation of Power and its Consequences." In *First World Interest Groups.* C. Thomas, cited above.

Zeigler, L. Harmon. 1963. "The Florida Milk Commission Changes Minimum Prices." In *State and Local Government: A Case Book,* ed. Edward W. Bock. Tuscaloosa: University of Alabama Press.

———. 1964. *Interest Groups in American Society.* Englewood Cliffs, N.J.: Prentice-Hall.

———. 1983. "Interest Groups in the States." In *Politics in the American States: A Comparative Analysis,* 4th ed. eds. Virginia Gray, Herbert Jacob, and Kenneth N. Vines. Boston: Little, Brown.

———. 1988. *Pluralism, Corporatism and Confucianism: Political Association and Conflict Regulation in the United States, Europe and Taiwan*. Philadelphia: Temple University Press.

———. 1993. "Switzerland: Democratic Corporatism in a Cosociational Society." In *First World Interest Groups*. C. Thomas, cited above.

Zeigler, Harmon, and Michael A. Baer. 1969. *Lobbying: Interaction and Influence in American State Legislatures*. Belmont, Calif.: Wadsworth.

Zeigler, L. Harmon, and G. Wayne Peak. 1972. *Interest Groups in American Society*. 2nd ed. Englewood Cliffs, N.J.: Prentice-Hall.

Zeigler. L. Harmon, and Hendrik van Dalen. 1976. "Interest Groups in the States." In *Politics in the American States: A Comparative Analysis*, 3rd ed., eds. Herbert Jacob and Kenneth N. Vines. Boston: Little, Brown.

Zeller, Belle. 1937. *Pressure Politics in New York: A Study of Group Representation Before the Legislature*. Englewood Cliffs, N.J.: Prentice-Hall. Reissued by Russell & Russell, 1967.

———. 1954. *American State Legislatures*, 2nd ed. New York: Thomas Y. Crowell.

Zisk, Betty H., ed. 1969. *American Political Interest Groups: Readings in Theory and Research*. Belmont, Calif.: Wadsworth.

———. 1973. *Local Interest Politics: A One-Way Street*. Indianapolis: Bobbs-Merrill.

———. 1992. *The Politics of Transformation: Local Activism in the Peace and Environmental Movements*. Westport, Conn.: Praeger.

Zuckerman, Edward. 1998. *Almanac of Federal PACs: 1998–99*. Arlington, Va.: Amward.

Zwier, Robert. 1979. "The Search For Information: Specialists and Nonspecialists in the U.S. House of Representatives." *LSQ* 4: 31–42.

Zysman, John. 1977. *Political Strategies for Industrial Order: State, Market and Industry in France*. Berkeley: UCAP.

———. 1983. *Governments, Markets and Growth: Financial Systems and the Politics of Industrial Change*. Ithaca, N.Y.: Cornell University Press.

Index

About the Editor and Contributors

THE EDITOR

Clive S. Thomas is Professor of Political Science and Chair of the Department of Social Science at the University of Alaska, Juneau. His publications include works on interest groups, legislative process, and U.S. state politics. He is Director of The Alaska Universities Legislative Internship Program, has been a volunteer lobbyist, and teaches seminars on lobby organization and tactics. During 1997 and 1998 and spring 2000 he was a Fulbright Senior Research Scholar in Brussels studying American interest groups operating in the European Union. He received a Senior Specialist Fulbright Award in 2004 to the Slovak Republic.

THE CONTRIBUTORS

Ali Abdullatif Ahmida is Associate Professor and Chair of Political Science at the University of New England, Biddeford, Maine. His publications focus on state formation, anticolonial resistance, and civil society in the Middle East and North Africa. He authored *The Making of Modern Libya* (1994) and edited *Beyond Colonialism and Nationalism in the Maghrib* (2000).

Michael G. Bath is an Assistant Professor of Political Science at Concordia College, Moorhead, Minnesota. His research interests include lobbying and think tank activity. He recently completed a study of female lobbyists with Anthony Nownes of the University of Tennessee.

Frank R. Baumgartner is Professor and Head of the Political Science Department at Pennsylvania State University. His most recent books include: *Basic Interests* (1998, coauthor with Beth L. Leech); and *Policy*

Dynamics (2002, coeditor with Bryan D. Jones). His work focuses on interest groups and public policy.

Robert C. Benedict is Associate Professor of Political Science at the University of Utah. His research focuses on political parties, interest groups, public opinion, and public policy—particularly environmental policy. He is coauthor of *Political Parties, Interest Groups and Political Campaigns* (1999) and has published several articles and chapters in books.

Jeffrey M. Berry is Professor of Political Science at Tufts University in Boston. His books include: *Lobbying for the People* (1977); *Feeding Hungry People* (1984); *The Interest Group Society* (3rd. ed., 1997); and *The Rebirth of Urban Democracy* (1993, coauthor). His most recent book is *The New Liberalism: The Rising Power of Citizen Groups* (1999).

Christopher J. Bosso is an Associate Professor of Political Science at Northeastern University in Boston. His publications include *Pesticides and Politics: The Life Cycle of a Public Issue* (1987). He also has written on environmental politics, the tactics and strategies pursued by U.S. national environmental organizations, and public policy-making dynamics in general.

Michael L. Boyer is an Assistant Professor of Law Sciences at the University of Alaska Southeast. He received his law degree from the University of Oregon. His research focuses on the intersection of law, politics, and social policy. He has published in *Judicature* and the *Southern California Interdisciplinary Law Journal*.

Paul Brace is Clarence L. Carter Professor of Political Science at Rice University. He authored *State Government and Economic Performance* (1993) and coauthored *Follow the Leader: Opinion Polls and the Modern Presidents* (1992). His articles appear in leading political science journals, and he has served on the editorial boards of several journals.

Richard Braunstein is an Assistant Professor of Political Science at the University of South Dakota. His research and teaching interests include state politics, empirical democratic theory, civil rights policy, and conflict resolution. He is also the executive director of a nonprofit organization that disseminates public voting information.

William P. Browne is a Professor of Political Science at Central Michigan University. He has published extensively on interest groups, particularly agricultural interests. His publications include: *Private Interests, Public Policy and American Agriculture* (1988); *Cultivating Congress: Constituents, Issues, and Interests in Agricultural Policymaking* (1995); and *Group Interests and U.S. Public Policy* (1998).

Kellie Butler is an Assistant Professor of Political Science at Pennsylvania State University. Her interest is in state politics, particularly government institutions and public policy. She has published in the *American Journal of Political Science* and *Justice Systems Journal.* Currently she is working on a book on agenda setting in the U.S. states.

Loree G. Bykerk is Professor of Political Science at the University of Nebraska at Omaha. Her publications include books and articles on organized interests in consumer politics and in insurance. Her current research focuses on interest advocacy, pension policy, and other financial issues.

Pamela G. Camerra-Rowe is an Assistant Professor of Political Science at Kenyon College in Gambier, Ohio. Her research focuses on the individual and collective lobbying efforts of firms in the European Union and on the effects of European integration on German domestic politics.

Elizabeth A. Capell holds a Ph.D. in political science from the University of California, Berkeley, and has worked in both the legislative and the executive branches of California state government. Since 1984 she has lobbied on behalf of the California Manufacturers Association, the California Nurses Association, and other groups. She is now a contract lobbyist.

Allan J. Cigler is the Chancellor's Club Teaching Professor of Political Science at the University of Kansas. His publications and research interests include interest groups, political parties, and political behavior. His current research focuses on the impact of outside funding on public interest group agendas.

John Constantelos is Associate Professor of Political Science at Grand Valley State University in Michigan. His research focuses on the politics of adjustment to European integration. He has written on French and Italian business responses to the Single European Act and to European economic and monetary union.

Christopher Cooper (Ph.D., University of Tennessee at Knoxville, 2002) is an Assistant Professor of Political Science at Western Carolina University. His research interests include legislative politics, voting behavior, and state politics.

Anne N. Costain is a Professor of Political Science at the University of Colorado, Boulder. She is the author of *Inviting Women's Rebellion: A Political Process Interpretation of the Women's Movement* (1992) and a number of other publications on social movements and interest group politics.

Maria Green Cowles is an Assistant Professor of Political Science at the American University, Washington, D.C. Her research focuses on multinational firms in European Union policy making and in transatlantic relations. She is the author of numerous refereed articles, coeditor of two books, and former Vice Chair of the European Union Studies Association (EUSA).

John H. Culver is Professor and former Chair of the Department of Political Science at California Polytechnic State University. His areas of teaching and research include state politics and judicial politics. He is a coauthor of both *Politics and Public Policies in California* (2001) and *The Politics of State Courts* (1992).

William De Soto is Associate Professor of Political Science at Southwest Texas State University. His publications include work on state Chambers of Commerce and local government lobbying in the states.

Polly J. Diven is an Associate Professor of Political Science at Grand Valley State University in Michigan where she teaches international relations, international organizations, and foreign policy. Her research focuses on the intersection between domestic and international politics, particularly the relationship between interest groups, public opinion, and U.S. foreign aid policy.

Michael J. Gorges, Ph.D., University of California at Berkeley, is a political consultant in Washington, D.C. From 1995 to 2002 he was an Assistant Professor of Political Science at the University of Maryland, Baltimore County. His publications focus on interest groups in the European Union and include *Euro-Corporatism? Interest Intermediation in the European Community* (1996).

Dennis O. Grady is Professor of Political Science and Director of the Energy Policy Center at Appalachian State University in North Carolina. His research focuses on comparative state politics, public administration, and intergovernmental relations. He has published in *Book of the States*, *Public Administration Quarterly*, *State and Local Government Review*, and *Western Political Quarterly*.

Virginia Gray is the Robert Watson Winston Distinguished Professor of Political Science at the University of North Carolina at Chapel Hill. Her research encompasses state politics, interest groups, and public policy. She has published numerous journal articles, two state politics textbooks, and a book on U.S. state interest groups with David Lowery.

Justin Greenwood is Jean Monnet and University Professor of European Public Policy at the Robert Gordon University, Aberdeen, Scotland. He has numerous publications on interest intermediation in the European Union, including *Inside the EU Business Associations* (2002) and *Interest Representation in the European Union* (2003). He is a former editor of *Current Politics and Economics of Europe*.

Steven H. Haeberle (Ph.D., Duke University) is an Associate Professor in the Department of Government and Public Service at the University of

Alabama at Birmingham. His research interests include urban politics; gay, lesbian, and bisexual politics; and public policy.

Glen A. Halva-Neubauer is Dana Associate Professor of Political Science and Director of the Christian A. Johnson Center for Engaged Learning at Furman University, Greenville, South Carolina. His published work is in the area of abortion politics and policy.

Keith E. Hamm is a Professor and former Chair of the Department of Political Science at Rice University. His research interests include state legislatures and interest groups. Among his publications are numerous articles and chapters in books on these and related subjects. He was a coeditor of *Legislative Studies Quarterly* from 1997 to 2002.

Eric S. Heberlig is an Assistant Professor of Political Science at the University of North Carolina, Charlotte. He was an American Political Science Association Congressional Fellow during 1997 and 1998. His several publications include *American Labor Unions in the Electoral Arena* (2001, coauthor) and *Classics in Congressional Politics* (1999, coeditor).

Brian Hocking is Professor of International Relations at Coventry University in England. His areas of interest are foreign policy and foreign economic policy processes. Among his writings are: *Localizing Foreign Policy* (1993); and *Beyond Foreign Economic Policy: The United States, the Single European Market and the Changing World Economy* (1997).

Daniel Hofrenning is Associate Professor of Political Science at St. Olaf College in Northfield, Minnesota. A specialist in American politics, he has published several articles and a book *In Washington But Not of It: The Prophetic Politics of Religious Lobbyists* (1995).

Robert E. Hogan is an Assistant Professor of Political Science at Louisiana State University. His major research focus is electoral politics in the states. He has published in *Legislative Studies Quarterly*, *Political Research Quarterly*, and *Social Science Quarterly*.

Ronald J. Hrebenar is Professor and Chair of the Political Science Department at the University of Utah. His research focuses on interest groups, political parties, public policy, and Japanese politics. He has published several books and articles including *Interest Group Politics in America* (3rd. ed., 1997). He was a Fulbright Scholar in Japan during 1982 and 1983.

Kennith G. Hunter is an Associate Professor of Public Administration at Jacksonville State University in Alabama. His teaching and research focuses on interest groups, public policy, research methods, and economic development. He has several publications on state interest groups, including *Interest Groups and State Economic Development Policies* (1999).

Henry J. Jacek is Professor of Political Science at McMaster University, Hamilton, Ontario. His publications include work on interest associations in Canada, the United States, and Western Europe. He has cochaired the Research Committee on Politics and Business of the International Political Science Association.

Grant Jordan is Professor of Politics and Head of the Department of Politics at the University of Aberdeen, Scotland. His interests focus on public policy making and interest groups. Among his many publications are: *Government and Pressure Groups in Britain* (1987, with J. J. Richardson); *Engineers and Professional Self-Regulation* (1992); *The Protest Business?* (1997, with W. A. Maloney); and *Shell, Greenpeace and the Brent Spar* (2001).

Stanley A. Kochanek is a retired Professor of Political Science from Pennsylvania State University. He has published several books and articles on interest groups in India, Pakistan, and Bangladesh and is currently working on a comparative study of interest groups in South Asia.

Ken Kollman is Associate Professor of Political Science and Senior Associate Research Scientist in the Center for Political Studies at the University of Michigan. He is the author of *Outside Lobbying: Public Opinion and Interest Group Strategies* (1998). His research focuses on party systems, voting systems, electoral competition, and lobbying.

Beth L. Leech is an Assistant Professor of Political Science at Rutgers University. She is coauthor (with Frank Baumgartner) of *Basic Interests* (1998). Her research focuses on interest group lobbying strategies and includes group use of the mass media.

Howard P. Lehman is an Associate Professor of Political Science at the University of Utah. His publications include a book, *Indebted Development: Strategic Bargaining and Economic Adjustment in the Third World* (1993); and articles in *World Politics*, *African Studies Review*, *Africa Today*, and *Political Science Quarterly*.

David Lewis is Lecturer at the Centre for Civil Society, London School of Economics, where he runs the M.S. degree in the Management of NGOs (nongovernmental organizations) program and researches NGOs and development issues. His publications include: *The Management of Nongovernmental Organisations* (2001); and *International Perspectives on Voluntary Action* (1999).

Pei-te Lien is an Associate Professor of Political Science and Ethnic Studies at the University of Utah. She is the author of *The Political Participation of Asian Americans* (1997). Her current research deals with the interrelationships of race, ethnicity, gender, and class within the Asian American political community.

Burdett A. Loomis is Professor of Political Science and Director of the Robert J. Dole Institute at the University of Kansas. His research focuses on legislative politics, organized interests, and policy making. His books include *The Sound of Money* (1999, coauthored with Darrell West) and six editions of *Interest Group Politics* (coedited with Allan J. Cigler).

David Lowery is Burton Craige Professor of Political Science at the University of North Carolina, Chapel Hill. His research interests include state politics, interest groups, budgetary politics, and bureaucracy. He has published numerous journal articles and has coauthored three books, including *The Population Ecology of Interest Representation* (1996, with Virginia Gray).

Michael C. MacLeod received his Ph.D. from Texas A&M University and is currently an organizational development consultant at Hewitt Associates. He is the coauthor of several journal articles focusing on the impact of interest groups and institutional structures and procedures on the policy-making process.

Andrew S. McFarland is Professor of Political Science at the University of Illinois at Chicago. His books include: *Public Interest Lobbies: Decision Making on Energy* (1976); *Common Cause: Lobbying in the Public Interest* (1984); and *Cooperative Pluralism: The National Coal Policy Experiment* (1993). He has also published several articles and chapters on interest groups.

Neil J. Mitchell is Professor and former Chair of the Department of Political Science, University of New Mexico. His teaching and research is in the area of comparative politics. He is the author of *The Conspicuous Corporation* (1997) and *Agents of Atrocity: Leaders, Followers, and the Violation of Human Rights in Civil War* (2004).

Brent F. Nelsen is Professor of Political Science at Furman University. His publications include: *The State Offshore* (1991); *Norway and the European Community* (1993); and *The European Union: Readings on the Theory and Practice of European Integration*, 3rd. ed. (2003, coedited with Alexander Stubb).

Martin A. Nie is Assistant Professor of Natural Resource Policy in the School of Forestry at the University of Montana. He received his Ph.D. in political science at Northern Arizona University. His research interests focus on environmental policy, including the role of interest groups.

Brian Noland, Ph.D., University of Tennessee at Knoxville, is Assistant Executive Director of Academic Affairs for the Tennessee Higher Education Commission, Nashville, Tennessee.

Anthony J. Nownes is an Associate Professor of Political Science, University of Tennessee, Knoxville, where he teaches courses on interest groups, political parties, and public opinion. His publications focus on interest group formation and maintenance and on lobbyists. He is the author of *Pressure and Power: Organized Interests in American Politics* (2001).

David M. Olson is Professor Emeritus of Political Science at the University of North Carolina at Greensboro, and serves as Cochair of the Committee of Legislative Specialists of the International Political Science Association. He was Fulbright Professor at Charles University in Prague in 1992 and at the University of Vilnius in Lithuania in 2002.

Susan M. Olson is Associate Vice President for Faculty Development and former Chair of the Department of Political Science at the University of Utah. Her publications include work on interest group litigation, attorney-client relations, attorney fee-shifting statutes, and legal consciousness and mobilization.

Sergei P. Peregudov is Professor at the Institute of World Economy and International Relations (IMEMO) of the Russian Academy of Sciences, Moscow. His publications include works on interest groups in Western countries, business interest groups and the state in the USSR, and interest groups and corporatist models in contemporary Russia.

Bert Pijnenburg, who passed away in 2001, was Lecturer in Political Science at the Erasmus University in Rotterdam, the Netherlands. His major fields of research were public affairs management, public environment analysis, pressure group politics, and lobbying. He published a coauthored book and several articles in academic journals and chapters in academic readers.

Dianne M. Pinderhughes is Professor of Political Science and Afro-American Studies at the University of Illinois, Urbana-Champaign. Her publications include studies of racial and ethnic politics in Chicago, the impact of African Americans in national politics, and the development of voting rights policy by civil rights interest groups.

A. Paul Pross is Professor Emeritus in Public Administration, Dalhousie University, Nova Scotia, Canada. He has written extensively on Canadian pressure groups, lobbying, and group regulation. His best-known book is *Group Politics and Public Policy* (1986 and 1992), a survey of Canadian interest group influence and behavior.

Jonathan Rosenberg is Associate Professor and Chair of the Political Science Department at the University of Alaska, Fairbanks, where he teaches United States and international political economy and comparative politics. He has published on Cuban political economy and the institutionalization of postrevolutionary regimes in Mexico and Cuba.

Laura C. Savatgy holds a Master's degree in Public Administration from the University of Alaska, Juneau, where she worked as a Research Assistant. Her professional experience is in human resource management. She has been an intern in the Alaska Legislature and is currently an analyst with the Department of Defense at the Pentagon in Washington, D.C.

Paul Schumaker is a Professor and Chair in the Department of Political Science at the University of Kansas. His research on urban interest groups has appeared in various scholarly journals and in his book, *Critical Pluralism, Democratic Performance and Community Power* (1991).

Irina S. Semenenko is Senior Researcher at the Institute of World Economy and International Relations of the Russian Academy of Sciences (IMEMO), Moscow. Her work focuses on interest groups—particularly business interests—in contemporary Russia, problems of social partnership, and business lobbying in the European Union.

Ronald G. Shaiko, who teaches at Dartmouth College, was an American Political Science Association Congressional Fellow (1993–94), Democracy Fellow at the United States Agency for International Development or USAID (1997–99), and a Fulbright Distinguished Chair at Warsaw University (2000–01). From 1992 to 1997 he was the founding academic director of The Lobbying Institute in Washington, D.C. He has many publications on interest groups.

Christine Marie Sierra is Associate Professor of Political Science at the University of New Mexico. Specializing in race, ethnicity, and gender in American politics, she has published on Latino interest groups, Latino political behavior, Chicanos/Latinos in politics, political mobilization strategies among Mexican Americans, and immigration policy.

Andrew Skalaban is a banking executive and formerly an Assistant Professor of Political Science at the University of California, Davis. His articles have appeared in the *American Journal of Political Science, Journal of Politics, British Journal of Political Science, Publius, Political Behavior,* and *Political Analysis.*

Kevin Snider is Executive Assistant to the President for Strategic Planning, Institutional Research, and Effectiveness at Indiana State University. He has a Ph.D. in Political Science from the American University in Washington, D.C. His dissertation dealt with foreign influence in American politics, and he continues to research and teach in this area.

David J. Sousa is Associate Professor and Chair of the Department of Politics and Government at the University of Puget Sound. His publications include work on U.S. congressional elections, electoral behavior, the domestic politics of international trade, and labor union politics. He is currently completing a book on the political consequences of union decline in the United States.

Wy Spano is a Ph.D. candidate in political science at the University of Minnesota and is coauthor of *Minnesota Politics and Government* (1999). He is a partner in the contract lobbying firm Spano & Janecek and publishes and coedits the subscription newsletter *Politics in Minnesota*.

Janie S. Steckenrider is an Associate Professor of Political Science at Loyola Marymount University. She has published articles on aging politics and is coauthor of *New Directions in Old Age Policies* (1998). She has received grants from the National Institute on Aging and has served on the boards of a hospital, a nursing home, and a senior citizens commission.

Jeffery C. Talbert is an Associate Professor of Public Policy at the University of Kentucky. His work has appeared in *American Journal of Political Science*, *American Political Science Review*, *Journal of Politics*, *Journal of Health Politics, Policy and Law*, *Political Research Quarterly*, and *Legislative Studies Quarterly*.

Paul Teske is Professor of Political Science at SUNY Stony Brook and an Affiliated Research Fellow at Columbia University's Institute for Tele-Information. He has written books and articles on state telecommunications and transportation regulation. He has also served as an expert witness in state telecommunications regulatory proceedings.

Patricia M. Thornton (Ph.D., University of California, Berkeley) is Assistant Professor of Political Science at Trinity College, Hartford, Connecticut. She has been a Fulbright Scholar at the Academia Sinica in Taipei and a post-doctoral fellow at Harvard University's Fairbank Center for East Asian Studies.

Rinus Van Schendelen is Professor of Political Science at Erasmus University, Rotterdam, the Netherlands. His main fields are politics and business and European-level lobbying, about which he has written many books and articles. He also presents seminars and training sessions on lobbying for various businesses and organizations.

John Warhurst is Professor of Political Science in the Faculty of Arts at the Australian National University. He has written individual studies of environmental, church, and business interest groups and of groups in election campaigns as well as several general accounts of the interest group system and lobbying in Australia.

Peter J. Williamson is Planning Director with the National Health Service in Tayside, Scotland. Previously he was an academic at Aberdeen University. His publications include two books on corporatist theory and practice. He has also written on policy implementation and organized interests in the economic and welfare fields and on health policy.

Franke Wilmer is a Professor of Political Science at Montana State University. Her publications include: *The Social Construction of Man, the State and War* (2002); *The Indigenous Voice in World Politics* (1993); and articles on indigenous peoples' issues and activism, ethnic identity, and conflict.

Laura A. Wilson is an Associate Professor in the School of Public Affairs at the University of Baltimore. Among her areas of interest are interest groups, welfare reform studies, program evaluation, and research into the efficacy of public management techniques.

Yael Yishai is a Professor of Political Science at the University of Haifa, Israel. Her publications include works on interest groups and public policy making in Israeli politics.